Social Marketing

Seventh Edition

This book is dedicated to all current and future social marketers working to change behaviors to improve health, decrease injuries, protect the environment, engage communities, support educational milestones, and enhance financial well-being.

We hope that you'll find that this 10-step strategic planning model enhances your success.

And to all instructors using the text, Nancy Lee offers you an opportunity for her to be "Skyped" in to your classroom for a 30- to 45-minute session to share her story about discovering social marketing and answer any questions students may have. She can be reached at nancyrlee@msn.com.

Sara Miller McCune founded SAGE Publishing in 1965 to support the dissemination of usable knowledge and educate a global community. SAGE publishes more than 1,000 journals and over 800 new books each year, spanning a wide range of subject areas. Our growing selection of library products includes archives, data, case studies, and video. SAGE remains majority owned by our founder and after her lifetime will become owned by a charitable trust that secures the company's continued independence.

Los Angeles | London | New Delhi | Singapore | Washington DC | Melbourne

Social Marketing

Behavior Change for Good

Seventh Edition

Nancy R. Lee

Social Marketing Services, Inc. and University of Washington

Philip Kotler

Kellogg School of Management, Northwestern University

Julie Colehour

C+C: A Communications Agency All About the Good

Los Angeles | London | New Delhi
Singapore | Washington DC | Melbourne

FOR INFORMATION:

SAGE Publications, Inc.
2455 Teller Road
Thousand Oaks, California 91320
E-mail: order@sagepub.com

SAGE Publications Ltd.
1 Oliver's Yard
55 City Road
London, EC1Y 1SP
United Kingdom

SAGE Publications India Pvt. Ltd.
Unit No 323-333, Third Floor, F-Block
International Trade Tower Nehru Place
New Delhi – 110 019
India

SAGE Publications Asia-Pacific Pte. Ltd.
18 Cross Street #10-10/11/12
China Square Central
Singapore 048423

Printed in the United States of America.

ISBN: 978-1-0718-5164-7

This book is printed on acid-free paper.

Acquisitions Editor: Lily Norton

Product Associate: Enawamre Ogar

Production Editor: Vijayakumar

Copy Editor: Christobel Colleen Hopman

Typesetter: TNQ Technologies

Indexer: TNQ Technologies

Cover Designer: Scott Van Atta

Marketing Manager: Jennifer Haldeman

23 24 25 26 27 10 9 8 7 6 5 4 3 2 1

BRIEF CONTENTS

DETAILED CONTENTS

FOREWORD

As an Adjunct Professor teaching "Social Marketing for Global Good" in Georgetown University's MBA program, I can heartily endorse the value of *Social Marketing: Behavior Change for Good* as a comprehensive guide to all of the key social marketing concepts students need to grasp. This textbook is easy to navigate, clearly written, and includes many illustrative examples that bring fundamental concepts to life. I find that it nicely complements my classroom lectures and the students' group project work, providing a clear structure to the process of understanding behavioral science theories, program planning models, audience segmentation, behavior change objectives, the "Four P's" elements, program management considerations, and monitoring and evaluation approaches.

This new, seventh edition of *Social Marketing: Behavior Change for Good* contains important updates and new content additions that reflect the evolving social marketing field and the most pressing issues of our time. There are 11 new cases and updates to 11 existing cases, with particular attention to "wicked problems" such as COVID-19, mass shootings, wildfires, democracy and voting, and youth mental health. Particularly noteworthy is the addition in each chapter of content addressing implications and examples related to diversity, equity, and inclusion.

New teaching tools include the addition of learning objectives at the beginning of each chapter, and an appendix that helps explain how the 10-Step Planning Framework relates to other behavioral science frameworks, including behavioral economics. Another welcome addition is an appendix that provides a template for a social marketing job description. My students appreciate the balanced attention in this textbook to social marketing concepts, "how-to" steps, applied examples, and practical resources such as sample worksheets, templates, and marketing plans.

As marketers, we know that our messages must resonate with our audience for change to occur. I can confirm that I have received enthusiastic and positive feedback from my students that this textbook enhances their learning in the classroom and in the real world. Multiple students have shared that they have applied what they've learned from this textbook and my course in their day jobs and social entrepreneurship endeavors. I am confident that this new edition will further enrich student learning and inform the next generation of social marketing solutions to the world's wicked problems.

Gael O'Sullivan, MBA
Adjunct Professor
Social Marketing for Global Good
Georgetown University | McDonough School of Business

ACKNOWLEDGMENTS

SAGE would like to thank the following reviewers:

Christopher J. Carpenter, *Western Illinois University*
Paul Christensen, *Saint Mary's University of Minnesota*
Timo Dietrich, *Griffith University*
Marie-Louise Fry, *Griffith University*
Tavis J. Glassman, *University of Toledo*
Christina Jones, *Ball State University*
Karen H. Smith, *Texas State University*
Susan E. Stein, *Drexel University*

ABOUT THE AUTHORS

Nancy R. Lee is President of Social Marketing Services, Inc., in Seattle, Washington, a strategic advisor for social marketing campaigns at C+C in Seattle, an affiliate instructor at the University of Washington, where she teaches social marketing. With more than 35 years of practical marketing experience in the public and private sectors, Ms. Lee has held numerous corporate marketing positions, including vice president and director of marketing for Washington State's second-largest bank and director of marketing for the region's Children's Hospital and Medical Center.

Ms. Lee has participated in the development of more than 250 social marketing campaign strategies for public sector agencies and consulted with more than 100 nonprofit organizations. Clients in the public sector include the Centers for Disease Control and Prevention (CDC), Environmental Protection Agency (EPA), Washington State Department of Health, Office of Crime Victims Advocacy, County Health and Transportation Departments, Department of Ecology, Department of Fisheries and Wildlife, Washington Traffic Safety Commission, City of Seattle, and Office of Superintendent of Public Instruction. Campaigns developed for these clients targeted issues listed below:

- Health: COVID-19, opioid overdose, teen pregnancy prevention, HIV/AIDS prevention, nutrition education, sexual assault, diabetes prevention, adult physical activity, tobacco control, arthritis diagnosis and treatment, immunizations, dental hygiene, senior wellness, and eating disorder awareness.
- Safety: texting and driving, drowning prevention, senior fall prevention, underage drinking and driving, youth suicide prevention, binge drinking, pedestrian safety, and safe gun storage.
- Environment: natural gardening, preservation of fish and wildlife habitats, grass fires, recycling, trip reduction, water quality, and water and power conservation.

She has conducted social marketing workshops around the world (Uganda, Jordan, South Africa, Ghana, Ireland, Scotland, Australia, Singapore, Canada, Indonesia, India, Bangladesh, Venezuela, Japan, and Haiti) for more than 4,000 public sector employees involved in developing behavior change campaigns in the areas of health, safety, the environment, and financial well-being. She has been a keynote speaker on social marketing at conferences for public health, improved water quality, energy conservation, family planning, nutrition, recycling, teen pregnancy prevention, influencing financial behaviors, wildfire prevention, litter control, and foodwaste reduction.

Ms. Lee has coauthored twelve other books with Philip Kotler: *Social Marketing: Improving the Quality of Life* (2002); *Corporate Social Responsibility: Doing the Most Good for Your Company and Your Cause* (2005); *Marketing in the Public Sector: A Roadmap for Improved Performance* (2006); *Social Marketing: Influencing Behaviors for Good* (2008 and 2011); *Social Marketing: Changing Behaviors for Good* (2016); *GOOD WORKS! Marketing and Corporate Initiatives That Build a Better World... And the Bottom Line* (2012); *Up and Out of Poverty: The Social Marketing Solution* (2009); *Social Marketing in Public Health* (2010); *Social Marketing to Protect the Environment* (2011); *Success in Social Marketing: 100 Case Studies From Around the Globe* (2022). She also authored a book *Policymaking for Citizen Behavior Change: A Social Marketing Approach* (2017) and Success in Social Marketing: 100 Case Studies from Around the Globe (2023). Ms. Lee has contributed articles to the *Stanford Social Innovation Review, Social Marketing Quarterly, Journal of Social Marketing*, and *The Public Manager*. (See more on Nancy Lee at www.socialmarketingservice.com.)

Philip Kotler is the S. C. Johnson & Son Distinguished Professor of International Marketing emeritus at the Kellogg School of Management, Northwestern University, Evanston, Illinois. Kellogg was twice voted Best Business School in *Business Week*'s survey of U.S. business schools. It is also rated Best Business School for the Teaching of Marketing. Professor Kotler has significantly contributed to Kellogg's success through his many years of research and teaching there.

He received his master's degree at the University of Chicago and his Ph.D. degree at MIT, both in economics. He did postdoctoral work in mathematics at Harvard University and in behavioral science at the University of Chicago.

Professor Kotler is the author or coauthor of 90 books including *Marketing Management*, the most widely used marketing book in graduate business schools worldwide; *Principles of Marketing; Marketing Models; Strategic Marketing for Non-Profit Organizations; The New Competition; High Visibility; Social Marketing; Marketing Places; Marketing for Congregations; Marketing for Hospitality and Tourism; The Marketing of Nations; Marketing 3.0; Good Works; Market Your Way to Growth; Winning Global Markets; Kotler on Marketing; Confronting Capitalism; Democracy in Decline: and Advancing the Common Good*. He has published over 170 articles in leading journals, several of which have received best-article awards.

Professor Kotler was the first recipient of the Distinguished Marketing Educator Award (1985) given by the American Marketing Association (AMA). The European Association of Marketing Consultants and Sales Trainers awarded him their prize for Marketing Excellence. He was chosen as the Leader in Marketing Thought by the Academic Members of the AMA in a 1975 survey. He also received the 1978 Paul Converse Award of the AMA, honoring his original contribution to marketing. In 1995, Sales and Marketing Executives

International (SMEI) named him Marketer of the Year. In 2012, he received the William L. Wilkie "Marketing for a Better World: Award of the American Marketing Association Foundation (AMAF)." In 2014, he was inducted into the AMA Marketing Hall of Fame. He was the first chosen Legend in Marketing and his work was published and reviewed in nine volumes.

Professor Kotler has consulted for such companies as IBM, General Electric, AT&T, Honeywell, Bank of America, Merck, and others in the areas of marketing strategy and planning, marketing organization, and international marketing.

He has been chairman of the College of Marketing of the Institute of Management Sciences, director of the American Marketing Association, trustee of the Marketing Science Institute, director of the MAC Group, former member of the Yankelovich Advisory Board, and a member of the Copernicus Advisory Board. He was a member of the Board of Governors of the School of the Art Institute of Chicago and a member of the advisory board of the Drucker Foundation. He has received 22 honorary doctoral degrees from Stockholm University, University of Zurich, Athens University of Economics and Business, DePaul University, the Cracow School of Business and Economics, Groupe H.E.C. in Paris, the University of Economics and Business Administration in Vienna, the Catholic University of Santo Domingo, the Budapest School of Economic Science and Public Administration, and several other universities.

He has traveled extensively throughout Europe, Asia, and South America, advising and lecturing to many companies and organizations. This experience expands the scope and depth of his programs, enhancing them with an accurate global perspective.

Julie Colehour is an owner of C+C, a 100-person social marketing firm with the purpose of creating campaigns that help take care of people and the planet (www.cplusc.com). She is also a founding board member of the Pacific Northwest Social Marketing Association (PNSMA) serving as the board's Vice President from 2014–2021. In 2011, she led a team of volunteers that created the annual PNSMA SPARKS conference which attracts hundreds of social marketers each year to learn about social marketing innovations and best practices.

Ms. Colehour has led teams to create social marketing campaigns that address COVID-19, climate, waste prevention, healthcare, STDs, substance use disorders, water conservation, wildfires, distracted driving, litter, suicide, and recycling. Most recently, she has been helping the Washington State Department of Health (WA DOH) with their COVID-19 response which has included a rapid-turn approach to increase adoption of COVID preventative behaviors and vaccine adoption. This work contributed to Washington State being the fourth lowest in the nation for COVID-19 deaths per 100K people. She has also helped support the EPA's ENERGY STAR® program for the past 25 years including coleading the original national launch plan that led to a 41 percent national awareness of the ENERGY STAR® label in just three years.

Ms. Colehour is frequently called upon to speak on social marketing at venues across the country and has helped hundreds of organizations with planning and implementing social marketing campaigns. She has conducted social marketing trainings sessions for many organizations including EPA, NOAA, Waste Management, Puget Sound Energy, the U.S. Department of Energy and the Consortium for Energy Efficiency, WaterSense, and WA DOH.

Ms. Colehour is coauthor of *The Environmental Marketing Imperative* (Probus Publishing) and for the social marketing chapter in the upcoming *Be the Change* textbook (Oxford Publishing). She led the charge in 2014 on two energy-efficient lighting social marketing pilot programs for ENERGY STAR for which the results were presented at the BECC conference and published in the *Social Marketing Quarterly Journal*. Ms. Colehour has received professional recognition for her work including being named the Puget Sound Chapter of PRSA 2021 PR Professional of the Year, the 2017 Person of the Year at the NW Marketing Awards, one of PRovoke's 2019 Top 25 Innovators and the one of The Puget Sound Business Journal's 40 under 40 young outstanding executives in 2001. Ms. Colehour's work has also been recognized with many awards (Silver Anvils, SABRES, PRWeek Awards, Addys, Emmys) including being recognized in 2021 for the COVID-19 work for the WA DOH by winning the Best of Silver Anvils award from PRSA and a Global SABRE award. In 2022, C+C was named the SMANA Outstanding Agency for its commitment to the elimination of social disparities at the USF Social Marketing Conference. This award recognized Ms. Colehour and her team's work on the Vacúnate Mijo/Mija campaign for WA DOH that helped increase COVID-19 vaccination rates among the Hispanic/Latino community.

PART I

UNDERSTANDING SOCIAL MARKETING

1 DEFINING AND DISTINGUISHING SOCIAL MARKETING

LEARNING OBJECTIVES

Upon reading this chapter, you should be able to:

1.1 Define social marketing and its impact on behavior.

1.2 Identify the origin of social marketing as a discipline.

1.3 Describe the differences between social marketing and commercial marketing.

1.4 Highlight the unique features of social marketing in comparison to related disciplines.

1.5 Identify the different organizations that utilize social marketing to influence public behaviors.

1.6 Explain alternative approaches to impacting social issues outside of social marketing.

1.7 Examine the ways social marketers can influence downstream, midstream, and upstream audiences.

Social marketing, as a discipline, has made enormous strides since its distinction in the early 1970s, and has had a profound positive impact on social issues in the areas of public health, injury prevention, the environment, community engagement, and more recently, financial well-being. Fundamental principles at the core of this practice have been used to help reduce tobacco use, decrease infant mortality, stop the spread of HIV/AIDS, prevent malaria, help eradicate polio, make wearing a bike helmet a social norm, decrease littering, stop bullying, increase recycling, encourage the homeless to participate in job-training programs, and persuade pet owners to license their pets and "scoop their poop."

Social marketing as a term, however, is still a mystery to most, misunderstood by many, and increasingly confused with other terms such as *behavioral economics* (a framework that can inspire social marketing strategies and is described later in this book), *social media* (one of many potential promotional tactics to choose from), and *health communications* (which only uses one of the marketing intervention mix tools … promotion). A few even worry about using the term with their administrators, colleagues, and elected officials, fearing they will associate it with socialism, manipulation, and sales. This chapter is intended to create clear distinctions and to answer common questions:

- What is social marketing?
- When did it originate?
- How does it differ from information/education campaigns?
- How does it differ from health communication?
- How does social marketing differ from commercial marketing, nonprofit marketing, and public sector marketing?
- What is its relation to behavioral economics, nudge, social change, community-based social marketing, community-based prevention marketing, social media, and cause promotion?
- Do people who do social marketing actually call themselves social marketers? Where do they work?
- What social issues can benefit from social marketing?
- When is a behavior change strategy considered social marketing? When is it something else?

We support the voices of many who advocate for an expanded role for social marketing and social marketers, challenging professionals to take this same technology "upstream" to influence other factors that affect positive social change, including laws, enforcement, public policy, built environments, school curricula, community organizations, business practices, celebrities, and the media. We also encourage distinguishing and considering "midstream" audiences, those influential others closer to our priority audiences, such as family, friends, neighbors, health care providers, teachers, and community leaders.

We begin this chapter, like the rest of the chapters in the book, with an inspiring case story; this one is from Massachusetts. We conclude with one of several Marketing Dialogues that feature discourses among practitioners seeking to shape, evolve, and transform this discipline.

CASE HIGHLIGHT

REDUCING DEATHS FROM DRUG OVERDOSES

Background

Drug overdoses are, as of 2020, the leading cause of accidental death in the United States, surpassing traffic accidents and gun violence, with more than 90,000 Americans dying from drug overdoses in 2020.[1] 1 Overdoses are also the leading cause of death in Americans under age 50.[2] This surge has been pushed to new heights primarily by the rising abuse of heroin and prescription painkillers, a class of drugs known as opioids. Robert Anderson, who has overseen death statistics at the Centers for Disease Control and Prevention (CDC), commented "I don't think we've ever seen anything like this. Certainly not in modern times."[3]

Promising strategies encouraged by CDC for states to focus on include: prescription drug monitoring programs, policy options relating to pain clinics, appropriate prescribing of opioid pain relievers, expanding first responder access to naloxone, supporting the use of CDC's guidelines for prescribing opioids for chronic pain, and increasing access to substance abuse treatment services.

This case highlights one community's creative and impactful social marketing effort to address this "wicked problem" with a unique focus on priority audiences most ready for change, providing them "Hope Not Handcuffs."

Priority Audience and Desired Behavior

In June of 2015, in Gloucester, Massachusetts, the then Police Chief Leonard Campanello told CNN's Sanjay Gupta he had "had enough."[4] He shared that this small community of 30,000 residents had just seen its fourth fatal drug overdose, the first Friday of March that year, surpassing the prior year's total number.[5] Campanello and his team had been fighting the drug war "the old-fashioned way," primarily targeting dealers and addicts in popular locations such as strip-mall parking lots and then arresting them and putting them in jail.

On the morning of May 4 that year, he decided to try a new approach, some described as a "defiant one."[6] He logged into the Gloucester Police Department's Facebook account for the first time and wrote, "Starting June 1, any addict who walks into the police station with the remainder of their drug equipment (needles, etc.) or drugs and asks for help will NOT be charged. I've never arrested a tobacco addict, nor have I ever seen one turned down for help."[7]

Marketing Intervention Mix Strategies

What Did "Help" Look Like?

When an addict came into the Gloucester Police Department asking for help, there was no arrest or jail sentence (*price*). An officer took them to a local hospital, where they were paired with a volunteer "ANGEL" who helped guide them through the process (*product*), including ensuring they received care from one of more than a dozen treatment centers that could receive them immediately (*place*). Working with partners in the community, the police department secured scholarships in order to fully fund in-patient programs for addicts (*price*). The department also developed an agreement with local drug stores to give people struggling with addiction access to free naloxone without a prescription (*place*).[8] The program was referred to as *Hope Not Handcuffs* and was promoted on the department's website, through social media (e.g., Facebook, Twitter), by word of mouth from fellow addicts, and in news stories (*promotion*).

Outcomes

The police chief's post instantly went viral, shared by more than 30,000 people, "liked" by 33,000, and viewed more than two million times.[9] Over the next few weeks, Campanello's office received notes of support, numerous thank you letters, and calls from reporters from around the world.

In 2016, a year and a half after opening the police department's doors for help, only two people had overdosed on opioids, close to 525 people had been placed into treatment programs, and there had been a 30% reduction in crimes associated with addiction: "breaking-and-entering, smash-and-grab, shoplifting." And on the national level, more than 200 law enforcement departments in 28 states had joined the movement.[10]

WHAT IS SOCIAL MARKETING?

Social marketing is a distinct marketing discipline, one that has been labeled as such since the early 1970s, more than 50 years ago. Early efforts adopting a social marketing approach were those focused on family planning, tobacco, and HIV/AIDS, and now include additional efforts to improve public health, prevent injuries, protect the environment, engage communities, and enhance financial well-being. Several definitions from social marketing veterans are listed in Box 1.1 of this chapter, beginning with one we have adopted for use in this text and one from the International Social Marketing Association (iSMA).

BOX 1.1

Definitions of Social Marketing From Social Marketing Veterans (Obtained via Personal Correspondence) and the International Social Marketing Association (iSMA)

Social Marketing seeks to develop and integrate marketing concepts with other approaches to influence behaviours that benefit individuals and communities for the greater social good. Social Marketing practice is guided by ethical principles. It seeks to integrate research, best practice, theory, audience and partnership insight, to inform the delivery of competition sensitive and segmented social change programmes that are effective, efficient, equitable and sustainable.

—*iSMA, 2014*[a]

Social Marketing is a process that uses marketing principles and techniques to change priority audience behaviors to benefit society as well as the individual. This strategically oriented discipline relies on creating, communicating, delivering, and exchanging offerings that have positive value for individuals, clients, partners, and society at large.

—*Nancy R. Lee, Michael L. Rothschild, and Bill Smith, personal communication*

Think of social marketing as the social change version of "Let's Make a Deal." We believe that all men and women have a right to determine what is valuable to them. Our job is not to change their values. That may be the mission of education or religion, but not of marketing. Our job is to offer people something they already value in exchange for a behavior which we believe will benefit not only them as individuals, but society as a whole. Our most fundamental principle, the principle of exchange, is radically democratic and populist.

Dr. Bill Smith, personal communication

Social Marketing is the application of commercial marketing concepts and tools to influence the voluntary behavior of target audiences to improve their lives or the society of which they are a part.

—Alan Andreasen (2014)

Social Marketing is a set of evidence- and experience- based concepts and principles that provide a systematic approach to understanding behaviour and influencing it for social good. It is not a science but rather a form of "technik"; a fusion of science, practical know-how, and reflective practice focusing on continuously improving the performance of programmes aimed at producing net social good.

—Jeff French (2014)

Social Marketing is a process that involves (a) carefully selecting which behaviors and segments to target, (b) identifying the barriers and benefits to these behaviors, (c) developing and pilot testing strategies to address these barriers and benefits, and, finally, (d) broad scale implementation of successful programs.

—Doug McKenzie-Mohr (2014)

Social Marketing is a way to reduce the barriers and increase the facilitators to behaviors that improve the quality of life for individuals and society. It uses concepts and planning processes from commercial marketing to make behaviors "fun, easy, and popular." It goes beyond communication, public service announcements, and education to give you a 360-degree view of potential causes and solutions for health and human service problems.

—Mike Newton-Ward (2014)

---

a. International Social Marketing Association, "Social Marketing Definition" (n.d.), accessed September 9, 2014, https://isocialmarketing.org/.

We believe that after you have reviewed these definitions, it will seem clear there are several common themes. Social marketing is about (a) influencing behavior change, (b) utilizing a systematic planning process that applies marketing principles and techniques, (c) focusing on priority audience segments, and (d) delivering a positive benefit for individuals and society. Each of these themes is elaborated upon in the next four sections.

We Focus on Behavior Change

Similar to commercial sector marketers' objective, which is to sell goods and services, social marketers' objective is to successfully influence behavior change. We typically want to influence priority audiences to do one of four things: (1) *accept* a new behavior (e.g., composting food waste); (2) *reject* a potentially undesirable behavior (e.g., starting smoking); (3) *modify* a current behavior (e.g., increase physical activity from three to five days of the week); or (4) *abandon* an old undesirable behavior (e.g., texting while driving). We may be encouraging a one-time behavior (e.g., installing a low-flow showerhead) or hoping to establish a habit and prompt a repeated behavior (e.g., taking a five-minute shower). More recently, Alan Andreasen suggested a fifth arena in which we want to influence people to *continue* a desired behavior (e.g., giving blood on an annual basis), and a sixth in which we want people to *switch* a behavior (e.g., take the stairs instead of the elevator).[11]

Although benchmarks may be established for increasing knowledge and skills through education, and although efforts may need to be made to alter existing beliefs, attitudes, or feelings, the bottom line for the social marketer is whether the priority audience actually adopts the behavior. For example, a specific behavior that substance abuse coalitions want to influence is women's use of marijuana during pregnancy. They recognize the need to inform women that marijuana may cause birth defects and convince them that this could happen to their baby. In the end, however, their measure of success is whether the expectant mother abstains from marijuana use.

Perhaps the most challenging aspect of social marketing (and also its greatest contribution) is that it relies heavily on "rewarding good behaviors" rather than "punishing bad ones" through legal, economic, or coercive forms of influence. And in many cases, social marketers cannot promise a direct benefit or immediate payback in return for adopting the proposed behavior. Consider, for example, the task of influencing gardeners to pull their dandelions instead of using harmful chemicals. It's tough to show the healthier fish their actions helped to support. And it's tough to convince youth who want to look good to use sunscreen so that they will (maybe) avoid skin cancer later in life. As you will read in subsequent chapters, this is why a systematic, rigorous, and strategic planning process is required—one that is inspired by the wants, needs, and preferences of priority audiences and focuses on real, deliverable, and near-term benefits. It should be noted, however, that many believe that this heavy reliance on individual voluntary behavior change is outdated and have moved on to applying social marketing technologies to influencing other change factors in the environment (e.g., public policies, media, and corporations). This is elaborated upon later in this chapter.

We Use Systematic Planning Processes

The American Marketing Association defines marketing as "the activity, set of institutions, and processes for creating, communicating, delivering, and exchanging offerings that have value for customers, clients, partners, and society at large."[12] For social marketing, the most fundamental principle underlying this approach is application of a *customer orientation* to understanding barriers that priority audiences perceive to adopting the desired behavior and benefits they want and believe they can realize. The process begins with alignment on the *social issue* to be addressed and an *environmental scan* to establish a purpose and focus for a specific plan. A *situation analysis* (SWOT) helps identify organizational strengths to maximize and weaknesses to minimize, as well as external opportunities to take advantage of and threats to prepare for. Marketers then *select* a *priority audience* they can best influence and satisfy. We establish clear *behavior objectives* and *target goals* the plan will be developed to achieve. *Formative research* is conducted to identify audience barriers, benefits, motivators, the competition, and influence others. This inspires the *positioning* of the offer, one that will appeal to the desires of the priority audience, and the game requires that we do this more effectively than the competition. We then consider the need for each of the major intervention tools in the marketer's toolbox, the "4Ps," to influence priority audiences: product, price, place, and promotion, also referred to as the *marketing intervention mix*. As will be noted several times in this text, not all 4P intervention tools are always needed for a given behavior change effort. They should, however, be considered in order to determine if they are needed to more effectively and efficiently reduce barriers to behavior change and provide personal desired benefits. An *evaluation* methodology is established, leading to a *budget* and *implementation* plan. Once a plan is implemented, ideally first with a pilot, results are *monitored* and *evaluated*, and strategies are altered as needed.

We Select a Priority Audience

Marketers know that the marketplace is a rich collage of diverse populations, each having a distinct set of wants and needs. We know that what appeals to one individual may not appeal to another and therefore divide the market into similar groups (market segments), measure the relative potential of each segment to meet organizational and marketing objectives, and then choose one or more segments (priority audiences) on which to concentrate our efforts and resources. The priority audience is always determined before selecting the desired behavior as the behavior most often varies by audience (e.g., physical activity behaviors for seniors are likely to differ from ones for teens). For each priority segment, a distinct mix of the 4Ps (Product, Price, Place, and Promotion) is considered, one designed to uniquely address that segment's barriers, benefits, motivators, competition, and influential others.

Considering, again, a more expanded view of social marketing, Robert Donovan and Nadine Henley (among others) advocate also targeting individuals in communities who have the power to make institutional policy and legislative changes in social structures (e.g., school superintendents). In this case, efforts move from influencing (just) an individual with a problem or potentially problematic behavior to influencing those who can facilitate behavior change in individuals.[13] Techniques, however, remain the same.

The Primary Beneficiary Is Society

Unlike commercial marketing, in which the primary intended beneficiary is the corporate shareholder, the primary beneficiary of the social marketing program is society. The question many pose and banter about is who determines whether the social change created by the program is beneficial? Although most causes supported by social marketing efforts tend to draw high consensus that the cause is good, this model can also be used by organizations that have the opposite view of what is good. Abortion is an example of an issue where both sides argue that they are on the "good" side and both use social marketing techniques to influence behavior change. Who, then, gets to define "good"? Some propose the United Nations' Universal Declaration of Human Rights (http://www.un.org/en/documents/udhr/) as a baseline with respect to the common good. Some share the opinion of social marketing consultant Craig Lefebvre, who posted the following on the Georgetown Social Marketing Listserve:

> "Good" is in the eye of the beholder. What I consider to be an absolute right and therefore worthy of extensive publicly funded social marketing campaigns, you may consider to be an absolute wrong. Organ donation is an absolute wrong for those whose religious beliefs preclude the desecration of bodies yet it is considered an important cause worthy of social marketing dollars by those not constrained by the same belief structure.[14]

Alan Andreasen's comments on the listserv focused on the role of the social marketing consultant versus the client or funder:

> We need to be clear that social marketers are "hired guns" (excuse the metaphor). That is, give us a behavior you want influenced and we have some very good ways of making it happen. Each of us is free to work on behavior-influence challenges with which we feel comfortable and "comfort" is both a matter of personal ethics and a matter of expertise. The decision about which behaviors ought to be influenced is not ours to make. Clients, or even societies or governments, make those judgments.[15]

WHERE AND WHEN DID SOCIAL MARKETING ORIGINATE?

When we think of social marketing as "behavior change for social good," it is clear that this is not a new phenomenon. Consider efforts to free slaves, abolish child labor, influence women's right to vote, and recruit women into the workforce (see Figure 1.1).

Launching the discipline formally more than 50 years ago, the term *social marketing* was first introduced by Philip Kotler and Gerald Zaltman, in a pioneering article in the *Journal of Marketing*, to describe "the use of marketing principles and techniques to advance a social cause, idea or behavior."[16] Their focus was on answering the question whether marketing could be used to persuade people to adopt behaviors that would be better for them, their families and friends, and the society in general. "We decided to call such marketing actions Social Marketing as a short term for Social Cause Marketing. Little did we know that Social Marketing would later be confused with Social Media Marketing."[17] In the intervening decades, interest in and use of social marketing concepts, tools, and practices has spread from the arena of public health and safety and into the work of environmentalists, community advocates, and poverty workers.

HOW DOES IT DIFFER FROM COMMERCIAL MARKETING?

There are a few important differences between social marketing and commercial marketing.

FIGURE 1.1 ■ "Rosie the Riveter," Created by the War Ad Council to Help Recruit Women

Source: Provided by the National Archives and Records Administration, Washington, DC.

In the commercial sector, the primary aim is selling goods and services that will produce a *financial gain* for the corporation. In social marketing, the primary aim is influencing behavior change that will contribute to *societal and individual gain*. Given their focus on financial gain, commercial marketers often favor choosing priority audience segments that will provide the greatest volume of profitable sales. In social marketing, segments are selected based on a different set of criteria, including prevalence of the social problem, ability to reach the audience, readiness for change, and other factors that will be explored in depth in Chapter 6 of this text. In both cases, however, marketers seek to gain the greatest returns on their investment of resources.

Although both social and commercial marketers recognize the need to identify and position their offering relative to the competition, their competitors are very different in nature. Because, as stated earlier, the commercial marketer most often focuses on selling goods and services, the *competition is often identified as other organizations offering similar goods and services*. In social marketing, *the competition is most often the current or preferred behavior of the priority audience* and the desired benefits associated with that behavior, including the status quo. This also includes any organizations selling or promoting competing behaviors (e.g., the tobacco industry).

For a variety of reasons, we believe social marketing is more difficult than commercial marketing. Consider the financial resources the competition has to make drinking alcohol look cool, yard cleanup using a gas blower easy, fried food look tasty, and bright green lawns the norm. And consider the challenges faced in trying to influence people to do any of the following:

- Give up an addictive behavior (e.g., stop smoking)
- Change a comfortable lifestyle (e.g., reduce thermostat settings)
- Resist peer pressure (e.g., be sexually abstinent)
- Go out of their way (e.g., take unused paint to a hazardous waste site)
- Be uncomfortable (e.g., give blood)
- Establish new habits (e.g., exercise five days a week)
- Spend more money (e.g., buy recycled paper)
- Be embarrassed (e.g., let lawns go brown in the summer)
- Hear bad news (e.g., get an HIV test)
- Risk relationships (e.g., take the keys from a drunk driver)
- Worry about unintended consequences (e.g., getting the COVID-19 vaccination)
- Give up leisure time (e.g., volunteer)
- Reduce pleasure (e.g., wear a mask)
- Give up looking good (e.g., wear sunscreen)
- Spend more time (e.g., flatten cardboard boxes before putting them in recycling bins)
- Learn a new skill (e.g., create and follow a budget)
- Remember something (e.g., take reusable bags to the grocery store)
- Risk retaliation (e.g., drive the speed limit)

Despite these differences, we also see many similarities between the social and commercial marketing models:

- *A customer orientation is critical.* The marketer knows that the offer (product, price, and place) will need to appeal to the priority audience by promising to solve a problem they have or satisfy a want or need.

- *Exchange theory is fundamental.* The priority audience must perceive benefits that equal or exceed the perceived costs they associate with performing the behavior.[18] As Bill Smith says in this chapter's opening quote, we should think of the social marketing paradigm as "Let's make a deal!"[19]
- *Marketing research is used throughout the process.* Only by researching and understanding the specific needs, desires, beliefs, and attitudes of target adopters can the marketer build effective strategies.
- *Audiences are segmented.* Strategies must be tailored to the unique wants, needs, resources, and current behaviors of differing market segments.
- *All 4Ps (product, price, place, and promotion) are considered.* A winning strategy requires an integrated approach, one utilizing all relevant intervention tools in the toolbox, not just relying on advertising and other persuasive communications.
- *Results are measured and used for improvement.* Feedback is valued and seen as "free advice" on how to do better next time.

HOW DOES SOCIAL MARKETING DIFFER FROM OTHER DISCIPLINES?

Social marketing is often confused or equated with several other related *disciplines* (nonprofit marketing, public sector marketing, and education), emerging behavior change *theories and frameworks* (behavioral economics, nudge, social change, community-based social marketing, and community-based prevention marketing), and popular *promotional tactics* (social media, advertising, and cause promotion). This section briefly helps distinguish 11 of these from the social marketing discipline, and the following section elaborates on the application of social marketing by corporations, nonprofit/nongovernmental organizations, and public sector agencies. Note as well that each of the behavior change theories and frameworks is elaborated on in Chapter 4 and that promotional tactics are described further in Chapter 13.

- *Nonprofit/NGO marketing.* Those responsible for marketing in the nonprofit/NGO sector most often focus on supporting utilization of the organization's programs and services (e.g., ticket sales for a new museum exhibit), purchases of ancillary products and services (e.g., at museum stores), volunteer recruitment (e.g., for museum docents), advocacy efforts (e.g., inviting elected officials to visit a museum), and fundraising (e.g., for expansion efforts).
- *Public sector marketing.* In this domain, marketing efforts are most often counted on to support utilization of governmental agency products and services (e.g., the post office, community clinics), engender citizen support (e.g., for road improvements),

and increase compliance (e.g., with policies regarding public health practices at farmers' markets).

- *Education.* Educational efforts designed to address social issues focus primarily on increasing awareness and understanding. Although social marketers may use education as a tactic (e.g., sharing information about why pet waste is dangerous for fish), it is rarely sufficient to actually influence behaviors as it does not often address major barriers, benefits, and motivators a priority audience has in regard to adopting the behavior (e.g., access to plastic bags to pick up pet waste).
- *Health communications.* Efforts with this label typically use only one of the marketing intervention strategies, those associated with promotion.
- *Behavioral economics.* This psychological framework proposes theories on why and when people make irrational choices and then focuses on how changes in the external environment can prompt and promote positive, voluntary, individual-level behavior change. Social marketers can (and do) explore these insights when developing social marketing strategies.
- *Nudge.* This framework, introduced by Richard Thaler and Cass Sunstein in 2009, proposes that behaviors that improve health, wealth, and happiness can be influenced by presenting choices (e.g., children in a school cafeteria can be influenced to choose healthier options by placing them at eye level and/or at the beginning of the food display). As Kotler noted in an article in July of 2020 titled "Marketing is the Original Behavioral Economics", Thaler and Sustein "recognized that people make many decisions by habit, or impulse, or irrational thinking."[20] This is an innovative strategy that can inspire social marketers.[21]
- *Social change.* We see social marketing as only one approach to creating positive social change. Others include advocacy (e.g., for gay marriage), innovation (e.g., electric cars), technology (e.g., the iPhone), infrastructure (e.g., bike lanes), science (e.g., a cure for HIV/AIDS), corporate business practices (e.g., calories posted on menu boards), funding (e.g., for malaria nets), and laws (e.g., prohibiting texting while driving). Although the focus of social marketing is on individual behavior change, you will read in the final sections of this chapter the role we see for social marketers to play in influencing these alternate social change strategies.
- *Community-based social marketing (CBSM).* This behavior change approach, developed by Doug McKenzie-Mohr in 1999, focused, at the time, primarily on behaviors to protect the environment. It emphasizes several of the steps in the 10-step social marketing planning model presented in this text: selecting behaviors, identifying barriers and benefits, developing strategies, piloting, and then broad-scale implementation and evaluation.[22]

- *Community-based prevention marketing.* This practice engages influential and relevant community members in the process of identifying problems, mobilizing resources, planning and implementing strategies, and tracking and evaluating progress toward objectives and goals. It is not focused just on achieving behavior change but also on building community.[23] Social marketers can (and do) benefit from this practice by engaging community members and organizations in the planning, implementing, and evaluation process.
- *Social media.* This is a communication channel that social marketers use and includes Facebook, Twitter, LinkedIn, Instagram, TikTok, YouTube, and other social networking sites. It is only one of numerous promotional tactics that social marketers use.
- *Cause promotion.* These promotional efforts are designed to increase awareness and concern for a social cause (e.g., climate change). Social marketers leverage these efforts by focusing on behaviors to alleviate these concerns.

WHO DOES SOCIAL MARKETING?

In most cases, social marketing principles and techniques are used by those on the front lines who are responsible for influencing public behaviors to improve public health, prevent injuries, protect the environment, engage communities, and, more recently, enhance financial well-being. It is rare that these individuals have a social marketing title. More often, they are program managers or those working in community relations or communication positions. Efforts usually involve multiple change agents who, as Robert Hornik points out, may or may not be acting in a consciously coordinated way.[24] Most often, organizations sponsoring these efforts are *public sector agencies*: international agencies such as WHO; national agencies such as the Centers for Disease Control and Prevention, the Ministries of Health, the Environmental Protection Agency, and the National Highway Traffic Safety Administration; state agencies such as departments of health, social and human services, and fish and wildlife; and local jurisdictions, including public utilities, fire departments, schools, parks, and community health clinics.

Nonprofit organizations and foundations also get involved, most often supporting behaviors aligned with their agency's mission. For example, the American Heart Association urges women to monitor their blood pressure, the Kaiser Family Foundation uses their Know HIV/AIDS campaign to promote testing, and the Nature Conservancy encourages actions that protect wildlife habitats.

Professionals working in for-profit organizations in positions responsible for corporate philanthropy, corporate social responsibility, marketing, or community relations might support social marketing efforts, often in partnership with nonprofit organizations and public agencies that benefit their communities and customers. Although the primary beneficiary is society, they may

FIGURE 1.2 ■ Home Depot's Arizona Stores Offered Weekend Workshops on Water Conservation Basics, Including Drought-Resistant Gardening. More Than 3,100 Consumers Attended

Source: Park and Company.

find that their efforts contribute to organizational goals as well, such as a desired brand image or even increased sales. Safeco Insurance, for example, provides households with tips on how to protect rural homes from wildfire; Crest supports the development of videos, audiotapes, and interactive lesson plans to promote good oral health behaviors; and thousands of customers at Home Depot's stores have attended weekend workshops focusing on water conservation basics, including drought-resistant gardening (see Figure 1.2).

Finally, there are marketing professionals who provide services to *organizations engaged in social marketing campaigns*, firms such as advertising agencies, public relations firms, marketing research firms, and marketing consulting firms—some that specialize in social marketing.

WHAT SOCIAL ISSUES CAN BENEFIT?

Table 1.1 presents 50 major social issues that could benefit from the application of social marketing principles and techniques. This is only a partial list, with data for the most part for the United States, but representative of the aforementioned five major arenas social marketing efforts usually focus on: health promotion, injury prevention, environmental protection, community engagement, and financial well-being. For each of the social issues listed, the status could improve if and when we are successful in increasing the adoption of desired related behaviors.

TABLE 1.1 ■ 50 Major Issues Social Marketing Can Impact in the United States Alone Unless Otherwise Noted.

Health-Related Behaviors to Impact	
Tobacco Use	Cigarette smoking is the leading cause of preventable disease and death in the United States, accounting for more than 480,000 deaths every year or one of every five deaths.[a]
Heavy/Binge Drinking	A third (33.0%) of 18–22 year old full-time college students reported binge drinking in the past month.[b]
Fetal Alcohol Syndrome	About 1 in 20 women (5%) take street drugs during pregnancy including cocaine, heroin, and ecstasy.[c]
Obesity	Almost half (46.7 %) of adults do not meet guidelines for aerobic physical activity levels.[d]
Teen Pregnancy and Sexually Transmitted Diseases	Only 9% of sexually active high school students used a condom + a more effective birth control method the last time they had sex.[e]
HIV/AIDS	13% of Americans living with HIV are unaware of their infection.[f]
Fruit and Vegetable Intake	Only 1 in 10 adults eat the recommended amount of fruits and vegetables each day.[g]
High Cholesterol	About 38% of American adults have high cholesterol.[h]
Breastfeeding	43% of mothers do not meet recommendations to breastfeed infants until they reach at least six months.[i]
Breast Cancer	Only a third (33.3%) of women over 40 have had a mammogram within the past two years.[j]
COVID-19	Only 49% of 18–24 year olds were fully vaccinated by the Fall of 2021.[k]
Colon Cancer	Only 32% of adults 50–75 years old are up-to-date with colorectal cancer screening.[l]
Birth Defects	60% of women of childbearing age are not taking recommended multivitamins containing folic acid.[m]
Immunizations	32% of 19- to 35-month-old children are not receiving all major recommended vaccinations.[n]
Skin Cancer	Only 9% of youth wear sunscreen most of the time.[o]
Oral Health	35% of adults do not visit a dentist or dental clinic annually.[p]
Diabetes	More than 1 in 3 American adults have prediabetes, and more than 84% of them don't know they have it.[q]

(Continued)

TABLE 1.1 ■ 50 Major Issues Social Marketing Can Impact in the United States Alone Unless Otherwise Noted *(Continued)*

Blood Pressure	Only about 1 in 4 adults (34%) with hypertension have their condition under control.[r]
Eating Disorders	57% of college students have cited cultural pressures as a cause of eating disorders.[s]
Injury Prevention-Related Behaviors to Impact	
Drinking and Driving	16.7% of high school students report having ridden one or more times in the past year in a car driven by someone who had been drinking.[t]
Texting or Emailing While Driving	39% of high school youth reported texting or emailing while driving.[u]
Bullying	15.7% of high school youth reported being bullied through texting, Instagram, Facebook, or other social media.[v]
Proper Safety Restraints for Children in Cars	43% of 8–12 year olds have not been buckled up, and 27% children less than 4 years old have not been properly restrained.[w]
Suicide	Suicide rates among 10–24 year olds increased by 57.4% from the year 2000 to 2018.[x]
Domestic Violence	More than 1 in 3 women (35.6%) and 1 in 4 men (28.5%) experience rape, physical violence, and/or stalking by an intimate partner.[y]
Gun Storage	Every year, nearly 1,800 children die from gun shootings, an average of more than 3 per day, and many more are seriously injured.[z]
Sexual Violence	10.8% of high school youth reported experiencing sexual violence in the past 12 months.[aa]
Fires	57% of reported home fire deaths resulted from fires in homes with no operational smoke alarm.[bb]
Falls	More than one out of four adults 65 and older fall each year, and one out of five falls causes a serious injury such as broken bones or a head injury.[cc]
Household Poisons	Medications are the leading cause of child poisoning. In 2017, over 52,000 children were seen in an emergency room for medicine poisoning. That's one child every 10 minutes.[dd]
Environmental Behaviors to Impact	
Waste Reduction	Only 50% of aluminum beer and soda cans, 31% of glass containers, and 17% of plastic containers and packaging are recycled.[ee]

(Continued)

TABLE 1.1 ■ 50 Major Issues Social Marketing Can Impact in the United States Alone Unless Otherwise Noted *(Continued)*

Wildlife Habitat Protection	Nearly 90% of global fish stocks are either fully fished or overfished.[ff]
Wildfires	In 2020, more than 46,000 fires burned over 8 million acres.[gg]
Toxic Fertilizers and Pesticides	An estimated 80% of households use harmful pesticides indoors.[hh]
Water Conservation	A leaky toilet can waste as much as 300 gallons of water a day.[ii]
Air Pollution From Automobiles	In 2019, prior to the COVID-19 pandemic, an estimated 75% of workers commuted to work by private vehicle.[jj]
Air Pollution From Other Sources	If every household in the United States replaced their five most frequently used light fixtures with bulbs that have the ENERGY STAR® label, more than 1 trillion pounds of greenhouse gas emissions would be prevented.[kk]
Composting Garbage and Yard Waste	An estimated 20%–30% of all trash that ends up in a landfill in the United States could have been composted.[ll]
Unintentional Fires	Nearly 85% of wildland fires are caused by humans from actions such as leaving campfires unattended, burning debris, and negligently discarding cigarettes.[mm]
Litter	In 2020, an estimated 50 billion pieces of litter appeared on U.S. roadways and waterways.[nn]
Watershed Protection	An estimated 40% of Americans don't pick up their dogs' waste.[oo]
Community Involvement Behaviors to Impact	
Organ Donation	As of October 2021, 106,708 men, women, and children were on a waiting list for an organ transplant.[pp]
Blood Donation	Only about 3% of age-eligible people donate blood yearly.[qq]
Voting	Only 61% of the eligible voting-age population voted in the 2016 U.S. presidential election.[rr]
Screen Time	In 2018, children 8–18 were averaging 6–9 hours of screen time each day.[ss]
Homelessness	In 2020, more than 500,000 people were experiencing homelessness on a single night.[tt]
Animal Adoption	Approximately 1.5 million dogs and cats in shelters are not adopted and are euthanized each year.[uu]

(Continued)

TABLE 1.1 ■ 50 Major Issues Social Marketing Can Impact in the United States Alone Unless Otherwise Noted *(Continued)*

Financial Behaviors to Impact	
Identity Theft	About 15 million U.S. residents have their identities used fraudulently each year, with financial losses totaling upward of $50 billion.[vv]
Establishing Bank Accounts	About 5.4% of households in the United States do not have a bank account.[ww]
Fraud	Each year, millions of elderly Americans are victimized by financial fraud and other schemes.[xx]

Source: Author.

Note: Statistics are estimated and approximate. Data are primarily for the United States. Most dates for these statistics are given in the table notes.

OTHER WAYS TO IMPACT SOCIAL ISSUES

Social marketing is clearly not the only approach to impacting a social issue, and social marketers are not the only ones who can be influential. Other forces and organizations, which some describe as upstream factors and midstream influential others can affect individual behaviors downstream. Included upstream are technological innovations, scientific discoveries, economic pressures, laws, improved infrastructures, changes in corporate business practices, new school policies and curricula, public education, and the media. Midstream influences include family members, friends, neighbors, church leaders, health care providers, entertainers, Facebook friends, and others our priority audiences listen to, observe, or look up to.

Technology: Many new gas pumps inhibit the ability to top off the tank, thus avoiding ozone-threatening spillage. Some cars have automatic seatbelts that wrap around the passenger when the door is closed. In some states, ignition locks require breathalyzers for serious offenders, and Mothers Against Drunk Driving (MADD) is advocating that automobile manufacturers be required to include high-tech alcohol sensors in all new cars. Imagine the impact on trip reduction if cars were designed to give feedback on how much that trip to the grocery store just cost, given the current price of a gallon of gas.

Science: Medical discoveries may eventually provide inoculations for certain cancers, such as the HPV vaccine released in 2009 for 11- to 26-year-olds to help prevent cervical cancer. And, in 2006, researchers at the Mayo Clinic announced that they felt they were close to discovering a shot that could be given that would help a smoker quit (if not ensure smoking cessation).[25]

Legal/political/policymaking/law enforcement: Sometimes when all else fails, the laws have to get tougher, especially when the vast majority of the market has adopted the behavior and only the most resistant are still holding out (late adopters and laggards, as they are labeled in marketing). As of August 2017, 44 states, the District of Columbia, Puerto Rico, Guam, and the U.S.

Virgin Islands have banned text messaging for all drivers.[26] All U.S. states now have a 0.08% blood alcohol level limit for drinking and driving, more strict than the prior 0.10%. Some states have considered laws requiring deposits on cigarettes similar to those requiring deposits on beverage containers (and rewarding their return). In a policy statement published in December 2006 in the journal *Pediatrics*, the American Academy of Pediatrics asked Congress and the Federal Communications Commission to impose severe limits on children-targeted advertising, including the banning of junk food ads during shows viewed predominantly by those under age eight.[27] In 2013, a law enforcement crackdown on sex trafficking rescued dozens of victims.[28] And of most current relevance was the adoption of a mandate in the Fall of 2021 requiring healthcare workers, police, and government employees to be vaccinated or lose their jobs,

Improved infrastructures and built environments: If we really want more people to ride bikes to work, we'll need more bike lanes, not just bike paths. If we really want to reduce cigarette butt littering on roadways, perhaps automobile manufacturers could help out by building in smoke-free cigarette butt containers so that disposing a cigarette inside the car is just as convenient as tossing it out the window. If we want to reduce electricity consumption, perhaps more hotels could ensure that lights in rooms can be turned on only when the room key is inserted in a master switch and therefore are automatically turned off when guests leave the room with their key. And if we want more people at work to take the stairs instead of the elevators, we may want to have elevators skip the first three floors except in cases of emergency or to accommodate those with a physical disability, and we certainly want to take a look at the cleanliness and lighting of the stairway. How about a little music? Social marketers can play a huge role in influencing policymakers and corporations to make these changes.

Changes in corporate policies and business practices: In 2010, the American Beverage Association announced their Clear on Calories initiative in support of First Lady Michelle Obama's anti-obesity campaign. Instead of printing the number of calories per serving on the back of the can in small print, members will print the number in large print on the front of the can—and the number will represent the total calories per container, versus per serving, since most consumers drink the entire can (see Figure 1.3).

Schools: School district policies and offerings can provide channels of distribution for social marketing efforts and contribute significantly in all social arenas: health (e.g., offering healthier options in school cafeterias and regularly scheduled physical activity classes), safety (e.g., requiring students to wear ID badges), environmental protection (e.g., providing recycling containers in each classroom), and community engagement (e.g., offering school gymnasiums for COVID-19 vaccinations).

Information/Education: As mentioned earlier, the line between social marketing and information/education is actually a clear one, with education serving a useful tool for the social marketer but one rarely working alone. Most often, education is used to communicate information and/or build skills but does not give the same attention and rigor to creating and sustaining behavior adoption. It primarily applies only one of the four marketing intervention tools, that of promotion. Many in the field agree that when the information is motivating and "new" (e.g., the finding that secondhand tobacco smoke increases the risk of sudden infant death syndrome), it can move a market from inaction—even resistance—to action very quickly. This, however, is unfortunately not typical. Consider the fact that death threats for tobacco use have been posted

FIGURE 1.3 ■ Making the Calories Per Container More Obvious

Source: Author photo.

right on cigarette packs for decades, and yet WHO estimates that 1 billion youth and adults (ages 15 and older) worldwide still smoke cigarettes.[29] Marketing (reducing barriers and offering benefits in exchange for behaviors) has often been missing in action.

Media: News and entertainment media exert a powerful influence on individual behaviors, as they shape values, are relied on for current events and trends, and create social norms. Many argue, for example, that the casual and sensational attitude of movies and television toward sex has been a major contributor to the problems we see among young people today.[30] On the flip side, the media were a powerful factor influencing people to donate time and resources to victims of the earthquake in Haiti, the tsunami in Japan, the shootings at Sandyhook Elementary school in Connecticut, the severe and destructive hurricane in New Jersey, and the brutal killing of George Floyd.

SOCIAL MARKETING UPSTREAM AND MIDSTREAM

As noted earlier, many believe that to date we have been placing too much of the burden for improving the status of social issues on individual behavior change and that social marketers should direct some of their efforts to influencing upstream factors and midstream influentials. We agree (See Box 1.2 for examples of audiences midstream and upstream.).

BOX 1.2

Examples of Potential Midstream and Upstream Audiences to Influence

Potential Midstream Audiences	Potential Upstream Audiences
Family members	Elected officials
Friends	Corporations
Neighbors	Media
Colleagues	Law enforcement
Health care providers	Celebrities
Pharmacists	School districts
Teachers	Nonprofit organizations
Librarians	Government agency directors
Community leaders	City and county governmental officials
Church members	State officers
Checkout clerks at retail stores	

Alan Andreasen describes this expanded role of social marketing well:

> Social marketing is about making the world a better place for everyone—not just for investors or foundation executives. And, as I argue throughout this book, the same basic principles that can induce a 12-year-old in Bangkok or Leningrad to get a Big Mac and a caregiver in Indonesia to start using oral dehydration solutions for diarrhea can also be used to influence politicians, media figures, community activists, law officers and judges, foundation officials, and other individuals whose actions are needed to bring about widespread, long-lasting positive social change.[31]

Consider the issue of the spread of COVID-19. *Downstream*, social marketers have focused on increasing protective behaviors among citizens including: wear a mask; social distance at least 6 feet apart; limit indoor gatherings to family members and outdoor gatherings to no more than 10; wash your hands frequently for at least 20 seconds; get tested if you are feeling sick; and get vaccinated. *Midstream* influencers have included healthcare providers encouraging their patients and colleagues to practice the protective behaviors; family members encouraging spouses to get vaccinated and their children to wear a mask; employers requesting that employees stay at home if feeling sick and offering hybrid work schedules to reduce employee contact; and teachers ensuring that students are sitting at least 6 feet apart and wearing their mask. And *Upstream* entities have promoted and established protective practices such as airlines and transit agencies requiring masks when onboard; retail stores requesting that customers at checkout lanes practice social distancing, guided by floor stickers placed 6 feet apart; universities requiring proof of vaccination in order for students to attend classes; restaurants limiting the number of indoor diners; healthcare clinics putting signs on chairs in waiting rooms to ensure patients were seated 6 feet apart; and pharmacies providing vaccines, many without appointments.

The marketing process and principles are the same as those used for influencing individuals: utilizing a customer orientation, establishing clear behavior objectives and target goals, conducting audience research, crafting a position statement, developing a marketing intervention mix, and conducting monitoring and evaluation efforts. Only the priority audience has changed.[32]

CHAPTER SUMMARY

Social marketing is a process that uses marketing principles and techniques to influence priority audience behaviors that will benefit society as well as the individual. This strategically oriented discipline relies on creating, communicating, delivering, and exchanging offerings that have positive value for individuals, clients, partners, and society at large.[33]

There are a few important differences between social marketing and commercial marketing. Social marketers focus on influencing behavior for societal gain, whereas commercial marketers focus on selling goods and services at a financial gain for the organization. Commercial marketers position their products against those of other companies, while the social marketer competes with the audience's current behavior and its associated benefits.

Social marketing is often confused or equated with several other related *disciplines* (nonprofit marketing, public sector marketing, education and health communications), emerging behavior change *theories and frameworks* (behavioral economics, nudge, social change, community-based social marketing, community-based prevention marketing), and popular *promotional tactics* (social media, cause promotion).

Social marketing principles and techniques are most often used to improve public health, prevent injuries, protect the environment, increase community engagement, and enhance financial well-being. Those engaged in social marketing activities include professionals in public sector agencies, nonprofit organizations, corporate marketing departments and advertising, public relations, and market research firms. A social marketing title is rare, and social marketing is most likely to fall within the responsibility of a program manager or community relations or communications professional.

Other approaches to behavior change and impacting social issues include technological innovations, scientific discoveries, economic pressures, laws, improved infrastructures, changes in corporate business practices, new school policies and curricula, public education, and the media. Many agree that influencing these factors and audiences is well within the purview of social marketers—and even their responsibility

We end this chapter with one of several Marketing Dialogues that feature discourses among practitioners seeking to shape, evolve, and transform this discipline.

MARKETING DIALOGUE

When Is Social Marketing "Social Marketing"?

In February 2010, a member of the Georgetown Social Marketing Listserve of 2,000-plus members sent a message with the subject line "To Stir the Pot." The message included a link to an announcement of a new type of speed bump unveiled in West Vancouver, Canada, one intended to persuade motorists to slow down in the vicinity of an elementary school. A pavement painting appears to rise up as the driver gets closer to it, reaching a full 3D image of a child playing, creating the illusion that the approaching driver will soon hit the child. As anticipated, several members were adamant that this effort was not social marketing: "This is not marketing. Where's the exchange? What does the driver get [benefit] in exchange for slowing down?" Counterarguments stressed that "by slowing down [the cost], the driver gets a great benefit—a reduced probability of hitting a child!" Some were troubled by unintended secondary effects ("cultivating resentful drivers not liking to be tricked"), and others weren't impressed with the potential efficacy, convinced that "it might work once but then wouldn't be sustainable." A few felt it met the basic criteria for social marketing: "Since social marketing's basic purpose is to change behavior for the good or betterment of society as a whole, I think this initiative seems to fit well into that criteria. However, I question whether or not it will work."

The authors of this text offer the following opinions on common questions and reactions, such as whether an effort is—or is not—social marketing. As will be apparent, we make a distinction between what defines social marketing, and what are its best practices:

- *Does the effort have to use all 4Ps in order to be called social marketing?* No, but your efforts will be more successful when you at least consider all four intervention tools to overcome audience barriers, increase benefits, consider audience-reported motivators, upstage the competition, and engage key influencers.
- *Does there have to be a narrowly defined and priority audience segment?* No, but this is also a best practice based on there being very few homogeneous populations, and the fact that different segments within these populations have different barriers and benefits and therefore require different interventions.
- *Is a communications-only campaign a social marketing campaign?* It might be. A campaign that is intended to influence a behavior (e.g., putting infants on their back to sleep) to benefit individuals and society (e.g., prevent sudden infant death syndrome) but uses only words (e.g., "Back to Sleep" printed on the strip of a newborn diaper) meets the basic criteria for a social marketing effort. However, it is more likely to be successful if other influence tools are used as well (e.g., demonstrations as part of a free class for new moms at a local hospital).
- *What needs to be present for an effort to be called social marketing?* An effort can be considered a social marketing effort when it is intended to influence a priority audience

behavior to benefit society as well as the individual. And we should keep in mind that the priority audience may be a school district or corporation upstream.

DISCUSSION QUESTIONS AND EXERCISES

1. How does social marketing, as described in this chapter, differ from what you thought it was in the past?
2. Share an example of a social marketing effort that you are aware of.
3. What is the biggest distinction between social marketing and commercial marketing?
4. How does social marketing differ from education? Health communications? Social media? Behavioral economics?
5. Reflect back on the Case Highlight. What was the key to success in influencing addicts to come to the police station for help?

2 10-STEP STRATEGIC PLANNING MODEL

LEARNING OBJECTIVES

Upon completion of this chapter, the reader should be able to:

2.1 List and explain the 10 steps to developing a compelling strategic social marketing plan.

2.2 Explain why systematic planning is important.

2.3 Describe how marketing research fits into the process.

Although most agree that having a formal, detailed plan for a social marketing effort "would be nice," that practice doesn't appear to be the norm. Social marketer Heidi Keller is eager for this to become a norm. "I find the social marketing 10-step model has a galvanizing effect on groups and coalitions that come together around a common goal. It is a logical, step-by-step process that makes sense. It provides a clear roadmap for how the project will be conducted, and the idea that their work will involve continuous monitoring reassures the team that their efforts will be measured and refined along the way as needed."[1]

We begin this chapter with an inspiring case that demonstrates the positive potential return on your investment in the planning process.

CASE HIGHLIGHT
WATERSENSE—AN EPA PARTNERSHIP PROGRAM

Source: WaterSense.

(2006–2020)[2]

Background

WaterSense® is a partnership program developed by the U.S. Environmental Protection Agency (EPA) with a *purpose* to make water saving easy and a *focus* on a label indicating certification as a water-efficient product. Water conservation is a growing concern in the United States, with water managers in at least 40 states expecting local, statewide, or regional water shortages to occur over the next few years.[3] WaterSense partners with manufacturers, distributors, and utilities to bring WaterSense-labeled products to the market, place, and also works with organizations that certify irrigation professionals to promote water-efficient irrigation practices. The program strategy is similar to EPA's successful ENERGY STAR® program that influences consumers to choose appliances, lightbulbs, computers, and more with the ENERGY STAR® label.

Priority Audiences and Desired Behaviors

The *priority consumer audience* are homeowners, especially those interested in saving money on their water bill, contributing to the environment, and making "green" purchases or behaviors when the choice is easy. The desired *behavior* is to choose water-consuming products for the home or yard that bear the WaterSense label and practice water-saving tips, such as turning off the water when shaving or brushing teeth.

Although the focus of this highlight is on consumers, the program also includes homebuilders, manufacturers, retailers, and distributors, utilities, commercial and institutional facilities, and irrigation professionals.

Audience Insights

Prior to launch, EPA conducted focus groups to help develop the WaterSense brand and further understand water-efficient product issues. This early research explored purchasing behaviors regarding water-using fixtures as well as preferences for water efficiency promotional messages and taglines.[4] In 2021, the program conducted additional quantitative research to evaluate brand awareness, attitudes toward water efficiency, and experience of consumers that had purchased WaterSense-labeled products. The online survey also identified barriers, benefits, and motivators related to the purchase of water-efficient products.[5] Findings showed aided brand awareness of 31% and also confirmed the value of having a label to look for when purchasing products. The 2021 research also reaffirmed the need shown in the original research to assure potential buyers that the products would also perform well (e.g., showerheads and faucets would still have adequate water pressure; toilets flush properly).

A pilot test in Atlanta, Georgia, helped verify consumer benefits when American Standard Brands provided WaterSense-labeled toilets, faucets, and showerheads to 21 volunteer households. Using detailed water usage reports, it was determined that participating households experienced an average reduction of 18%–27% in total water use, all without any noticeable difference in water pressure or performance. Families reported strong satisfaction with the fixtures, most commenting they didn't notice a difference in water pressure, and many families commenting they appreciated the attractive styling, greater comfort, and increased functionality of the WaterSense products.[6]

These findings helped to confirm and strengthen the brand's marketing intervention mix strategy going forward.

Marketing Intervention Mix Strategies

Product

Major consumer product categories for certification and labeling include toilets, faucets, showerheads, flushing urinals, spray sprinkler bodies, and irrigation controllers that use weather or soil moisture conditions to control watering, turning the system on and off to tailor watering schedules to actual conditions. In order for a product to receive certification and display the WaterSense label, they are certified by a third party to ensure that the product conforms to WaterSense criteria for efficiency, performance, and label use. Certifiers also conduct periodic market surveillance.

Price

Strategies emphasize savings on water bills. For example:

- "Bathrooms are the main source of water use in homes, accounting for more than half of residential indoor water consumption."[7]
- "Consumers can reduce their water and energy bills by as much as 30% by using WaterSense-labeled products."[8]
- "By replacing old, inefficient toilets with WaterSense-labeled models, the average family can reduce water used for toilets at least 20%—that's 13,000 gallons of water savings for your home every year! They could also save more than $170 per year in water and sewer costs, and $3,400 over the lifetime of the toilets."[9]
- "The average family spends nearly $1,100 per year in water costs but can save nearly $350 from retrofitting with WaterSense-labeled fixtures and ENERGY STAR®-qualified appliances."[10]

Contributions to the environment are made concrete: "Nationally, if all old, inefficient toilets in the United States were replaced with WaterSense-labeled models, we could save 360 billion gallons of water per year across the country or the amount of water that flows over Niagara Falls in about 9 days."[11] A "Rebate Finder" on the WaterSense website provides information on rebate programs for purchases of WaterSense products, helping consumers find programs in their local communities. In 2020, more than 257,000 searches were conducted on the Rebate Finder tool.

Place

All major U.S. manufacturers of bathroom fixtures pursue the WaterSense label for their water-efficient products. This means WaterSense-labeled products are available at all major big box retail and plumbing showrooms nationwide, as well as online, in a wide variety of styles, colors, and price points. WaterSense-labeled products can easily be found nationwide as there are more than 36,000 product models in the marketplace.

Promotion

Key messages, as mentioned in the prior *Price* section, emphasize water and cost savings. There are also key messages assuring that products perform as well or better than their less-efficient counterparts, and that this is determined by an independent, third-party verification.

WaterSense benefits from earned media including public service announcements; features on programs such as *CNN*, *Today*, and *Good Morning America*; and articles in newspapers including *USA Today* and magazines including *Newsweek*, *National Geographic*, and *Consumer Reports*. The program owes much of its promotional success to the more than 2,100 utilities, government entities, nonprofit organizations, manufacturers, retailers, and builders who have helped promote the WaterSense label and spread the word about the importance of water efficiency (see Figure 2.1.).

FIGURE 2.1 ■ A Graphic in the WaterSense Toolkit That Can Be Used by Partners Such as a Utility Bill Statement Stuffer

Source: Colehour + Cohen.

FIGURE 2.2 ■ Total WaterSense-Labeled Product Models

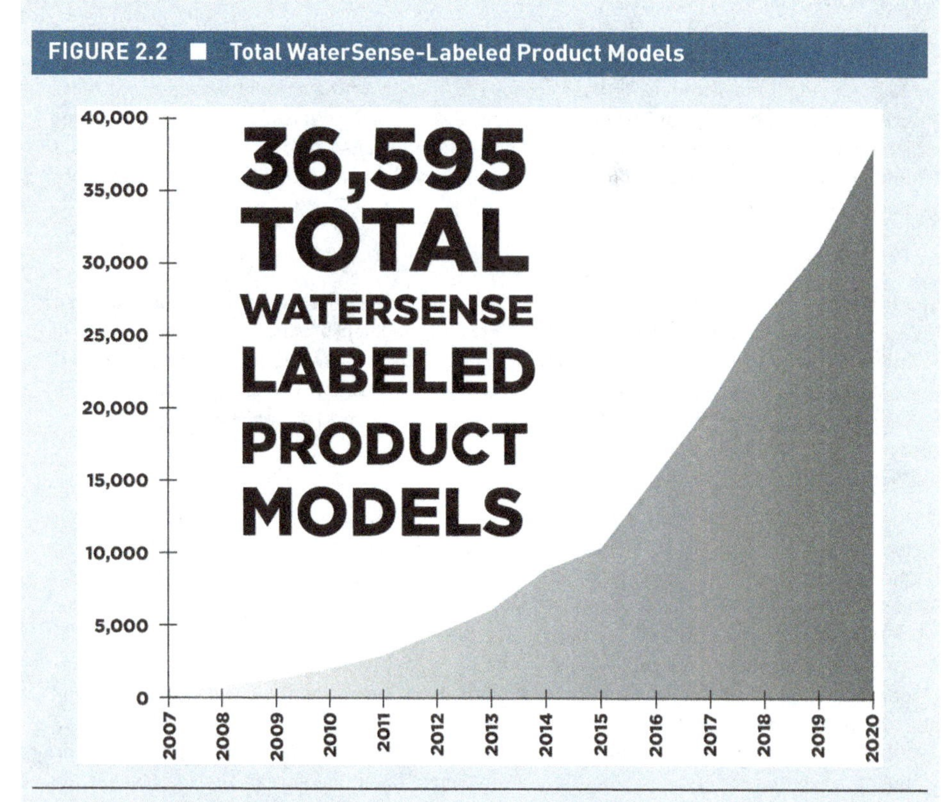

Source: EPA WaterSense.

Social media tactics include utilizing Facebook and Twitter, engaging nearly 37,000 fans. In 2012, WaterSense hosted its first annual "Fix a Leak Week" Twitter party. In 2016, the Twitter party garnered more than 2,200 contributors, with 3.5 million impressions. During COVID-19, partners pivoted to promote Fix a Leak Week with additional tactics including online webinars and workshops to show people how to find and fix household leaks.

Results

In terms of *outcomes*, as indicated in Figure 2.2, certifications for WaterSense-labeled products have accelerated steadily over the past four years, reaching more than 36,000 product models labeled in 2020, as all major manufacturers have water-efficient product lines with WaterSense-labeled fixtures.

What about *impact*? A 2020 Accomplishments Report estimates that since the program's launch in 2006, WaterSense has helped consumers save 5.3 trillion gallons of water and more than $108 billion in water and energy bills. And use of these products since 2006 has contributed to reductions of 603 billion kilowatt-hours of electricity.[12]

A 10-STEP PLANNING MODEL

Our first of several primers in this book is presented in Table 2.1, outlining the 10 distinct and important steps to developing a strategic social marketing plan. They are described briefly in this chapter, with Chapters 5-16 providing more detailed information on each step. Worksheets are presented in Appendix A (a downloadable version is available at www.socialmarketingservice.com), and sample plans using this model are presented in Appendix B. It is noted that other planning models of interest include: The Logic Model, CDCenergy, PRECEDE-PROCEED, People and Place Model of Social Change, and the Creative Brief.

Although this outline for the most part mirrors marketing plans developed by product managers in for-profit organizations, three aspects of the model stand out:

1. Priority audiences are selected before objectives and goals are established. In social marketing, our objective is to influence the behavior of a priority audience, making it important to identify the priority segment (e.g., seniors) before determining the specific behavior the plan will promote (e.g., joining a walking group).
2. The competition isn't identified in the situation analysis. Because we haven't yet decided the specific behavior that will be encouraged, we wait until Step 4, when we conduct audience research related to the desired behavior.
3. Goals are the quantifiable measures of the plan (e.g., number of seniors you want to join a walking group) versus the broader purpose of the plan. In this model, the plan's purpose statement (e.g., increase physical activity among seniors) is included in Step 1. Certainly, labels for any part of the plan can and probably should be changed to fit the organization's culture and existing planning models. The important thing is that each step be taken and developed sequentially.

TABLE 2.1 ■ Social Marketing Planning Primer

Executive Summary

Brief summary highlighting the social issue the plan is intended to impact, and its purpose, focus, priority audience(s), major marketing objectives and goals, desired positioning, marketing mix strategies (4Ps), and evaluation, budget, and implementation plans.

1.0 Social issue, DEI considerations, organization(s), background, purpose, and focus

- **1.1** Social issue plan is intended to impact
- **1.2** Diversity, equity, and inclusion (DEI) considerations relevant to the social issue being addressed
- **1.3** Organization(s) involved in developing and implementing plan
- **1.4** Background information leading to the development of this plan
- **1.5** Purpose of this effort, relative to the social issue
- **1.6** Plan focus, approach that will be used to contribute to the purpose

2.0 Situation analysis (SWOT)

- **2.1** Organizational strengths (e.g., management priority)
- **2.2** Organizational weaknesses (e.g., funding limitations)
- **2.3** External opportunities (e.g., levels of societal concern)
- **2.4** External threats (e.g., advocates for competing issues)
- **2.5** Key learnings from a review of similar prior efforts and additional exploratory market research

3.0 Priority audiences

- **3.1** Descriptions of priority audience(s), including demographics, geographics, readiness to change, relevant behaviors, values and lifestyle, social networks, and community assets relative to the plan's purpose and focus
- **3.2** Additional important audiences that you will need to influence as well

4.0 Behavior objectives and target goals

- **4.1** Behavior objective, one that the priority audience(s) will be influenced to adopt
- **4.2** Knowledge objective, what they need to know in order to be more likely to act
- **4.3** Belief objective, what they need to believe in order to be more likely to act
- **4.4** SMART (specific, measurable, achievable, relevant, time-bound) goals quantifying levels of desired behavior change outcomes as well as changes in knowledge, beliefs, and behavior intent

5.0 Priority audience barriers, benefits, motivators; the competition; and influential others

- **5.1** Perceived barriers and costs associated with adopting the desired behavior
- **5.2** Desired benefits the priority audience wants in exchange for performing the desired behavior
- **5.3** Potential strategies the priority audience identifies that might motivate them to perform the behavior
- **5.4** Competing behaviors/forces/choices
- **5.5** Others who have influence with the priority audience

6.0 Positioning statement

How you want the priority audience to see the targeted behavior, highlighting unique benefits and the value proposition

TABLE 2.1 ■ Social Marketing Planning Primer

Executive Summary

7.0 Marketing intervention mix (4Ps)

7.1 Product: *Benefits from performing behaviors and features of goods or services offered to assist adoption*

Core product: Audience-desired benefits promised in exchange for performing the behavior (e.g., native plants require less maintenance, fertilizing, and watering)

Actual product: Features of any goods or services offered/promoted (e.g., 100 native plants to choose from)

Augmented product: Additional goods and services to help in performing the behavior or increase appeal (e.g., workshops on how to design a native plant garden)

7.2 Price: *Costs that will be associated with adopting the behavior and price-related tactics to reduce costs*

Costs: money, time, physical effort, psychological, lack of pleasure

Price-related tactics to decrease costs and increase benefits:

- Monetary incentives (e.g., discounts, rebates)
- Nonmonetary incentives (e.g., pledges, recognition, appreciation)
- Monetary disincentives (e.g., fines)
- Nonmonetary disincentives (e.g., negative public visibility)

7.3 Place: *Convenient access*

Creating convenient opportunities for audience(s) to engage in the desired behaviors and/or access goods and services, including developing partnerships for distribution channels and reinforcing desired behaviors

7.4 Promotion: *Persuasive communications highlighting the offer: product, price, and place strategies*

Decisions regarding messages, messengers, creative strategies, and communication channels

Consideration of incorporating prompts for sustainability

8.0 Plan for monitoring and evaluation

8.1 Purpose for evaluation

8.2 Audience for whom evaluation is being conducted

8.3 What will be measured: inputs, outputs, outcomes (from Step 4), and (potentially) impact and return on investment

8.4 How measures will be taken

8.5 When measurements will be taken

8.6 How much evaluation will cost

9.0 Budget

Costs of implementing the marketing plan, including additional research and monitoring/evaluation plan

Any anticipated incremental revenues, cost savings, or partner contributions

10.0 Plan for implementation and sustaining behaviors

Who will do what, when, for how much—including partners and their roles (pilot projects are strongly encouraged prior to full implementation)

Note: This is an iterative, nonlinear process, with numerous feedback loops (e.g., barriers to a behavior may be determined to be so significant that a new behavior is chosen). Marketing research will be needed to develop most steps, especially exploratory research for Steps 1 and 2, formative research for Steps 3 through 6, and pretesting for finalizing Step 7.

Developed by Philip Kotler and Nancy Lee with input from Alan Andreasen, Carol Bryant, Craig Lefebvre, Bob Marshall, Mike Newton-Ward, Michael Rothschild, and Bill Smith in 2008.

The Importance of Diversity, Equity, and Inclusion Considerations in the Social Marketing Planning Process

Before we jump into the details of the steps, it is important that we reflect upon the need to include a focus on diversity, equity, and inclusion (DEI) in any social marketing program. Traditional marketing and advertising efforts in the United States are built upon the same structures, institutions, and systems that have perpetuated racism. In order to break this cycle, we need to be sure that we are reflecting upon DEI issues during each stage of the social marketing planning process. A recent open letter by Sonya Grier and Sonja Martin Pool, 2020, published in Social Marketing Quarterly challenges social marketers to ask themselves these five questions during the planning process:[13]

1. Are we acknowledging the pervasiveness of racism in our individual psyches, culture, systems, and institutions, and building our expertise in racial equity issues, so we understand how they may influence the design, content, or implementation of a particular social marketing intervention?
2. Are we considering the ways in which Whiteness is centered in our framing of the social problem or how we interpret effectiveness in social marketing interventions?
3. Whose narratives are we using to inform the development of social marketing interventions, research, and evaluations?
4. Are we applying concepts and translating approaches from a wide cross-section of disciplines and community partners to develop social marketing strategy?
5. Are we recognizing the unique ways in which targets and other stakeholders experience privilege and oppression as a result of overlapping social stratification?

Applying this thinking can help ensure that social marketing programs are helping move our society forward in the fight against structural racism.

Steps in the planning process are described briefly in the following sections and illustrated using excerpts from a social marketing plan to reduce litter in Washington state.

Step 1: Describe Social Issue, DEI Considerations, Background, Purpose, and Focus

Begin by noting the social issue the project will be addressing (e.g., carbon emissions) and then summarize factors that have led to the development of the plan. What's the problem? What happened? The problem statement may include epidemiological, scientific, or other research data related to a public health crisis (e.g., increases in obesity), a safety concern (e.g., increases in cell phone use while driving), an environmental threat (e.g., climate change), or need for community involvement (e.g., need for more blood donations). The problem may have been precipitated by an unusual event such as increased wildfires or may simply be fulfilling an organization's mandate or mission (e.g., to promote sustainable seafood).

Next, develop a purpose statement that briefly clarifies the benefit of a successful campaign (e.g., improved water quality). Then, from the vast number of factors that might contribute to this purpose, select one focus (e.g., reducing the use of pesticides).

Litter Plan Excerpt: In the early 2000s, it was estimated that every year in Washington state, over 16 million pounds of "stuff" was tossed and blown onto interstate, state, and county roads. Another six million pounds was tossed into parks and recreation areas. Programs funded through the Department of Ecology (Ecology) spent over $4 million each year, but staff estimated that only 25%–35% was picked up. Litter creates an eyesore, harms wildlife and their habitats, and is a potential hazard for motorists, who may be struck by anything from a lit cigarette to an empty bottle of beer, or even a bottle of "trucker's pee." In 2001, Ecology developed a three-year social marketing plan with the *purpose* of decreasing littering and a *focus* on intentional littering on roadways.

Step 2: Conduct a Situation Analysis

Now, relative to the purpose and focus of the plan, conduct a quick audit of factors and forces in the internal and external environments that are anticipated to have some impact on or relevance in subsequent planning decisions. Often referred to as a SWOT (strengths, weaknesses, opportunities, and threats) analysis, this audit recognizes organizational *strengths* to maximize and *weaknesses* to minimize, including factors such as available resources, expertise, management support, current alliances and partners, delivery system capabilities, the agency's reputation, and priority of issues. Then make a similar list of external forces in the marketplace that represent either *opportunities* your plan should take advantage of or *threats* it should prepare for. These forces are typically not within the marketer's control but must be taken into account. Major categories include cultural, technological, natural, demographic, economic, political, and legal forces.[14] Time taken at this point to contact colleagues, query listservs, and conduct a literature—even Google—search for similar campaigns will be well spent. Lessons learned from others regarding what worked and what didn't should help guide plan development, as should reflection on prior similar campaigns conducted by the organization sponsoring this new effort.

Litter Plan Excerpt: The greatest organizational strengths going into the plan development included the state's existing significant fines for littering, social marketing expertise on the team, management support, and other state agency support, including critical involvement and buy-in from the state patrol and Department of Licensing. Weaknesses to minimize included limited financial resources, competing priorities faced by law enforcement (traffic safety issues such as drinking and driving and use of seatbelts), and lack of adequate litter containers in public areas.

External opportunities to take advantage of included the fact that litterers were not always aware of the significant fines for littering (as indicated by formative research), the strong environmental ethic of many citizens, and many businesses that were "part of the problem" but also potential campaign sponsors (e.g., fast-food establishments, beverage companies, and minimarts). Threats to prepare for included the argument that litter was not a priority issue and that litterers were not motivated by environmental concerns.

Step 3: Select Priority Audiences

In this critical step, select the bull's-eye for your marketing efforts. Provide a rich description of your priority audience using characteristics such as stage of change (readiness to act), demographics, geographics, related behaviors, psychographics, social networks, community assets, and size of the market. A marketing plan ideally focuses on a priority audience, although additional secondary markets (e.g., strategic partners and opinion leaders) are often identified and strategies included to influence them as well. As you will read further in Chapter 6, arriving at this decision is a three-step process that involves first segmenting the market (population) into similar groups, then evaluating segments based on a set of criteria, and finally choosing one or more as the focal point for determining a specific desired behavior, positioning, and marketing intervention mix strategies.

Litter Plan Excerpt: Surveys indicate that some of us (about 25%) would never consider littering. Some of us (about 25%) litter most of the time. Almost half of us litter occasionally but can be persuaded not to.[14,15] There were two major audiences for the campaign: litterers and nonlitterers. Priority audiences for littering include the five behavior-related segments creating the majority of intentional litter on roadways: (a) motorists or passengers who toss (1) cigarette butts, (2) alcoholic beverage containers, and (3) food wrappers and other beverage containers out the window, and (b) those who drive pickup trucks and are (1) not properly covering or securing their loads and (2) not cleaning out the backs of their pickup trucks before driving on roadways. Campaign plan strategies were also developed and aimed at nonlitterers traveling on Washington state roadways to influence their reporting of littering.

Step 4: Set Behavior Objectives and Goals

Social marketing plans always include a *behavior* objective—something we want to influence the priority audience to do. It may be something we want them to accept (e.g., start composting food waste), reject (e.g., purchasing a gas blower), modify (e.g., water deeply and less frequently), abandon (e.g., using fertilizers with harmful herbicides), switch (e.g., to cooking oils lower in saturated fat), or continue (e.g., donating blood on an annual basis). Often our research indicates that there may also be something the audience needs to know or believe in order to be motivated to act. *Knowledge objectives* include information or facts we want the market to be aware of (e.g., motor oil poured down the street drain goes directly to the lake)—including information that might make them more willing to perform the desired behavior (e.g., where they can properly dispose of motor oil). *Belief objectives* relate more to feelings and attitudes. Home gardeners may know the pesticide they are using is harmful, and even that it works its way into rivers and streams, but they may believe that using it once or twice a year won't make "that much difference."

This is also the point in the marketing plan where we establish quantifiable measures (goals) relative to our objectives. Ideally, goals are established for behavior objectives, as well as any knowledge and belief objectives—ones that are specific, measurable, attainable, relevant, and time-bound (SMART). You should recognize that what you determine here will guide your subsequent decisions regarding marketing intervention strategies. It will also have significant implications for your budgets and will provide a clear direction for evaluation measures later in the planning process.

Litter Plan Excerpt: Campaign strategies were developed to support three separate objectives: (a) a short-term objective to create *awareness* that there were significant fines associated with littering and that there was a (new) toll-free number to report littering, (b) a midterm objective to convince litterers to *believe* that their littering would be noticed and that they could be caught, and (c) a long-term objective to influence litterers to *change their behaviors*: to dispose of litter properly, cover and secure pickup truck loads, and clean out the backs of their trucks before driving on roadways. Telephone surveys were conducted to establish a baseline of public awareness and beliefs about the littering, and field research was done to measure current quantities and types of litter.[16]

Step 5: Identify Priority Audience Insights

At this point, you know who you want to influence and what you want them to do. You (theoretically) even know how many, or what percentage, of your priority audience you are hoping to persuade (goal). Before rushing to develop a positioning and marketing intervention mix for this audience, however, take the time, effort, and resources to understand what your priority audience is currently doing or prefers to do (the competition) and what real and/or perceived barriers they have to this proposed behavior, what benefits they want in exchange, and what would motivate them to "buy" it. In other words, what do *they* think of your idea? What are some of the reasons they are not currently doing this or don't want to (barriers)? What do they come up with when asked "What can you imagine would be in it for you to do this behavior (benefits)?" Do they think any of your potential strategies would work for them, or do they have better ideas (motivators)? Their answers should be treated like gold and considered a gift.

Litter Plan Excerpt: Focus groups with motorists who admitted to littering (yes, they came) indicated several perceived barriers to the desired behaviors of disposing of litter properly, covering pickup loads, and cleaning out backs of trucks: "I don't want to keep the cigarette butt in the car. It stinks." "If I get caught with an open container of beer in my car, I'll get a hefty fine. I'd rather take the chance and toss it." "I didn't even know there was stuff in the back of my truck. Someone in the parking lot keeps using it as a garbage can!" "The cords I have found to secure my load are just not that effective." "What's the problem, anyway? Doesn't this give prisoners a way to do community service?"

And what strategies can they imagine and would motivate them? "You'd have to convince me that anyone notices my littering and that I could get caught." "I had no idea the fine for littering a lit cigarette butt could be close to a thousand dollars! And if I thought I could get fined, I wouldn't do it." (Notice their concerns were not about helping keep Washington green!)

Step 6: Develop Positioning Statement

In brief, a positioning statement describes how you want your priority audience to see the behavior you want them to buy relative to competing behaviors. Branding is one strategy to help secure this desired position. Both the positioning statement and brand identity are inspired by your description of your priority audience and its list of competitors, barriers, benefits, and motivators to action. The positioning statement will also guide the development of a strategic marketing intervention mix. This theory was first popularized in the 1980s by advertising executives Al Ries and Jack Trout, who contended that positioning starts with a product, but not what you do to a product: "Positioning is what you do to the mind of the prospect. That is, you position the product in the mind of the prospect."[17] We would add, "where you want it to be."[18]

Litter Plan Excerpt: "We want motorists to believe that they will be noticed and caught when littering and that fines are steeper than they thought. In the end, we want them to believe disposing of litter properly is a better, especially cheaper, option."

Step 7: Develop Strategic Marketing Intervention Mix (4Ps)

This section of the plan describes your product, price, place, and promotional strategies. As noted in Chapter 1, the 4Ps are the intervention tools, those you consider to influence, even help, your priority audience to adopt the desired behavior. Some suggest adding to this list other important components of a social marketing plan that start with a *p* (where each of these components fit in this strategic model is noted in parentheses): pilot (an implementation strategy); partners (potential messengers, funding sources, distribution channels, and/or implementation strategies); prompts (potential services, and promotions); and policymakers (a priority audience or influential others). The Marketing Dialogue at the end of this chapter discusses this in more detail.

It is the blend of these elements that constitutes your marketing intervention mix, also thought of as the determinants (independent variables) used to influence behaviors (the dependent variable). Be sure to develop the marketing intervention mix in the sequence presented, beginning with the product and ending with a promotional strategy. After all, the promotional tool is the one you count on to ensure that priority audiences know about your product, its price, and how to access it. These decisions obviously need to be made before promotional planning.

Product

Describe core, actual, and augmented product levels. The *core product* consists of benefits the priority audience values that they believe they will experience as a result of acting and that you will highlight. Your list of desired benefits and potential motivators and positioning statement are a great resource for developing this component of the product platform. The *actual product* describes, in more detail, features of the desired behavior (e.g., how a pickup load should be secured) and any tangible goods and services that will support the desired behavior. The *augmented product* refers to any additional tangible goods and/or services that you will include in your offer or that will be promoted to the priority audience (e.g., guaranteed anonymity when reporting litterers).

Litter Plan Excerpt: It was determined that a new service, a toll-free number, would be launched for motorists who witnessed people throwing trash from vehicles or losing materials from unsecured loads. When they called the hotline, they would be asked to report the license number, a description of the vehicle, time of day, type of litter, whether it was thrown from the passenger's or driver's side of the car, and approximate location. Within a couple of days, the registered owner of the car would receive a letter from the state patrol, alerting the owner, for example, that "a citizen noticed a lit cigarette butt being tossed out the driver's side of your car at 3 p.m. on Interstate 5, near the University District. This is to inform you that if we had seen you, we would have pulled you over and issued a ticket for $1,025." All "Litter and it will hurt" campaign materials, from road signs (see Figure 2.3) to litterbags, stickers, and posters, would feature the campaign slogan and the litter hotline telephone number.

FIGURE 2.3 ■ Road Sign for Reporting Littering

Source: Courtesy of Washington State Department of Ecology.

Price

Mention here any program-related *monetary costs* (fees) the priority audience will pay (e.g., cost of a gun lockbox) and, if offered, any *monetary incentives* such as discount coupons or rebates that you will make available. Also note any *monetary disincentives* that will be emphasized (e.g., fines for not buckling up), *nonmonetary incentives* such as public recognition (e.g., plaques for backyard sanctuaries), and *nonmonetary disincentives* such as negative public visibility (e.g., publication of names of elected officials owing back taxes). As you will read in Chapter 11 on pricing, arriving at these strategies begins with identifying major costs the priority audience associates with adopting the behavior—both monetary (e.g., paying for a commercial car wash vs. doing it at home) and nonmonetary (e.g., the time it takes to drive to the car wash).

Litter Plan Excerpt: Fines for littering would be highlighted in a variety of communication channels, with an emphasis on desired behaviors (lit cigarette butts $1,025, food or beverage container $103, unsecured load $194, and illegal dumping $1,000–$5,000 plus jail time), with notes that fines would be subject to change and might vary locally. The image in Figure 2.2 was used on billboards, posters, and litterbags.

Place

In social marketing, place is primarily where and when the priority audience will perform the desired behavior and/or acquire any campaign-related tangible goods (e.g., rain barrels offered by a city utility) or receive any services (e.g., tobacco quitline hours and days of the week) associated with the campaign. Place is also referred to as a delivery system or distribution channel, and you will include here any strategies related to managing these channels. Distribution channels are distinct from communication channels, which are where promotional messages will appear (e.g., billboards, outreach workers, and websites).

Litter Plan Excerpt: The hotline would be available 24 hours a day, seven days a week, as would a website where littering could be reported (www.litter.wa.gov/c_hotline.html). Litterbags (printed with fines for littering) were to be distributed at a variety of locations,

FIGURE 2.4 ■ Washington State's Litter Campaign Focused on a Hotline and Stiff Fines

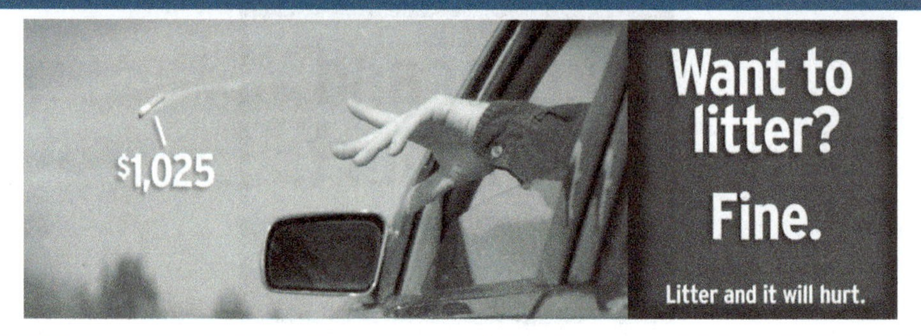

Source: Courtesy of Washington State Department of Ecology.

including fast-food restaurant windows, car rental agencies, and vehicle licensing offices. A litterbag was also enclosed with each letter sent in response to a litter hotline report.

Promotion

In this section, describe persuasive communication strategies, covering decisions related to *key messages* (what you want to communicate), *messengers* (any spokespersons, sponsors, partners, actors, or influential others you will use to deliver messages), *creative elements* (any logos, taglines, and graphics), and *communication channels* (where promotional messages will appear). Information and decisions to this point will guide your development of the promotional plan—one that will ensure that your target audiences know about the offer (product, price, and place), believe they will experience the benefits you promise, and are inspired to act.

Litter Plan Excerpt: Communication channels selected to spread the "Litter and it will hurt" message included roadway signs, television, radio, publicity, videos, special events, websites, and messages on state collateral pieces, including litterbags, posters, stickers, and decals. There were even special signs to be placed at truck weigh stations targeting one of the state's "most disgusting" forms of litter—an estimated 25,000 jugs of urine found on the roadsides each year (see Figure 2.5).

Step 8: Develop Evaluation Plan

Your evaluation plan outlines what measures will be used to evaluate the success of your effort and how and when these measurements will be taken. It is derived after first clarifying the purpose and audience for the evaluation and referring back to goals that have been established for the campaign—the desired levels of changes in behavior, knowledge, and beliefs established in Step 4. This plan is developed before devising a budget plan, ensuring that funds for this activity are included. Measures typically fall into one of four categories: *input* measures (resources contributed to the campaign), *output* measures (campaign activities), *outcome* measures (audience responses and changes in knowledge, beliefs, and behavior), and *impact* measures (contributions to the effort's purpose, e.g., improved water quality).

FIGURE 2.5 ■ Washington State's Litter Poster at Truck Weigh Stations

Source: Washington State Department of Ecology.

Litter Plan Excerpt: A baseline survey of Washington state residents was planned to measure and then track (a) awareness of the stiff fines associated with littering and (b) awareness of the toll-free number for reporting littering. Internal records would be used to assess the number of calls to the hotline, and periodic litter composition surveys would be used to measure changes in the targeted categories of roadway litter.

Step 9: Establish Budgets and Funding

On the basis of draft product benefits and features, price incentives, distribution channels, proposed promotions, and the evaluation plan, summarize funding requirements and compare them with available and potential funding sources. Outcomes at this step may necessitate revisions of strategies, the audience prioritized, goals, timeframes, or the need to secure additional funding sources. Only a final budget is presented in this section, delineating secured funding sources and reflecting any contributions from partners.

Litter Plan Excerpt: Major costs would be associated with campaign advertising (television, radio, and billboards). Additional major costs would include road signs, signage at governmental

FIGURE 2.6 ■ Summary of Marketing Planning Steps and Research Input

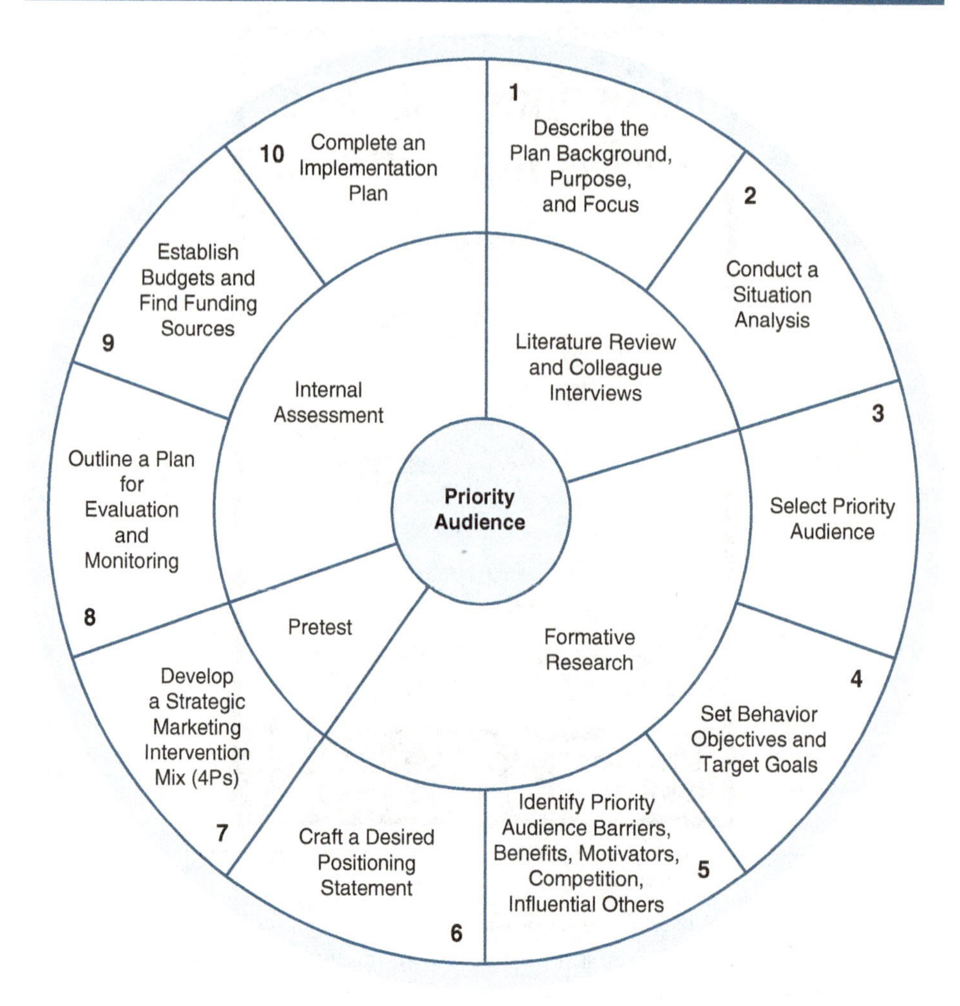

facilities, and operation of the toll-free litter hotline number. Funding for litterbag printing and distribution and retail signage was anticipated to be provided by media partners and corporate sponsors who would augment advertising media buys.

Step 10: Complete Implementation Plan

The plan is wrapped up with a document that specifies *who* will do *what, when,* and for *how much.* It transforms the marketing strategies into specific actions. Some consider this section "the real marketing plan," as it provides a clear picture of marketing activities (outputs), responsibilities, time frames, and budgets. Some even use this as a stand-alone piece that they can then share with important internal groups. Typically, detailed activities are provided for the first year of a campaign along with broader references for subsequent years.

Litter Plan Excerpt: Three phases were identified for this three-year campaign plan. In summary, first-year efforts concentrated on awareness building. Years 2 and 3 would sustain this effort as well as add elements key to belief and behavior change.

A news release from the Department of Ecology in May 2005 regarding the results of Washington state's litter prevention campaign touted the headline "Ounce of Prevention Is Worth 4 Million Pounds of Litter." The results from a litter survey three years into the campaign found a decline from 8,322 tons to 6,315 tons (24%) compared with a baseline survey. This reduction of more than 2,000 tons represented four million pounds less litter on Washington's roadways. And calls to the hotline were averaging 15,000 a year.

WHY IS SYSTEMATIC PLANNING IMPORTANT?

Only through the systematic process of clarifying your plan's *purpose and focus* and *analyzing the marketplace* are you able to select an appropriate priority audience for your efforts? Only through taking the time to *understand your audience* are you able to establish realistic behavior *objectives and goals*? Only through developing an *integrated strategy* will you create real behavior change—an approach that recognizes that such change usually takes more than communications (promotion) and that you need to establish what product benefits you will be promising, what tangible goods and services are needed to support desired behaviors, what pricing incentives and disincentives it will take, and how to make access easy? Only by taking time up front to establish how you will measure your performance will you ensure that this critical step is budgeted for and implemented?

The temptation, and often the practice, is to go straight to advertising or promotional ideas and strategies. This brings up questions such as these:

- How can you know whether ads on the sides of buses (a communication channel) are a good idea if you don't know how long the message needs to be?
- How can you know your slogan (message) if you don't know what you are selling (product)?
- How can you know how to position your product if you don't know what your audience perceives as the benefits and costs of their current behavior compared to the behavior you are promoting?

Although planning is sequential, it might be more accurately described as spiral rather than linear in nature. Each step should be considered a draft, and the planner needs to be flexible, recognizing that there may be a good reason to go back and adjust a prior step before completing the plan. For example:

- Research with priority audiences may reveal that goals are too ambitious, or that the current priority audience should be reconsidered because you may not be able to meet its unique needs or overcome its specific barriers to change with the resources you have.
- What looked like ideal communication channels might turn out to be cost prohibitive or not cost-effective during preparation of the budget.

TABLE 2.2 ■ Aligning Additional and Alternative "Ps" With the 10-Step Planning Model

A. Additional and Alternative "Ps"	B. Aligning With the 4P Intervention Tools Step 7: Strategic Marketing Mix Product, Price, Place, and Promotion	C. Aligning With Other Steps in the 10-STEP Model
Packaging	Product	
Participation		Step 5: Audience insights Step 10: Implementation plan
Partnership		Step 10: Implementation plan
People		Step 3: Priority audience
Perspective		Step 5: Audience insights
Philosophy		Step 5: Audience insights
Physical environment	Place	Step 5: Audience insights
Physical evidence		Step 1: Background, purpose, and focus Step 2: Situation analysis Step 5: Audience insights
Planning		Steps 1–10
Process		Steps 1–10
Proposition	Product, price, place, and promotion	Step 5: Audience insights
Policy		Step 3: Priority audience Step 4: Desired behavior
Positioning		Step 6: Positioning statement
Politics	Promotion (e.g., messengers and messages)	Step 3: Priority audience
Purse strings		Step 9: Budget
Publics		Step 3: Priority audiences Step 5: Audience insights
Public opinion		Step 2: Situation analysis Step 5: Audience insights
Public relations	Promotion	
Press releases	Promotion	

TABLE 2.2 ■ Aligning Additional and Alternative "Ps" With the 10-Step Planning

A. Additional and Alternative "Ps"	B. Aligning With the 4P Intervention Tools Step 7: Strategic Marketing Mix Product, Price, Place, and Promotion	C. Aligning With Other Steps in the 10-STEP Model
Alternatives to 4Ps		
Co-creation		Research and planning approach
Collaboration		Research, planning, and implementation approach
Communication	Promotion	
Creative	Promotion	
Customer benefit	Product (core product)	
Customer-oriented		Step 5: Audience insights

WHERE DOES RESEARCH FIT IN?

You may have questions at this point regarding where marketing research fits into this process, other than at the step noted for conducting research to determine barriers, benefits, motivators, competitors, and influential others. As you will read further in Chapter 3, and as is evident in Figure 2.6, research has a role to play in the development of each step. And properly focused marketing research can make the difference between a brilliant plan and a mediocre one. It is at the core of success at every phase of this planning process, providing critical insights into the priority audience, the marketplace, and organizational realities. For those concerned (already) about the resources available for research, we will discuss in Chapter 3 Alan Andreasen's book *Marketing Research That Won't Break the Bank.*[19]

CHAPTER SUMMARY

Marketing planning is a systematic process, and a 10-step model is recommended for developing social marketing plans. You begin by identifying the social issue your plan will address and clarifying the purpose and focus of your plan. You should be ready to integrate DEI considerations throughout the process. You then move on to analyzing the current situation and environment; identifying priority audiences; establishing marketing objectives and goals; understanding audience barriers, benefits, and motivators as well as competing alternatives and influential others; determining a desired positioning for the offer; designing a strategic marketing intervention mix (4Ps); and then developing evaluation, budget, and implementation plans.

Although planning is sequential, the process is more accurately described as spiral rather than linear—a draft the first time around—as you may need to go back and adjust a prior step before completing the plan. Given the customer-centered nature of all great marketing programs, planning efforts will revolve around the priority audience, and research—both external and internal—will be essential to your success.

MARKETING DIALOGUE

The 4Ps—Aren't There More?

Nancy R. Lee

As presented in this chapter, the 4Ps are *intervention tools*, ones considered and then developed to motivate behavior change, based on audience insights (barriers, benefits, motivators, competition, and influencers). As Mike Rothschild once described, they are the independent variables (product, price, place, and promotion) used to influence the dependent variable (the desired behavior). It is important to note, as well, that these 4Ps do not represent all tools (or Ps) available to the social marketer when developing a strategic social marketing plan. There are also tools for conducting research, choosing priority audiences, selecting desired behaviors, developing a brand, and more. Most of these will be discussed in relevant chapters.

Over the past decades, social marketers have frequently expressed views regarding the limitations of the 4Ps presented in this chapter. We have even had "The Big Debate" regarding the 4Ps at one of the World Social Marketing Conferences. To provide content for this Marketing Dialogue, in the Fall of 2017, I posted a message on the Social Marketing Listserve inviting other social marketers to share their thoughts on additional and alternative "Ps." The list appearing in Table 2.2, Column A, includes ones suggested by Nedra Kline Weinreich, Craig Lefebvre, Stephen Holden, Tom Beall, Jim Mintz, and Ed Maibach. Column B offers a perspective on where the suggestion fits within this 4P framework, and Column C suggests where they are "covered" in the 10-step planning model.

DISCUSSION QUESTIONS AND EXERCISES

1. Reflect back on Table 2.1 (Social Marketing Planning Primer). Review the order of the 10 steps and discuss any that are not in a sequence you are familiar with using, or that you question.

2. Similarly, reflect back on the sequence of determining the 4Ps: product, price, place, and promotion. Why is it recommended they be determined in this order?
3. Reflect back on the litter campaign example. Why did they develop the toll-free number for reporting litterers? If the letter that violators get isn't a ticket, why does it appear that it worked to deter littering?
4. Reflect back on the Marketing Dialogue. What additional "P" have you thought about and where might it fit in this 10-step model?

3 RESEARCH OPTIONS

LEARNING OBJECTIVES

Upon reading this chapter, you should be able to:

3.1 Understand commonly used research terms and their distinctions.

3.2 Identify the major steps involved in developing a research plan.

3.3 Describe a few ways that research can be conducted at a reasonable price point.

Alan Andreasen, a renowned marketing professor and social marketer at Georgetown University, captures the mood of many regarding research with his list of common myths below—coupled with his counterpoints for each:[1]

> Myth 1: "*I'm already doing enough research.*" Almost always, they aren't, but there are simple decision frameworks that will help you find out.
>
> Myth 2: "*Research is only for big decisions.*" Research is not only for big decisions, and sometimes big decisions don't even need it.
>
> Myth 3: "*Market research is simply conducting surveys, and surveys are expensive.*" All research is not surveys, and even surveys can be done inexpensively.
>
> Myth 4: "*Most research is a waste.*" Research can be a waste, but it need not be, especially if you use a systematic approach to developing a plan, beginning with determining key decisions to be made using the research results.

This chapter precedes the in-depth chapters on each of the 10 steps in the planning model, as it is intended to serve as a reference guide, as well as inspire and prepare you to apply appropriate research activities in the development of a social marketing plan. As illustrated in Chapter 2, some form of research is applicable at each step in the planning process. It is notably most critical when exploring audience insights: barriers, benefits, motivators, influential others, and the competition (Step 5). More-detailed research case stories appear at the end of this and all remaining chapters, intended to cover the range of research methodologies as well as applications for social marketing campaigns.

We open with a case that demonstrates the power of developing a strategic plan based on a clear understanding of audience barriers, desired benefits to highlight, and motivating interventions.

CASE HIGHLIGHT

INCREASING VOTER TURNOUT

(2018–2020)

Source: Information for this Case Highlight was provided by Dr. Linsey Grove, a consultant to the League of Women Voters, St. Petersburg Area, Florida.[2]

Background, Purpose, and Focus

Although in the City of St. Petersburg, Florida, voting has historically been relatively strong compared to state and national averages, there are significant disparities in voter registration and voter turnout by race and place. An effort in 2020 was developed and implemented with a *purpose* to increase equitable voter turnout in St. Petersburg and a *focus* on Vote By Mail participation. Partners included the Urban League, Delta Sigma Theta, Pinellas Ex-Offender Re-Entry Coalition (PERC), Mt. Zion Progressive Missionary Baptist Church, Community Development and Training Center (CDAT), and the National Council of Negro Women.

Priority Audience and Desired Behavior

Historically, precincts with the lowest voter turnout in St. Petersburg are clustered in communities of color and low socioeconomic status. A *priority audience* selected for this effort in 2020 were registered female voters of color in low voter turnout precincts who were heads of households and had access to phones. The *desired behavior* was for them to Vote By Mail.

Audience Insights

Focus groups and personal interviews with registered female voters of color provided the following inspiring insights:

Barriers:

- Low trust and faith that institutions are going to listen, even if citizens participate
- Lack of trust in Vote By Mail ballots being counted
- Lack of understanding about how to Vote By Mail
- Lack of stamps
- Lack of transportation to Supervisor of Elections' office on voting day to drop off

Desired Benefits:

- Making my voice heard
- Doing something for my community/family

- Recognizing it's easier to make an informed decision when can fill out ballot while studying candidates
- Not having to worry about the weather
- Making it easier for working people
- Keeping me and my family physically safe from COVID-19
- Influencing policy and laws that impact me
- Not worrying about uncertainty of COVID-19 impact on polling places

Motivators:

- Assuring Vote By Mail is safe and secure
- Making it really easy and convenient
- Modeling positive behavior for young people at home, church, and community

Influential audiences:

- Churches, community activists, popular radio show hosts, community organizations, elected officials, local business owners, and local artists

Positioning Statement

Based on audience insights, organizers concurred they wanted active female voters of color living in low voter turnout precincts in South St. Petersburg, Florida, to see requesting a Vote By Mail ballot and sending in on time as a *secure and convenient way to ensure their voice is heard, their family and community will be kept safe from COVID-19, and that they will set an inspiring example for young people in their family and neighborhood.*

Marketing Intervention Mix Strategies

Product: The actual product was the Vote By Mail ballot with augmented products including stamps and reminder postcards. The campaign also included a mock kid's ballot that could also be filled in and mailed, and final numbers were counted and reported on via social media and other communication channels.

Price: The County paid for postage for all Vote By Mail ballots with support from the City of St. Petersburg, and those who voted by mail received a sticker (nonmonetary incentive) to recognize their action as well as help increase participation of others in the community.

Place: Given the audience desire for ease and convenience, ballots could be obtained over the phone, by mail, online, or in person. Once the request was made, the ballot would arrive by mail. Completing the ballot could happen in the comfort of the voter's home, and there were many options for the finished ballot including putting it in the mail, taking it early in person to one of the designated sites, or taking it on the day of the election to the Supervisor of Election's offices. Given the priority audience's key influencers, the team worked to help ensure faith institutions and places of worship would provide designated spaces for ballot drop-offs.

Promotion: The campaign was branded Democracy Starts at Home and slogans to support Key Messages included:

- "Suppress your cough not your vote."
- "Your Voter Disaster Kit"
- "My polling place is my couch and my poll workers are my family members."
- "Continue the Tradition and Keep Your Family Safe"
- "It's easier than you think."
- "Social Distance Voting"

Messengers included key influencers: church leaders, a variety of community organizations, radio hosts, and social media influencers in their community. *Creative elements* focused on real photos of families in the community filling out ballots together in their homes, on their couches (see Figure 3.1). *Communication channels* included a launch event with a com-

FIGURE 3.1 ■ Image Used for Vote By Mail Promotional Materials

Source: League of Women Voters, St. Petersburg area Florida.

missioned mural, podcasts, social media, radio news features, a texting campaign, and community networks (faith-based community, food banks, and childcare centers).

Results

The 2020 General Election generated an increase in voter turnout compared with 2016 (presidential election) and 2018 (mid-term election). Overall, the voter turnout in St. Petersburg in 2020 was 77.7% with increased turnout in communities of color. Approximately 70% of

Black voters and 71.9% of Hispanic voters voted in the 2020 general election. This was an 8% increase from 2018 for Black voters and a 15.3% increase among Hispanic voters. Most relevant to this case highlight, in 2020, there was a 66% increase in the number of Vote By Mail ballots compared with 2016.[3]

MAJOR MARKETING RESEARCH TERMINOLOGY

The first primer in this chapter presents some of the most commonly used research terms (see Table 3.1). They have been grouped according to whether they refer to the *objective* of the research, *when* the research is conducted in the planning process, the *source* of data and information, the *technique/methodology* used, or approaches to *collecting* primary data. More-detailed descriptions and an illustrative example are presented in the next several sections.

Research Characterized by Research Objective

Exploratory research has as its objective to gather preliminary information that helps define the problem.[4] It would be most characteristic of research conducted at the beginning of the marketing planning process, when you are seeking to determine the purpose and focus of your plan. Exploratory research should also be used to help you define the equity considerations that are related to your purpose. A city wanting to persuade restaurants to recycle their cooking oil, for example, might begin by reviewing data on the estimated amount of cooking oil that is currently being dumped down drains or put in garbage cans and the impact it is having on infrastructures and the environment.

Descriptive research has as its objective to describe factors such as the market potential for a specific behavior change or the demographics and attitudes of potential priority audiences.[5] It would be expected, for example, that the city developing the cooking-oil-recycling campaign would want to know the numbers, types, and locations of restaurants in the city that were generating the most cooking oil and where and how they were currently disposing of the oil.

Causal research is done to test hypotheses about cause-and-effect relationships.[6] We can now imagine the city managers "running the numbers" to determine how much in oil disposal costs they might be able to defray if they concentrate on Chinese restaurants in Phase 1 of their efforts and how this potential outcome stacks up against the suggested funding at various cooperation (market penetration) levels.

Research Characterized by Stage in Planning

Formative research, just as it sounds, refers to research used to help form strategies, especially to select and understand priority audiences and draft marketing strategies. It may be qualitative or quantitative. It may be new research that you conduct (primary data), or it may be research conducted by someone else that you are able to review (secondary data). In June 2002 in Washington state, for example, formal observation studies indicated that 82% of drivers wore seatbelts. Although some might think this market share adequate, others, such as the Washington Traffic Safety Commission, were on a mission to save more lives and wanted

TABLE 3.1 ■ A Marketing Research Primer

Marketing research is the systematic design, collection, analysis, and reporting of data and findings relevant to a specific marketing situation facing the organization.[a]

Characterized by research objective

Exploratory research helps define problems and suggest hypotheses.

Descriptive research is used to describe existing characteristics of a population, situation, or market, but does not offer causes or predictions.

Causal research tests hypotheses about cause-and-effect relationships.

Characterized by stage in planning process

Formative research is used to help select and understand priority audiences and develop the draft marketing mix strategy.

Pretest research is used to evaluate draft marketing mix strategies and then make changes prior to finalizing the marketing plan and communication elements.

Monitoring research provides ongoing measurement of program outcomes through periodic surveys.

Evaluation research most often refers to research conducted at the conclusion of a campaign pilot or effort.

Characterized by source of information

Secondary data were collected for another purpose and already exist somewhere.

Primary data are freshly gathered for a specific purpose or for a specific research project.

Characterized by approach to collecting primary data

Key informant interviews are conducted with colleagues, decision makers, opinion leaders, technical experts, and others who may provide valuable insight regarding target markets, competitors, and strategies.

Focus groups usually involve 8–10 people gathered for a couple of hours with a trained moderator who uses a discussion guide to focus the discussion.

Surveys use a variety of contact methods, including face-to-face, mail, telephone, online/Internet, intercept, and self-administered surveys, asking people questions about their knowledge, attitudes, preferences, and behaviors.

Crowdsourcing is, in part, a technique that taps online communities for formative, pretest, and evaluative research efforts (crowd research). It also refers to efforts for fundraising (crowdfunding), to recruit workers (crowd labor), and to generate creative elements, typically for a communications strategy (creative crowdsourcing).[b]

Participatory action research is a collaborative approach to research that involves community members and organizations in the research process, the objective being to determine the most effective actions in the community for positive social change.

Human-centered design research builds upon participatory action research by involving the priority audience for a behavior change effort in all stages of the planning process, including evaluation.

TABLE 3.1 ■ A Marketing Research Primer *(Continued)*

Experimental research efforts, such as randomized controlled trials (RCTs), are used to capture cause-and-effect relationships; primary data are gathered by selecting matched groups of subjects, giving them different treatments, controlling related factors, and checking for differences in group responses.[c]

Observation is the gathering of primary data by observing target audiences in action, in relevant situations.

Ethnographic research is considered a holistic research method, founded in the idea that to truly understand priority audiences, the researcher will need an extensive immersion in their natural environment.

Mystery shoppers pose as customers and report on strong or weak points experienced in the buying process.

Mobile technology research efforts use mobile phones for conducting surveys; this is of particular interest in developing nations where utilization of mobile phones is pervasive and Internet infrastructures and landlines in homes are lacking.

The Zaltman metaphor elicitation technique (ZMET) is an in-depth interviewing technique developed by Professor Gerald Zaltman that seeks to tap the right brain and unconscious and explore what deep metaphors reveal about the minds of consumers.[d]

Neuromarketing is a relatively new field of marketing research that studies the brain's response to alternate marketing stimuli, the objective being to inform development of product features and promotions that have the most positive appeal.

Characterized by rigor of the technique

Qualitative research is exploratory in nature, seeking to identify and clarify issues. Sample sizes are usually small, and findings are not usually appropriate for projections to larger populations.

Quantitative research refers to research that is conducted in order to reliably profile markets, predict cause and effect, and project findings. Sample sizes are usually large, and surveys are conducted in a controlled and organized environment.

---

[a] Philip Kotler and Gary Armstrong, *Principles of Marketing*, 9th ed. (Upper Saddle River, NJ: Prentice Hall, 2001), 140.

[b] Claudia Parvanta, Yannig Roth and Heidi Keller, "Crowdsourcing 1010: A Few Basics to Make You the Leader of the Pack," *Health Promotion Practice* 14, no. 2 (January 8, 2013): 163–167, doi: 10.1177/1524839912470654.

[c] Philip Kotler and Armstrong, *Principles of Marketing*, 146.

[d] Philip Kotler, *Marketing Insights From A to Z* (New York, NY: Wiley, 2003), 117–118.

to increase this rate. Formative research helped select priority audiences and form strategies. Existing data from the National Highway Traffic Safety Administration helped identify populations with the lowest seatbelt usage rates (e.g., teens and men 18–24, among others). Focus groups conducted around the state with citizens who didn't wear seatbelts on a regular basis presented clear findings that current positive coaching messages, such as, "We love you. Buckle up," were not motivating. A primary seatbelt law, tougher fines, and increased enforcement were what they said it would take (although they wouldn't like it). As of 2019, Washington has been able to maintain a high rate of seat belt use (93%–98%) in the years since 2002 by continuing to support enhanced enforcement programs in conjunction with public education effort.[7]

Pretest research is conducted to evaluate a short list of alternative strategies and tactics, ensure that potential executions have no major deficiencies, and fine-tune possible approaches so that they speak to your priority audiences in the most effective way.[8] It is typically qualitative in nature (e.g., focus groups and intercept interviews), as you are seeking to identify and understand potential responses your priority audiences may have to various campaign elements. It is most powerful when you can participate in, or at least observe, the interviews. Referring back to the Washington state seatbelt story, potential slogans, highway signs, and television and radio ad concepts were developed based on findings from the formative research and then shared once more with focus groups. Among the concepts tested was a successful campaign from North Carolina called "Click It or Ticket." Although focus group respondents certainly "didn't like it" (i.e., that they would be fined $86 for not wearing a seatbelt and that a part of the effort included increased law enforcement), their strong negative reaction indicated that it would certainly get their attention and likely motivate a behavior change. Findings indicated that elements such as roadside images utilized in the North Carolina television and radio spots, however, left people with the impression that the enforcement effort was happening somewhere else in the country, and thus they could psychologically dismiss the message. Advertisements were developed locally to counteract this.

Monitoring research provides ongoing measurement of program outputs and outcomes and is often used to establish baselines and subsequent benchmarks relative to goals. Most important, it can provide input that will indicate whether you need to make course corrections (midstream), alter any campaign elements, or increase resources in order to achieve these goals. Once launched, the state's Click It or Ticket campaign was monitored using several techniques, including reviewing data from the state patrol on the number of tickets issued, analyzing news media coverage, and, most important, conducting periodic formal observation studies the first year. Findings indicated that in the first three months after the campaign was launched, seatbelt usage rates increased from 82% to 94%. Even though strategies appeared to be working, the decision was made to increase the fine from $86 to $101, and more grants were provided to support increased enforcement in hopes of reaching a goal of zero traffic deaths and serious injuries by 2030 (Target Zero). In 2007, data from research and monitoring efforts turned the state's attention to nighttime drivers, whose seatbelt usage was lower; motorists driving at night had a death rate about four times higher than that of those driving during the day. Twice-yearly law enforcement and publicity mobilizations stressed the importance of buckling up at night and that special patrols "were watching." *Evaluation research*, distinct from monitoring research, according to Andreasen "typically refers to a single final assessment of a project or program and may or may not involve comparisons to an earlier baseline study."[9] Important attempts are made in this effort to measure and report in the near term on campaign outcomes and in the longer term on campaign impacts on the social issue being addressed—both relative to campaign outputs. (Both monitoring and evaluation techniques will be discussed in depth in Chapter 14.) Each year, a nationwide observational seatbelt survey is conducted. In Washington state, over 90,000 vehicle drivers and passengers are observed. Summarizing the results of the seatbelt campaign in Washington state, a press release in August 2006 from the Washington Traffic

Safety Commission reported that results from the latest observational research survey of seatbelt use had shown that the use rate had climbed to 96.3%. It was the highest seatbelt use rate in the nation and the world, and research indicated that buckling up was attributable to seatbelt road signs, aggressive local law enforcement, and educational activities at all levels of government. And, by 2012, the numbers were getting even better, reaching 96.9%.

Research Characterized by Information Source

Secondary research, or secondary data, refers to information that already exists somewhere, having been collected for another purpose at an earlier time.[10] It is always worth a first look. The agency's internal records and databases will be a good starting point. Searching through files for information on prior campaigns and asking around about what has been done before and what the results were is time well spent. It is likely, however, that you will need to tap a wide variety of external information sources, ranging from journal articles to scientific and technical data to prior research studies conducted for other, similar purposes. Some of the best resources are peers and colleagues in similar organizations and agencies around the world, who often have information on prior similar efforts that they are willing to share. Unlike commercial marketers competing fiercely for market shares and profits, social marketers are known to rally around social issues and to treat each other as partners and team players. Typical questions to ask peers responsible for similar issues and efforts include the following:

- What are the systemic equity issues that impact the focus area? How were these addressed in program planning?
- What priority audiences did you choose? Why? Do you have data and research findings that profile these audiences?
- What behaviors did you promote? Do you have information on what benefits, costs, and barriers your priority audience perceived? Did you explore their perceptions regarding competing alternative behaviors?
- What strategies (4Ps) did you use?
- What were the results of your campaign?
- What strategies do you think worked well? What would you do differently?
- Are there elements of your campaign that we could consider using for our program? Are there any restrictions and limitations?

There are also relevant e-mail lists to query (e.g., the Social Marketing Association of North America's Social Marketing Listserv, the International Social Marketing Association, and the Fostering Sustainable Behavior Listserv), online database services (e.g., LexisNexis for a wide range of business magazines, journals, and research reports), and Internet data sources (e.g., the Centers for Disease Control and Prevention's Behavioral Risk Factor Surveillance System, which will be described further in Chapter 7).

Primary research, or primary data, consists of information collected for the specific purpose at hand, for the first time. This journey should be undertaken only after you have exhausted potential secondary resources. A variety of approaches to gathering this data will be described in the following section. A hypothetical example of a water utility interested in a sustainable water supply will be used throughout.

Research Characterized by Approach to Collecting Primary Data

Key informant interviews are conducted with decision makers, community leaders, technical experts, and others who can provide valuable insights regarding priority audiences, competitors, and potential strategies. They can be useful in helping to interpret secondary data, explain unique characteristics of the audience (e.g., in a country other than where you live), shed light on barriers to desired audience behaviors, and provide suggestions for reaching and influencing targeted populations. Though typically informal in nature, a standard survey instrument (questionnaire) is often used to compile and summarize findings. For example, a water utility interested in persuading households to fix leaky toilets to conserve water might interview engineers on staff to understand more about what causes toilets to leak and what options customers have to fix them. They might then want to interview a few retail managers of home supply and hardware stores to learn more about what types of questions customers come to them with regarding leaky toilets and what advice they give them.

Focus groups are a very popular methodology for gaining useful insights into priority audiences' thoughts, feelings, and even recommendations on potential strategies and ideas for future efforts. Perceived as a group interview, a focus group usually involves 8–10 people "sitting around a table" or "online via Zoom" for a couple of hours participating in a guided discussion—hence the term *focus group*. In terms of numbers of groups to conduct, Craig Lefebvre offers:

> My rule of thumb is to plan to do as many as you can afford *only* for segments that you will truly develop a specific marketing mix for. The advice I have gotten is to do at least three for any segment, but stop once you start hearing the same thing.[11]

This chapter's second primer highlights focus group terminology and key components (see Table 3.2). For the leaky toilet project, focus groups with homeowners could help identify reasons they did not test their toilets (*barriers*), what they would want in exchange for doing the behavior (*benefits*), and what it would take to persuade them (*motivators*). Households in targeted areas of the city might be contacted by a market research firm that would screen potential participants and then invite to the upcoming group those with the following profile: homeowner, person in the home most responsible for household maintenance and repairs, having a toilet older than 1994 that has not been checked for leaks in the past five years, and having some concern about whether or not his or her toilet has a leak and what should be done.

Surveys use a variety of contact methods and include in-person interviews, mail, telephone, online/Internet, intercept, and self-administered surveys, asking people questions about their knowledge, attitudes, preferences, and behaviors. Findings are typically quantitative in nature, as the intent of the process is to project findings from a representative segment of the population to a larger population and to then have large enough sample sizes to enable the researcher

TABLE 3.2 ■ Focus Group Primer

Focus Groups: A research methodology where small groups of people are recruited from a broader population and interviewed for an hour to an hour and a half utilizing a focused discussion led by a trained moderator. Results are usually considered qualitative in nature and therefore not projectable to the broader population.

Planning: The first step in the focus group planning process is to establish the purpose of the group. What decisions will this research support? From there, informational objectives are delineated, providing guidance for discussion topics.

Participants: The ideal number of participants is between 8 and 12. With fewer than 8 participants, discussions may not be as lively nor input as rich. With more than 12 participants, there is not typically enough time to hear from each person in depth.

Recruitment: Ten to 14 participants are usually recruited in order to be assured that 8–12 will show up. A marketing research firm is often involved in recruiting participants, using a screener developed to find participants with the desired demographic, attitudinal, and/or behavioral profile.

Discussion guide: This detailed outline of discussion topics and related questions distributes the 60–90 minutes to ensure informational objectives are achieved. It usually begins with a welcome, statement of purpose, and ground rules and concludes with opportunities for the moderator and participants to summarize highlights of the discussion. It is likely to include time for numerous probes (e.g., "Please say more about that") to achieve the intended in-depth understanding and insights.

Moderator: The group facilitator is usually (but doesn't have to be) a trained professional. Important characteristics include strong listening and group dynamics skills, knowledge of the topic, genuine curiosity about the findings, and ability to synthesize and report on findings relative to research objectives.

Facility: Many groups are held in designated focus group rooms at market research firms, which include two-way mirrors so that observers (e.g., the client for the research) can witness participants' expressions and body language as well as slip notes to the moderator regarding additional questions or probes. Groups are often audiotaped and sometimes videotaped in order to prepare reports and share findings with others. Many focus groups are now conducted online, via video conferencing.

Incentives: Participants are usually provided monetary incentives for their time (e.g., $50–$60) and offered light refreshments when they arrive. The opportunity to share opinions and even contribute to an important social issue is a strong motivator as well.

Analysis: Given the qualitative nature of focus groups, analysis is focused on identifying "themes" versus priorities and percentages. These themes can then inform the informational objectives and questions for follow-up quantitative surveys.

to conduct a variety of statistical tests. These samples are designed by determining first *who* is to be surveyed (sampling unit), then *how many* people should be surveyed (sample size), and finally how the people will be *chosen* (sampling procedure).[12] It is important to consider that there are some cultural and racial communities that tend to participate less in research and may not participate in traditional surveys or focus groups. If your program is seeking to reach diverse audiences, it is important to think about alternate ways to gather the needed insights from these audiences (e.g. partnerships with community-based organizations or one-on-one in-language interviews). Back to our leaky toilet example. A telephone survey might be conducted following the focus groups to help prioritize and quantify barriers and benefits identified by participants in the groups. Findings might also be used to identify the demographic and attitudinal profile of priority audiences (those most likely/ready to test their toilets) and to test potential marketing strategies. How would interest increase (or not) if the utility were to host demonstrations on how to fix leaky toilets (*product*), provide monetary incentives for replacing old high-water-use toilets with new water-efficient ones (*price*), and offer to pick up old toilets (*place*)?

Crowdsourcing is, in part, a technique that taps online communities for formative, pretest, and evaluative research efforts (crowd research). A vivid example in the private sector of crowdsourcing as a formative research technique is one conducted by Starbucks, where a special website (My Starbucks Idea) is dedicated to sharing, voting on, and discussing ideas. Examples of ideas posted for new products include a raspberry and caramel frappe; for enhanced experiences, more comfy leather chairs; and for corporate social responsibility, a tree-planting campaign. For social marketers working to increase timely immunizations, a pretesting idea using crowdsourcing would be to post alternative campaign endorsements on a popular "mommy's blog" to solicit ratings on messenger credibility. And for evaluation, social marketers could consider engaging clients at Supplemental Nutrition Program for Women, Infants, and Children (WIC) clinics to provide feedback online as to how they were treated at the farmers' market when using their coupons.

Participatory action research is most distinguished by its involvement of priority audiences for the campaign, along with professional researchers, in the formative research process. The method is considered unique in that the participants are regarded (and listened to) as "experts," sharing their personal knowledge, attitudes, and behaviors relative to a behavior change effort. And professional researchers have significant opportunities throughout the process to conduct studies to test and verify potential behavior change approaches. Methods range from focus groups to personal interviews to online research communities.

Human-centered design research builds upon participatory action research by significantly involving priority audiences in developing strategies (interventions) for behavior change. It is helpful to think of them as an advisory group, participating in all phases of the planning process including selecting a desired behavior, identifying barriers, benefits and influential others, and then, most importantly, providing input for marketing intervention mix strategies. These audiences are also often involved in providing feedback once an effort has been launched to then enhance the effort. Melinda Gates was once asked "What innovation do you think is changing the most lives in the developing world?" She responded: human-centered design. Meeting people where they are and really taking their needs and feedback into account. When you let people participate in the design process, you find that they often have ingenious ideas about what would really help them."[13]

Experimental research efforts, sometimes referred to as controlled experiments, involves the gathering of primary data to capture cause-and-effect relationships by selecting matched groups of respondents (similar on a variety of characteristics), giving them different treatments (exposing them to alternative marketing strategies), controlling related factors, and checking for differences in group responses.[14] Some call it a *pilot*, where you measure and compare the outcomes of one or more potential strategies among similar market segments. For example, let's assume the utility was trying to decide whether they needed to provide homeowners with dye tablets to use to test for a leak or whether it worked just as well to provide instructions on how to use ordinary food coloring from the household pantry. If the incidence of testing for leaks is not higher among households who have been mailed a tablet than those who have simply been mailed instructions, the utility will likely decide to roll out the campaign without the added costs of the tablet.

Observational research, not surprisingly, involves gathering primary data by observing relevant people, actions, and situations. In the commercial sector, consumer packaged-goods marketers visit supermarkets and observe shoppers as they browse the store, pick up products, examine the labels (or not), and make purchase decisions.[15] In social marketing, observational research is more often used to provide insight into difficulties people have performing desired behaviors (e.g., recycling properly), to measure actual versus self-reported behaviors (e.g., seat-belt usage), or to simply understand how consumers navigate their environments in order to develop recommended changes in infrastructures (e.g., removing their computers from their bags as they approach airport security screeners). It would be useful for the managers working on the leaky toilet project to watch people at local home supply stores as they check out repair kits for their toilets.

Ethnographic research is considered a holistic research method, founded in the idea that to truly understand priority audiences, the researcher will need an extensive immersion in their natural environment. It often includes observation as well as face-to-face interviews with study participants. For example, the utility might want to actually observe and interview people in their homes as they test their toilets for leaks and (if warranted) make decisions regarding repair or replacement. Findings can then be used to develop instructional materials that will be most helpful to others as they then engage in these behaviors.

Mystery shoppers pose as customers and report on strong or weak points experienced in the buying process. This technique may include interfacing with an agency's personnel with an interest in observing and reporting what the target audience sees, hears, and feels during the exchange and how personnel respond to their questions. For example, utility managers may want to call their own customer service center and ask questions regarding the mailer on testing for leaky toilets "they" received as well as questions regarding options for repairing and replacing the toilets. They may also want to visit the website for the project, post a comment or question, and note how quickly their question is acknowledged.

Mobile technology research efforts use mobile phones for conducting surveys. This method is increasingly popular in developing nations where utilization of mobile phones is pervasive and Internet infrastructures and landlines in homes are lacking. Some survey methods use talking on the phone, some use SMS, some leverage social media platforms, and others include a mixed mode, using a combination of telephone, SMS/social media, and web during interviews.

The *Zaltman metaphor elicitation technique (ZMET)* is an in-depth interviewing technique developed by Professor Gerald Zaltman that seeks to tap the right brain and unconscious and explore what deep metaphors reveal about the minds of consumers.[16] Research study participants are usually asked to collect a set of pictures that represent their thoughts and feelings about the topic of interest and then discuss these in an interview. A study that Olson Zaltman Associates conducted for the Robert Wood Johnson Foundation

(RWJF), for example, helped create a new framework for discussing health care issues that would resonate across the political spectrum. As a result, RWJF discontinued using language of inequality in its communications and developed a framing that appealed to both Republicans and Democrats. The tagline "Health starts where you live, work, and play" has helped RWJF gain bipartisan support for initiatives in areas including childhood obesity, access to health care, and healthy family eating.[17]

Research Characterized by Rigor

Sometimes a research project is characterized as either a qualitative or a quantitative study. The differences between these two techniques are described in the following section and illustrated by a research effort conducted to inform the development of a social marketing campaign to combat the spread of HIV/AIDS in Ethiopia, where the infection rate is one of the world's highest.

Qualitative research generally refers to studies where samples are relatively small and the findings are not reliably projected to the greater population. That isn't their purpose. The focus instead is on identifying and seeking clarity on issues and understanding current knowledge, attitudes, beliefs, and behaviors of priority audiences. Focus groups, personal interviews, observations, and ethnographic studies are commonly used, as they are often qualitative in nature.[18]

In October 2005, an article titled "Managing Fear in Public Health Campaigns" by Cho and Witte appeared in *Health Promotion Practice*, a journal of the Society for Public Health Education (SOPHE).[19] It described, in depth, the role that formative research played in the development of strategies to influence HIV/AIDS-preventive behaviors among teens and young adults (aged 15–30) living in Ethiopia. This research was grounded in a fear appeal theory called the Extended Parallel Process Model.[20] Thus, the variables studied were not selected at random but were purposely chosen. Once the researchers discovered what people believed regarding these variables, they would have specific guidance from the theory about how to influence their beliefs in the direction providing the most behavior change.

Focus groups were conducted first to better understand urban youths' perceptions about HIV/AIDS-prevention issues by exploring, among other factors, their current knowledge, attitudes, beliefs, and behaviors regarding HIV/AIDS and condom use. Four focus groups were conducted in the two most populous towns in each of five regions in Ethiopia. Of specific interest were perceptions of consequences associated with HIV/AIDS. Participants in groups identified a variety: dysentery, weight loss, family breakdown, increase in orphans, social stigma, long-term disability, and death. The groups also revealed negative perceptions of condoms, including embarrassment, reduction of sexual pleasure, breakage during sexual intercourse, reduction of faithfulness between partners, and a perception among some that condoms actually spread HIV/AIDS. Also interesting was who participants considered to be most at risk for HIV infections: commercial sex workers, drivers, soldiers, youth in and out of school, government employees, and sexually active young adults. Most importantly, "participants expressed that condom promotion campaigns were either absent or ineffective in most of their localities" and that some totally ignored the HIV/AIDS-prevention messages.[21]

Quantitative research refers to studies conducted to reliably profile markets, predict cause and effect, and project findings. This reliability is created as a result of large sample sizes, rigorous sampling procedures, and surveys conducted in a controlled and organized environment.

For the HIV/AIDS-prevention study in Ethiopia, a quantitative effort followed the qualitative focus group phase. The study plan included a sample of 160 households per region, for a total of 800 households, drawn from a representative sample. A total of 792 household participants ages 15–30 years were interviewed from the 10 towns of priority regions. Of interest was the measurement and analysis of levels of agreement on a five-point scale (*strongly agree, agree, neutral, disagree,* and *strongly disagree*), with statements related to four beliefs often considered to be predictive of behavior change:

- Perceived susceptibility: "I am at risk of getting infected with HIV/AIDS."
- Perceived severity: "Getting infected with HIV/AIDS would be the worst thing that could happen to me."
- Perceived response efficacy: "Condoms work in preventing HIV/AIDS infection."
- Perceived self-efficacy: "I am able to use condoms to prevent HIV/AIDS infection."

Next, the data were analyzed within the theoretical framework. Based on previous research, the researchers knew they needed high levels of each of the four variables listed above to promote behavior change. If just one of the variables was at a low level, then they knew they had to focus on that variable in a subsequent campaign. The authors of the article embarked on five steps to analyze the data:

1. Examine the frequency distribution of each variable (agreement levels for each of the four variables).
2. Compare the mean score for each variable (average level of agreement) to assess whether average beliefs are all at high levels (i.e., 4 or 5).
3. Categorize the four variables into weak, moderate, and strong belief categories. Perceived severity was strong, and thus there was no need to address it in a campaign. However, perceived susceptibility was weak and response and self-efficacy moderate, thus needing to be strengthened in a subsequent campaign.
4. Strengthen targeted beliefs by examining the psychological, social, cultural, and structural bases of these beliefs to determine what caused low perceived susceptibility and only moderate levels of self-efficacy and response efficacy. For example, the researchers found that simply talking with partners about condom use was one key to increasing perceived self-efficacy.
5. Then the research was entered into a chart of key beliefs to introduce, change, and reinforce. This chart guided writers and program planners in the development and production of a 26-week radio soap opera.[22]

STEPS IN DEVELOPING A RESEARCH PLAN

Andreasen recommends that we begin our research journey with the end in mind. He calls this "backward research" and states, "the secret here is to start with the decisions to be made and to make certain that the research helps management reach those decisions."[23]

Nine traditional steps to take when planning a research project are described in the following section, beginning with a critical purpose statement. We'll use an example to illustrate this process from an article in the *Social Marketing Quarterly* (SMQ) in March 2022, "Using Formative Research to Develop a Social Marketing Campaign to Understand Food Shopping Behaviors in Young Mothers."[24]

1. *Purpose:* What decisions will this research help inform? What questions do you need this research to help answer?

This research effort was conducted to first gain insight into factors influencing food choices and grocery shopping behaviors of women with children on a limited budget who participate in the Supplemental Nutrition Assistance Program (SNAP) in the United States. These insights would then inform development of interventions to influence better adherence to Federal Dietary Guidelines for Americans.

2. Audience: For whom is the research being conducted? To whom will it be presented?

Research was intended to inform social marketing efforts of SNAP and was conducted by a team at the University of North Carolina Center for Health Promotion and Disease Prevention.

3. *Informational objectives:* What specific information do you need to make this decision and/or answer these questions?

Respondents were selected and research methods were designed to identify barriers, benefits, motivators, competition, and influencers to make it more likely that these SNAP recipients would develop and maintain the adoption and use of a *healthy food budget.*

4. *Respondents:* From whom do you need information? Whose opinion matters?

The focus of the study was on women with children, on a limited budget, who utilize or are eligible for SNAP program benefits.

5. *Technique/survey instrument:* What is the most efficient and effective way to gather this information? Do you need to consider alternative research techniques to reach diverse populations?

The research team conducted in-person interviews, as well as a journey mapping exercise.

6. *Sample size, source, and selection:* How many respondents should you survey, given your desired statistical confidence levels? Where will you get names of potential respondents? How do you select (draw) your sample from this population to ensure that your data are representative of your target audience?

Members of the research team screened women in the waiting room of their local Department of Social Services to determine whether they met eligibility requirements for the study which included: being at or below the age of 45, sharing a household with children, and receiving SNAP or WIC benefits. Independent interviews were ultimately conducted with 19 women meeting these eligibility requirements, including two women that were identified as actively practicing the desired behavior of budgeting for and purchasing healthy foods.[25]

7. *Pretest and fielding:* With whom will the survey instrument (e.g., questionnaire, focus group discussion guide) be pretested? Who will conduct the research, and when?

Research was developed and then led by a team at the University of North Carolina at Chapel Hill.

8. *Analysis:* How and by whom will data be analyzed to meet the planners' needs? A variety of statistical procedures will be considered and applied. This chapter's third primer, on basic statistical terminology, is presented in Table 3.3.

Data collected from the interviews and journey mapping exercise were analyzed by the team, leading to identification of interventions that aligned with the audience insights, especially barriers.

9. *Report:* What information should be included in the report, and what format should be used for reporting?

Final reports yielded from the interviews and journey mapping exercise included "tips and tricks" that would influence mothers to budget for and purchase health foods.

RESEARCH THAT WON'T "BREAK THE BANK"

Alan Andreasen's book *Marketing Research That Won't Break the Bank* has more than 250 pages of suggestions for reducing research costs, a few of which are described in the following section.

- Use available data because they are almost always cheaper to gather than new data and are often "simply lying about as archives waiting to be milked for their marketing and management insights."[26] One place to look is at prior primary research projects conducted for your organization but not analyzed thoroughly or with your new research questions in mind. There may also be existing internal records or documents, such as attendance levels at events, tallies of zip codes, and ages of clients, and anecdotal comments captured by telephone customer service staff. Externally, there are commercial enterprises that sell major marketing research data (e.g., *Advertising Age* magazine), and there are also free options, often easily found on the web (e.g., Centers for Disease Control and Prevention's Behavioral Risk Factor Surveillance System).

TABLE 3.3 ■ A Statistical Primer

Statistics are numbers that help make sense of data. Statistical procedures are tools that are used to organize and analyze the data in order to determine this meaning. The following terms are described very briefly and are only a few among those used in the field.[a]

Terms describing the distribution of the data

Mode: The response or score that occurs with the greatest frequency among findings.

Median: The value (score) halfway through the ordered data set, below and above which lies an equal number of values.

Mean: The simple average of a group of numbers, often thought of as the one number that best describes the distribution of all other numbers/scores.

Range: Determined by subtracting the lowest score from the highest score.

Terms describing measures of variability

Margin of error: A measure indicating how closely you can expect your sample results to represent the entire population (e.g., plus or minus 3.5%).

Confidence interval: A statistic plus or minus a margin of error (e.g., 40% plus or minus 3.5%).

Confidence level: The probability associated with a confidence interval. Expressed as a percentage, usually 95%, it represents how often the true percentage of the population lies within the confidence interval.

Standard deviation: A measure of the spread of dispersion of a set of data. It gives you an indication of whether all the data (scores) are close to the average or whether the data are spread out over a wide range. The smaller the standard deviation, the more "alike" the scores are.

Terms describing analytical techniques

Cross-tabs: Used to understand and compare subsets of survey respondents, providing two-way tables of data with rows and columns allowing you to see two variables at once (e.g., the percentage of men who exercise five times a week compared to the percentage of women who exercise five times a week).

Factor analysis: Used to help determine what variables (factors) contribute (the most) to results (scores). This analysis, for example, might be used to help determine the characteristics of people who vote (or don't) in every election.

Cluster analysis: Used to help identify and describe homogeneous groups within a heterogeneous population, relative to attitudes and behaviors used to identify market segments.

Conjoint analysis: Used to explore how various combinations of options (alternatives features, prices, distribution channels, etc.) affect preferences and behavior intent.

Discriminant analysis: Used to find the variables that help differentiate between two or more groups.

Terms describing samples

Population: A set that includes all units (people) being studied, usually from which a sample is drawn.

Sample: A subset of the population being studied.

TABLE 3.3 ■ A Statistical Primer *(Continued)*

Probability sample: Based on some form of random selection. Each population member has a known chance of being included in the sample. This chance measure helps determine the confidence level to be used when interpreting data.
Nonprobability sample: A sample that was not selected in a random fashion. As a result, results are not representative of the population, and a confidence level cannot then be determined and used when interpreting data.

[a] Webster's New World Dictionary (Cleveland, OH: William Collins, 1980); R. J. Senter, *Analysis of Data: Introductory Statistics for the Behavioral Sciences* (Glenview, IL: Scott, Foresman, 1969); A. R. Andreasen, *Marketing Research That Won't Break the Bank* (San Francisco, CA: Jossey-Bass, 2002); D. Rumsey, *Statistics for Dummies* (Indianapolis, IN: Wiley, 2003); P. Kotler and G. Armstrong, *Principles of Marketing*, 9th ed. (Upper Saddle River, NJ: Prentice Hall, 2001); Ellen Cunningham of Cunningham Environmental Consulting.

- Conduct systematic observations, as they represent "the ultimate in cheap but good research."[27] And just because they're "free" doesn't dismiss the need for using a systematic and objective process to collect and interpret the data. For example, a state drowning coalition may decide they want to measure increases in life vest usage among children as a result of their campaign by observing toddlers on beaches in public parks. A standardized form for volunteers to use and a designated time and day of the week to conduct the research will be important to ensure reliability of the data when comparing pre- and postcampaign measures.
- Try low-cost experimentation, a technique often used in the private sector and referred to as "test marketing." In the social sector, it may be more familiar as a "pilot." In either case, the objective is to try things out before rolling them out. There are several advantages, including the ability to control the intervention so that it closely matches the strategic options under consideration. If your experiment is carefully designed, you can control extraneous variables and findings can be used to confirm (or not) cause and effect. And this approach is also "often speedier and more efficient than many other approaches."[28]
- Use quota sampling instead of the more costly probability sampling method by developing a profile of the population to be studied and then setting quotas for interviewers so that the final sample matches the major profile of the broader population. For example, a researcher who wanted a projectable sample of opinions of mental health care providers regarding various recovery models might control interviews to match the types of health care organizations in the state (e.g., clinical settings vs. hospital settings vs. school-based programs). Some maintain that these results can still be projectable to the larger similar population "if the quotas are complex enough and interviewers are directed not to interview just easy or convenient cases."[29]

Additional options to consider include *participating in shared cost studies*, sometimes called omnibus surveys. With these studies, you can pay to add a few additional questions to a survey being conducted by a research firm for a variety of other organizations, targeting an audience you are interested in. A county department of natural resources, for example, may want to estimate the percentage of households who might be willing to drop off unused prescription drugs at local pharmacies (market demand). They might then take advantage of a marketing research firm's offer to add that question to their monthly countywide survey that queries households on a variety of questions for similar clients. Another option is to *ask professors and students* at universities and colleges to volunteer their assistance. They may find your research proposal to be of interest and benefit to their current projects and publication goals. A third option is to partner with community-based organizations and compensate them or help conduct research or gather data from the communities they represent.

CHAPTER SUMMARY

It may be easiest for you to remember (even understand) familiar research terms by recognizing the criteria used to categorize them:

- By research objective: exploratory, descriptive, and causal
- By stage in planning process: formative, pretest, monitoring, and evaluation
- By source of information: secondary and primary
- By approaches to collecting primary data: key informant, focus groups, surveys, experimental research, observational research, ethnographic research, and mystery shoppers
- By rigor of the technique: qualitative and quantitative

There are nine steps for you to take when developing a research plan, beginning "with the end in mind":

1. Get clear on the purpose of the research.
2. Determine the audience for the research findings.
3. Identify informational objectives.
4. Determine respondents for the research.
5. Find the best technique given the above, taking into account the best ways to include diverse audiences.
6. Establish sample size and source, and how it will be drawn.
7. Draft survey instrument, pretest, and field.
8. Create an analytical approach.
9. Outline contents and format for reporting, helping to ensure that the methodologies will provide the desired management information.

RESEARCH HIGHLIGHT

Reducing Youth Suicide

Using *Existing Survey Data* to identify the profile of youth most at risk for suicide and *Formative Research* to select a priority audience, desired behavior, and positioning.

(2016)

This case highlights the important role that research played in helping a work team draft and then refine key components of a social marketing plan to reduce youth suicide attempts. Information for this case was provided the Washington State Department of Health, Suicide Prevention Program.[30]

Background

Suicide is the second leading cause of death for Washington state teens 15–19 years old, and according to the 2014 Washington State Healthy Youth Survey, 10th graders reported the following:[31]

- 20% have seriously considered suicide in the past 12 months
- 16% have a plan as to how they would attempt suicide
- 10% have actually attempted suicide

In 2016, the Washington State Department of Health led an effort to develop a social marketing plan to decrease these statistics, with partners including local school districts, nonprofit organizations focused on youth suicide prevention, and a social marketing firm. The team initially established a campaign *purpose* to reduce youth suicides, with a *focus* on suicide attempts. Of initial interest among team members was to understand more about predictive factors for suicide attempts. What characteristics/factors distinguish the 20% of youth who seriously considered suicide in the past year from the 80% who reported they had not? Existing data from the state's anonymous Healthy Youth Survey, containing more than 100 questions and completed by more than 8,000 respondents in the 10th grade, provided a more in-depth profile of this audience, with a few of the major distinguishing characteristics summarized in Table 3.4. Results suggested that suicidal youth were more likely to be female; identify as gay, lesbian, or bisexual; use alcohol, tobacco, marijuana, and drugs; have been physically abused by an adult or a boyfriend/girlfriend; and have experienced being bullied.

Priority Audience: Original and Revised

Preliminary discussions regarding the campaign's priority audience began with an inclination to focus on the suicidal youth. A *situation analysis*, however, that included a review of findings from prior and similar efforts was noteworthy. Most of the campaigns emphasized focusing on the close friends of suicidal youth versus the suicidal youth. To confirm whether or not the plan should shift in this direction, team members conducted one-on-one interviews with high school youth, asking for their advice. The findings were clear. The most powerful intervention would be a close friend of the suicidal youth, one who would know "something was up" and would be seen as someone it would be comfortable to open up to.

TABLE 3.4 ■ Some of the Major Distinguishing Characteristics of Suicidal Youth[32]

Survey Question	Group A (n =6,842) 79.5% of Respondents	Group B (n =1,759) 20.5% of Respondents
During the past 12 months, did you ever seriously consider attempting suicide?	No	Yes
Gender		
Female	47%	69%
Sexual orientation		
Identify as gay, lesbian, or bisexual	5%	22%
Alcohol, tobacco, marijuana, drug use Past 30 days		
Smoked cigarettes	5%	18%
Used e-cigarettes	16%	28%
Drank alcohol	8%	19%
Used marijuana	15%	30%
Used a painkiller to get high	2%	13%
Used a prescription drug not prescribed to me	5%	18%
Sexual behavior		
Have had sexual intercourse in my lifetime	23%	44%
Safety/violence		
I have been hurt on purpose by an adult	21%	50%
I have been physically hurt by a girlfriend or boyfriend	4%	15%
School climate: in past 30 days		
I have been bullied in past 30 days	18%	42%
I have been bullied because of my perceived sexual orientation	6%	24%
I have been bullied because of my race/ethnicity	9%	18%

Source: Washington State Department of Health, "Healthy Youth Survey" (2014), accessed November 24, 2017, https://www.doh.wa.gov/DataandStatisticalReports/DataSystems/HealthyYouthSurvey.

Desired Behavior: Original and Revised

The next question before the team was to select a desired behavior for this friend. What very specific behavior did we want to influence them to do? The team decided to test the action of "Ask your friend who seems depressed, hopeless, or unusually angry 'Are you thinking about suicide?'"

Personal interviews with youth indicated clearly that the behavior was "too much of a leap":

- It would be awkward
- It might put the thought in their head and they might do it
- It's too big of a jump

Based on the interviews, the desired behavior was refined to be to:

FIGURE 3.2 ■ Social Media Encouraging a Conversation

Source: Washington State Department of Health.

- First, KNOW the warning signs
- Then, SHOW you care by asking "What's going on?"
- Finally, ASK "Are you thinking about killing yourself?"

Positioning and Strategic Marketing Intervention Mix

Research conducted to identify desired benefits and potential motivators led to a positioning statement that: "We want friends of a classmate who seems very depressed, hopeless, or unusually angry, to know it's *okay, even necessary*, to ask if their friend is thinking of killing themselves and that this *courageous act* can *save the life of their friend*."

Campaign strategies, then focused on getting this conversation started. Strategies included promoting a free (*price*) app branded "A Friend Asks" (*product*), a lifeline and texting resource (*product*), and friends would be encouraged to have the conversation in private (*place*). *Promotional* strategies focused on stories from friends who helped save the life of a suicidal friend (see Figure 3.2); in-school messaging including a one-day cafeteria "takeover" combined with posters and clings in hallways and bathrooms; and a simple online landing page using Tumblr that would outline the warning signs, conversation starters, hotline information, and where and how to download an app.

Summary Comments

As noted in the introduction, this research highlight is intended to confirm that this strategic planning process is more spiral than linear in nature. Decisions such as priority audiences and desired behaviors should be considered drafts until formative audience research can be conducted to either confirm choices or inspire changes.

And as of 2021, the program continues, with tailored efforts emerging in several parts of the state including one branded "The Native and Strong" campaign that features the images and voices of Native American youth from tribes and communities throughout Washington state.[33]

DISCUSSION QUESTIONS AND EXERCISES

1. What, in your experience, are the biggest barriers to conducting research for a social marketing effort?
2. What type of research is most often conducted: formative, pretest, or monitoring/evaluation? Which is least often conducted? Why?
3. Why do the authors strongly recommend that a research project begin with asking the question, "What decisions will you be making that this research is intended to inform?"
4. Crowdsourcing is a relatively new research technique. Are you familiar with any application of this?
5. In the Research Highlight, what were the two major shifts in decisions that the research informed?

4 BEHAVIOR CHANGE THEORIES, MODELS, AND FRAMEWORKS

LEARNING OBJECTIVES

Upon completion of this chapter, you should be able to:

4.1 Recognize major theories, models, and frameworks that can contribute to the selection of priority audiences.

4.2 Understand how major theories, models, and/or frameworks help inform the selection of behavior objectives.

4.3 Identify major theories, models, and frameworks that can provide audience insights.

4.4 Be familiar with what theories, models, and frameworks can inspire development of intervention strategies.

This chapter appears before in-depth explanations of the 10-step planning process as it is intended to provide a convenient reference guide to 20 major theories, models, and frameworks listed below that can inspire social marketers and inform social marketing campaign development.

Theories	Models
1. Diffusion of Innovation Theory	8. Social Determinants Model
2. Self-Control Theory	9. Health Belief Model
3. Goal-Setting Theory	10. Stages of Change Model
4. Self-Perception Theory	11. Service-Dominant Logic Model
5. Social Cognitive Theory/Social Learning Theory	12. Ecological Model
6. Theory of Reasoned Action/Planned Behavior	13. Community Readiness Model
7. Exchange Theory	14. Community-Based Prevention Marketing
	15. Hierarchy of Effects Model Frameworks
	16. Social Norms
	17. Behavioral Economics & Nudge Tactics
	18. Science of Habit Framework
	19. Carrots, Sticks, and Promises
	20. Triggers and Shikakeology

Although most of these theories, models, and frameworks can inform multiple steps in the strategic planning process, we have grouped them in this chapter by their strongest applicability, that is, by which of the following categories they are most applicable:

1. Selecting priority audiences
2. Setting behavior objectives and goals
3. Understanding audience barriers, benefits, motivators, the competition, and influential others
4. Developing marketing intervention mix strategies

This chapter's opening case highlights the power of an intervention based on a unique human behavior change opportunity.

CASE HIGHLIGHT
INCREASING BEHAVIOR CHANGE RATES USING TRIGGERS

This case highlight, in part, summarizes an article titled "Shikakeology: Designing Triggers for Behavior Change," coauthored in 2014 by Naohiro Matsumara at Osaka University in Japan and Renate Fruchter and Larry Leifer at Stanford University.[1] Three brief case examples from the article are highlighted, ones demonstrating clearly how a small trigger can cause a big difference and how, as the authors proclaim, "Changing behavior has enormous possibilities for creating a better world."[2] A concluding section makes a connection between these triggers and marketing intervention tools and principles for success presented in this text.

What Is Shikakeology?

Shikake is a Japanese word with various meanings, depending on the context. It can be seen as a noun (e.g., a mechanism) or a verb (e.g., set up). Shikakeology is described by the authors as the "science of shikake," one that uses an integrated approach and includes the following three characteristics:

(1) shikake is a trigger for behavior change

(2) the trigger is designed to inspire a specific behavior

(3) the behavior helps to alleviate a social or personal problem

Authors emphasize that it should not be seen as a "trap to force or trick people" but rather a way to encourage behavior change by presenting an alternative behavior, either explicitly or implicitly. Given that the aim of a shikake approach is to solve a problem through behavior change, the alternative desired behavior needs to be carefully selected and designed, one that when chosen by the priority audience will have a positive impact on the problem to be solved.

A shikake is seen as having two aspects: a psychological trigger and a physical trigger. A good combination of these two types of triggers leads to an effective shikake to change people's behavior, with psychological triggers affecting our psychological preference and physical triggers working directly to actually "prompt" the behavior change.

Shikake Examples and Mechanisms

The following are summaries and brief commentaries on three of the six examples presented in the article.

- *Increasing Proper Recycling*: This example discussed a case from Japan, one featuring a trigger to increase proper disposable of trash. Consider, for a moment, difficulties you have, or have observed others having, when disposing of trash. Those with intentions to put the right items in the right bin are often seen staring at the imprint on a plastic bottle and going back and forth reading the (often small) labels on the bins. By contrast, in this case from Japan, trash bins were designed to help people know quickly what goes where by creating bins with transparent windows on the sides, with the items people throw away highly visible to others (see Figure 4.1). This not only makes it easier for the placement of an item in the proper bin, the authors see this as also potentially eliciting "pro-social" behaviors with people not wanting their self-esteem compromised. Authors also note that the mechanism was so successful that the Central Japan Railway Company replaced about 1,600 ordinary trash bins with transparent ones.

FIGURE 4.1 ■ Examples of Bins With Transparent Windows Similar to Those in Japan

Source: ©iStock.com/Ratana21.

- *Reducing the "Splash" from Urinals*: This trigger was designed to decrease the "splash back" in urinals (for men in this case) and thereby increase the sanitation of public restrooms. Evidently, etching a graphic in the size and physical shape of a fly in a strategic "sweet spot" in the urinal causes a psychological trigger to aim at it by instinct, reducing the amount of splash (see Figure 4.2). In Thaler and Sunstein's book *Nudge*, this tactic was noted as one that first launched in Amsterdam airport urinals and was evaluated to have reduced spillage by 80%.[3] And since that time, these "flies" have been reported in locations around the world including Singapore, Moscow, Munich, and Seattle.

FIGURE 4.2 ■ A Fly Etched in a Urinal to Reduce Splash

Source: Gustav Broennimann via Wikimedia Commons/Creative Commons, CC BY 3.0 CH https://creativecommons.org/licenses/by/3.0/ch/legalcode.fr.

- *Reducing Speeding on Roadways*: Another shikake the authors note is one to reduce injuries and deaths from auto crashes—a digital speed camera on the side of the road that lets the driver know how fast they are going, as well as posting the actual speed limit for that zone (see Figure 4.3). The system is not connected to a police officer, and there are

FIGURE 4.3 ■ A Speed Camera to Provide Feedback to Prompt Slowing Down

Source: ©iStock.com/jhorrocks.

no other enforcement strategies at the scene compelling rivers to slow down. However, the feedback of the car's speed to the driver acts as a psychological trigger to slow down if exceeding the speed limit.

In some communities in the United States, these signs have been expanded to include a digital message such as "Slow Down" for those over the limit and a "Thank you" for those at or below the limit.

Commentary

Shikakes, or triggers, could be considered similar to the behavioral economics framework and nudge tactics described in more detail in this chapter, with behavioral economics a growing body of science that looks at how environmental and other factors prompt personal decisions and nudges going beyond the psychology-oriented behavioral economics framework to suggest concrete tactics that can inspire behavior change, such as those presented in this highlight.

How do triggers fit in the 10-step social marketing planning process presented in this text? First, they can often be categorized as *augmented products*, goods (e.g., transparent trash bins), and/or services (e.g., a speed monitoring display) designed to help the priority audience perform the desired behavior. Their selection and design are inspired by psychological factors such as self-esteem and motivators such as social norms. Triggers are sometimes similar to *prompts*, reminding our priority audience of a behavior they are perhaps committed to (e.g., notice of an annual immunization due) and are also aligned with a powerful media principle discussed in Chapter 13 to "be there at the point-of-decision-making." Note that for each of the examples described in this highlight, the intervention takes place at a juncture and were designed to influence the desired behavior change choice.

INFORMING SELECTION OF PRIORITY AUDIENCES

The Diffusion of Innovations Theory

Some believe, like Craig Lefebvre, that "the diffusion of innovations theory offers one of the most robust theories for taking innovations in ideas, behaviors, and practices to scale."[4] Everett Rogers first conceptualized this theory in the early 1960s, and in the fifth edition of his book *Diffusion of Innovations* (2003), Rogers defines diffusion as a process by which (a) an innovation (b) is communicated through certain channels (c) over time (d) among the members of a social system. Innovation diffusion research suggests that different types of adopters accept an innovation at different points in time. Five groups have been identified:

1. *Innovators* are motivated by a need for novelty and a need to be different.
2. *Early adopters* are drawn by the product's intrinsic value.
3. The *early majority* perceive the spread of a product and decide to go along with it out of their need to match and imitate.
4. The *late majority* jump on the bandwagon after realizing that "most" are doing it.

5. *Laggards* finally follow suit as the product attains popularity and broad acceptance.

The implication for social marketers is that for a relatively new behavior, you start by prioritizing innovators and early adopters and then, once that adoption is successful, move to the early majority and then the late majority. After these groups are on board, the assignment gets easier, as the laggards will be "outnumbered." Beginning in January 2010 in Washington, D.C., for example, a 5-cent tax was charged for grocery bags. Later, in October of that year, the *Wall Street Journal* reported on outcomes. Retail outlets went from handing out 68 million bags per quarter to only 11 million. The article, however, attributed this success to something more than the 5-cent tax. "No one got bags automatically anymore. Instead, shoppers had to ask for them—right in front of their fellow customers."[5] The article concluded that the magic ingredient was not the financial incentive; it was peer pressure.

The Stages of Change/Transtheoretical Model

The stages of change model was originally developed by Prochaska and DiClemente in the early 1980s[6] and has been tested and refined over the past decades. It describes six stages that people go through to change their behavior. These stages create unique audience segments:

1. *Precontemplation.* "People at this stage usually have no intention of changing their behavior, and typically deny having a problem."[7]
2. *Contemplation.* "People acknowledge that they have a problem and begin to think seriously about solving it."[8]
3. *Preparation.* "Most people in the Preparation Stage are (now) planning to take action ... and are making the final adjustments before they begin to change their behavior."[9]
4. *Action.* "The Action Stage is one in which people most overtly modify their behavior and their surrounds. They stop smoking cigarettes, remove all desserts from the house, pour the last beer down the drain, or confront their fears. In short, they make the move for which they have been preparing."[10]
5. *Maintenance.* "During Maintenance (individuals) work to consolidate the gains attained during the action and other stages and struggle to prevent lapses and relapse."[11]
6. *Termination.* "The Termination stage is the ultimate goal for all changes. Here, a former addition or problem will no longer present any temptation or threat."[12]

For social marketers selecting a priority audience, the most attractive segments may be those in the action, preparation, and/or contemplation stages (in that order), assuming that the size of the segment is large enough to meet targeted behavior adoption goals. The rationale for this is that those in these stages at least know about the behavior and are open to it. You don't need to spend scarce resources waking up those in precontemplation or convincing them that your idea is a good one. The three priority groups "simply" have barriers we need to address and/or benefits we need to assure and help provide.

INFORMING BEHAVIOR OBJECTIVES AND GOALS

Self-Control Theory

Self-control theory encourages planners to consider that individuals have a limited resource of self-control strength to use for various exertions such as resisting temptations or breaking "bad," but pleasurable, habits.[13] According to this theory, exerting self-control can be "exhausting," and as a result, individuals are prone to performing more poorly on concurring or subsequent tasks that require self-control. Implications for selecting behaviors for a social marketing effort are that you may want to avoid efforts to influence a priority audience to take on more than one challenging behavior at a time. Rather, intervention success is likely to be greater when behavior changes are initiated sequentially rather than simultaneously.[14]

For example, consider efforts by a physician to influence a 45-year-old male patient who had recently suffered from a heart attack to stop smoking cigarettes and resist consumption of fast foods. The self-control theory suggests that instead, we recommend that the patient focus first and solely on one behavior (smoking cessation) and ignore weight management until he is confident that he will not relapse.

The Goal-Setting Theory

The goal-setting theory offers insight into crafting a behavior objective that is both motivating and instructional. Dr. Edwin Locke's pioneering research in the late 1960s found that specific, clear goals that are realistically achievable are more effective than ambiguous and easy ones.[15]

Consider the difference between an effort to "eat more fruits and vegetables a day" and "5 a Day"; between "exercise regularly" and "exercise five days a week at least thirty minutes at a time"; between "take shorter showers" and "take a five-minute shower"; between "pick up pet waste in your yard" and "pick up pet waste in your yard on a daily basis and put it in the trash"; or between "don't idle except when in traffic" and "don't idle more than 10 seconds except when in traffic." Behaviors that are specific, measurable, achievable, realistic, and time-bound (SMART) work to first communicate what it is we want the priority audience to do and second to assist them (and you) in knowing if they have accomplished it. This is consistent with "helping" the audience perform the desired behavior by overcoming any audience barriers regarding understanding the behavior (e.g., exercise five days a week) and providing a sense of accomplishment and pride in having performed the behavior "properly" (at least thirty minutes at a time).

Self-Perception Theory

Self-perception theory suggests that the more we engage people in a behavior category (e.g., healthy behaviors, environmentally friendly behaviors), the greater the chances they will sustain these behaviors and even take on more. This happens as they begin to perceive themselves as the type of person who participates in these types of actions, which, upon reflection, alters their beliefs about themselves.[16]

Doug McKenzie-Mohr suggests we leverage this tendency by providing convenient opportunities for people to initiate and engage in a behavior.

> He cites an example where prior to curbside recycling being introduced, most individuals had no strongly held beliefs regarding the importance of waste reduction. However, when these same individuals received their new curbside containers and began to recycle, their participation in recycling led them to come to view themselves as the type of person who believed that waste reduction was important. Furthermore, it is likely these beliefs will be most strongly held when the opportunity exists to engage in these actions frequently.[17]

When someone engages, for example, in repetitive actions such as sorting and disposing of garbage properly, this is likely to increase his or her belief in the importance of waste reduction. And imagine the impact if an employee received a thank you card from their employer, not just acknowledging them for recycling but actually thanking them for "being" a good recycler.

DEEPENING UNDERSTANDING OF AUDIENCE BARRIERS, BENEFITS, MOTIVATORS, THE COMPETITION, AND INFLUENTIAL OTHERS

Social Determinants Model

This model alerts us to consider the behavioral influences of conditions in which people are born, grow, live, work, and play that affect a wide range of behaviors and outcomes. For public health, as an example, CDC sites five key health-related determinants: Healthcare Access and Quality; Education Access and Quality; Social and Community Context; Economic Stability; and Neighborhood and Build Environments.[18] For social marketers developing a campaign to influence annual medical checkups and immunizations, it will be critical to consider barriers and motivators that low income communities may have to accessing health services and then develop interventions that address their unique situations.

The Health Belief Model

Kelli McCormack Brown clearly describes the model originally developed by social psychologists Hochbaum, Kegels, and Rosenstock, who were greatly influenced by the theories of Kurt Lewin:

The Health Belief Model states that the perception of a personal health behavior threat is itself influenced by at least three factors: general *health values*, which include interest and concern about health; specific health beliefs about *vulnerability* to a particular health threat; and beliefs about the *consequences* of the health problem. Once an individual perceives a threat to their health and is simultaneously cued to action, and their perceived benefits outweigh their perceived costs, then that individual is most likely to undertake the recommended preventive health action. Key descriptors include:

- Perceived Susceptibility: Perception of the likelihood of experiencing a condition that would adversely affect one's health.
- Perceived Severity: Beliefs a person holds concerning the effects a given disease or condition would have on one's state of affairs: physical, emotional, financial, and psychological.
- Perceived Benefits of Taking Action: The extent to which a person believes there will be benefits to recommended actions.
- Perceived Barriers to Taking Action: The extent to which the treatment or preventive measure may be perceived as inconvenient, expensive, unpleasant, painful, or upsetting.
- Cues to Action: Types of internal and external strategies/events that might be needed for the desired behavior to occur.[19]

This model suggests that you would benefit from reviewing or conducting research to determine each of these forces (susceptibility, severity, benefits, barriers, and perceptions of effective cues to action) *before* developing campaign strategies. The National High Blood Pressure Education Program (NHBPEP) understands this well, as illustrated in the following highlight of their social marketing efforts and successes.

More than 65 million American adults, one in three, had high blood pressure in 2006, and less than 30% were controlling their condition.[20] Key to influencing desired behaviors (increasing monitoring and lifestyle and medication plans) is an understanding of perceived susceptibility, seriousness, and barriers such as the following:

- "It is hard for me to change my diet and to find the time to exercise."
- "My blood pressure is difficult to control."
- "My blood pressure varies so much; it's probably not accurate."
- "Medications can have undesirable side effects."
- "It's too expensive to go to the doctor just to get my blood pressure checked."
- "It may be the result of living a full and active life. Not everybody dies from it."

As you read on, you can see how messages in NHBPEP materials and related strategies reflect an understanding of these perceptions:

- "You don't have to make all of the changes immediately. The key is to focus on one or two at a time. Once they become part of your normal routine, you can go on to the next change. Sometimes, one change leads naturally to another. For example, increasing physical activity will help you lose weight."[21]
- "You can keep track of your blood pressure outside of your doctor's office by taking it at home."[22]
- "You don't have to run marathons to benefit from physical activity. Any activity, if done at least 30 minutes a day over the course of most days, can help."[23]

The year the program began in 1972, less than one fourth of the American population knew of the relationship between hypertension, stroke, and heart disease. By 2001, more than three fourths of the population were aware of this connection. As a result, virtually all Americans were having their blood pressure measured at least once, and three fourths of the population were having it measured every six months.

The Theory of Reasoned Action, the Theory of Planned Behavior, and the Integrated Behavioral Model

The theory of reasoned action (TRA), developed by Ajzen and Fishbein in 1975 and restated in 1980, suggests that the best predictor of a person's behavior is their intention to act. This intention is determined by two major factors: a person's beliefs about the outcomes associated with the behavior and their perceptions of how people they cares about will view the behavior in question. Using language from other theories presented throughout this text, one's likelihood of adopting the behavior will be greatly influenced by perceived benefits, costs, and social norms. In 1988, Ajzen extended the TRA to include the influence of beliefs and perceptions regarding control—beliefs about one's ability to actually perform the behavior (e.g., self-efficacy). This successor is called the theory of planned behavior (TPB).[24] Stated simply, a priority audience is most likely to adopt a behavior when they have a positive attitude toward it, perceive that "important others" would approve, and believe they will be successful in performing it (see Figure 4.4 and the Research Highlight at the end of this chapter).

It is worth mentioning that in the early 2000s, a third iteration of the model, the integrated behavioral model, suggested four additional behavior influence components. In this iteration, picture four additional boxes in Figure 4.4, ones also pointing to the *Behavior* box: (1) knowledge and skills to perform the behavior; (2) salience of the behavior (e.g., degree to which it is noticeable, stands out); (3) environmental constraints; and (4) habit.[25]

FIGURE 4.4 ■ Theory of Planned Behavior

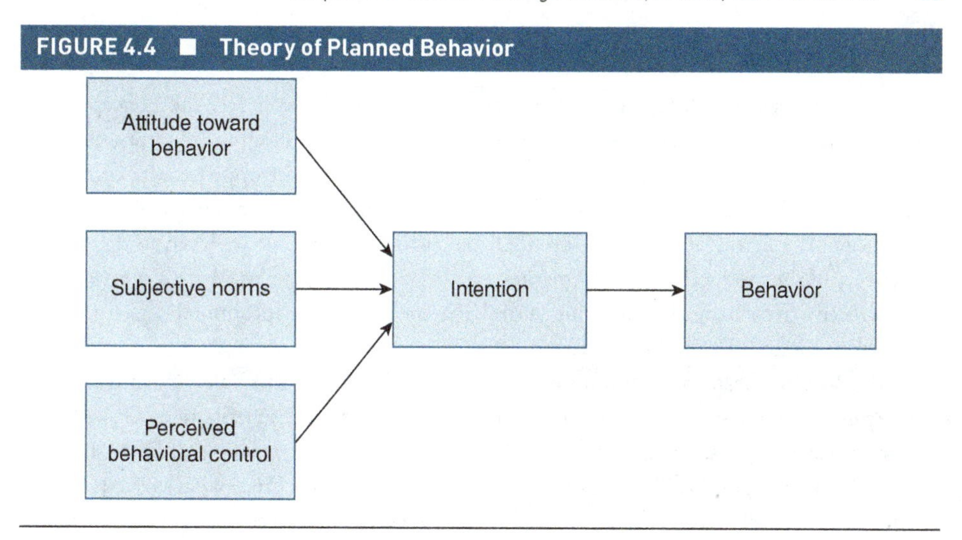

Source: I. Ajzen, "The Theory of Planned Behavior," *Organizational Behavior and Human Decision Processes* 50(1991): 179–211.

The Social Cognitive Theory/Social Learning

Fishbein has summarized Bandura's description of the social cognitive theory, also referred to as the social learning theory:

> The Social Cognitive Theory states that two major factors influence the likelihood that one will take preventive action. First, like the Health Belief Model, a person believes that the benefits of performing the behavior outweigh the costs (i.e., a person should have more positive than negative outcome expectancies). [This should remind you of the exchange theory mentioned frequently throughout this text.] Second, and perhaps most important, the person must have a sense of personal agency or self-efficacy with respect to performing the preventive behavior,... [and] must believe that he or she has the skills and abilities necessary for performing the behavior under a variety of circumstances.[26]

Andreasen adds that this self-efficacy comes about at least in part from learning specific skills and from observing social norms, hence the name "social learning." This learning of specific new behaviors, he explains, has three major components: sequential approximation, repetition, and reinforcement. Sequential approximation acknowledges that individuals do not often instantly leap from not doing a behavior to doing it. They may prefer to work their way up to it. For example, one way of teaching smokers how to adopt a nonsmoking lifestyle is to reduce their consumption step by step, perhaps one cigarette at a time, starting with the easiest behavior to give up and working up to the most difficult. Encouraging repetition (practice) and providing reinforcement strategies will then make it more likely that the behavior will become a "part of a permanent behavioral repertoire."[27]

The Service-Dominant Logic Model

In a seminal article in 2004, Steve Vargo and Robert Lusch proposed the concept of a service-dominant logic model, asserting that a product (whether a tangible good or a service) has value only when a customer "uses" it, and that when they do, it improves the condition or well-being of that person in some way. They also stress that this value is determined by the customer, not the marketer, and therefore that the customer should be involved in the design and delivery of the product.[28] In social marketing, this is equivalent to the *benefit* the audience wants to receive in exchange for engaging in the behavior that is being promoted (e.g., for fixing a leaky toilet, a reduced water bill).

In the 10-step social marketing model outlined in this book, this value is equivalent to the *core product* and best determined when conducting barriers and benefits research with the priority audience. As described in more depth in Chapter 10, determining a product strategy includes three decisions. We'll use family planning as an example. First, what is the primary benefit (value) the priority audience wants in exchange for adopting the behavior (e.g., having children when they can best provide for them)? This becomes the *core product*. Second, what tangible good or service will you be promoting, the *actual product* (e.g., birth control pills)? And, third, what additional goods and services (*augmented product*) will you be offering that will make it more likely that the priority audience will acquire the actual product (e.g., family planning counselors)? The core product (desired benefit/value) then inspires product branding (e.g., the family welfare vitamin),[29] as well as additional promotional messages.

INSPIRING DEVELOPMENT OF MARKETING INTERVENTION MIX STRATEGIES

Social Norms

Social norms are most commonly thought of as the "rules" that a group uses to determine appropriate and inappropriate behaviors as well as values, beliefs, and attitudes.[30] Several related terms include the following:

- *Injunctive norms* are behaviors a group perceives as being approved or disapproved of by others in the group.
- *Descriptive norms* are perceptions of what behaviors others are actually, or normally, engaged in, regardless of whether or not these are approved by others.
- *Explicit norms* are those that are written or openly expressed.
- *Implicit norms* are those that are not openly stated but understood to be the norm for a group.
- *Subjective norms* are expectations that individuals think valued others will have about how they will behave.

- *Personal norms* are an individual's standards for their own behavior.

Linkenbach describes the social norms approach to prevention, which has clear potential implications for strategy development that highlights the potential benefit of understanding perceived versus actual behaviors among priority audiences. Results may signal an opportunity to correct the perception:

> The social norms approach to prevention emerged from college health settings in the mid-1980s in response to the seemingly intractable issue of high-risk drinking by college students. Wesley Perkins and Alan Berkowitz, social scientists at Hobart, Williams, and Smith Colleges, discovered that a significant disparity existed between actual alcohol use by college students and their perceptions of other students' drinking. Simply put, most college students reported that they believed drinking norms were higher than they really were.
>
> The major implication of these findings is that if a student believes that heavy alcohol use is the norm and expected by most students, then regardless of the accuracy of the perception, they are more likely to become involved in alcohol abuse—despite their own personal feelings. Perkins came to call this pattern of misperception the "reign of error" and suggested that it could have detrimental effects on actual student drinking. According to Berkowitz, if students think "everyone is doing it," then heavy drinking rates rise due to influence from "imaginary peers."[31]

Efforts to increase handwashing behaviors are also ones that can benefit by the application of social norms. In the following case example, the focus was on enhancing perceptions of an injunctive norm.

> In October of 2017, in advance of Global Handwashing Day the 15th, Carolyn Moore, Secretariat Director of the Global Handwashing Partnership, shared in a blog post how "research improved hand washing programs by uncovering drivers of behavior change."[32] She cited a notable research effort in rural Zimbabwe conducted to understand the differences between "doers" (people who wash their hands at 9 out of 10 recommended times) and "non-doers" (people who wash their hands less often). One of the largest differences between the two groups was that the "doers" were significantly more motivated by others' approval. This finding led researchers to develop a behavior change program to increase perceptions of consistent handwashing as a social norm, in particular, a source of others' approval. The program led to increased handwashing after defecating by close to 30%.[33]

A final example in this section on the power of incorporating social norm theories into project planning is from Australia, one that was featured in the *Journal of Social Marketing* in 2016.[34] It illustrates well the potential behavior change impact of the social norming tactic of increasing visibility for the desired behavior within the community of the priority audience.

The *purpose* of the social marketing effort that was described and evaluated in the article was to increase the number of primary (elementary) school children aged between 5 to 12 years who walked to and from school, with a *focus* on increasing the visibility of those walking to school among a *priority audience* of caregivers. The campaign was branded *Walk to School* and was implemented by VicHealth. Rather than just "telling" the priority audience through mass media channels about the importance of physical activity for children, the campaign utilized more community-based channels including social media tactics to spread the word about walk to school programs (smartphone apps, Facebook, and Twitter). Participating schools supported the effort by encouraging children and their caregivers to participate in organized activities such as "walking buses" from landmarks close to the school, and weekly gatherings such as community breakfasts. Rigorous evaluative measures showed that increasing the visibility of the desired behavior of walking to school influenced positive change in perceived social norms in the context of children walking to and from school. In 2020, the program continues, with a special media release in July of 2020 announcing a National Walk Safely to School Day, encouraging primary school aged children across Australia to start incorporating regular walking back into their daily routine, following the ease of COVID-19 restrictions.[35]

The Ecological Model

One criticism of many theories and models of behavior change is that they emphasize the individual behavior change process but pay little attention to sociocultural and physical environmental influences on behavior—the ecological perspective.[36] The ecological approach places significant importance on the role of supportive environments, and four are typically cited: *individual* factors (demographics, personality, genetics, skills, religious beliefs), *relationship* factors (friends, families, peers, colleagues), *community* factors (schools, work sites, health care organizations, media), and *societal* factors (cultural norms, laws, policies, governance). This model argues that the most powerful behavior change interventions are those that simultaneously influence these multiple levels and that this will lead to greater and longer-lasting behavioral changes. The key to success is to assess each of these levels of influence and determine what is needed that will provide the greatest influence on the desired behavior.[37]

The Behavioral Economics Framework and Nudge Tactics

Behavioral economics is a growing body of science that looks at how environmental and other factors prompt personal decisions. The core idea that humans don't behave like rational economic agents was introduced several decades ago by Daniel Kahneman, Amos Tversky, and others. The central thesis is that people move between states of emotional hot and cold. As it sounds, when in a hot state, we are emotionally aroused (irrational), and in a cold state, we are calm or neutral (rational). And as might be expected, arousal, more often than not, overrides reason. A young person watching their budget may think before to buy the athletic shoes they heard were 50% off. When they go to purchase them and see the newer model with enhanced features, however, they are likely to succumb to their desires and pay full price.

Bill Smith argues in an article in the Summer 2010 *Social Marketing Quarterly* that "we have a new ally in Behavioral Economics"—one he is particularly excited about, as it has the potential to encourage the government "to arrange the conditions of life... and build policy contingencies so that it is fun, easy, and popular for people to make the right decision."[38]

To distinguish behavioral economics from social marketing, Philip Kotler offered the following thoughts in an article titled "Behavioral Economics or Social Marketing? The Latter!":

> Behavioral economics does not come with a rich tool box for influencing individual and group behavior ... Behavioral economics is mainly interested in demonstrating the irrationality of human decision making, not finding a more comprehensive system to influence individual and group behavior .... Behavioral economics is simply another word for "consumer behavior theory" as used by marketers ... and the bottom line is that those who want to influence social behavior for the good of the individual and society need to apply social marketing thinking, a much larger system than behavioral economics.[39]

In their book *Nudge*, Professors Richard Thaler and Cass Sunstein go beyond the more psychology-oriented behavioral economics theory to suggest concrete tactics this can inspire and improve public policy. They call them "nudges." Consider, for example, organ donation in Europe. In Germany, they note, only an estimated 12% of citizens consent to organ donation when getting or renewing their driver's license. By contrast, in Austria, nearly everyone (99%) does.[40] Why the difference? In Germany, citizens must "opt in"—check a box indicating they agree to be an organ donor. By contrast, in Austria, citizens need to "opt out"—check a box indicating they don't agree. The same "choice architecture," as the authors call it, could be used to bolster retirement-savings plans (companies automatically enroll employees unless told otherwise) or to increase the chances that students in school cafeterias will choose healthier foods (healthy options are at the beginning of the line).

To distinguish nudge from social marketing, Jeff French offers the following thoughts in *Think Paper: Autumn 2010*, a publication of Strategic Social Marketing:

> Nudging people into better health or away from criminality will seldom be enough to result in population level improvements because in many situations, evidence and experience make it clear that there is a need for other forms of intervention. Therefore, Nudges should be seen as a helpful part of the solution but not a magic bullet... and do not represent a full toolbox of possible forms of intervention... The selection of which form of intervention or combination of intervention types should always be driven by evidence and target audience insight.[41]

Daniel Read, Professor of Behavioral Science at Warwick Business School in the United Kingdom, offers this perspective on the contributions that behavioral economics can make to social marketers:

Achieving behavioural change requires a flexible toolkit of possible solutions, because each situation presents its own, previously unsolved challenges. The remarkable growth of behavioural-economics based interventions such as nudging has increased the size and potential effectiveness of the toolkit available to social marketers, a toolkit that has a strong theoretical and empirical justification, and (we should not underestimate this) one that makes social marketing sexy and exciting.[42]

Relative to the 10-step model presented in this text, nudge tactics can usually be categorized as one of the 4P intervention tools and are therefore only one of numerous interventions available, with the ideal strategies being those that consumer insight research or pilots indicate would have the most success in removing barriers, increasing benefits, and providing motivators for your priority audience. The following nudge tactics are among some of the most familiar:

- A *product* nudge: Streamlining applications for financial aid for college education.
- A *price* nudge: Offering lower minimum amounts for workplace savings plans.
- A *place* nudge: Placing the "good food" at the beginning of the school lunch line.
- A *promotion* nudge: Having potential organ donors opt "out" versus opt "in".

Our hope is that program managers involved in developing behavior change strategies will recognize that "nudges" are simply one of a bundle of potential behavior change marketing intervention tools, ones that Jeff French describes as being more automatic or unconscious in nature.[43]

The Science of Habit Framework

Charles Duhigg's 2008 article in the *New York Times*, "Warning: Habits May Be Good for You," encourages those interested in influencing "good behaviors" to take a lesson from the playbooks of the Proctor & Gambles and Unilevers of the world:

> If you look hard enough, you'll find that many of the products we use every day—chewing gums, skin moisturizers, disinfecting wipes, air fresheners, water purifiers, antiperspirants, colognes, teeth whiteners, fabric softeners, vitamins—are results of manufactured habits. A century ago, few people regularly brushed their teeth multiple times a day. Today... many Americans habitually give their pearly whites a cavity-preventing scrub twice a day.[44]

How is this useful to social marketers? Consider opportunities to "manufacture" new habits (e.g., walking a new puppy 30 minutes a day) or try embedding a new behavior into an existing habit (e.g., flossing your teeth while watching your favorite late-night show).

FIGURE 4.5 ■ The Hierarchy of Effects Model: Six Steps From Awareness to Purchase

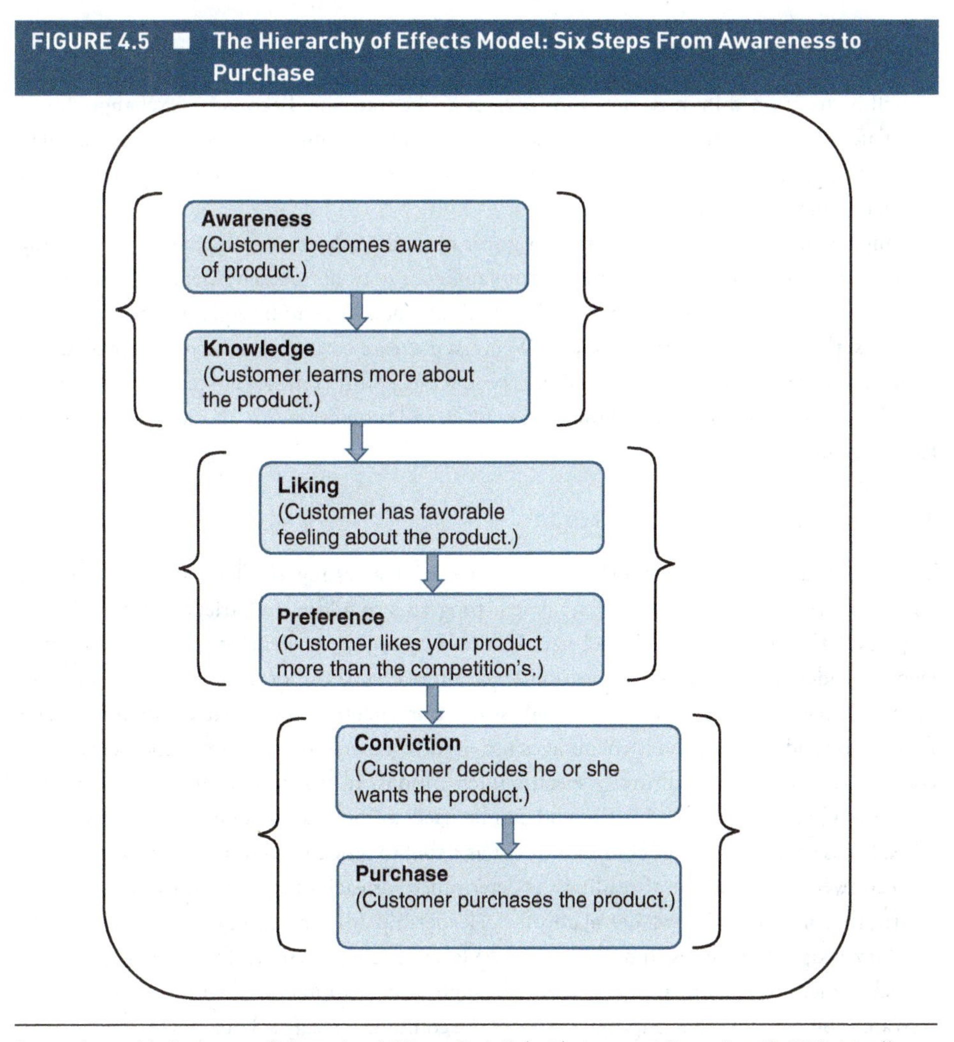

Source: Learn Marketing.net, "Hierarchy of Effects Model" (n.d.). Accessed December 17, 2013, http://www.learnmarketing.net/hierarchy_of_effects_model.html.

The Hierarchy of Effects Model

The hierarchy of effects, a communications model created in the early 1960s by Robert Lavidge and Gary Steiners, suggests that there are six steps that a potential customer experiences from first viewing a product promotion to the end state, product purchase (see Figure 4.5).[45]

Implications for the social marketer are that promotional strategies should be designed to target the "buyer readiness" stage the priority audience is in relative to adopting the behavior and moving them to the next step.

The Exchange Theory

As will be mentioned in more detail in Chapter 8, the traditional economic exchange theory postulates that for an exchange to take place, priority audiences must perceive benefits (value) in the offer equal to or greater than perceived costs. In other words, they must believe they will get as much or more than they give.

Implications for social marketers are significant and guide the development of marketing intervention mix strategies, for if the priority audience does not perceive benefits of adopting a behavior (e.g., exercise five times a week, 30 minutes at a time) to be equal to or greater than the costs, the marketer has "work to do." We must decrease costs and/or increase benefits, and we have four major tools to accomplish this: product (e.g., fun exercise classes for seniors), price (e.g., free), place (e.g., at a local community center), and promotion (e.g., positioned as a way to feel better and live longer).

The Community Readiness Model

The community readiness model offers a process for assessing the level of readiness that a community has to develop and implement programs to address a variety of public health (e.g., COVID-19, drug and alcohol use, HIV/AIDS), injury prevention (e.g., domestic violence, suicide), environmental protection (e.g., alternative transportation modes), and community engagement (e.g., animal control) issues. Proponents suggest that communities have found this model helpful, as it encourages use of local experts and resources and helps create community-specific and culturally specific interventions. It was developed at the Tri-Ethnic Center at Colorado State University and can be used as "both a research tool to assess levels of readiness across a group of communities or as a tool to guide prevention efforts at the community level."[46] Assessment of readiness is determined for each of six key dimensions: (a) past efforts, (b) community knowledge of efforts, (c) leadership, (d) community climate, (e) community knowledge of the issues, and (f) resources. A level-of-readiness score, from 1 to 9, is assigned to each dimension. Scores are determined through in-depth interviews with key informants, who are chosen to represent important parts of the community (e.g., school, government, medical). Strategy development is based on these community readiness scores, with dimensions with the lowest levels of readiness typically being addressed first.

The Community-Based Prevention Marketing

Many social change agents realize that interventions designed and directed by community members are far more likely to succeed than those planned and executed by outsiders. For this reason, social marketers at the University of South Florida have developed and evaluated a community-driven social marketing approach called *Community-Based Prevention Marketing* (CBPM).[47]

In the CBPM approach, a coalition of local public health professionals, other local health and education agency representatives, lay leaders and activists, representatives of local businesses, churches, voluntary organizations, and residents guides every step in program planning, implementation, and evaluation. Social marketers collaborate with these community members to critically analyze community problems, set preventive health goals, conduct formative research, and use results to develop an integrated marketing plan that guides intervention design, implementation, and evaluation.

Since 1998, CBPM has been used to guide behavior change program development,[48] policy change,[49] and system-wide interventions.[50] Additional information about these applications and materials used to train community coalitions to apply social marketing principles and techniques is available at the website for the Florida Prevention Research Center at the University of South Florida.

In 2021, the Washington State Department of Health created a new community grant program to help increase COVID-19 protective behaviors among communities that had been disproportionately impacted by COVID-19. The program was created with the recognition that "community-rooted and community-led organizations and groups are better positioned and equipped to listen, understand, and respond to the needs of their community members in the most culturally relevant and linguistically appropriate way."[51] The program provided funding and assistance to these groups to create social marketing interventions to address behaviors like mask wearing and vaccination. While the model continues to evolve, these pilot tests suggest that community control of the social marketing process enhances program integration into existing community structures and a sense of local ownership, making them more effective and sustainable.

The Carrots, Sticks, and Promises Framework

Michael Rothschild, an emeritus professor for the School of Business at the University of Wisconsin, "shook" the social marketing world in a seminal article in the *Journal of Marketing* in October 1999 titled "Carrots, Sticks, and Promises: A Conceptual Framework for the Management of Public Health and Social Issue Behaviors."[52] The framework distinguishes three very distinct tools that governments can rely on to influence behaviors: marketing (the carrot), law (the stick), and education (the promise) and expresses concern that "current public health behavior management relies heavily on education and law while neglecting the underlying philosophy of marketing and exchange."[53]

Education, Rothschild writes, refers to messages that attempt to inform and/or encourage voluntary behaviors. They can create awareness about existing benefits of adopting the behavior but cannot deliver them. *Law* involves coercion to achieve the behavior or threatens punishment for noncompliance or inappropriate behavior. *Marketing*, however, influences behaviors by offering incentives for voluntary exchange.

> The environment is made favorable for appropriate behavior through the development of choices with comparative advantage (products and services), favorable cost–benefit relationships (pricing), and time and place utility enhancement (channels of distribution). Positive reinforcement is provided when a transaction is completed.[54]

Triggers and Shikakeology

As mentioned in the opening Marketing Highlight, Matsumara, Fruchter, and Leifer describe Shikakeology as the "science of shikake," one that includes three characteristics: (1) a shikake is a trigger for behavior change; (2) the trigger is designed to inspire a specific behavior; and (3) the behavior helps to alleviate a social or personal problem. Trigger categories include motivators such as challenge, negative expectation, positive expectation, reward, self-esteem, being watched, social norm, and social proof.[55]

Themes From All

Fishbein's summary of behavior change interventions melds themes from most of the theories, models, and frameworks presented in this chapter and provides a quick reference for gauging whether your priority audience is "ready for action"—and, if not, what might be needed to help them out.[56]

Generally speaking, it appears that in order for a person to perform a given behavior, one or more of the following must be true:

1. The person must have formed a strong positive intention (or made a commitment) to perform the behavior.
2. There are no environmental constraints that make it impossible to perform the behavior (even better, there are "nudges" in the environmental infrastructure that make it more likely that the audience will choose the desired behavior).
3. The person has the skills necessary to perform the behavior.
4. The person believes that the advantages (benefits, anticipated positive outcomes) of performing the behavior outweigh the disadvantages (costs, anticipated negative outcomes).
5. The person perceives more social (normative) pressure to perform the behavior than to not perform the behavior.
6. The person perceives that performance of the behavior is more consistent than inconsistent with their self-image, or that its performance does not violate personal standards that activate negative self-actions.
7. The person's emotional reaction to performing the behavior is more positive than negative.
8. The person perceives that they have the capability to perform the behavior under a number of different circumstances.

Based on the science of habit framework, we would add a ninth point: The person is encouraged to form a *new habit* by connecting the new behavior with an existing one or new environmental cue.

COVID-19 Social Marketing Example

In this, and subsequent chapters, we feature something we saw, read, or heard about that is an example of an application of a social marketing theory, principle, or intervention related to influencing protective behaviors to reduce the spread of COVID-19.

In May of 2020, a stone statue outside a grocery store in a small town appears intended to help "trigger" bypassers to see wearing a mask as a social norm (See Figure 4.6).

FIGURE 4.6 ■ Public Statue Decorated to Help Create a Positive Social Norm for Mask Wearing

Source: Author photo.

TABLE 4.1 ■ Reference Guide for Applying Theories, Models, and Frameworks in the 10-Step Planning Process

Step	Description	Most Applicable Theories, Models, and Frameworks
3	Selecting Priority Audiences	Diffusion of Innovations Theory Stages of Change Model/Transtheoretical Model
4	Setting Behavior Objectives	Self-Control Theory Goal-Setting Theory Self-Perception Theory
5	Understanding Audience Barriers, Benefits, Motivators, Competition, and Influential Others	Social Determinants Model Health Belief Model Theory of Reasoned Action/Theory of Planned Behavior Service-Dominant Logic Model
7	Developing Marketing Intervention Mix Strategies	Social Norms Ecological Model Behavioral Economics Framework Nudge Tactics Science of Habit Framework Hierarchy of Effects Model Exchange Theory Community Readiness Model Community-Based Prevention Marketing Carrots, Sticks, and Promises Framework Triggers

CHAPTER SUMMARY

This chapter is intended to be used as a quick reference guide for identifying and understanding theories, models, and frameworks that can inform and inspire development of audience-driven social marketing strategies, summarized in Table 4.1.

As a practical tip, we recommend that you review these theories, models, and frameworks as you begin developing the relevant steps in the planning model. Not only will they be inspirational as you develop these steps, but your references to them will also help build confidence in your proposed strategies among funders, decision makers, and partners.

RESEARCH HIGHLIGHT

Reducing Obesity in Indonesia

When planning campaigns, social marketers often have several questions regarding the theory of planned behavior (TPB), described earlier in this chapter. If the ultimate objective is to move our priority audience to behavioral intention, the predictor of actual behavior change, do we need to influence all three variables seen as key to impacting intention (*attitudes, subjective norms*, and *perceived behavioral control*), or do we distribute resources based on our desired behavior and priority audience's unique characteristics? This study provides a few insights to address this query.

Information for this Research Highlight was provided by Denni Arli, Ph.D., Senior Lecturer, Department of Marketing, Griffin University. The study in 2006 was inspired by an interest in investigating the potential of the theory of planned behavior to inform campaigns to reduce obesity. It is one of the first few studies exploring obesity in Indonesia, with implications for social marketers related to priority audience selection, intervention strategies, and allocation of resources based on levels of obesity.

Background

Indonesia is the fourth most populous nation with 261 million people (2016).[57] Despite having the fifth highest number of stunted children in the world, in 2014, Indonesia became the 10th most obese country with the number of overweight and obese adults doubling in the last decade.[58]

Theory of Planned Behavior

This study was developed incorporating the original three major constructs of the TPB, as described by Ajzen in 1991 mentioned earlier in this chapter:[59]

- *Attitude* refers to the degree to which an individual has a favorable or unfavorable belief about the benefit of the proposed behavior, with the more favorable the attitude toward the behavior, the stronger the individual's intention will be to adopt the behavior.
- *Subjective norms* refer to the levels of perceived social pressure to perform or not perform the behavior and are described in this study as the expectation of other important persons' opinion(s) and the degree to which this individual is willing to adopt the behavior.

- *Perceived behavioral control* refers to the perceived difficulties or ease of performing the behavior.

Methodology

Data for the study were collected from a large university in Indonesia in three different cities. Several research assistants distributed the survey to students and staff at those universities, as well as to staff in a large private hospital. A total of 575 surveys were collected, with 499 usable responses. Respondents were required to enter their height and weight in order for their BMI to be calculated, and the sample was then divided into three BMI levels: 55% normal weight, 27% overweight, and 18% obese according to BMI calculations. It is noted that samples were higher than the national average of obesity in Indonesia, at the time 12.3%.

Informational objectives included the following measurement items, with language and scales translated into Indonesian language:

1. *Attitude*: "For me, losing weight in the next six months is __________." (Scale 1 = good; 7 = bad)
2. *Subjective norms*: "People who are important to me think I should lose weight." (Scale 1 = strongly agree; 7 = strongly disagree)
3. *Perceived behaviors control*: "How much control do you feel you have over losing weight over the next six months?" (Scale 1 = extremely easy; 7 = extremely difficult)
4. *Intention to lose weight*: "I intend to lose weight in the next six months." (Scale 1 = strongly agree; 7 = strongly disagree)
5. *Intention to exercise*: "I intend to exercise in the next 7 days." (Scale 1 = extremely unlikely; 7 = extremely likely)
6. *Intention to eat healthy*: "I intend to eat more healthfully in the next 7 days." (Scale 1 = extremely unlikely; 7 = extremely likely)

Findings

Researchers concluded the study provided empirical support for continued use of the theory of planned behavior as a guiding framework to understand how to influence weight loss in the context of a developing country. Highlights of results leading to this conclusion included:

- *Attitude* had the greatest influence on intention to lose weight for all body weights.
- *Subjective norm influences* were greatest for those who were overweight and obese.
- *Intention to lose weight* was more positively correlated to *intention to exercise* than *intention to eat healthy.*
- Results highlight the importance of a person's social network in maintaining or achieving a healthy weight.

Implications for Marketing Intervention Strategies

These researchers recommend that social marketers keep the following in mind when developing intervention strategies for efforts to decrease obesity:

- Focus on the positive aspects of weight loss such as feeling better about self, improved energy and vitality, avoiding type 2 diabetes (Relative to the 10-step planning model for this text, the implications are for the core product, the desired benefit.).
- A focus on physical activity may be more successful in increasing intention to lose weight than a focus on healthier eating.
- Encourage audiences to support each other to live a healthier lifestyle.
- Encourage having regular healthy meals; suggest family meals during adolescence.
- Consider creating a health-related online community, with social support interactions such as play among members of Internet weight-loss communities.
- Policymakers need to help ensure easy access to affordable healthy food ingredients.

DISCUSSION QUESTIONS AND EXERCISES

1. Which of the 20 theories, models, and frameworks do you find most inspiring? Why?
2. Why do you think behavioral economics has gained more visibility to date than social marketing? In your own words, how does it differ from social marketing? What do the authors argue are the distinctions between social marketing and behavioral economics?
3. Referring back to Table 4.1, for each of the steps, point out one of the theories/frameworks/models that you see as potentially useful and how it could inspire your development of that step.

PART II

DETERMINING PLAN PURPOSE, FOCUS, AUDIENCE, BEHAVIORS, AND INSIGHTS

5 STEP 1: SOCIAL ISSUE, DEI CONSIDERATIONS, PURPOSE, FOCUS, AND STEP 2: SITUATION ANALYSIS

LEARNING OBJECTIVES

Upon reading this chapter, you should be able to:

5.1 Understand and distinguish components of Step 1: social issue, diversity, equity, and inclusion (DEI) implications, purpose, and focus.

5.2 Understand and distinguish components of Step 2: situation analysis.

5.3 Explain what components of Step 2 that exploratory research can assist in determining.

5.4 Identify major ethical issues that should be considered when determining a *focus* for your plan, and why they are important.

With this chapter, the strategic marketing planning process begins, following the 10-step model presented in Chapter 2. Whether you are a student developing a plan for a course assignment or a practitioner working on a project for your organization, this practical approach is intended to guide you in creating a final product destined to "do good." (In Appendix A, you will also find worksheets that follow this planning outline; you can also download an electronic version of this document from www.socialmarketingservice.com.) For those among you who are reading this "just for fun," the process is illustrated with a variety of examples to make it come to life.

This chapter presents:

- Step 1: Describe the social issue, background, purpose, and focus of your plan
- Step 2: Conduct a situation analysis (SWOT)

Since both of these first two steps are relatively brief, they will be covered together in this chapter. As mentioned earlier, this model begins "with the end in mind," inspiring your decision-making audiences with the problem your plan will address and the possibility it intends to realize. With this background, you will then paint a vivid picture of the marketplace where you will be engaging and will be honest about the challenges you face and what you will need to address and prepare to be successful.

In our opening Case Highlight, a compelling purpose leads to a focus that inspires a lifesaving marketing strategy.

CASE HIGHLIGHT
OUR HEALTH IN OUR HANDS[1]

Combating Diabetes in New York City

(2010–2015)

Background

In 2012, 35% of Black Americans and 27.9% of Hispanic Americans were "obese."[2] Obesity can lead to diabetes which poses significant health challenges that can impact the health and well-being of individuals, families, and communities.

Part of the core issue driving this problem is targeted marketing that directs communities of color toward unhealthy eating practices. US fast-food giants (e.g. McDonalds, Wendy's, and Dominos) are top advertisers on Spanish-language TV and Black-targeted marketing channels. Yet, less than one percent of all advertising of fruits, vegetables, water/low-calorie juices target Black and Hispanic communities.[3] This creates larger health disparities in these communities, contributing to higher rates of diabetes, unhealthy weight, and hypertension.

Purpose and Focus

This Case Highlight will address the Brooklyn Partnership to Drive Down Diabetes' (BP3D) *Our Health is in Our Hands* campaign in New York City. BP3D was established in 2010 and is a partnership between Greater Brooklyn Health Coalition and CAMBA. The campaign's *purpose* was to decrease diabetes with a *focus* on healthy eating and physical activity among Black and Hispanic residents in Central Brooklyn and East New York.

SWOT Analysis

Organizational Strengths to Take Advantage Of:

The community partnership approach was a significant strength in the development of this campaign. The *Our Health is in Our Hands* social marketing campaign created a community coalition comprised 57 community members, leaders, researchers, medical staff, and social workers to ensure representation of each community's lived experiences in the campaign planning and implementation. This team met bimonthly to ensure equity and true community visibility in:

1. Concepting for images and messaging
2. Campaign research and messages in English, Creole, and Spanish

3. Survey development
4. Reviewing data
5. Creating the campaign distribution strategy

Organizational Weaknesses to Minimize:

This was one of the first social marketing campaigns developed and implemented tailored for Black and Hispanic communities aimed at creating healthier lifestyle choices that could lead to a decrease in diabetes. In a pilot campaign like this, trial and error can lead to mistakes from both a marketing and equity lens. The coalition and community-centered approach helped address this weakness by ensuring equity and inclusion were built into the campaign development process.

External Opportunities to Take Advantage Of:

The seriousness of the health impacts facing the community provided the opportunity for BP3D to create a campaign with a purpose and focus to test intervention strategies that could have a meaningful impact on obesity and diabetes. In addition, opportunities for collaboration with community partners, transit agencies, and trusted healthcare professionals ensured the campaign would reflect the community's lived experiences.

External Threats to Prepare For:

Campaign priority audiences have factors that made it more difficult to practice the desired behaviors including less availability of affordable, healthy food in their neighborhoods, higher stress levels, and fewer, convenient options for physical activity.

Priority Audiences

This campaign's priority audiences were Black and Hispanic people aged 18–64 living in Central Brooklyn and East New York, two of the most impoverished, high-need communities in New York City.[4]

Desired Behavior

BP3D's *Our Health is in Our Hands* campaign's behavior objectives were to address the dual threats of obesity and type 2 diabetes, by influencing these behaviors:

1. Attend nutritional programming
2. Make healthier eating choices
3. Attend a fitness class
4. Advocate for local food markets to have fresh fruits and vegetables

Audience Insights

About one third of the priority audience included families living below the poverty line, and about 22% did not have access to health insurance. In addition, about one third also viewed their health as fair or poor.[5] These factors contributed to barriers that the campaign would need to overcome. Benefits of practicing the desired behaviors included improved personal health and overall community health. The campaign coalition partners provided motivators, including free exercise classes, free nutritional education, and resources for healthy living and eating.

Message testing was conducted through intercept interviews to test advertising concepts with priority audience members. Cultural competency of the campaign was evaluated through key informant interviews and focus groups.

Marketing Intervention Mix Strategies

This community-based campaign promoted each desired behavior through community engagement, media outreach, transit advertising, in-language educational print materials, social media, and online resources. In addition, campaign sponsors offered classes and programming to help people engage with and try the desired behaviors. This included utilizing trusted community educators to disseminate information through community-led diabetes prevention programming (see Figure 5.1).

FIGURE 5.1 ■ Sponsor-Led Classes

SIX WEEKS TO FITNESS

Invigorating 6-week fitness and nutrition classes for adult men and women!

Choose your neighborhood, Choose your Night!!

Bedford Stuyvesant

Wednesday January 11, 2012 5:30 - 7pm
Bedford Stuyvesant Family Health Center 1413 Fulton Street
btwn Marcy and Tompkins Ave.
C to Kingston-Troop, B25 or B26 bus
Or

East New York

Wednesday January 18, 2012 4:30—6pm
I.S. 292/The UFT Elementary Charter School
301 Vermont Street Brooklyn, NY 11207
Cnr of Vermont and Pitkin A/C to Van Siclen or B20/B83 to Pitkin

Participants MUST RSVP with
Stephen Beasley, BP3D Program Coordinator
Stephenb@camba.org
718.282.2500

Source: CAMBA.

The campaign used local ethnic media outlets such as Caribbean Life and radio outlets like WNYC to reach community members in their preferred method of communication.

A partnership with New York's Metropolitan Transit Authority (MTA) transit led to placement of advertisements inside and outside of buses, subways, and bus stops in Central Brooklyn and East New York. These advertisements empowered community members to "take health into their own hands," using imagery of what healthy eating can look like parallel to what unhealthy eating looks like on a plate and how consumption can alter one's physical appearance.

FIGURE 5.2 ■ Social Media Posts and Written Materials From Community Partners

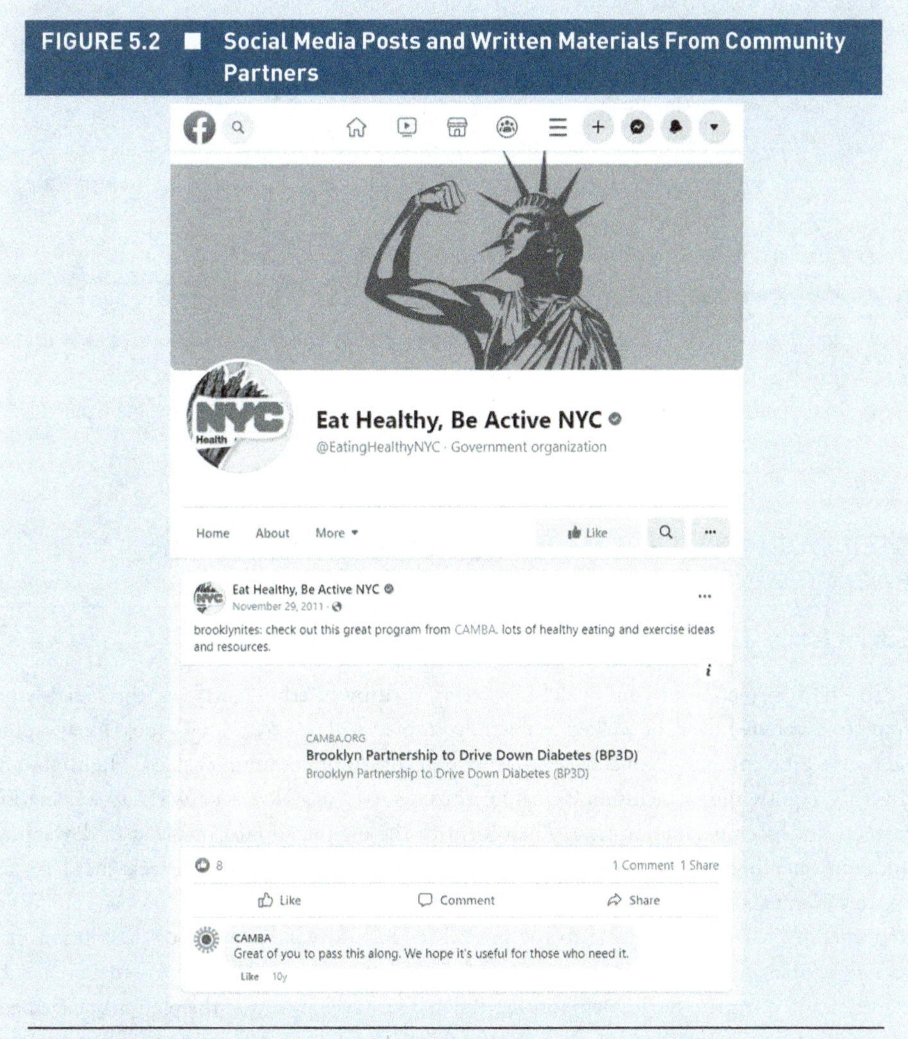

Source: CAMBA.

Social media posts were also utilized on partner social channels, like at Bedstuy Neighborhood's Food and Family Health Summit and the Brooklyn Labor Day Parade (see Figure 5.2).

Results

The campaign was evaluated through a survey (171 participants) and by looking at the reach of the campaign's promotional strategies:[6]

Campaign outcome metrics:

- 45.7% of respondents reported recognizing the campaign. Of these:
  - 40% said that the campaign was imperative in understanding nutritional scales and influenced their eating habits including eating more fruit and vegetables, less red meat, and overindulging less.
  - 17% were inspired to demand healthier foods at their local markets.
  - 31% said they had contacted BP3D to learn more.

Campaign output metrics

- From 2011 to 2013, there were over 11,000 social media engagements.
- MTA ran ads for 10 weeks including four free weeks, due to community value and buy-in.
- Significant media coverage distributed campaign messaging in publications read by priority audience groups.
- Community partners amplified the campaign e-mail campaigns, blogs, social media, and community boards.

STEP 1: DESCRIBE SOCIAL ISSUE, DEI CONSIDERATIONS, BACKGROUND, PURPOSE, AND FOCUS

Social Issue, DEI Considerations, and Background

Begin the first section of your social marketing plan by briefly identifying the social issue, sometimes referred to as the wicked problem, your plan will be addressing—most likely a public health problem, safety concern, environmental threat, or community need. Highlight any diversity, equity, and/or inclusion factors for consideration (e.g., lower COVID-19 vaccination rates in low-income communities). Then identify the organization(s) involved in developing and implementing the plan, and then move on to present information and facts that led your organization to take on the development of this plan. What's the problem? How bad is it? What happened? What is contributing to the problem? How do you know? This description may include epidemiological, scientific, or other research data from credible sources—data that substantiate and quantify the problem for the reader. The development of the plan may have been precipitated by an unusual event, such as a school shooting, or it may simply be a means of fulfilling one of your organization's mandates. In either case, this section should leave the reader understanding why you have developed the plan and wanting to read on to find out what you are proposing to do to address the social issue.

It wouldn't be surprising, for example, to find the first paragraph of the following illustration in the social issue and background section of a social marketing plan developed to reduce air pollution in China. It also gives a glimpse of the subsequent intended purpose and chosen focus.

In September 2013, an article in the *New York Times*[7] described the Chinese government's new plan to curb air pollution (*social issue*). *Background* information described how Chinese cities suffer from some of the worst air pollution in the world, and residents in China's largest cities "grapple with choking smog that can persist for days and even weeks." Some estimate that air pollution accounts for 1.2 million premature deaths a year, that it is changing everyday lives, and that face masks are becoming ubiquitous.[8] For years, evidently, China had a variety of strict environmental standards, and leaders seemed concerned about the need to improve the environment, but enforcement was lax. Interestingly, the article mentions that one impetus for this new plan was a Twitter feed from the United States Embassy that was publishing the hourly fine particulate matter level, known as PM 2.5, and that Chinese citizens increased the pressure on the government to have cities start to release their PM 2.5 levels, considering how deeply it penetrates the lungs and enters the bloodstream.

The article goes on to describe the government's intention to reduce this pollution (*purpose*). One of two plans would seek to reduce this pollution by curbing coal burning (*focus*). Evidently, China burns half of all the coal consumed in the world.[9] A second plan has a *focus* on removing all high-polluting "yellow-label" vehicles, those failing to meet China's national fuel standards. It is probably obvious that a social marketing plan with a focus on curbing coal burning would be very different than one removing high-polluting vehicles, which is why a focus is determined at the first step of the planning process. And an update in 2022 on the country's effort focused on curbing coal burning is encouraging with a report that: "Air pollution in 339 Chinese cities improved in 2021" and was attributed in part to "a concerted effort to cut coal consumption for heating while driving industries to improve efficiencies and install cleaner technologies."[10]

Purpose

Given this background, you now craft a broad purpose statement for the campaign. It answers the questions, "What is the potential impact of a successful campaign?" and "What difference will it make?" This statement is sometimes confused with objective or goal statements. In this planning model, it is different from each of these. An *objective* in a social marketing campaign is what we want our priority audience for the effort to do (behavior objective) and what they may need to know (knowledge objective) or believe (belief objective) to be persuaded. Our *goals* establish a desired level of behavior change as a result of program and campaign efforts. They are quantifiable and measurable, similar to sales goal-setting in commercial marketing. The campaign *purpose*, by contrast, is the ultimate impact (benefit) that will be realized if your priority audience performs the desired behaviors at the intended levels. Typical purpose statements, like the background information, should inspire support for the plan. They don't need to be long or elaborate at this point. The following are a few examples:

- Decrease the spread of COVID-19
- Reduce the amount of time it takes to get through airport security
- Improve water quality in Lake Sammamish
- Increase the percentage of spayed and neutered pets in the county
- Eliminate the stigma surrounding mental illness

A plausible social marketing plan addressing pedestrian injuries in China illustrates this sequential thought process. The background section of this plan would likely include statistics describing pedestrian-related injury rates, locations where injuries occurred, and populations most affected, including an estimated number of traffic injuries that claimed the lives of children ages 14 and under. And that further analysis of motor vehicle collisions typically shows two main reasons for child traffic injuries: children (a) suddenly running into driveways or (b) crossing a street behind or just in front of a car. Surveys also indicate that 65% of children ages 8–10 walk to school but only 15% are accompanied by adults. And among the 40% of children surveyed who had problems crossing roads, lack of traffic signs and crosswalks were the major problems.[11]

Several related *purpose* statements might then be considered, including *increasing proper use of crosswalks by students* and *decreasing accidents among children in driveways*. As you can probably tell, each of these purpose statements will lead to a different focus, with the crosswalk problem being more likely solved by a focus on infrastructures such as flashing lights and the driveway problem being more likely addressed by a focus on parents walking with children to school and teaching them about navigating driveways. In the end, one would be chosen as the purpose for the plan (as a start).

Focus

Now, to narrow the scope of the plan, a *focus* is selected from the vast number of potential options that could contribute to the plan's *purpose* (e.g., decreasing accidents among children in driveways). This decision-making process can begin with brainstorming several major potential approaches (*foci*) that might contribute to the plan's *purpose*. These may be approaches that the agency has discussed or undertaken in the past; they may be new for the organization, recently identified as areas of greatest opportunity or emerging need; or they may be approaches other organizations have used that should be considered for your organization. Table 5.1 lists different social issues and possible foci of each. The areas of potential focus may be behavior-related, population-based (although a priority market segment has not yet been chosen), or a broad intervention mix strategy (e.g., a product that will be promoted such as life vests or face masks). Several criteria can be used to choose the most appropriate focus from your initial list of options:

- *Behavior change potential:* Is there a clear behavior within this area of focus that can be promoted to address the issue?
- *Market supply:* Is this area of focus already being addressed adequately in this way by other organizations and campaigns?

TABLE 5.1 ■ Identifying Potential Focuses for Your Campaign

Social Issue (and Hypothetical Sponsoring Organization)	Campaign Purpose	Options for Campaign Focus
Family planning (nonprofit organization)	Decrease teen pregnancies	• Condoms • Birth control pills • Abstinence • Sexual assault prevention • Talking to your child about sex
Traffic injuries (state traffic safety commission)	Decrease drinking and driving	• Designated drivers • Underage drinking and driving • Advocating tougher new laws with policymakers • Military personnel • Repeat offenders
Air pollution (regional air quality council)	Reduce fuel emissions	• Carpooling • Mass transit • Walking to work • Telecommuting • Not topping off gas tanks • Gas blowers
Senior wellness (city department of neighborhoods)	Increase opportunities for community senior wellness gatherings	• Tai chi classes in parks • Walking groups in pedestrian malls • Strength and balance exercise classes at community centers

- *Organizational match:* Is this a good match for the sponsoring organization? Is it consistent with its mission and culture? Can the organization's infrastructure support promoting and accommodating the behavior change? Does it have staff expertise to develop and manage the effort?
- *Funding sources and appeal:* Which focus area has the greatest funding potential?
- *Impact:* Which area has the greatest potential to contribute to the social issue?

TABLE 5.2 ■ Potential Rationale for Choosing a Campaign Focus

Campaign Purpose	Campaign Focus	Rationale for Focus
Decrease teen pregnancies (nonprofit organization)	Abstinence	• Recent governmental funding for campaigns promoting abstinence in middle schools and high schools • Controversial nature of "safe-sex" campaigns in school environments
Decrease drinking and driving (state traffic safety commission)	Designated drivers	• Opportunities to work with restaurants and bars • Familiarity with brand, yet little recent promotion in past several years
Reduce fuel emissions (regional air quality council)	Not topping off gas tanks	• Consumer research in other regions revealing a high level of willingness to stop topping off gas tanks after hearing the (low) costs and potential benefits • Ease of getting the message out in partnership with gas stations
Increase opportunities for community senior gatherings (city department of neighborhoods)	Tai chi classes in parks for seniors	• Availability of space at parks and existing roster of tai chi instructors • Increasing popularity of this form of exercise and camaraderie for seniors

The best focus for a social marketing campaign would then have high potential for behavior change, fill a significant need and void in the marketplace, match the organization's capabilities, have high funding potential, and contribute most to alleviating the social issue (see Table 5.2).

STEP 2: CONDUCT SITUATION ANALYSIS AND REVIEW PRIOR EFFORTS

Now that you have a purpose and focus for your plan, your next step is to conduct a quick audit of organizational strengths and weaknesses and external opportunities and threats that are anticipated to have some impact on or relevance for subsequent planning decisions. It is also the time to explore prior similar campaigns that may inform development of this new effort. As may be apparent, it is critical that you selected a *purpose* and *focus* for your plan first, as they provide the context for this exercise. Without it, you would be scanning all aspects of the environment versus just the strengths, weaknesses, opportunities, and threats (SWOT) relevant to your specific plan. It would be overwhelming indeed.

Figure 5.3 presents a graphic overview of the factors and forces that are anticipated to have some impact on your priority audience and therefore your efforts. As indicated, picture your priority audience at the center of your planning process. (A specific segment of the population

FIGURE 5.3 ■ Organizational Factors (Microenvironment) and External Forces (Macroenvironment)

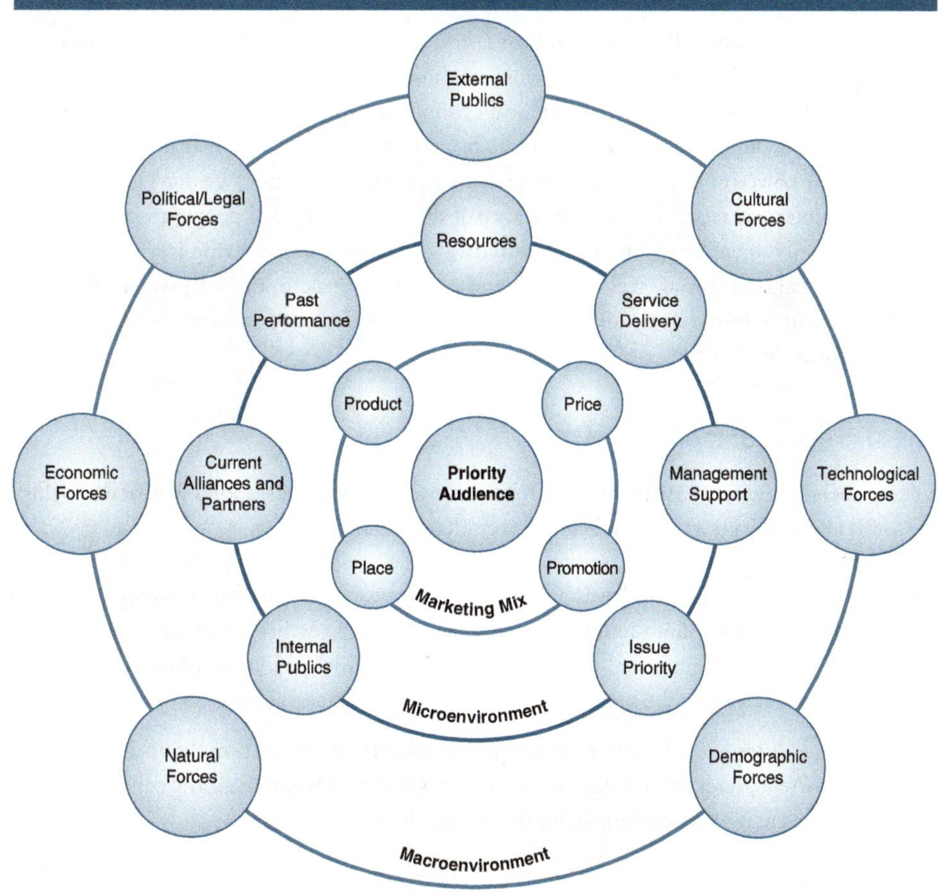

you will be prioritizing will be selected in Step 3, in part based on this analysis.) In the first concentric circle are the 4Ps, the variables that you as a marketer have the most control over. Next, a little farther away from the priority audience, are factors associated with the sponsoring organization for the campaign, thought of as the *microenvironment*. The outer concentric circle depicts the *macroenvironment*, forces the marketer has little or no control over but that have influence on your priority audience and therefore your effort. Christine Domegan, a Professor at the National University of Galway, Ireland, offers the following inspirational perspective on the importance on considering these influences, especially the macroenvironment:

> Two young fish were swimming across the lake one day, when they met an older fish swimming in the other direction. The old fish nodded at the youngsters as he passed and said, "Good morning, boys, the water is lovely today, isn't it?" The two young fish had been well-raised, so politely replied, "Yes the water is lovely sir, thank you." They

swam on in silence for a couple of minutes, then one young fish looked over at the other and asked: "What the heck is water?"[12]

David Wallace, who tells us the two little fish story, explains that the most ubiquitous and powerful influences on our behaviors are those closest to us—the ones we take for granted, do not even realize are there, and cannot discuss or describe. Our immediate environment and the system we live in is to us as the water is to the little fish, and it has an equally powerful impact on our lives whether we realize it or not. We don't get a full picture unless we recognize the importance of the system—a set of people and market structures interconnected producing patterns of behaviors; we are living it with all its political, cultural, social, technological and economic, structural, and psychological characteristics. Importantly, different systems produce their own patterns of behavior and choices over time.[13]

The Microenvironment

The microenvironment consists of factors related to the organization(s) sponsoring or managing the social marketing effort—ones therefore considered internal:

- *Resources:* How are your levels of funding for the project? (If funding amounts are already established, it should be recognized at this step and kept in mind throughout the planning process.) Is there adequate staff time available? Do you have access to expertise related to the social issue or priority populations that you can easily tap?
- *Service delivery capabilities:* Does the organization have distribution channels available for current goods and services or ones you might develop? Are there any concerns with the current or potential quality of this service delivery?
- *Management support:* Does management support this project? Have they been briefed on it?
- *Issue priority:* Within the organization, is the social issue your plan will be addressing a priority for the organization? Are there other issues you will be competing with for resources and support, or is this one high on the list?
- *Internal publics:* Within the organization, who is likely to support this effort? Who might not? Are there groups or individuals whose buy-in will be needed for the campaign to be successful?
- *Current alliances and partners:* What alliances and partners does the sponsoring organization have that could potentially provide additional resources such as funding, expertise, access to priority populations, endorsements, message delivery, and/or material dissemination?
- *Past performance:* What is the organization's reputation in regard to projects such as this? What successes and failures are relevant?

Strengths

Make a (bulleted) list of major organizational strengths relative to this plan, based at least in part on an audit of these seven internal factors. These points will be ones your plan will want to *maximize*. You may not have something to note for each of the factors. You should be aware that this list will guide you in many subsequent decisions, such as which priority audiences you can best reach and serve, what products (goods and services) you have the resources and support to develop, prices you will (need to) charge, incentives you will be able to afford to offer, and existing alliances you might be able to tap for delivery of products, services, promotional materials, and messages.

For another brief illustration from China, consider a plan with the purpose of reducing energy consumption and a focus on reducing commercial electrical use.[14] We can imagine that a national group charged with the responsibility of developing this plan would begin fully aware of one of their major strengths to maximize—that as a result of historic blackouts experienced in dozens of provincial-level power grids, energy saving had topped the government agenda (In the end, this may have led to changes in infrastructure, such as self-activated escalators in hotel lobbies and hotel rooms that require room keys to be inserted for lights to go on. And of course, lights then go off as guests leave the room with the key that they will need when they return.) The team's pitch to leadership would remind the government of earlier responses and successes.

Weaknesses

On the flip side, a similar list is made of factors that don't look as positive for your effort—ones you may need a few action items, even strategies, to *minimize*. This bulleted list is constructed by reviewing each of the same seven internal factors, noting ones that stand out as potential concerns in developing and implementing a successful plan. Most frequently for governmental agencies and nonprofit organizations (the likely sponsors of a social marketing effort), concerns involve resource availability and issue priority, as in the following example.

Consider organizational factors challenging those charged with developing a plan to reduce smoking in China, especially among teens.[15] In 2022, a report on the "Current Progress and Challenges to Tobacco Control in China" notes that even though there are bans for tobacco advertisements on mass media, in public places, on public transports, and outdoors, presently there are still tobacco advertisements and promotions at sales points and Internet-based media, and about two thirds of the public indicating they have seen smoking scenes in movies or TV series as well.[16]

The Macroenvironment

The macroenvironment is the set of forces typically outside the influence of the social marketer that must be taken into account, as they either currently have an impact on your priority audience or are likely to in the near future. In each of the following seven categories, you will be noting any major trends or events you may want to take advantage of (*opportunities*) or prepare for (*threats*). Remember, you are interested in those related to the purpose and focus of your plan and may not have one in each category.

- *Cultural forces:* Trends and happenings related to values, lifestyles, preferences, and behaviors, often influenced by factors such as advertising, entertainment, media, consumer goods, corporate policies, fashion, religious movements, health concerns, and environmental concerns. This is also where you should ask yourself how systemic racism impacts your issues. What are the racist elements of the structures and systems you are working within? How does the history and current realities of race impact your issue and your audiences?
- *Technological forces:* Introduction or potential introduction of new technologies and products that may support or hinder your effort.
- *Demographic forces:* Trends and changes in population characteristics, including age, ethnicity, race, household composition, employment status, occupation, income, and education.
- *Natural forces:* Forces of "nature," including famine, fires, drought, hurricanes, energy supply, water supply, endangered species, tsunamis, and floods.
- *Economic forces:* Trends affecting buying power, spending, and perceptions of economic well-being.
- *Political/legal forces:* Potential or new laws and actions of governmental agencies that could affect campaign efforts or your target audience.
- *External publics:* Groups outside the organization other than current partners and alliances, including potential new partners, that could have some impact on your efforts (good or bad) and/or your priority audience.

As discussed in Chapter 1, it is important to note that social marketing experts are now recommending that you also consider the role you can play in influencing decision makers who can impact these upstream forces (e.g., focusing on school district administrators to increase formal physical activity programs in elementary schools).

Opportunities

A major purpose for scanning the external environment is to discover opportunities that you can take advantage of and build into your plan. Your activities can be leveraged by benefiting from the visibility and resources that other groups may be bringing to your issue or the increased awareness and concern that you find is already out there in the general public, as it was in the following example.

Relative to an effort to increase pet adoption in China, external factors a program could leverage include support from organizations such as the country's Ministry of Health and the International Fund for Animal Welfare, and an emphasis on the positive cultural-related factors including the continued promotion of the *Year of the Dog* celebrations that have helped establish having a pet as a symbol of prosperity. In addition, some have attributed the popularity of pets to a growing sense of loneliness among city dwellers, particularly the elderly living alone and single white-collar workers (demographic).[17]

Threats

On the other hand, some of these forces will represent potential threats to your project, and you will want your plan to address or prepare for them. Understanding the influences on your priority population can provide insight, as shown in the following example.

Referring again to the problem with tobacco use in China, early efforts to reduce teen smoking were challenged by then powerful and entrenched cultural economic, and legal forces operating at the time in the marketplace:[18]

- People begin smoking at an early age, especially in tobacco-planting areas.
- Parents and teachers smoke in front of children.
- China is the world's largest tobacco producer and consumer, so smoking is accepted, even supported, given the close relationship between the production and consumption of tobacco and the national economy.
- Cigarette companies are still allowed to advertise their brands.
- There are no national laws or regulations in China to forbid selling cigarettes to youngsters.

Review Prior Efforts

One social marketing principle for success is to begin your marketing planning with a search and review of prior efforts undertaken by your organization and similar campaigns planned and launched by others. When reviewing past efforts, you are looking for examples of priority audiences, behaviors selected, intervention strategies employed, and lessons learned. What worked well? What didn't? What did evaluators think should have been done differently? What was missing? One of the benefits of working in the public and nonprofit sectors is that your peers and colleagues around the world often can and will help you. They can share research, plans, campaign materials, outcomes, and war stories. (It should be emphasized, though probably understood, that citations acknowledging the source should be noted in campaign plans, and formal permissions are often needed for replicating campaign materials.) Finding these resources (and people) can be as simple as searching the website of social marketing journals and those of major organizations with missions related to your campaign purpose (e.g., searching Environmental Protection Agency's website for water quality improvement campaigns or Centers for Disease Control and Prevention's website for physical activity campaigns). It could be helpful to join social marketing listservs and posting a comment such as: "Does anyone know of social marketing campaigns to increase consumption of fruits and vegetables among food stamp recipients?" It can also be as simple as watching what others have done, as illustrated in this next example from China.

FIGURE 5.4 ■ Wide Bicycle Lanes

Nations and communities around the world interested in increasing bicycling (especially as a mode of commuting) could benefit from observing what China has done over the decades to make bicycling a social norm. They provide bike lanes, not just paths, that are protected from cars that might be opening a door (see Figure 5.4). At many intersections, there's a traffic signal—just for cyclists—that gives them their own time and space (see Figure 5.5). In Beijing,

FIGURE 5.5 ■ Traffic Signals Including Ones for Bicycle Lanes

Source: Author photo.

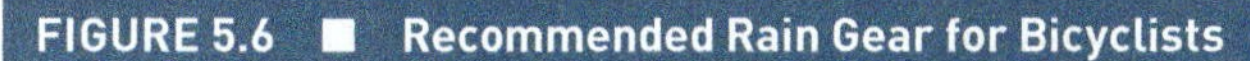

FIGURE 5.6 ■ Recommended Rain Gear for Bicyclists

Source: Author photo.

there are sports coliseums for biking events, adding to the excitement (and status) of bikers. For those concerned about "overexertion," electric bicycles costing about the same as a cell phone and getting the equivalent of 1,362 miles per gallon of gas are common and certainly not a "sign of weakness." For those concerned about costs, the government makes the competition (cars) very unattractive through escalating gas prices and high fees for vehicle licensing.[19] And for those concerned about rain, they've thought of everything, including form-fitting heavy-duty ponchos that protect legs, heads, packages—even two riders (see Figure 5.6).

THE ROLE OF EXPLORATORY RESEARCH WHEN CHOOSING FOCUS

As mentioned in Chapter 3, exploratory research is conducted to describe the marketplace relative to the *social issue* you are addressing, a process that assists in making decisions regarding the *purpose* and *focus* of your plan (Step 1). Consider, for example, a state public health social marketing manager developing a plan to address high outbreaks of COVID-19 among those attending large gatherings, such as social, recreational, entertainment, and sporting events. Exploratory research can help determine a purpose and focus for the plan by answering several important questions: (a) How do the positive testing rates vary by location, type, and size of the event? (b) What tactics are currently in place at these different locations to limit the spread of COVID-19 (e.g., proof of vaccinations, requirements to wear a mask, and safe distancing)? Findings may point to prioritizing a social marketing plan with a purpose of decreasing the spread of COVID-19, with a focus on indoor sports events, with data indicating the highest incidence of positive tests, and fewest guidelines enforced.

Exploratory research also assists in identifying *organizational strengths and weaknesses* (Step 2) by assessing such factors as levels of support from management and key internal publics, resources available for the effort, the organization's past performance on similar efforts, and the capacity for incremental service delivery. For example, this research would be insightful for a large metropolitan hotel interested in increasing water conservation (*purpose*) with a *focus* on water utilized for laundering guest towels and sheets. Before selection of priority audiences and desired behaviors, a work team would be interested in knowing the levels of behaviors influenced by existing cards in bathrooms that encourage guests to leave towels on the rack if they don't need a clean one and a card on a pillow if sheets don't need to be changed. They would also be curious about any feedback from guests and anecdotal comments from staff regarding the program.

Exploratory research will enrich the identification of external forces that represent *opportunities* as well as *threats*. A citizen advocacy group interested in having the state legislature pass a law making texting while driving a primary, versus secondary, offense will find it useful to conduct informal interviews before speaking at a senate subcommittee hearing. What if they heard, for example, that four of the eight members of the committee were planning to recommend against the bill? This potential threat would certainly guide their selection of a priority audience (Step 3) and underscore the urgent need to conduct subsequent formative research with these four to identify perceived barriers, desired benefits, and potential motivators (Step 5) relative to a "yes" recommendation.

Finally, a search for prior similar efforts addressing the focus for this plan is time well spent and may be accomplished by secondary research including literature reviews, key informant interviews, and queries on social marketing listservs. Christine Domegan, a professor at the National University in Galway, recommends we also consider a collaborative model such as the collective intelligence model, a group methodology for complex problems, also known as interactive management.[20] This model facilitates multiple stakeholders from various sectors and settings to simultaneously work together to scope possible causes of and solutions to social issues, providing perspectives that can inform subsequent steps in the planning model.

ETHICAL CONSIDERATIONS WHEN CHOOSING FOCUS

Conscientious social marketers will no doubt face ethical dilemmas and challenges throughout the planning and implementation process. Although ethical considerations are varied, several themes are common: social equity, unintended consequences, competing priorities, full disclosure, responsible stewardship, conflicts of interest, and whether the end justifies (any) means.

For each of the planning steps covered in this text, major potential ethical questions and concerns will be highlighted at the completion of most chapters, beginning with this one. We present more questions than answers, with the intention of increasing awareness of "ethical moments" and the chances that your decisions will be based on a social conscience that leads all of us to "higher ground."

As was illustrated in the Case Highlight at the beginning of this chapter, many times racist systems and structure that are embedded in our society create ethical challenges for campaigns. For example, a campaign to encourage healthy eating only works in a community where there is access to healthy, affordable food choices. You can imagine a campaign created by a well-meaning social marketer to encourage the consumption of more fruits and vegetables. If they don't take into account that some communities don't have convenient access to fresh produce, and work to overcome that barrier, they may inadvertently leave out a large segment of their audience that needs the campaign the most. The *Our Health is in Our Hands* case highlight showed how BP3D addressed this potential ethical pitfall by using partnerships and advocacy behaviors to help overcome access barriers.[21] In another example, think about when you brainstormed potential focuses and then picked one for your current plan, your first ethical question and challenge probably popped up: "What will happen to the ones we didn't pick?" For decreasing drunk driving, potential foci include choosing designated drivers, promoting a tougher new law, and focusing on specific populations, such as military personnel or repeat offenders. Since each of these choices would lead to a different marketing strategy, you can only (effectively) deal with one at a time. One potential way to address this challenge is to present a comprehensive organizational plan for the social issue, indicating when important areas of focus will be handled and why they have been prioritized as such.

An additional common question and challenge regarding your focus may also come up, often from a colleague or peer: "If you are successful in accomplishing this, won't you make it tougher for me to accomplish mine?" Some argue, for example, that if you choose the focus of increasing the number of teens who choose a designated driver, won't you increase the number of teens who drink? Won't it look like "the government" approves of teen drinking? Good questions. And to answer, you will want to be prepared with your background and SWOT data as well as outcomes from prior similar efforts conducted by other agencies in other markets that support your decisions.

COVID-19 Social Marketing Example

As noted earlier, a COVID-related example will be given at the end of each of the remaining chapters, one that illustrates the application of the featured step in the planning process.

The vast majority of initial COVID-related campaign efforts reflected a *Purpose of Reducing the Spread of COVID-19*, with a *Focus on Protective Behaviors*. Clearly, research data helped determine that there were, in fact, several major protective behaviors that would have reduced the spread, and that social marketing efforts should focus on creating them to be a norm.

CHAPTER SUMMARY

This chapter has introduced the first two of the 10 steps in the social marketing planning model.

Step 1 is intended to help you (and others) clarify why you are embarking on this project and, in broad and brief terms, what you want to accomplish and where you will focus your efforts. This will include:

- Identifying the social issue your plan will address

- Exploring any diversity, equity, and inclusion considerations
- Noting the organization(s) that will be sponsoring the effort
- Gathering and presenting background information relative to the social issue
- Choosing a campaign purpose
- Brainstorming and then selecting a focus for this plan

Step 2 provides rich descriptions of the marketplace where you will be vying for your customers and entails creating a common understanding of the organizational and external challenges you will face by conducting an analysis of:

- *Organizational strengths* to maximize and *weaknesses* to minimize related to organizational resources, service delivery, management support, issue priority, internal publics, current alliances and partners, and past performance
- *External opportunities* to take advantage of and *threats* to prepare for related to cultural, technological, demographic, natural, economic, and political/legal forces, as well as external publics other than current partners and alliances
- *Prior similar campaigns*, with an interest in lessons learned as well as opportunities for using existing research, plans, and materials developed by others

Exploratory research informs the process of identifying a purpose and focus and conducting a situation analysis, and also provides a rationale for your decisions.

RESEARCH HIGHLIGHT

INCREASING HEALTHY FOOD CHOICES IN MILITARY DINING HALLS OBSERVATIONAL RESEARCH

This research case highlights the strength of using an observational research methodology to evaluate and compare multiple intervention strategies, a method that can often remove biases inherent in self-reported surveys. Information for this case was provided by Julia Carins and Sharyn Rundle-Thiele at Griffith University in Australia, coauthors of the more comprehensive article on the study "Delivering Healthy Food Choice: A Dual-Process Model Enquiry," which appeared in the *Social Marketing Quarterly* in 2017.[22]

Background

Military personnel are often chosen and called upon to perform at their best, both physically and cognitively. However, many military personnel consume a diet that is low in recommended foods like fruit and vegetables and high in fat and/or sugar-rich foods. Concern has also been expressed about the level of obesity in military forces in many nations.[23]

Authors of the study first conducted a variety of research efforts related to influencing healthier eating in military dining facilities including:

- a literature review to discover successful strategies used with other audiences that might translate to a military audience;

- conducting in-depth interviews with military personnel to identify barriers and motivators to healthy eating;
- a food audit of military dining facilities and nearby commercial outlets to determine how well the environment supports healthy eating; and
- an observational study of food choice behavior in a military dining hall.

Findings indicated that a primary motivator to eat well was to support performance, rather than health, and that the dining environment layout and a fast-paced choice process was not optimal for healthy eating. This case highlights the relative impact of two programs developed to influence healthier choices in the military dining environment, with an intention for findings to inspire global practices to achieve increased desired behavior changes.

Intervention Strategies Tested

Based on these findings, the GO FOOD program theme was then developed with a focus on linking military personnel motivations (e.g., improved performance) to the foods available, rather than emphasizing the nutritional content of the food (see Figure 5.7). Two programs were developed for testing:

Communications-only program: Designed to be positive and included three key messages:

- GO LEAN: Stay lean and keen with protein
- GO FRESH: Gain an edge with crisp fruit and salads
- GO ENERGY: Complex carbs for slow burn energy

Messages appeared in highly visible spots in the dining room, and materials included a combination of posters, placards, floor stickers, and food labels.

Broader social marketing program. This program used the same GO FOOD communication elements but enhanced the program by changing the dining hall environment to reduce barriers to healthier food choices noted during the formative research. To increase convenience and prominence of healthy choices, the salad counter was moved to be more visible, and a new Express Bar was created to provide premade wraps, sandwiches, juice, and fruit, and was conveniently located to provide a faster traffic flow.

Methodology

The field research was a collaborative effort between Griffith University and the Defence Science and Technology Group. Each program was tested concurrently in two separate, but similarly sized, military dining halls in Australia. In both dining halls, catering staff indicated to diners they could make one main entrée choice but were free to choose any number of selections from the hot vegetable, salad, or sandwich/fruit bars.

A quasi-experimental prepost design technique was used to test the programs over a six-week period. Lunch and dinner meals were observed on each data collection day, providing for four meals in the preimplementation observation period at each site and four meals in the postimplementation period.

Observational methods were developed to measure food selection behaviors.[24] Prior to each meal, researchers noted all choices available for that meal, clarifying with catering staff to ensure each dish (or side dish) was captured and adequately described. Up to eight observers were stationed in the dining room, and observers recorded each selection a diner made. This method produced counts of selections for each dish. To provide additional

FIGURE 5.7 ■ Point-of-Decision Making Signage for the GO FOOD Brand

Source: Sharyn Rundle-Thiele.

insight and more detailed information to compare results between the two dining halls, a second method utilized photographs. As diners exited the food counters, a photographer asked if they could take a photograph of their plate. Examination of each photograph provided more detail on food selections. Correlation analyses were used to examine the relationship between the observed data and the photographic data, and analysis was performed for all food categories.

A total of 4,400 diners (an average of 280 diners per meal) were observed over the course of the experiment.

Findings

Results indicated that although both programs resulted in statistically significant increases in the selection of healthier foods, the broader social marketing program (communications and layout changes) was more effective than the communications-only approach.

Implications

This study, by intention, contributes to military health efforts. Authors note that:

> social marketing programs staged in real-world settings have been dominated by education, communication, or promotion strategies. This is true of the nutrition domain, in reducing alcohol consumption, and in the wider social marketing field... Overall, the results from this direct test of "communication" and "communication plus more" show that while the communication was successful, the broader program achieved even stronger gains.[25]

DISCUSSION QUESTIONS AND EXERCISES

1. What is the distinction between a social issue and a campaign purpose?
2. Identify four potential areas of focus for an effort to decrease youth gun violence.
3. How are strengths and weaknesses distinguished from opportunities and threats?
4. Give an example of a campaign that is "already out there" that an organization planning a similar effort could take advantage of.

6 STEP 3: SELECTING PRIORITY AUDIENCES

LEARNING OBJECTIVES

Upon completion of this chapter, you should be able to:

6.1 Describe the three steps to follow when selecting a priority audience.

6.2 Explain the major variables used for developing potential audience segments.

6.3 Identify the major criteria used for evaluating potential audience segments.

6.4 Note the three recommended steps to finally selecting a priority audience.

6.5 Recognize what ethical considerations are relevant when selecting priority audiences.

Selecting priority audiences probably makes sense to you by now and sounds good in theory. It is, however, the practice that creates the greatest angst for many, reflected in these common musings addressed in this chapter:

- "We're a governmental agency and expected to treat everyone the same. How can we justify allocating a disproportionate share of our resources to a few population segments? Even worse, how can we justify eliminating some segments altogether?"
- "I keep hearing about 'the low-hanging fruit' and that we should go after them first. In my community clinic, I interpret that to mean that we focus our resources on clients who are ready to lose weight, ready to exercise. I don't get it. Don't the ones who aren't ready need us the most to convince them they should?"
- "If a marketing plan is built around and for a particular segment of the population, does that mean we'll need separate and multiple marketing plans for every audience we try to influence? That seems over the top."
- "Sometimes this just sounds like fancy language for something that never really happens. When we do a billboard for organ donation, everyone in town sees it. How is that priority audience marketing?"

In this chapter, you'll read in depth about the benefits of segmentation and learn this three-step process for selecting a priority audience for a specific program effort:

1. Segment a population into homogeneous groups
2. Evaluate segments based on a variety of factors
3. Choose one or more segments as a priority for a program or campaign plan being developed

We believe this inspiring opening case can help dissuade common segmentation concerns by illustrating how multiple segments can be addressed by a social marketing effort, with only a few tailored, but critical, interventions to meet unique audience needs and desires.

CASE HIGHLIGHT

Decreasing Wasted Food By "Forking It Over"

Oregon State's Department of Environmental Quality (DEQ) envisions that in 2050, Oregonians *produce and use materials responsibly*, with an important material being *food*, both in terms of its environmental impact as well as connection to well-being.[1] A strategic plan developed to address this issue was one with a purpose of *preventing waste of food* with a focus on *contributing "perfectly good surplus food" to those in need*, rather than an emphasis on proper disposal solutions. Planners were clearly inspired by background data indicating:[2]

- Up to 40% of the food grown or imported for consumption is not eaten and then disposed of.
- One in seven people living in the United States are food insecure.

This case highlights a program strategy launched by the Portland Metro government that was branded *Fork It Over!* Two priority audiences, *restaurants* and *schools*, are featured in this case story, each with a common purpose, focus, and desired behavior (donate surplus, edible food), but, not surprisingly, unique barriers, benefits, and motivators, leading to customized marketing interventions. More than 150 agencies were identified as recipients of donated foods, including food banks, churches, Boys & Girls Clubs, senior centers, shelters for the homeless, and more.[3] And the program utilized all 4P marketing intervention tools to "help" priority audiences, as well as food banks and other agency recipients, make this happen.

Restaurants as a priority audience: In depth audience research was conducted with over 70 restaurant businesses to identify barriers and desired benefits to donating their surplus food to food agencies.[4] Major concerns were related to knowing whether the food was safe (e.g., perfectly good); how to store it properly; the amount of time it might require to select, store, and deliver the food; and whether they would be liable if there was any harm caused by the food items they donated. They also had questions regarding whether or not they could choose the agency their food would be donated to, and how to get items for donation to them. Interestingly, their primary desired benefit was not the potential financial benefits of tax write-offs. They were most motivated by the purpose and focus of the effort to help reduce waste and at the same time help fight hunger.[5]

All four marketing intervention tools were needed and utilized to make this happen.

- *Products* included local government specialists to help businesses get set up. An interactive website was developed to provide: online program instructions for identifying food items that could be donated; ways to package and equipment needed to store them; and resources for selecting agencies of choice to receive their donations.
- *Price* strategies included nonmonetary incentives, with an emphasis on obtaining a written and public commitment from restaurants to donate food regularly. These commitments were then reinforced through publicized print advertising, web postings, and earned media. Monetary incentives included grants to purchase refrigerated trucks, coolers, and freezers, and other equipment needed to store food to be donated.
- *Place:* A portal on the *Fork It Over!* website would make it easy for donors to enter their business location, the food they wished to donate, and to then select from a list of closest food rescue agencies the ones they were interested in supporting. For delivery, an option for many is a nonprofit organization Waste Not Food Taxi, which has a network of volunteer drivers who will pick up commercial leftovers and deliver them to a partner hunger-relief agency. They provide an online tool to communicate and coordinate pick-ups, at times that work for the restaurants, as well as the food agencies.[6]
- *Promotion*: Restaurant inspectors agreed to distribute *Fork it Over!* brochures during their regular annual inspections, as well as leaving behind durable magnets with information on how to learn more about the program. Brochures and posters provided detailed program information for potential restaurant participants, and pioneer donors were recruited as spokespersons, addressing major concerns by assuring that donations were "safe, simple, and the right thing to do." Advertisements were placed in the food section of daily newspapers; ads were placed in industry publications; and special events were held. Ads were even placed in telephone directories under restaurant and catering listings to remind patrons to ask for and to acknowledge businesses to *Fork it Over!*[7]

Results: A measurement of campaign outcomes between 2003 and 2005 indicated that an estimated total of 9,000 tons (18,000 pounds) was "forked over" annually. By 2005, the campaign had expanded participation by signing on 59 new businesses in the first six months. "Visits to the program's website increased from 34 in May of 2004, a month before the campaign began, to 948 for the month of July 2004, nearly a 2700% increase."[8]

Schools as a priority audience: A motivating statistic that ignited *Fork It Over!* to consider public schools as a priority audience included an example in one school district where over 70% of the food thrown away during lunch in several elementary schools was completely avoidable waste.[9] In 2004, Portland Public School System began working with nonprofits near the schools to coordinate quarterly food collection before long school holidays. In addition, DEQ worked with "demonstration" school kitchens to implement practices around reducing the wasting of food. Activities also include opportunities to teach students about the impacts of wasted food, such as one offered by a nonprofit organization, StopWaste, that provides free class programs introducing students to becoming "Garbologists," and to conduct waste audits at the schools.[10]

In 2014, the Portland Public School System reported that over the past ten years, about 92 tons of less perishable foods such as fruit, bread, juice, and breakfast bars had been "forked over."[11]

STEP 3: SELECT PRIORITY AUDIENCES

At this point in the planning process, you have established the following components of your plan (illustrated using a utility as a hypothetical example):

- *Purpose* (e.g., decrease landfill and hauling costs)
- *Focus* (e.g., residential backyard composting of food waste)
- *Strengths* to maximize (e.g., as a utility, access to the customer base)
- *Weaknesses* to minimize (e.g., the utility's curb side yard waste collection service just started accepting food waste, an internal competitor for the food waste)
- *Opportunities* to capture (e.g., continued community interest in natural gardening)
- *Threats* to prepare for (e.g., potential to increase rodent populations)
- Possible discovery of *existing campaigns* that will be useful for your efforts (e.g., one from a list of success stories on a state department of ecology's website)

You are now ready to select a priority audience for your campaign, defined by commercial marketers as *a set of buyers sharing common needs or characteristics that the company decides to serve*. They are subsets of the larger group (population) that may also be exposed to your efforts. In the utility example, residential households are the population of focus for the backyard composting campaign but not the priority audience. Your marketing strategy will be crafted to be particularly effective with a subset of these diverse residents.

It is noted there are several terms that are also used to describe these subsets of a population for a social marketing effort including *priority audience, target audience*, and *priority group*. In recent years, social marketers have moved away from using the term "target" audience due to concerns over the aggressive and violent connotation that term implies. Instead the term "priority" is used to describe audiences, people or groups that are the focus of a specific social marketing program.

STEPS IN SELECTING PRIORITY AUDIENCES

Determining a priority audience for your program or campaign plan is a three-step process involving *segmentation, evaluation*, and then *selection*. Each of these steps is described briefly in the following section and elaborated upon in the remaining sections of the chapter.

Segment the Market

First, the most relevant (larger) population for the campaign is divided into smaller groups who will likely require unique strategies in order to be persuaded to change their behavior. The groups you end up with should have something in common (needs, wants, barriers, desired benefits, motivations, values, culture, behavior, demographics, lifestyles, etc.)—something that makes them likely to respond similarly to your offer. Based on background information about attitudes toward composting indicating that avid gardeners are the most interested in composting, this city utility might identify three market segments among avid gardeners to consider. As you will see, their segmentation is based initially on a combination of values, lifestyle, and behavior variables:

- Avid gardeners putting most of their food waste in their *yard waste container to be hauled off*
- Avid gardeners putting most of their food waste in the *garbage containers to be hauled off*
- Avid gardeners putting most of their food waste down the drain with a garbage disposal

Evaluate Segments

Each segment is then evaluated based on a variety of factors described later in the chapter, ones that will assist you in prioritizing (perhaps even eliminating some) segments. For the food-waste-composting scenario, planners should be very eager to know more about each of these segments, beginning with *size* (number of households in the group) as a way to understand the impact that the segment is having on the solid waste stream. They should also consider their *ability to reach* each identified segment and *how receptive* they might be to the idea of composting food waste in their backyard.

Select a Priority Segment

Ideally, you are able to select only one or a few segments as a priority audience for the campaign and then develop a rich profile of their distinguishing characteristics that will inspire strategies to uniquely and effectively appeal to them. Keep in mind that if you select more than one audience, it is likely that you will need a different marketing intervention mix strategy for each. A campaign to influence avid gardeners who are currently putting their food waste in their yard waste container to be hauled off, to instead put it in a backyard compost pile or container would have different incentives and messages, and perhaps even communication channels, than one intending to persuade those who currently put their food waste down the drain using a garbage disposal, or in their garbage containers.

This segmentation and prioritization process, though sometimes tedious and complex, provides numerous benefits—ones long familiar to corporate sector marketers who "know that they cannot appeal to all buyers in their markets, or at least not all buyers in the same way":[12]

- *Increased effectiveness:* Outcomes (numbers of behaviors successfully influenced) will be greater, as you have designed strategies that address your priority audience's unique wants and preferences and therefore "works." (It's like fishing. If you use the bait that the fish you want like, you're more likely to catch the ones you want... and more of them!)

- *Increased efficiency:* Outcomes relative to outputs (resources expended) are also likely to be greater, again as a result of prioritizing your efforts and resources toward market segments with a higher likelihood of responding to your offer. (And back to the fish analogy. You are also likely to catch all these fish in a shorter time and with less bait.)
- *Input for resource allocation:* As a result of evaluating each of the segments, you have objective information that will assist you in distributing your resources and providing this rationale to others.
- *Input for developing strategies:* This process will leave you with detailed profiles of a segment that will then provide critical insights into what will influence a specific audience to buy your behavior.
- *Addressing equity:* Most of the programs and issues that social marketers work on are impacted by social equity issues. It is important to understand how your issue, program, and audiences are influenced by the systems and structures in our society that perpetuate racism and inequity. Dealing with systems and structures is almost never the quickest or most cost-effective path to behavior change, but it may be the right path to make the long-term change you are seeking. Factoring this thinking into your segmentation strategy and priority audience selection is an important part of addressing equity issues in social marketing programs.

Even if, for a variety of purposes, programs are developed for all markets, segmentation at least organizes, prioritizes, and provides a framework for developing strategies that are more likely to be successful with each of the markets.

VARIABLES USED TO SEGMENT MARKETS

Potential variables and models for segmenting a market are vast and still expanding. Traditional approaches used by commercial marketers for decades are described in this section, as are unique models successfully applied by social marketing theorists and practitioners, expanding on those mentioned in Chapter 4.

Keep in mind that in this initial segmentation process, before you have actually chosen a priority audience, your objective is to create several potential segments for consideration. You will select variables to characterize each group that are the most meaningful predictors of market behavior, ending up with groups that are likely to respond similarly to your offer (*products, price*, and *place*) and your promotional elements (*messages, messengers, creative elements*, and *communication channels*).

Traditional Variables

Traditional segmentation variables used to categorize and describe consumer markets are outlined in Table 6.1. Each is applicable to a social marketing environment (marketplace) as well.[13]

TABLE 6.1 ■ Traditional Segmentation Variables for Consumer Markets

Variable	Sample Classifications
Geographic	
World, region, or country	North America, Canada, Western Europe, Middle East, Pacific Rim, China, India, Brazil
Country or region	Pacific, Mountain, West North Central, West South Central, East North Central, East South Central, South Atlantic, Middle Atlantic, New England
City or metro size	Under 5,000; 5,000–20,000; 20,000–50,000; 50,000–100,000; 100,000–250,000; 250,000–500,000; 500,000–1,000,000; 1,000,000–4,000,000; over 4,000,000
Density	Urban, suburban, exurban, rural
Climate	Northern, southern
Demographic	
Age	Under 6, 6–11, 12–17, 18–24, 25–34, 35–49, 50–64, 65 and over
Gender	male, female, nonbinary
Family size	1–2, 3–4, 5, or more
Family life cycle	Young, single; married, no children; married with children; single parents; unmarried couples; older, married, no children under 18; older, single; other
Income	Under $10,000; $10,000–$20,000; $20,000–$30,000; $30,000–$50,000; $50,000–$100,000; $100,000–$250,000; over $250,000
Occupation	Professional and technical; managers, officials, proprietors; clerical, sales; craftspeople; supervisors; service providers; gig-economy workers; farmers; retired; students; homemakers; unemployed
Education	Grade school or less, some high school, high school graduate, some college, college graduate
Religion	Catholic, Protestant, Jewish, Muslim, Hindu, other
Race/ethnicity	White, Hispanic/Latino, Black/African American, Asian American Indian/Alaska Native, Pacific Islander/Native Hawaiian, Multiple Races
Generation	Baby Boomer, Generation X, Millennials, Generation Z, Gen Alpha
Disability	Physical, mental, emotional, neurodiverse
Psychographic	
Lifestyle	Achievers, strivers, strugglers
Personality	Compulsive, outgoing, authoritarian, ambitious
Peer crowds	Mainstream, Popular, Hip Hop, Alternative, Country
Values	Conservative, liberal, independent
Behavioral	
Occasions	Regular occasion, special occasion, holiday, seasonal
Benefits	Quality, service, economy, convenience, speed
User status	Nonuser, ex-user, potential user, first-time user, regular user
Usage rate	Light user, medium user, heavy user
Loyalty status	None, medium, strong, absolute
Readiness stage	Unaware, aware, informed, interested, desirous, intending to buy
Attitude toward product	Enthusiastic, positive, indifferent, negative, hostile

Source: Kotler, Philip T.; Armstrong, Gary, Principles of Marketing, 9th Ed., ©2001. Reprinted by permission of Pearson Education, Inc., New York, NY.

Demographic segmentation divides the market into groups on the basis of variables common to census forms: age, gender, marital status, family size, income, occupation (including the media, legislators, physicians, etc.), education, religion, ethnicity, and nationality. Sometimes referred to as sociodemographic, diversity, or socioeconomic factors, these are the most popular bases for grouping markets, for several reasons. First, they are some of the *best predictors* of needs, wants, barriers, benefits, and behaviors. Second, this type of information about a market is *more readily available* than it is for other variables, such as personality characteristics or attitudes. Finally, these are often the easiest ways to *describe and find a priority segment* and to share with others working to develop and implement program strategies.

Example: A demographic basis for segmentation could be quite appropriate in planning an immunization campaign because immunization schedules vary considerably according to age. Planners might understandably create unique strategies for each of the following population segments in their local community:

- Parents of children age birth to 2 years
- Parents of children age 3–6 years
- Parents of children age 7–17 years
- Adults, 18–64 years
- Seniors, 65 years and over

Geographic segmentation divides a market according to geographic areas, such as continents, countries, states, provinces, regions, counties, cities, schools, and neighborhoods, as well as related elements, such as commute patterns, places of work, and proximity to relevant landmarks.

Example: An organization focused on reducing the number of employees driving to work in single-occupant vehicles might find it most useful to develop strategies based on *where employees live* relative to the worksite, current van pools, current carpools, and each other. The planner might then decide that the first four groups represent the greatest opportunity for connecting employees with attractive alternative and/or existing forms of transportation:

- Employees living on current van pool routes
- Employees living within five miles of current carpools
- Employees living within five miles of each other
- Employees living within walking or biking distance of the workplace
- All other employees

Psychographic segmentation divides the market into different groups on the basis of lifestyle, values, culture, or personality characteristics. You may find that your market varies more by a personal value, such as concern for the environment, than by some demographic characteristic, such as age.

Behavior segmentation divides the market into different groups on the bases of historic and current related behaviors.

Example: A blood donation center may increase efficiency by prioritizing resource allocation according to donation history, allocating the most resources to loyal donors (those who have given in the past):

- Gave more than 10 times in the past five years
- Gave 2–10 times in the past five years
- Gave only once, less than five years ago
- Gave only once, more than five years ago
- Never gave at this blood center

In reality, marketers rarely limit their segmentation to the use of only one variable as we did to illustrate each of these variables. More often, they use a combination of variables that provide a rich profile of a segment or help to create smaller, better-defined primary audiences.[14] Even if, for example, the blood center decided to prioritize those who had given more than once in the past five years, they might further refine the segment by blood type if a particular type was in short supply and high demand.

Stages of Change Variables

The *stages of change model*, mentioned in Chapter 4 and referred to as the *transtheoretical model*, was originally developed by Prochaska and DiClemente in the early 1980s[15] and has been tested and refined over the past decades. In a 1994 publication, *Changing for Good*, Prochaska, Norcross, and DiClemente describe six stages that people go through to change their behavior.[16] As you read about each one, imagine the implications for a specific population you are working with or, if you are a student, one you have chosen for the focus of a class project.

Precontemplation: "People at this stage usually have no intention of changing their behavior and typically deny having a problem."[17] Relative to the behavior you are "selling," you could think of this market as "sound asleep." They may have woken up and thought about it at some point in the past, but they have gone back to sleep. In the case of an effort to convince people to quit smoking, this segment is not thinking about quitting, doesn't consider their tobacco use a problem, or tried once in the past but decided not to try again.

Contemplation: "People acknowledge that they have a problem and begin to think seriously about solving it."[18] Or they may have a want or desire and have been thinking about fulfilling it. They are "awake but haven't moved." This segment of smokers is considering quitting for any number of reasons but hasn't definitely decided and hasn't taken any steps.

Preparation: "Most people in the Preparation Stage are (now) planning to take action and are making the final adjustments before they begin to change their behavior."[19] Back to our analogy, they are "sitting up"—maybe they even have their feet on the floor. In this segment, smokers have decided to quit and may have told others about their intentions. They probably have decided how they will quit and by when.

Action: "The Action Stage is one in which people most overtly modify their behavior and their surroundings. They stop smoking cigarettes, remove all desserts from the house, pour the last beer down the drain, or confront their fears. In short, they make the move for which they have been preparing."[20] They have "left the bed." This segment has recently stopped smoking cigarettes. However, it may not be a new habit yet.

Maintenance: "During Maintenance, individuals work to consolidate the gains attained during the action and other stages and struggle to prevent lapses and relapse."[21] Individuals in this segment have not had a cigarette for perhaps six months or a year and remain committed to not smoking. However, at times they have to work to remind themselves of the benefits they are experiencing and distract themselves when they are tempted to relapse.

Termination: "The Termination stage is the ultimate goal for all changers. Here, a former addiction or problem will no longer present any temptation or threat."[22] This segment is not tempted to return to smoking. They are now "nonsmokers" for life.

One of the attractive features of this model is that the authors have identified a relatively simple way to assess a market's stage. They suggest four questions to ask, and, on the basis of responses, respondents are categorized in one of the four stages.[23] Table 6.2 summarizes the groupings by stage of change on the basis of the four responses.

In the model shown in Box 6.2, the "name of the marketer's game" is to move segments to the next stage.

Figure 6.1 is Prochaska et al.'s graphic representation of the more likely patterns of change, a spiral one.

BOX 6.1

Stages of Change Progression

Precontemplation ⇒	Contemplation ⇒	Preparation ⇒	Action ⇒	Maintenance ⇒	Termination

Diffusion of Innovation: Social Marketing Version

As described in Chapter 4, social marketers often now use a "custom" version of the Diffusion of Innovation Model, one that is described in Box 6.2.

FIGURE 6.1 ■ The Spiral of Change

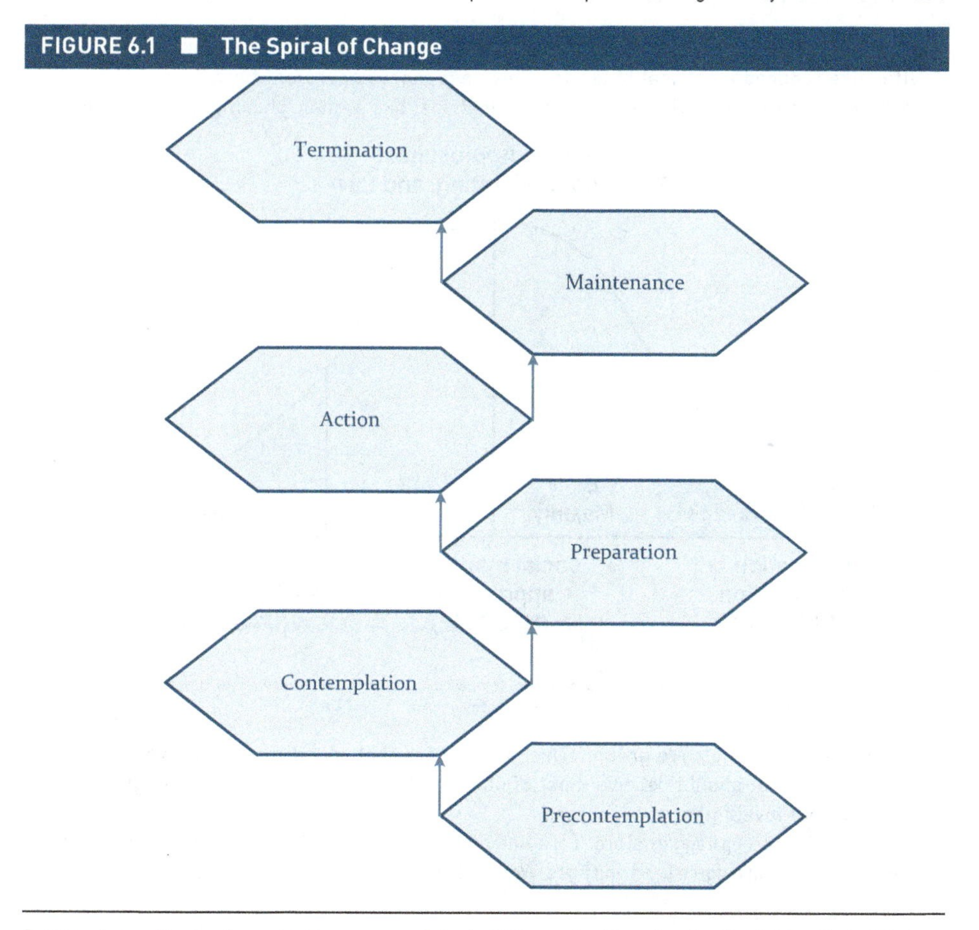

Source: James Prochaska, John Norcross, and Carlo DiClemente, Changing for Good (New York, NY: Avon Books, 1994), 40–56.

BOX 6.2

"Show Me"/"Help Me"/"Make Me": A Social Marketing Version of the Diffusion of Innovation Model

When a new behavior is introduced into the marketplace, the first two groups (innovators and early adopters) usually only need someone to show them what to do to be healthy, prevent injuries, protect the environment, and contribute to their communities. Information and education are typically all it takes with this group, so we call them the "just *Show Me* group."

The two middles, and typically largest, groups (early and late majority) have some interest in doing the behavior or at best are not opposed to it. But they have barriers to action and may not be convinced the benefits outweigh the costs. They need goods and services to stop smoking, like tobacco quitlines. They need incentives to insulate their attic, like reduced electrical bills. And they need more convenient times and locations to recycle their unwanted prescription medications, like at their pharmacy. We call this

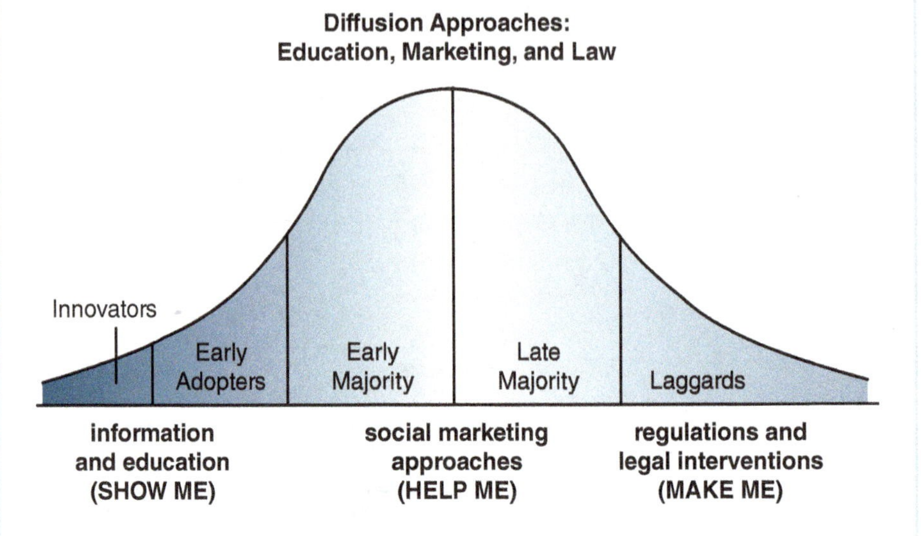

Source: Graphic based on Everett Rogers's diffusion of innovations model, reinterpreted by Jay Kassirer, Mike Rothschild, Dave Ward, and Kristen Cooley, and graphically designed by C+C in Seattle.

group the "please *Help Me* group." This is the group that social marketers were "born for," the one that should receive most of our attention, as we can expect the greatest return on our investment of resources.

And the final group (laggards) aren't at all interested in doing the behavior, and most likely won't unless we pass and enforce laws and fines. We call them the "you'll have to *Make Me* group."

TABLE 6.2 DETERMINING STAGE OF CHANGE (EXCLUDING TERMINATION STAGE)

Decision/ Response Taken	Decision/Response Taken By:				
	Precontemplation Segment	Contemplation Segment	Preparation Segment	Action Segment	Maintenance Segment
I solved this problem more than six months ago	No	No	No	No	Yes
I have taken action within the past six months	No	No	No	Yes	Yes
I intend to take action in the next month	No	No	Yes	Yes	Yes
I intend to take action in the next six months	No	Yes	Yes	Yes	Yes

TABLE 6.3 ■ Healthstyles Segmentation System, American Healthstyles Audience Segmentation Project

Decent Dolittles (24%)
They are one of the less health-oriented groups. Although less likely to smoke or drink, they also are less likely to exercise, eat nutritiously, and work to stay at their ideal weights. Decent Dolittles know that they should be performing these behaviors to improve their health, but they do not feel that they have the ability. Their friends and family tend to avoid these behaviors as well. They describe themselves as "religious," "conservative," and "clean."
Active Attractives (13%)
They place a high emphasis on looking good and partying. Active Attractives are relatively youthful and moderately health oriented. They tend not to smoke and limit their fat intake more than do other groups. They are highly motivated, intending to exercise and keep their weight down, but they do not always succeed at this. Alcohol consumption is an important part of their lifestyle, and Active Attractives often are sensation seekers, constantly looking for adventure. They describe themselves as "romantic," "dynamic," "youthful," and "vain."
Hard-Living Hedonists (6%)
They are not very interested in health and tend to smoke and drink alcohol more heavily and frequently than do other groups. They also enjoy eating high-fat foods and do not care about limiting their fat intake. Despite this, they tend not to be overweight and are moderately physically active. Although they are the group least satisfied with their lives, they have no desire to make any health-related changes. Hard-Living Hedonists also are more likely to use stimulants and illicit drugs than are other segments. They describe themselves as "daring," "moody," "rugged," "independent," and "exciting."
Tense But Trying (10%)
They are similar to the more health-oriented segments except that they tend to smoke cigarettes. They are average in the amount of exercise they get and in their efforts to control their fat intake and weight. They have a moderate desire to exercise more, eat better, and control their weight more effectively as well. The Tense but Trying tend to be more anxious than other groups, with the highest rate of ulcers and use of sedatives and a higher number of visits to mental health counselors. They describe themselves as "tense," "high-strung," "sensitive," and "serious."
Noninterested Nihilists (7%)
They are the least health oriented and do not feel that people should take steps to improve their health. Accordingly, they smoke heavily, actively dislike exercise, eat high-fat diets, and make no efforts to control their weight. Despite this, they tend to drink alcohol only moderately. Of all the groups, Noninterested Nihilists have the highest level of physical impairment, the most sick days in bed, and the most medical care visits related to an illness. They describe themselves as being "depressed," "moody," and "homebodies."
Physical Fantastics (24%)
They are the most health-oriented group, leading a consistently health-promoting lifestyle. They are above average in not smoking or drinking, exercising routinely, eating nutritiously, and making efforts to control their weight. They tend to be in their middle or latter adult years and have a relatively large number of chronic health conditions. Physical Fantastics follow their physicians' advice to modify their diets and routinely discuss health-related topics with others.

(Contiunued)

TABLE 6.3 ■ Healthstyles Segmentation System, American Healthstyles Audience Segmentation Project *(Continued)*

Passive Healthy (15%)
They are in excellent health, although they are somewhat indifferent to living healthfully. They do not smoke or drink heavily and are one of the most active segments. Although they eat a high amount of dietary fat, they are the trimmest of all the groups. The Passive Healthy do not place much value on good health and physical fitness and are not motivated to make any changes in their behaviors.

Source: Reprinted by permission of Sage Publications Ltd. from Edward W. Maibach, Keren Ladin, and Don Slater, "Translating Health Psychology Into Effective Health Communication: The American Healthstyles Audience Segmentation Project," *Journal of Health Psychology*, I, pp. 261–277. As appeared in Weinreich, N., *Hands-On Social Marketing: A Step-by-Step Guide* (p. 55).

Healthstyles Segmentation

Another segmentation model used for health-related program planning appears in Table 6.3. This system incorporates several segmentation variables, including demographics, psychographics, knowledge, attitudes, and current behaviors related to personal health. Resulting segments provide planners with a rich and memorable picture of each potential priority audience, aiding in the development of winning strategies for that market. For example, a physical activity campaign wanting to influence *Decent Dolittles*, who may not have confidence in their ability to exercise, might emphasize the benefits of moderate physical activity, how it can fit into everyday life and activities, and the opportunities to "hang out with friends" while doing it. By contrast, a strategy to influence the *Tense but Trying* segment would switch the emphasis to the health benefits of exercise, especially for stress-related illnesses.

Environmental Segmentation

Professor Ed Maibach at George Mason University is passionate about audience segmentation:

> Selecting the right audience may be the most important decision you make. For both upstream and downstream social marketing programs, it is critically important to identify the people who you can influence, and who, if you succeed in influencing them, will make the biggest difference in improving the situation you seek to improve.[24]

With the goal of improving climate change public engagement initiatives, Maibach, Leiserowitz, and Roser-Renouf conducted a national study to identify distinct and motivationally coherent groups within the American public.[25] In the fall of 2008, they conducted a nationally representative web-based survey to measure Americans' climate change beliefs, issue involvement, policy preferences, and behaviors. Using market segmentation techniques, they identified six distinct groups and described them as follows (see also Figure 6.2):

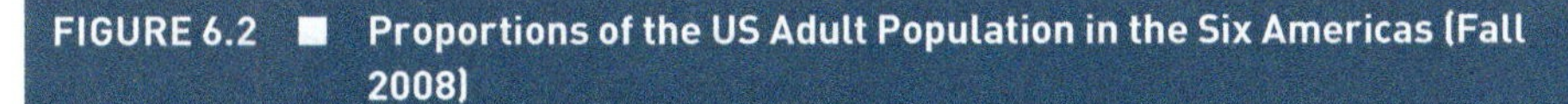

FIGURE 6.2 ■ Proportions of the US Adult Population in the Six Americas (Fall 2008)

Proportion represented by area

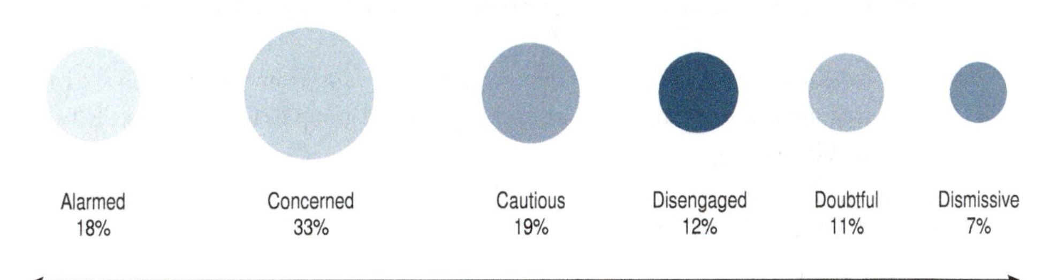

Highest Belief in Global Warning
Most Concerned
Most Motivated
n = 2,129

Lowest Belief in Global Warning
Least Concerned
Least Motivated

Source: Anthony Leiserowtiz and Edward Maibach, *Global Warming's "Six Americas": An Audience Segmentation* (Fairfax, VA: George Mason University, Center for Climate Change Communication, 2010).

- The *Alarmed* (18%) are the segment most engaged in the issue of global warming. They are completely convinced it is happening, caused by humans, and a serious and urgent threat. The Alarmed are already making changes in their own lives and support an aggressive national response.
- The *Concerned* (33%) are moderately convinced that global warming is a serious problem, but while they support a vigorous national response, they are distinctly less involved in the issue and less likely than the Alarmed to take personal action.
- The *Cautious* (19%) also believe that global warming is a problem, although they are less certain that it is happening than the Alarmed or the Concerned. They don't view it as a personal threat and don't feel a sense of urgency to deal with it through personal or societal actions.
- The *Disengaged* (12%) haven't thought much about the issue. They are the segment most likely to say that they could easily change their minds about global warming, and they are the most likely to select the "don't know" option in response to every survey question about global warming where "don't know" is presented as an option.
- The *Doubtful* (11%) are evenly split among those who think global warming is happening, those who think it isn't, and those who don't know. Many within this group believe that if global warming is happening, it is caused by natural changes in the environment, that it won't harm people for many decades into the future, if at all, and that America is already doing enough to respond to the threat.

- The *Dismissive* (7%), like the Alarmed, are actively engaged in the issue, but on the opposite end of the spectrum. The large majority of the people in this segment believe that global warming is not happening, is either not a threat to people or is not caused by humans, and is not a problem that warrants a personal or societal response.

As of 2022, these surveys are conducted twice yearly, with results from the survey in the Fall of 2021 indicating significant changes with the size of Alarmed group nearly doubling (33% in 2021 vs. 18% in 2008) (see Figure 6.3).

Generational Segmentation

Some researchers and theorists point to the power of market segmentation on the basis of generation. Every generation is profoundly influenced by the times in which it grows up—the music, movies, politics, technological advances, economics, and defining events of the period (e.g., the Great Depression, 9/11, COVID-19 Pandemic). Demographers refer to generational groups as *cohorts*, members of which share similar major cultural, political, and economic experiences.[26] The six groups in Table 6.4 are a blend of several popular generational segmentation typologies.[27]

Of significance to social marketers is that these cohort segments and characteristics may provide unique insight into current beliefs, attitudes, and other behavioral influences. Kotler and Keller suggest, however, that we consider the impact that additional variables have on these cohorts. For example, two individuals from the same cohort (Baby Boomers) may differ in their *life stages* (e.g., one recently divorced and the other never married); *physiographics*,

FIGURE 6.3 ■ Proportions of the U.S. Adult Population in the Six Americas (Fall 2021)

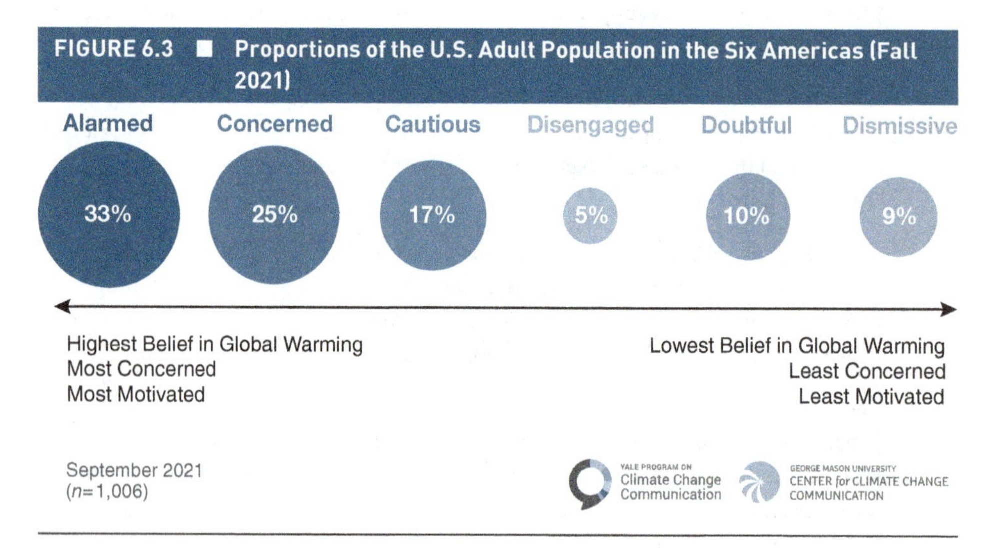

Source: Anthony Leiserowtiz and Edward Maibach, Global Warming's "Six Americas": An Audience Segmentation (Fairfax, VA: George Mason University, Center for Climate Change Communication, 2010 and 2021).

TABLE 6.4 ■ Generational Segments

Born	Name	Major Characteristics
1927–1945	Traditionalists	Loyal, hardworking, disciplined, patriotic, civic-minded
1946–1964	Baby boomers	Optimistic, driven, competitive, career-centered
1965–1977	Generation X	Cynical, self-starters, independent, resourceful, media savvy
1978–1994	Generation Y	Edgy, focused on urban style, more idealistic than Gen-X
1995–2002	Millennials	Tech-savvy, multicultural, grew up in affluent society
2003–2019	Generation Z	Currently described as a generation that will be more global, social, and technological
2020–2025, 2028	Gen Alpha	First to be born in the 21st century with childhood dominated by smart technology

that is, conditions related to a person's age (e.g., one coping with hair loss and the other diabetic); and/or *socioeconomics* (e.g., one having recently lost a job and the other having received an inheritance).[29]

Segmenting Midstream and Upstream

To this point, we have been focusing on market segmentation variables for those we are interested in prioritizing for adoption of a behavior, sometimes referred to as downstream audiences. As you read in Chapter 1, however, real social change strategies also often benefit from (even depend on) influencing markets midstream and/or upstream from the individual:

- *Midstream audiences* include family members, friends, neighbors, church leaders, healthcare providers, teachers, law enforcement, retail clerks, entertainers, media, Facebook friends, and others closer to your priority audience, especially ones they listen to, observe, or look up to.
- *Upstream audiences* include policymakers, school districts, corporations, foundations, and other groups with decision-making power and/or resources for creating infrastructures, business practices, and environments that support behavior change (e.g., bike lanes, labeling of serving sizes on packages, breathalyzers in bars, and placement of healthy foods in school cafeterias).

The segmentation process is the same for these populations, but the variables are likely to differ. Family members, for example, may be segmented by spouses versus children, and healthcare providers may be segmented by pharmacists versus pediatricians. Politicians might be segmented by what committees they serve on or by political party. The corporate market will more likely be segmented by industry type, schools by administrative level, and foundations by areas

TABLE 6.5 ■ Segmentation Synchronizing Five of the Stages of Change and *Show Me. Help Me. Make Me.* Model as Primary Bases for a Hypothetical Population of People Who Smoke in Their Cars

Stage of Change	The Make Me's (Precontemplation)	The Help Me's (Contemplation)	The Help Me's (Preparation for or in Action)	The Show Me's (Maintenance)
Behavior and intent	Throw cigarette butts out the window and aren't concerned about it.	Throw cigarette butts out the window, feel bad about it, and have been thinking about not doing it.	Sometimes throw cigarette butts out the window and sometimes use ashtray. Trying to increase use of ashtray.	Never throw cigarette butts out the window; use ashtray instead.
Size	20%	30%	30%	20%
Geographics (residence)	Rural (10%) Suburban (40%) Urban (50%)	Rural (8%) Suburban (55%) Urban (37%)	Rural (6%) Suburban (65%) Urban (29%)	Rural (5%) Suburban (70%) Urban (25%)
Demographics (age)	16–20 (60%) 21–34 (25%) 35–50 (10%) 50+ (5%)	16–20 (43%) 21–34 (22%) 35–50 (15%) 50+ (10%)	16–20 (45%) 21–34 (20%) 35–50 (20%) 50+ (15%)	16–20 (30%) 21–34 (18%) 35–50 (27%) 50+ (25%)
Psychographics (environmental ethic)	Environmentally: Concerned (10%) Neutral (30%) Not concerned (60%)	Environmentally: Concerned (15%) Neutral (45%) Not concerned (40%)	Environmentally: Concerned (30%) Neutral (40%) Not concerned (30%)	Environmentally: Concerned (60%) Neutral (30%) Not concerned (10%)

of focus. Once the market is segmented, you will still proceed to the next two steps of evaluation and selection.

Combination of Variables

As noted earlier, it is rare that a market will be segmented using only one variable. However, one base is often used as a primary way to group a market (e.g., age for immunization); then each segment is further profiled using descriptive variables (e.g., related behaviors) and perhaps narrowed by using additional important and relevant variables that predict response to strategies (e.g., education and income levels within each of the age segments for immunization).

"The most appropriate segmentation variables are those that best capture differences in the behavior of priority adopters."[30] For social marketing planning, we encourage you to consider using the *Show Me. Help Me. Make Me.* variables as the primary base for segmenting the market, similar to the ones in the stages of change model described earlier. Segments are then profiled using other meaningful variables. Table 6.5 illustrates a hypothetical profile of market segments that a planner might compile at this stage in the planning process. References to how these relate to the diffusion model are noted. This profile uses Andreasen's version of the stages of change model, which collapses the six stages to four, a model more manageable for some programs. The issue is litter on roadways. The market is people who smoke in cars.[31]

CRITERIA FOR EVALUATING SEGMENTS

Once the marketplace has been grouped into meaningful population segments, the next task is to evaluate each segment in preparation for decisions regarding selection of priority audiences.

For social marketers, Andreasen cites nine factors for evaluating segments relative to each other.[32] A list of these factors follows, with typical questions that might be asked to establish each measure. To further illustrate each factor, a situation is described in which a state health agency is deciding whether middle school students would be the most attractive segment for promoting safe sex. This segment would then be compared to a similar evaluation of high school students and college students.

1. *Segment size:* How many people are in this segment? What percentage of the population do they represent? (How many middle school youth are sexually active?)
2. *Problem incidence:* How many people in this segment are either engaged in the "problem-related behavior" or not engaged in the "desired behavior"? (What percentage of middle school youth are having unprotected sex?)
3. *Problem severity:* What are the levels of consequences of the problem behavior in this segment? (What is the incidence of sexually transmitted diseases and pregnancy among middle school youth?)

4. *Defenselessness:* To what extent can this segment "take care of themselves" versus needing help from others? (What percentage of middle school youth have easy access to condoms?)

5. *Reachability:* Is this an audience that can be easily identified and reached? (Are there communication channels and other venues that we can use for safe-sex messages specifically for middle school youth?)

6. *General responsiveness:* How "ready, willing, and able" to respond are those in this segment? (How concerned are middle school youth about sexually transmitted diseases and pregnancy? How do they compare with high school students or college students in this regard? Which group has been most responsive to similar campaign messages in the past?)

7. *Incremental costs:* How do estimated costs to reach and influence this segment compare with those for other segments? (Are there free or inexpensive distribution channels for condoms for middle school youth? How does this compare with those for high school and college students? Are there campaigns from other states that have been proven to work well with middle school youth, or will we need to start from scratch?)

8. *Responsiveness to marketing intervention mix:* How responsive is this market likely to be to marketing intervention strategies (product, price, place, and promotion)? (What are the greatest influences on middle school youths' decisions relative to their sexual activity? Will the parents of middle school youth, more so than those of high school or college students, be concerned about potential programs and messages?)

9. *Organizational capabilities:* How extensive is our staff expertise and the availability of outside resources in terms of assisting in the development and implementation of activities for this market? (Is our experience and expertise with middle school youth as strong as it is with high school and college students?)

HOW PRIORITY AUDIENCES ARE SELECTED

Market segmentation has identified and described relevant market segments. *Evaluation activities* provide information on each segment that will help you take the next step: deciding which segment will be *the priority audience* for the campaign or program being planned.

Most organizations involved in social marketing (public sector agencies and nonprofit organizations) are faced with limited budgets. Segments will need to be prioritized, with a disproportionate amount of resources being allocated to the most effective and efficient segments. Some segments will need to be eliminated from the plan.

Priority audiences (markets of greatest opportunity) emerge as those with the greatest need, are the most ready for action (Help Me's), easiest and least costly to reach, and best match for the organization. Evaluation criteria used to assess each of these are as follows:

- *Greatest need* (*Evaluation Criteria #1, #2, #3, and #4*): size, incidence, severity, and defenselessness
- *Greatest readiness for action (Evaluation Criteria #6):* readiness, willingness, and ability to respond
- *Easiest and least costly to reach (Evaluation Criteria #5 and #7):* identifiable venues available for distribution and communication
- *Best match (Evaluation Criteria #9):* organizational mission, expertise, and resources

It is important to note that those with the greatest need may conflict with the other criteria on the list (e.g. readiness for action, easiest, and least costly). It is often harder and more expensive to reach those with the most need. This dynamic often comes into play with programs that have embedded equity considerations. If this is the case for your program, you will need to decide how to weigh the various factors when choosing audiences. It might be the case that while it is harder and will take longer to reach a particular audience, doing so better aligns with your campaign purpose and achieving your long-term goals. A great example of this is the COVID-19 vaccines. The Black/African American community has been disproportionately impacted by COVID-19 deaths and serious illness (Evaluation Criteria #3). They also have had slower adoption of the COVID-19 vaccine driven by barriers such as mistrust of the medical community and government due to historic discrimination and limited access to vaccine sites (Evaluation Criteria #2). Public health officials across the country have faced the dilemma of how to increase vaccination rates among the Black/African American population knowing that it may be harder to reach this audience, that the audience is less receptive, and it may take more time and be more costly than efforts to vaccinate other populations (Evaluation Criteria #5, #6, #7, and #8). But in this case, for many communities, the severity of the need outweighs the other factors leading to a public health imperative to try and increase vaccination rates among the Black/African American population.

In addition, prioritizing audiences with the *greatest market opportunity* may run counter to a social marketer's natural desire and inclination (or mandate) to either (a) ensure that all constituent groups are reached and served (markets are treated equally) or (b) focus resources on segments in which the incidence and severity of the problem are the gravest (markets of greatest need). Concerns can be addressed by emphasizing that this is the most effective and efficient use of scarce resources, reassuring others that segmentation allows plans to be developed that are likely to succeed with individual segments, and explaining that additional segments can be addressed over time. You are simply prioritizing efforts in an objective and systematic way to achieve the greatest return on investment of resources.

ETHICAL CONSIDERATIONS WHEN SELECTING PRIORITY AUDIENCES

The musings at the beginning of the chapter expressing concern regarding resource allocation represent well the ethical dilemma at this phase in the planning process. In campaigns in which a majority of resources have been allocated to one or a few market segments, how do you address concerns about social inequity? Or what about reverse situations in which resources are allocated equally, when in fact only one or a few market segments have the greatest need? For example, a state water conservation effort may send messages to all residents in the state to voluntarily reduce water usage by a goal of 10% over the next six months: Take shorter showers. Flush one less time. But what if water levels and resources are actually adequate in half the state? Should residents on one side of the mountain (where it rains "all the time") be asked to make these sacrifices as well? What is fair?

Our recommendation, as it was when selecting a focus for your campaign, is that you provide objective data regarding the rationale for selection of the intended priority audience. This is also a good place to introduce the important topic of understanding where your data comes from. This will be discussed further later in the book, but understanding the sources of your data and identifying gaps can help ensure you are making good decisions (e.g. did the racial make-up of your data set mirror the racial composition of your geographic segment? If not, what can you do to fill the gaps in your data set?). With comprehensive data in hand, you should present (or at least mention) a long-range plan that will eventually address groups you are not addressing in this phase.

A last point to make in helping you identify ethical consideration is to make sure you pause to check your own implicit bias. We all have bias and the tendency to make assumptions about our audiences based on our own lived experiences is very strong. As social marketers, it is our job to consistently try and be objective—being thoughtful to recognize our own implicit bias and that of others that are helping plan a program. For example, when determining lowest hanging fruit/easiest to reach audiences, are you basing that decision on your own perception or on audience data? If on data, what data did you use or seek out? Did you confirm with others to make these decisions? Was the community or members of the potential priority group involved? Asking yourself these questions will help you keep unintended bias in check and lead to a better designed social marketing program.

COVID-19 Social Marketing Example

The week of 19 July 2021, a TV news reporter shared that he had come up with a new name for those who were hesitant to get vaccinated, "*The Movable Middle.*" He elaborated that this was a group that was hesitant, and did not see themselves as vulnerable, and that he had noticed many messages lately were being used to increase perceptions of vulnerability.[33]

From a social marketing perspective, this is very similar to the "Help Me" group, a group that is not "against" a behavior, but has barriers to adopting it, or doesn't see the benefit as outweighing the cost.

CHAPTER SUMMARY

Selecting priority audiences is a three-step process: (1) segment the market and population, (2) evaluate segments, and (3) choose one or more segments as the campaign's priority. Traditional variables used to describe consumer markets include demographics, geographics, psychographics, and behavior variables. Five additional models frequently used by social marketing practitioners include stages of change, diffusion of innovation (*Show Me. Help Me. Make Me.*), health styles segmentation, environmental segmentation, and generational segmentation.

Priority audiences are evaluated based on efficiency and effectiveness measures, using nine variables outlined by Andreasen and presented in this text: segment size, problem incidence, problem severity, defenselessness, reachability, general responsiveness, incremental costs, responsiveness to marketing mix, and organizational capabilities.

Three common prioritizing approaches include undifferentiated marketing (same strategy for all segments), differentiated marketing (different strategies for different audiences), and concentrated marketing (only a few key segments are targeted and with unique strategies).

It is recommended that the markets of "greatest opportunity" be recognized as those that have the greatest need, are most ready for action (*Help Me's*), are easiest and least costly to reach, and are the best match for the organization (see Appendix A for a worksheet on prioritizing audiences.).

RESEARCH HIGHLIGHT

Decreasing Gun Violence Exploratory Research

This Research Highlight features the nature and benefits of conducting Exploratory Research, in this case one reviewing prior efforts addressing the "wicked problem" of gun violence.

Assume, as you read this, that you are a Social Marketing Program Manager for a county sheriff's department. Your job includes identifying and recommending strategic approaches for reducing deaths and injuries from gun violence, and developing social marketing campaigns focused on voluntary behavior change. In researching reducing gun violence success stories online, one of your findings is a report in 2019 from the Police Executive Research Forum titled "*Reducing Gun Violence: What Works, and What Can be Done Now.*"[34] Findings from this 60-page report make clear how a literature review of prior similar efforts can inspire a plan's Purpose, Focus, Priority Audience, and Behavior Objective.

The report opens with an Executive Summary titled "Gun Violence Is 4 Different Problems," elaborating that "because each type of gun violence has different causes, victims, types of guns that are typically used, and other characteristics, the solutions will be different."[35] It then provides relevant background information for each of the four gun violence categories, outlined in Table 6.6.

TABLE 6.6 ■ Four Categories of Gun Violence in the United States in 2017[36]

Category	#1. Suicides	#2. Criminal Homicides	#3. Domestic Violence Homicides	#4. Mass Shooting Fatalities
Annual fatalities	23,854	14,542	1,000–2,000	117
Most common victims	White males, ages 50+ Youth at high risk of attempts	Black males, ages 18–34	Females	Varied
Most common type of gun used	Legal handguns	Illegally possessed handguns	Handguns originally purchased legally, but due to criminal convictions are illegal to possess	A larger portion of rifles than in other categories of shooting
Additional relevant background	Suicides are often impulsive. Firearms used in attempted suicides by youth usually belong to a parent.[37]	These include drug-related and gang-related violence and killings as part of robberies or other crime.[38] Many altercations start with insults on social media.[39]	The majority of intimate partner homicides involve a gun.[40] Many survivors have shared things like, "I'm not sure if it's a crime. I'm not sure if I have any rights here."[41]	Many mass shootings occur in schools, churches, movie theaters, and other entertainment venues. One study indicated that, in 81% of the school shootings, other kids knew about the shooter's plans.[42]

The majority of the report shares ideas based on various presentations at the Forum regarding "What Can Be Done to Reduce Shootings." Presenters provided detail on case stories in their communities for one of the four categories and highlighted strategies they had determined worked. Recommendations included types of *laws, policies, and programs* they believed would have the greatest impact in reducing fatalities. Table 6.7 uses our social marketing planning framework to provide examples of what the social marketing program planner might have gleaned from the report for developing *program* strategies versus laws and policies. It is noted that these are examples of strategies that might be proposed by the program manager after reading the report.

In the end, the social marketing program planner might then make a recommendation based on internal resources, as well as external opportunities and threats, to choose one of the four as a priority effort for a social marketing plan, and then recommend timeframes for other potential campaigns.

It should be clear that this review, even of just one document, can inspire efforts for prioritizing and then developing a social marketing plan.

TABLE 6.7 ■ Potential Purpose, Focus, Audience, and Behavior Inspired by Background Information

Social Issue	Deaths From Gun Violence			
Purpose	#1. Reduce suicides	#2. Reduce criminal homicides	#3. Reduce domestic violence homicides	#4. Reduce mass shootings fatalities
Focus	Safe gun storage	Social media postings	Incidence of repeated violence	A central reporting mechanism
Audience	Parents with youth living at home	Active users of social media	Victims of domestic violence	Students aware of a potential threat for gun violence
Behavior	Use gun safes and locks to ensure firearms cannot be taken	Report suspicions gun violence-related postings	Accept the assistance of social services such as victim advocates	Report, anonymously, concerns to via school website, dedicated smart phone application, or other mechanism

DISCUSSION QUESTIONS AND EXERCISES

1. In your own words, what is the difference between a population and a priority audience? Give an example of each.
2. What segmentation variables are you most familiar with and/or use the most? Which new variables did you read about that interest you for future audience segmentation?
3. What are the major criteria you would use to select among major potential priority audiences?

7 STEP 4: BEHAVIOR OBJECTIVES AND TARGET GOALS

LEARNING OBJECTIVES

Upon completing the chapter, you should be able to:

7.1 Define and distinguish between behavior, knowledge, and belief objectives.

7.2 Explain behavior objectives in depth.

7.3 Describe knowledge and belief objectives in depth.

7.4 Describe the nature, components, and ethical considerations of goals for social marketing campaigns.

7.5 Identify ethical considerations when setting objectives and goals.

We recognize the challenges, even resistance, some of you may have when it comes to this section in the planning process—that of setting campaign objectives (desired behavior) and target goals (levels of behavior change). Do any of the following sound familiar?

- "I always have trouble choosing among the numerous optional good behaviors we want to promote. Why do we need to (once more) narrow our focus, as we did with priority audiences? It seems to me the more we can get them to do, the better."
- "When I look at this model and the use of the terms 'objective' and 'goal', I get confused, even discouraged. We were taught in public health programs that goals were what we were trying to accomplish, like decrease obesity. This model says that goals are the quantifiable measure of your objective. Does it matter?"
- "This goal setting is nice in theory but near to impossible, in my experience. If we have not done this behavior change campaign before, how could we know what kind of a target goal or milestone to set?"

In this chapter, steps will be outlined to address these concerns, as well as outline tasks involved in Step 4:

- Selecting a specific behavior your effort is intended to promote

- Identifying any knowledge and belief objectives your effort will need to address to influence the desired behavior
- Setting target goals for levels of behavior change because of your effort

It is understood that some may have alternative definitions or applications for the terms *objectives* and *goals*. In this model, *objectives* are the dependent variables (behavior, knowledge, belief) that we will design our independent variables (the marketing intervention mix) to influence. And *goals* are like "sales goals" in commercial marketing, setting the levels of behavior change that we will develop campaign strategies to achieve, which is why they are determined at this early phase in the planning process. We chose this opening case to highlight the importance of selecting a behavior that will have a significant impact on a "wicked problem."

CASE HIGHLIGHT
REDUCING WILDFIRES

Background

Driven by climate change and drying conditions, wildfires have been a critical threat to communities in Washington state. Annual acres burned in Washington have grown from an average of 189,000 in the 2000s to an average of 488,000 over the last five years. In 2020, 812,000 acres burned.[1] The Washington State Department of Natural Resources (DNR) is responsible for fighting fires as well as helping communities prepare for wildfire risks. In 2021, DNR launched a social marketing pilot program called Wildfire Ready Neighbors with a purpose of reducing loss of life and destruction of property due to wildfires, with a focus on building community resiliency to wildfires.[2]

Priority Audiences

Priority audiences for the campaign were residents in three high-risk counties (Chelan, Okanogan, and Spokane Counties). The program had a focus on homeowners but also had offerings for all residents. These counties have substantial populations of Hispanic/Latinx residents, so the pilot program was created and implemented in both English and Spanish. Influencer audiences included community partners such as local fire departments, conservation districts, and tribal nations.

Objectives and Target Goals

Behavior Objective: Conduct specific activities to make their home and property more wildfire resilient. Note that this was ultimate priority behavior in a behavior chain as follows:

- Sign up for Wildfire Ready Neighbors program
- Answer some questions and receive a free *Wildfire Ready Plan*
- Schedule a home visit
- Attend the home visit and get customized recommendations

- Conduct activities recommended in their plan around their home to make it more wildfire resilient (e.g., clear/prune brush near home, store fuel and gas away from home)

Knowledge Objective: Residents were aware of wildfire risk but unsure where to start to prepare for wildfires. The pilot program needed to build knowledge of how to prepare for wildfires in simple steps that met the individual needs of the resident and their property.

Belief Objective: Their community can reduce its' wildfire risk if they all work together to make individual changes on their properties.

Goals (by the end of the pilot campaign):

- 1,800 Wildfire Ready Neighbors sign-ups
- Distribute tailored *Wildfire Ready Plans* to residents
- Get six hundred residents to sign-up for home visits
- Engage Fire Districts + community partners to implement and deliver the campaign
- Garner commitments to complete wildfire preparedness actions at their homes/on their property

Audience Insights

Research was employed to understand the dynamics in the three high-risk counties with the aim to understand the individual community needs/barriers to wildfire preparedness and identify who the community trusted most to deliver the campaign. Key learnings included:

- Time and money were large barriers. Residents needed simple, low-cost options (with easy-to-follow steps).
- Residents were open to receiving an in-person property visit to get advice from an expert.
- Residents would only trust local experts—not the government—to conduct the program.
- The word "neighbor" evoked community trust. For research participants, it encompassed everyone from the person who lives next door to a trusted community organization to their local fire department.

Marketing Intervention Strategies

Based on the research, the Wildfire Ready Neighbors pilot program plan was developed. The plan was designed to make it easy for all residents to prepare for wildfires, allowing everyone in a community to participate regardless of income and/or time constraints. The campaign was unified with easy behavior change: *Get your free Wildfire Ready Plan*. It also offered residents the additional support of a home visit from an expert. The campaign included:

- **Wildfire Ready Neighbors Website**: Program websites were created in English and Spanish (WildfireReady.com and ListosParaIncendios.com), where residents could sign up for the program, take a quick survey to get their *Wildfire Ready Plan*, sign up for a home visit, and learn about wildfire risks.
- **Trusted Messengers**: The project team worked to secure support and participation of a coalition of community partners, including local fire departments, conservation districts,

and tribal nations. A promotional toolkit was created to help these partners implement and socialize the campaign.

- **Community Captains**: DNR enlisted neighborhood captains to be the "early adopters" of Wildfire Ready Neighbors. These captains agreed to encourage their surrounding community to sign up for Wildfire Ready Neighbors and served the significant role providing social diffusion for the campaign. The Community Captains put a local face on the campaign and became community storytellers in earned and social media stories.
- **Feedback and Social Norms**: Progress toward goals for each county was shared on the website through a goal thermometer that tracked individual sign-up. Every resident that became a "Wildfire Ready Neighbor" moved the thermometer up for their community.
- **Incentives**: The Wildfire Ready Neighbors campaign included both individual and community incentives. The individual incentives were the free *Wildfire Ready Plan* and home visits. At the community level, incentives included resources that would help people act on becoming more wildfire ready like free dumpsters for community clean-up days and wood chipping days to get rid of debris on properties.
- **Commitments**: Commitments to do wildfire preparedness actions were built into the program structure being included in the online *Wildfire Ready Plan* and into the home visit process.
- **Communications**: The program was promoted through paid advertising, earned media outreach, and direct mail in each community (see Figure 7.1).

FIGURE 7.1 ■ Bi-lingual Direct Mail Program Recruitment Postcard

Source: Washington State Department of Natural Resources.

Results

The pilot program delivered the following results against its' goals:

- 2,201 program sign-ups (22% above goal).
- 1,138 home visit requests (78% above goal).

- 30,000 tailored *Wildfire Ready Plans* were distributed to residents—in English and Spanish—with attainable, concrete steps to prepare regardless of property size, financial ability, language, or experience.
- A coalition of over seventeen community partners helped implement the pilot, including local fire departments, conservation districts, and tribal nations. As trusted local voices, these partners were critical to socializing the campaign, conducting home visits, addressing barriers firsthand, and offering valued expertise on the ground.
- More than 8,000 wildfire preparedness actions were committed to by residents.

Based on the success of the pilot, the program will continue in 2022 in Chelan, Okanogan, and Spokane and will also expand to three additional high-risk counties in Washington.

STEP 4: SET BEHAVIOR OBJECTIVES AND GOALS

Once a priority audience for a campaign has been selected, your next step is to establish *campaign objectives*, with the primary objective always being the extremely specific *behavior* you want to influence your audience to accept, modify, abandon, reject, switch, or continue. As you will read, the key to success is to select single, doable behaviors—and then explain them in simple, clear terms.

This chapter presents examples of the three types of objectives associated with a social marketing campaign:

1. *Behavior objectives* (what you want your audience to **Do**)
2. *Knowledge objectives* (what you want your audience to **Know**)
3. *Belief objectives* (what you want your audience to **Believe or Feel**)

A social marketing campaign always has a behavior objective. When and if you determine there is something your audience needs to know or believe to "act," that objective is identified and incorporated as well. As will become clear, campaign behavior objectives (e.g., conducting activities around their home to make it more wildfire resilient) are different from the campaign purpose (e.g., to reduce loss of life and destruction of property due to wildfires), defined earlier in this model as the ultimate impact of a successful campaign on the social issue being addressed.

After determining campaign objectives, campaign *target goals* are established that are specific, measurable, attainable, relevant, and time sensitive (SMART).[3] Ideally, they specify targeted rates of change in behaviors, such as the desired increase in numbers of those in the priority audience who will be performing the desired behavior at some future date. They may also establish desired changes in knowledge and belief, especially in cases where behavior change may be a long-term effort. We recognize that in some models, such as those used in public health, goals are the nonquantifiable components of a campaign. These, however, are usually referred to as "overarching goals." Target goals at this step in the planning process refer to campaign goals. This social marketing model is based on commercial marketing models, where goals are expressed as "sales goals." We recommend, however, that you feel free to reverse these labels to match your organization's language and culture.

Remember from Chapter 2 that this planning model should be considered spiral in nature. Objectives and goals established at this point should be considered *draft behavior objectives* and *target goals*. You may learn in Step 5, for example, when you "talk" with your priority audience about these desired behaviors that your objectives and target goals are not realistic, clear, or appropriate for them and should be revised. Your audience may express a misconception that will require an additional knowledge objective, or an attitude that a new belief objective will need to address. Or you might find when developing preliminary budgets that you will need to reduce your goals because of funding realities.

As a final overview of this step, keep in mind that objectives and goals will affect your campaign evaluation strategy. Given that campaign goals represent the foundation for campaign evaluation, it is crucial that goals be relevant to campaign efforts and able to be measured.

Table 7.1 illustrates key concepts that will be presented in this chapter, using an example of an effort that might be undertaken by a state department of transportation to reduce traffic injuries and deaths caused by drivers distracted while texting.

BEHAVIOR OBJECTIVES

Ed Maibach recommends that we "Focus. Tackle one 'non-divisible' behavior at a time. As the name suggests, and Doug McKenzie-Mohr describes, a non-divisible behavior is one that cannot be further divided into more specific behaviors. This is critical, as barriers and benefits differ dramatically for different behaviors."[4]

All social marketing campaigns should be designed and planned with a specific behavior objective in mind. Even if the planner discovers that the campaign needs to include additional knowledge and belief objectives, a behavior objective will need to be identified that these additional elements will support. As you develop and consider potential behavior objectives for your efforts, the following five criteria, ones adapted from Doug McKenzie-Mohr's framework,

TABLE 7.1 ■ Example of a Campaign's Purpose, Focus, Objectives, and Goal

Campaign Purpose	Reduce Traffic Injuries and Deaths
Focus	Texting while driving
Campaign Objectives	
Behavior Objective	To wait until you arrive at your destination to text
Knowledge Objective	To know the percentage of traffic crashes involving someone texting while driving
Belief Objective	To believe that texting while driving is a significant distraction
Target Goal	Decrease the number of traffic crashes associated with texting while driving by 25% in one year

should help you choose one with the greatest potential for meaningful change, or at least assist you in prioritizing them:

1. *Impact*: If your audience adopts the behavior, how much difference will it make relative to the purpose of your campaign (e.g., decreasing teen pregnancies)? How does this compare with other behaviors being considered?
2. *Willingness*: Has your priority audience heard of doing this behavior before? How willing or interested are they in doing this behavior? Do they perceive it will solve a problem or concern they have, or will it satisfy an unfulfilled need?
3. *Measurability*: Is the behavior measurable, either through observation, record keeping, or self-reporting? You should be able to "picture" your priority audience performing the behavior (e.g., removing the plastic insert from the cereal box before sorting for recycling). And your priority audience should be able to determine that they have performed the behavior (e.g., placing infants in cribs on their backs to reduce the risk of infant death).
4. *Market opportunity*: How many in the priority audience are not currently doing the behavior? What, in other terminology, is the current penetration of this behavior in the priority audience segment? A behavior that few have adopted would garner a high score in terms of market opportunity.
5. *Market supply*: Does the behavior need more support? If some other organization is already "doing all that can be done" to promote this behavior, perhaps a different behavior would be more beneficial to the social issue.

It is also important to consider racial and cultural factors that could impact your behavior objective. Does the behavior you are seeking to influence have different framing for members of the community based on history, societal structures, and systems or cultural heritage of some members of your priority audience? If so, you will need to be sure to define your behavior, knowledge, and belief objectives in ways to encompass these differences.

At the end of Al Gore's book *An Inconvenient Truth*, 30 specific desired behaviors to reduce carbon emissions were listed. Ten were selected for a handout titled "Ten things to do" and make an interesting prioritization exercise that could be approached using a grid like the one in Table 7.2.[5] Assume that once launched, efforts would then focus on highlighting two behaviors each year based on scores for each of the five criteria just mentioned. To keep it simple, each behavior could be rated on each criterion as high (3), medium (2), or low (1), as illustrated in the first row. Ideally, these ratings would be determined using objective information (e.g., citizen surveys, scientific data). The ratings might be more subjective in nature—which is still better than prioritizing behaviors using less rigorous means, such as informal conversations or hunches.

To increase the rigor (and value) of the exercise, you could also weigh the criteria. For example, you could understandably decide that "Impact" was more important than other criteria and decide to double the score (2 × 2 = 4). That way, something that was minimal impact (1) but had the highest scores on other criteria would not automatically surface as the number-one priority.

TABLE 7.2 ■ Process for Prioritizing 10 Behavior Objectives for Addressing Climate Crisis: High (3), Medium (2), Low (1)

Behaviors	Impact	Willingness	Measurability	Market Opportunity	Supply	Average
Change a light	2	3	3	3	1	2.4
Drive less						
Recycle more						
Check your tires						
Use less hot water						
Avoid products with a lot of packaging						
Adjust your thermostat						
Plant a tree						
Turn off electronic devices						
Spread the word						

A behavior objective should be distinguished from several other planning components. It is not the same as a campaign slogan or campaign message, although it is used to develop both (e.g., "Eat five or more fruits and vegetables a day" became "5 a Day the Color Way"). It is not quantifiable as we are defining it. The target goal is the quantifiable, measurable component that has implications for strategies and budget decisions and provides a benchmark for monitoring and measuring program success (e.g., Did the average consumption of the number of fruits and vegetables increase from 2.5 to 4 per day by 2018?).

If you are familiar with logic models, you may be curious where social marketing objectives fit in the model. They should be noted as "outcomes" in the traditional model, reflecting behaviors changed as the result of program "outputs."

For those not familiar with logic models, these are visual schematics that show links between program processes (inputs, activities, and outputs) and program outcomes and impact. This tool will be discussed in more depth in Chapter 14, which covers evaluation.

Although a campaign may promote more than one behavior, it should be recognized that different tactics or strategies may be necessary to promote each one (e.g., getting people to use a litterbag will take different strategies than getting people to cover their loads in pickup trucks). Table 7.3 presents examples of potential behavior objectives in our

TABLE 7.3 ■ Examples of Potential Behavior Objectives for Specific Audiences

Improving Health	Behavior Objective
Immunizations	Get recommended COVID-19 vaccinations.
Tobacco use	Don't start smoking.
Heavy/binge alcohol drinking	Drink less than five alcoholic drinks at one sitting.
Alcohol and drug use during pregnancy	Don't drink alcoholic beverages if you are pregnant.
Diabetes prevention	Exercise moderately 30 minutes a day, five days a week, at least 10 minutes at a time.
Breast cancer	Learn the proper procedure for examining your breasts.
Prostate cancer	Talk with your health care provider about an annual prostate exam if you are 50 years of age or older.
Preventing Injuries	
Drinking and driving	Keep your blood alcohol level below 0.08% if you are drinking and driving.
Seatbelts	Buckle your seatbelt before you put your vehicle in gear.
Domestic violence	Have a plan that includes a packed bag and a safe place to go.
Gun storage	Store handguns in a lockbox or safe or use a reliable trigger lock.
Fires	Replace smoke alarm batteries every six months, at the same time you change clocks.
Protecting the Environment	
Waste reduction	Buy bulk and unpackaged goods rather than packaged items.
Wildlife habitat protection	Stay on established paths when walking through forests.
Forest destruction	Use materials made from recycled tires and glass for garden steps and paths.
Toxic fertilizers and pesticides	Follow instructions on labels and measure precisely.
Water conservation	Replace old toilets with new low-flow models.
Air pollution from automobiles	Don't top off the gas tank when refueling your car.
Involving the Community	
Volunteering	Give five hours a week to a volunteer effort.
Mentoring	Encourage and support caring relationships between your child and a nonparent adult.

(Continued)

TABLE 7.3 ■ Examples of Potential Behavior Objectives for Specific Audiences (*Continued*)

Improving Health	Behavior Objective
Acts of terrorism	If you see something, say something.
Enhancing Financial Well-Being	
Bank accounts	Open a checking account.
Savings	Build a savings account equivalent to six months of income.
Using credit	Establish a monthly budget and follow it.

familiar arenas of health, injury prevention, the environment, community, and financial well-being. Box 7.1 presents a commentary by Doug McKenzie-Mohr regarding the concept of behavioral chains.

BOX 7.1

Behavioral Chains

Doug McKenzie-Mohr[6]
McKenzie-Mohr & Associates
2018

Many behaviors that protect the environment or promote public health and safety can be broken into smaller activities that constitute a behavioral chain. For example, composting's behavior chain consists of transporting oneself to a hardware store to pick out a composter, purchasing a composter, transporting the composter back home, putting the composter together, siting the composter in the yard, finding a container to place kitchen scraps in, placing scraps in the container, taking the kitchen scrap container out to the composter on an ongoing basis, adding yard waste to the composter, stirring the composter repeatedly, and finally, harvesting the finished compost and placing it on lawns or gardens. Unpacking an overarching behavior into the smaller actions that make up the behavioral chain has several benefits. First, the barriers exist at the level of these small individual actions that make up the behavioral chain. For example, the barriers to purchasing a composter and transporting it back home are completely different than taking the kitchen scrap container out to the composter. Second, we can identify which items in the behavioral chain need more attention than others. If many households have composters but are not using them, a program to promote composting would look vastly different than if households do not have composters. Third, articulating the behavior chain can lead to the identification of segments of the chain that can be addressed to make the activity much more convenient. Using composting again as an example, the segment related to transporting oneself to a hardware store, picking out and purchasing a composter and transporting it back home can be eliminated if composters instead are delivered directly to households by a municipality. Develop more effective behavioral change programs by first identifying whether the overarching behavior that you wish to promote is made up of a behavioral chain.

KNOWLEDGE AND BELIEF OBJECTIVES

When gathering background data and conducting the strengths, weaknesses, opportunities, and threats (SWOT) analysis, you probably learned from existing secondary research or from prior similar campaigns that typical audiences need a little "help" before they are willing, sometimes even able, to act. They may need to have some *knowledge* (information or facts) and/or *belief* (values, opinions, or attitudes) before they are convinced that the action is doable and/or worth the effort. Those in the precontemplation stage, for example, typically don't believe there is a problem that needs their attention. Those in the contemplation stage may not have made up their mind that the effort (cost) is worth the gain (benefit). Even those in the action stage may not be aware of their accomplishments and therefore be vulnerable to relapses.

Knowledge objectives are those related to statistics, facts, and other information and skills your priority audience would find motivating or important. Typically, the information has simply been unavailable to the audience or gone unnoticed. Here are examples:

- Statistics on risks associated with current behavior (e.g., percentage of obese women who have heart attacks vs. those not medically obese)
- Statistics on benefits of proposed behavior (e.g., the amount of money you will have saved in a year by making small monthly deposits)
- Facts on attractive alternatives (e.g., lists of flowering native plants that are drought and disease resistant)
- Facts that correct misconceptions (e.g., cigarette butts are not biodegradable and can take more than 10 years to disintegrate completely)
- Facts that might be motivating (e.g., moderate physical activity has been proven to have some of the same important medical benefits as vigorous physical activity)
- Information on how to perform the behavior (e.g., how to prepare a home for an earthquake)
- Resources available for assistance (e.g., phone numbers where battered women can call to find temporary shelter)
- Locations for purchase of goods or services (e.g., locations where handgun lockboxes can be purchased)
- Current laws and fines that may not be known about or understood (e.g., a fine of $1,025 can be imposed for tossing a lit cigarette)

Belief objectives are those related to attitudes, opinions, feelings, or values held by the priority audience. The priority audience may have current beliefs that the marketer may need to alter for them to act. Belief objectives are another area where you should pause and apply a racial equity and cultural consideration lens. To do this, look back at the "Five Questions for a Racial

Equity Mindset"[7] as was outlined in Chapter 2. Use these questions as prompts to examine if your belief objectives are appropriate across races and cultures. You may also find that an important belief is missing, such as one of the following:

- That they will personally experience the benefits from adopting the desired behavior (e.g., increased physical activity will help them sleep better)
- That they are at risk (e.g., they currently believe they are capable of driving safely with a blood alcohol level of over 0.08)
- That they will be able to successfully perform the desired behavior (e.g., talk to their teenager about thoughts of suicide)
- That their individual behavior can make a difference (e.g., taking mass transit to work)
- That they will not be viewed negatively by others if they adopt the behavior (e.g., not accepting another drink)
- That the costs of the behavior will be worth it (e.g., establishing a bank account vs. cashing pay checks at check-cashing services and pawn shops)
- That there will be minimal negative consequences (e.g., that organ donation information won't be shared with third parties)

These knowledge and belief objectives provide direction for developing subsequent strategies (positioning and the marketing intervention mix). They have important implications *especially for developing a brand identity and key messages* that provide the information and arguments that will be most motivating. Advertising copywriters, for example, will reference these objectives when developing communication slogans, script, and copy. There are also opportunities for other elements of the marketing intervention mix to support these additional objectives: for instance, an immunization product strategy that incorporates a free downloadable app to ensure that parents know the recommended schedule; an incentive offered by a utility for trading in gas mowers for mulch mowers as a way to convince homeowners of their harm to the environment; or a special website dedicated to purchasing booster seats, sponsored by a children's hospital, as a testimonial to the safety concern. Table 7.4 provides examples of each of the objectives described. It should be noted that even though each campaign illustrated has a knowledge and belief objective, this is neither typical nor required. As stated earlier, the behavior objective is the primary focus.

TARGET GOALS

Ideally, target goals establish a desired level of behavior *change* because of program efforts (e.g., from 10% of homeowners who check for leaky toilets on an annual basis to 20% in one year). To establish this target for the amount or percentage of change, you will, of course, need to know current levels of behavior among your priority audience. In this regard, you are like commercial

TABLE 7.4 ■ Purpose, Audience, and Objectives

Campaign Purpose	Priority Audience	Behavior Objective	Knowledge Objective	Belief Objective
Reduced senior falls	Seniors 75 and older	Exercise five times a week, including strength and balance exercises.	One in three adults aged 65 and older falls each year.	Risk of falling can be reduced by strengthening muscles and improving balance.
Reduced child injuries from automobile accidents	Parents with children ages 4 to 8	Put children who are ages 4 to 8 and weigh less than 80 pounds in booster seats.	Traffic accidents are the leading cause of death for children ages 4 to 8.	Children ages 4 to 8 weighing less than 80 pounds are not adequately protected by adult seatbelts.
Improved water quality	Small horse farmers within 5 miles of streams, lakes, or rivers	Cover and protect manure piles from rain.	Storm water runoff from piles can pollute water resources.	Even though your manure pile is small, it does contribute to the problem.
Increased number of registered organ donors	People renewing driver's licenses	Register to be an organ donor when you renew your driver's license.	Your family may still be asked to sign a consent form for your donation to occur.	Information will be kept private and can be accessed only by authorized officials.
Decreased number of unbanked in San Francisco	Residents relying on check cashers, pawn shops, and other fringe financial services charging high fees and interest rates	Open a Bank on San Francisco account, one established by a public-private partnership.	These accounts offer a low- or no-cost product with no minimum balance; consular identification cards are accepted as primary identification.	Participating banks will be easy to find; you will feel welcomed.

marketers, who establish sales goals for their products when developing annual marketing plans and then develop strategies and resource allocations consistent with these goals. Consider how the specificity and time-bound nature of the following goals would inspire and guide your planning and eventually help justify your resource expenditures:

- Increase by 25% in a 24-month period the percentage of women over the age of 50 in the country who get annual mammograms
- Decrease the amount of glass, paper, aluminum, and plastic litter on interstate roadways by four million pounds in two years

Target goals may also be set for knowledge and belief objectives, as illustrated in Table 7.5. Although the goals are hypothetical for the purposes of this illustration, the effort to increase the intake of folic acid to prevent birth defects is real. The U.S. Public Service and the March of Dimes recommend that all women of childbearing age consume 400 micrograms of folic acid per day in a multivitamin in addition to eating a healthy diet (see Figure 7.2).

This process is difficult or impractical for many social marketing programs. Baseline data on current levels of behavior for a priority audience may not be known or may not be available in a timely or economically feasible way. Projecting future desired levels (goal setting) often depends on data and experience from years of tracking and analyzing the impact of prior efforts. Many social marketing efforts are being conducted for the first time, and historical data may not have been recorded or retained.

There are several excellent resources in the public health arena you can explore, however, that may provide data that guide efforts to establish baselines as well as goals.

- The Behavioral Risk Factor Surveillance System (BRFSS) was developed by the Centers for Disease Control and Prevention (CDC), headquartered in Atlanta, Georgia. It is used

TABLE 7.5 ■ Hypothetical Objectives and Target Goals

Purpose	Behavior	Knowledge	Belief
Reduce birth defects	What we want them to do	What they may need to know before they will act	What they may need to believe before they will act
Objective	Get 400 micrograms of folic acid every day	For it to help, you need to take it before you become pregnant, or during the early weeks of pregnancy.	Without enough folic acid, the baby is at risk for serious birth defects.
Target goal	Increase the percentage of women ages 18 to 45 who take a daily vitamin containing folic acid from 39% in 2008 to 50% by 2014.	Increase the percentage of women ages 18 to 45 who know folic acid should be taken before pregnancy from 11% in 2008 to 15% by 2014.	Increase the percentage of women ages 18 to 45 who believe folic acid prevents birth defects from 20% in 2008 to 30% by 2014.

FIGURE 7.2 ■ Promoting Daily Use of a Vitamin Before Pregnancy

Get the "B" Attitude

That's "B" for the B vitamin folic acid.

Get the attitude by taking it every day. Folic acid may help save your baby from birth defects of the brain and spinal cord. But you have to take it every day *before* you get pregnant and in the first few weeks of your pregnancy for it to help.

B vitamin folic acid — Why you need it

A baby needs folic acid right after it's conceived, *before* you even know you're pregnant. Folic acid helps the baby's brain and spinal cord develop properly. Without enough, the baby could have serious birth defects called neural tube defects.

March of Dimes

Saving babies, together

Source: Copyright © March of Dimes Birth Defects Foundation (1999). Reprinted with permission.

throughout the United States to measure and track the prevalence of major risk-related behaviors among Americans, including tobacco use, sexual behavior, injury prevention, physical activity, nutrition, and prevention behaviors, such as breast, cervical, and colorectal cancer screening. Details on this system are highlighted in Box 7.2.

- *Healthy People 2030* is managed by the Office of Disease Prevention and Health Promotion within the U.S. Department of Health and Human Services. It is a set of objectives with 10-year target goals designed to guide national health promotion and disease prevention efforts to improve the health of all people in the United States (see Box 7.3). It is used as a strategic management tool by the federal government, states, communities, and other public and private sector partners. Its set of objectives and targets is used to measure progress for health issues in specific populations and serves as a foundation for prevention and wellness activities across various sectors and within the federal government, as well as a model for measurement at the state and local levels.[8] Of interest to social marketers is the inclusion, for the first time in 2020, of three objectives related to social marketing (see Box 7.4).

- Explore the availability of data from peers in other agencies who may have conducted similar campaigns.
- Often nonprofit organizations and foundations with a related mission (e.g., the American Cancer Society) may have excellent data helpful in establishing meaningful campaign goals.

BOX 7.2

The CDC's Unique State-Based Surveillance

In the early 1980s, the CDC worked with the states to develop the Behavioral Risk Factor Surveillance System (BRFSS). This state-based system, the first of its kind, made available information on the prevalence of risk-related behaviors among Americans and their perceptions of a variety of health issues.

Now (2022) active in all 50 states as well as the District of Columbia and three U.S. territories, BRFSS completes more than 400,000 adult interviews each year and continues to be the primary source of information on major health risk behaviors among Americans. State and local health departments rely heavily on BRFSS data to:

- Determine priority health issues and identify populations at highest risk
- Develop strategic plans and target prevention programs
- Monitor the effectiveness of intervention strategies and progress toward achieving prevention goals
- Educate the public, the health community, and policymakers about disease prevention
- Support community policies that promote health and prevent disease

In addition, BRFSS data enable public health professionals to monitor progress toward achieving the nation's health objectives as outlined in *Healthy People 2030: National Health Promotion and Disease Prevention Objectives*. BRFSS information is also used by researchers, volunteer and professional organizations, and managed care organizations to target prevention efforts.

The benefits of the BRFSS for states include the following:

- Data can be analyzed in a variety of ways. BRFSS data can be analyzed by a variety of demographic variables, including age, education, income, and racial and ethnic background. The ability to determine populations at highest risk is essential in effectively targeting scarce prevention resources.
- The BRFSS is designed to identify trends over time. For example, state-based data from the BRFSS have revealed a national epidemic of obesity.
- States can add questions of local interest.

- States can readily address urgent and emerging health issues. Questions may be added for a wide range of important health issues, including diabetes, oral health, arthritis, tobacco use, folic acid consumption, use of preventive services, and health care coverage.

Although the BRFSS is flexible and allows for timely additions, standard core questions enable health professionals to make comparisons between states and derive national-level conclusions. BRFSS data have highlighted wide disparities between states on key health issues. In 2016, for example, the prevalence of current smoking among U.S. adults ranged from a low of 8.8% in Utah to a high of 24.5% in Kentucky. These data have also been useful for assessing tobacco control efforts. For instance, BRFSS data revealed that the annual prevalence of cigarette smoking among adults in Massachusetts declined after an excise tax increase and an antismoking campaign were implemented.

BOX 7.3

Healthy People 2030: Health Conditions

These topic areas of *Healthy People 2030* identify and highlight specific health conditions. Each topic area is assigned to one or more lead agencies within the federal government that is responsible for developing, tracking, monitoring, and periodically reporting on objectives.

1. Addiction
2. Arthritis Adolescent health
3. Blood Disorders
4. Cancer
5. Chronic Kidney Disease
6. Chronic Pain
7. Dementias, including Alzheimer's disease
8. Diabetes
9. Foodborne Illness
10. Health Care-Associated Infections
11. Heart Disease and Stroke
12. Infectious Disease
13. Mental Health and Mental Disorders
14. Oral Conditions
15. Osteoporosis
16. Overweight and Obesity
17. Pregnancy and Childbirth
18. Respiratory Disease
19. Sensory of Communication Disorders
20. Sexually Transmitted Infections

Source: U.S. Department of Health and Human Services, Office of Disease Prevention and Health Promotion, https://health.gov/healthypeople/objectives-and-data/browse-objectives.

BOX 7.4

https://health.gov/healthypeople/objectives-and-data/browse-objectives/health-communication/increase-number-state-health-departments-use-social-marketing-health-promotion-programs-hchit-d01

Healthy People 2020: Health Communications and Health Information Technology Objectives Related to Social Marketing

#13 To increase social marketing in health promotion and disease prevention:

13.1 Increase the number of state health departments that report using social marketing in health promotion and disease prevention programs.

13.2 Increase the proportion of schools of public health and accredited Master of Public Health (MPH) programs that offer one or more courses in social marketing.

13.3 Increase the proportion of schools of public health and accredited MPH programs that offer workforce development activities in social marketing for public health practitioners.

Source: HealthyPeople.gov, "Health Communication and Health Information Technology," https://www.healthypeople.gov/2020/topicsobjectives2020/overview.aspx?topicid=18.

Health Communication and Health Information Technology | Healthy People 2020

https://www.healthypeople.gov/2020/topics-objectives/topic/health-communication-and-information-technology/objectives

Pilots to Set Goals

Piloting is most often used to identify and address problems prior to campaign rollout and/or to test various potential strategies to determine which one(s) would be most effective. Pilots can also be used as a reference point for setting target goals. For example, a campaign to influence parents not to smoke around their children, with a focus on distribution of materials for children in elementary schools to take home to their parents, could be piloted at one school in a school district. A quantitative follow-up survey with parents regarding any changes in their behavior could help determine reasonable goals to set for campaign rollout in other schools. The advantages of this approach are not only the feedback you get from the priority audience regarding the campaign but also the reduced evaluation research-related costs and the increased credibility your effort will have with funders, providing an expected rate of return on their investments in terms of anticipated levels of behavior change. Methods for conducting pilots will be presented in Chapter 16.

Alternatives for Goal Setting for Behaviors

If baseline data are not available and setting target goals relative to behavior change is not practical or feasible at the time, the following alternatives might be considered for goal setting:

- Establish target goals for **campaign awareness** and recall. For example, a state-wide tobacco prevention program establishes a goal for the first three months of an advertising campaign that 75% of the priority audience (adults who smoke) will correctly recall the campaign slogan and two of the four television ads on an unaided basis. Results will then be presented to the state legislature to support continued funding of the campaign.

- Establish target goals for **levels of knowledge**. For example, a program for improved nutrition among low-income families sets a goal that 50% of women participating in a pilot project will correctly identify and describe the recommended daily servings of fruits and vegetables.
- Establish goals for **acceptance of a belief**. For example, a chain of gas stations is conducting a pilot project to influence customers not to top off their gas tanks and establishes a goal that 80% of customers, versus 25% prior to launch of the campaign, will report that they believe topping off a gas tank can be harmful to the environment.
- Establish target goals for a **response to a campaign component**. For example, a water utility will consider a campaign a success if 25% of residential customers call a well-publicized toll-free number or visit a website for a listing of drought-resistant plants.
- Establish target goals for **intent to change behavior**. For example, a state coalition promoting moderate physical activity is eager to know if a brief six-week pilot program increased interest in physical activity. They establish a goal that states their "reported intention to increase physical activity in the next six months from 20% to 30%, a 50% increase in behavior intent."
- Establish target goals for the **campaign process**. For example, a school-based program promoting sexual abstinence has a goal that 40 abstinence campaigns will be developed and implemented by youth in middle schools and high schools around the state during the upcoming school year.
- Establish target goals for **influencing an audience currently engaged in a behavior to have a conversation with three others regarding the benefits of having engaged in a behavior** (e.g., sharing with neighbors how well the organic fertilizer was working on their lawn).

In situations such as these, in which campaign goals are not specifically related to behavior change, it should be emphasized that campaign objectives should still include a behavior objective. Alternative goals relate to some activity that supports and promotes the desired behavior.

Objectives and Goals Are Drafts

In Step 5 of this planning process, you will deepen your understanding of your priority audience. You will learn more about their knowledge, beliefs, and current behaviors relative to objectives and goals established at this point, as well as their perceived barriers, desired benefits, potential motivators, and key influencers. It is often necessary to then revise and finalize objectives and goals to make them more realistic, clear, and appropriate.

Objectives and Target Goals Used for Campaign Evaluation

One of the last steps (Step 8) in developing a social marketing plan will be to develop an evaluation plan, a process covered in Chapter 14. It is important to emphasize at this point, however, that the planner will need to return to Step 4 of the plan, setting campaign objectives and goals, and select methodologies and develop plans to measure these stated goals. Examples of items that would need to be measured include:

- Number of mammograms among women in the pilot community
- Number of people stopped at checkpoints wearing seatbelts
- Pounds of specific types of litter on roadways
- Number of women in childbearing years taking folic acid
- Number of bank accounts opened by the unbanked in San Francisco

The message is simple. Establish a goal that is meaningful to campaign efforts and that will be feasible to measure.

ETHICAL CONSIDERATIONS SETTING OBJECTIVES AND GOALS

What if trends indicate that a behavior objective you are planning to support (e.g., putting food waste in curbside pickup containers) conflicts with the desired behaviors of other agency programs (e.g., backyard composting)? Coordination and further discussions of potential impact would be helpful. Or what if your research reveals that the goals that your funders or sponsors would like to support are not realistic or attainable for your priority audience? For example, a community clinic may know they are to encourage pregnant women to quit smoking—completely. But what if research has shown that cutting down to nine cigarettes a day would have significant benefits for those not able to quit? Can the clinic consider their efforts a success if they persuade pregnant women to decrease from 24 cigarettes a day to nine? Do they suggest a more attainable behavior (maybe using the foot-in-the-door technique) for this segment instead of just sending a "quit" message? Seeking confirmation from experts in the field may be important to solving dilemmas of this nature.

COVID-19 Social Marketing Example

Behavior Objectives

Perhaps one of the most social marketing-related strategies of COVID-19 campaigns and communications has been the consistent use of clear and specific desired public behaviors:

- Stay 6 feet apart from others.
- Wear a mask when out in public.

- Wash your hands frequently for 20 seconds.
- Get tested for COVID-19 if you feel sick.

In keeping with principles emphasized in this chapter, these behavior statements are not only singular and specific, they are also measurable, with updated statistics on compliance often reported on daily news features.

CHAPTER SUMMARY

The primary objective of a social marketing campaign is behavior change. All social marketing campaigns should be designed and planned with a specific behavior objective in mind—something we want our priority audience to do. Behavior objectives should be clear, simple, doable acts—ones that can be measured and that the priority audience will know they have completed.

Social marketers also need to consider the need for one or two additional objectives. *Knowledge objectives* (something you want your priority audience to know) are those related to statistics, facts, and other information your audience would find motivating or important. *Belief objectives* (something you want your priority audience to believe) are those related to attitudes, opinions, or values held by the priority audience, including current beliefs that the marketer will need to alter for them to act, or an important belief may be found missing.

Target goals are quantifiable, measurable, and relate to the specific campaign focus, priority audience, and time frame. Ideally, they establish a desired level of behavior change because of program and campaign efforts. When establishing and measuring behavior change is not practical or economically feasible, alternatives can be considered, including measuring campaign awareness, response, process, and/or increase in knowledge, beliefs, and intention.

RESEARCH HIGHLIGHT

Decreasing Bulkheads on Waterfront Properties

(2015–Present)

This research case highlights the power of (and need for) different behaviors for different priority audiences, often revealed through secondary, as well as primary research. Information was provided by C+C in Seattle, a partner in the development of this campaign, along with Futurewise, Applied Research Northwest, and Coastal Geologic Services.

Background

In 2015, more than 25% of the Puget Sound shoreline in Washington state had bulkheads or other "hard armor" instead of a natural waterfront, damaging delicate habitats crucial to the survival of coastal species, from insects and seabirds to salmon and orcas.[9] A program branded *Shore Friendly* was launched in 2016, funded through the National Estuary Program by the Washington Departments of Fish and Wildlife and Natural Resources. The *purpose* of the social marketing effort was to reduce the amount of hard armor on marine shorelines, with a *focus* on residential properties.

The program selected two distinct priority audiences and unique behaviors for each: (1) shoreline owners currently without hard armoring on their waterfront but considering adding some type of armoring, with a desired behavior to *leave their shoreline unarmored*; and (2) homeowners interested in voluntarily removing all or part of their old waterfront bulkhead, with a desired behavior to *replace the armor with soft shore protection* (e.g., rocks, logs, native plants). Next steps were, of course, to identify their respective barriers, desired benefits, and motivators for the behaviors and for program planners to develop independent, though coordinated, strategies that would leverage and strengthen the Shore Friendly brand.

TABLE 7.6 ■ Different Behaviors for Different Priority Audiences

Priority Audience	Desired Behavior	Major Barriers	Marketing Intervention Tools
1. No current Armor, low, or medium erosion potential	Leave shore unarmored	Concern that erosion/storms, waves, or tides might reduce or change the shoreline	Free site erosion assessment Free informational site visits with trained volunteers Workshops and "How To" Packets
2. Current hard Armor on property with low to medium erosion potential	Remove all or a portion of their Armor Replace Armor with soft shore protection (if needed)	Concern with erosion	Free site erosion assessment Free informational site visits with trained volunteers Workshops and "How To" packets
		Expense of removing Armor	Inform regarding current property tax breaks Mini grants to assist with qualified bulkhead removal projects
		Complicated nature of regulatory and permitting process to remove Armor	Assistance navigating the permit process

Methodology

To inspire campaign strategies, two major research efforts were developed and executed.

The first was a detailed analysis of *existing databases* regarding characteristics of marine shoreline properties on the Puget Sound, including current types and levels of armoring, potential for erosion, and location near forage fish spawning areas. Existing data records were also used to profile owner characteristics including whether owner-occupied, legal structures (e.g., trusts), and property value. This provided program planners with the ability to size and locate parcels meeting the two audience type parameters.

The second was a formative research effort utilizing *focus groups* as well as more than 400 *telephone surveys* to assess current knowledge, attitudes, and behaviors related to shoreline armoring among the two priority audiences. These surveys were designed, more specifically, to identify major barriers, desired benefits, and motivators related to the desired behavior for each audience, with a few highlights of findings summarized in Table 7.6.

Findings and Implications

Inspired by audience insights, program planners developed multiple marketing intervention tools (4Ps), also noted in Table 7.6. Major themes inspiring these strategies included:

- The easiest behavior to change will be to encourage audiences to not add shoreline armoring to their shorelines. The research showed that compared to removing Armor,

FIGURE 7.3 ■ Real Photos and Real Stories to Address a Desired Beauty of the Waterfront Property Posted on Shore Friendly Websites: Before Removal of Hard Shoreline Armor

Source: Kirvie Mesebeluu-Yobech http://shorefriendlykitsap.com/gallery/.

  the barriers to this behavior were low and could be overcome (erosion concerns) and the potential motivators very high (save money, natural look, access to beach). This finding meant that resources for the campaign should be focused first on avoiding new shoreline armoring being added, rather than on removal of existing armoring.

- Changing shore Armor behaviors would require *face-to-face interaction* with shoreline property owners, with calls to action in promotional materials to get people into a face-to-face environment where their questions and concerns about shoreline armoring and erosion could be addressed.

FIGURE 7.4 ■ Real Photos and Real Stories to Address a Desired Beauty of the Waterfront Property Posted on Shore Friendly Websites: After Removal of Hard Armor

Source: Kirvie Mesebeluu-Yobech http://shorefriendlykitsap.com/gallery/.

- Face-to-face education would need to come from a *trusted source*, with people suspicious about contractors or professionals that may be trying to sell them something.
- Decisions about armoring are usually made immediately after an erosion event, or when a property has just been purchased. *Outreach activities should be timed around these decision points.*
- People want to see and hear about successes from *real stories* from other shoreline property owners in using alternatives to shoreline Armor (see Figures 7.3 and 7.4.).
- Shoreline property owners have a desire and capacity for detailed, science-based information about their shorelines. They want to learn more and do the right thing. A *centralized education resource* would be beneficial.
- *Changing the social norm* about armoring will be critical to success. Armor is currently seen by many as a desirable element in protecting shoreline properties. In fact, many landowners believe that Armor enhances their property value. Shifting this perception will take presenting facts regarding property value, tapping into a desire for a natural-looking beach, wanting access to shoreline, and seeing it as their personal responsibility to help protect the health of Puget Sound.

More About the Shore Friendly Campaign

Intervention tools were designed to help shoreline property owners change their armoring behaviors, bundled under the umbrella concept of the Shore Friendly campaign, creating a consistent Puget Sound—wide look and feel for shoreline armor reduction efforts, and providing a rally point for localized efforts. Unlike other behavior change initiatives, the excessive cost of removing armor and, if needed, using soft shore protection can be challenging for landowners. In some cases, achieving desired behaviors can require significant financial assistance for landowners. The process of educating landowners, offering incentives, securing necessary permits, and ultimately removing armoring can also take several years. Early results of these programs, however, have shown that behavior change programs can effectively reduce the amount of hard armor on residential shoreline properties across Puget Sound.

Results

In 2014, five recent programs began applying Shore Friendly strategies and tools at the local level. Program elements have included informative workshops, free on-site technical assistance, permitting and design assistance, financial incentives, and outreach to secondary influencing audiences, namely realtors and shoreline contractors. To support these programs, a Shore Friendly website was launched to educate interested landowners and to provide a centralized source of information about local incentive programs.

By early 2018, almost 600 shoreline landowners participated in educational workshops to learn about the impacts of hard armor and alternatives to protect their property. More than 400 landowners also received on-site assistance to explore options for their properties, many resulting in technical reports from engineers or other experts assessing the conditions of the site and making recommendations for the property. Ultimately, more than 1,000 linear feet of hard shoreline armor have been removed, and this amount is expected to rise as many more potential projects have been identified.[10]

In 2020, the program received nearly $2.5 million in funding for the Shore Friendly 2021–2023 biennium.[11] And, as of 2022, the program continues to offer valued resources. A website includes links to connect landowners to relevant upcoming workshops in their area, submit a request for a site visit, and gain a free permit-ready design for their shoreline improvement.

DISCUSSION QUESTIONS AND EXERCISES

1. Why do the authors stress that behaviors need to be specific, or as Doug McKenzie-Mohr says, "non-divisible"?
2. For a campaign addressing the social issue of suicide, share a potential purpose, focus, priority audience, behavior objective, and target goal.
3. What is your experience with the use of the term *goal*?

8 STEP 5: AUDIENCE INSIGHTS

LEARNING OBJECTIVES

8.1 Explain the fifth step of identifying audience insights and the exchange theory.

8.2 Describe information you need to know about priority audience.

8.3 Explain the research tactics for learning more about priority audience.

8.4 Illustrate how insights help develop strategy.

8.5 Describe how potential revisions may be made to correctly understanding priority audiences.

8.6 Describe the ethical considerations when researching priority audiences.

By the time you reach this stage in the planning process, you may (understandably) just want to "get going." You will probably be eager to design the product, brainstorm incentives, search for convenient locations, dream up clever slogans, and envision beautiful billboards. After all, you have conducted a SWOT analysis, selected a priority audience, and know what you want that audience to do. And you may think you know what they need to know or believe in order to act. The problem is you are not your priority audience, so you don't know how they really feel about what you have in mind for them or what they may be thinking when approached to behave in ways such as these:

- Put all your liquids in a quart-sized resealable plastic bag before reaching security checkpoints.
- Reduce grass lawns by half.
- Eat five or more fruits and vegetables a day, the color way.
- Wear a mask in public places.

You may not know what's really in the way of their taking you up on your offer. This is the time to find out. Five audience insights are important and will be described and illustrated in this chapter:

- *Perceived barriers*. Reasons your priority audience hasn't done the behavior in the past, might not want to do the behavior, or don't think they can.
- *Desired benefits*. What your priority audience says is "in it for them" if they do the behavior.
- *Potential motivators*. Your priority audience's ideas on what someone could say to them, show them, do for them, or give to them that would increase the likelihood that they would adopt the behavior.
- *The competition*. Behaviors your priority audience prefers to do instead behaviors they have been doing "forever," and/or organizations and individuals who send messages that counter or oppose the desired behavior.
- *Influential others*. Those your priority audience listens to, watches, and/or looks up to, relative to the desired behavior.

And by conducting this investigation well, the rest of your planning process will be grounded in reality and guided by the customer's hand, as it was in the following opening case (see Figure 8.1).

CASE HIGHLIGHT

Decreasing Vaping Among Youth

(2018–Present)

FIGURE 8.1 ■

Source: Rescue Agency.

Background, Priority Audience, and Desired Behavior

In 2018, teen vape use was declared a public health epidemic in the United States.[1] Alarmingly, lower risk youth who might not otherwise use tobacco were vaping, potentially serving as a gateway to combustible cigarette use.[2] Dozens of vaping prevention efforts have been implemented in response to this crisis. Thanks to improved knowledge and higher risk perceptions associated with vape use from these varied public health efforts, an increasing number of vape users are now (2022) trying to quit, with a recent study suggesting that 45% of teens who vape were seriously considering quitting.[3] To address this need, *Quit The Hit* was developed as a vape cessation program tailored to support teens (ages 13–17) and young adults (18–21) interested in quitting to *participate in a virtual cessation program*.

Audience Insights

Critical audience insights to inform program development were obtained through a series of focus groups and interviews with over 380 young people to inform Marketing Intervention Strategies.

Barriers to Quitting

- *Low perceived negative health and addiction risk to vaping:* Young people who vape perceive themselves to be uniquely different from combustible cigarette users, who were perceived to have serious nicotine addiction and negative health risks.
- *Stress and anxiety coping strategy:* Young people who vaped reported a pleasant, relaxing buzz from using vapes, which they believed helped them deal with the stresses and anxieties of daily life, especially during COVID lockdown.
- *Lack of knowledge regarding the quitting process*: A significant number of young people who vaped believed they could quit whenever they wanted to without any cessation support and were not aware of evidence-based cessation strategies that would help them quit successfully.
- *Perceived social norms.* Vaping was perceived to be common and socially acceptable by young people. In fact, vape initiation commonly occurred during social interactions and gatherings when a peer casually offered "a hit."
- *Lack of support to quit*: Many vape users noted that adults in their lives (e.g., parents, teachers, coaches) were not aware of their vape use and felt like they would not have anyone to talk to who would be supportive.
- *Lack of relevant and accessible cessation services:* Many believed that available tobacco cessation services were geared toward adults and/or cigarette users with serious nicotine addiction, and thus traditional phone-based quitlines were not designed for them. They noted that calling a quitline counselor would feel too formal, too serious, too big of a commitment, and not a natural way for them to communicate.

Benefits (to quitting): Young people who vape believed that quitting would help them be healthier overall, save money they would otherwise spend on vapes, and take more control of their lives. They also mentioned that it would be a relief to no longer have to hide their vape use from the adults in their lives.

Motivators (to getting help to quit): Respondents noted texting and/or social media as the preferred methods of communication for help in quitting.

Competition (to quitting): Frequent social media usage exposed this audience to disingenuous vape promotion tactics and reinforced vape use as part of the lifestyle and image that young people find desirable.

Marketing Interventions

Quit The Hit (https://www.instagram.com/quitthehit/, https://quitthehitnow.com/) was strategically developed based on audience insights and co-created with priority audiences as an innovative and interactive Instagram-based vaping cessation intervention. It was a collaborative effort between the University of California, San Francisco (UCSF) Center for Tobacco Control Research and Education; Hopelab, a social innovation lab focused on improving the health of young people; and Rescue Agency, a behavior change agency that leverages social marketing principles for public health efforts. The framework for *Quit The Hit* was based on UCSF and Rescue's previous collaboration on a successful Facebook-based cigarette cessation program for young adults called Smokefree Social (https://www.facebook.com/communesmokefreesocial/).

Product: *Quit The Hit* is a 5-week virtual cessation program delivered fully on Instagram, facilitated by a highly trained, compassionate, and relatable cessation coach. Program participants receive evidence-based daily cessation multimedia content (video, audio, pictures, text only, games) to increase motivation to quit and support participants throughout their quit journey, with facilitated prompts (see Figure 8.2). Each cohort of 12–15 participants are engaged in a group direct message (DM) on Instagram, fostering a network of accessible social support where participants openly share and support each other's authentic experiences in their quit journey based on facilitated prompts from the cessation coach.

Price: There is no monetary cost to participants. They simply need a free Instagram account to join. Program costs such as counselor compensation and evaluation costs are covered by organizations sponsoring cessation programs in the area. Participants receive monetary incentives for completing the built-in evaluation surveys and for referring a friend to participate after they complete the program.

Place: Based on audience insights, it is critical for the intervention to be available on an accessible and familiar platform to young people that does not require additional effort to access. Additionally, teens were experiencing unprecedented social isolation due to the COVID-19 lockdown and spent more time on social media platforms, such as Instagram, to socialize. *Quit The Hit* is comprehensively administered on Instagram from promotion to program sign-up to interactive content to pre/post evaluation surveys.

Promotion: Targeted Instagram advertisements are posted to recruit cohorts of young people in a certain geographic area where *Quit The Hit* is implemented.

Results[4]

As of 2022, *Quit The Hit* has been piloted in five locales (San Diego in California, South Carolina, Oklahoma, Minnesota, and Kansas), funded by government grants or public health departments. Baseline data from pilot programs in South Carolina and San Diego show that *Quit The Hit* has successfully recruited the right priority audience with 88% of participants vaping

FIGURE 8.2 ■ *Quit The Hit* Instagram Promotion Example

Source: Rescue Agency.

within 60 minutes of waking up, 76% trying to quit in the past year but failed, and 90% indicating a strong desire to quit. Teens who expressed the highest level of confidence in successfully quitting vaping significantly increased from 16% at baseline to 40% at follow-up. Most importantly, past 30-day vape use significantly decreased from 100% at program intake to 81% at follow-up. *Quit The Hit* will continue to expand in other locales as a subscription-based intervention that can be licensed by organizations working to address teen vaping. *Quit The Hit* continues to be supported by updated formative research for fresh audience insights and will be further customized to address the unique needs of higher risk populations such as LGBTQ+ young adults.

STEP 5: IDENTIFY AUDIENCE INSIGHTS

In the marketing game, the winners almost always have one "maneuver" in common: a customer-centered focus. The best have a genuine curiosity, even hunger, to know what the potential customer thinks and feels about their offer. This fifth step in the planning process is designed to do just that—deepen your understanding of your priority audience.

This chapter will first identify and discuss what priority audience perspectives will be helpful for you to know and understand. You then will read about how to gather this information and, finally, how you will use these insights in developing your strategies. First, a word about the exchange theory, another marketing cornerstone—one that will help you envision this "deal-making" process.

The Exchange Theory

As mentioned in Chapter 4, the traditional economic exchange theory postulates that for an exchange to take place, priority audiences must perceive benefits equal to or greater than perceived costs.[5] In other words, they must believe they will get as much or more than they give. If perceived benefits are less than perceived costs, the consumer is less likely, even unlikely, to buy. And the term "perceived" is critical to this understanding. It all depends on how the audience defines the benefits and the costs. In 1972, Philip Kotler published an article in the *Journal of Marketing* asserting that exchange is the core concept of marketing and that exchange takes place when the priority audience believes they will get as much or more than they give.[6]

And earlier, in 1969, Kotler argued that exchange theory applies to more than the purchase of tangible goods and services, that it can in fact involve intangible or symbolic products (e.g., recycling), and that payments are not limited to financial ones (e.g., time and effort may be the only major perceived costs).[7] In 1974 and 1978, Richard Bagozzi broadened this framework by adding several ideas, including that more than two parties may be involved in the transaction and that the primary beneficiary of an exchange may in fact be a third party (e.g., the environment).[8] This is certainly consistent with the definition of social marketing used throughout this text, as it acknowledges that the intent is always to better society as well as the priority audience. We like to speak of it as "Behavior Change for Social Good."

Given this, five priority audience perspectives identified at the beginning of the chapter (barriers, benefits, motivators, competition, and influential others) are crucial and will be elaborated upon in the next section of this chapter.

WHAT YOU NEED TO KNOW ABOUT YOUR PRIORITY AUDIENCE

Perceived Barriers

Barriers are revealed in audience responses to a variety of questions. Actual questions in focus groups or personal interviews could include the following:

- How has this behavior been perceived in your family and/or cultural?

- What are some of the reasons that you haven't done this behavior in the past?
- What are some of the reasons you might not do this in the future?
- What do you think you will have to give (up) in order to perform this behavior?
- Do you think you can do it?
- Why, if applicable, did you quit doing it?

These could also be thought of as the "costs" the priority audience perceives. Doug McKenzie-Mohr, the environmental psychologist highlighted in Chapter 7, notes that barriers may be *internal* to the individual, such as lack of knowledge or skill needed to carry out an activity, or *external*, as in structural changes that need to be made in order for the behavior to be more convenient. He also stresses that these barriers will differ by priority audience and by behavior. In our planning process, that is why priority audiences and the desired behavior (activity) are identified early in the planning process.[9]

Barriers may be related to a variety of factors, including knowledge, beliefs, skills, abilities, infrastructures, technology, economic status, or cultural influences. They may be *real* (e.g., taking the bus will take longer than driving alone to work) or *perceived* (e.g., people who take the bus can't really afford any other mode of transportation). In either case, they are always from the priority audience's perspective and often something you can address. It is also important to consider cultural and racial foundations that may create unique barriers for priority audience groups. For example, early in the COVID-19 pandemic, wearing a mask in public posed real safety concerns around racial profiling and police harassment for members of the African American community. In addition to using primary research to identify barriers for each priority audience, barriers can also sometimes be identified by reviewing prior and existing social marketing efforts and exploring social marketing listserves, journals, websites of major governmental organizations, and relevant news stories.

Desired Benefits

Benefits are something your priority audience wants or needs and therefore values and that the behavior you are promoting has the potential to provide.[10] What social marketers will need to address are any doubts their audience has that they will, in fact, experience these benefits. Again, these will be benefits in the eyes of the customer—not necessarily the same as yours.

Example: Benefits to Saving the Crabs in Chesapeake Bay.[11] For centuries, Chesapeake Bay blue crabs were considered the best blue crabs in the world, but in 2003, the Chesapeake harvest hit a near historic low. With this knowledge at hand, a planned campaign theme of "saving the seafood" was born. While people in the Washington, DC area might have only limited concern for the bay, many are passionate about their seafood, as is evidenced by the many thriving seafood restaurants throughout Washington, DC and its Maryland and Virginia suburbs. Reframing the problem of a polluted bay as a *culinary, not an environmental, problem* was the cornerstone of the campaign developed by the nonprofit Academy for Educational Development (AED).

Branded "Save the Crabs. Then Eat'em," promotional messages focused on a behavior to skip the spring fertilizing. Three television ads were developed, each encouraging viewers to wait until fall to fertilize their lawns and each using humor to lighten the message. One ad explained that "no crab should die like this," and as a man bites into a lump of crabmeat, opines that "they should perish in some hot, tasty butter." Print ads ran in the *Washington Post* and in a free tabloid handed out at metro stops (see Figure 8.3). Drink coasters were printed and distributed without charge for local seafood restaurants to use and hand out to patrons (see Figure 8.4).

To monitor campaign outcomes early on, random-digit-dial telephone surveys were administered to measure behavior intent before and after the campaign was launched. Interviews were completed with 600 area residents who reported they cared for their lawn or hired someone to do it. In 2004, prior to the campaign, 52% of those surveyed reported that they planned to

FIGURE 8.3 ■ Out-of-Home Ad Promoting Fertilizing in the Fall

Source: Academy of Educational Development for Chesapeake Bay Club.

fertilize that spring. In 2005, after the campaign had launched, that number had dropped to 39%, a 25% improvement.

Potential Motivators

Motivators are distinct from audience benefits. They are ideas your priority audience shares with you, ones they think would make it more likely that they would adopt the desired behavior. Their answers to four questions will provide insight regarding intervention strategies (the 4Ps):

(1) "What could someone *say* to you that would make it more likely that you would consider adopting this behavior?"

FIGURE 8.4 ■ Drink Coasters Distributed to Local Seafood Restaurants

Source: Academy of Educational Development for Chesapeake Bay Club.

(2) "What could someone *show* you that would make it more likely that you would adopt this behavior?"

(3) "Is there anything someone could *give* you that would help you adopt this behavior?"

(4) "Is there anything someone could *do* for you that would help you adopt this behavior?"

Responses are likely to fall into one of the 4P categories. We'll use an example of an effort to influence shoreline property owners to remove all or portions of seawalls and bulkheads on beaches to improve water quality and protect wildlife habitats, elaborating on the case example mentioned in the Chapter 7 Research Highlight. Audience members may mention that you could give them the native plants they would need to help decrease erosion as well as technical assistance with a design (*product strategies*). Further, having these plants delivered to their home, and having the technical assistance provided there, would be ideal (*place strategies*). They may suggest that it would be motivating for them if they could get a decrease in property taxes in exchange for removing shoreline seawalls (*price strategy*). And they may mention that it would be persuasive to hear promising positive impacts on habitat protection determined by a pilot project (*message*), as well as to hear from other homeowners in the area with satisfaction stories (*messengers*) at a special event (*communication channel*).

It should be noted that in this idea-generating interview process, you can also test ideas you have been thinking of that respondents don't mention. This is different from a formal pretest effort, which is recommended after strategies have been drafted based on these audience insights but prior to implementation.

Example: Motivators for Breastfeeding. Studies show that babies who are breastfed for six months are less likely to develop ear infections, diarrhea, and respiratory illnesses. And some studies suggest that infants who are not breastfed have higher rates of obesity, diabetes, leukemia, and asthma. Yet, in 2004 in the United States, only about 33% of mothers were breastfeeding at the recommended six months postpartum, one of the lowest breastfeeding rates in the developed world.[12] The *Healthy People 2010* goal was to raise this to 50%. The U.S. Department of Health and Human Services, Office of Women's Health took on this challenge, inspired by audience input.

Precampaign research findings provided a direction and focus for the campaign, revealing that there was no clear understanding of the duration goal for breastfeeding and that there were no known major perceived advantages of breastfeeding. Campaign messages were designed to address this confusion and to highlight advantages that would be most motivating. A media campaign was launched in June 2004 with the support of the Ad Council, using ads driving home the message "Babies were born to be breastfed" and highlighting real health advantages—with a little humor (see Figure 8.5).[14]

In addition to mass media and the Internet, resources were directed to supporting community-based demonstration projects (CDPs) throughout the country. These projects involved funding local coalitions, hospitals, universities, and other organizations so that they could offer breastfeeding services, provide outreach to their communities, train health care providers, implement the media aspects of the campaign, and track breastfeeding rates in their communities.

Research after the first year of the campaign was encouraging. Awareness about breastfeeding had risen from 28% to 38%. More than half of respondents (63%) either correctly identified six months as the recommended length of time to exclusively breastfeed a baby or said the recommended duration was longer than six months. The number agreeing that babies should be exclusively breastfed in the first six months increased from prewave (53%) to postwave (62%). And, most important, more of the women surveyed had breastfed a child (any duration) in the 2005 study (73%) than in the 2004 study (63%). An updated "report card" ten years later, in 2016, indicates that breastfeeding rates were on the rise, with breastfeeding at six months having increased to 51.8% and the *Healthy People 2020* objective having now been set at 60.6%.[15]

FIGURE 8.5 ■ Poster for a Breastfeeding Campaign in Partnership With the Ad Council[13]

Source: U.S. Department of Health and Human Services.

The Competition

Identifying the Competition

The fourth area you'll want to explore with your priority audience is the competition. Simply stated, in social marketing, the competition is primarily the behavior your priority audience is doing instead of the one you are promoting. It is actually similar to commercial marketing where the competition is what the consumer is buying instead of your product to satisfy a want or need. It may be a similar product (e.g., different brand for a purse), or a substitute product (e.g., a backpack), that satisfies the same need. Social marketers have tough competitors because we define *the competition* as follows:

- Behaviors our priority audience would prefer over the ones we are promoting (e.g., eating high calorie foods is more gratifying than eating of fruits and vegetables).
- Behaviors they have been doing "forever," such as a habit that they would have to give up (e.g., driving alone to work or taking long showers).
- Organizations and individuals who send messages that counter or oppose the desired behavior (e.g., flavored vaping products).

Table 8.1 illustrates the challenges you (will) face. Consider the pleasures and benefits you are asking your priority audience to give up. Consider the economic power of organizations and sponsors that are sending messages countering those you are sending. Consider the persuasiveness and influence of typical key messengers. And consider that the competition may even be your own organization! We call this "friendly" competition, where one program within the organization (e.g., a needle exchange program) may in fact potentially erode the success of another (e.g., a drug use reduction program).

Another potential framework (and way to identify the competition) is offered by Sue Peattie and Ken Peattie of Cardiff University in Wales.[16] They suggest that in social marketing, the competition is better thought of as a "battle of ideas" and that these competing ideas can come

TABLE 8.1 ■ What and With Whom You May Be Competing

Behavior Objective	Competing Behaviors	Competing Messages and Messengers
Drink less than five drinks at one sitting	Getting really "buzzed"	Budweiser
Wear sunscreen	Tanning	Fashion ads showing "beautiful" tan people
Give five hours a week to a volunteer effort	Spending time with family	The audience member's kids
Compost organic food waste	A habit of pushing scraps down the drain when cleaning dishes	Neighbors who say the backyard composter will attract rats

from four sources that can be considered potential competitors: (1) *commercial countermarketing* (e.g., cigarette companies), (2) *social discouragement* of your desired behavior (e.g., anti-gun-control activists), (3) *apathy* (e.g., when considering whether to vote), and (4) *involuntary disinclination* (e.g., physical addictions).

Identifying Perceived Barriers and Benefits of the Competition

Once competitors are identified, there is more you want to know while you're at it. McKenzie-Mohr and Smith provide a useful framework for capturing your research findings—one that will prepare you for developing your product's positioning and 4Ps marketing intervention mix strategy in Steps 6 and 7. The name of this marketing game is to change the ratio of benefits to barriers so that the target behavior becomes more attractive. McKenzie-Mohr and Smith propose four ways (tactics), which are not mutually exclusive, to accomplish this:

1. Increase the benefits of the target behavior
2. Decrease the barriers (and/or costs) of the target behavior
3. Decrease the benefits of the competing behavior(s)
4. Increase the barriers (and/or costs) of the competing behaviors[17]

Table 8.2 is a simple illustration of what in reality (ideally) would include a more exhaustive list of benefits and barriers/costs created from audience research. Keep in mind that there is likely to be more than one preferred or alternative behavior identified as the competition.

An important component of this research process will include attempting to prioritize these benefits and barriers/costs within each of the quadrants. You are most interested in the "higher values"—the key benefits to be gained or costs that will be avoided by adopting the desired behavior. In the example in Table 8.2, your research won't be complete until you determine how your priority audience ranks benefits and barriers in each quadrant (e.g., what is the number-one benefit for using a litterbag?).

Example: Highlighting Costs of Not Adopting Pets. On Saturday morning, October 14, 2006, an interview on a Seattle, Washington radio station with a spokesperson for the Humane Society for Tacoma and Pierce County certainly highlighted the costs of doing nothing: "We have over a hundred cats and kittens that are likely to be euthanized tonight if they are not adopted today." Television news programs, newspaper articles, and blogs also helped spread the word to "skadoodle over to Kittenkaboodle and help us end the heartache of euthanasia by adopting a homeless cat or kitten." The event promised to be festive and was decked out with balloons and offered free face paintings for kids. An incentive topped off the offer—a $20 discount on the regular adoption fee, which ("today only") included spaying or neutering, a veterinary exam, a cat carrier, and even a cat toy.

On the following Monday, it was announced that a record-breaking 180 shelter pets had found homes in just eight hours! Evidently, the shelter had made the cost of "doing nothing" (apathy) real and significant. Follow-up news stories and website postings assured those who

TABLE 8.2 ■ Identifying Perceived Barriers and Benefits of the Competition

Audience Perceptions	Desired Behavior: Use a Litterbag in the Car	Competing Behavior: Tossing Fast-Food Bags Out the Window
Perceived benefits	• It's good role modeling for my kids. • I am doing my part for the environment. • I help save tax dollars. • I don't feel as guilty.	• It's easier. • I avoid the smell of old food in my car. • I avoid the trash all over my car. • It's okay because it will biodegrade. • It gives prisoners a job to do.
Perceived barriers/costs	• Having to find one and remember to put it in the car. • Having liquid spill out of it. • It will smell up my car. • I won't remember to empty it.	• I might have to do community service and pick up litter. • I could get caught and fined. • I'm contributing to the litter on the roadways that looks bad and will have to be picked up.

missed out, "No problem. The shelter will be open all week, and there is sure to be a new and ample supply of adoptable animals."[18]

Influential Others

The fifth area to consider at this point is those your priority audience listens to, watches, and/or looks up to, especially related to the desired behavior you have in mind. We think of them as midstream audiences, and they include social groups your priority audience belongs to (e.g., a moms' support group or Facebook friends) as well as coworkers, classmates, neighbors, family members, physicians, counselors, pharmacists, the media, and entertainers. In some cases, it may be individuals the priority audience finds trustworthy, likable, and as having expertise (e.g., a highly regarded scientist or entertainer). Knowing what these groups and individuals are saying and doing (or might say and do) regarding the desired behavior will have significant implications, especially for promotional strategies, perhaps warranting an additional priority audience for your plan.

Example: An Influencer for Energy Conservation.[19] During an energy crisis on the U.S. West Coast in the winter of 2001, a popular, well-respected radio talk show host, Dave Ross of 97.3 FM KIRO in Seattle, Washington, was intrigued when he heard of a successful conservation effort in Israel more than 20 years before. He then tried a similar strategy with his listening audience of several hundred thousand.

The campaign in Israel had taken place immediately after a popular television show dramatized Israel's overuse of electricity. The show's host asked the audience to leave the room and go around the house and turn off all extra lights. The viewers then saw the impact of their actions on their television screens, from a camera focused on the Israeli Electric Company's electricity consumption gauges. Within a few seconds, the gauges dropped sharply. This experiment that helped alter the belief that "my lights don't make a difference" saved an estimated 6% in aggregate electricity consumption during the eight months of the campaign.[20]

Taking a similar approach, Dave announced on a preview for his show that he would try an experiment at 11:30 that morning and would be asking listeners to turn off and unplug anything electric that wasn't being used. He emphasized that he didn't want people to make any sacrifices; he just wanted them to turn off what they didn't need. At 11:28, the city's electric utility staff were standing by and read the current level of megawatts in use: "We're at 1,400 megawatts." At 11:30, the talk show host said, "Go!" and for the next five minutes, he walked around the studios of the station with a handheld microphone and turned off conference room lights and computer monitors in empty offices. He then called his wife at home to make sure she was participating, all as an example for the listening audience.

At 11:35, the city utility public information officer came back on the air and reported impressive results. Usage had dropped by 40 megawatts to 1,360. The decrease was enough to power 40,000 homes and represented $300,000 worth of electricity. Excitement over the success generated an hour-long program the next day on ways to conserve electricity (e.g., doing laundry in non-peak hours and purchasing energy-saving appliances). Dave was presented a conservation award on air (an energy-saving lightbulb) by a member of the Seattle city council. For several weeks thereafter, local home and garden supply stores featured energy-saving appliances and lightbulbs.

HOW TO LEARN MORE ABOUT PRIORITY AUDIENCE

Formative research, as described in Chapter 3, and as the name implies, will help deepen your understanding of your customer—even develop empathy and compassion. It will help you gain insights into audience barriers, benefits, and motivators; the competition; and influential others that will then assist you in developing draft strategies to pretest.

Resources for Audience Insights

As usual, you should begin with a search and review of existing literature and research (e.g., social marketing journals, governmental publications) and through discussions with peers and colleagues (e.g., social marketing listserves). If, after this review, informational gaps still exist, it may be important to conduct original research using qualitative methods, such as focus groups and personal interviews, to identify barriers, benefits, motivators, the competition, and important influential others. Quantitative instruments, such as telephone and web-based surveys, would then be very helpful in prioritizing these benefits and barriers to, say, using a litterbag, such as those listed in Table 8.2. It is important to note that traditional research tools (surveys, focus groups, etc.) do not work for all audience groups. There is usually underrepresentation of cultural, racial, and ESL groups in these types of research. If one of your priority audience groups falls into one of these categories, you should consider nontraditional research techniques to gather information (e.g. partnerships with community organizations, one-on-one interviews in the audiences preferred language or intercept interviews at places members of the audience gathers).

One popular survey model to consider is the knowledge, attitudes, practices, and beliefs (KAPB) survey. As described by Andreasen,

> these are comprehensive surveys of a representative sample of the target population designed to secure information about the social behavior in question and on the current status of the target audience's Knowledge, Attitudes, Practices, Beliefs. KAPB studies are relatively common in social marketing environments, especially in the area of health. They are very often carried out routinely by local governments, the World Bank, or the United Nations. For this reason, they are sometimes available to social marketers as part of a secondary database.[21]

For example, a KAPB-type study has been conducted annually by the Gallup Organization for the March of Dimes, beginning in 1995, and is supported by the Centers for Disease Control and Prevention.[22] Telephone surveys conducted nationwide among women ages 18–45 are designed to track knowledge and behavior related to the importance of taking folic acid before becoming pregnant to decrease the chances of birth defects. Consider how these summary findings in the year 2008 would shape campaign strategies and priorities:

- Nine out of 10 women (89%) did not know that folic acid should be taken prior to pregnancy.
- Eight out of 10 women (80%) did not know that folic acid could help prevent birth defects.
- Only about one in three women (39%) not pregnant at the time of the survey reported consuming a multivitamin containing folic acid daily.

An example of a more qualitative research approach to understanding a priority audience was one conducted by Michael Jortner, an MBA candidate at the Institute for Social Marketing at the University of Stirling. Michael was interested in answering the question, "What desired benefits influence dog walkers in urban parks to keep their dogs on a leash [the preferred behavior] compared to those who don't?" He learned through personal interviews that dog walkers who leashed their dogs valued the "peace" in their walk, while those who didn't leash their dogs were looking for "joy" in their outing.[23] Perhaps those wanting to influence "nonleashers" to become "leashers" will want to challenge themselves to ask priority audiences the question, "How can we put more joy for you in walking a dog on a leash?"

HOW INSIGHTS HELP DEVELOP STRATEGY

If you understand (better yet, empathize with) your priority audience's real and perceived barriers, benefits, motivators, competitors, and influential others relative to your desired behavior, it will be akin to having a guiding hand as you craft your positioning statement and 4Ps strategies. We'll illustrate this application and process with a brief case.[24]

In 2006, the Washington State Department of Health developed a social marketing plan with the purpose of decreasing falls among seniors and a focus on developing fitness classes that could be offered by a variety of community organizations. The priority audiences for the pilot (first year) were seniors ages 70–79 living in one county of the state. Formative research with key informants and seniors in the priority audience identified the following major perceived benefits, barriers, motivators, competition, and important others influencing seniors regarding joining and attending classes:

- Benefits desired: "It could improve my strength, balance, and fitness, and then perhaps I can live independent longer. I also want it to be fun and a chance to make new friends."
- Barriers to joining: "It depends on how much it will cost, where the class is located, the time of day it is offered, and who will be leading the class. I don't want some young instructor I can't relate to!"
- Barriers to attending regularly: "I'd probably drop out if it's too strenuous, I hurt myself, or I couldn't keep up. And I'd need to see improvements in my fitness for it to seem worthwhile."
- Motivators to attend regularly: "If the class is less than $50 a month, is located near my home, has free parking, includes others in the class like myself, and is taught by an instructor who understands seniors."
- Competition: "I can probably just do my own thing at home for free, at my own pace, by watching an exercise video or going out for a walk. I guess the advantage of the class, though, is that it's a way to make sure I do it!"
- Influential others: "My neighbor who is my age says that the gym instructor is our age, and really energetic, and she thinks I can easily keep up!"

A *positioning* statement, as you will read in Chapter 9, describes how you want your priority audience to see your desired behavior, especially relative to the competition. Planners wanted the fitness classes to be seen by their priority audience of 70- to 79-year-olds as

> a fitness class for seniors that *works*, as it will improve strength and balance; is *safe*, as it has experienced skilled instructors offering tested exercises; and is *fun*, as it offers an opportunity to meet others and get out of the house. It is an important and worthwhile activity for seniors wanting to stay *independent, be active*, and *prevent falls.*

The *product* platform includes a description of the core, actual, and augmented product, all inspired by your benefits, barriers, motivators, and competitive research. For the fitness classes, the *core* product (benefits of the classes) was subsequently refined to be "staying active, independent, and preventing falls." The *actual* product (features of the classes) would be one-hour fitness classes, with up to 20 participants, meeting three times a week. The classes would include strength exercises with wrist and ankle weights, balance exercises, and moderate aerobics.

The exercises could be done standing or sitting, and the instructor would be a certified fitness instructor with special training in strength and balance exercises for seniors. The *augmented* product (extras to add value) would include a booklet giving information on fall prevention and describing how to conduct a self-assessment for fall risk and determine readiness to exercise (see Figure 8.6). External safety effectiveness assessments would be available as well.

Pricing strategies include *costs* for products, *fees* for services, and any *monetary* and *nonmonetary incentives* and *disincentives*. Based on priority audience comments, it was determined that the recommended fee per class should be $2.00–$2.50, enough to help cover the cost of the instructors, add to perceived value, and build commitment. It was also recommended that a coupon be offered for a free first class as well as a punch card giving 12 classes for the price of 11,

FIGURE 8.6 ■ Brochure Cover for a Fall-Prevention Class for Seniors

Source: Washington State Department of Health.

and it was suggested that organizers build in a reward of a free class to participants who attended at least 10 classes in a month.

Place strategies refer to where and when behaviors are performed and tangible goods and services are accessed. For the exercise classes, nine sites were selected, eight of them at senior centers and one at a senior retirement facility. Suggested ideal start times were 9 or 10 a.m. or 1, 2, or 3 p.m. There was to be free, adjacent parking at each site.

Promotional elements include messages, messengers, creative elements, and communication channels. The recommended name of the program was S.A.I.L. (Stay Active and Independent for Life), with a tagline of "A strength and balance fitness class for seniors." Consistent with the desired positioning, key messages to incorporate in promotional materials included the following:

- "It works. You'll be stronger, have better balance, and feel better, and this will help you stay independent and active and prevent falls."
- "It's safe. Instructors are experienced and skilled, and exercises have been tested with seniors."
- "It's fun. You'll meet other seniors and make new friends, and this will get you out of the house three days a week."
- Types of media channels to promote the class would include flyers, posters, articles in newsletters and local newspapers, packets for physicians, website information, sandwich board signs at senior centers, and a Q&A fact sheet for senior center staff.

POTENTIAL REVISIONS

This new in-depth understanding of priority audiences may signal a need to revise priority audiences (Step 3) and/or objectives (Step 4) because it may reveal one or more of the following situations:

- One distinct segment of the priority audience (men in their early 70s) has beliefs that you would have a difficult time changing or may not want to: "Moderate physical activity like this is wimpy, and I'd rather increase vigorous activity from two to three days a week if I do anything more."
- The desired behavior has too many insurmountable barriers for one or more audiences: "I can't get to the farmers' market to use my coupons because they close before I get off work."
- The audience tells us the behavior objective isn't clear: "I don't understand what reducing my BMI means."
- Perceived costs are too high: "Quitting smoking while I'm pregnant looks impossible, but I might be able to cut down to a half a pack a day."

- The behavior objective has already been met: "My child already has five caring adult relationships outside the home, so for you to suggest I go find one caring adult for my child says you're not talking to people like me."
- A major knowledge objective isn't needed but a belief objective is: "I already know that tobacco kills one out of three users. I just believe I'll be one of the two out of three who make it!"
- The original behavior objective isn't the solution to the problem: "I always cover the load in the back of my pickup truck with a tarp. The problem is, it still doesn't keep stuff from flying out. What we need is a net or cable that holds the tarp down."
- The goal is too high: "The latest survey shows that 1 in 5 teens has used marijuana in the past month so decreasing the the use of marijuana by 50% looks impossible with this groups.!"

ETHICAL CONSIDERATIONS WHEN RESEARCHING PRIORITY AUDIENCE

Perhaps the greatest ethical concern when conducting activities to learn more about your priority audience is the research process itself. Concerns range from whether questions will make respondents uncomfortable or embarrassed to deceiving respondents regarding the purposes of the research to assurance of anonymity and confidentiality.

Institutional review boards (IRBs) have been formed to help avoid these ethical problems. An IRB is a group formally designated to review and monitor behavioral and biomedical research involving human subjects. The purpose of IRB review is to ensure that appropriate steps are taken to protect the rights and welfare of humans participating as subjects in a research study. In the United States, IRBs are mandated by the Research Act of 1974, which defines IRBs and requires them for all research that receives funding, directly or indirectly, from the Department of Health and Human Services (HHS). These IRBs are themselves regulated by the Office for Human Research Protections within HHS and may be based at academic institutions or medical facilities or conducted by for-profit organizations.[25]

COVID-19 Social Marketing Example

In January of 2022, a *Seattle Times* columnist wrote that "Most of Seattle area's 200,000 unvaccinated adults say they will 'definitely not' get COVID shots."[26] This was in spite of the fact that Seattle was, at the time, one of the most vaccinated major metro areas in the nation, with more than 90% of the 18-and-older population in the state's three largest counties having received at least one dose of the vaccine.[27] Relevant to this chapter on audience insights, the article proceeded to share the results of a survey to identify the major (multiple) reasons for not getting fully vaccinated, ones we'll label as barriers that program planners would consider their "assignment" to address:

- 60% concerned with possible side effects
- 55% not trusting the government
- 45% not believing they need a vaccine
- 41% planning to wait and see if it is safe
- 36% not trusting COVID-19 vaccines

CHAPTER SUMMARY

In this important step in the marketing planning process, you take time out to deepen your understanding of your priority audience. What you are most interested in knowing are (their) perceived *barriers, benefits, motivators, competitors*, and *influential others*. What you are most interested in feeling are compassion and a desire to develop marketing intervention strategies that decrease these barriers, increase benefits, are inspired by what the priority audience says will motivate them, upstage your competition, and engage influential others.

These insights may be gathered through a literature review or other secondary research resources including organizational websites and social marketing listserves and journals. They are more likely to involve at least some qualitative surveys, such as focus groups or personal interviews. Quantitative surveys, such as a KAPB (knowledge, attitudes, practices, and beliefs) survey, will help you prioritize your findings and provide sharp focus for your positioning and marketing intervention strategies. You should also consider nontraditional research methods to reach any priority audience groups that are underrepresented in your secondary and traditional research methods.

RESEARCH HIGHLIGHT

Reducing Cardiac Death Risks Among Firefighters

Inspired by Formative Research

This Research Highlight "makes real" the inspirational value of formative research. In this case, a multi-methods research approach was used to identify, for an audience of frontline firefighters: cultural norms, unique barriers, desired benefits, motivators, and competing behaviors relative to engaging in regular physical activity. It is only a summary of a more detailed article authored by John Staley, PhD, MSEH, that appeared in the *Social Marketing Quarterly* in 2009.[28]

Background

Firefighters, as an occupational group, are known to be at increased risk for cardiac-related injuries, with 44% of deaths among fire fighters while on duty due to sudden cardiac death.[29] Significantly, firefighters also have a high prevalence of sedentary lifestyle, obesity, hyper-tension, and high total cholesterol. At the time this article was published in 2009, research into physical fitness programs for firefighters revealed mixed success, and there were no national-level policies mandating firefighters participate in workplace fitness programs. The major question the research addresses is what are the cultural determinants and beliefs that firefighters hold regarding physical fitness, ones that would inspire a motivating and successful program.

Methodology

A mixed-methods study in North Carolina was employed to identify individual factors (e.g., self-efficacy), environmental factors (e.g., lack of adequate space and equipment), and organizational attributes (e.g., workplace culture and norms) that impacted physical fitness activities among firefighters. Major efforts included the following:

Personal Interviews: Researchers talked with approximately 100 frontline firefighters and administrators about physical fitness practices, health and fitness norms, and cardiac risk awareness. They met as well as with firefighters from across the state during two annual state fire conferences.

Focus Groups: This phase built upon personal interview findings through six focus-group discussions, exploring the normative expectations for overall fitness and current efforts for participation.

Quantitative Survey: Results from the focus groups informed the design of a survey administered to 1,000 firefighters in the state to identify and prioritize perceived barriers, potential motivators, and, perhaps most importantly for this case, competing factors related to personal and organizational fitness programs.

Findings

Inspiring themes were revealed:

Barriers: When time is available to exercise, many firefighters found doing so by traditional means (e.g., treadmill, bicycle, weight lifting) to be neither interesting nor beneficial. Yet participation in team sports was considered both enjoyable and a great way to build crew camaraderie.

Motivators: The most cross-cutting and key motivating factor across all age and experience levels for the fitness intervention was a team-sport-oriented approach, one capitalizing on the inherent competitive nature of most firefighters.

The Competition: Several factors readily compete with the time provided for firefighters during the organization's fitness period including: mandatory activities such as emergency or disaster response activities, continuing education, public relations events, and job tasks scheduled by the organization during the departments' committed time for exercise. Additional competing elements included intrapersonal factors (e.g., spending time checking personal emails) and perceived lack of fitness norms. Broader community factors also existed, such as local government's limited ability to offer new fitness activities. From the frontline firefighter's perspective, these factors conflicting with the exercise period were considered major indicators of management's lack of support and priority for good physical fitness.

Marketing Intervention Strategies

In 2008, the research team met with the fire chief, a captain overseeing department physical fitness, six seasoned firefighters, and representatives from the town administration to develop the intervention strategy. A subsequent pretest meeting followed with firefighters (n = 190) in midspring 2008 to introduce the study and answer any questions or concerns about developing/and or implementing a competitive team sports intervention. Participating firefighters chose the name *Get Firefighters Moving* for the interventions, seen as a valued concept from the firefighters' perspective. In keeping with the sports-oriented theme, the intervention used elements of the National Football League's structure, with crews competing in team-sport activities over a six-month period to improve physical fitness outcomes. At the end of the competition period, the top ranked teams competed in a playoff format, with the winning ("Super Bowl") team having the most wins at six months. Additionally, the most physically fit team was recognized in terms of the best overall fitness outcome measures. Key features of the marketing intervention strategy included:

Product: A variety of team sports were offered including basketball, volleyball, ultimate frisbee, and flag football. Guidelines helped ensure good sportsmanship, proper structure of teams and activities, rules of play, and safety, with injury prevention guidelines a key priority.

Price: No monetary outlays were required of the firefighters, as competition took place during the workday, and all necessary equipment was provided free of charge. Considerable attention, however, was given to competition (nonmonetary) incentives, including awarding winners a "Challenge Coin," designed by the firefighters themselves and considered an iconic symbol of the strength and valor of the fire service.

Place: Teams competed within their own districts, allowing for quick response to any emergency event. Competition locations rotated through different fire stations to provide the added appeal of the "home team versus the away team."

Promotion: Key messengers promoting the competition were role-model firefighters, those individuals within the fire department who were respected for consistently promoting good health and safety behaviors, having demonstrated positive physical fitness habits by "talking the talk" and "walking the walk."

Results

The impact measures of the pilot for this study were promising, as paired t-test analyses of mean differences in pre- and postintervention (six months) measures demonstrated improvement in systolic blood pressure, cardiovascular class, flexibility, and body-fat percentage as a measure of body composition.

Conclusions

Organizers concluded that "Our focus on both downstream fitness behavior of frontline firefighters and upstream management influences greatly enhanced intervention design and implementation.... This study has shown the critical importance of understanding the priority audience of any occupational group and the perceptions and values they hold, including work practices and competing behaviors, prior to designing any workplace intervention."[30]

DISCUSSION QUESTIONS AND EXERCISES

1. It is argued in this chapter that benefits to the priority audience for performing a proposed behavior are likely to be different than those identified by the campaign sponsor. What might be primarily "in it" for homeowners to use organic fertilizers? How might this differ from what environmental organizations supporting the use of organic fertilizers want?
2. What is the difference between perceived benefits and potential motivators? Why do you need to know both?
3. What are some nontraditional forms of research that can be used to reach underrepresented audience groups?
4. Why is Audience Insights Step 5 in the planning process?

DEVELOPING MARKETING INTERVENTION STRATEGIES

9 STEP 6: CRAFTING A DESIRED POSITIONING

LEARNING OBJECTIVES

Upon completion of this chapter, you should be able to:

9.1 Describe what a positioning statement is and what it is intended to accomplish.

9.2 Write a positioning statement.

9.3 Distinguish between positioning and branding.

9.4 Recognize any ethical considerations when developing a positioning statement.

Back in the early 1970s, a couple of advertising executives, Al Ries and Jack Trout, started a small revolution—a marketing revolution, that is, they introduced the concept and art of positioning. It was more than a new approach. It was, as they described it, a creative exercise.

Positioning starts with a product—a piece of merchandise, a service, a company, an institution, or even a person. But positioning is not what you do to a product. Positioning is what you do to the mind of the prospect. That is, you position the product in the mind of the prospect.[1]

And as you, no doubt, have discovered, or at least have read so far in this text, different markets have different needs, and your challenge is to position your offer "perfectly" in the mind of your desired prospect (priority audience). It should be noted, and explained, that developing a positioning statement (Step 6) prior to determining the marketing intervention mix (Step 7) is intentional. Your positioning statement will help guide the development of your offer (product, price, place) and especially promotional elements. It is sometimes confused with branding, a distinction which is also made in this chapter.

The positioning exercise you will explore in this chapter will help provide that clarity and will illustrate the following positioning strategies:

- Behavior-focused positioning
- Barriers-focused positioning
- Benefits-focused positioning
- Competition-focused positioning

- Repositioning
- Positioning-inspired brands

And in the following Case Highlight, you'll experience the power this can have.

CASE HIGHLIGHT

ENERGY STAR: THE POWER OF A BRAND TO CHANGE BEHAVIOR

Background

Climate change is one of the defining issues of the 21st century. The world's reliance on burning fossil fuels to generate energy increases carbon in the earth's atmosphere, contributing to climate change. In the United States, scientists expect that climate change will lead to more droughts and heat waves, stronger hurricanes, sea level rise, and water supply shortages in communities.[2] As a result, stopping the acceleration of climate change is an increasingly urgent challenge and the mission of the ENERGY STAR Program.

Purpose and Focus

In the early 1990s, the U.S. Environmental Protection Agency (EPA) was looking for innovative ways to help address climate change. They knew that there was significant promise to reduce carbon emissions by reducing the amount of energy used to power products through energy-efficient technologies. They created a bold approach, centered on partnering with industry, to change purchasing behaviors toward greater energy efficiency, leveraging the entire supply chain—from manufacturers to retailers, to utilities, and to consumers. The approach was ENERGY STAR (see Figure 9.1)—an overwhelmingly successful public-private partnership that brought market forces together to change the trajectory of energy efficiency in the United States[3]

The ENERGY STAR products program has a purpose to *reduce greenhouse gas emissions* with a focus to *improve energy efficiency of products*.

Priority Audience, Desired Behavior

This public-private partnership includes several priority audiences and a chain of desired behavior changes[4]:

- Manufacturers would make products that met ENERGY STAR specifications.
- Utilities would provide education about and rebates for products meeting ENERGY STAR specifications.
- Retailers would carry and promote ENERGY STAR certified products.
- Consumers would purchase and use ENERGY STAR certified products.

Branding Through Partnership

This case highlights the story of how a partnership branding strategy was the foundation for helping spur desired behavior changes for each priority audience. ENERGY STAR has all the ingredients of a strong brand[5]:

FIGURE 9.1 ■ ENERGY STAR Label

Source: U.S. EPA.

- Relevance: The brand provides benefits to each priority audience group.
- Differentiation: The brand clearly differentiates energy-efficient products.
- Consistency: The brand has a simple overarching message that has been consistently communicated over time.
- Credible: The brand is backed by EPA providing important third-party credibility.

Barriers, Benefits, and Motivators

In the early years of the program, each priority audience group needed to see the pragmatic business value of ENERGY STAR. Manufacturers needed to believe that if they made energy-efficient products, consumers would buy them. Retailers needed to believe there would be an incremental sales value if they promoted ENERGY STAR. Utilities needed to see ENERGY STAR as a way to help them achieve energy efficiency goals. And consumers needed to understand that ENERGY STAR could help them save money on their energy bills while also protecting the environment. The early major barrier across all audiences was that the concept was not yet proven. To address this, EPA worked to prove to the marketplace that ENERGY STAR provided benefits to all market actors while also helping reduce greenhouse gas emissions. As the partners experienced the value of ENERGY STAR, they increased their participation and marketing support leading to brand awareness and consumer adoption.

Recognition has served as an important motivator for partner action. Each year, EPA gives out ENERGY STAR Partner of the Year Awards to top performers. Not only have these awards-driven market actions, including the development of energy-efficient technologies and sales and promotion of certified products, but they have given winners impetus to promote their ENERGY STAR Award broadly among all audiences, further increasing awareness and driving behavior change. Studies demonstrate the customer-relations value of the ENERGY STAR Award, including higher JD Power scores.

Messaging and Positioning[6]

ENERGY STAR has built a strong value proposition. The brand is more than a mark of energy efficiency and cost savings; it is also a symbol of trust, quality, and environmental protection. The ENERGY STAR brand message strategy has included these pillars:

- **Protects the environment**. In early years, consumers did not link home energy use to environmental impact. "If it runs on electricity, it runs on fuel" was used in messaging to connect the dots. As the program matured, ENERGY STAR was positioned as the right choice to fight global warming and protect the environment for future generations.
- **Saves energy and money**. A home outfitted with ENERGY STAR certified products can save up to 25%.
- **Efficiency and performance**. Backed by EPA, ENERGY STAR is a credible way to ensure products are energy efficient and well perform as well as their less efficient counterparts.
- **An easy/simple choice**. ENERGY STAR is the simple way to know if a product is energy efficient.

Marketing Intervention Tools[7]

The communications approaches deployed in support of ENERGY STAR can be broken into the 4Ps: Product, Price, Place, and Promotion. It is important to note that partnership drove the success of ENERGY STAR's marketing efforts. EPA supported the brand nationally, while partners used their own resources to run ENERGY STAR campaigns.

Product: High efficiency is defined through specifications for 75 product categories.

Price: ENERGY STAR certified products result in energy savings, and therefore reduce utility bills. In addition, utilities use ENERGY STAR as their basis for energy efficient product rebates and do tax credits and tax holidays on energy-efficient products/equipment. These cost savings have played an instrumental role in ENERGY STAR's success since it is one of the few environmentally friendly actions that actually save homeowners' money—a strong motivational factor.

Place: Products are available in retail stores and online and are easily identified by the ENERGY STAR label.

Promotion: The following core promotional strategies have been used to support the brand:

- **Partnerships Marketing**: Working in partnership to promote the brand has traditionally been the core promotional strategy for ENERGY STAR. The significant reach of ENERGY STAR partners is leveraged through nationally coordinated campaigns. Retail, manufacturer, and utility partners devote resources to paid advertising featuring ENERGY STAR, including newspaper circulars, in-store signage, and television ads, and EPA supports their investments with direct-to-consumer outreach and education.
- **Partner Marketing Toolkits**: Easy-to-use toolkits were created for partners with EPA-developed marketing materials to educate Americans about the value of ENERGY STAR, including customizable ads, signage, press releases, and social media assets.
- **Media relations**: Media tours, events, and pitching were used to help spur news coverage of the ENERGY STAR brand and key messages and milestones.

- **Events**: Special events such as a one-month, coast-to-coast bus tour (see Figure 9.2) put thousands of ENERGY STAR certified, energy-efficient bulbs into the hands of consumers, engaging utility and business partners at each stop, and garnering media coverage in each market.

FIGURE 9.2 ■ ENERFY STAR Change a Light Bus Tour

Source: U.S. EPA.

- **Social media**: A robust social media strategy has been employed to support ENERGY STAR brand messaging (see Figure 9.3).

Results

By staying true to its brand strategy, ENERGY STAR has been embraced by the marketplace as the preeminent differentiator for energy efficiency. Metrics include:

- ENERGY STAR Purpose: Reduce greenhouse gas emissions[8]
  - Since 1992, the program has helped save five trillion kilowatt-hours of electricity, avoid more than $450 billion in energy costs, and achieve four billion metric tons of greenhouse gas reductions.
  - U.S. consumers have purchased more than seven billion ENERGY STAR certified products.

FIGURE 9.3 ■ Social Media Graphic

Source: U.S. EPA.

- 75,000 product models have met ENERGY STAR specifications.
- 91% national brand awareness.
- 70% of ENERGY STAR purchasers indicate brand loyalty.
- More than 3,000 national retail and manufacturer partners actively promote ENERGY STAR.[11]

- ENERGY STAR Products Focus: Improve energy efficiency of products[9]
- ENERGY STAR brand[10]

POSITIONING DEFINED

Positioning is the act of designing the organization's actual and perceived offering in such a way that it lands on and occupies a distinctive place in the mind of the priority audience—where you want it to be.[12] Keep in mind that your offering, which you will design in the next three chapters, includes your product, its price, and how it is accessed—place. The desired positioning is then supported by promotional components including messages, messengers, creative elements, and communication channels.

Think of your priority audience as having a perceptual map that they will use to locate your offer. Consider further that they have a different map for each product category (one each for cars, airlines, fast food, beverages, etc., and, more relevant for social marketers perhaps, one each for exercise, workplace safety, recycling, organ donation, etc.). Figure 9.4 illustrates a simplified version of a perceptual map, showing which brands are perceived as being similar and which are competing against each other. Most perceptual maps for goods and services use data from consumer surveys evaluating each on specific attributes.

There is a good reason we present and recommend you take this step *after* you have selected and researched your priority audience and *before* you develop your marketing intervention mix strategy. Since offers are positioned differently for different audiences (e.g., exercise for tweens

FIGURE 9.4 ■ A Perceptual Map

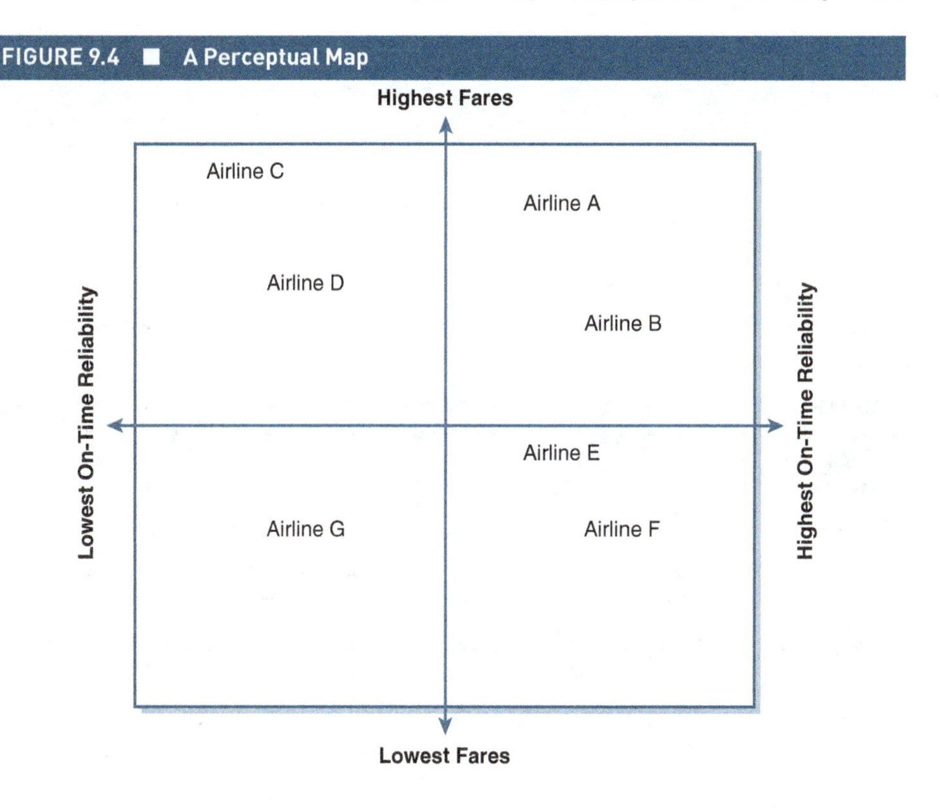

vs. seniors), choosing an audience comes first. And since your product, price, place, and promotion will determine (to a great extent) where you land, it makes sense to know your desired destination.

Positioning in the Commercial Sector

Perhaps because the commercial sector has embraced this positioning concept for decades, great examples of clear positioning and the value proposition are easy to find, as suggested in Table 9.1, and a version for social marketing is shown in Table 9.2. In the Focus column, we have linked these value propositions to social marketing theories and models we have discussed in prior chapters: benefits, barriers, and competition. One new option, now that we have introduced the positioning concept, would be a focus on repositioning—where a brand manager is interested in moving a product from its current location in the mind of priority audiences to a new, more desirable one (see Figure 9.5).

Commercial marketers also often consider and establish *points of difference* and *points of parity*, which are described by Kotler and Keller.[13] Points of difference are attributes or benefits consumers strongly associate with a brand and believe they could not find with a competing brand. Examples include FedEx (guaranteed overnight delivery), Costco (lower costs for similar products), and Lexus (quality). Points of parity, by contrast, are associations that are not necessarily unique to the brand but may be considered essential to a legitimate offering within a

TABLE 9.1 ■ Commercial Sector Brand-Positioning Examples

Category	Brand	Focus	Value Proposition
Car	Volvo	Benefits	Safety
Fast food	Subway	Barriers	Fresh, healthy options
Airline	Southwest	Competition	No frills, lower costs
Beverage	Milk	Repositioning	From boring to cool

TABLE 9.2 ■ Social Marketing Examples With Brand Names Supporting Positioning

Category	Brand	Focus	Value Proposition
Health	5 a Day	Behavior	Better health and easy to remember
Injury Prevention	Take It to Make It	Benefits	Using a flag at pedestrian crossings will help you be seen
Environmental protection	WaterSense	Competition	Reduce water bills and help protect the environment
Community engagement	Meet Your Match	Repositioning	A way to save a pet's life and find the best pet for you

certain goods or service category (e.g., a bank needs to at least offer access to ATM machines, online banking services, and checking accounts in order to be considered a bank). Competitive points-of-difference positioning might instead or also work to negate the competitors' points of difference. One good example Kotler and Keller highlight is a Miller Lite advertising strategy that ends with the tagline, "Everything you've always wanted in a beer and less."[14]

STEP 6: DEVELOP POSITIONING STATEMENT

Positioning principles and processes for social marketing are similar to those of commercial marketing. With the profile of your priority audience in mind, including any unique demographic, , geographic, psychographic, cultural considerations, and behavior-related characteristics and the findings from your research on perceived barriers, benefits, motivators, competitors, and influential others, you will now "simply" craft a positioning statement.

One way to develop a positioning statement is to fill in the blanks to this phrase, or one similar to it:

> We want [PRIORITY AUDIENCE] to see [DESIRED BEHAVIOR] as [ADJECTIVES, DESCRIPTIVE PHRASES, SET OF BENEFITS, OR WHY THE DESIRED BEHAVIOR IS BETTER THAN COMPETING BEHAVIORS]

FIGURE 9.5 ■ Repositioning Milk as "Cool"

Source: National Dairy Council.

Keep in mind that this positioning statement is "for internal use only." It is not your ultimate message to your priority audience. It will, however, be shared with others working with you on your effort to develop your marketing intervention mix strategy and help to unify and strengthen decision making. Consider how agreement on the following statements would guide these teams:

- "We want pregnant women to see breastfeeding exclusively for the first six months as a way to bond with their child and contribute to their health and as more important than concerns about nursing in public."
- "We want homeowners who love gardening to see composting food waste as an easy way to contribute to the environment and create great compost for their garden at the same time, and to see that this is better for the environment than putting it in the garbage, which then goes to the landfill, or down the kitchen disposal and into water that has to be treated."
- "We want people shopping for a puppy to visit the Humane Society's website first to see if the pet they have in mind is just waiting for someone to adopt it, and that this is likely to be a less expensive and more convenient option than going to the classified ads."

Inspiration for your descriptive phrase will come from the lists of barriers, benefits, and motivators identified in your research. As you may recall, the ideal research will have included a prioritization of barriers and benefits, giving you a sense of what factors would be most important to highlight. You are searching for the "higher value," the key benefits to be gained or costs that will be avoided by adopting the desired behavior.

To leverage prior steps in the planning model, you may find it advantageous to consider a focus for your positioning statements, choosing from among those that drive home specific *behaviors*, highlight *benefits*, overcome *barriers*, upstage the *competition*, or *reposition* an "old brand." More detail on each of these options is presented in the next five sections, with a couple of brief examples and one longer illustration.

Behavior-Focused Positioning

For some social marketing programs, especially those with a new and/or very specific desired behavior in mind, you may benefit from a behavior-focused positioning. In these cases, a description of your behavior will be highlighted, as shown in this example:

- In the fall of 2014, it was announced that Washington state had the highest property crime rate in the country during the year 2013. The City of Mercer Island, with the leadership of Chief of Police Ed Homes, decided to explore a new approach to reducing residential crime, the *Help Me* approach. After determining that the method of entry for 41% of home burglaries was an unlocked door or window, and that one of the three top reasons (*barriers*) cited by citizens for not always locking their doors and windows was that they forget to check the doors before leaving home, a clear behavior emerged. To promote the desired behavior, the team developed a branded campaign *Lock It or Lose It* and distributed a laminated door hanger similar to those in hotel rooms, one that would be a timely reminder at the point of decision making (see Figure 9.6).[15]

In these cases, making sure priority audiences know the specifics of the desired behavior is key to successful outcomes, as illustrated in the following example.

Example: 5 a Day. In 1991, the National Cancer Institute (NCI), in cooperation with the Produce for Better Health Foundation, created "5 a Day for Better Health," a national program that approaches Americans with a simple, positive message: "Eat five or more servings of vegetables and fruit daily for better health" (see Figure 9.7).

This key message has been repeated using a well-integrated strategy and a multitude of venues over the years: plastic produce bags, grocery bags, in-store signage and displays, produce packaging labels, supermarket tours, recipe cards, brochures, grocery store flier ads, magazine articles, newspaper ads, news stories, the Internet, radio news inserts, television news inserts (cooking/recipe spots), radio public service announcements (PSAs), television PSAs, billboards, nutrition newsletters, patient nutrition education materials, pay stubs, school curricula, preschool programs, food assistance program materials, church bulletins and newsletters, posters, restaurant menus, Girl/Boy Scout badges, 4-H materials, food bank program materials, health fairs, county fairs, cookbooks, children's coloring books, and videotapes. In 2006, a new slogan, "The Color Way," was added to promote more variety in the 5 a Day mix we choose.

FIGURE 9.6 ■ Door Hanger Distributed to Citizens as a Reminder to Lock Doors

Source: Author photo.

FIGURE 9.7 ■ The Produce for Better Health Foundation's Behavior-Focused Positioning

Source: Produce for Better Health Foundation.

Barriers-Focused Positioning

With this type of focus, you want your offer's positioning to help overcome or at least minimize perceived barriers, such as concern about self-efficacy, fear, or perceived high costs associated with performing the behavior:

- For tobacco users who want to quit, quitlines are often positioned as hopeful and encouraging, as in the following poem (perhaps more like a rap) that appeared on the Washington State Department of Health's website in 2007:

  In the New Year, make smoking a thing of the past
  Put yourself first and your habit last
  Start the year right; start out on top
  And make '07 the year that you stop
  Tobacco products will harm your health
  They'll deplete your energy as well as your wealth
  Although smoking is a hard habit to break
  With determination and support it's a change you can make
  Call the Washington State Tobacco Quit Line to learn how
  A quit coach will assist you at 1–800–QUIT–NOW
  A customized plan and one-on-one counseling you'll get
  To help make '07 smoke-free, and your best year yet
  The call is confidential, the service is free
  And can double your chance of quitting successfully
  More than 80,000 Washingtonians have made the call
  For free counseling and quit kits available for all
  Don't hesitate; call the quit line today
  And in the New Year, you'll be well on your way![16]

In the following illustration, the positioning reflects and addresses audience concerns about time, effort, cost, and "know-how."

Example. In 2012, the City of Chicago launched an initiative to support solar power installation and branded the campaign *Chicago Solar Express*, with audience barriers and motivators in mind. To make installation cheaper, group discounts were offered, helping, for example, owners of single-family homes to pool their buying power. Permit fees were reduced by 25%; and the permitting process was also streamlined and standardized, with residents acquiring permits for their installations in one day, compared to 30 days or more previously. Zoning policies were rewritten to give clearer guidance on designing solar projects in accordance with the city's ordinance, providing the ability to potentially forgo a more intensive zoning review, saving both time and money. The city also developed separate steps for small versus large rooftop systems. The program was considered a success with over 2,100 people registering, resulting in over 600 kW of newly contracted solar capacity.[17]

Benefits-Focused Positioning

When the best hook seems to be related to the WIFM ("what's in it for me") factor, perceived benefits become the focus of the positioning:

- Natural yard care practices, such as pulling weeds versus spraying them, are positioned as ways to ensure the health of your children and pets.

- Moderate physical activity, such as raking leaves and taking the stairs instead of the elevator, is positioned as something you can fit into your daily routine.
- Reading to your child 20 minutes each night is positioned as a way to help ensure he or she will do well in school.

In the following illustration of benefit-focused positioning, the focus is once more on benefits your priority audience wants.

Example: Road Crew. Michael Rothschild, professor emeritus at the University of Wisconsin, believes that good positioning begins with a clear understanding of the priority audience and their competitive choices. He also believes that when developing this positioning, a marketer needs to learn about the priority audience, current usage patterns, and why existing competitive brands are succeeding. And that is what a team he led in Wisconsin in the spring of 2000 did for the Wisconsin Department of Transportation.

The "assignment" was to reduce alcohol-related crashes in rural Wisconsin. There was ample prior evidence that the group of people most likely to drink, drive, and crash were 21- to 34-year-old single men. The team conducted 17 focus groups, 11 with the priority audience and six more with those who observed the priority audience (e.g., bar owners, law enforcement ambulance drivers, judges). Meetings with the priority audience were held in the back of local taverns so that respondents would feel comfortable discussing the issues. By asking the priority audience why they drove after drinking, the team learned about reasons for driving drunk: to get home; to avoid the hassle of coming back in the morning to get the vehicle; everybody does it; at 1:00 a.m., they are fearless; and there is a low risk of getting caught. When asked to help design a ride program that they would use, they asked for:

- Vehicles that were at least as nice as their own
- A ride from home to the bar, between bars, and then home again, as they wouldn't want to leave their cars behind and wanted to go between bars
- The right to smoke and drink in the vehicles

This is exactly what they were then offered. The resulting service uses limousines and other luxury vehicles to pick people up at their home, business, or hotel; take them to the bar of their choice; take them between bars; and then take them home at the end of the evening. As allowed by local ordinances, passengers may smoke and drink in the vehicles. The cost to the passenger is $15–$20 for the evening.

Figure 9.8 shows the initial poster that was used to raise awareness. It doesn't tell people not to drive drunk; it focuses on Road Crew's position. That is, it tells people that they can have more fun if they use Road Crew than if they drive themselves. Research had shown that the priority audience wanted to have fun and that drinking was a part of having fun. The priority audience didn't feel that driving drunk was fun but that it was necessary in order to have fun earlier in the evening.

FIGURE 9.8 ■ Repositioning Road Crew as a Cool Way to Get Around and Have Fun

Source: Road Crew, University of Wisconsin.

By 2008, the program was operating in 32 small communities in rural Wisconsin and had provided over 97,000 rides and prevented an estimated 140 alcohol-related crashes and six alcohol-related fatalities. The costs incurred from an alcohol-related crash are approximately $231,000, but the cost to avoid a crash through the use of Road Crew is approximately $6,400. This means that it is about 37 times more expensive to incur a crash than it is to avoid one. Total net savings through the use of Road Crew has been more than $31 million. Of special note is that research shows that while driving behavior has changed dramatically, people are not drinking more as a result of getting rides. After receiving seed money to begin the program, communities are able to self-sustain from ride fares and tavern contributions.[18] Road Crew has succeeded because it is well positioned relative to its competition. Rather than being told that drunk driving is bad, people are told that using Road Crew is more fun than the competitive choice. Road Crew offers more benefits than driving. In the past, driving was often the only choice available; anyone who admitted to not being able to drive home was seen as a "wimp." But now, choosing the Road Crew is a sign of being cool (For more insights on Road Crew, go to www.roadcrewonline.org.).

Competition-Focused Positioning

A fourth option for focus is the competition, one quite appropriate when your priority audience finds "their offer" quite appealing and your offer "a pain":

- Taking a shorter shower to save water may have a desired end benefit of saving a vital resource for future generations, but it comes at the cost of personal sacrifice for many who relish the relaxation a long hot shower can bring.
- Consequences of tobacco use are often positioned as gross, realistic, and shocking (see Figure 9.9).

Because consumers typically choose goods and services that give them the greatest value, marketers work to position their brands on the key benefits that they offer relative to competing brands. Kotler and Armstrong illustrate this with six possible value propositions, as shown in Table 9.3.[19]

An additional model for developing competitive advantage focuses on creating *competitive superiority*, a more rigorous objective. Four tactics are used in tandem, as illustrated in Table 9.4. A *benefit-to-benefit superiority* tactic appeals to values higher than those perceived for the competition (e.g., a child who wants and needs a parent is compared to the short-term pleasures of smoking). A *cost-to-benefit superiority* tactic focuses on decreasing costs of or barriers to adopting the desired behavior and, at the same time, decreasing perceived benefits of the competition (e.g., success stories from cessation classes include a testimonial from a spouse about how nice it is to have clean air in the house). A *benefit-to-cost superiority* tactic emphasizes the benefits of the desired behavior and the costs of the competing behavior(s) (e.g., abilities of teen athletes who don't smoke as compared to those of teen athletes who do). A *cost-to-cost superiority* tactic relies on a favorable comparison of costs of the desired behavior relative to those of the competition (e.g., short-term nicotine withdrawal symptoms are compared with living with emphysema).

FIGURE 9.9 ■ Positioning Tobacco Use

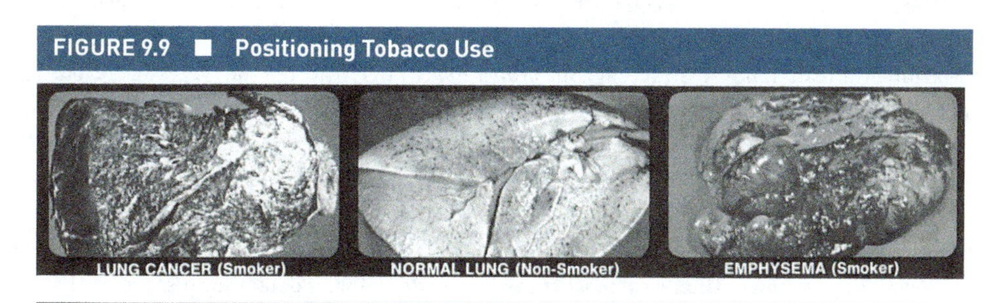

Source: Pilgrim Plastics, Brockton, MA.

TABLE 9.3 ■ Illustrating Value Propositions Based on Price and Product Quality

More for More	Starbucks
More for the Same	Lexus versus Mercedes Benz
Same for Less	Amazon
Less for Much Less	Motel 6
More for Less	Costco
Less for Much Less	Southwest Airlines

TABLE 9.4 ■ Creating Competitive Superiority

Competing Behavior	Desired Behavior	
	Increase Benefits	Decrease Costs/Barriers
Decrease Benefits	Tactic A: Benefit-to-benefit superiority tactic	Tactic B: Cost-to-benefit superiority tactic
Increase Costs/ Barriers	Tactic C: Benefit-to-cost superiority tactic	Tactic D: Cost-to-cost superiority tactic

Example: Broccoli's Makeover[20]. A six-page article in the November 3, 2013, *New York Times* magazine announced that broccoli was about to get a serious makeover by ad agency Victors & Spoils, which had created campaigns for some of the biggest brands in the food industry, including Coca-Cola. Michael Moss, the author of the *Times* article, followed the team's vision quest for a campaign and at the beginning challenged them with a couple of questions: "How would you get people to want to buy and eat broccoli?. What would you do that all the well-intentioned government-funded campaigns have failed to do for generations?"[21]

From there, the firm's team set out on a research journey to get a handle on what the public felt about broccoli—a crowdsourcing exercise. Impressions shared included "overcooked, soggy"; "hiding under cheese"; "told not to leave the table until I eat it"; and "brown, squishy, and smelly." When asked what an epitaph for broccoli might be, the team heard comments like, "Good-bye, poor friend" and "I hardly spent time with you, mainly because I didn't like you." They heard from a chef that broccoli wasn't thought of as much as a food as it was as a divider in the display case between meat and fish. And when looking through various food and cooking magazines, the team ran across a recent issue of *Bon Appétit* that featured the "vegetable revolution" and 10 different vegetables. Broccoli didn't even make the list.

Back in the firm's conference room for a brainstorming session, potential positioning and message strategies were considered, including that perhaps it should be seen as a flower and you could give someone broccoli bouquets. Or maybe they should change its name, or at least have Italians pronounce it!

Their "Aha!" moment finally came when, as they reviewed sales data, they discovered that broccoli ranked 20th among vegetables, doing far better than kale in 47th place, which had been rocketing to fame over the past several years. "Let's pick a fight with kale!"—just like the great soda war between Pepsi and Coca-Cola. From there, the team created multiple slogans, including "Broccoli: Now 43 Percent Less Pretentious Than Kale" and "Eat Fad Free: Broccoli v. Kale."

Repositioning

What happens when your program has a current positioning that you feel is in the way of your achieving behavior change goals? Several factors may have contributed to this wake-up call and the sense that you need to "relocate." For instance, you might need to attract *new audiences* to sustain your growth, and these new markets may not find your current position appealing. For example, adults over 50 not engaged in regular physical activity may have tuned out messages regarding exercise long ago, as they could hear only the "vigorous aerobic" recommendation. Planners would be more successful emphasizing moderate physical activity with this group.

Or you may be suffering from an image problem. When bike helmets were first promoted to youth, they balked. Making the behavior "fun, easy, and popular" for the audience is Bill Smith's recommendation and could well describe the strategy in Figure 9.10. These three words focus program managers on how to change behavior by giving people what they want along with what we feel they need.

- *Fun* in this context means to provide your audience with perceived benefits they care about.
- *Easy* means to remove all possible barriers to action and make the behavior as simple and accessible as possible.
- *Popular* means to help the audience feel that this is something others are doing, particularly others the audience believes are important to them.[22]

Or you may have just received (as do lots of others) the results of an *evaluation* indicating disappointing outcomes as a result of your current positioning strategy, as was the case in the following example.

The Black Lives Matter (BLM) movement has greatly increased people's awareness of police brutality and racial profiling issues. Support for BLM peaked after the murder of George Floyd on May 25, 2020.[23] The movement is consistent with many of the strong positive values that many Americans share. When the "Defund the Police" movement was introduced as a way to help make progress, public support for that idea was hard to garner. People assumed defunding would make communities less safe, rather than safer. If the campaign had been positioned with a positive message around investing in community safety offices and resources, it may have had more success. Instead, after public opinion research showed the problem with the Defund the Police positioning, BLM leaders had to spend their time explaining why defund the police was not what its name implied.

FIGURE 9.10 ■ Positioning of Wearing Protective Gear as Fun, Easy, and Popular

Source: Newsweek.

BLM co-founder Alicia Garza appeared June 7, 2020, on NBC's "Meet the Press" to explain that growing calls to "defund the police" were not about eliminating police departments but about reinvesting funds toward "the resources that our communities need."[24]

Having to try and refocus the narrative took precious time and effort away from building BLM's intended message. If the positioning had a more positive handle—like #Community Officers[25], it may have been easier to build the needed public support to change the way policing resources are invested in communities.

HOW POSITIONING RELATES TO BRANDING

Although the concept of the brand and the branding process will be covered in future chapters featuring Products and Promotions, you may have immediate questions regarding positioning and how it relates to branding that we will address briefly at this point. It helps to see a brand as the way audiences think and feel about a company, organization, cause, or set of related behaviors. A brand is manifested in a name, term, sign, symbol, tagline, and/or design that identifies the maker or seller of the product (e.g., ENERGY STAR® identifies products that are energy efficient), but the brand essence comes from how it is perceived by its priority audience groups. This perception is built over time by all the interactions that a brand has with its audiences.

Your positioning statement is something you and others can count on to provide parameters and inspiration for developing your desired brand identity—how you want the desired behavior to be seen by the priority audience. It will provide strong and steady guidance for your decision making regarding your marketing intervention mix, as it is the 4Ps that will determine where your offer lands in the minds of your priority audience. And when your brand image doesn't align with your desired positioning (brand identity), you'll look to your 4Ps for "help" in repositioning the brand.

ETHICAL CONSIDERATIONS FOR DEVELOPING A POSITIONING STATEMENT

When developing your positioning statement, several ethical questions may (and actually should) come to your mind. You will notice that many of these relate to the familiar "truth in advertising" code.

If your positioning statement is *behavior focused*, ensure that your recommendations are accurate. For example, in the case of the *Lock It or Lose It* campaign we discussed earlier in this chapter that aimed to reduce property crime, you'd want to make sure the home resident knows to place the hanger on an entry door and include detailed information on the door hanger as to why this helps. If your positioning statement focuses on *benefits* for the priority audience, you will want to be certain that you can really deliver these benefits. A campaign promoting moderate physical activity should make it clear to potential "buyers" what levels and types of physical activity are needed to achieve any health gains promised, and at what levels.

If your positioning statement focuses on how the priority audience will be able to overcome their *barriers*, you will want to be certain you paint a realistic picture. Communications promoting quitlines as a way to quit smoking should be certain to include rates of success and the fact that not all those who call will be able to quit. If you reread the poem from the Washington State Department of Health's website, note that the quitline delivers on its positioning as "hopeful and encouraging" but doesn't mention any guarantees.

If your positioning statement focuses on the *competition*, be certain that what you say about them is really true and not exaggerated. New York City, for example, has promised better and "seamless" service when you call 311 rather than 911 for a missing car. It wouldn't take many citizens not getting quick help to spread the word that 911 will get you better service faster.

And if your positioning statement focuses on *repositioning* the brand, be sure your offer is really "new and improved." The Police as Guardian program will need to be obviously distinct from the prior program.

In all cases, it is also important to consider cultural nuance and interpretation in your positioning statement. Make sure you are not making references or allusions to things that would not be applicable across cultures. It's important to avoid gender stereotypes or "gendering" and figurative phrases or idioms that are solely associated with one culture. Also, be careful about visual cues that may not work across cultures. An example of a brand positioning where this went wrong is when Pampers started communicating in multiple countries with the brand visual of the stork carrying a baby. The idea and image of a stork does not have meaning in all cultures and caused brand confusion in several countries and for many potential Pampers' customers.

COVID-19 Social Marketing Example

Relative to positioning, though not formally stated as such, most communications from governmental agencies such as CDC and Health Departments want citizens to see following COVID-19 safe practices (e.g., immunizations, masking up, social distancing) as *a way to help stop the spread of COVID-19 and protect yourself and those you care about.*

CHAPTER SUMMARY

Positioning is the act of designing the organization's offering in such a way that it lands on and occupies a distinctive place in the mind of the priority audience—where you want it to be. Step 6 in the marketing planning process recommends that you develop a positioning statement at this point. The research on your audience's barriers, benefits, motivators, competitors, and influential others in Step 5 will provide the inspiration you need. It will also help build consensus among your colleagues and partners, ensuring fewer surprises and disappointments as you move forward to developing your strategies.

Positioning statements may be focused on behaviors, barriers, benefits, the competition, and/or repositioning. Your decisions will reflect your value proposition, a reason why the priority audience should buy the product—from you!

Take time and care to develop this statement, as you will refer to it frequently when developing each of the 4Ps. This will help ensure the "proper landing" you have in mind.

RESEARCH HIGHLIGHT
INCREASING BLOOD DONATIONS[26]

Background

Blood collection agencies in Australia, as well as globally, are challenged to recruit and retain enough blood donors to meet needs for sustainable patient blood supplies. In 2015, for example, Australian data indicated that only 63.4% of first-time whole blood donors returned to donate within two years.[27] This research case study highlights the results of a pilot effort of Australian Red Cross Lifeblood, formerly Australian Red Cross Blood Service, in 2015 to test a new strategy for donor retention, one that was strategically designed with *a new positioning* to motivate the remaining almost 40% of donors to frequently return.

Priority Audience for the Study

Return donors were a priority for the agency to explore, as they offer several advantages. They are a more cost-effective group, given the reduced costs for recruitment, blood typing, and health status testing. Studies have also shown that repeat donors tend to have healthier lifestyles, carry less risk of infectious disease than new donors, and offer a supply of blood with known record of safety.

Positioning

Historically, strategies for encouraging first time donors to return have focused on *prompts*, encouraging them to schedule a future appointment, as well as a reminder of the appointment via a short messaging service (SMS).

In 2015, the marketing department of Australian Red Cross Lifeblood tried something new. Instead of a reminder to make, or keep, an appointment (e.g., a request), they focused on a tangible, motivational benefit, that of assuring them that their behavior resulted in a *desired benefit* in exchange, confirmation, and recognition that their donation was on the way to help save a life. They would receive an SMS that would inform them that his or her blood donation was already being used and named the hospital, or location, to which their donation had been sent (see Figure 9.11).

FIGURE 9.11 ■ Example of SMS Sent to Donors

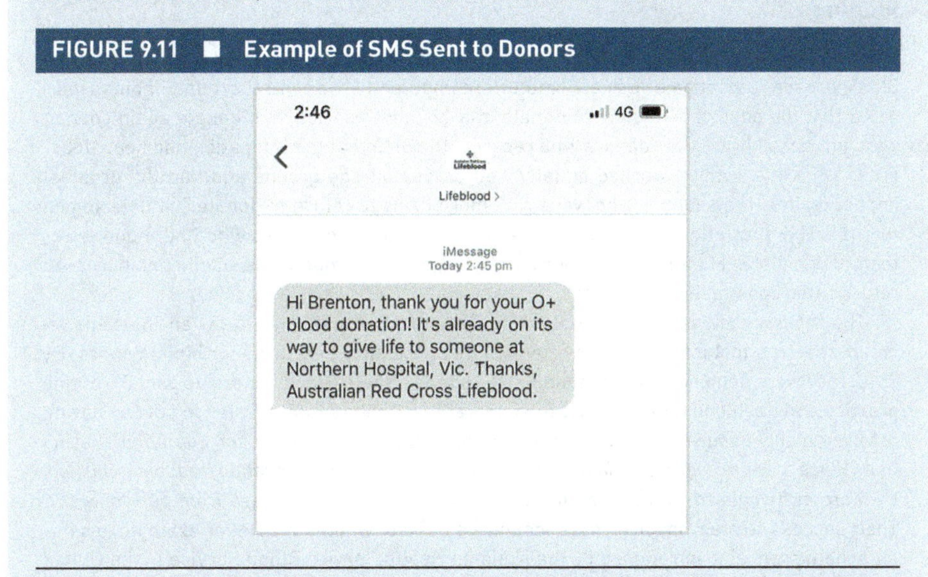

Source: Australian Red Cross Lifeblood.

Research Objectives

A rigorous research study was designed with an objective to investigate whether receipt of this new message positioning had a positive impact on the percent of donors who then returned to donate over the following 12 months. It was also to inform program planners as to whether response rates varied by factors such as gender, age, or prior donation experience. The study was also to inform the ideal point in time to send the SMS after donation.

Research Design and Methods

The new post donation SMS was tested with donors (n = 2647) who donated at one of six donor centers and was sent between one and 41 days after donating. Donors included in the analysis of the trial were ones who had successfully donated but had left the center without making a future appointment. A control group of donors (n = 1796) consisted of donors who had donated at the same six donor centers during the trial period and met criteria to receive the SMS but did not receive one. Both groups continued to receive the same postdonation communications as was the usual business practice, which may have included e-mails and phone contact to encourage them to return.

Data routinely collected for Lifeblood were extracted for donors in both the SMS and control groups to determine any significant differences in return donation behavior over the subsequent 6- and 12-month periods. Additional data collected included variables such as date of donation, number of prior donations, blood type, gender, age, whether they experienced an adverse event at their last donation, and whether they had donated at an established or mobile donor site. Statistical analyses were then performed to evaluate whether there was a statistical significance of the intervention.

Findings

Analyses were conducted to determine if receipt of the benefits-oriented positioning of the SMS increased retention at 6 and 12 months, compared to the control group. Findings indicated that the odds of returning to donate in a 12-month period, and donate again sooner, were increased by 49% for donors who received the SMS that their donation had been delivered.[28] The intervention worked equally well across all age groups and had the greatest impact on first-time donors who were 73% more likely to return to donate.[29] It determined that the SMS was effective for first-time donors, as well as donors who had made fewer than 10 donations. More frequent doors, however, did not demonstrate significant increased return rates upon receiving an SMS.

The study concluded that a motivating SMS had the potential to be an inexpensive, broad-reaching tool for increasing retention and frequency of returns for blood donors. By 2018, they were sending a postdonation SMS to most Whole Blood donors as part of routine practice and Lifeblood implemented the intervention nationally, motivated in part by having received highly positive feedback from donors, with a spokesperson for Lifeblood sharing that "*When the campaign was trialed in New South Wales last year, donation frequency doubled. We were overwhelmed-we received more than 10,000 positive responses from our donors.*"[30] Their success strategy inspired other countries as well, where, in 2016 for example, a similar scheme was also introduced by the National Health Service Blood Service in the United Kingdom.[31]

DISCUSSION QUESTIONS AND EXERCISES

1. How would you describe positioning to someone who asked?
2. What does positioning inform?
3. One exercise that can inspire repositioning is to complete the following grid.

If your agency/program were a dog, what dog would your key publics say you are? What dog do you want to be? Do the same for "a car" and "a famous person."

	today	desired
a dog		
a car		
a famous person		

10 STEP 7.1: PRODUCT

Creating a Product Platform

LEARNING OBJECTIVES

Upon completion of this chapter, you should be able to:

10.1 Describe what a product is in a social marketing framework.

10.2 Identify and distinguish the three major levels of a product platform.

10.3 Give examples of a social marketing "tangible good" that might be promoted.

10.4 Give examples of a social marketing "service" that might be promoted.

10.5 Understand the meaning of the term "branding" and its application for social marketing.

You are (finally) ready to develop your marketing intervention strategy.

- You have identified a priority audience and developed rich descriptions using relevant demographic, geographic, psychographic, cultural, and behavioral variables.
- You know what you want your audience to do and what they may need to know and/or believe in order to act, and you've come to some agreement on levels of desired behavior change that you will develop a plan to achieve.
- You know what benefits and barriers your audience perceives relative to the desired behavior you have in mind and who and what might motivate them to adopt the desired behavior.
- You know how this stacks up against the competition—most often your priority audience's current or preferred behavior or the programs and organizations sponsoring it.
- You are aware of others your priority audience considers influential.
- You have a positioning statement that will align and guide your team's decision-making regarding the marketing intervention mix (4Ps).

It is time to decide how you will influence your priority audience to adopt the desired behavior. You have four intervention tools (product, price, place, and promotion) to help make this happen. And you'll probably need all of them to reduce barriers and create and deliver the value your priority audience expects in exchange for this new behavior.

This chapter will focus on developing your product strategy, with an emphasis on exploring opportunities for goods and services that will support desired behaviors. You will read in this chapter about the three decisions you will make regarding the product offered:

1. *Core product*: The major benefit the audience wants in exchange for performing the behavior.
2. *Actual product*: Any tangible goods and services your campaign will focus on promoting that your audience acquire (e.g., a life vest for a toddler), consume (e.g., five fruits and vegetables a day), participate in (e.g., senior strength and balance exercise classes), utilize (e.g., mass transit), or prepare (e.g., an emergency preparedness kit).
3. *Augmented product*: Additional goods and services your campaign will provide and/or promote to support the desired behavior change (e.g., a life vest loaner station at docks). These are often considered *optional* but may make the difference in whether your audience is motivated to adopt the desired behavior, even acquire or utilize an actual product (e.g., an app that provides real-time arrivals and departures for buses).

We begin with a case story where the product strategy is key to saving lives . . . of dogs and cats!

CASE HIGHLIGHT
INCREASING PET ADOPTION

(2004–Present)

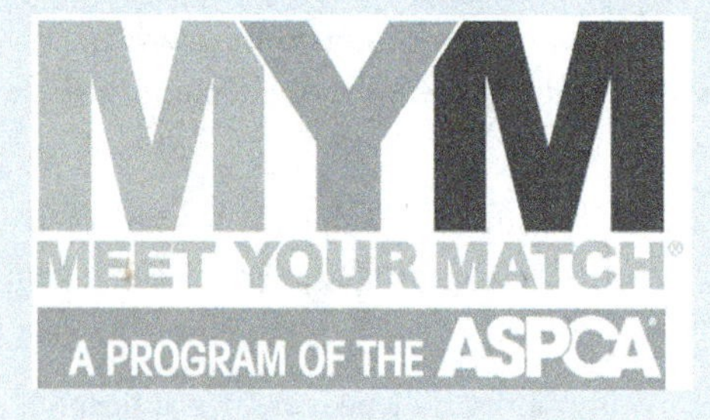

Source: American Society for the Prevention of Cruelty to Animals.

Background

The American Society for the Prevention of Cruelty to Animals (ASPCA) estimates that approximately 6.5 million cats and dogs entered shelters in 2016. Although adoption rates increased more than 18% since 2011 and 3.2 million cats and dogs were adopted, an estimated 1.5 million were euthanized.[1] The 2017–2018 American Pet Products Association survey found that only 44% of dogs and 47% of cats are adopted from shelters (vs. other sources).[2] And although some pets in shelters are sick or have behavioral issues, The Humane Society of the United States estimates that about 80% of the animals euthanized "were healthy and treatable and could have been adopted into new homes."[3] Most animals are "destroyed simply because there is no one to adopt them."[4]

Strategies to increase adoptions have ranged from rescue groups concentrating on saving and rehoming specific dog breeds (*product*) to waving adoption fees (*price*), to offsite adoptions at stores like PetSmart (*place*), to branding strategies such as renaming animal shelters as pet adoption centers (*promotion*).

We think the strategy highlighted in this case is a great example of a product designed to significantly decrease barriers to pet adoption and deliver on desired benefits. Information for this case was provided by Caryn Ginsberg, author of *Animal Impact: Secrets Proven to Achieve Results and Move the World*.[5]

Audience Insights

Maddie's Fund, a charitable foundation, identifies two obstacles to more shelter adoptions: fear and uncertainty.

> Many people believe shelter pets are "damaged goods." They're worried that they'll come with too much baggage, that they're sick or have serious behavior problems. They think of shelters as depressing and can't handle selecting one pet while worrying that those they don't choose will die. What should be a happy family occasion starts to feel like a prison visit.[6]

A research study conducted by Ipsos Marketing for PetSmart Charities in 2011 showed that people who had recently acquired an animal other than from a shelter gave five top reasons they chose not to adopt from an animal shelter (see Table 10.1).

TABLE 10.1 ■ Top Five Reasons for Not Adopting From a Humane Organization

Reason	%
My local pet organization/shelter did not have the type of dog/cat I was looking for.	36%
I want a purebred dog/cat.	34%
I feel that pets from pet organization/shelters have behavioral problems.	13%
The adoption process (application) is too difficult.	12%
I do not know very much about pet adoption.	12%

Note: Percentages add to more than 100 because multiple responses allowed.

Source: PetSmart Charities, Attitudes on pet homelessness are changing: 2014 U.S. shelter pet report, https://www.petsmartcharities.org/sites/default/files/PetSmart%20Charities%202014%20U.S.%20Shelter%20Pet%20Report_2014Oct1.pdf.

Shelter personnel, the other audience for the effort, were interested in improved strategies to increase adoptions, as these then would reduce euthanasia, and potentially lead to shorter lengths of stay for animals. Increased adoptions and an enjoyable process to make this happen would also contribute to higher staff and volunteer moral. A strategy that would significantly increase adoption rates also had the potential to generate media interest and, therefore, increased awareness and visits to the shelters.

Strategies

Dr. Emily Weiss, ASPCA's vice president of equine welfare, was always interested in animals. In college, she had a mentor who encouraged her to become a behaviorist, leading her to study everything from mice to elephants to Komodo dragons. Her work at the ASPCA has ranged from developing enrichment programs for animals in shelters to researching and advancing the adoption and rehoming of horses.

In 2004, Dr. Weiss created an innovative way to address the concerns of potential pet parents and to increase adoptions. She developed models to predict how dogs and cats would behave in the home based on behaviors that could be measured in the shelter. It was branded *Meet Your Match* and was designed to scientifically match a shelter dog's personality, traits, and behavior characteristic with the traits and characteristics that adopters are seeking in a new animal companion. (We could perhaps think of this a pet version of eHarmony.com!) There were two priority audiences for program design: (1) shelter personnel who would be involved in assessing and characterizing the pets, as well as working with potential adopters; and (2) potential adopters. *Canine-ality* was piloted with one shelter and launched nationally in 2004. *Feline-ality* followed in 2006 after a pilot with five shelters. Their marketing intervention mix strategy is summarized in Table 10.2.

TABLE 10.2 ■ The *Meet Your Match* Marketing Intervention Mix Strategy

Priority Audience	Shelter Personnel	Potential Adopters
Desired Behavior	Facilitate potential adopters in finding their best match.	Adopt a pet from a shelter, one that will be the best match for you.
The 4Ps:		
• Product	*The Canine-ality and Feline-ality Assessments* These programs assess friendliness, playfulness, energy level, motivation, and drive. Results place dogs into one of nine color-coded Canine-alities and cats into one of nine color-coded Feline-alities (see Figure 10.1). Staff are also provided a training, talking points, and more that help personnel work with adopters.	*Dog Adopter Cat Adopter Surveys* Survey consists of 18 questions to help determine which pet in the shelter best matches adopter expectations, experience, lifestyle, and home environment. Once completed, adopters receive a colored card that directs them to dogs with cage cards that match the color of their guest passes. Shelter personnel provide individualized attention to the potential adopter.
• Price	ASPCA does not charge any fee for shelters to use the program.	Shelters do not charge a fee for administering the adopter survey.

TABLE 10.2 ■ The *Meet Your Match* Marketing Intervention Mix Strategy

Priority Audience	Shelter Personnel	Potential Adopters
• Place	Assessments are administered at the shelters.	Shelters administer the adopter survey on paper in the facility, or online prior to a visit.
• Promotion	Key messages include testimonials answering the question "What do you like about the program?" "We were using a very long, two-page application that made the adopter feel like the enemy. We required background checks, personal references, and we often made people go home empty handed while we did our research. After talking to Emily and going to a training, we learned to see the adopter as a friend."[a] "We get a lot of black Labrador retrievers and lab mixes that look alike ... Now, rather than a black lab, one dog may be a 'teacher's pet,' another may be a 'life of the party,' each with different characteristics written out."[b] The ASPCA introduced the Meet Your Match program primarily through one-on-one contact. Initial outreach included via the ASPCA pro website for shelters and at conferences. The programs are now available entirely online. Most shelters are able to proceed with self-paced training and implementation.	Key Messages as adapted by one shelter include:[c] "You could be gazing at the animal of your dreams." "The Meet Your Match program wouldn't let you go home without knowing who's in that carrier or on that leash." "This is the only method in existence today that evaluates an animal's behavior and interests and matches them to an adopter's preferences." Descriptions of specific personalities are appealing: "*Life of the Party.* I think everything is fun, interesting and meant for play, especially you. Anything you do, I'll want to do too. With my own brand of surprises, life with me will keep you constantly on your toes, and the fun is guaranteed. (Socially motivated.)"[d] The ASPCA provides a how-to publicity guide with tips and tools, such as sample media releases and pitch letters, to help shelters generate awareness.

[a] Maddie's Fund, "Meet Your Match: Does It Deliver?" (2006), http://www.maddiesfund.org/Maddies_Institute/Articles/Meet_Your_Match.html.

[b] Ibid.

[c] The Washington Animal Rescue League, "Meet Your Match" (n.d.), http://www.warl.org/adopt/meet-your-match/.

[d] ASPCA, "Meet the Canine-alities" (n.d.), http://www.aspca.org/adopt/meet-your-match/meet-canine-alities.

[e] ASPCA, "MYM Mesmerizes Media at Jacksonville Humane" (n.d.), http://www.aspcapro.org/node/72096.

FIGURE 10.1 ■ The Nine Feline-alities

meet the feline-alities

Source: American Society for the Prevention of Cruelty to Animals.

Outcomes

The *Meet Your Match* program provides measurable results with participating shelters achieving gains in adoption often reaching more than 15%, even 40%–60% gains during heavy publicity.[7] As of 2022, it is implemented at adoption agencies all across the United States.[8] Emily Weiss, Vice President of ASPCA writes that "When we tally up the increases in adoptions, decreases in returns, decreases in euthanasia, and decreases in length of stay from shelters who have implemented the program, we are looking at literally tens of thousands of lives saved!"[9]

TABLE 10.3 ■ Examples of Existing and New Social Marketing Goods and Services

Potential Actual Products	Goods	Services
Existing Products Promoted to Acquire or Utilize	Condoms Breast pumps Home blood pressure monitors Immunizations Lockboxes for handguns at home Low-flow showerheads Organic fertilizers	Mammography Gym membership Mass transit Blood donation Pet neutering Home energy audits Septic tank inspections
New Products Developed to Support Behaviors	Home tests for COVID-19 Breathalyzers at bars An app for youth suicide prevention resources Drug test kits for parents of teens Collapsible grocery carts suitable for walking to and from the store Food waste containers for under the sink Tablets to test for leaky toilets	Tobacco quitline Home visits for early learning Workshops on natural gardening Veggie Mobiles for inner-city residents Walking school bus programs Amber Alert for missing children

PRODUCT: THE FIRST "P"

A product is anything that can be offered to a market to satisfy a want or need.[10] It isn't, as many typically think, just a tangible offering like soap, tires, or hamburgers. It can be one of several types: physical goods, a service, an experience, an event, a person, a place, a property, an organization, information, or an idea.[11]

At this point, it is beneficial to distinguish between what we consider goods and what we consider services. We also distinguish between existing products and new products, as depicted in Table 10.3. While goods are usually "consumed" or "utilized" and are purchased or obtained for personal use (e.g., organic fertilizers), services are a product form that is essentially intangible and does not result in the ownership of anything (e.g., a workshop on natural yard care).[12] These distinctions are important primarily so that you are inspired to consider all four categories when developing a product strategy. Additional relevant terms often associated with product strategy in the commercial sector are presented in Table 10.4.

STEP 7.1: DEVELOP THE SOCIAL MARKETING PRODUCT PLATFORM

Traditional marketing theory propounds that from the customer's perspective, a product is more than its features, quality, name, and style and identifies three product levels you should consider when developing your product: *core product, actual product*, and *augmented product*.[13] This platform is illustrated in Figure 10.2, and each of these levels will be described in detail

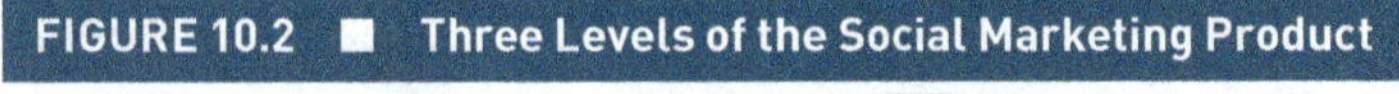
FIGURE 10.2 ■ Three Levels of the Social Marketing Product

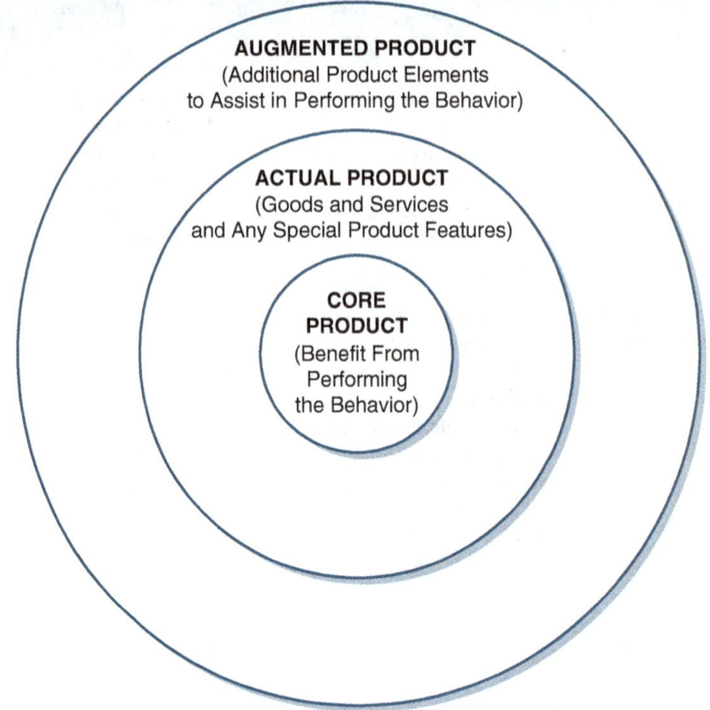

in the next three sections of this chapter. This will be helpful to you in conceptualizing and designing your product strategy.

Briefly, your *core product* is the benefit the priority audience wants and expects in exchange for performing the behavior. The *actual product* is any goods or services you will be influencing your priority audience to "buy or get." And the *augmented product* includes any additional product elements that you may develop, distribute, sell, or just promote. Examples are presented in Table 10.4.

Core Product

The core product, the center of the product platform, answers the following questions: What's in it for the customer to adopt the behavior? What benefits will customers receive? What needs will the desired behavior satisfy? What problems will it solve? The core product is not the behaviors or accompanying goods and services you will be developing, providing, and/or promoting. It is the benefits your audience wants and expects to experience when they perform the behavior—benefits *they say* are the most valuable to them (e.g., "moderate physical activity will make me feel better, look better, and live longer"). The great Harvard marketing professor Theodore Levitt was known to have told his students, "People don't want to buy a quarter-inch drill. They want a quarter-inch hole!" And Charles Revson, of Revlon, also provided a memorable quote illustrating the difference between product features (actual product) and product benefits (core product): "In the factory we make cosmetics; in the store, we sell hope."[14]

TABLE 10.4 ■ Examples of Three Product Levels

Behavior Objective (What you want your audience to do)	Core Product (What your audience wants in exchange for performing the behavior)	Actual Product (Major tangible goods or services that will be promoted and any special product features)	Augmented Product (Additional tangible goods or services that might make it more likely will adopt the behavior)
For Improved Health			
Get tested for COVID-19 as close as possible to attending an in-person event (e.g., grandmother's birthday celebration).	Protecting others you care about such as your grandmother	COVID-19 test	Home test results in 15 minutes
For Injury Prevention			
Do not text while driving	Preventing injuries and death	An app that disables messaging while driving	Passenger's ability to view a message by tapping "I'm not driving."
To Protect the Environment			
Reduce home energy consumption	Saving money and reducing carbon emissions	Home energy audits	Findings from the audit of potential anticipated savings
For Community Involvement			
Sign up to become an organ donor	Saving someone's life	Organ donor registry	Form that makes it clear that in the event of death, any family members will be asked to give final approval
To Enhance Financial Well-Being of the Poor			
Make regular deposits to a savings account	Children's education	Lockbox to keep at home for depositing money	Bank personnel make home visits to collect the money and deposit in a savings account

FIGURE 10.3 ■ A Testimonial Used to Persuade Youth That Tobacco Is Addictive

Source: Centers for Disease Control and Prevention's Media Campaign Resource Center.

Decisions about the core product focus primarily on what potential benefits should be stressed. This process will include reviewing (from Step 5) audience perceptions of (a) benefits from the desired behavior and (b) perceived costs of the competing behaviors that the desired behavior can help the priority audience avoid. You may have even identified this core product when constructing your positioning statement (in Step 6). Decisions are then made regarding which of these should be emphasized in a campaign. And keep in mind, the key benefit you should highlight is the benefit the priority audience perceives for performing the behavior—not the benefit to your organization or agency.

Example. Interviews with teens often reveal several perceived benefits youth associate with not smoking: doing better in school, doing better in sports, being seen as smart, and looking and feeling good. They may also reveal the following perceived costs of smoking: You could get addicted and not be able to quit, you might die, you'll stink, and you won't be as good in sports. Further discussions may indicate that one of these (e.g., fear of addiction) is most concerning and should be highlighted in the campaign (see Figure 10.3).

Actual Product

Surrounding the core product are the *specific tangible goods or services* you want your audience to acquire, consume, participate in, and/or utilize—those related to the desired behavior. As noted earlier, it may be existing goods or services offered by a for-profit company (e.g., fruits and vegetables), a nonprofit organization (e.g., blood donations), or a governmental agency (e.g., COVID-19 tests). Or it may be goods or services your organization develops or advocates for development (e.g., Road Crew). The following example illustrates this principle well.

Example. At the 2013 World Social Marketing Conference, Shiraz Latiff, CEO of Hummingbird International, shared an inspiring "product development" story from Sri Lanka, an island nation in the Indian Ocean known to be one of the best and largest producers of black tea in the world. It is also known for its very high diabetes-related death rate, attributed in part to the two to three teaspoons of sugar added to several traditional cups of tea a day. In celebration of World Diabetes Day in 2011, the Diabetes Association of Sri Lanka piloted a new product, one designed to decrease sugar consumption. They called it a F'Poon, as in fact it was a "serrated"

FIGURE 10.4 ■ The F'Poon: A Product Designed to Make it Easier to Have Less Sugar With a Cup of Tea

Source: Hummingbird International.

spoon that looked and functioned more like a fork than a spoon (see Figure 10.4). On this day, the F'Poon was distributed across a chain of leading restaurants and tea houses in the Colombo district, replacing the regular spoons in sugar bowls. Within six hours, over 1,500 tea drinkers used the F'Poon; 65% less sugar was consumed; and 100% of tea drinkers spoke with representatives of the Diabetes Association, most expressing that "it was a good idea" rather than a complaint. The success of the pilot with the major restaurants and tea houses was featured in the local electronic and print media and was commended by major governmental and nongovernmental institutions for its classic innovative concept and outcome. By 2013, all major restaurants in three country districts had adopted the F'Poon at their own cost, with plans being discussed to roll this out among medium-scale and low-end tea boutiques across the island nation at no cost by 2015.

Example. Every year in the United States, an estimated 20,000–25,000 children die before their first birthday,[15] and one in every eight babies is born prematurely.[16] To address this public health crisis, the National Healthy Mothers, Healthy Babies Coalition (HMHB) has created text4baby, a free mobile information service providing pregnant women and moms whose babies are less than a year old with information to influence them to perform behaviors that will give their babies the best possible start in life.

Augmented Product

This level of the product platform includes any *additional product elements* you will be providing and/or promoting along with the actual product. Although they may be considered optional, they are sometimes exactly what else is needed to provide encouragement (e.g., a walking buddy), remove barriers (e.g., a detailed resource guide and map of local walking trails and organized walking programs), or sustain behavior (e.g., a journal for tracking exercise levels). They may also provide opportunities to brand and to "tangibilize" the campaign, creating more attention, appeal, and memorability for priority audiences.[17]

Example. In 2019, an article in the *Business Standard* titled "Global Handwashing Day: Low-cost 'social' robot teaches Kerala children hygiene lessons" described an impactful augmented product strategy in India, a hand-shaped speaking robot, named Pepe, teaching students of the Wayanad Government Primary School how to wash their hands in accordance with WHO Standards. Pepe is mounted on a wall above a handwashing station, and "speaks" to the pupils and draws their attention to a nearby poster outlining the steps of effective handwashing. A set of moving "eyes" helps create the illusion that Pepe is paying attention to the children's actions. Researchers reported that "the robot helped the children wash their hands more effectively and consistently, boosting their rates of handwashing by 40 percent."[18]

DECISIONS REGARDING TANGIBLE GOODS

You will face several decisions in regard to developing or enhancing tangible goods that your campaign will encourage audiences to acquire, utilize, or consume.

Is there a need for new tangible goods that would greatly support the behavior change? For example, many adults with diabetes conduct finger-prick blood tests to monitor their blood sugar levels. A painless, needle-free mechanism that would provide reliable readings would be a welcome innovation and might result in more regular monitoring of blood sugar levels. It happened in 2021 when a new monitoring device, the DEXCOM G6 Continuous Glucose Monitoring System, became available, one with no need for fingersticks and that showed your glucose numbers at a quick glance on your mobile device. Not all new products will require retooling or significant research and development costs, as illustrated in the following example.

Example. In December 2012, news around the world featured the story of a 23-year-old student in Delhi, India, who was gang-raped on a public bus. She died 13 days later. The attacks sparked not only mass anger and demonstrations but also the imagination and determination of three engineering students from the SRM Institute of Science and Technology in Tamil Nadu, India, who then created electronic underwear they believed would help protect women from sexual assault. The lingerie (actual product) will deliver electric shock waves of 3,800,000 volts to an attacker, is designed to track the wearer's location by GPS, and can send text message alerts to police and/or family in case of emergencies.[19] The protective underwear, named Society Harnessing Equipment (SHE), won the 2013 Gandhian Young Technology Innovation Award and is expected to be mass produced and distributed.[20]

Do current tangible goods need to be improved or enhanced? For example, typical compost bins require the gardener to use a pitchfork to regularly turn the yard waste to enhance compost development. New and improved models that a social marketing campaign might make known to priority audiences are suspended on a bracket that requires only a regular "tumble."

Consider that until recent years, most users (and especially nonusers) have perceived life vests as bulky and uncomfortable. Teens have raised concerns about tan lines and the "ugly" orange color. New options are vastly improved, with a look similar to that of suspenders and a feature for automatic inflation using a pull tab. Consider also the clear need for an improved product within a product category in the next example.

Example. An environmental scan of bullying prevention apps available in 2013 conducted by the Substance Abuse and Mental Health Services Administration (SAMHSA) identified something

TABLE 10.5 ■ Examples of Innovative Products to Support Behavior Change

Product Type	Example
Gamification	*Don't Turn a Night Out into a Nightmare* An online game where you move around a game board and encounter a variety of people, places, and situations. "It'll be up to you to decide if your night out will become a nightmare."[22]
Apps	*Smoke Wise* An EPA citizen science project using a mobile app that brings wildfire smoke and health resources to the palm of your hand. With the app, users make a personal connection to wildfire smoke as an environmental exposure and are encouraged to adopt individual-level health protective behaviors.
Artificial Intelligence	*Alexa Devices* "Alexa, can I put bones in the food-waste compost?"
Wearables	*Digital Tattoos* MIT and Harvard Medical School developed a color-changing tattoo ink that responds to changes in the body, such as blood sugar and sodium levels to monitor diabetes.
GPS	*Smart Dog Collar* An attachment for a dog collar that tracks locations and levels of physical activity.

critical missing. Most bullying prevention apps available focused on reporting bullying incidents, by either the person being bullied or a bystander. Some also provided educational content (e.g., signs of bullying and what actions to take). And yet, formative research with technical experts indicated that children look (more) to their parents and caregivers for guidance on tough choices, peer pressure, and making decisions. And that parents and caregivers who spend at least 15 minutes a day talking with their child can build the foundation for a strong relationship and offer reassurance that he or she can come to them for any problem. A new bullying prevention app was designed by SAMHSA to fill this product gap. It aids parents and caregivers prevent bullying by helping them to:

- Understand bullying and how to recognize warning signs
- Learn pointers on talking with a child about bullying
- Set reminders to talk with a child
- Establish a profile for a child so they can easily navigate to age-appropriate content and manage reminders
- Share conversation tips, advice, and resources from the app with others via Facebook, Twitter, email, and text message.[21]

Table 10.5 highlights a few additional innovative products that would support social marketing efforts:

Is there a need or opportunity for a substitute product?[23] A substitute product is one that offers the audience a "healthier and safer" way to satisfy a want, fulfill a need, or solve a problem. The key is to understand the real benefit (core product) of the competing behavior and to then develop and/or promote products offering the same or at least some of the same benefits. These include, for example, food and beverages such as nonalcoholic beers, garden burgers, fat-free dairy products, nicotine-free cigarettes, and decaffeinated coffee; natural fertilizers, natural pesticides, and ground covers to replace lawns; an older sibling (vs. a parent) taking a younger teen to a community clinic for STD screening; and a package containing a can of chicken soup, tissues, and aspirin "prescribed" to patients suffering from colds, in an effort to reduce the overuse of antibiotics.

DECISIONS REGARDING SERVICES

Services are often distinguished as offerings that are intangible and do not result in the ownership of anything.[24] In the social marketing environment, examples of services that support the desired behavior change might include *education-related services* (e.g., parenting workshops on how to talk to your kids about sex), *personal services* (e.g., escorts for students back to their dorms at night), *counseling services* (e.g., a crisis line for people considering suicide), *clinical services* (e.g., community clinics for free immunizations), and *community services* (e.g., hazardous waste mobiles for disposal of toxic waste products). It should be noted that services that are more sales oriented in nature (e.g., demonstrations on the efficiency of low-flow toilets) fall into the promotional category and will be discussed in Chapter 13. You will also face several decisions regarding any services you offer.

Should a new service be developed and offered? For example, given the apparent success and popularity of toll-free tobacco quitlines to support smoking cessation in other states, a community without one might want to develop and launch a line to accompany mass-media campaigns encouraging adults to quit smoking. A new service might also be inspired by a new unique version of an existing popular service, one described in the following example.

Example. In his 2017 autobiography *My Adventures in Marketing*, Philip Kotler described the accomplishments of one of his students at Northwestern University who took seriously his call for businesses to use business and marketing to create a better world. Xavier Lopez developed an amazing new theme park in Mexico called *KidZania*, one like Disneyland, providing rides and fun for kids, usually ages 4–14, but differing by also adding learning to their experience. Most kids ages 4–14 know little about the world of work, or what they might want to do someday. Kids visiting KidZania can experience what it would be like to work in a variety of micro-settings such as a hospital, hotel, bank, TV station, police station, fire station, law court, cooking school, and more.

> I watched a group of children wearing doctors' uniforms operate on a "dummy" patient in the virtual hospital. I watched a trial taking place in a courtroom with an accused person, prosecuting and defending attorneys, a judge, and a jury. I watched a building on fire with young firemen spraying the building to put out the fire.[25]

KidZania is now (2022) located in over 15 countries with 25 facilities from Mexico City to Tokyo to London, receiving more than 9 million visitors a year.[26]

Does an existing service need to be improved or enhanced? For example, what if customer surveys indicate that an estimated 50% of callers to the state's 800 number for questions about recycling hang up because they typically have to wait more than five minutes on hold? And, as illustrated in the following example, would a service such as providing feedback on current behaviors increase chances more would "take on" the desired behavior?

Example. Doug McKenzie-Mohr is an environmental psychologist specializing in designing programs that support sustainable behaviors. One of the tools he encourages social marketers to use is making norms visible: "Norms guide how we should behave. If we observe others acting unsustainably . . . we are more likely to act similarly. In contrast, if we observe members of our community acting sustainably, we are more likely to do the same."[27] One example that demonstrates this is Opower, an energy efficiency and smart grid software company, which has developed a program whereby residents receive information about their own level of household energy consumption compared with the norm for their local community. They say their company was "founded on a simple premise: It's time to engage the 300 million Americans who are in the dark about their energy use."[28] One of their products is a home energy report that not only provides the utility's customers information and trends on their energy usage but also features comparisons to their neighbors, including the use of symbolic "smiley faces" (see Figure 10.5). According to Opower, leading utilities across the country provide home energy reports to nearly one million households nationwide, and these utility customers have cut their annual gas or electricity usage by 1.5%–3.5% annually after receiving these reports.[29]

Design Thinking

Tim Brown, CEO and president of IDEO, a leading design company, frequently writes and speaks about design thinking, and in a 2009 TED talk in Oxford, he described the difference between

FIGURE 10.5 ■ Home Energy Report Comparing "You" to Your Neighbors

November Neighbor Comparison | You used **28% MORE** energy than your efficient neighbors.

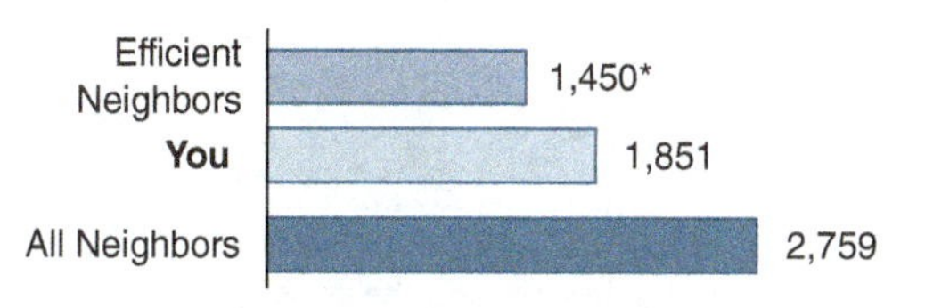

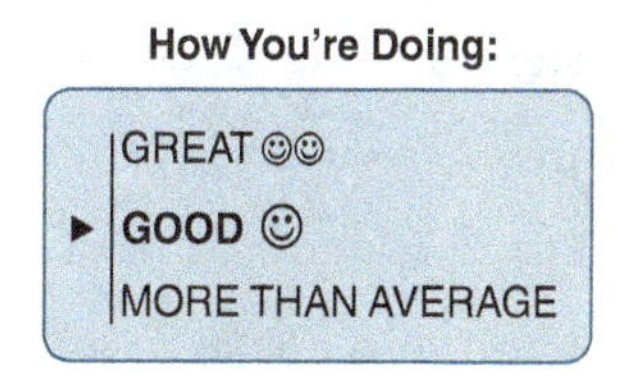

* This energy index combines electricity (kWh) and natural gas (thorme) into s single measurement.

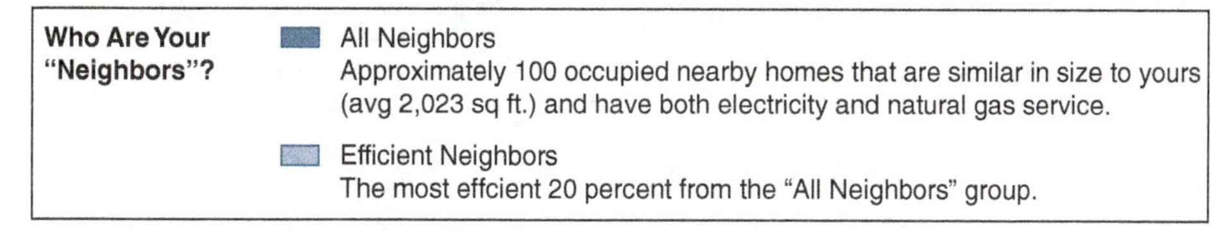

design and *design thinking.* Design, as he describes it, focuses on making a product attractive, easy to use, and ultimately more marketable. By contrast, design thinking focuses less on an object and more on an approach to designing products that fulfill human desires, solve problems, and create world-changing innovations. He calls for a shift to a more local, collaborative, and participatory process to fully understand what humans need, test preliminary ideas with prototypes, and then design products that fulfill human needs and desires.[30] Design thinking is very consistent with the product platform outlined in this chapter, where we begin with determining the core product, the value the priority audience wants in exchange for adopting the behavior. What benefits do *they* say they want the behavior to provide? We then, and only then, move on to determining the features of tangible goods and services (actual and augmented products). In the Research Highlight at the end of this chapter, you'll read about "The Lucky Fish," another great example of using design thinking, this time to reduce anemia in Cambodia.

BRANDING

Branding of products in the commercial sector is pervasive and fairly easy to understand and recognize. A brand, as mentioned earlier, is a name, term, sign, symbol, or design (or a combination of these) that identifies the maker or seller of a product (see Table 10.6).[31] You have contact with brands when you start your day with a Starbucks, search for directions on your iPhone, drive your Volvo, listen to music on your iPod, like a friend's post on Facebook, tweet a Super Bowl score on Twitter, use Microsoft Word, run in your Nikes, and TiVo the CBS News.

TABLE 10.6 ■ A Branding Primer
Brand is a name, term, sign, symbol, or design (or a combination of these) that identifies the maker or seller of a product or service.
Brand Identity is how you (the maker) want consumers to think, feel, and act with respect to your brand.
Brand Image is how your target audience actually does think, feel, or act with respect to your brand.
Branding is the process of developing an intended brand identity.
Brand Awareness is the extent to which consumers recognize a brand.
Brand Promise is the marketer's vision of what the brand must be and do for consumers.
Brand Loyalty refers to the degree to which a consumer consistently purchases the same brand within a product class.
Brand Equity is the value of a brand, based on the extent to which it has high brand loyalty, name awareness, perceived quality, strong brand associations, and other assets such as patents, trademarks, and channel relationships. It is an important, although intangible, asset that has psychological and financial value to a firm.
Brand Elements are those trade markable devices that serve to identify and differentiate the brand.

Source: Kotler, P., & Lee, N. Marketing in the public sector: A roadmap to improved performance (Wharton School, 2006).

Branding in social marketing is not as common, although we would like to encourage more of it, as it helps create visibility and ensure memorability. Branding is covered again in this chapter, as it is most often inspired by the finalized product platform and becomes synonymous with the actual product being promoted (ENERGY STAR®). As mentioned in Chapter 9, your positioning statement (Step 6) will inform the development of your brand (the name, term, sign, symbol, and/or design that identifies your campaign). The following list includes a few of the stronger social marketing brands, noted in bold. In these cases, brand names that have been used to identify programs and products are used consistently in an integrated way. Many cleverly highlight the desired behavior (Designated Skipper); some focus on a desired benefit (Meet Your Match); a few adopt, and stick with, a mascot (Smokey Bear); and others draw attention to the competition (Mr. Yuk). Most are then accompanied by additional brand elements, including graphics and taglines developed at the promotional phase in campaign development:

- Wildfire prevention: **Smokey Bear**
- Commute reduction: **Just One Trip**
- Poison prevention: **Mr. Yuk**
- Maternal and child health: **Text4Baby**
- Nutrition: **5 a Day**
- Traffic safety: **Click It or Ticket**
- Physical activity: **VERB**
- Suicide prevention: **Asking Saves Lives**
- Crime protection: **McGruff the Crime Dog**
- Safe produce: **USDA Organic**
- Sustainable seafood: **Seafood Watch**
- Waste reduction: **Reduce. Reuse. Recycle**
- Drinking and driving: **Road Crew**
- Tobacco prevention: **truth®**
- Litter prevention: **Don't mess with Texas**
- Pet waste: **Scoop the Poop**
- Youth drug prevention: **Parents. The Anti-Drug**
- Voting: **Rock the Vote**
- SIDS: **Back to Sleep**
- Water conservation: **Water—Use It Wisely**

- Water quality: **Chesapeake Club**
- Energy conservation: **ENERGY STAR®**
- Schoolchildren's safety: **Walking School Bus**
- Senior fall prevention: **S.A.I.L. (Stay Active and Independent for Life)**
- Anemia: **Lucky Fish**
- Sugar reduction: **F'Poon**
- Boat related drownings: **Designated Skipper**
- Pet adoption from animal shelters: **Meet Your Match**
- Heroin overdose: **Help Not Handcuffs**
- Property crime: **Lock It or Lose It**
- Light duty jobs for injured workers: **Stay at Work**
- Water pollution from automobile oil leaks: **Don't Drip & Drive**
- Erosion on shorelines: **Shore Friendly**

Ethical Considerations for Product Platform

One way to highlight ethical considerations relative to product decisions is to revisit each component of the product platform.

The *core product* promises the audience a benefit they will receive (or cost they will avoid) if they perform the behavior. Can you be sure? How much should you disclose about the probability of success? Tobacco prevention specialists emphasize the health costs of smoking cigarettes, and yet how many times have you seen or read the research that claims that much of the physiological damage done by smoking during the first 10–20 years will be repaired by the body if and when you quit? Should this information be prominently displayed?

For the *actual product*, decisions are made relative to a specific behavior you will be promoting (e.g., 5 A Day) and any name and sponsors that will be associated with the behavior (e.g., Produce for Better Health Foundation). Perhaps one major ethical consideration here is whether you make the actual sponsor/funder of the project very visible or not. For example, should the funder of the campaign be visible on a teen pregnancy prevention campaign poster? And consider this product introduced in January 2011 in Placer, California. Law enforcement and schools there began offering parents a home alcohol and drug screening kit at a deeply discounted price. The kit included a 10-panel drug screening for $10, which would sell for about $40 in stores; alcohol test strips sell for $2. A deputy who launched the program said authorities were not asking parents to turn in kids who tested positive for illicit drugs and that it was meant to help keep kids safe. Are you as concerned as one representative of the New York–based Drug Policy Alliance, who noted that "asking kids to urinate in a cup could further erode a rocky relationship with parents"?[32] This may be where the rule of thumb "do more good than harm" can help you decide.

For the *augmented product*, decisions regarding additional tangible goods and services are similar to those in the private sector, although in this case you are often dealing with taxpayer-funded programs, a different constituent group with agendas different from those of shareholders. Does your product "perform as promised"? If your community is offering safe injection sites or free Naloxone for opioid overdoses, do you get push back from community members that feel like this is condoning the use of illegal drugs? In terms of services, can you deliver and provide good service if you are successful in generating demand?

COVID-19 Social Marketing Example

From launch in 2020–2022, a variety of products were noticed, with a few mentioned in Table 10.7:

TABLE 10.7 ■ Examples of COVID-19 Related Product Strategies

Core Product	Actual Products	Augmented Products
Helping stop the spread of COVID-19 and protecting yourself and those you care about	• Immunizations • Masks • Hand sanitizers • Workers personal protective equipment • Exposure notification tools for smart phones • At-home COVID-19 test kits	• Signs on floors noting 6 feet • Chairs in classrooms, offices and healthcare facilities spaced 6 feet apart. • Telemedicine • Support groups for widows and widowers • Contact tracing • Vaccine verification QR codes

CHAPTER SUMMARY

The *product* platform has three levels: the core product (the benefit of the behavior), the actual product (major goods and/or services your effort will be developing or promoting that the audience acquire or consume), and the augmented product (any additional product elements needed to support behavior change).

Decisions are faced at each level. At the core product level, decisions will need to be made regarding what potential benefits should be stressed. At the actual product level, you will consider whether existing goods (e.g., bike helmets) or services (e.g., home energy audits) should be promoted or whether new or improved products are needed to support behavior adoption (e.g., a tobacco quitline or a bullying app for parents). We encourage you to also consider whether there are additional product elements (augmented products) that would provide support for the priority audience, ones not "required" but that might make the difference in whether the audience is moved to action (e.g., life vests available for loan at beaches).

RESEARCH HIGHLIGHT
REDUCING ANEMIA IN CAMBODIA[33]

By Louise Brown*

November 12, 2011

University of Guelph grad student Chris Charles helped in the development of this iron fish that poor village women in Cambodia put in their cooking pots, allowing iron to leach into the food and therefore raising the levels of iron in their bodies. They tried several designs but finally chose a lucky fish (see Figure 10.6).

GUELPH—At the heart of this tale is a lucky little fish.

How it became the answer to a dire medical problem deep in the Cambodian jungle is something University of Guelph researcher Christopher Charles swears is no fish tale.

It began three years ago when this science whiz from Milton, who had just graduated from Guelph with a bachelor in biomedical science, took on a gritty little summer research gig in Cambodia. The task was to help local scientists try to persuade village women to place chunks of iron in their cooking pots to get more iron in their diet and lower the risk of anemia. Great in theory, but the women weren't having it.

FIGURE 10.6 ■ The Lucky Fish

Source: Author Photo. https://images.search.yahoo.com/search/images;_ylt=Awr9Ik.46zxiKRIAfgNXNyoA;_ylu=Y29sbwNncTEEcG9zAzQEdnRpZAMEc2VjA3Nj?p=lucky+fish+cambodia+iron&fr=mcafee.

It was an enticing challenge in a country where iron deficiency is so rampant, 60% of women face premature labor, hemorrhaging during childbirth, and poor brain development among their babies.

A disease of poverty, iron deficiency affects 3.5 billion people in the world. This was frontier research. Chris Charles was hooked—but he was also due to start his master's back in Guelph.

Mere weeks before he was to leave, Charles called his academic adviser to pull the plug on his master's in hormone research. To his credit, his adviser refused to let him quit. Instead, he told Charles he had found his true master's project.

From his new base in a bamboo hut on stilts, Charles took on the task with two researchers from Research Development International in Cambodia, with funding from the University of Guelph, the International Development Research Centrein Ottawa and the Canadian Institutes of Health Research's doctoral research award.

"Some nights I wondered what I had got myself into; here I was in a village with no running water, no electricity and no way to use my computer—it was like a (research) baptism by fire," he recalled.

The people they worked with—"the poorest of the poor"—can't afford red meat or pricey iron pills, and the women won't switch to iron cooking pots because they find them heavy and costly. Yet a small chunk of iron could release life-saving iron into the water and food. But what shape would the women be willing to place in their cooking pots?

"We knew some random piece of ugly metal wouldn't work ... so we had to come up with an attractive idea," he said. "It became a challenge in social marketing."

The research team tried a small circle of iron. The women wouldn't use it.

They crafted iron shaped like a lotus flower. The women didn't like that either.

But when Charles's team came up with a piece of iron shaped like a local river fish believed to be lucky? Bingo. Women were happy to place it in their cooking pots and in the months that followed, the iron levels in the village began to climb.

"We designed it about 3 or 4 inches long, small enough to be stirred easily but large enough to provide up to about 75 per cent of the daily iron requirement," said Charles. They found a local scrap metal worker who could make them for $1.50 each, and so far they have been reusing the fish roughly three years.

"We're getting fantastic results; there seems to be a huge decrease in anemia and the village women say they feel good, no dizziness, fewer headaches. The iron fish is incredibly powerful."

In three years, Charles has discovered an answer to the iron problem that is stunning in its simplicity, is likely to save lives, and has earned him a master's and very nearly his Ph.D. Along the way, the 26-year-old learned the Khmer language, mastered the art of taking a blood sample from someone sitting in a dugout canoe while balancing in a second canoe, and caught dengue fever.

Today, Charles is back at Guelph, crunching numbers, preparing to submit the research for publication, and putting final touches on his Ph.D.

Almost as excited is the adviser he called three years ago: endocrinology professor Alastair Summerlee, who also happens to be president of the university.

Summerlee knew he had taken a chance when he let Charles change academic gears.

"We were flying by the seat of our pants, Chris working in a field placement where he had to learn everything (including Khmer) by trial and error and me worrying about whether or not this was the right decision. Did he have the skills to pull it off?" recalled Summerlee.

"But his results are spectacular. He has presented his findings in Asia, Europe and North America to acclaim, and there is a serious possibility that this simple discovery will have a profound influence on the health status of women in Asia."

One more lesson Charles learned? That marketing is the flip side of science.

"You can have the best treatment in the world, but if people won't use it, it won't matter."

2018 Update

In 2013, the Lucky Iron Fish Enterprise (LIFE) was founded to disseminate this simple innovation worldwide, working with registered nonprofits and health clinics around the world to distribute the Lucky Iron Fish and provide support in impact assessment and evaluation. By 2018, 500,000 Lucky Iron Fish have been distributed to people around the globe, including to those in the countries of Peru, India, Nicaragua, Mozambique, the Democratic Republic of Congo, Somalia, Haiti, Uganda, Pakistan, Canada, the United States, and more. And thanks to their buy-one-give-one program, they have distributed 50,000 to people in need in the past year alone (2017).[34]

2022 Update

In 2022, the Lucky Iron Fish website reports that the program is currently active in 88 countries.[35]

DISCUSSION QUESTIONS AND EXERCISES

1. In the opening highlight addressing pet adoption, there were two priority audiences. Why did program planners develop a strategy for the animal shelters as well as potential adopters?
2. How do the authors define *core product*? What is its relation to *service-dominant logic*?
3. How would you describe the difference between an actual product and an augmented product?
4. What examples could you add to the list of social marketing brands, even if they are not well known?

STEP 7.2: PRICE

Determining Incentives and Disincentives

LEARNING OBJECTIVES

Upon completion of this chapter, you should be able to:

11.1 Describe what the priority audience considers the price of adopting a behavior to be.

11.2 Identify the six attachments to the price tool and their distinctions.

11.3 Explain why commitments and pledges increase likelihood of behavior change.

11.4 Explain social marketers' role and ethical considerations in setting prices for tangible goods and services.

This chapter introduces "price," the second tool in your marketing intervention toolbox and one you may find especially helpful in overcoming financial barriers associated with adopting your behavior. You will find it useful in "sweetening the pot"—and not necessarily just monetary incentives that could add significant costs to your program budget. You may also find it effective in reducing the appeal of the competition's offer. As Dr. Stephen Dann at Australian National University shared with us: "Social marketers need to use the whole of the marketing mix to win their priority audience's business—there's no use tying one hand behind your back and only using promotion when the competition has price, distribution, and, more often than not, a better product."[1] You'll read how others have used creative monetary and nonmonetary incentives to add value, sometimes just enough to tip the exchange in their favor:

- How coupons helped increase the use of bike helmets from 1% to 57% in one community.
- How a social marketing approach succeeded in persuading legislators to toughen the laws and fines for texting while driving.
- How a group of teens convinced their peers to postpone having sex by sharing the pain of pubic lice (crabs).
- How hand washing was increased using the price tool in India.

You'll read that the price tool has six "attachments", with the major four being:

1. Monetary incentives (e.g., discount coupons)
2. Nonmonetary incentives (e.g., personal pride and positive public recognition)
3. Monetary disincentives (e.g., fines)
4. Nonmonetary disincentives (e.g., negative public recognition)

When describing Step 5 (audience insights) in Chapter 8, audience benefits were noted as the "what's in it for me (WIFM)?" phenomenon. In this chapter on *price*, we consider the other side of the equation that identifies, "What am I willing to pay?" In the following case highlight, the answer to this question inspired a unique audience and behavior selection, as well as marketing intervention mix.

CASE HIGHLIGHT
DECREASING DROWNINGS FROM BOATING UNDER THE INFLUENCE (BUI)

(2016–2021)

Source: Courtesy of Sea Tow Foundation.

Information for this Marketing Highlight was provided by Michael Wesolowski, Executive Director in 2016 of the Sea Tow Foundation in New York. It illustrates the application of two strong social marketing principles: (1) selecting a single, simple, doable behavior for a priority audience and (2) leveraging the power of prior similar, successful efforts. An update was provided in 2022 by a new Executive Director, Gail Kulp.

Background, Purpose, and Focus

In 2016, the U.S. Coast Guard reported that alcohol use is the leading contributing factor in fatal boating accidents where the primary cause was known and that between 2005 and 2015, there were a total of 1,368 deaths attributed to boating under the influence (BUI), an average of 115 deaths per year. Further, 17% of all fatal boating accidents are the result of boat operators using alcohol.[2]

In 2015, the Sea Tow Foundation, in partnership with Sea Tow Services International, local Sea Tow franchises, and the Washington State Parks Department, developed a social marketing plan launched in 2016, one with a *purpose* of reducing the number of skippers driving boats while under the influence of alcohol and drugs, with a *focus* on designating a sober skipper. The familiar branded campaign Designated Driver and the acronym DUI are, of course, the prior effort this campaign leveraged.

Priority Audiences

Using historic accident and death incident data to prioritize audiences, the population of boaters was segmented using variables including demographics and current related boating behaviors, with the priority audience for the 2016–2018 season identified as:

- Males 36–54 years old
- Skippering a vessel 14–16 feet (primarily trailered vs. moored)
- On lakes
- Boating between noon and 8 p.m. on weekends, especially between 4:30 p.m. and 6:30 p.m. on Saturdays

Since the idea of designating a sober skipper was relatively new to most boaters, the team prioritized, for the launch of the campaign, those within this group that would be "early adopters," helping to create a social norm.

Behavior, Knowledge, and Belief Objectives

Campaign objectives established were to influence the skipper of the boat to "do, know, and believe" the following:

Behavior Objective: Designate someone (even yourself) before leaving the dock to be the Designated Skipper for the trip, one who is trained to handle the boat, will respect the legal alcohol limit to remain sober, and will be responsible for all passengers.

Knowledge Objective: Alcohol use is the primary contributing factor to accidents and deaths on the water. Being the Designated Sober Skipper will allow you to not only be aware of what is happening on your boat but also the action of other boaters; on a boat, wind vibration, noise, and the sun can intensify the effects of alcohol and impair balance and coordination.

Belief Objective: It is just as smart a choice to designate a sober skipper as it is to designate a sober driver; you can still have fun on the water, even if you are sober, and other people's lives are in your hands.

Audience Insights

Survey research identified three major reasons the priority audience had not designated a skipper in the past or might not in the future:

- It's hard to know if someone is sober or not.
- I believe it's safer to drink on the water than on the land.

- I won't remember to do it.

The planning team was also inspired by their responses to what would motivate them including convincing them it's such a big problem, knowing what the laws are regarding a BUI, and having something that would prompt them to remember to designate a skipper.

Marketing Intervention Strategies

Product Strategies: Yellow wristbands, floating key tags.

Price: Proposed plans included pledges to be the Designated Skipper (see Figure 11.1) and discounts provided at select convenience stores, marinas, restaurants, and other retailers to skippers wearing a yellow Sober Skipper wristband.

Place: Wristbands and floating key tags were to be made available at a variety of channels including convenience stores, marinas, nonprofit organizations, schools, restaurants, and fuel docks.

Promotions: Key messages included ones encouraging boaters to "designate a sober skipper before leaving dock" and to believe that "designating a sober skipper on the water is just like designating a sober driver on land." Potential communication channels recommended included a website, signage at marinas and docks, signs at marine stores, social media, and news releases.

The Designated Sober Skipper strategies are intended to be flexible, allowing for participating organizations to use them in a way that suits their local marketplace. Two examples include the Lake George community in Lake George, New York, and

FIGURE 11.1 ■ Pledging to be a Designated Skipper

Source: Sea Tow Foundation.

the Seafair organization in Seattle, Washington, each having similar goals to reduce drinking among operators of paddle and power vessels. Their tactics differed, however, with the Lake George business, civic, and municipal leaders distributing Sober Skipper messages on key dates during the boating season and making yellow Sober Skipper wristbands and printed materials available from sites around the lake. The Seafair organization distributed yellow Sober Skipper wristbands and printed materials to power boaters that rent space around the boat race and from a tent located in the vendor section of the event during the event weekend.

Results

After the launch of the Designated Skipper program at the 2015 Seafair on Lake Washington, results for the pilot were indeed encouraging, with Seafair having its first zero fatality or major injury since its beginning in the early 1950s.[3]

Case Update 2019–2021[4]

As a result of the COVID-19 pandemic, an update was made to the Sober Skipper's Social Marketing Plan that provided alternate ways to reach boaters without connecting with them at in-person events. Major strategies focused on utilizing social media and installing custom-made signage at boat ramps and marinas for boaters to easily see. One activity in 2020, for example, was a social media contest that encouraged boaters to Take the Sober Skipper Pledge online, and those who took the pledge were entered to win a $3,000 prize pack from a participating partner, KICKER Marine Audio. These media channels and other promotional efforts "led to 119.6 million impressions valued at $13.7 million which is 114 times the amount of grant funding that this project was awarded and represent a strong Return on Investment (ROI)."[5]

PRICE: THE SECOND "P"

Price is the cost that the priority audience associates with adopting the desired behavior. Traditional marketing theory has a similar definition: "The amount of money charged for a product or service, or the sum of the values that consumers exchange for the benefits of having or using the product or service."[6]

Associated costs for behavior change may be *monetary* or *nonmonetary* in nature. Monetary costs in a social marketing environment are most often related to *goods and services* associated with adopting the behavior (e.g., buying a life vest or paying for a swim class for toddlers). Nonmonetary costs are more intangible but are just as real for your audience and often even more significant for social marketing products. They include costs associated with the *time, effort, and energy* required to perform the behavior, *psychological risks and losses* that might be perceived or experienced, and any *physical discomforts* that might be related to the behavior. You probably discovered most of these nonmonetary costs when you conducted barriers research, identifying concerns your priority audience had about adopting the desired behavior. There may be more to add to the list, however, as you may have decided you want to include goods and services such as those listed in Table 11.1. This is the time to do that.

TABLE 11.1 ■ Potential Costs for Performing the Desired Behavior

Type of Cost	Examples
Monetary: Goods	• Nicotine patches • COVID-19 home tests • Blood pressure monitoring equipment • Condoms • Bike helmets, life vests, and booster seats • Breathalyzers • Earthquake preparedness kits • Smoke alarm batteries • Food waste compost tumblers • Natural fertilizers (vs. regular fertilizers) • Recycled paper (vs. regular paper) • Energy-saving lightbulbs • Electric mulch mowers
Monetary: Services	• Fees for family-planning classes • Smoking cessation classes • Athletic club fees • Suicide prevention workshops • Taxi rides home from a bar
Nonmonetary: Time, Effort	• Cooking a balanced meal • Driving to a COVID-19 testing site and perhaps waiting in line • Pulling over to use the cell phone • Taking the food waste outside to a composter
Nonmonetary: Psychological	• Finding out whether a lump is cancerous • Finding out if you test positive for COVID-19 • Having a cup of coffee without a cigarette • Feeling "dorky" carrying a flag across a crosswalk • Listening to the chatter of others in a car pool • Asking your child whether he is considering suicide • Telling your spouse you think they drink too much • Using sunscreen and coming back from Hawaii "pale" • Letting your lawn go brown in the summer

TABLE 11.1 ■ Potential Costs for Performing the Desired Behavior *(Continued)*

Type of Cost	Examples
Nonmonetary: Physical Discomfort	• Exercising • Wearing a COVID-19-protective mask • Pricking a finger to monitor blood glucose • Having a mammogram • Lowering the thermostat • Taking shorter showers

If your organization is actually the maker or provider of these tangible goods (e.g., rain barrels) or services (e.g., home energy audits), you will want to be involved in establishing the price your customer will be asked to pay. This is the time to do that as well, before developing the incentives that are the emphasis of this chapter. A section at the end of this chapter presents a few tips on price setting.

STEP 7.2: DETERMINE INCENTIVES AND DISINCENTIVES: SIX OPTIONS TO CONSIDER

Your objective and opportunity with this second marketing tool is to develop and provide *incentives* that will increase benefits and/or decrease costs (It should be noted that *product* and *place* tools will also be used to increase benefits and decrease costs. The *price* tool is unique in its use of monetary incentives, as well as nonmonetary ones including keeping commitments, recognition, appreciation, and reward.) The first four of the six price-related tactics focus on the desired behavior and the last two on the competing one(s).

1. Increase monetary benefits for *the desired behavior.*
2. Increase nonmonetary benefits for *the desired behavior.*
3. Decrease monetary costs for *the desired behavior.*
4. Decrease nonmonetary costs for *the desired behavior.*
5. Increase monetary costs for *the competing behavior.*
6. Increase nonmonetary costs for *the competing behavior.*

The next six sections of this chapter explain each of these in more detail and provide illustrations for each.

Increase Monetary Benefits for Behavior

Monetary rewards and incentives can take many forms familiar to you as a consumer and include *rebates, gift cards, allowances, cash incentives*, and *price adjustments* that reward customers for adopting the proposed behavior. Some are rather "tame" in nature (e.g., 5-cent credit for reusing grocery bags), others a little more aggressive (e.g., quit-and-win contests that offer a chance to win a $1,000 prize for successfully stopping smoking for at least one month,[7] a $20 annual license fee for a neutered dog vs. $60 for an unaltered one), and a few quite bold (e.g., offering voters a chance at a $1 million lottery just for showing up at the polls). In the following example, you'll read how motivating a monetary incentive can be.

Example: Monetary Incentive for Tobacco Cessation[8]. A field experiment in the Philippines funded by the World Bank and conducted by researchers Xavier Gine, Dean Karlan, and Jonathan Zinman tested the viability and effectiveness of monetary, as well as nonmonetary incentives, to influence current smokers, aged 15 years and older, to quit. Of significance was the research indicating that 72% of these smokers reported they wanted to stop smoking, influenced by concerns with serious health effects, as well as the fact that they were spending approximately US$2 per week on cigarettes, representing nearly 15% of their monthly income. They were clearly a great priority audience for testing viability of monetary incentives.

The offer researchers tested was a voluntary commitment savings program, one branded *A Commitment Contract for Smoking Cessation* (CARES), also referred to by the researchers as "Put Your Money Where Your Butt Is." A smoker wanting to quit would sign a commitment contract and open a savings account (*product*) at Green Bank, a participating partner, with an initial deposit of about US$1 and would deposit the money they would normally have spent on cigarettes into this account each week for six months (*price*). The savings account would not yield interest, and clients could only make deposits to, and not withdraw from, the CARES account during the six-month commitment period. Every week, a Green Bank field staff would collect the money and deposit it in one of the bank's microfinance branches, saving him or her the weekly trip to the bank (*place*). If, at the six-month milestone, a nicotine test proved that the client was "tobacco free," the entire savings would be given back. If not, he or she would be required to give up the money and donate it to a charity.

Individuals participating in the CARES Contract group were 3.3–5.8 percentage points more likely to pass the six-month urine test than the control group, representing a 35% increase in likelihood of smoking cessation compared to baseline.[9]

Increase Nonmonetary Benefits for Behavior

There are also ways to encourage behavior change that don't involve cash or free/discounted goods and services with significant monetary value. Instead, they provide a different type of value. In the social marketing environment, they often take the form of a *pledge/commitment, recognition*, and/or *appreciation* acknowledging the adoption of a desired behavior. In most cases, the benefit is psychological and personal in nature. By signing and keeping a pledge or commitment, a participant receives (in return) increased self-respect. If the pledge is made public, the value increases, with public respect increasing perceived value even further, as illustrated in the following example.

Example. In 2021, the S.A.F.E. Group and Psychology Club at the Mercer Island High School in Washington state had been busy working on projects to decrease impaired driving. A major event they held is a great example of a nonmonetary incentive tactic. A campaign branded "I DONUT drive impaired" included a special event in the high school's hallways which included students encouraging fellow students to sign a pledge not to drive impaired, one that was posted for all to see. And those who signed the pledge were given a free donut!

Decrease Monetary Costs for Behavior

Methods to decrease monetary costs are also familiar to most consumers: discount coupons, gift cards, trial incentives (e.g., eight free rides on a network of bus routes), cash discounts, quantity discounts, seasonal discounts, promotional pricing (e.g., a temporary price reduction), and segment pricing (e.g., price based on geographic locations). Many of these tactics are also available to you as a social marketer to increase sales. In July 2013, for example, a pet adoption extravaganza in Seattle waived adoption fees for cats one year and older and reduced fees for kittens, resulting in 203 adoptions in one weekend and breaking a 116-year history.[10] You yourself may have used a discount coupon from a utility for compost, taken advantage of a weekend sales event for water-efficient toilets, or received a discount on parking at work because you are part of a car pool. The social marketing organization may be involved in subsidizing the incentive, distributing coupons, and/or getting the word out, as illustrated in the following example. It is noted that this example is one from the late 1990s, but it is shared to confirm how a discount coupon was key to inspiring significant behavior change that then led to a new and sustainable (to this day) norm.

Example: Bike Helmet Coupons. The website of the Harborview Injury Prevention and Research Center (HIPRC) reported in February 2000 that "more bicyclists in Seattle wear helmets than bicyclists in any other major city in the country where laws do not require it." The Washington Children's Helmet Bicycle Campaign had been launched in 1986 by physicians at Harborview Medical Center in Seattle, who were alarmed at the nearly 200 children they were treating each year with bicycle-related head injuries.[11] "Although bicycle helmets were available in 1985, just one child in 100 wears one." HIPRC physicians conducted a study to understand why parents didn't buy bike helmets for their children and what factors influenced whether children actually wore them.

> The results from a survey of more than 2,500 fourth graders and their parents shaped the eventual campaign. More than two thirds of the parents said that they had never thought of providing a helmet and *another third cited cost as a factor* [italics added].

A campaign was designed around "four key objectives: increasing public awareness of the importance of helmets, educating parents about helmet use, overcoming peer pressure among children against wearing helmets, and lowering helmet prices."

The HIPRC formed a coalition of health, bicycling, and helmet industry and community organizations to design and manage a variety of promotions. As a result, parents and children heard about helmets on television, on the radio, in the newspapers, in their doctors' offices, at school, and at youth groups. The advertised discount coupons cut helmet prices by half, to $20. Nearly 5,000 helmets were distributed at no or low cost to needy families.

By September 1993 (seven years later), helmet use had jumped from 1% to 57% among children in the greater Seattle area, and adult use had increased to 70%. Five years into the campaign, an HIPRC evaluation revealed its ultimate impact: Admissions at five Seattle-area hospitals for bicycle-related head injuries had dropped by approximately two thirds for children 5–14 years old.

Decrease Nonmonetary Costs for Behavior

Tactics are also available for decreasing *time, effort,* and *physical* or *psychological* costs. Fox suggests reducing usage time by "embedding" a new behavior into present activities.[12] Thus, people might be encouraged to floss their teeth while they watch television. People can also be encouraged to "anchor" a new behavior to an established habit.[13] To encourage physical activity, for example, you can recommend that people climb the stairs to their third-floor office instead of taking the elevator.

Gemunden proposed several potential tactics for reducing other nonmonetary costs in this model:

1. Against a perceived psychological risk, provide social products in ways that deliver *psychological rewards such as public recognition.*
2. Against a perceived social risk, gather *endorsements from credible sources* that reduce the potential stigma or embarrassment of adopting a product.
3. Against a perceived usage risk, provide target adopters with *reassuring information* on the product or with a free trial of the product so they can experience how the product does what it promises to do.
4. Against perceived physical risk, solicit *seals of approval* from authoritative institutions, such as the American Dental Association, the American Medical Association, or other highly respected organizations.[14]

Example: Redeeming Farmers' Market Checks. Offices of the Supplemental Nutrition Program for Women, Infants, and Children (WIC) often distribute checks to qualified families to purchase fresh fruits and vegetables at local farmers' markets. Yet clients often face significant nonmonetary costs that lead to lower redemption rates than many WIC offices would like to see. Many experience increased *effort* in finding the market and parking, *embarrassment* around other shoppers when using a WIC check, *difficulty* in identifying qualified produce when signs are inconsistently displayed or hard to see, *concern* about not getting change back from checks, *frustration* with misplacing checks that are often stored in drawers or forgotten in strollers, and *fear* of what the WIC counselor will think if they decline the checks, even though their chances of using them are minimal, given work schedules that conflict with market hours.

These costs could be overcome with a variety of tactics related to the price tool as well as to the other Ps:

- Detailed maps showing the way to the market and parking areas printed on the backs of checks
- Electronic debit cards in place of the checks
- Signs on poles above the stands that display some recognizable logo that doesn't "brand" the client, such as the 5 a Day logo
- Printing checks in lower amounts, such as $1 denominations
- Packaging checks in sturdy check folders
- Offering hesitant clients fewer checks and more if they use them all

Increase Monetary Costs for Competing Behaviors

In the social marketing environment, this tactic is likely to involve influencing policymakers, as the most effective monetary strategies against the competition often require *increasing taxes* (e.g., on gas-guzzling cars), *imposing fines* (e.g., for not recycling), and/or *decreasing funding* (e.g., if a school doesn't offer an hour of physical education classes). As Alan Andreasen lays out in his book *Social Marketing in the 21st Century*, these policy changes may be critical to significant social change, and the social marketer can play a role in making this happen. "Our models and frameworks are flexible enough to guide efforts aimed at this kind of upstream behavior, especially for the many smaller organizations, especially at the local level, that cannot afford lobbyists."[15] Andreasen proposes that you use familiar components of the social marketing model. You can segment the potential audience using the stages of change model, and in the legislative environment, this may be translated into those who are opponents, undecideds, or supporters. You will then benefit from identifying and understanding your priority audience's BCOS factors: *benefits, costs*, and *others* in the priority audience's environment and their influence and *self-assurance* (perceptions of opportunity and ability).[16] These should sound familiar as well.

In the following example, a social marketing approach upstream helped pass a law to influence behaviors downstream, one expected to save lives.

Example: *Persuading Legislators*. As of January 2010, only 15 states and the District of Columbia had made it a primary offense to **text and drive**, and only five states and the District of Columbia had made it a primary offense to talk on handheld cell phones while driving. Washington state was one of the states where this was only a secondary offense, meaning a driver must have done something else wrong (e.g., weaving across lane markers) to be ticketed.[17] Two state legislators and a volunteer citizen task force stepped up efforts to persuade the legislature and the governor to pass a new law (*desired behavior*), one that would allow the police to pull over drivers talking on their cell phones or texting while driving. They used a social marketing approach, and their first step was to understand concerns legislators had about voting yes. Several major barriers were identified. A few are presented in Table 11.2, along with responses presented at testimonies to legislative committees.

Washington's new law was passed and went into effect on June 10, 2010, and is still enforced as of 2022. Tickets are $124 for talking on handheld cell phones while driving or texting while

TABLE 11.2 ■ Addressing Barriers to Passing a Primary Cell Phone and Texting Law

Major Concerns Expressed by Legislators	Responses From Advocates
"My constituents will argue that talking on a cell phone is no more dangerous than putting on makeup or eating food. They'll claim laws against this will be next."	Human factors experts tell us that there are three kinds of driving distractions. The first is visual—eyes off the road. The second is mechanical—hands off the wheel. The third is cognitive—when our mind is not fully engaged on the task of driving. Talking on a handheld cell phone or texting involves all three. As a result, one study shows that drivers talking on cell phones are as impaired as drunk drivers who have a 0.08% blood alcohol level and those texting while driving are equivalent to those with a 0.24% blood alcohol level.
"I don't understand how talking on a phone is any different than talking with a passenger in the vehicle."	There is one very important difference. A passenger in a vehicle is aware of the driving situation and can even serve as an additional lookout for hazards. He or she also understands when there is a needed pause in a conversation.
"A law like this would not be enforceable."	Although we won't see all offenders, this law would give us the important ability, though after the fact, to assess additional penalties on those who have chosen to act recklessly or irresponsibly.

driving. Drivers must use hands-free devices, and teens with intermediate driver's licenses or learner permits may not use a wireless device at all while driving, including a hands-free device, unless they're reporting an emergency.

Increase Nonmonetary Costs for Competing Behavior

Nonmonetary tactics can also be used to increase actual or perceived nonmonetary costs associated with choosing the competing behavior. In this case, you may be creating or emphasizing negative public recognition. In the spring of 2013, dog owners in a village near Madrid, for example, started receiving unpleasant home deliveries if they failed to pick up their pets' waste on the streets. It worked like this: Volunteers waited for someone to abandon their dog's poop on the streets. While some of the volunteers snatched up the poop without being seen, others approached the dog owner and found out the dog's name and breed. Volunteers would then search the town's pet registration database to find the owner's address. The pet's waste was then dropped off at the corresponding address in a box labeled "Lost Property." One report on results indicated that the amount of dog poop seen on the streets of Brunete decreased by 70%.[18]

In Tacoma, Washington, a website features properties not in full compliance with municipal codes. They call it "The Filthy 15," and although property owners' names do not appear on the website, it does include photos of each building, specific reasons the property is on the list, and what is next in the cleanup process, including something a neighbor or other concerned citizen could track.[19]

And in Denver, Colorado, in 2008, a judge tried a new nonmonetary disincentive to decrease noise ordinance violators, many of them teenagers. In addition to the normal fine, they were required to sit in a room and listen to music they did not like, that of Barry Manilow. Some characterized it as "cruel and unusual punishment" for this age group.[20]

In a different scenario, you might be highlighting the downsides of the competition, as illustrated in the following example in which research was key to understanding what costs should be highlighted.

Example: Encouraging Teen Abstinence. The Teen Aware Project is part of a statewide effort to reduce teen pregnancy and is sponsored by the Washington State Office of Superintendent of Public Instruction. Funds are allocated through a competitive federally funded grant process to public middle/junior and senior high schools for the development of media campaigns to promote sexual abstinence and the importance of delaying sexual activity, pregnancy, and childbearing. This campaign example shows how nonmonetary costs can be used to encourage a behavior. However, it is important to note that recent research has shown that abstinence—only sex education tends not to be effective and can be counterproductive to the health and wellness of teens by withholding potentially life-saving information on HIV and other sexually transmitted diseases.[21]

These campaigns were substantially designed and produced by students. Student media products include video and radio productions, posters, theater productions, print advertising, multimedia, T-shirts, buttons, and websites. Campaign messages are distributed in local project schools and communities.

This particular research effort was conducted by teens at Mercer Island High School, a grant recipient. A team of nine students from marketing, health, and communications classes volunteered to develop the campaign, from start to finish. Several teachers and outside consultants served as coaches on the project.[22] At the time this research effort was undertaken, the team had chosen their campaign focus (abstinence), purpose (reducing teen pregnancies), priority audience (eighth-graders), and campaign objective (to persuade students to "pause and think in a heated moment"). Information from existing student surveys indicated that about 75% of eighth-graders—but only 25% of seniors—were abstinent. It was decided that the campaign bull's-eye would be eighth-graders, who were seen as being the most vulnerable in terms of making choices regarding sexual activity.

The team of juniors and seniors wanted to refresh their memories about middle school years. As one student expressed it, "It's been a long time since I was an eighth-grader, and I don't have a clue what they know and think about sex these days." The primary purposes of their research were to (a) help with decision-making regarding which benefits of abstinence and costs related to sexual activity should be highlighted in the campaign and (b) provide input for selecting a slogan for the campaign. More specifically, the study was designed to determine major perceived benefits of abstinence, costs associated with being sexually active, and messages (and tone) that would be most effective in influencing an eighth-grader to consider abstinence.

Each of the nine students agreed to conduct casual interviews with at least five eighth-graders over a one-week period. They used an informal script that explained the project and assured respondents that their comments would be anonymous. They recorded and summarized responses to the following three open-ended questions:

1. What's the most important reason you can think of for delaying having intercourse until you are older?
2. What are the worst things you can think of that can happen to you if you have intercourse before you are ready?
3. What would you say to your best friend if she or he told you that they thought they were going to have sex for the first time tonight?

Interviews were conducted, with district permission, before and after classes at the middle schools as well as at informal settings such as sports events, after-school programs, and friends' homes. Students returned to class the following week, shared summaries of their findings, and were guided to identify the following themes for each of the informational areas:

- Major reasons for delaying sex:
    - You won't get sexually transmitted diseases (STDs).
    - You can save it for someone special.
    - You won't get pregnant.
- The worst things that can happen:
    - They could drop you later for someone else.
    - You could get pregnant, and childbirth really hurts.
    - You can get really bad STDs, like crabs.
- Words for a friend:
    - "You should wait until you are older."
    - "Are you sure he really loves you?"
    - "Do you have protection?"
    - "Are you ready for all the things that could happen?"

The team used this input to develop a campaign centered around three "gross" consequences of having sex before you're ready. They developed the campaign slogan "Are you ready?" and followed the question with each of the three consequences. Graphic, in-your-face images were reflected on the posters and depicted in radio scripts (see Figures 11.2–11.4).

Radio spots that were played on the high school radio station followed the three gross consequence themes. In one, a male voice says,

> I remember the day I learned what an STD really was. I had seen little things crawling around in my... hair. I woke up in the middle of the night, my... you know... was burning from an itch. My entire crotch was swarming with miniature crabs. Finally, I had to get help. If you think you're going to have sex, ask yourself, "Are you ready for that?"
>
> *(see Figure 11.2)*

In another approach, a girl graphically recounts the pain of giving birth (see Figure 11.3). And in the third spot, a girl sadly yet frankly relates how the guy she slept with immediately told everyone at school and found a new girlfriend. It took her years to trust a guy again (see Figure 11.4).

FIGURE 11.2 ■ Abstinence Campaign Poster

Source: Washington State Office of Superintendent of Public Instruction.

MORE ON COMMITMENTS AND PLEDGES

As noted earlier, we consider commitments and pledges as nonmonetary incentives, adding value to adopting a desired behavior, most often in the form of increased self-respect and/or public reputation. In terms of distinctions between commitments and pledges, many use the term *pledge* when referring to actually signing a form or clicking a box on a website, expressing the *commitment*.

Doug McKenzie-Mohr distinguished four forms of commitments in a workshop in 2017 at the World Social Marketing Conference: verbal, written, public, and durable. He encouraged the use of public (vs. private) and durable (vs. only visible temporarily) commitments, as they are the most likely to motivate individuals to keep their as well as foster social diffusion. An

FIGURE 11.3 ■ Abstinence Campaign Poster

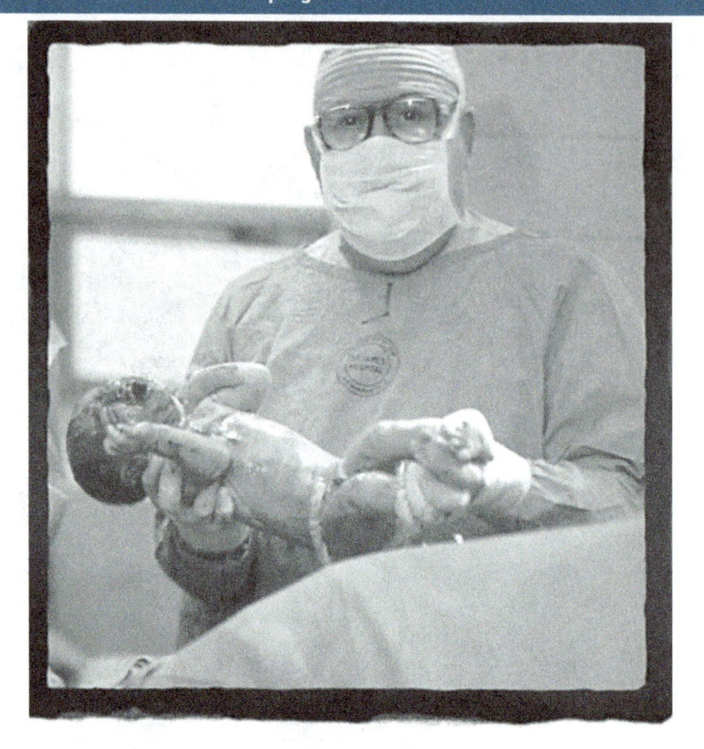

Source: Washington State Office of Superintendent of Public Instruction.

example of a public and durable commitment might be a sticker on top of a garbage bin, one with a graphic of a dog and the phrase "We Scoop the Poop and Place It in the Trash" visible to neighbors while placing their bin on the same curb. Doug also stressed that commitments can be a key tactic to help move an audience from intention to behavior. An example might be where a dog owner attending the special event described in the opening case highlight indicated they were interested in the upcoming *Leave It* trainings. A call or email asking if they planned to attend the session next month would certainly increase the likelihood they would, especially if they said "Yes."

In April 2022, we asked members of the Georgetown and International Social Marketing Association listserves for examples of the use of commitments and pledges in social marketing efforts and received the following examples

FIGURE 11.4 ■ Abstinence Campaign Poster

Are you ready?

Mercer Island Teens For Delaying Sex

Source: Washington State Office of Superintendent of Public Instruction.

- Jennifer Tabanico, President of Action Research, shared about an effort in 2022, working with the Orange County Stormwater program (H_2OC) to reduce litter at skateparks with a focus on youth skaters who were leaving items behind when returning to skate or leaving the park. Interviews informed and inspired a campaign to influence skaters to make a *public, written, and durable commitment* to check for their trash and throw it away before leaving the park. Youth were asked to sign their name on a commitment sticker placed on a poster and displayed at the park. Participants were then given a sticker to put on their skateboard or helmet to serve as a prompt. A pilot test gained a **commitment participation rate of 85.2%**, and observations of litter during the weeks before and after the event showed a **57% reduction in the litter accumulation** rate following the pilot event. Note that three variations of the commitment stickers were used, each representing a unique skate character.

The characters were designed to represent common California species impacted by pollution of local waterways—an octopus, shark, and heron. Skaters could choose whichever character sticker they liked best.[23]

- Jacqueline Devine, a Social and Behavior Change Advisor in Maryland, shared about **stickK**, a platform created by behavioral economists at Yale University to help people leverage the power of incentives and accountability. The model supports users to develop a 3 step plan-of-action: (1) define their goal; (2) pick a timeline to accomplish it; and (3) put something at stake. As the **stickK** website elaborates, "So whether you'd like to lose weight, quit smoking or spend more time with your grandkids, **stickK** is the go-to- goal-setting tool for you."[24]
- Taylor Rhoades, a project manager at Action Research, provided information about a fishing line recycling project run by the Plastic Pollution Prevention Partnership (P3P) in Texas, with a purpose to decrease animals and birds ingesting or becoming entangled in plastic debris, with a focus on discarded (littered) fishing lines, one of the biggest threats identified. Intentions were to create a sustainable behavior, one not only easy for anglers to adopt, but "easy to practice again and again." To encourage this, anglers were asked to pose for a photo and sign it, pledging to recycle their fishing line to help save sea turtles. These photos were then publicly posted on a bulletin board near the entrance of their fishing site. Anglers committing to recycling their line are then given a sticker to put on their tackle box, serving as a prompt (see Figure 11.5). Pledge stickers were printed in Vietnamese, Spanish, and English to represent the three dominant languages spoken by anglers in the area. After four months of testing at a mini-pilot site, there was a 32% increase of line in the bins versus on the ground.[25]

FIGURE 11.5 ■ A Public Commitment and Prompt for Recycling Fishing Lines Placed on Tackle Boxes

Source: Taylor Rhoades.

SETTING PRICES FOR TANGIBLE GOODS AND SERVICES

Prices for tangible goods and services involved in social marketing campaigns are typically set by manufacturers, retailers, and service providers. Social marketers are more often involved in helping to decide what tangible goods and services would be beneficial in facilitating behavior change, recommending discount coupons and related incentives and then promoting their use.

When a social marketer gets involved in the price setting, however, several principles can guide decision-making. Three options to consider include the following:

1. *Cost-based pricing*, where prices are based on a desired or established profit margin or rate of return on investment (e.g., condoms are sold at community clinics at prices to cover purchase costs).
2. *Competitive-based pricing*, where prices are more driven by the prices for competing (similar) products and services (e.g., a life vest manufacturer partnering on a drowning prevention campaign offers discount coupons to make pricing similar to less expensive vests that are not Coast Guard approved).
3. *Value-based pricing*, where prices are based on an analysis of the target adopters' "price sensitivity," evaluating demand at varying price points (e.g., food waste composters that require simple spinning are priced higher than those requiring manual tossing).

Ethical Considerations for Pricing Strategies

Ethical considerations related to pricing strategies include issues of *social equity* (e.g., fixed vs. sliding scale fees), *potential exploitation* (e.g., encouraging abstinence only knowing that it may increase rates of HIV and STDs among teens, like a program in North Carolina to reduce teen pregnancy, giving a dollar for each day not pregnant to teens who have never been pregnant, want to attend college, and have a sister who gave birth as a teen), impact and fairness of *public shame* tactics (e.g., what if owners of one of the Filthy 15 buildings have lost their job, and this explains why they haven't repaired their dilapidated building), and *full disclosure* of costs (e.g., requirements to toss food composters daily in order to receive stated benefits). In the case of promoting farmers' markets to WIC clients, each of these issues might apply. Should clients receive additional checks if they use all of their first set, making it necessary to give some clients only half a pack? What do we do about the fact that many items at the market are less than the $2 check denomination and yet change cannot be given? Are we consistent about telling our clients that they will probably need to pay $3 for parking while at the markets?

COVID-19 Social Marketing Example

An article written in 2022 by the National Academies of Sciences, Engineering, and Medicine, Division of Behavioral and Social Sciences and Education[26], included the following incentive-related recommendations (primarily monetary-related), ones that social marketers could consider for Price tool interventions related to COVID-19 containment:

- *The incentive is known and well-advertised.*

(e.g., social media)

- *The incentive is delivered immediately.*

(e.g., gift card received at the vaccination site)

- *The incentive is valued.*

(e.g., a hunting license for rural residents getting vaccinated)

- *The incentive is cost-effective.*

(e.g., lotteries, given individuals tend to overestimate chances of winning)

- *The incentive meets ethical and health equity criteria.*

(e.g., modest cash awards could unfairly induce those who are least well-off)

It is also important to remember that incentives will have varying impacts on different priority audience groups. In the case of the COVID-19 vaccine, the Washington State Department of Health found that for People with Conservative Values and members of the Black/African American Community offering an incentive (lottery, money, and gifts) actually decreased willingness and intent to get the vaccine. This was because people felt that there must really be something wrong with the vaccine if the government needed to "bribe" them to get it. This points to the importance of doing research with your priority audience segments prior to setting your incentive strategy.

CHAPTER SUMMARY

The price of a social marketing product is *the cost that the priority audience associates with adopting the new behavior.* Costs may be monetary or nonmonetary in nature. Your task is to use this second tool to help ensure that what you offer the audience (*benefits*) is equal to or greater than what they will have to give (*costs*). As noted, the *product* and *place* tools are also used to increase benefits and decrease costs (e.g., providing more convenient locations to recycle is a *place* strategy). Your objective (and opportunity) with the *price* tool is to develop and offer *incentives* that can be used to provide one or more of the following six impacts. The first four tactics focus on the desired behavior and the last two on the competing one(s):

1. Increase monetary benefits for *the desired behavior.*
2. Increase nonmonetary benefits for *the desired behavior.*
3. Decrease monetary costs for *the desired behavior.*
4. Decrease nonmonetary costs for *the desired behavior.*
5. Increase monetary costs for *the competing behavior.*
6. Increase nonmonetary costs for *the competing behavior.*

Although most prices for tangible goods and services are established by manufacturers, retailers, and service providers, several principles can guide a social marketer faced with price-setting decisions, beginning with establishing pricing objectives. What do you want the price to accomplish for you? Once that is defined, you will likely decide to establish your price based on cost, the competition, or the perceived value that the product holds for your priority audience.

RESEARCH HIGHLIGHT
INCREASING THE HABIT OF HANDWASHING IN INDIA

2016–2018

This Research Highlight explores the potential impact of both monetary and nonmonetary incentives on habit formation. Reshmaan Hussam, an assistant professor at Harvard Business School, and her colleagues conducted a randomized field experiment in rural West Bengal, India, that provided sound conclusions, ones the authors of the study considered "a clean victory."[27]

Background

Every year more than a million children under the age of five die from diarrheal diseases and pneumonia.[28] Regular handwashing with soap is believed to have a substantial impact on child health in the developing world. Unfortunately, most handwashing campaigns sponsored by major health organizations in the developing world have been primarily education campaigns and have failed to establish and maintain a regular practice (habit) of handwashing.[29]

When Hussam and her fellow researchers conducted their formative research, including an initial survey of several thousand rural households in West Bengal, India, they discovered that

> people don't wash their hands with soap for the same reason most of us don't run three miles every morning or drink eight glasses of water every day, despite our doctors lecturing us on the benefits of cardiovascular exercise and hydration. It's not that we are uniformed, unable, or lazy. It's that we're just not in the habit.[30]

In fact, this preliminary survey in the study area also showed that although 79% of mothers could articulate, without being prompted, that the purpose of soap is to kill germs, only 8% said they used soap before cooking and only 14% before eating. And confirming preliminary assumptions, some 57% of the respondents reported that the reason they didn't wash their hands was simply because "I do not have the habit."[31]

Research Objectives

With this in mind, researchers designed a field experiment to answer the following more specific questions:

1. Is handwashing with soap a potentially habit-forming behavior?
2. If so, can the habit be induced by interventions?
3. Will the habit continue after the interventions cease?

Methodology

The first intervention was a simple wall-mounted soap dispenser (*product*) with a time-stamped sensor hidden inside, designed in partnership with engineers at the MIT Media Lab. The sensor allowed the team to determine not only how often people were washing their hands (*nonmonetary incentive*) but also whether they were doing so before dinner, seen as critical to an effective intervention. This approach allowed researchers the ability to isolate the various interventions in a way that self-reports or observation research could not do reliably.

A second intervention was a *monetary incentive* in the form of a ticket for each day they washed their hands. Tickets could be accumulated and cashed in for various goods and gifts in a prize catalog.

The experiment included 3,763 young children and their parents in 2,943 households across 10 villages in West Bengal, where women traditionally manage both cooking and childcare. At rollout, all households received a basic information campaign regarding the importance of washing hands with soap, especially prior to eating. Researchers then randomly divided households into two groups, those that would receive dispensers and those that would not, approximately 1,400 each. The group receiving dispensers were then randomly divided into six groups:

Group A: Dispensers and Monitoring Only

1. Told their handwashing would be tracked from the get go and that they would receive feedback reports on their soap usage
2. Told their behavior would be tracked in a few months
3. (Control group for monitoring) Not told their soap use would be tracked

Group B: Dispensers, Monitoring, and Incentives

1. Told they would receive one ticket for each day they washed their hands
2. Told they would receive one ticket each day for washing their hands with soap and in two months would begin receiving three tickets every day they used the dispenser
3. (Control group for incentives) Were not told of the possible incentives

Findings

Authors of the study concluded the following:[32]

- Both monitoring and monetary incentives increased handwashing relative to receiving only a dispenser.

- ○ Households aware they were being monitored were 23% more likely to use soap if they knew they were being monitored.
- ○ Seventy percent of households receiving the tickets (*monetary incentives*) used their soap dispensers regularly throughout the experiment, compared with 30% of households that received the dispensers without incentive.

- These effects persist after monitoring or incentives were removed.
- The anticipation of monitoring increases handwashing rates significantly.

In terms of impact of the dispensers, when compared with households that did not have soap dispensers, the intervention resulted in healthier children in households that received a soap dispenser, with a 20% decrease in acute respiratory infections and a 30%–40% decrease in loose stools. In addition, the children with soap dispensers ended up weighing more and even growing taller.[33]

Commentary

In a concluding comment, Hussam shared, "Wherever we go, habits define much of what we do. This work can help us understand how to design interventions that help us cultivate the good ones."[34]

DISCUSSION QUESTIONS AND EXERCISES

1. One of the concerns that has been expressed regarding the use of monetary incentives is their "durability," meaning that behaviors that are influenced primarily through monetary incentives might revert back once the incentive is removed, perhaps even dropping below initial levels. What is an example you can think of that used monetary incentives to launch an effort, and you question whether the behavior would be sustainable once incentives are removed?
2. Discuss pledges or commitment programs you have used or are aware of.
3. In the Research Highlight in India, what was the nonmonetary incentive and what did you think about the evidence that showed it made a difference? Were you surprised?

12 STEP 7.3: PLACE

Making Access Convenient and Pleasant

LEARNING OBJECTIVES

Upon completion of this chapter, you should be able to:

12.1 Describe the meaning of Place for social marketing efforts.

12.2 Explain what 10 Place strategies can make behavior change more likely.

12.3 Discuss what ethical considerations are relevant when developing a Place strategy.

Store-based retailers often say that the three most important things in the success of their businesses are "location, location, location!" You may find this true for many social marketing efforts as well. Consider how much lower the following scores would be without the convenient-access component of these programs:

- *Recycling.* In 2018, Americans recycled an estimated 50% of aluminum cans, and 31% of glass containers.[1] Although this is certainly not as much as we would like to see, imagine how grim the statistics would be without curb side recycling and recycle containers in office buildings and most public places.
- *Pet waste pickup.* Although an estimated 40% of dog owners in the United States do not pick up their dog's waste, at least 60% do, and without bag dispensers and waste bins (*products*) being made available in parks and public properties around the country (*place*), we can imagine that number would be smaller.[2]
- *Tobacco quitlines.* The prevalence of smoking among adults in the United States declined from about 25% in 1990 to 12.5% in 2020.[3] Most tobacco users across the states have access to quitlines (*product*), which provide telephone counseling to help them quit, and in some cases, these lines provide limited access to medication. Quitlines overcome many barriers to traditional smoking cessation classes as they require no transportation and are available at the smoker's convenience (*place*).
- *Organ donations.* Many initiatives around the world aim to increase the number of organs obtained from deceased donors. Convenience of registering as an organ donor is one important strategy, with many countries now offering registration through

driver's license bureaus or departments of motor vehicles (*place*), where individuals can designate their wish to be an organ donor on their license, whether obtaining one for the first time, or upon renewal.[4]

In this chapter, you'll read about 10 strategies for increasing convenience of access and making the desired behavior easier and more pleasant to carry out. The following Case Highlight presents four innovative uses of the *place* intervention tool, underscoring the power, applicability, and diversity of this third "P."

CASE HIGHLIGHT
FOUR INNOVATIVE USES OF THE PLACE TOOL

Cutting Shower Times in Switzerland

In Switzerland in 2012, water heating was the second largest residential energy end use, and showering accounted for more than 80% of this hot water demand.[5] A pilot program in 2012 and 2013 led by Dr. Verena Tiefenbeck at ETH Zurich, a STEM university, was developed with a *purpose* to reduce shower times and a *focus* on providing feedback to residents regarding their hot water and energy usage related to showers. Although feedback on energy use had been implemented in the past and had provided information about usage levels, it had not focused on a single, energy-intensive activity such as showering. Most of these historic feedback programs consisted of monthly or quarterly reports that were mailed to households, leading to substantial time lags in providing feedback and insubstantial savings.

The pilot program, branded *ewz-Amphiro study*, was designed to promote showering behavior that reduced energy and water use by providing convenient access to real-time, engaging, and nonjudgmental feedback. Marketing interventions included:

- *Product:* Participants in the pilot were provided a monitoring device that was quite simple to install in any shower with a handheld showerhead, which most people have in Europe. It could be installed without any tools.
- *Place:* The shower meter hung at eye level, providing easy-to-read, real-time information, displaying current water temperature and how much water and energy had been used since the water was turned on.
- *Promotion:* The shower meter also displayed a short animation of a polar bear standing on an ice flow, depicting that if you took a long shower, the ice flow shrank and eventually the animation would disappear (see Figure 12.1).

Relative to a control group, treatment groups reduced their shower time by an average of roughly 20%, which reduced water consumption by 21% and energy consumption by 22%.[6]

Increasing Use of Sunscreen

Skin cancer is the most common cancer in the United States, with more skin cancers diagnosed each year than all other cancers combined.[7] Most are caused by too much exposure to ultraviolet (UV) rays, with most of this coming from the sun. The good news is that exposure to UV radiation is the most preventable risk factor for all types of cancer, including melanoma. And yet CDC found in 2022 that only 25.7% of men and 48.1% of women ages 25+_reported that they extensively use sunscreen on both their face and other exposed

FIGURE 12.1 ■ Shower Meter Providing Real-Time Water and Energy Use, as Well as an Animated Display of the Ice Melting Below the Polar Bear as the Shower Goes On

Source: Verena Tiefenbeck.

skin.[8] Although for some a barrier is the competition, "wanting to get a tan," many report that "sunscreen is expensive" or "I forgot to bring it with me." Could the *place* tool help? What about convenient access to free sunscreen?

In 2014, the nonprofit **Impact Melanoma** and the company Bright Guard launched a partnership to help make this happen, having installed since 2017 over 2,000 free sunscreen dispensers across all 50 states in a variety of locations including beaches, parks, schools, and special events.[9] At one special event in Minnesota, for example, an observation research study at the annual state fair estimated that 17,000 persons used the sunscreen over the course of the event and concluded the public was clearly highly receptive to easy and free access to sunscreen.[10] It removed their barriers!

The **Impact Melanoma** program continues to expand across the United States, supported by special virtual fundraising events such as "Martinis for Melanoma" in May of 2022, which included live music performances.[11]

Increasing Bike Sharing

In March of 2022, Doug McKenzie-Mohr's *Fostering Behavior Change Minute* featured programs that were "Making Biking Convenient", sharing a milestone that as of August 2021, 57 years after the first bike-sharing program was launched in Amsterdam in 1965, there were "nearly 10 million shared bikes and 3,000 bike-sharing systems across the world."[12] As he noted, "the concept is disarmingly simple" providing easy and appealing access:

- Bikes are provided at numerous convenient stations or locations.
- Users can register to use the bike at the station or online.
- Registrations can be for as short as a day, or as long as a year.

- Once registered, riders then obtain their bike by either entering a code, swiping a registration card, or using their phone.
- They then drop off the bike at another station or leave it parked close to their destinations.

Increasing Family Planning in Uganda

In Uganda, as of 2016, 44% of pregnancies were unplanned.[13] One intervention strategy that the Uganda Health Marketing Group (UHMG) employs to meet unmet needs for family planning (FP) services focuses on reducing access barriers for working couples, often challenged by a lack of time to travel to FP clinics to partake in counseling and receiving FP products. UHMG addresses this barrier by taking products and services to workplaces throughout the country, with services varying by whether a factory or nonfactory setting. In the factories, given the diverse nature of staff, service providers conduct discussions and counseling sessions focused on family planning with all staff, then set up service points for those in need of immediate services. They use a mobile clinic or bus (see Figure 12.2) and a tent to offer injectables, pills, IUDs, and implants. In the nonfactor settings such a banks, markets, and plantations, customer care call centers are set up with services including a midwife who presents the various family planning options.

FIGURE 12.2 ■ Male Workers at Pramukh Steel Rolling Mills Accessing Condoms From the Mobile Clinic

Source: Uganda Health Marketing Group.

Through these workplace activations approach, UHMG reached 120 workplaces between July 2016 and October 2017 across Uganda, reaching 5,503 individuals with the family planning methods of their choice.[14]

PLACE: THE THIRD "P"

Place is where and when the priority audience will perform the desired behavior, acquire any related goods, and/or receive any associated services.

We live in a convenience-oriented world in which many of us highly value our time, trying to save some of it for our families, friends, and favorite leisure activities. As a social marketer, you'll want to be keenly aware that your priority audience will evaluate the convenience of your offer relative to other exchanges in their lives. You'll also want to be cognizant of the access barriers that are inherent in our communities that limit equitable place-based access (think of access to transit services, larger grocery stores that carry fresh food choices, parks, safe places to exercise, healthcare facilities, mental health services, etc.). If your program is one where access is inequitable for some people, you can use place-based strategies to help provide equitable access.

The convenience bar has been raised over the past decades for all marketers by companies such as Starbucks, McDonald's, Federal Express, 1–800–Flowers, Netflix for online movie rentals, and, of course, Amazon.

In commercial sector marketing, place is often referred to as the distribution channel, and options and potential examples for social marketing are pervasive:

- *Physical locations:* Recycle stations at retail outlets
- *Phone:* Domestic violence helpline
- *Mobile phone apps:* To find out when the next bus arrives
- *Mail:* Postage-paid plastic bags for recycling mobile phones
- *Email:* An agreement to quit smoking signed online by both patient and physician and forwarded to a quitline
- *Internet:* Rideshare matching
- *Mobile units:* For hazardous waste
- *Where people shop:* Mammograms in a department store
- *Where people spend time together:* HIV tests at gay bars
- *Drive-throughs:* For COVID-19 vaccinations at medical centers
- *Home delivery/house calls*: Home energy audits
- *Kiosks:* For determining blood pressure
- *Vending machines*: Condoms
- *Application forms:* A box on a driver's license form where you can select to become an organ donor

It is important to clarify and stress that place is *not the same as communication channel*, which is where your communications will appear (e.g., social media, brochures, radio ads, news stories, and personal presentations). Chapter 13 presents a detailed discussion of communication channels.

STEP 7.3: DEVELOP PLACE STRATEGY

Your objective with the place marketing intervention tool is to develop strategies that will make it as convenient and pleasant as possible for your priority audience to perform the behavior, acquire any goods, and/or receive any services. It is especially helpful in reducing access-related barriers (e.g., lack of transportation) and time-related barriers (e.g., being at work all day). It can also break down psychological barriers (e.g., providing needle exchange programs on street corners vs. at a community health clinic). You will also want to do anything possible and within reason to make the competing behavior (seem) less convenient (e.g., the lack of convenient and available parking spots for single occupant vehicles vs. carpools at work sites). The next sections of this chapter will elaborate on 10 successful strategies for you to consider.

1. Make the Location Closer

Example: A Dental Office on Wheels. Many children don't get the regular dental care they need. They may be struggling with language barriers, poverty, rural isolation, or homelessness. A mobile clinic called the SmileMobile travels to communities across Washington state. This modern dental office on wheels brings dental services directly to children aged 13 and younger

FIGURE 12.3 ■ Making Dental Care for Children More Accessible

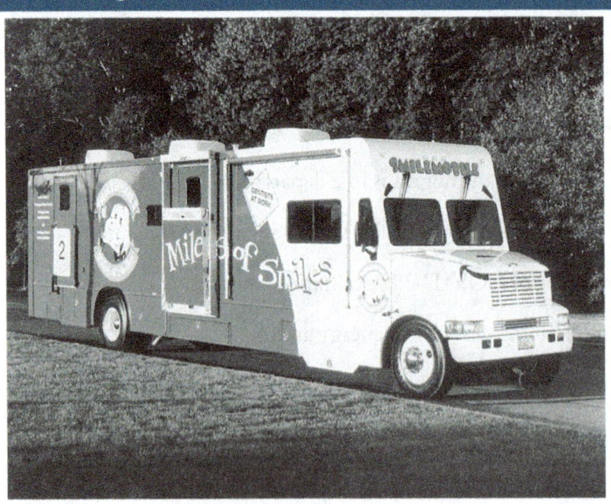

Source: Reprinted with permission from the Washington Dental Service Foundation, Making Dental Care for Children More Accessible. SmileMobile was developed by Washington Dental Service (WDS), the Washington State Dental Association (WSDA), and the Washington Dental Service Foundation (WDSF).

who don't otherwise have access to care. Children enrolled in Medicaid have no out-of-pocket expenses, and other children are charged on a sliding fee schedule. Families may even enroll in Medicaid at the SmileMobile.

The SmileMobile was developed by Washington Dental Service, the Washington State Dental Association, and the Washington Dental Service Foundation (see Figure 12.3). Staff work closely with local health departments and community, charitable, and business organizations to coordinate visits to cities and towns throughout the state. Every effort is made to reach the neediest children and provide translators for non-English-speaking patients and their families. The mobile clinic first hit the road in 1995 and by 2022 had treated more than 44,000 children throughout the state.[15]

Additional examples illustrating ways to save your priority audience a little time, effort, and travel include the following:

- Exercise facilities at work sites
- COVID-19 vaccinations offered at grocery stores
- Print cartridges recycled at office supply stores
- Litter receptacles that make it easy to drive by and deposit litterbags
- Dental floss kept in the TV room or, better yet, attached to the remote control
- Christmas tree recycling drop-off at the local high school
- Bins for unwanted clothing placed in residential buildings
- Mobile libraries reaching rural areas

2. Extend Hours

Example: Vote by Mail: A survey of 15,167 citizens who had not voted in the 2008 presidential election in the United States indicated that the number-one reason for this was that they were "too busy or had a conflicting schedule." "Oregon, however, had one of the highest voter turnouts in the nation, with 86% of registered voters voting in the 2008 presidential election.[16]" Perhaps this is because voting is so convenient, with Oregonians *voting only by mail.* There are no polling places, and election day is just a deadline to turn in your ballot and has been that way since 1998, when nearly 70% of Oregonians approved the Vote by Mail initiative. Some believe it is the most "effective, efficient and fraud-free way to conduct an election."

Oregon, as of 2020, continues to have one of the highest rankings in terms of voter turnout, with a Vote by Mail system that is simple, straightforward, and most of all, convenient. Ballots are mailed to registered voters 14–18 days before an election. Voters can complete the ballot "in the comfort of their own home" and on their own schedule. They have two weeks to return the ballot through the mail, or they can drop it off at one of many official conveniently located sites, including ones in a downtown park (see Figure 12.4). And there are additional advantages as well, including reduced election costs (since there are no polling places) and the fact that some

FIGURE 12.4 ■ One of Oregon's Conveniently Located Ballot Boxes in a Park in Downtown Portland

Source: Author photo.

feel voters give more thought to how they mark their ballots, having access to campaign materials at their fingertips.[17]

Additional examples of strategies that offer priority audiences more options in terms of time and day of the week include the following:

- Vending machines in shelters for the homeless that have donations from supermarkets, accessible with a key card for a limited number of items a day
- Licensed childcare searches online (vs. calling a telephone center during normal business hours)
- Twenty-four-hour helplines for counseling and information
- Hand sanitizers available at entry to restaurants
- Natural yard care workshops offered weekday evenings

3. Be There at the Point of Decision-Making

Many social marketers have found that an ideal moment to speak to the priority audience is when they are about to choose between alternative, competing behaviors. They are at a fork in the road, with your desired behavior in one direction and their current behavior, or a potential undesirable one, in the other. Presenting the offer at a priority audience's point of decision-making can be powerful, giving you one last chance to influence their choice.

Example: Ecstasy Pill Testing at Nightclubs. DanceSafe is a nonprofit organization promoting health and safety within the rave and nightclub community, with local chapters throughout the United States and Canada. They report that they neither condone nor condemn the use of any drug. Rather, they engage in efforts to reduce drug-related harm by providing health and safety information and on-site pill testing to those who do use drugs.[18] Among other programs and services, volunteers in communities with chapters offer *on-site pill testing* to ecstasy users at raves, nightclubs, and other public events where ecstasy is being used socially. Users who are unsure of the authenticity of a pill they possess can bring it to a booth or table where trained harm-reduction volunteers will test it for use. DanceSafe reports on its website that volunteers staff booths at raves, nightclubs, and other dance events, where they also provide information on drugs, safe sex, and other health and safety issues concerning the dance community (such as driving home safely and protecting one's hearing).[19]

Other creative solutions that can influence decision-making "just in time" include the following:

- Place a glass bowl of fruits and vegetables at eye level in the refrigerator versus in closed drawers on the bottom shelf.
- Negotiate with retailers to place natural fertilizers in a prominent display at the beginning of the aisle.
- Place a small, inexpensive plastic magnifier on fertilizer jugs so that gardeners can read the small print, including instructions for safe usage.
- Use an "opt-out" versus "opt-in" strategy such as automatically registering a person to vote when they get their driver's license unless they "opt-out."

4. Make Location More Appealing

Example: Bicycle Paths and Lanes in Los Angeles. One of the major barriers a potential bicyclist will cite for not commuting by bike to work is the lack of safe, pleasant, and interconnected bike paths and lanes. In 1994, the City of Los Angeles, led by its Department of City Planning, developed its first-ever comprehensive Bicycle Plan. It was adopted by the city council in 1996 and then provided the Department of Transportation a template for bicycle paths, lanes, and myriad bicycle amenities and policies to be implemented throughout the city.

And the plan has a goal, that of increasing bicycle travel in the city to *5% of all utilitarian trips taken* by 2025, the year the plan is expected to be fully implemented. By 2014, the city had installed 56 miles of bicycle paths, 119 miles of bicycle routes, and 348 bike lanes (see Figure 12.5). In addition, the Los Angeles Department of Transportation had installed over 5,500 U style bicycle racks and had developed and distributed over 500,000 comprehensive city bicycle maps.[21]

Additional examples of enhanced locations include the following:

- Conveniently located teen clinics that have reading materials and decor to which the market can relate

FIGURE 12.5 ■ Making Bicycling More Appealing and Safer in Los Angeles, With the Orange Line Bike Path Built in Conjunction With a Metro Bus Rapid Transit Project[20]

Source: Author photo.

- Stairways in office buildings that employees would want to take instead of the elevator—ones that are well lit, carpeted, and have art exhibits on the walls that get changed out once a month
- Organized walking groups for seniors in shopping malls

5. Overcome Psychological Barriers With Place

Example: Pets on the Net. Estimates in 2021 were that more than six million dogs and cats end up in shelters across America every year and that only about 40% get adopted.[22] Potential pet owners have several considerations (*barriers*) associated with visiting animal shelters to see what pets are available. In addition to the time it takes to travel to a center, some describe the psychological risk—a concern that they might take home a pet that isn't what they were really looking for. They worry they won't be able to say no. Viewing pets available for adoption on the Internet can help reduce both costs.

Many humane societies across the country have created websites where all or some of the pets currently available for adoption are featured, 24 hours a day, seven days a week. As illustrated in the photo on Sacramento's Pets on the Net website (see Figure 12.6), detailed information on the pet includes a personality profile based on information provided by the previous owner. Website visitors are told that adoptions are offered on a first-come, first-served basis, and directions to the facility are provided.[23] Some websites include features such as daily updates, an opportunity to put a temporary hold on an animal, information on how to choose

FIGURE 12.6 ■ Pets on the Net Reduces Concern About Not Being Able to Say No

Name: **Jake**

Sex: Neutered Male

Age: 3 yrs

Breed: German Shepherd/Boxer

Color: Brown/Black, Bicolor

Personality Profile:
Hey there! I'm Jake. I'm a friendly and playful young dog in need of a good home, and a little love and guidance from someone special like you! I walk well on a leash and I like to ride in the car, so maybe we could run errands together! Please come and adopt me and give me the chance I deserve.

CASE: 47862A

Source: Courtesy of SSPCA.

the right shelter pet, and reasons the pet was given up for adoption. A few national sites offer the ability to search nationwide for a pet by providing criteria such as desired breed, gender, age, size, and geographic locale.

Additional examples of strategies that reduce psychological barriers regarding place include the following:

- A website to help youth quit smoking, with an option to email a counselor instead of calling—an option some research with youth indicates just "isn't going to happen"
- Aiding military service members overseas in the election voting process, including a call center and robust website, "Americans can vote. Wherever they are."[24]
- Breastfeeding at designated rooms at airports

6. Be More Accessible Than Competition

Example: School Lunch Line Redesign. Brian Wansink, a professor at Cornell University, argues that "the ideal lunchroom isn't one that eliminates cookies. The ideal lunchroom is the one that gets children to choose an apple instead of a cookie, but to think it's their own choice."[25] Wansink's Center for Behavioral Economics and Childhood Nutrition at Cornell aims to provide schools with research-based solutions that encourage healthier eating in the lunchroom. In an October 2010 article in the *New York Times*, Wansink and his colleague, David Just, shared a dozen strategies that they found nudge students toward making better choices on their own by changing the way their options are presented. Several are place-related strategies, highlighted in bold:

1. **Place nutritious foods at the beginning of the lunch line.**
2. Use more appealing words to label healthy foods (e.g., "creamy corn" rather than "corn").
3. Give choices (e.g., carrots or celery vs. just carrots).
4. **Keep items like ice cream out of sight in the freezer with an opaque top.**
5. **Pull the salad bar away from the wall.**
6. Have cafeteria workers ask children, "Do you want a salad?"
7. Provide food trays, as they appear to increase the likelihood of taking a salad.
8. Decrease the size of cereal bowls.
9. **Place the chocolate milk behind the white milk.**
10. **Place fruit in glass bowls rather than stainless-steel pans.**
11. Lunch tickets should cover fruit as a dessert, but not cookies.
12. **Provide a "healthy express" checkout line for those not buying chips or desserts.**

Other examples in which the desired behavior is made more accessible relative to the competition include the following:

- Family-friendly lanes in grocery stores where candy, gum, and adult magazines have been removed from the checkout stand;
- High-occupant vehicle lanes that reward high-occupant vehicles with less traffic congestion (often).

7. Make Access to the Competition More Difficult, Unpleasant

Example: Tobacco's "25-Foot Rule". On December 8, 2005, Washington became the fifth state to implement a comprehensive statewide law prohibiting smoking in all indoor public places and workplaces, including restaurants, bars, taverns, bowling alleys, skating rinks, and nontribal casinos. But this law went further than any state had up to that time. Unlike Washington's measure, most statewide bans exempt some businesses, such as bars, private clubs, card rooms, and cigar lounges. And no state at the time had a deeper no-smoking buffer than Washington's 25-foot rule that prohibits smoking within 25 feet of entrances, exits, windows that open, and ventilation intakes that serve indoor public places or places of employment.

Other examples of limiting access to competitive behaviors include the following:

- Offering coupons for lockboxes for safe gun storage and distributing brochures listing convenient retail locations for purchase
- Distributing padlocks for home liquor cabinets to reduce alcohol access for minors; better yet, advocating with home builders to make these standard in new homes
- Pruning bushes in city parks so that youth are not able to gather in private and share their cigarettes and beer

8. Be Where Priority Audience Shops

Example: *Mammograms in the Mall.* The following excerpt from an article in the *Detroit Free Press* in 1999 provides an example of reducing barriers through improving access and location appeal.[26] Although this article was published more than 20 years ago, at the time of this text update in 2022, it is still an inspiring example of providing a distribution channel where a priority audience already goes frequently.

> Many women already pick up birthday gifts, grab dinner, and get their hair cut at the malls, so why not schedule their annual mammograms there, as well? With a concept that screams "no more excuses," the Barbara Ann Karmanos Cancer Institute will open a cancer prevention center at the Somerset Collection South in Troy in September. A first for Michigan and the Detroit Institute, the mall-located screening center will provide a comfortable, spa like atmosphere for patients in a less intimidating setting than a traditional doctor's office or hospital.

Other examples of similar opportunities to provide services and tangible objects where your priority audience is already shopping include the following:

- Distributing sustainable seafood guides at the fish counter of fish markets
- Providing litterbags at gas pumps, like pet waste bags in parks
- Giving demonstrations on how to select a proper life vest at sporting goods stores
- Offering beauty salon clients laminated cards to give to customers to hang on a shower nozzle with instructions and reminders to conduct a monthly breast self-exam

9. Be Where Priority Audience Hangs Out

Example: HIV Tests in Gay Bathhouses. A headline in the *Chicago Tribune* on January 2, 2004, exemplified this ninth-place strategy: "Rapid HIV Tests Offered Where Those at Risk Gather: Seattle Health Officials Get Aggressive in AIDS Battle by Heading Into Gay Clubs, Taking a Drop Of Blood and Providing Answers in 20 Minutes." The article described a new and aggressive effort for Public Health–Seattle & King County, one that included administering rapid result HIV tests in bathhouses and gay sex clubs.[27] Up to this point in time, it had been common for health counselors to visit bathhouses to administer standard HIV testing. Although this certainly made taking the test more convenient, it didn't address the place barrier associated with getting the results. Those who took advantage of these services would still need to make an appointment at a medical clinic and then wait at least a week to hear the results, a critical step in the prevention and initial treatment process that was not always taken. With this new effort, counselors would be with clients to present their results within about 20 minutes of taking the test. To address concerns about whether people carousing in a nightclub could handle the sudden news if it turned out they were HIV positive, counselors would refuse to test people who were high, drunk, or appeared emotionally unstable.

Apparently, the bathhouse and sex club owners initially expressed concern with health officials about whether this effort might offend customers or even drive them away. A tracking effort between July 2003 and February 2007 revealed that 1,559 rapid HIV tests were administered to gay male patrons of these bathhouses, identifying 33 new cases, a rate of 2.1%. In general, new-case-finding rates of greater than or equal to 1% are considered cost effective, and screening in the baths has substantially exceeded that threshold.[28] Perhaps the fact that in 2022 (18 years later), one of the clubs still touts the availability on its website of free and anonymous rapid HIV tests is an indication of how things turned out.[29]

By contrast, consider these dismal results when the place wasn't right. In Denmark in 2009, a government-sponsored pilot program was launched in Copenhagen to supply people that used drugs with free heroin. You would think this offer would be welcomed. It included a doctor's prescription that guaranteed users a pure dose. But the addicts weren't "biting." Out of Denmark's estimated 30,000 heroin addicts, only 80 took the government's offer. The problem was the "place." Users had to show up daily at a medical clinic to get the heroin, which was then administered and supervised by a doctor. Evidently, this place took all the "fun and freedom" out of it.[30]

10. Work With Existing Distribution Channels

Example: Influencing the Return of Unwanted Drugs to Pharmacies. In the fall of 1999, in response to a request from British Columbia's minister of the environment, pharmaceutical industry associations voluntarily created an organization to administer a medications-return program in British Columbia, Canada. The program provides the public with a convenient way to return (at no charge) unused or expired medications, including prescription drugs, nonprescription and herbal products, and vitamin and mineral supplements. Easy-to-find links for participating pharmacies are on the association's website, and information promoting the program is provided on annual recycling calendars, brochures, flyers, bookmarks, and posters. By 2018, 95% of pharmacies were participating, providing convenient access at over 1,098 locations. Many of the pharmacies have extended open hours, and most offer easy access to those with special needs. All containers returned from a pharmacy are tracked by pickup date, weight, and location and stored in a secure location until ready for safe destruction at a licensed destruction facility. The association's annual report indicated that in 2018, 86,632 kg of medication were collected.[31]

Social Franchising

Social franchising can be described as the application of the principles of franchising originating in the commercial sector for companies like Starbucks and Subway to the nongovernmental organization (NGO) and public sectors... for social good. Fundamentally, it is a way to increase distribution channels for an existing program or product, which then increases utilization by offering convenience of access and quality assurance for users. It is a way of scaling up successful solutions and often builds on existing private sector infrastructures including private clinics, pharmacies, and community providers.

The first significant implementation of social franchising was conducted in the 1990s by Population Services, International (PSI), when they created the Greenstar franchise in Pakistan, which provides family planning, sexual and reproductive health services, maternal and child health services, and tuberculosis diagnosis. As noted on their website in 2022, Greenstar products and services are now distributed through a nationwide network of over 7,000 franchised clinics and 75,000 retail outlets and community-based distribution sites.[32] Franchising has grown rapidly around the world in the past 20 years, primarily in the health sector, addressing a widely recognized gap in accessibility and quality, especially in low-income countries. Franchise networks most frequently provide services and products related to family planning, sexual and reproductive health services, maternal and child health services, HIV/AIDS diagnosis and treatment, tuberculosis diagnosis and treatment, diarrhea treatment, malaria treatment, and respiratory infections.

The International Centre for Social Franchising, as of 2022 rebranded to Spring Impact, often refers to an inspirational quote from former President Bill Clinton: "Nearly every problem has been solved by someone, somewhere. The frustration is that we can't seem to replicate (those solutions) anywhere else."[33] The organization's mission is to take this challenge on by helping to replicate the most successful social impact projects. The following example demonstrates this well.

Example. Nature Conservation in Nepal. Launched in 1986, the Annapurna Conservation Area Project (ACAP) is the first conservation area and largest protected area in Nepal. It is home to over 100,000 residents of diverse cultural and linguistic groups as well as being rich in biodiversity with a treasure house for 1,226 species of flowering plants, 102 unique mammals, 474 birds, 39 reptiles, and 22 amphibians.[34] Its social franchising model is seen to deliver systematic replication of best practices to increase environmental impact. The management team at ACAP is the franchisor, with seven local conservation offices (franchisees) serving as the "watchdog" for conservation issues in its area and then implementing activities on the ground in cooperation with local subcommittees.[35] Initial funding was secured through donations from international institutions, with internal funding derived from entry fees and trekking tourists eventually constituting more than 70% of the annual budget.[36]

Managing Distribution Channels

In situations in which goods and services are included in your campaign or program, a network of intermediaries may be needed to reach priority audiences through the distribution channel.

Kotler and Roberto describe four types of distribution levels to be considered, illustrated in Figure 12.7.[37] In a *zero-level channel*, there is direct distribution from the social marketer to the priority audience. Tangible goods and services are distributed by mail, over the Internet, door to door, or through outlets managed by the social marketing organization. In a *one-level channel*, there is one distribution intermediary, most commonly a retailer. In a *two-level channel*, you would be dealing with the local distributor as well as the retailer. In a *three-level channel*, a national distributor finds local distributors.

FIGURE 12.7 ■ Distribution Channels of Various Levels

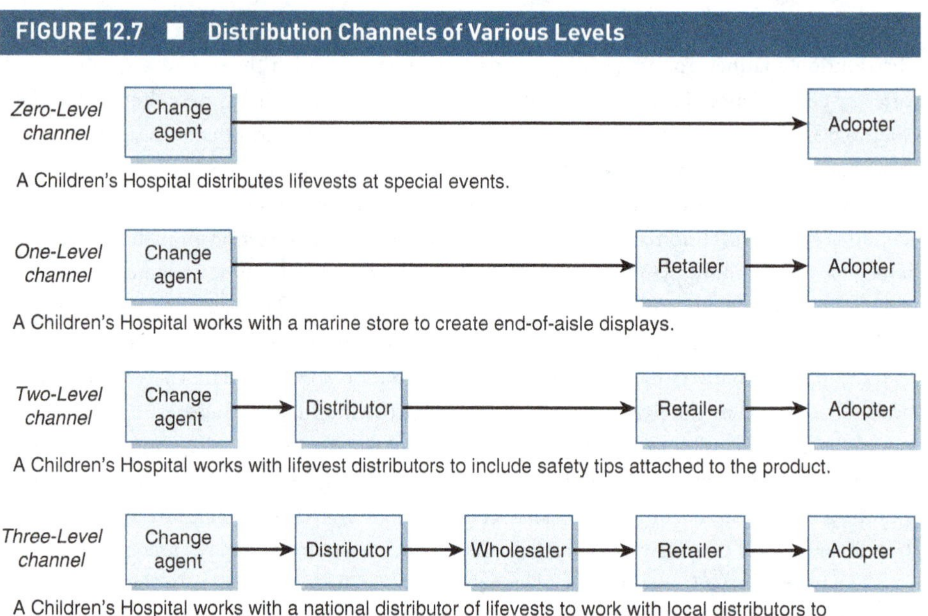

In the following example from Malcom Gladwell's book *The Tipping Point*, program planners found they had the "perfect" distribution channel and the "perfect" distributors:[38]

> In Baltimore, as in many communities with a lot of drug addicts, the city sends out a van stocked with thousands of clean syringes to certain street corners in its inner-city neighborhoods at certain times in the week. The idea is that for every dirty, used needle that addicts hand over, they can get a free clean needle in return.

To analyze how well the needle program was working, researchers at Johns Hopkins University began, in the mid-1990s, to ride along with the vans to talk to the people handing in needles. What they found surprised them. They had assumed that addicts brought in their own dirty needles for exchange, that IV drug users got new needles the way that you or I buy milk: going to the store when it is open and picking up enough for the week. But what they found was that a handful of addicts were coming by each week with knapsacks bulging with 300 or 400 dirty needles at a time, which is obviously far more than they were using themselves. These men were then going back to the street and selling the clean needles for $1 each. The van, in other words, was a kind of syringe wholesaler. The real retailers were these handfuls of men—these *super exchangers*—who were prowling around the streets and shooting galleries, picking up dirty needles, and then making a modest living on the clean needles they received in exchange. Those super exchangers sound as though they have the skills to bridge the chasm between the medical community and most drug users, who are hopelessly isolated from the information and institutions that could save their lives.

ETHICAL CONSIDERATIONS WHEN SELECTING DISTRIBUTION CHANNELS

Issues of equity and unintended consequences are common when planning access strategies. How do working mothers get their children to the free immunization clinic if it is only open on weekday mornings? How do drug addicts get clean needles if they don't have transportation to the exchange site? What if bike sharing locations are only located in more affluent areas of your city? In these cases, "more" of this place tool may be just the answer, with mobile units, for example, traveling to villages and neighborhoods to reach more of the priority population. It is particularly important that you ask yourself if there are structural access barriers in place for some members of your priority audience that will make it harder for them to practice your desired behavior. If this is the case, you should plan you "place" strategies to help overcome those access barriers.

Do critics of the ecstasy-testing volunteers at dance clubs have legitimate and higher-priority concerns that this will increase use of the drug? What about those who argue that restricting access (e.g., of alcohol to teens in their homes) leads to more profound consequences (e.g., driving home drunk)? And does a safe gun storage campaign that distributes coupons for lockboxes send a message that having guns is a norm and thereby increase ownership? One strategy to consider when addressing the potential for unintended consequences is to conduct a pilot and measure actual behavior changes, both intended and unintended. These data can then be used to conduct a cost-benefit analysis and help guide decision-making for future efforts and potentially a quantifiable rationale for a sustainable effort and expanded markets.

COVID-19 Social Marketing Example

On May 3, 2021, ABC NEWS announced a splendid example of the tactic to be where your priority audience "hangs out." The article shared that "Seventy one fans got vaccinated during the Milwaukee Bucks versus Brooklyn Nets basketball game Sunday, marking the latest effort by health departments to make COVID-19 vaccines convenient and even fun. The Bucks game vaccination pop-up, a partnership with the Milwaukee Public Health Department, was open to fans at least 16 years of age and is part of a series of mobile vaccination pop-ups the health department has hosted at community centers, churches, businesses and neighborhood events, according to Emily Tau, a health department spokesperson."[39]

CHAPTER SUMMARY

Place, the third "P," is where and when the priority audience will perform the desired behavior, acquire any related tangible goods, and receive any associated services.

Distribution channels, as they are often referred to in the commercial sector, include more than physical locations, with other alternatives that may be more convenient for your priority audience, including phone, mail, fax, Internet, mobile units, drive-throughs, home delivery, kiosks, and vending machines.

Your objective with the *place marketing intervention tool* is to develop strategies that will make it as convenient and pleasant as possible for your priority audience to perform the behavior, acquire any goods, and receive any services. You are encouraged to consider the following winning strategies:

1. Make the location closer.
2. Extend hours.
3. Be there at the point of decision-making.
4. Make the location more appealing.
5. Overcome psychological barriers related to "the place."
6. Be more accessible than the competition.
7. Make accessing the competition more difficult.
8. Be where your priority audience shops or dines.
9. Be where your priority audience hangs out.
10. Work with existing distribution channels.

And, finally, since this tool is often misunderstood, it is worth repeating that place is *not the same as the communication channel*, which is where your communications will appear (e.g., social media, brochures, radio ads, news stories, personal presentations).

RESEARCH HIGHLIGHT
REDUCING OPIOID OVERDOSE DEATHS

(2018–2022)

This Research Highlight focuses on the nature and value of conducting secondary research (e.g., literature review) to inform and inspire marketing intervention mix strategies, in this case for efforts to reduce opioid overdose deaths (*purpose*). In the planning process, this is most often conducted in Step 2 when current and prior efforts are explored. In keeping with this chapter's discussion of the *place* tool, our *focus* will be on identifying recent intervention strategies related to increasing convenience and appeal of access, the Place tool objective.

In March of 2018, the National Institute on Drug Abuse published an article citing the statistic that every day more than 115 Americans die after overdosing on opioids.[40] The CDC estimates the economic burden of prescription opioid misuse alone in the United States is $78.5 billion a year, including costs of healthcare, lost productivity, addiction treatment, and criminal justice involvement.[41] And on April 4, 2018, the launch of the HEAL (Helping to End

Addiction Long-term) Initiative[42] was announced by the National Institutes of Health, with the top two priorities being: a) improving access to treatment and recovery services and b) promoting use of overdose-reversing drugs. Further secondary research provides five examples where the *place* tool is being used to support these potential (although sometimes controversial) areas of focus.

1. *Allow and encourage more people to carry the opioid overdose-reversing drug Naloxone.* In fact, on April 5, 2018, the U.S. surgeon general issued an advisory encouraging this, given the fact that the drug, commonly known as Narcan, can very quickly restore normal breathing in someone suspected of overdosing on opioids, including heroin and prescription pain medications. A literature review on the topic indicates that when Narcan hit the market a few decades ago, it had to be applied intravenously, and only paramedics were equipped with it. In recent years, a nasal spray solution was developed and EMTs and police have been equipped with it too. This new recommended policy would expand this "convenience of access" strategy even further, with the surgeon general noting that most states already offer training to use naloxone properly to people who are, or who know someone, at risk for opioid overdose.
2. *Open safer drug consumption sites*, also called supervised injection facilities (SIFs), where users could inject and use drugs in a supervised manner with a goal of stopping overdoses and reducing disease rates. There are now (2018) 100 SIFs in at least 66 cities around the world in nine countries, with the first site in North America opening in 2003 in Vancouver, Canada. According to the Drug Policy Alliance, these sites have been researched and evaluated with conclusive evidence that they reduce overdose deaths, exposure to public injections, discarded syringes, HIV and hepatitis transmission risks, as well as increase the number of people who enter drug treatment.[43]
3. *Support retail outlets to sell Narcan without a prescription.* In 2017, for example, Walmart announced it would have Naloxone behind its pharmacy counters for sale or for dispensing by a pharmacist in all states where pharmacy practice laws support its ability to do so.[44]
4. *Create more space availability in treatment facilities.* Others advocate that while drugs like Narcan are invaluable for saving lives, the real key to tackling the epidemic could lie in expanding treatment, including access to services and beds in rehab facilities. Advocates stress that patients need also to be able to access care quickly in places where they can receive medicine-based treatment on the same day. This is in sharp contrast to what many health care institutions require which often involve lengthy screening processes and multiple doctor visits.
5. *Increase access to existing medication-assisted treatment programs*, such as ones using methadone and suboxone. Patients in recovery can take these drugs to taper off opioids. Suboxone, for one, is said to not only stop withdrawal but also block users from being able to get high for days after it is administered and is taken regularly.[45]
6. *Increase access to naloxone by installing vending machines.* In January 2022, an article in THE HILL noted that a nonprofit organization in New York was in the process of installing 10 Public Health Vending Machines that will dispense sterile syringes, naloxone, and additional health supplies. A guiding principle for the selection of locations included the perspective that "Racial equity does not mean simply treating everyone equally, but rather, allocating resources and services in such a way that explicitly addresses barriers imposed by structural racism."[46]

In summary, by conducting this type of secondary research/literature review where prior and current similar strategies are explored, planners will be inspired to consider programs that others have employed, potentially reducing some development costs (e.g., gaining permits to use existing promotional materials) and having access to evaluation data that can be used to support a proposed direction.

DISCUSSION QUESTIONS AND EXERCISES

1. To further explore the strategy of being where your priority audience hangs out, imagine places where these priority audiences hang out that you might consider distribution channels for the services or tangible goods associated with your campaign:
   - **a** Where could you find groups of seniors so you can give them small, portable pedestrian flags to keep and wave when entering crosswalks?
   - **b** What would be a good place to distribute COVID-19 vaccine booster shots to people that had "just not gotten around to getting it yet"?
   - **c** To increase voting among college students, where could you distribute voter registration packets?
   - **d** Where could you efficiently provide dog owners a mail-in pet licensing form?
2. These questions were posed in the ethical considerations section of this chapter. Discuss responses to the following:
   - **a** Do critics of the ecstasy-testing volunteers at dance clubs have legitimate and higher-priority concerns that this will increase use of the drug?
   - **b** What about those who argue that restricting access (e.g., of alcohol to teens in their homes) leads to more grave consequences (e.g., driving home drunk)?
   - **c** Does a safe gun storage campaign that distributes coupons for lockboxes send a message that having guns is a norm and thereby increase ownership?
   - **d** Regarding social franchising, what opportunities do you see that might be considered for existing programs or products?

13 STEP 7.4: PROMOTION

Deciding on Messages, Messengers, Creative Strategies, and Communication Channels

LEARNING OBJECTIVES

Upon completion of this chapter, you should be able to:

13.1 Apply the four components of the fourth "P" (promotion strategy) to a social marketing campaign.

13.2 Create a message strategy that will resonate with your priority audiences.

13.3 Explain how to choose appropriate messengers for your campaign.

13.4 List the 12 tips that can help guide development of creative assets.

13.5 Use pretesting to evaluate the effectiveness of campaign messages and creative concepts with priority audiences.

13.6 Describe the four types of communications channels.

13.7 Apply the eight factors to help guide the communication channel mix that is right for your campaign.

13.8 Evaluate and make decisions around ethical dilemmas related to creative concepts and promotional strategies.

Consider for a moment the fact that this chapter on promotion is the 13th of 16 chapters in this book. Twelve chapters precede it. It is placed more than two thirds of the way into the journey to complete a social marketing plan. Those who started this book thinking, as many do, that marketing *is* promotion are probably the most surprised. However, we imagine and hope that, after reading the first 12 chapters, you understand that you wouldn't have been ready before now to explore or use this final tool in the marketing intervention mix.

Many of you who are following the planning process are probably eager for the more creative, often fun-filled exercises associated with brainstorming slogans, sketching out logos, crafting a social media post, even screening potential actors. Others find this the most intimidating, even dreaded, process of all, having experienced in the past that it can be fraught with internal battles over words, colors, and shapes, and in the end, having experienced disappointment and frustration with their final materials or radio and television spots.

This time will be different. You have help. You know your priority audience and a lot about them. You have clear behavior objectives in mind and understand what your potential customers really want out of performing the behavior and the barriers that could stop them in their tracks. You know now that this understanding is your inspiration, a gift—one that has already helped you craft a powerful positioning statement, build a product platform, find incentives, and select distribution channels.

In this chapter, you will read about the components of a promotional campaign: (1) deciding on intended messages, (2) choosing credible messengers, (3) 12 tips to consider when developing creative elements of your campaign, and (4) selecting communication channels. We think you'll be inspired by the diversity of possible promotional tools you can use to help change people's behaviors and achieve your program's goals.

CASE HIGHLIGHT
VACCINATE WA

Information in this case study was provided by Kristen Haley, Health Promotion & Education Supervisor at the Washington State Department of Health.
(2020–2022)

Background

The Washington State Department of Health (WA DOH) created a social marketing initiative called Vaccinate WA (see Figure 13.1) to increase COVID-19 vaccination rates. WA DOH was particularly interested in ensuring that typically underserved populations were proactively considered as campaign priority audiences. Understanding the attitudes, beliefs, barriers, benefits, and motivators regarding the vaccine was fundamental to choosing promotional tools and creating an effective campaign. The campaign was grounded in significant research (see Research Highlight at the end of the chapter).

Purpose, Goals, and Objective

The purpose of the campaign was to save lives and reduce serious illness related to COVID-19. The goal was to get 70% of WA adults (aged 18+) to initiate vaccination. Objectives included to:

FIGURE 13.1 ■ Vaccinate WA Logos

Source: WA State Department of Health.

- Create an inclusive campaign that reached all Washingtonians.
- Increase intent to get vaccinated (before vaccine roll-out).
- Drive traffic to the Phase Finder, Vaccine Locator, and DOH vaccine information websites.
- Increase vaccination rates among hesitant populations.

Desired Behavior Changes

The desired behavior changes for the Vaccinate WA campaign were broken out into three stages:

Education: The campaign started in late 2020 before the vaccines were available with a baseline multimedia effort to educate about the basics of vaccines.

Intent: Once vaccines became available, the Vaccinate WA campaign launched. This included an online tool called Phase Finder where people could find out their vaccine eligibility phase. This stage was designed to help build vaccine intention.

Action: The bulk of the campaign focused on getting Washingtonians vaccinated:

- When the vaccine became available to all adults, WA DOH launched a vaccine locator website where people could find a vaccine location near them.
- In mid-2021, the strategy shifted to focus on audience groups with lower vaccination rates.
- As the vaccine became available to different aged children, the campaign encouraged parents to get their children the vaccine.

Priority Audiences and Message Strategy

Priority audiences were all adults in Washington with a special focus on populations with lower vaccination rates: young adults, people with conservative values (PWCVs), people living in rural counties, and members of the Black/African American and Hispanic/Latinx communities. To ensure inclusivity and accessibility, the campaign was also created in 36 languages.

The message strategy for the campaign evolved over time as the pandemic progressed as shown in Table 13.1:

Communications Channels

A wide suite of tactics supported the campaign strategy. Campaign materials were created in 36 languages with 28 languages incorporated into the paid media buy.

- *Paid advertising* reached audiences through a wide variety of channels: TV, radio, digital video, social, billboards, and mobile. For young adults, channels included TikTok, Snapchat, Reddit, Twitch, dating apps, and bar coasters. Microcommunity media reached diverse segments of the population (cultures, languages, LGBTQ+, etc.).
- Both *organic and paid social media* were integral to the campaign, with new daily content as well as engaging with and responding to the public.
- A *Google Search* strategy drove 1.5 million clicks to DOH vaccine websites.

TABLE 13.1 ■ Campaign Timeline

Start Date	Campaign Phase	Messaging Strategy
October 2020	Vaccine education	To set the stage for the coming COVID-19 vaccine, educational messaging was created that focused on how vaccines work in your body, how the COVID-19 vaccines were being developed, and how to know if you can trust information about vaccines.
February 2021	Gratitude	When vaccine supplies were limited, a series of messages thanked people for their patience and highlighted the work of all the medical professionals and volunteers that were working to get the vaccine to people in the community.
March 2021	Together We Will	The *Together We Will* campaign shared people's vaccine stories and encouragement messages from trusted medical experts and community members.
May 2021	Social norms	The campaign reported back to the public periodically about how many people in the community were vaccinated. The message strategy was designed to establish that there was a social norm around getting vaccinated and to try and urge the people that wanted to "wait and see" to go ahead and get the vaccine.
May 2021	Parents	Message strategies to encourage parents to vaccinate their children started with making sure that parents knew kids were eligible, then a *Vax to School* campaign encouraged vaccination before the school year started, and next messaging focused on why the vaccine was important from the perspective of parents, kids, and pediatricians (see Figure 13.2).
June 2021	Young adults	A high energy messaging strategy was employed letting them know that getting vaccinated was a way to get back to doing all the things they love to do (see Figure 13.3).
September 2021	Counties with lower vaccination rates	Rural counties with lower vaccination rates had unique barriers and motivators. Customized campaigns for these communities changed the call to action from vaccine locator to asking people to talk to their healthcare provider, featured stories from local trusted messengers, and added the benefit of protecting children as a motivator.
November 2021	Latinx/ Hispanic	Members of the Hispanic/Latinx community worked on all aspects of campaign and message development They developed messaging that empowered undecided Latinx/Hispanic community members to choose the vaccine by addressing misinformation with straight facts presented in culturally relevant ways. WA DOH worked with Hispanic/ Latinx healthcare providers, community members, and leaders to create content that highlighted how they made their vaccination decision. The *Mijo/Mijo* campaign featured an "abuela" as the main character—an emotionally charged, nostalgic grandmother-like figure in many Hispanic/Latinx families who acts as *the* trusted source. A lighthearted *Mentira Mariachi* campaign was created that featured a local mariachi band signing a song that addressed key vaccine misinformation.

TABLE 13.1 ■ Campaign Timeline *(Continued)*

Start Date	Campaign Phase	Messaging Strategy
March 2022	Black/ African American	WA DOH used community research to inform a campaign created by a team of Black creatives, health educators, and community engagement specialists. This was a unique messaging approach where WA DOH was not driving the conversation, but supporting it to happen. The messaging created by the community was designed to start a new conversation and build trust by elevating the voices of the Black community through the sharing of their real stories (see Figure 13.4).

FIGURE 13.2 ■ Child Eligibility Social Ad

Source: WA State Department of Health.

- More than 55 paid *social media influencers* created content that reached priority audiences.
- *Partnerships* with many organizations delivered additional reach:
    - Every major Washington state sports team partnered with the campaign. The Seattle Seahawks' Coach Carroll provided footage for a PSA, teams communicated with fans

FIGURE 13.3 ■ Young Adult Digital Ad

Source: WA State Department of Health.

and staff through various channels, and all teams provided footage of players and coaches.

- WA DOH partnered with eight local health jurisdictions in counties with lower vaccination rates to create and place custom messaging and materials.
- Organizations such as large-scale employers, the Latino Center for Health, transit agencies, AARP, Fred Hutch, and many others sent campaign messaging through their channels.

- *Expert panel webinars* were held once a month in both English and Spanish.
- *Materials and resources were created* for everyone to access:
    - An online partner toolkit with materials and web content in 36 languages.
    - An online portal where vaccine providers and businesses could order free vaccine materials (stickers, signage, handouts, buttons, etc.).

FIGURE 13.4 ■ Here for Us Social Ad

Source: WA State Department of Health.

Evaluation

The purpose of the campaign was to save lives and reduce the risk of serious illness from COVID-19. As of March 2022, Washington ranked as the sixth lowest state in terms of lowest cases per 100K population and fifth in terms of deaths.

Goal: Get 70% of WA adults (aged 18+) to initiate vaccination.

Result: As of April 2022, 85.5% of WA adults aged 18+ have initiated vaccination (22% above goal). The campaign closed the gap in vaccination rates among hesitant populations and adults 18+ as follows (May 2021–April 2022):

- *9.7% for young adults* (rates went from 16% behind to just 6.5% behind)
- *9.8% for Hispanic/Latinx* (rates went from 32% behind to 22.2% behind)
- *18.4% for Black/African American* (rates went from 26.5% behind to just 8.1% behind)

Objectives:

- The campaign was inclusive, reaching all Washingtonians through materials in 36 languages as well as messaging for the Black/African American, Hispanic/Latinx, LGTBQ+, Ethiopian, Somali, Japanese, Filipino, Indian, Pacific Islander/Native Hawaiian, Chinese, Vietnamese, Russian, and Korean communities.

- Paid media tactics drove:
  - 1.2 billion completed video views.
  - Drove 4.6 million clicks to WA DOH vaccine websites and 1.8 million Phase Finder submissions.
  - More than 475,000 social media engagements.
  - 3.5 billion media impressions.
- Intent to vaccinate increased 14 points between December 2020 and February 2021 (from 65% to 79% intending to get vaccinated).

PROMOTION: THE FOURTH "P"

Promotions are persuasive communications designed and delivered to inspire your priority audience to action. You will be highlighting their desired benefits for performing the behavior (*core product*), and any associated tangible goods and services. You will be touting any monetary and nonmonetary incentives. And you will be letting priority adopters know where and when they can access any tangible goods and services included in your program's effort and/or where you are encouraging them to perform the desired behavior (e.g., recycle motor oil). In this step, you create the voice of your brand and decide how you will establish a dialogue and build relationships with your customer.[1]

Developing this promotion strategy is the final component of Step 7, developing a strategic marketing intervention mix. Your planning process includes four major decisions:

1. *Messages:* What you want to communicate, inspired by what you want your priority audience to do, know, and believe
2. *Messengers:* Who will deliver your messages or be perceived to be sponsoring or supporting your offer
3. *Creative strategy:* What you will actually say and show and how you will say it. This is also the point in the planning process when the actual brand (e.g., name, graphic elements) is developed.
4. *Communication channels:* Where and when your messages will appear (distinct, of course, from distribution channels)

A Word About Creative Briefs

One of the most effective ways to establish clear messages, choose credible messengers, inspire winning creative strategies, and select effective communication channels is to develop a document called a creative brief, usually one to two pages in length.[2] It helps ensure that communications will be meaningful (pointing out benefits that make the product desirable), believable (the

TABLE 13.2 ■ Creative Brief for a Youth Tobacco Prevention Campaign

Purpose and focus:

Reduce tobacco use among youth with a focus on addictive components.

Priority audience description and insights:

Middle school and high school youth who don't currently smoke, vape, or chew tobacco, although they may have experimented with it in the past. They are vulnerable, however, to using tobacco because they have family members and friends who use tobacco products. They know many of the facts about the consequences of using tobacco. They've been exposed to them in health classes, and may even have experienced the reality with family members who have smoking-related illnesses or who have died from smoking. The problem is, they don't believe it will happen to them. They don't really believe they will get addicted. There is much peer pressure to fit in by smoking. These youth have also heard that smoking and vaping are a great stress relief and are an appealing way to pass the time. Some think kids who smoke look older and cool.

Communication objectives:

To do: Refuse to try cigarettes, vape, or chew.

To know: Addiction is real and probable.

To believe: Smoking-related illnesses are shocking, "gross," and painful.

Benefits to promise:

You will have a longer, healthier, and happier life, free of tobacco addiction.

Supports to promise:

Real stories from real people who started smoking or vaping at a young age

Stories of personal loss involving a family member's dying or living with or dying from a smoking-related illness

Graphic visuals depicting real, shocking, and "gross" consequences to the body

Real facts from the American Cancer Society and surgeon general

Style or tone:

Credible, realistic, and serious

Openings:

Engaging in social media including Facebook, Instagram, and Twitter

Playing video games

Listening to the radio

Watching television

Surfing the Internet

Talking with friends

Positioning:

People who smoke are risking their health and hurting their future, families, and friends. It's not worth it.

product will deliver on the promised benefits), and distinctive (how your offer is a better choice than competing behaviors).[3] Its greatest contribution is that it helps ensure that all team members, especially those in advertising and public relations firms working on the campaign, are in agreement with communication objectives and strategies prior to more costly development and production of communication materials. Typical elements of a creative brief are illustrated in the following section, and a sample creative brief is featured in Table 13.2.

Purpose of communications: This is a brief statement that summarizes the purpose and focus of the social marketing effort, taken from Step 1 in your plan.

Priority audience: This section presents a brief description of the priority audience in terms of key variables determined in Step 3. Most commonly, it will include a demographic, geographic, and psychographic profile of the priority audience. It is helpful to include what you know about your audience's current knowledge, beliefs, perceived barriers, cultural foundations, and behaviors relative to the desired behavior as well as to competing ones. Ideally, it describes the priority audience's current stage of change and anything else that you think is special about them.

Communication objectives: This section specifies what you want your priority audience to *do* (behavior), *know* (think), and *believe* (feel), based on exposure to your communications. This can be taken directly from decisions made in Step 4. (Social marketing campaigns will always have a behavior objective and often have both a knowledge and belief objective.)

Positioning statement: The product positioning established earlier in Step 6 is presented here. This provides guidance to those selecting images and graphics and developing script and copy points.

Benefits to promise: Key benefits the audience hopes they will receive from adopting the behavior were identified as the *core product* when developing the product platform in Step 7. The primary benefit is sometimes expressed in terms of a cost that the audience can avoid by adopting the desired behavior (e.g., stiff penalties for drinking and driving).

Support for the promise: This section refers to a brief list of additional benefits and highlights from product, price, and place strategies established earlier in Step 7. The ones to be highlighted are those that would most help convince the priority audience that they can perform the desired behavior, that the benefits are likely, and that they exceed perceived costs. This section also includes any available testimonials.

Style and tone: Come to some agreement on any recommended guidelines about the style and tone for creative executions. Also note whether there are any existing graphic standards or related efforts that should be taken into consideration (e.g., the logo and taglines used for any current similar or competing efforts).

Openings: This final important section will be helpful to those selecting and planning communication channels. Siegel and Doner describe openings as "the times, places, and situations when the audience will be most attentive to, and able to act on, the message."[4] Input for this section will come from profiles and audience behaviors explored in Step 5 (barriers, benefits, and motivators). Additional input may come from secondary and expert resources on the priority audience's lifestyle and media habits.

MESSAGE STRATEGY

At this point, you are focused on the content of your communications, not the ultimate slogans, scripts, or headlines. That comes later. What those developing your creative strategies need to know first is what responses you want from your priority audience. In our social marketing model, you've already done the hard work here and can simply fill in the blanks to the following by refining and elaborating on campaign objectives established earlier in Step 4 and referencing barriers, benefits, motivators, and your competition from Step 5.

What You Want Your Priority Audience to Do

What specific desired behavior is your campaign focused on (e.g., get an HIV test three to six months after having had unprotected sex)? It will include any immediate calls to action (e.g., call this toll-free number for locations in your area for free, rapid HIV tests). If your behavior objective was stated in fairly broad terms (e.g., practice natural yard care techniques), this is the time to break these down into more single, simple, doable messages (e.g., leave grass clippings on the lawn).

What You Want Them to Know

Select key facts and information regarding your offer that should be included in campaign messages. If you are offering tangible goods or services related to your campaign (e.g., free quart-sized resealable plastic bags at security checkpoints), you will want messages that inform priority audiences *where and when they can be accessed*. There may be key points you want to make on *how to perform* the behavior (e.g., the limit for carry-on liquids is three ounces, and they must fit in a quart-sized resealable plastic bag). To highlight benefits of your offer, you may decide that a key point you want your audience to know relates to *statistics on risks* associated with competing behaviors (e.g., makeup and other liquids not in these bags will be taken and discarded) and *benefits you promise* (e.g., having liquids in the appropriate containers ahead of time can save you and fellow passengers up to 20 minutes in lines).

What You Want Them to Believe

This question is different from what you want your priority audience to know. This is about what you want them to believe and/or feel as a result of your key messages. Your best inspiration for these points will be your barriers, benefits, and motivators research. What did they say when asked why they weren't planning to vote (e.g., "My vote won't make a difference")? Why do they think they are safe to drive home after drinking (e.g., "I've done it before and was perfectly fine")? Why are they hesitant to talk with their teen about suicide (e.g., "I might make them more likely to do it")? These are points you will want your communications to counter. And what was their response when you asked what would motivate them to exercise five days a week (e.g., "believing I would sleep better"), fix a leaky toilet (e.g., saving 200 gallons of water a day), or take the bus to work (e.g., having Wi-Fi available for the duration)? These are points you'll want to put front and center.

Example: Reducing Binge Drinking

To further illustrate these communication objectives, we will use a campaign developed by students at Syracuse University, one that won first prize in the 2009 National Student Advertising Competition sponsored by the Century Council, in which over 140 schools competed. The assignment was to develop and present a campaign to curb the dangerous overconsumption of alcohol on college campuses. (A full description of contest entry materials can be found at http://www.centurycouncil.org/binge-drinking.)[5] The student teams' formative research included 1,556 in-depth surveys reaching all 50 states, with 75 expert interviews and 15 journals documenting sober and drunk weekends. The first revelation was a "difference of opinions," with 92% of college students rejecting the definition of "binge drinking" as having five or more drinks (male) or four or more drinks (female) in about two hours. Students were quick to mention, however, that they were well aware of the negative consequences of drinking too much, and that there was definitely a line between "drinking" and "drinking too much." As one student put it, "There's always that one drink—that one shot that I wish I didn't have. It always makes things go downhill. Always." The problem, as students defined it, was knowing when they "crossed the line." That's when things went wrong.

The team found out what didn't work—statistics and authoritarian messages. And they learned that students got smarter about how they consumed alcohol by the time they were juniors and seniors. The team saw their job as getting students to progress more quickly to that ability to moderate. Their message strategy was developed to do just that.

What Did They Want Students to Do? Refuse that "next drink," the one that would take them "over the line."

What Did They Need Them to Know? Recognize that the point between drinking and drinking too much is actually... a drink.

What Did They Need Them to Believe? By refusing that drink that would take them over the line, they would avoid negative consequences, ones their research indicated were "all too familiar" and made them feel stupid: "sending drunk texts"; "blacking out"; "getting a DUI"; "ending up in an unwanted hookup"; "throwing up"; "arguing with my girlfriend"; "falling down stairs"; "acting like an idiot."

With this as their inspiration, the students developed a creative strategy, one that would identify and stigmatize the one drink that would separate enjoyable drinking from the negative consequences of "drinking too much." They called it "The Stupid Drink" (see Figure 13.5).

Messages Relative to Stage of Change

Messages will also be guided by your priority audience's current stage of change. As mentioned in Chapter 5 on priority audiences, the marketer's role is to move priority adopters to the next

FIGURE 13.5 ■ The Stupid Drink Campaign Poster

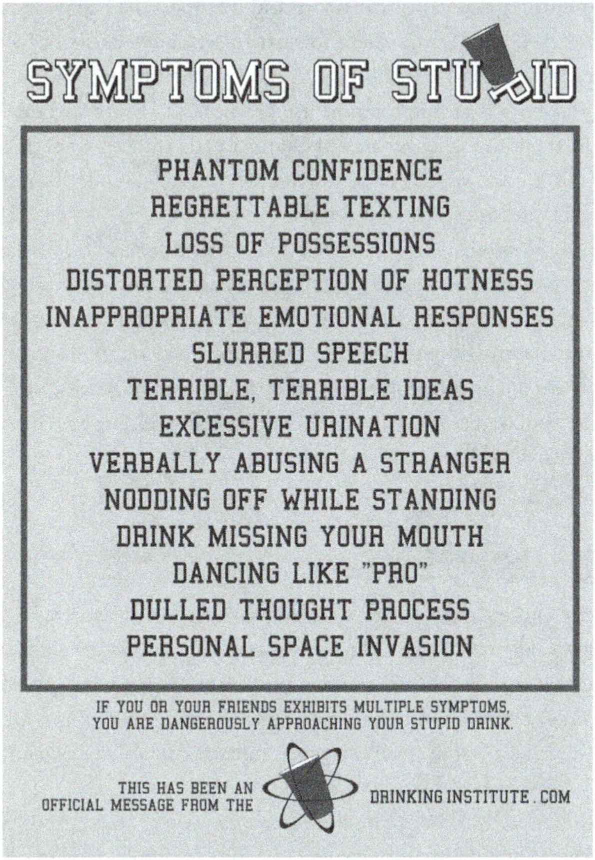

SYMPTOMS OF STUPID

PHANTOM CONFIDENCE
REGRETTABLE TEXTING
LOSS OF POSSESSIONS
DISTORTED PERCEPTION OF HOTNESS
INAPPROPRIATE EMOTIONAL RESPONSES
SLURRED SPEECH
TERRIBLE, TERRIBLE IDEAS
EXCESSIVE URINATION
VERBALLY ABUSING A STRANGER
NODDING OFF WHILE STANDING
DRINK MISSING YOUR MOUTH
DANCING LIKE "PRO"
DULLED THOUGHT PROCESS
PERSONAL SPACE INVASION

IF YOU OR YOUR FRIENDS EXHIBITS MULTIPLE SYMPTOMS,
YOU ARE DANGEROUSLY APPROACHING YOUR STUPID DRINK.

THIS HAS BEEN AN
OFFICIAL MESSAGE FROM THE

DRINKINGINSTITUTE.COM

Source: Courtesy of the Century Council.

stage, influencing precontemplators to become contemplators, contemplators to take action, and those in action to make it a habit (maintenance). Most important, there are different recommended message strategies for each stage.[6]

For *precontemplators*, your major emphasis is on making sure your priority audience is aware of the costs of competing behaviors and the benefits of the new one. These are often stated using statistics and facts, especially those that your priority audience was not aware of—ones that serve as a wake-up call. When these facts are big news, they can often move some priority audience members very quickly through subsequent stages—all the way to maintenance in some cases (e.g., when it was discovered that aspirin given to children for flu is related to a potentially fatal disease called Reye's syndrome).

For *contemplators* (now that they are "awake"), your message options include encouraging them to at least try the new behavior and/or restructure their environment to make adoption easier (e.g., put a compost container under the kitchen sink). You'll want to dispel any myths (e.g., air bags are as good as seatbelts) and potentially address any barriers, such as a concern they have about their ability to successfully perform and maintain the behavior.

For those *in action*, you'll want them to start to see the benefits of having "gotten out of bed." Perhaps you will be acknowledging that they reached targeted milestones (e.g., 30 days without a cigarette) or persuading them to use prompts to ensure sustainability (e.g., put the laminated card to track monthly breast self-exams in the shower) or sign pledges or commitments to "keep up the good work." Your messages will target a tendency to return to old habits and at the same time prepare them to create a new one.

For those in *maintenance*, you still have a role to play, for as you learned earlier, behavior change is spiral in nature, and we can easily regress back to any of the stages—even go "back to sleep." This is the group whose behavior you want to recognize, congratulate, feature, and reward. You want to be sure they are realizing the promised benefits, and you may want to occasionally remind them of the long-term gains they are bound to receive or contribute to (e.g., a message on a utility bill that selectively thanks residents for helping to reduce peak hour electrical consumption by 6%).

MESSENGER STRATEGY

Who your priority audience perceives to be delivering your message and what they think of this particular messenger can make or break the deal. And this is the right time to be choosing the messenger, as this decision will have important implications when you develop the creative strategy as well as select communication channels. You have six major messenger options (sole sponsor, partners, spokespersons, endorsements, midstream audiences, and mascot), described next, followed by considerations for choosing.

The sponsoring organization can be the *sole sponsor*, with campaign communications highlighting the organization's name (somewhere). A quick audit of social marketing campaigns is likely to indicate a public sector agency sponsor (e.g., the Environmental Protection Agency promoting energy-efficient appliances) or a nonprofit organization (e.g., the American Cancer Society urging colon cancer screenings). Although it is not as common, the sole sponsor might be a for-profit organization (e.g., Safeco Insurance promoting "10 Tips to Wildfire Defense").

For many efforts, there will be *partners* involved from the beginning in developing, implementing, and perhaps funding the campaign. In this scenario, priority audiences may not be certain of the main or actual sponsors. These partners may form a coalition or just a project, one where the priority audience may or may not be aware (or clear) what organizations are sponsoring the effort (e.g., a water quality consortium that includes utilities, departments of health, and an environmental advocacy group). In 2006, for example, a public, private, and nonprofit partnership was formed to influence 10,000 of the estimated 50,000 unbanked households in San Francisco to open a bank account. Estimates were that the average unbanked household was spending 5% of its income per year on check cashing alone, relying on check cashers, pawnshops, payday lenders, and other fringe financial services charging high fees and interest rates. City officials were able to persuade 75% of the banks and credit unions in the city to offer what were branded Bank on San Francisco accounts. Even those with a poor banking history were encouraged to open these "second-chance" accounts offering a low- or no-cost product with no minimum balance requirement, accepting consular identification, and waiving one set of overdraft fees per client. Two years after the program launched, more than 31,000 Bank on San Francisco accounts had been opened.[7]

Some organizations and campaigns make effective use of *spokespersons* to deliver the messages, often achieving higher attention and recall as well as increased credibility. In 2006, for example, Barack Obama traveled to Kenya and received a public HIV test. He then spoke about his trip on World AIDS Day:

> So, we need to show people that just as there is no shame in going to the doctor for a blood test or a CAT scan or a mammogram, there is no shame in going for an HIV test. Because while there was once a time when a positive result gave little hope, today the earlier you know, the faster you can get help. My wife Michelle and I were able to take the test on our trip to Africa after the Centers for Disease Control informed us that by getting a simple 15-minute test, we may have encouraged as many as half-a-million Kenyans to get tested as well.[8]

Some programs have used entertainers to draw attention to their effort (e.g., Willie Nelson for the Don't Mess with Texas litter prevention campaign). The best choice would be someone highly recognized and appropriate for the effort. This strategy is not without risk, however, as there is a chance the celebrities you choose might lose popularity or, even worse, get caught in a scandal or embarrassing situation, as when Willie Nelson was arrested for drug possession.[9] You may want to include *endorsements* from outside organizations, which are often then seen as one of the messengers. These can range from simply including an organization's name or logo in your communications to displaying more formal testimonials in support of your campaign's facts and recommendations (e.g., the American Medical Association's verifying that a public health department's statistics on the dangers of secondhand tobacco smoke are scientifically based).

It may be very advantageous to engage *midstream audiences*, who typically have a closer relationship with your audience, to be your messengers. Soul Sense of Beauty, for example, is an outreach program that trains hairstylists, considered confidants by many, to talk to their clients about health issues such as the threat and prevention of breast cancer. Hair salons hold special meaning for African American women, the priority audience for this effort. To many, the salons represent a place where women can go to be pampered and cared for consistently. Although the salon setting is important to the delivery of health messages, including videos and printed material, it is the relationship between the client and her stylist that creates the magic. After all, this confidant is likely to be someone she has had a personal history with for years, and since she "generally stands 6–8 inches from a woman's ear, who better to whisper some potentially lifesaving pearls of wisdom?"[10]

Finally, there is always the option of creating a *mascot* to represent the brand, like Smokey Bear or McGruff the Crime Dog. Others have used current popular characters such as Sesame Street's Elmo, who is featured in a *Ready, Set, Brush Pop-Up Book* intended to feature the fun side of good oral health habits (e.g., a wheel shows how much toothpaste you should use, and there is a pop-up whose teeth can be brushed with an attached toothbrush).[11]

How Do You Choose?

In the end, you want your priority audience to see the messenger, or messengers, as a credible source for the message. Three major factors have been identified as key to source credibility: expertise, trustworthiness, and likability.[12]

Expertise is the perceived knowledge the messenger has to back the claim. For a campaign encouraging 12-year-olds to receive the new human papillomavirus (HPV) vaccine to help prevent cervical cancer, the American Academy of Pediatrics was an important messenger, in addition to local healthcare providers. *Trustworthiness* is related to how objective and honest the source is perceived to be. Friends, for example, are more trusted than strangers, and people who are not paid to endorse a product are viewed as more trustworthy than people who are paid.[13] This is why for-profit organizations often need the partnership or at least the endorsement of a public agency or nonprofit organization, with priority audiences being innately skeptical about the commercial sector's motive (e.g., a pharmaceutical company encouraging childhood immunizations). *Likability* describes the source's attractiveness, with qualities such as candor, humor, and naturalness making a source more likable.

The most credible source, of course, would be the option scoring highest on all three dimensions. Perhaps that's what inspired the strategy in the following example.

Example: Meth Project in Montana

The United Nations has identified methamphetamine abuse as a growing global pandemic. Law enforcement departments across the United States rank meth as the number-one crime problem in America. In response to this growing public health crisis, Montana rancher Thomas

FIGURE 13.6 ■ The Primary Messengers for This Successful Effort Are Youth Meth Users

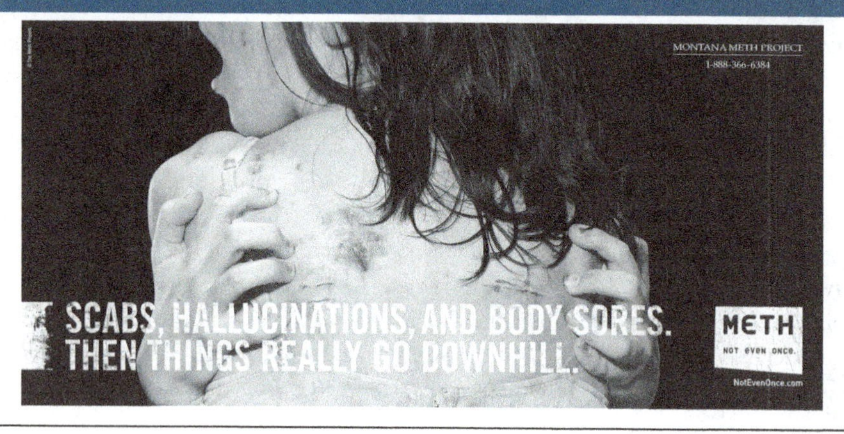

Source: Montana Meth Project (website), accessed March 26, 2007.

M. Siebel established the Meth Project to significantly reduce meth use through public service messaging, community action, and public policy initiatives.[14]

The state of Montana, where the Meth Project was first initiated, ranks among the top 10 states nationally in treatment admissions per capita for methamphetamine. The social costs reported on the project's website are staggering and the human costs incalculable: 52% of children in foster care are there because of meth, costing the state $12 million a year; 50% of adults in prison are there because of meth-related crime, costing the state $43 million a year; and 20% of adults in treatment are there for meth addiction, costing the state $10 million a year.

The Meth Project, launched in 2005, focuses on informing potential meth consumers about the product's attributes and risks. The integrated program consists of an ongoing, research-based marketing campaign—supported by community outreach and public policy initiatives—that realistically and graphically communicates the risks of methamphetamine use.

At the core of the Meth Project's effort is research-validated, high-impact advertising with the tagline "Not Even Once" and bold images that communicate the risks of meth use. Television, print, radio, and a documentary feature testimonials from youth meth users (see Figure 13.6). Approaching meth use as a consumer product marketing problem, the project aims to unsell meth. It organizes a broad range of community outreach programs to mobilize the people of Montana to assist in meth awareness and prevention activities. Through its Paint the State art contest, thousands of teens and their families were prompted to create highly visible public art with a strong antimeth message. As of 2018, the project was a program of the national nonprofit organization The Partnership at Drugfree.org and has been adopted by six states, including Colorado, Georgia, Hawaii, Idaho, Montana, and Wyoming.

CREATIVE STRATEGY

Your creative strategy will translate the content of your desired messages to specific communications. These will include everything from logos, typeface, taglines, headlines, copy, visuals, and colors in designed materials to script, actors, scenes, and sounds in broadcast media. You will be faced with choosing between informational appeals that elaborate on behaviors and their benefits and emotional appeals using fear, guilt, shame, humor, love, or surprise. Your goal is to develop (or approve) communications that will capture the attention of your priority audience and persuade them to adopt the desired behavior. We present 12 tips in these next sections for you to consider and to help you and others decide.

Creative Tip 1: Keep It Simple and Clear

Given a social marketing campaign's inherent focus on behaviors, try to make your instructions simple and clear.[15] Assume, for a moment, that your priority audience is interested in adopting, even eager to adopt, the behavior. Perhaps it was something you said or something they were already inclined to do, and they are just waiting for clear instructions. Messages like this are probably familiar to you. "Eat five or more fruits and vegetables a day." "Wash your hands long enough to sing the Happy Birthday song twice." "Move right for sirens and lights." "Check your

FIGURE 13.7 ■ This Landfill Is Where I'll End Up If I Don't Find a Home

Source: Shannon Jonhstone, Meredith College.

fire alarm batteries when you reset your clocks in the fall and spring." Consider how easy these messages make it for you to know whether you have performed the desired behavior and can therefore count on receiving the promised benefits.

Creative Tip 2: Focus on Audience Benefits

Since, as Roman and Maas suggest, people don't buy products but instead buy expectations of benefits,[16] creative strategies should highlight benefits your priority audience wants (most) and expects in return for costs associated with performing the behavior. This will be especially effective when the perceived benefits already outweigh perceived costs. The priority audience just needs to be prompted and reminded, as they were in the following example shared by Mary Shannon Johnstone, a photographer and a tenured associate professor at Meredith College in Raleigh, North Carolina, with a passion for saving the lives of homeless dogs.

Example: Landfill Dogs

> These are not just cute pictures of dogs. [See Figure 13.7] These are dogs who have been homeless for at least two weeks, and now face euthanasia if they do not find a home. Each week for 18 months (late 2012–early 2014) I bring one dog from the county animal shelter and photograph him/her at the local landfill. The landfill site is used for two reasons. First, this is where the dogs will end up if they do not find a home. Their bodies will be buried deep in the landfill among our trash. These photographs offer the last opportunity for the dogs to find homes. The second reason for the landfill location is because the county animal shelter falls under the same management as the landfill. This government structure reflects a societal value; homeless cats and dogs are just another waste stream. However, this landscape offers a metaphor of hope. It is a place of trash that has been transformed into a place of beauty. I hope the viewer also sees the

beauty in these homeless, unloved creatures. As part of this photographic process, each dog receives a car ride, a walk, treats, and about 2 hours of much needed individual attention. My goal is to offer an individual face to the souls that are lost because of animal overpopulation, and give these animals one last chance. This project will continue for one year, so that we can see the landscape change, but the constant stream of dogs remains the same.[17]

Creative Tip 3: When Using Fear, Provide Solutions and Credible Sources

Social marketers frequently debate whether or not to use "fear appeals." Some researchers suggest that part of the reason is the lack of distinction between a fear appeal and what might better be called a "threat appeal."[18] They argue that threats simply illustrate undesirable consequences of certain behaviors (e.g., cancer from smoking) and that the emotion triggered may in fact not be fear, which some worry can immobilize the audience.

Rob Donovan, Professor of Behavioral Research at Curtin University in Australia, posted on the Georgetown Social Marketing Listserv in 2013 that "the issue is not so much whether fear, disgust, etc., work or not—but under what conditions and for whom are they appropriate, and when might they be counterproductive."[19] Kotler and Roberto point to research by Sternthal and Craig suggesting that decisions to execute fear-based messages should take several factors into account:[20] A strong fear-based appeal works best when it is accompanied by solutions that are both effective and easy to perform. Otherwise, you may be better off with a moderate appeal to fear (see Figure 13.8).

FIGURE 13.8 ■ A Fear Appeal Followed by a Solution

Source: Children's Hospital and Regional Medical Center, Seattle, Washington.

FIGURE 13.9 ■ A Fear Appeal From a Credible Source: "The Surgeon General Warns That Smoking is a Frequent Cause of Wasted Potential and Fatal Regret"

Source: Image courtesy of www.adbusters.org.

- A strong fear-based appeal may be most persuasive to those who have previously been unconcerned about a particular problem. Those who already have some concern may perceive a message of fear as going too far, which will inhibit their change of attitudes or behaviors.

- An appeal to fear may work better when it is directed toward someone who is close to priority audience. This may explain some research indicating that fear appeals are more effective when they are directed toward family members of the priority audience.[21]
- The more credible the source, the more persuasive the fear-based appeal. A more credible source reduces the chances that the audience will discount or underestimate the fear-based appeal (see Figure 13.9).

Creative Tip 4: Messages That Are Vivid, Concrete, and Personal

McKenzie-Mohr and Smith believe one of the most effective ways to ensure attention and memorability is to present information that is vivid, personal, and concrete.[22] They point to a variety of ways to make this happen.

Vivid information, they explain, increases the likelihood that a message will stand out against all the other information competing for our attention. Furthermore, because it is vivid, we are more likely to remember it at a later time. For example, one assessor conducting home energy audits was trained to present vivid analogies:

> You know, if you were to add up all the cracks around and under these doors here, you'd have the equivalent of a hole the size of a football in your living room wall. Think for a moment about all the heat that would escape from a hole that size.[23]

FIGURE 13.10 ■ A Vivid, Personal, and Concrete Creative Strategy

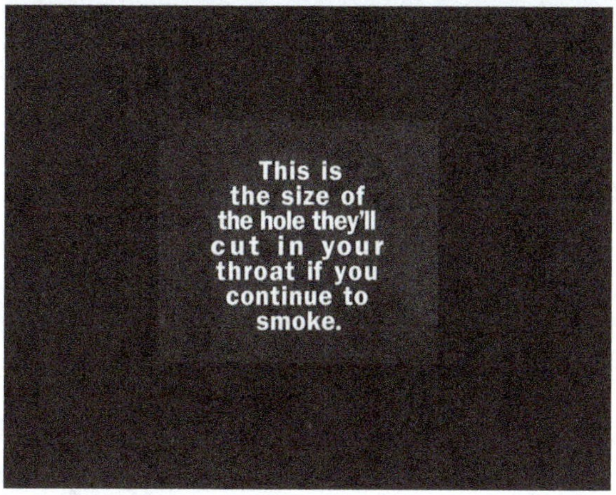

Source: Washington Department of Health.

TABLE 13.3 ■ Sample Ad Taglines

Brand Theme	Ad Tagline
Our hamburgers are bigger.	Where's the Beef? (Wendy's restaurants)
Our tissue is softer.	Please, Don't Squeeze the Charmin (Charmin bathroom tissue)
No hard sell, just a good car.	Drivers Wanted (Volkswagen automobiles)
We don't rent as many cars, so we have to do more for our customers.	We Try Harder (Avis auto rental)
We provide long-distance phone service.	Reach Out and Touch Someone (AT&T telecommunications)

Source: Philip Kotler and Kevin Lane Keller, *Marketing Management*, 12th ed. (Upper Saddle River, NJ: Prentice Hall, 2005), 545.

Information that is *personalized* uniquely addresses your priority audience's preferences, wants, and needs, fully informed by their perceived barriers to and benefits of doing the behavior. For example, McKenzie-Mohr and Smith have a suggestion for utilities on how they might promote energy conservation: show the percentage of home energy by use item. Rather than using bars for the graph, replace them with a picture of the item itself (furnace, water heater, major appliances, lighting, etc.) and the corresponding energy use in the home.[24]

McKenzie-Mohr and Smith also illustrate information that is *concrete* with an example of a more powerful way to depict waste. Instead of stating that Californians each produce 1,300 pounds of waste annually, Shawn Burn at California Polytechnic State University depicts

Californians' annual waste as "enough to fill a two-lane highway, ten feet deep, from Oregon to the Mexican border."[25]

We think the postcard shown in Figure 13.10, used for a youth tobacco prevention campaign in Washington state, demonstrates that a creative strategy can be vivid, personal, and concrete.

Creative Tip 5: Make Messages Easy to Remember

The magic of persuasive communications is to bring your messages to life in the minds of the priority audience. And as Kotler and Keller reveal, every detail matters. Consider, they suggest, how the legendary private sector ad taglines listed in Table 13.3 were able to bring to life the brand themes listed on the left. Consider, as well, how familiar many or most of them (still) are to you.

In their book *Made to Stick: Why Some Ideas Survive and Others Die*, the Heath brothers suggest six basic traits of sticky ideas—ones that are understood and remembered.[26] Note that they even make the six traits sticky by having them almost, but not quite, spell the word *success*:

1. **S**implicity: The Golden Rule
2. **U**nexpectedness: Southwest: the low-cost airline
3. **C**oncreteness: John Kennedy's "A man on the moon by the end of the decade"
4. **C**redibility: Ronald Reagan's "Before you vote, ask yourself if you are better off today than you were four years ago."[27]
5. **E**motions: "Don't Mess with Texas"
6. **S**tories: David and Goliath

A quick audit of familiar, perhaps even "famous," social marketing messages provides a few additional clues as to what seems to help priority audiences remember what to do, especially when your communications aren't close at hand:

- Try rhyming techniques such as "Click It or Ticket" and "If it's yellow, let it mellow; if it's brown, flush it down."
- Those that surprise you may be more likely to stick with you, such as "Save the Crabs. Then Eat 'em."
- Create a simple and memorable mental picture, such as "Drop. Cover. Hold" in case of an earthquake.
- Connect the timing to some other familiar event, such as a birthday, as in "Get a colonoscopy when you turn 60."

- Leverage the familiarity of another brand or slogan, as "Just Say No" did with Nike's "Just Do It."

Creative Tip 6: Have a Little Fun Sometimes

Having fun with social marketing promotions is often as controversial as using fear-based appeals. We suggest that the key here is to know when it is an appropriate and potentially effective solution—and when it isn't. A host of variables will impact your success, including your priority audience (e.g., demographics, psychographics, and geographics), whether the social issue is one that your audience can "laugh about," and how a humorous approach contrasts with what has been used in the past to impact this issue. Consider, for example, results of a research study led by Brian Wansink at Cornell University to explore whether more appealing names for vegetables would increase selections of vegetables in school cafeterias. Results indicated that alternative names such as the following significantly increased vegetable purchases among the kids:[28]

- Crunchy Yummy Carrots
- Power Punch Broccoli
- Silly Dilly Beans

The following successful example suggests the "fun" boundaries can be stretched further than we might think.

In 2007, the Bill & Melinda Gates Foundation announced that Thailand's Population and Community Development Association (PDA) had received the 2007 Gates Award for Global Health in recognition of its pioneering work in family planning and HIV/AIDS prevention. The prize honored Mechai Viravaidya, founder and chairman of the PDA and an ex-senator in Thailand with a passion for reducing unplanned pregnancies and the spread of HIV/AIDS in the country. He had decided to popularize condoms, thinking a "little fun" might make them more acceptable. His creative promotional strategies supported the "fun" theme:

- He spoke at a variety of events, proclaiming, "The condom is a great friend. You can do many things with it… You can use different colors on different days—yellow for Monday, pink for Tuesday, and black when you are mourning."[29]
- He organized condom "balloon-blowing" contests with prizes for kids and adults. He also made sure the media would take photos that he hoped would end up on the front page or on the evening news.
- He influenced tollbooths to hand out condoms with their tickets.
- He created a Cops and Rubbers program in which traffic police were given boxes of condoms to distribute on New Year's Eve.
- He had monks bless condoms so that Thais would be assured there would be no ill effects after using them.

FIGURE 13.11 ■ A Welcome Approach in a Subway in New York City

Source: Author photo.

- He added condoms to fashion shows, with runs of condoms in different colors.
- He opened new restaurants branded "Cabbages and Condoms" with the slogan "Our food is guaranteed not to cause pregnancy"—and a condom, instead of a mint, comes with the bill.

In general, humorous messages are most effective when they represent a *unique approach* to the social issue. For example, consider how surprised and perhaps delighted you would be to read a sign in a subway in New York like the one in Figure 13.11. There are probably opportunities for humor whenever your priority audience would get a kick out of *laughing at themselves or with others*. The WA State Department of Health campaign that was highlighted in the case highlight at the beginning of this chapter also incorporated some humor into its COVID-19 campaigns. They felt that at certain points in the pandemic when people were feeling burned out, a little humor might help reengage people with the desired behaviors. Examples included fun animated ads to promote safer game-day gatherings and a vaccine ad that tied into Star Wars Day: May the Fourth Be With You (see Figure 13.12).

On the other hand, humorous messages are not as effective for *complex messages*. There would be no benefit, and perhaps even a detriment, to a campaign to influence parents to child-proof their home, an effort involving multiple, specific instructions. Nor is it appropriate for issues with *strong cultural, moral, or ethical concerns* (e.g., child abuse or domestic violence).

FIGURE 13.12 ■ Social Media Ads That Employed Humor

Source: WA State Department of Health.

FIGURE 13.13 ■ Part of a Big Campaign Idea

Source: Ad Council.

Creative Tip 7: Try for a "Big Idea"

A "big idea" brings the message strategy to life in a distinct and memorable way.[30] In the advertising business, the big idea is thought of by some as the Holy Grail, a creative solution that in just a few words or one image sums up the compelling reason to buy.[31] It takes message strategy statements that tend to be plain, straightforward outlines of benefits and desired positioning and transforms them into a compelling campaign concept.[32] It might be inspired by asking yourself, if you had only "one thing" you could say about your product, how would you say it and how would you show it? Others suggest that getting the big idea is not a linear process, but rather a concept that might emerge while in the shower or in a dream. At Porter Novelli, a global public relations firm, the big idea is described as one that has a head, heart, hands, and legs.

> Not only can the Big Idea straddle across a period of time through several campaigns but also at the same time, it can stand astride any channel we choose. The Big Idea brings campaigns and channels together, rather than working as disconnected executional elements.[33]

Examples in the commercial sector to model include the well-known "Got milk?" campaign that has been adopted for a variety of celebrities and nondairy products (e.g., "Got junk?"). A great social marketing example is one developed by the U.S. Department of Health and Human Services' Office on Women's Health's national breastfeeding campaign. The big idea for this campaign will seem more obvious when you see two of their ads, ones intended to increase knowledge about the benefits of breastfeeding exclusively for the first six months (see Figure 13.13).

Creative Tip 8: Consider a Question Instead of a Nag

Are you going to drink eight glasses of water today? Are you going to vote tomorrow? Some believe the very act of asking these questions can be a force for positive change, a technique referred to as the "self-prophecy effect," or the behavioral influence of a person making a self-prediction. Research conducted by Eric Spangenberg, professor of marketing, and Dave Sprott, assistant professor of marketing, both at Washington State University, has led them to believe that having people predict whether they will perform a socially normative behavior increases their probability of performing that target action. These researchers have even demonstrated successful application of self-prophecy through mass-communicated prediction requests.[34] They have also found theoretical support for a dissonance-based explanation for self-prophecy.

Spangenberg and Sprott's studies show that when people predict they will do something, they are more likely to do it. These authors' analysis of the technique showed an average effectiveness rate of 20% immediately following the asking of the question, and sometimes behavior change would last up to six months after people predicted their behavior.[35] Specific studies have shown that self-prophecy has increased voter turnout in elections, improved attendance at health clubs, increased commitment to recycling aluminum cans, and increased the chances that a family will eat dinner together. The researchers believe this result can be explained by the phenomenon of cognitive dissonance that uncomfortable feeling we humans sometimes get when we say we'll do something and then we don't (Some of us would probably call it guilt.). This uncomfortable feeling then drives us to act consistently with our predictions. In other words, the prediction becomes a self-fulfilling prophecy.

FIGURE 13.14 ■ A Message Intended to Help Make Scooping the Poop and Placing It in the Trash a Norm

Source: Author photo.

Spangenberg stresses that for this to be successful, the priority audience must see the behavior as a social norm and be predisposed to the behavior, or at least not have strong commitments to the other, undesirable one. For example, asking a group of drug users, "Are you going to stop using today?" is probably not going to work.[36]

Creative Tip 9: Make Norms (More) Visible

Social norms marketing, as mentioned in earlier chapters, is based on the central concept of social norms theory—that much of people's behavior is influenced by their perceptions of what is "normal" or "typical." When a behavior is not (yet) a social norm, however, one strategy is to increase perceptions that others are engaged in the behavior. In Figure 13.14, for example, note the sign on the curbside garbage container that states, "We Scoop." The sticker is there not only to forewarn the garbage collectors as they dump the container but also to "spread" the idea to other pet owners around the neighborhood.

Creative Tip 10: Tell Real Stories About Real People

Perhaps one of the reasons that real stories told by real people is such a great creative strategy is that they embody many of the message and messenger best practices mentioned in this chapter. The messenger, because they are a real person telling their own story, is viewed as *credible* and usually *likable*. And the messages, when they are true stories, have more possibility for providing *concrete* examples and creating *emotion*, two of the "sticky" principles. The Vaccinate WA

FIGURE 13.15 ■ Social Media Ad Featuring a Community Messenger

Source: WA State Department of Health.

campaign also includes a great example of telling real stories from real people that were trusted messengers (doctors, nurses, community members, priests, etc.) as is illustrated in Figure 13.15.

Creative Tip 11: Try Crowdsourcing

As noted in Chapter 3, crowdsourcing is often used to tap online communities for formative, pretest, and evaluative research efforts. It can also be used to generate creative elements, as Johnson & Johnson did for its Campaign for Nursing's Future, a multiyear corporate social marketing effort to underscore the value of the nursing profession and help increase the nursing workforce. One component the campaign undertook was the Art of Nursing: Portrait of Thanks Mosaic Project, designed to thank nurses for their hard work and dedication and to commemorate the campaign's 10th anniversary in 2012. Nurses from around the world were encouraged to upload a photo and brief information on the campaign's website, Discovernursing.com. The photo could be from on the job, a social event, or even a family outing. Photos were then compiled to create a single digital (mosaic) image, one intended to be a symbol of pride for nurses everywhere (see Figure 13.16). The mosaic includes nearly 10,000 photos submitted by nurses

FIGURE 13.16 ■ The Johnson & Johnson's Campaign for Nursing's Future Portrait of Thanks. Once on the site, you can search through nearly 10,000 individual photos by keyword: name, hometown, specialty.

Source: Johnson & Johnson.

and nursing students. For every photo that was submitted to the project, the campaign pledged to donate $1 to fund student nursing scholarships.

Creative Tip 12: Appeal to Psychographic Characteristics

Psychographic traits such as personality, lifestyle, values, interests, and attitudes can often lead us deeper into persuasive factors than demographics alone. Curtis Carey, an adjunct professorial lecturer at American University, shared the following inspirational application.

If someone asks you about your best friend's defining characteristics, you are unlikely to start with where she lives or her age. Instead, you might explain that she's motivated, that she always reads something interesting in the book club, and that she is the first person to help out friends and family. You might even talk about the interesting activities and things she shares on Facebook or Twitter or the time she asked you to go water skiing. If she truly is your best friend, you'll tell us about her as a motivational and maybe inspirational person, not as a demographic.

PRETESTING

Appropriate Reasons for Testing

The primary purpose for pretesting potential messages and creative executions is to *assess their ability to deliver* on the strategies and objectives developed in Step 4 and highlighted in your creative brief. When faced with several potential executions, the process can also help you *choose the*

FIGURE 13.17 ■ Recycling Cart Hangers

Source: C+C.

most effective options or eliminate the least effective. It provides an opportunity to *refine materials* prior to production and distribution.

In addition, it helps identify any red flags—something about the potential ad or message that might interfere with communications or send the wrong message. This often happens when planners and campaign developers are too close to their work or don't have the same profile and characteristics as the priority audience. For example, a potential tobacco prevention ad targeting teens with the fact that "all it takes is 100 cigarettes to become addicted" raised a couple of red flags when several youths commented, "Well, then I'll just have 99" and others expressed the idea that 100 cigarettes (to a nonsmoker) "sounds like a lot!"

Lastly message and concept testing allow you to check for cultural resonance and applicability. Ads can sometimes use references or nuance that do not make sense cross-culturally. A recent example of this is a waste management company that wanted to place cart hangers on recycling bins to give feedback to residents about how they were doing with recycling. The bins would be "checked" and the cart hanger would be left with a letter grade marked and a "congratulations" if the recycling looked good or "tips for improvement" if they saw contamination in the cart. The cart hangers would be bilingual in Spanish and English. In message testing, it was discovered that using a letter grade did not make sense to many recent immigrants that spoke Spanish as letter grading systems were not a part of the culture they grew up in. As a result, the campaign was changed to instead focus on emojis (happy, surprised) which did show in pretesting to have universal understanding among the priority audience groups (see Figure 13.17).

Potential Pretesting Techniques

Techniques used for pretesting are typically qualitative in nature, and most include *focus groups* or *personal interviews* and *professional review* of materials for technical accuracy and readability (i.e., literacy levels). An additional more recent technique, *neuromarketing research*, uses medical technologies such as functional magnetic resonance imaging (fMRI) to study the brain's responses to marketing stimuli such as messages, messengers, and creative elements. When a more quantitative, controlled approach is required, methodologies may include *theater* or *natural exposure testing* (e.g., ads are embedded between other spots or in the middle of programming) and/or a *larger number of focus groups, intercept interviews, self-administered surveys*, and *A/B testing* (e.g., you run two versions of digital or social ads online for a short period of time and compare results). This more extensive testing is often warranted when (a) interested parties are divided on their initial assessments of creative executions, (b) there will be significant economic and political implications to choices, and (c) the campaign needs to have a longer-term shelf life (e.g., years vs. months).

Often these techniques vary according to stages in the pretest process. At early stages, when concepts and draft executions are being tested, qualitative instruments are usually most appropriate. After concepts have been refined, quantitative techniques may be important to help you choose from several potential executions.

The purpose of pretesting is to evaluate if concepts and messages are believable (does the audience find it credible?), relevant (does the audience think it's applicable to them personally?), engaging (does it catch the audience's attention and make then want to learn more?), informative (does it convey they information you intend?), and motivating (is it likely to cause the audience to do the desired behavior change?). In addition, pretesting can also help you look for cultural resonance and elasticity—does the message or concept work across multiple cultures? Typical topics explored with respondents to uncover these things and assess the ability of potential executions to deliver on the strategy are listed as follows (responses are then compared with intentions developed in the creative brief).

1. "What is the main message you get from this (promotional material)?"
2. "What else are they trying to say?"
3. "What do you think they want you to know?"
4. "What do you think they want you to believe or think?"
5. "What action do you think they want you to do?"
6. If the respondent doesn't mention the desired behavior, say, "actually, the main purpose of this (promotional material) is to persuade you and people like you to..."

7. "How likely do you think it is that this (promotional material) will influence you to take this action?"
8. "What about this (promotional material) works well for that purpose?"
9. "What doesn't work well for that purpose?"
10. "How does this (promotional material) make you feel about [doing this behavior]?"
11. "Where is the best place to reach you with this (promotional material)? Where would you most likely notice it and pay attention to it? Where are you when you make decisions about [this behavior]?"

SELECTING COMMUNICATION CHANNELS

There are a wide variety of communications channels that can be employed as part of your social marketing campaign. It can be quite overwhelming to figure out which ones to choose. This section will give you the tools you need to help make those choices. As you might expect, the key is to take an audience-centric approach to finding the right communications channels to reach them at the right time and in the right place when they are receptive to your message.

Communications channels can be broken into four buckets:

- Paid: Paid channels are those that would be included in a media buy (such as TV, online ads, and transit boards).
- Shared: Shared channels are those that allow you to engage two ways with your audience. These include things like organic media posts and personal selling.
- Earned: Earned channels are those a third part does for you at no cost (like placing story in the news media or a public service announcement (PSA) that runs for free on TV).
- Owned: Owned channels are those that you create and control the platform and message. This includes websites and promotions materials.

A brief explanation of many of the communications channel options follows (see Table 13.4).

Communication Vehicles

Within each of the major communication channels (media types), there are specific vehicles to select. Which social media platform, TV stations, radio programs, magazines, websites, mobile technologies, and bus routes should you choose? At what events should you sign up for a booth? When are road signs warranted? Where should you put your fact sheets?

TABLE 13.4 ■ Major Social Marketing Communication Channels

PAID	
Advertising	
Broadcast:	*Outdoor/out of home:*
Video (network and cable TV, steaming video)	Billboards (printed and digital)
Audio (traditional radio, digital audio, and streaming)	Transit boards
Print:	Bus shelter/subway displays
Newspaper	Taxis
Magazine	Vinyl wraps on cars and buses
Direct-to-home:	Sports sponsorships
Direct mail	Poster and banner placement
Pay check and other stuffers	Postcard racks; paid poster placement
Door hangers	Kiosks
Digital/social/mobile	Restroom stall ads
Banner ads (online and mobile)	Truck side advertising
Social media ads	Airport billboards and signage
Video preroll	Backs of tickets and receipts
SMS texting	Ads in theaters
Search	Paid social media influencers
Product integration in media/programming	
Product or behavior placement in TV shows or movies	
Behavior integration with toys or curriculum	
SHARED	
Organic social media	
Social media platforms such as Facebook, Twitter, Instagram, Snapchat, TikTok, Pinterest, and LinkedIn	Virtual worlds
Text messaging	Memes and GIFs
YouTube	Apps
Personal selling	
Face-to-face meetings, presentations, speakers' bureaus	
Telephone/personal texting	

(Continued)

TABLE 13.4 ■ Major Social Marketing Communication Channels *(Continued)*

Community events and fairs	
Workshops, seminars, and training sessions	
EARNED	
Public relations	
Stories on television and radio	Lobbying
Articles in newspapers and magazines	Press releases
Op-eds	Media advocacy
Public affairs/community relations	Authored articles
Public service announcements	
TV, radio, print, and outdoor ads	
Media partnerships	
Special events	
Meetings	Exhibits
Speakers' bureaus	Community events
Conferences	Demonstrations
OWNED	
Materials	
Videos	Podcasts
Brochures	Calendars
Newsletters	Envelope messages
Flyers	Booklets
Posters	Bumper stickers
Catalogs	Static stickers
Websites and online	
Websites	Blogs and microblogs
Microsites	Widgets
Banner ads	Apps
E-mail blasts and alerts	SEO (organic search)
Special promotional items	
Clothing:	*Functional items:*

TABLE 13.4 ■ Major Social Marketing Communication Channels *(Continued)*

T-shirts	Key chains
Baseball hats	Flashlights
Diapers	Refrigerator magnets
Bibs	Water bottles
Temporary items:	Litterbags
Coffee sleeves	Pens and pencils
Bar coasters	Bookmarks
Lapel buttons	Book covers
Temporary tattoos	Notepads
Balloons	Tote bags
Stickers	Mascots
Sports cards	e-Cards
Signage and displays	
Road signs	
Signs and posters on government property	
Retail displays and signage	
Popular and entertainment media	
Songs	Public art
Comic books and comic strips	Flash mobs
Video games	Gamification

Communication Timing

Timing elements include decisions regarding months, weeks, days, and hours when campaign elements will be launched, distributed, implemented, and/or aired in the media. Your decisions will be guided by when your audience is most likely to be reached or when you have your greatest windows of opportunity for being heard (e.g., a drinking-and-driving campaign aimed at teens might be most effective immediately prior to and during prom and graduation nights).

Paid Communication Channels

Advertising

Defined formally, advertising is "any paid form of nonpersonal presentation of ideas, goods, or services by an identified sponsor."[37] Advertising channels include television, *social media, online/*

mobile, radio, newspapers, magazines, direct mail, and a variety of *outdoor* (out-of-home) channels such as billboards, transit signage, and kiosks. A newer advertising approach is *paid social influencer outreach*. This is when you pay people with a large social media following that reaches your priority audience group to create and post content about your issue or program.

Advertising today has the ability to deliver broad reach through mass media channels as well as to directly reach many priority audience groups. With the wide use of social media, mobile phones, and the Internet, you can purchase advertising that reaches subsegments of the population based on very specific criteria (e.g., demographics, geography, hobbies, interests, affiliations, and values). For example, if you want to reach people that fish for crabs in a specific water body, you can create a Facebook and Instagram ad buy that reaches your desired geography with people that have an interest in crabbing. The benefit of this is that you can avoid message waste—only delivering your ads to the people that the message is relevant to (your priority audience group).

It is also possible to deliver ads in multiple languages reaching audience that do not speak English. Almost all media channels can be purchased to reach Spanish-speaking people. But, in addition, community media, social media, and banner ads can be purchased to reach multiple other languages (30+ languages at last count on social media platforms).

If advertising is part of your promotional mix, you should likely involve a media buying expert to help ensure that you are creating an advertising buy that uses your media budget in the most efficient manner possible. A professional media buyer will look at your budget, your campaign goals, and your priority audience segments and recommend the best channels to reach your audience with your message. They will analyze the buy to ensure it delivers the optimum reach (the percentage of your audience group you reach) and frequency (number of times you deliver the message to your audience).

Example: Denver Water's Conservation Advertising Campaign. From 2002 to 2006, Denver Water's 1.2 million customers reduced their water usage by about 20% each year. The Denver mayor, however, wanted to continue this trend and announced a partnership in July 2006 to reduce use by 22% a year over the next decade, including a $500,000 advertising campaign intended to help make this happen. The campaign, with the tagline "Use Only What You Need," appeared in community newspapers, magazines, billboards, transit, and other

FIGURE 13.18 ■ A Creative Campaign and Use of Outdoor Advertising for Denver Water

Source: Denver Water.

FIGURE 13.19 ■ ONIE Facebook Promotion

Source: ONIE Project.

out-of-home media (see Figure 13.18). The ads also appeared in places you might not expect, such as on 20,000 drink coasters that went to local restaurants and bars, offering water conservation tips such as "Be a real man and dry shave, tough guy."[38] And in 2013, the campaign sent out a "Thank you for Using Even Less" message to customers, announcing they had exceeded their goal of reducing water use 10% throughout the summer: "Without your efforts, providing a secure water future is an exercise in futility."[39]

Another example that illustrates the power of Facebook's advertising platform comes from Robert John, Professor of Health Promotion Sciences at the University of Oklahoma. He shared how they used Facebook as a primary channel to reach low-income Oklahomans.[40]

The Oklahoma Nutrition Information and Education (ONIE) project is a SNAP-Education program focused on nutrition behaviors consistent with the dietary guidelines for Americans and physical activity consistent with current public health knowledge. Our priority group is low-income Oklahomans with income below 185% of the federal poverty level. In recent years, we have expanded our efforts disseminating nutrition education and physical activity materials throughout Oklahoma through our project website in Spanish and English (onieproject.org), our Facebook pages (Proyecto ONIE and ONIE Project), our weekly blog in English and Spanish posted to Facebook and Instagram, and other nutrition education materials such as

FIGURE 13.20 ■ Barbie Modeling the "Scoop the Poop" Behavior for Her Dog Tanner

Source: Author photo.

healthy recipes distributed through social media (primarily Facebook and Pinterest; see Figure 13.19).

Facebook advertising is used on a weekly basis to promote the ONIE blog (in English and Spanish) and other ONIE project goals such as promoting SNAP-accepting farmers markets in the state. The project has also used social media as part of broader multichannel interventions to promote the consumption of 1% low-fat milk, cooking meals at home, and to promote an easy way to reduce salt in the diet. Our messages routinely reach 4,000–5,000 weekly.

Social media presents an opportunity for the ONIE project to segment advertising to precise audiences. To identify and reach our priority audience, Facebook provides segmentation variables for demographic characteristics such as age, gender, or geographic location, but also for essential psychographic characteristics such as preferences, interests, and specific behaviors such as cooking, family activities, or healthy food. Once the advertisement is placed, Facebook analytics provide evidence of audience engagement including the number of people reached, clicks, likes, and shares.

Product Integration

In the commercial sector, product placement is a specialty of its own, with marketers finding inventive ways to advertise during actual television programs and movies especially. You probably recognize this when you see a familiar logo on a cup of coffee in an actor's hand or the Swoosh on a star's baseball cap. In the James Bond film *Die Another Day*, for example, 7UP,

Aston Martin, Finlandia, Visa, and Omega all spent an estimated $100 million for product placement rights, with some critics nicknaming the film *Buy Another Day*.[41]

More relevant for social marketing is the integration of your desired behaviors into commercial products or their packaging. Sometimes corporations decide "all on their own" to take on an initiative. In the fall of 2006, for example, the toymaker Mattel unveiled Tanner, Barbie's new pet dog. Tanner comes with little brown plastic "biscuits" that he can be fed simply by lifting his tail. When he "releases them," Barbie can then scoop them up using her new, magnetic pooper scooper and place them in the little garbage can included in the package (see Figure 13.20).

More often, the social marketing organization approaches the corporation for support, as Seafood Watch did with Warner Home Video, who then agreed to include the 2007 Seafood Watch pocket guide in every copy of the Academy Award–winning animated film *Happy Feet* when millions of DVD copies became available in March 2007.

Shared Communication Channels

Social Media

Social media platforms are a necessary part of any social marketer's toolkit. In 2021, social media platforms were used by 72% of the U.S. population (up from 5% in 2025)[42] with Facebook and YouTube being the most used channels. Several platforms have significant reach among segmented audiences like TikTok and Snapchat reaching younger people and LinkedIn reaching professionals. The first step when looking at organic social media as a communications channel is to evaluate which platforms make sense for your organization or cause. You can do this by finding out which channels your priority audiences use. It's a good idea to start with just a few channels since you will need to maintain activity and engagement on any channels you create, posting new content frequently, and engaging with comments from the public.

Twelve lessons learned that the Centers for Disease Control and Prevention (CDC) hopes will benefit others as they develop, implement, and evaluate social media efforts include the following:[43]

1. "Make strategic choices" based on the audience's profile and your communication objectives.
2. "Go where the people are" by reviewing user statistics and demographics.
3. "Adopt low-risk tools first," such as podcasts and videos.
4. "Make sure messages are science based," ensuring accuracy and consistency.
5. "Create portable content," such as widgets and online videos that can easily be shared.
6. "Facilitate viral information sharing" through sites such as Facebook, YouTube, and Twitter.
7. "Encourage participation," especially through two-way conversations.

8. "Leverage networks" such as Facebook, where many in your target audience may have more than 100 "friends."
9. "Provide multiple formats" to increase accessibility, reinforce messages, and provide preferred ways to interact.
10. "Consider mobile phones," since 90% of adults in America subscribe to mobile services.
11. "Set realistic goals," as social media alone are unlikely to achieve aggressive communication or behavior change goals.
12. "Learn from metrics and evaluate efforts," an advantage afforded by digital communications.

Examples of the use of several major social media types for social marketing are featured in this next section.

Facebook

Facebook is a platform that most organizations, brands, and causes need to have. This is because 69% of U.S. adults use Facebook, and seven in ten of those people use it daily[44]. It has become an integrated part of how people get information and engage with their networks making it an important communications channel for most organizations.

An example of using Facebook to help leverage a campaign's reach comes from Lifebuoy. In 2013, a Warc Prize for Social Strategy was awarded to Lifebuoy, a corporation with a social mission (and corporate social marketing effort) to help more children reach their fifth birthday by supporting good hand-washing habits around the world. Every year, they report, two million children fail to reach their fifth birthday because of diseases like diarrhea and pneumonia, diseases that could (in part) be prevented by healthy hand-washing habits.[45] Program strategies include working directly with schoolchildren, new moms, and community groups to encourage hand washing with soap before eating, after using the toilet, and when bathing. The campaign was launched with an inspiring three-minute video (http://www.youtube.com/watch?v=GVhCQNSGF1w), one that offers a real, personal, and powerful perspective through the story of a father's journey to celebrate his son's fifth birthday. Those viewing the video are encouraged to share on Facebook, with Lifebuoy making a contribution to the effort for every posting. With over six million views (as of 2013), the video has sparked strong emotions and is expected to increase hand-washing behaviors. And in 2016, Lifebuoy launched their "High Five for Handwashing" campaign in Nairobi, with a commitment to change the handwashing behaviors of 12 million Kenyans by 2020.[46]

YouTube

YouTube is the most used social media channel with 81% of U.S. adults reporting they use YouTube[47]. Having a YouTube channel allows you to post and share video content.

FIGURE 13.21 ■ Encouraging U.S. Citizens to Vote From Abroad

Source: Photo by Salter Mitchell.

Example: Letting YouTube Bury the Argument for Brochures. As a sponsor of landmark menu-labeling legislation, the California Center for Public Advocacy in 2008 contracted with Brown Miller Communications to increase support for the nation's first statewide menu-labeling law, one that would require chain food facilities to disclose calories for each standard menu item directly on the menu next to the actual item. The fast-food industry was backing an alternative bill opting instead for nutrition brochures. Based on the old saying that a picture is worth a thousand words, the agency spent an afternoon filming people standing in line with fast-food outlets' complex brochures, trying, unsuccessfully, to quickly find simple information for the item they wanted. They then created a lighthearted man-on-the-street video showcasing their difficulties and posted it on YouTube (http://www.youtube.com/watch?v=zD4m6WN3Tlg) and sent it directly to fast-food industry representatives, legislators, and their staff, advocates, and the media. The secretary of health and human services and the governor were shown the video in one-on-one meetings. The YouTube video garnered over 5,000 views the first week, and over 80% of the comments directly attacked the fast-food industry's bill. Featured on the *New York Times* editorial blog, the video reached beyond the confines of YouTube. The resulting public backlash prompted the fast-food industry to withdraw its legislation. State legislators who had previously been skittish about the bill and supportive of the fast-food industry's bill passed the first statewide menu-labeling law. The governor signed it into legislation, and California became the first state to pass statewide menu-labeling legislation.[48]

Twitter

While Twitter is a less used channel (with 22% of U.S. adults using it)[49], it can be an important tool for showing thought leadership and engaging with certain demographics.

Example: In May 2018, Maggie Lawrence of Marketing for Change and Lynne Doner Lotenberg of Elucidate Change shared with the social marketing listserv an example of using

Twitter to increase voting among U.S. citizens overseas, including military personnel. The social media campaign Marketing for Change, branded "I Voted from Abroad," developed a web tool that allowed overseas U.S. citizens to create and share their own "I Voted From" sticker featuring the country from which they're casting their ballot (see Figure 13.21). By doing so, they could both show their pride as American voters abroad and raise awareness of the overseas voting process and absentee-voting assistance offered by the Federal Voting Assistance Program. The campaign in 2016 generated 5,000 shares on Twitter alone.[50]

Texting

More than 85% of Americans own a smartphone.[51] Not only do they own them, their phones are with them most of the time and they interact with them throughout the day. This has provided an opportunity for marketers to reach their audiences through their smartphones. One way this is done is through texting campaigns.

Example: South Africa has more HIV-positive citizens than any country in the world; in some provinces, more than 40% of the population is infected.[52] With many seeking care only after becoming symptomatic with end-stage AIDS, an ambitious initiative undertaken by Project Masiluleke is tackling this issue using text messaging to get the word out about testing for the virus. Cell phones are abundant in South Africa, with more than 90% of the population (including the young and the poor) using some kind of mobile technology.[53] The developers of Project Masiluleke struck a unique deal with a South African cellular company to send out messages accompanying one million "please call" messages each day for a year. Similar to a PSA, these messages are inserted in the unused space of a "please call me" (PCM) text message, which is a special free form of SMS text widely used in South Africa, substituting a call for a paid text message. One message read, "Frequently sick, tired, losing weight and scared that you might be HIV positive? Please call AIDS Helpline 0800012322." For each PCM message, an accompanying script and frequently asked questions have been provided to helpline operators to ensure consistent and accurate information. Project Masiluleke's PCM campaign is reported to have increased calls to the National AIDS Helpline in Johannesburg by 300%, and project managers believe the potential is to mobilize several hundred thousand South Africans to get tested.[54]

Instagram

Instagram is owned by Facebook allowing for integration between the two platforms (easy to share content and cross-post). It works well for shorter more visually oriented posts. While Instagram is used by just 37% of U.S. adults, it skews younger being used by Maluleka's 71% of 18–29-year-olds.[55]

Example: The following example using Instagram as a communication channel was provided by Carrie Clyne at Rescue/the Behavior Change Agency.[56] *Fresh Empire* is a tobacco prevention campaign designed to prevent and reduce tobacco use among at-risk youth who identify with the hip-hop peer crowd (African American, Hispanic, and Asian American/Pacific Islander youth ages 12–17). As described in Chapter 6, the hip-hop teen peer crowd is one unified by a belief that the odds are stacked against them and they cannot succeed through traditional pathways for success, so they must carve their own path. With research indicating that these teens are 50% more likely to use tobacco than mainstream youth, and a culture promoting imagery and messages portraying tobacco use as a desirable behavior, the campaign sought to shift these perceived norms. In an effort to maximize engagement on social channels, Rescue launched The New Wave rap competition in which hip-hop teens voted for their favorite up and coming tobacco-free artist to be the Leader of The New Wave. The New Wave Instagram content included videos, images, and live stories combining relevant and relatable facts about tobacco usage with culturally authentic insights, reinforced by personal stories and beliefs. Not only did the content run on the Fresh Empire Instagram channel, artists also utilized their own social media channels to encourage their fans to vote and engage with the competition. Results were encouraging, with almost six million impressions, 765,517 exploratory engagements (views, clicks, likes, reactions, and web visits), and 250,979 active engagements (votes, shares, comments, and use of #TheNewWave).

Personal Selling

Perhaps the oldest promotional channel is that of face-to-face selling. Kotler and Keller see this tool as being the most effective at later stages of the buying process and as one that helps build buyer preference, conviction, and action. They cite three distinctive qualities this tool provides: (a) personal interaction—involving an immediate and interactive relationship; (b) cultivation—permitting relationships to grow; and (c) response—making the buyer feel under some obligation for having listened to the "sales talk."[57] And, as illustrated in the following example, the experience doesn't have to be unpleasant.

Example: One Man Helping to Clear the Air Over China. Ma Jun, a well-known Chinese environmentalist who spoke at the 2013 World Social Marketing Conference in Toronto, was named by *Time* magazine in 2006 as one of the world's 100 most influential people. He has also been called an eco-warrior, an innovator, and a modern-day hero.[58] He must be what Margaret Mead had in mind with her famous quote: "Never doubt that a small group of thoughtful committed citizens can change the world. Indeed it's the only thing that ever has." Ma's strategy isn't typical, though, of an activist who is more often drawn to communication channels such as sit-ins or demonstrations. Instead, he personally calls on corporate decision makers and shows them data that provide evidence of environmental pollution and then persuasively talks about the benefits of change.

Although China had penalties for polluters, according to Ma, companies have found it "easier and cheaper to simply pay fines for polluting than to clean up their acts."[59] Concluding in 2006 that credible and "shocking" information was a primary motivator for change, Ma founded the Institute of Public and Environmental Affairs, an agency that gathers data from the government concerning water, air, and hazardous waste and then "exposes" this information. As of April 2013, Ma and his team had exposed more than 120,000 violations by multinational and local companies in China. At least 900 have made efforts to change their techniques,[60] including Apple, which made major efforts to clean up environmental violations in the company's supply chain.[61]

Earned Communication Channels

Public Relations

Public relations is distinguishable by its most favorable outcome—free visibility for your campaign.[62] Successful activities generate free, positive *mentions of your programs in the media*, most commonly as news and special programming on radio and television and as stories, articles, and editorial comments online and in newspapers and magazines. Many refer to these accomplishments as *earned media*, contrasting it to paid media. Additional typical efforts in this channel include planning for *crisis communications* (e.g., responding to adverse or conflicting news), *lobbying* (e.g., for funding allocations), *media advocacy* (e.g., working with the media to take on and advance your social issue), and managing *public affairs* (e.g., issue management). Although some organizations hire public relations firms to handle major campaigns, it is more common for internal staff to handle day-to-day media relations.

Some believe this is one of the more underutilized channels, and yet a well-thought-out program coordinated with other communications-mix elements can be extremely effective. It provides more in-depth coverage of your issue than is often possible with a brief commercial and is often seen as more objective than paid advertising. Tools used to generate news coverage include proactive media pitching, press releases, press kits, news conferences, editorial boards, letters to the editor, and strong personal relationships with key reporters and editors. Siegel and Doner recommend several keys to success:

Build relationships with the media by first "finding out who covers what and then working to position yourself and your initiative as an important, reliable source of information so that the reporters will call you when they are running a story on your topic."[63]

Frame the issues with the goals of the media in mind, "to appeal to the broadest number of audience members possible, and... tell a compelling story that is relevant to their audience and in the public's interest."[64]

Create news by convening a press conference, special event, or demonstration. Consider a technique mastered by the Center for Science in the Public Interest (CSPI) in which their studies create "news that applies pressure to decision makers. For example, after [CSPI's] analysis of the nutrient content of movie popcorn was reported in the media, many major movie chains began using oils lower in saturated fat or offering air-popped options."[65]

Public Service Announcements

As a social marketer working for a public sector or nonprofit organization, you will also have opportunities for *unpaid advertising*, something you know of as PSAs. An obvious advantage of PSAs, of course, is the cost (often free, or at least deeply discounted); the disadvantage is that you do not have the same level of control over where the ad will actually appear in the media or during what program or time of day it will air on television or radio. This perhaps is why some refer to a PSA as "people sound asleep."

In the past, media companies were required by the Federal Communications Commission to run a certain number of PSAs at no charge. This is no longer the case. Because of this, it can be hard to convince a media company to place PSAs. Your best bet is to either go to them with a

FIGURE 13.22 ■ Inside the Prevent Cancer Super Colon™

Source: Janet Hudson, Manager, Exhibit Services, Prevent Cancer Foundation, www.PreventCancer.org.

limited advertising budget and ask for them to match or provide free space as part of the buy. It can also be effective to partner with a private sector organization that is aligned with your cause (and that has a media budget) and approach the media together.

Another option is to try and work with the Ad Council. The Ad Council[66] is an organization that recruits ad agencies and media companies to create and run PSA campaigns. They pick a few issues to work on each year, and their campaigns are created with sponsors that represent the issues (government agencies and non-profits). Media companies do provide free advertising space to the Ad Council to run their campaigns. For large-scale national campaigns addressing high-profile societal issues, it would be worth exploring if an Ad Council partnership is an option for your cause.

Special Events

Special events can also generate visibility for your effort, offering the advantage of interaction with your priority audience and allowing them to ask questions and express attitudes about your desired behaviors that you probably need to hear. The event may be a part of a larger public gathering such as a county fair, or it may be something you have organized just for your campaign. It might include a demonstration (e.g., car seat safety checks), or it might be a presentation at a location where your priority audience shops, dines, or commutes, such as the one in the following example.

Example: An Unusual Tour for Colon Cancer Prevention. Times Square in New York City is a cultural hub featuring upscale hotels, broadway theaters, music, nightlife, quality shops, and gargantuan promotional icons. In 2009, it added one more feature: a giant colon. Since 2003, the Prevent Cancer Foundation had been sponsoring the Prevent Cancer Super Colon™ exhibit, featuring a tour of an inflatable tube, 20 feet long and 8 feet tall—one that most could easily walk through. On February 27, it arrived in New York City to honor March as Colon Cancer

FIGURE 13.23 ■ A Weekly Calendar Intended to Increase Safety Practices on Construction Job Sites

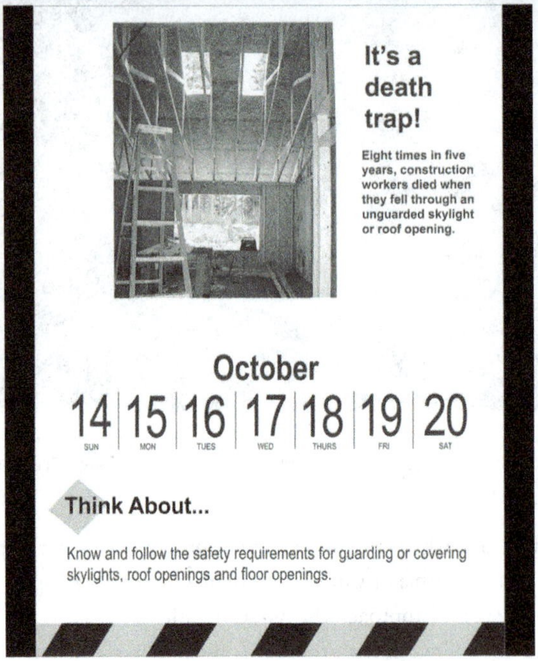

Source: Washington State Department of Labor and Industries.

Awareness Month, with the purpose of increasing timely colon cancer screening. As visitors take the tour, they get an up-close look at healthy colon tissue, tissue with nonmalignant colorectal disease, colorectal polyps, and various stages of colorectal cancer (see Figure 13.22). The Prevent Cancer Super Colon attracted over 1,500 visitors that week in Times Square, and then throughout 2009, traveled across the nation reaching out to people in small towns as well as big cities, stopping at health fairs, hospitals, and cancer centers.[67] As of 2014, the Super Colon has visited 49 states, the District of Columbia, and Puerto Rico.[68]

Owned Communication Channels

Materials

This is one of the most familiar and utilized communication channels for social marketing campaigns. *Videos, brochures, newsletters, booklets, flyers, calendars, bumper stickers, door hangers, and catalogs* provide opportunities to present more detailed information regarding the desired behavior and the social marketing program. Sometimes, but not as often as you might like, priority audiences hold on to these materials, and ideally even share them with others. In some cases, special materials are developed and distributed to other key internal and external groups, such as program partners and the media. Included in this channel category are any collateral pieces associated with the program, such as *letterheads, envelopes*, and *business cards*.

Example: A Calendar to Increase Workplace Safety "Keep Washington safe and working," the mission statement of the Washington State Department of Labor & Industries (L&I), also serves as the title of the annual calendar produced by L&I's Division of Occupational Safety and Health. First published in 2007, the calendar explains job hazards and provides safety tips. In 2009, the calendar began featuring real Washington state businesses and employees in a variety of industries. This educational tool brings important safety messages to employers and workers 365 days a year. L&I produces and distributes 12,000 copies a year (see Figure 13.23).

Websites and Online

To increase visibility for your website, *search engine marketing* has evolved immensely in the past several years, and many of us are not fully exhausting recommended strategies to increase the visibility of our website when someone conducts a Google-type search (e.g., "natural gardening"). There are paid options to ensure a ranking, often with a "pay per click" fee structure, a strategy that probably makes more business sense in the for-profit sector. There are also numerous unpaid options to improve the chances that your site will make the first results page, if not the top of that page (i.e., your site's ranking). Ranking can be improved by enhancing a website's structure, content, and keyword submissions.

Websites are a critical "touch point" for your customer, one that not only impacts awareness and attitudes toward your organization but also makes a difference in whether your audience is inspired and supported to act (e.g., to pledge to keep a lawn pesticide free). Some even believe your website could be "the third place," a term referring to social surroundings different from

FIGURE 13.24 ■ A Posting on the Website From Ananda pledging Pledging to Use Biodegradable Detergents (http://westmauikumuwai.org/take-the-pledge/)

Source: West Maui Kumuwai.

the two usual social environments of home and the workplace (customers of Starbucks, for example, might classify their coffee spot as one of their third places).

Blogs are another online tool that can be "owned" with the author controlling the message and the distribution of the content.

To maximize the influence of your website, experts advise that you pay attention to your site's (a) ease of navigation, (b) ability to tailor itself to different users, (c) availability of related links, and (d) potential for two-way communications as illustrated in the following example.[69]

Example: A Website to Highlight Citizens Taking Action to Protect Ocean Health. West Maui Kumuwai is a movement to protect the ocean through inspiring personal action and community collaboration, a movement with many moving parts. Just Googling the name provides a glimpse of the multiple platforms that feature their work as well as their website, including Twitter, YouTube, Facebook, and Instagram. A core strategy is to feature individuals in the West Maui community taking personal action to reduce polluted runoff and to share their stories on the website along with photos of the individual and a personal quote. An example from Julie is typical:

I was in Ace Hardware Hawaii in Lahaina, debating about what fertilizer to buy and I noticed a sticker that read "Ocean Preferred." It really helped, and was the deciding factor in my purchase. I appreciate Ace making it easy for customers to choose more environmentally responsible products. Mahalo!

Additional features on the website include opportunities to participate in volunteer activities (e.g., help clear invasive plants) and to post a pledge to take one of eight specific actions (e.g., use a drip water system), even showing individuals holding up a sign of what they have pledged (see Figure 13.24).

Special Promotional Items

You can reinforce and sometimes sustain campaign messages through the use of special promotional items, referred to by some in the industry as "swag." Among the most familiar are messages on *clothing* (e.g., T-shirts, baseball hats, diapers, and bibs), *functional items* (e.g., key chains, water bottles, litterbags, pens and pencils, notepads, bookmarks, book covers, and

FIGURE 13.25 ■ A Promotional Item, a Flashlight, That Also Helps Overcome Barriers to "Scooping the Poop" in the Dark

Source: Author Photo.

FIGURE 13.26 ■ A Temporary Tattoo Signaling "Good Job, Aja!"

Source: Author photo.

FIGURE 13.27 ■ Sign in a Public Park

Source: Author photo.

refrigerator magnets), and more *temporary mechanisms* (e.g., bar coasters, stickers, temporary tattoos, coffee sleeves, sports cards, and lapel buttons). Some campaigns, such as the one in the following example, create a treasure chest of these items.

Example: Temporary Tattoos and More for Pooper Scoopers. In Snohomish County, Washington, Dave Ward of the Snohomish County Public Works Department understood the difference between an awareness campaign and a social marketing campaign. He also understands how important it is to research priority audiences' current attitudes and practices regarding picking up pet waste and to focus on creative strategies to promote very specific behaviors by solving the customer's problem.

His research among pet owners revealed that 42% picked up their dog's waste regularly and disposed of it properly in the trash; 42% were picking it up regularly but not disposing of it properly (e.g., they were burying it on their property); and 16% were picking it up only sometimes or not at all. To promote "proper behaviors," the county created concrete and vivid communications: "More than 126,000 dogs live in Snohomish County, producing waste equivalent to a city of 40,000 people. More than 20 tons of dog waste are dropped in Snohomish County backyards every day." Observation research then helped define the problem even further. Although citizens appeared to be fairly reliable in picking up pet waste on public property such as sidewalks and parks (where they could be seen), they were less judicious in their own backyards.

Ask dog owners why they don't pick up their dog's waste in their yard, and you might hear what Dave did: "When I come home from work at night and let the dog out to go, it's too dark to see where they go." To address this barrier, a free functional promotional item was developed, a small flashlight that could be left by the door, serving not only as a way to follow the pet around the yard but also as a prompt for the desired behavior on a regular basis (see Figure 13.25). And to spread the word and recognize these pooper scoopers, another promotional item, a temporary tattoo for the hand with the words "I'm a pooper scooper," was especially popular among youth (see Figure 13.26).[70]

Signage and Displays

Many social marketing campaigns rely on signage and displays to launch and, especially, sustain campaign messages. Examples of those more permanent items include *road signs* warning against drinking and driving, reminding people to use a litterbag, and asking motorists to "move right for sirens and lights." *Signs on government property and establishments regulated by the government* can be used to target messages, such as signs in forests asking people to pick up pet waste (see Figure 13.27), plaques in bars with messages warning about the dangers of alcohol when pregnant, and signs at airports urging us to remove computers from our bags before reaching the checkpoint. Displays and signage can also be used at point of purchase in *retail environments* (e.g., for life vests, tarps for covering pickup loads, energy-saving lightbulbs, and natural pesticides). In this case, preparing signage and special displays will include selling the idea to distribution channel decision makers and coordinating distribution of any special signage and accompanying materials.

Popular Entertainment Media

A less well-known and underused media category employs popular forms of entertainment to carry behavior change messages, referred to as popular entertainment media by some and edutainment by others. These include movies, television series, radio programs, comic books, comic strips, songs, theater, video games, and traveling entertainers such as puppeteers, mimes, and poets. Social marketing messages integrated into programming, scripts, and performances have included topics such as drinking and driving, use of condoms, eating disorders, recycling, youth suicide, organ donation, HIV testing, avoiding loan fraud, and sudden infant death syndrome.

Alan Andreasen sees this approach as a very effective one in overcoming the problems of selective exposure and selective attention on the part of indifferent target audiences. "This has come to be called the Entertainment Education Approach.[71] It began in the 1960s with a soap opera in Peru called *Simplemente Maria*, which discussed family planning, among other topics."[72] And John Davies, an international social marketing consultant who refers to these initiatives as "edutainment."[73] One more current example illustrating this application is the inclusion of financial messages in 7 of 35 episodes of a Mexican Soap opera, Mucho Corazon. The World Bank worked with the show's producers to include content related to several themes including creating a budget, saving, investing, and avoiding financial abuse.[74] On a local level, you might try persuading local celebrities popular with the priority audience to develop special promotional products (e.g., songs on their CDs) to perform at special events or to be featured in advertisements. In a national award–winning television spot for Mississippi's antilitter campaign, for example, former first lady Pat Fordice magically appears in the cab of a pickup truck between two "Bubbas," one of whom has gleefully tossed trash out the window. Pinching the ears of the driver and his offending pal, Fordice admonishes the pair for littering Mississippi highways. The former first lady continued as a spokesperson and representative of the campaign with the tagline "I'm Not Your Mama! Pick It Up, Mississippi!"[75]

Efforts to make this happen on a large scale, however, are likely to be substantial and costly and may include lobbying and partnership efforts with the entertainment industry. The CDC, for example, often partners with Hollywood executives and academic, public health, and advocacy organizations to share information with writers and producers about the nation's pressing health issues. Knowing that an estimated 88% of people in America learn about health issues from television, they believe prime time and daytime television programs are great outlets for health messages. To facilitate this, they provide tip sheets for TV writers and producers, conduct expert briefings for writers, and respond to inquiries for health information. They arrange expert briefings for the entire writing staff of a TV show, set up one-on-one conversations between a producer and a health expert to explore storyline possibilities, and help find real people who deal with health issues firsthand. They also present awards and acknowledgments for exemplary portrayal of health issues, as they did in 2013 when they awarded a Sentinel for Health Award to HBO's *Enlightened* for its depiction of a character's struggle during drug rehab and why people relapse.[76]

Another impressive trend is also seen as an opportunity for popular media. By 2007, video games had surpassed movie rental, music, and box office films in terms of time and dollars spent. In fact, since 2005, an annual Games for Change Conference has been held in New York City to inspire organizations to use video games to further social change, and there is now a website (http://www.gamesforchange.org/) that provides a listing and description of over 175 games (2018) intended to support change for social good, including ones to increase literacy and decrease bullying.

You have, no doubt, experienced public art intended to advocate a cause (e.g., white crosses in a park to protest a war), attract tourists (e.g., Cows on Parade in Chicago), or raise money for a nonprofit organization (e.g., quilts for AIDS victims). But what about public art intended to actually influence behaviors—behaviors to improve health, safety, the environment, or financial well-being? We think it is another emerging and untapped channel, with unique potential to sustain behaviors, create media attention, and be seen as a credible messenger. Channel types include *sculptures, exhibits, murals, paintings*, and "*flash mobs.*"

Example: To help make real the problem that millions of tons of plastic enter the ocean each year affecting the health of marine wildlife, ecosystems, and humans, a traveling exhibit *Washed Ashore* features large sculptures of marine life constructed out of plastic debris collected at beaches. Sculptures are colorful and detailed and use a variety of objects made with plastic including those most familiar such as plastic bottles, straws, and plastic bags, as well as those not often thought of including golf balls, flip flops, balloons, toys, and fishing gear. In the end, exhibits are intended to inspire more people to think of ways to reduce their own plastic footprint.[77]

FACTORS GUIDING COMMUNICATION CHANNEL DECISIONS

Clearly, you have numerous channel options available for getting your messages to priority audiences. Choices and decisions can be guided by a few important factors, eight of which are described in the following sections, in no particular order, since each is an important consideration. Some are even deal breakers.

Factor 1: Campaign Objectives and Goals

In Step 4 of your planning process, you ideally set a quantifiable goal for changes in behavior, behavior intent, awareness, and/or attitudes. Those measures/targets are now your guide for selecting communication channels.

For example, it makes sense that if you want 50 homes in a neighborhood of 500 homes on a river to be stream stewards, you will have a very different outreach (communication) strategy than if you want five million residents of a state to be aware of an *Escherichia coli* outbreak. Confirming these numbers ahead of time with funders and team members will help you make the case for the strategies that you then propose.

Factor 2: Desired Reach and Frequency

Kotler and Armstrong describe *reach* as "a measure of the percentage of people in the priority audience who are exposed to the ad campaign during a given period of time" and *frequency* as "a measure of how many times the average person in the target audience is exposed to the message."[78] This will be an important decision. For example, a state health department may want radio and television spots to reach 75% of youth aged 12–18 living in major metropolitan areas at least nine times during a two-month campaign. Media representatives will then use computer programs to produce media schedules and associated costs to achieve these objectives. The media planner often looks at the cost of the plan and calculates the cost per contact or exposure (often expressed as the *cost per thousand*—the cost of reaching 1,000 people using the medium).

Factor 3: Your Priority Audience

Perhaps the most important consideration when planning media strategies will be the *priority audience's profile* (demographics, psychographics, geographics, and behaviors) and their *media habits*. This will be especially important when selecting among social media platforms and using paid advertising and selecting specific media vehicles, such as radio stations, television programs, sections of the newspaper, magazines, and direct mail lists. Ideally, these were identified as "openings" when developing the creative brief. In 2017, for example, the U.S. Food and Drug Administration announced an adult smoking cessation campaign encouraging cigarette smokers with an intention to quit with messages displayed in and around gas stations and convenience stores, locations where smokers face a multitude of triggers, including cigarette ads. Messages including "Every Try Counts" encourage these smokers to rethink their next pack of cigarettes at the most critical of places[79] (see Figure 13.28). Again, media representatives will be able to provide audience profiles and recommendations. The goal will be to choose general media types, specific vehicles, and the timing most likely to reach, appeal to, and influence priority audiences. *Compatibility* of the social marketing program and associated messages will also be key and will contribute to the ultimate impact of the given medium. For example, a

FIGURE 13.28 ■ Encouraging Smokers With an Intention to Quit at Points of Purchase

Source: EveryTryCounts.gov.

message regarding safe gun storage is more strategically aligned with a parenting magazine than one on home decorating, even though both may have readerships with similar demographic profiles. And the timing of this ad would be best linked to special issues on youth violence or campus shootings.

Factor 4: Being There Just in Time

Many social marketers have found that an ideal moment to speak to the priority audience is when they are about to choose between alternative, competing behaviors. They are at a fork in the road, and the social marketer wants a last chance to influence this decision. Tactics demonstrating this principle include the following:

- The use of the ♥ symbol on menus signifying a smart choice for those interested in options that are low in fat, cholesterol, and/or calories
- Calories posted on menu boards
- The familiar forest fire prevention signs that give updates on the current level of threat for forest fires in the park
- A message on the backs of diapers reminding parents to turn their infants over, onto their backs, to sleep
- The idea of encouraging smokers (in the contemplation stage) to insert their child's photo under the wrappers of cigarette packs
- A sign at a beach that makes the benefit of a life vest clear (see Figure 13.29)
- A key chain for teens with the message "You Don't Have to Be Buzzed to Be Busted"
- A card on a table in a university library warning students not to leave their belongings unattended (see Figure 13.30)

Factor 5: Being There "In the Event Of"

Communicators also want to prepare for events that are likely to motivate priority audiences to listen, learn more, and alter their behaviors. Examples would include an earthquake, a teen suicide in a small community, the listing of an endangered species, threats of drought and power blackouts, a famous female entertainer diagnosed with AIDS, a governor injured in an automobile accident while not wearing a seatbelt, a college student sexually assaulted after a rave party, or a politician diagnosed with prostate cancer. Events such as these often affect levels of awareness and belief relative to costs and benefits associated with behavior change.

The amount of time it will take to learn about and prepare a home for a potential earthquake will seem minor compared with suffering the costs and losses in a real earthquake. Though such events are often tragic, the silver lining is that priority audiences in the precontemplation stage are often moved to contemplation, even action, and the social marketer can take advantage of the momentum created by heightened publicity and the need for practical information. Just as

FIGURE 13.29 ■ A Sign at a Beach Shows the Benefit of a Life Vest

Source: Author photo.

FIGURE 13.30 ■ A Business-Size Card Left at a Table in the Library When a Student Left the Table Unattended

Source: Author photo.

public relations professionals prepare for crisis communications, the social marketer wants to prepare for these *opportunity communications*.

Example: A Timely Message on Earthquake Preparedness. On Sunday, 13 March 2011, three days after the 8.9 earthquake off the coast of Japan, a front-page headline in the *Seattle Times* read "GETTING READY FOR DISASTER. See Page A13 for a clip-and-save guide to make sure your family are ready if disaster strikes." Editors had likely been ready long before the quake with the full-page checklist, including tips on storing copies of important documents such as birth certificates, making a family emergency plan, having a list of important phone numbers, and knowing how and when to turn off the gas, as well as a list of supplies for the home as well as the car. Publishing this when readers "were awake" to the reality of disasters certainly ensured that more would look at the list—even clip it out and start checking off completed items.

Factor 6: Integrated Marketing Communications

Commercial marketers routinely invest millions of dollars in marketing communications, and this experience has led many companies to adopt the concept of *integrated marketing communications* (IMC), "where a company carefully integrates and coordinates its many communication channels to deliver a clear, consistent, and compelling message about the organization and its products."[80]

With IMC, you achieve consistency in the use of slogans, images, colors, font types, key messages, and sponsor mentions in all media vehicles and customer touch points. It means that statistics and facts used in press releases are the same as those in printed materials. It means that television commercials have the same tone and style as radio spots and that print ads have the same look and feel as the program's social media.[81]

In addition, IMC points to the need for a graphic identity and perhaps even a statement or manual describing graphic standards. The integrated approach also addresses the need for coordination and cooperation among those developing and disseminating program materials and, finally, calls for regular audits of all customer touch points.

Benefits of an integrated approach are significant, including (a) increased efficiency in developing materials (e.g., eliminating the need for frequent debates over colors and typefaces and incremental costs of developing new executions) and (b) increased effectiveness of communications, given their consistent presentation in the marketplace.

Example: Friends Don't Let Friends Drive Drunk. In the early 1990s, the Ad Council and the U.S. Department of Transportation's National Highway Traffic Safety Administration introduced a new campaign encouraging friends to intervene in order to prevent a drunk person from getting behind the wheel. It was originally designed to reach 16- to 24-year-olds, who accounted for 42% of all fatal alcohol-related car crashes.[82] Eighty-four percent of Americans recall having

FIGURE 13.31 ■ Magazine Insert From a Memorable Campaign

Source: Courtesy of the US Department of Transportation and the Ad Council.

TABLE 13.5 ■ Profiles of Major Media Types

Medium	Advantages	Disadvantages
Newspapers	Flexibility, timeliness, good local market coverage, broad acceptability, high believability	Short life, poor reproduction quality, small pass-along audience
Television	Good mass-market coverage; low cost per exposure; combines sight, sound, and motion; appealing to the senses	High absolute costs, high clutter, fleeting exposure, less audience selectivity
Direct mail	High audience selectivity, flexibility, allows personalization	Relative high cost per exposure, "junk mail" image
Radio	Good local acceptance, high geographic and demographic selectivity, low cost	Audio only, fleeting exposure, low attention ("the half-hear" medium); fragmented audiences
Magazines	High geographic and demographic selectivity, credibility, and prestige; high-quality reproduction; long life; good pass-along readership	Long ad purchase lead time, high cost, no guarantee of position
Outdoor	Flexibility, high repeat exposure, low cost, low message competition, good positional selectivity	Little audience selectivity, creative limitations
Social media	Timeliness, ability to leverage target audience networks, provides for interactions and feedback, ability to personalize, ability to prompt and reinforce behaviors	Resource intensive, primarily audience controlled Clutter
Websites	High selectivity, low cost, immediacy, interactive capabilities	Small, demographically skewed audience; relatively low impact
Sales promotions	Attention getting, stronger and quicker buyer response, incentives add value	Short life, potential image of "trinkets and trash"
Public relations	High credibility, ability to catch prospects off guard, ability to reach prospects preferring to avoid salespeople and advertisements	Less audience reach and frequency
Events and experiences	Relevance, high involvement and active engagement, "softer sell"	Less audience reach, high cost per exposure
Personal selling	Effective for understanding consumer objections and for building buyer preference, conviction, action, and relationships	Audience resistance, high cost

Source: Adapted from Philip Kotler and Gary M. Armstrong, *Principles of Marketing* (Upper Saddle River, NJ: Prentice Hall, 2001), 553. Reprinted with permission.

seen or heard a PSA with the now famous "Friends Don't Let Friends Drive Drunk" tagline. More impressive, nearly 80% report they have taken action to prevent a friend or loved one from driving drunk, and 25% report they have stopped drinking and driving as a result of the campaign.[83] This hard-hitting campaign was instrumental; it is reported, in achieving a 10% decrease in alcohol-related fatalities between 1990 and 1991—the single largest one-year drop in alcohol-related fatalities ever recorded.[84] Communication channels have been consistent in their use of the tagline, emotional themes, and memorable stories of "innocent victims" and have included PSAs produced for TV, radio, print, out-of-home, and online media outlets and, more recently, social media including Facebook (see Figure 13.31). As of 2018, the Ad Council's website reports more than 68% of Americans have tried to prevent someone from driving after drinking.[85]

Factor 7: Advantages and Disadvantages of Media Types

Media decisions should also be based on the advantages and limitations of each unique media type and should take into consideration the nature and format of key messages established in the creative brief. For example, a brief message such as "Choose a designated driver" can fit on a key chain or bar coaster, whereas a complex one such as "How to talk with your teen about suicide" would be more appropriate in a video, website, or on a special radio program. Table 13.5 presents a summary of advantages and limitations for each of the major advertising categories.

Factor 8: Your Budget

Even when all other factors are considered, resources and funding may very well have the final say in determining communication channels. In the ideal scenario, as we have discussed, media strategies and associated budgets are based on desired and agreed-upon campaign goals (e.g., reach 75% of youth at least nine times). In reality, plans are more often influenced by budgets and available funding sources. For example, first estimates of a draft media plan to achieve the above goal may indicate that costs for the desired reach and frequency exceed actual and fixed budgets. In this (all-too-common) scenario, you will need to prioritize and allocate funding to media types and vehicles judged to be most efficient and effective. In some cases, it may then be necessary and appropriate to reduce campaign goals (e.g., reach 50% of youth at least nine times) and/or create a phased approach to campaign implementation (e.g., achieve the reach and frequency goals in half the state).

ETHICAL CONSIDERATIONS RELATED TO PROMOTION STRATEGIES

Many of the ethical issues regarding communications seem straightforward. Information should be accurate and not misleading. Language and graphics should be clear and appropriate for audiences exposed to the communications. Gray areas are hard to avoid, however, and what and whose criteria should be used to decide whether something is appropriate? Is this tagline in a teen sexual assault prevention campaign too risky—"If you force her to have sex, you're screwed"—even though it tested well with the priority audience? Should someone blow the whistle on a local television station promoting the TV sitcom *Friends* on an outdoor billboard by featuring photos of the three slender stars and the headline "Cute Anorexic Chicks"? These two examples illustrate instances that may work well for one priority audience group but may also offend or trigger trauma in others. It is important to evaluate the potential impact of messages on all people that may see them.

Ethical considerations will also be a factor when choosing communication channels. Does the end justify the means in a case where antiabortionists block the entrance to clinics and threaten the lives of doctors? Or what about a case in which activists threaten (but do not physically harm) a person wearing a fur coat? Considerable mention has been made of channels involving access to computers, emails, and the Internet. What about the fact that many members of a priority audience don't have this access, or even the skills, to fully utilize and benefit from these new media campaigns?

Organizations, understandably, have ethical and legal concerns about the use of social media, especially regarding security, staff productivity, and negative postings from readers. To address this, many organizations develop and distribute formal policy and best-practice statements.

In most cases, the funders of the effort will likely be the ones to make the final call but as a social marketer, it is your job to identify the potential impacts and solutions when these ethical dilemmas arise.

And here's one to ponder: Is it wrong to advertise for a kidney donor? In 2010, in the United States, 19 people on average die each day waiting for an organ transplant, 10 of them waiting for a kidney.[86] MatchingDonors.com is a nonprofit organization trying to improve the odds of finding an organ donor for patients needing transplants. Reportedly, they have the world's largest database of available altruistic donors, ones who are not allowed to receive any financial benefit from organ donation. Some physicians wage campaigns against such websites, believing the practice is unethical and should be illegal, as it "bypasses" the national organ donor list. Proponents of the website argue that those on the organ donor list get organs harvested only from cadavers and that there are currently 70,000 people waiting for a kidney and that half of those on this list will die while waiting.[87]

COVID-19 Social Marketing Example

For this chapter, examples of COVID-19 efforts are featured in the Case and Research Highlights.

CHAPTER SUMMARY

Promotion is persuasive communication and the tool we count on to ensure that the priority audience knows about the offer, believes they will experience the stated benefits, and is inspired to act. There are four major components of a communications strategy:

- *Messages:* What you want to communicate, inspired by what you want your priority audience to do, know, and believe
- *Messengers:* Who will deliver your messages or be perceived to be sponsoring or supporting your offer
- *Creative strategy:* What you will actually say and show and how you want to say it, including any brand name developed for the campaign
- *Communication channels:* Where and when your messages will appear (distinct, of course, from distribution channels)

Several tips are suggested to assist you in evaluating and choosing a creative strategy:

1. Keep it simple and clear.
2. Focus on audience benefits.
3. When using fear, follow up with solutions and use credible sources.
4. Try for messages that are vivid, personal, and concrete.
5. Make messages easy to remember.
6. Have a little fun sometimes.
7. Try for a "big idea."
8. Consider a question instead of a nag.
9. Make norms (more) visible.
10. Tell real stories about real people.
11. Try crowdsourcing.
12. Appeal to psychographics.

Before producing campaign materials, you are encouraged to pretest messages and creative concepts, even if informally. You will be testing their ability to deliver on the objectives for your campaign, especially those outlined in your creative brief. Potential pitfalls in testing are real and can be minimized by carefully constructing questioning and briefing respondents as well as colleagues and clients.

Communication channels, also referred to as media channels, can be categorized as one of four types:

- Paid
  - Advertising
  - Product integration in media/programming
- Shared
  - Organic social media

  - Personal selling

- Earned
  - Public relations
  - Public service announcements
  - Special events

- Owned
  - Materials
  - Websites and online
  - Special promotional items
  - Signage and displays
  - Popular and entertainment media

In addition, eight factors are presented to guide your selection of communication types, vehicles, and timing:

Factor 1: Your campaign objectives and goals

Factor 2: Desired reach and frequency

Factor 3: Your priority audience

Factor 4: Being there just in time

Factor 5: Being there "in the event of"

Factor 6: Integrated marketing communications

Factor 7: Knowing the advantages and disadvantages of media types

Factor 8: Your budget

RESEARCH HIGHLIGHT
VACCINATE WA

(2022)

The Vaccinate WA team at the WA DOH used ongoing research with varied methodologies to inform all stages of campaign promotional strategy development. This started by analyzing trusted secondary research sources to inform initial primary research. Subsequently, five types of research were used to inform the Vaccinate WA campaign strategy, messages, and creative concepts:

- **Gates Foundation Statewide Polling**: WA DOH partnered with the Gates Foundation to poll 1,000+ Washingtonians to inform on vaccine intent, behavior, barriers, benefits, and motivators.

- **2020 Qualitative Research**: Conducted a four-day, online qualitative research study with 120 research participants, 12 from each of 10 audience segments (e.g., Rural, LGBTQ+, college students, etc.).

- **In-language Stakeholder Interviews**: Conducted 1:1 interview in 15 languages every other month throughout the campaign. Community members served as interview moderators.
- **2021–2022 Market Research Online Community (MROC)**: WA DOH created a MROC with more than 850 Washington residents. An MROC is a community of research participants that are available to quickly provide input on an ongoing basis. This community has informed the campaign throughout 2021–2022 with two to three quantitative and/or qualitative research exercises per week. Research activities include open-ended questions, projective techniques, feedback on messaging/concepts, and ranking/rating barriers, benefits, and motivations.
- **Focus Groups and Community Research**: Focus groups and in-community research were employed to reach audience segments that were hard to reach through the other research methodologies. This included an advisory board of young adults that met eight times throughout 2021, focus groups with PWCVs, people that were a "hard-no" about getting the vaccine, young adults and members of the Hispanic/Latinx community. The team also conduct 1:1 interviews and community conversations with members of the Black/African American community.

Table 13.6 provides examples of research findings and how they informed the campaigns:

TABLE 13.6 ■ Research Findings Informing Vaccinate WA Campaign

Research Findings	How They Were Applied
Mixed emotions dominated by anxiety, worry, and nervousness drive a vaccine *"wait and see" mentality.*	Used social norming techniques to try and spur the "wait and see" audience to get vaccinated. This included sharing numbers of how many people had been vaccinated and sharing the stories and experiences from many different types of people who had gotten the vaccine.
The *biggest barrier was concern over the safety* of the vaccine. Political involvement and mistrust of "big pharma" contribute to this concern.	Shared the data about and partnered with trusted experts from the medical community to talk about the vaccine's safety.
Experience with systemic racism added level of mistrust around vaccines for some audiences.	Addressed these concerns by being direct and transparent and discussing the issue openly. Held expert panels and developed detailed content like blogs that talked about the history of vaccines and medical testing that create mistrust among audiences.
Doctors and other *healthcare providers were by far the most trusted source* for vaccine information.	Local doctors, nurses, and other healthcare providers have been prominently featured in all aspects of the Vaccinate WA campaign.
The desire to *protect loved ones, community members, and the vulnerable* was a strong motivator.	Protecting the community was a central message in many of the campaign messages.

TABLE 13.6 ■ Research Findings Informing Vaccinate WA Campaign

Research Findings	How They Were Applied
"Operation Warp Speed" increased concern: parallel vaccine production and testing was not intuitive to the audience and was seen as concerning rather than encouraging.	Did not focus on "Operation Warp Speed" or rapid development in our messaging strategy.
Young adults were getting vaccinated at slower rates, not due to hesitancy, but due to a lack of urgency and not being that concerned about getting COVID-19. Their primary motivator was getting to go back to doing all the things they love to do.	Two high-energy campaigns (*Get Ready for Summer* and *Do More of Whatever You're Into*) were launched letting young adults know that getting vaccinated was a way to get back to doing all the things they love to do.
Members of *the Black/African American community had deep levels of mistrust around the vaccine* that were being exacerbated by perceived government efforts to force or bribe people to take the vaccine. There was also a feeling that it was developed too fast leading to unknowns around potential risks and side effects.	Worked with members of the community to create two campaigns (*Here for Us* and *WeConsider*) that told the stories of people in the community with their own voices, with the goal of inspiring people to make their own choice about the vaccine.
The majority of PWCV who had not yet gotten the vaccine were hesitant due to safety and efficacy concerns. They wanted *to make the decisions for themselves based on straightforward scientific information about the vaccine.* They were distrustful of government information sources and became less likely to get the vaccine if they felt they were being convinced or coerced into making the decision.	We delivered straightforward messaging to communities with large number of PWCV. We sourced information so that people could go learn more for themselves about the vaccine.
People that had *made a "hard-no" decision did not appear to be persuadable* to get the vaccine.	Did not pursue communications to this audience segment knowing that doing so was likely to have the opposite impact we were seeking, making them even more resistant to get the vaccine.
Parents primarily had safety concerns about getting their children the COVID-19 vaccine and the most trusted messenger for information about vaccinating their child was their child's pediatrician. Many had also been skipping regular child check-ups during COVID-19 so were not being prompted by their pediatrician to get their child vaccinated.	Partnered with pediatricians to talk about the safety of the vaccine among children and also created messaging from both kids and parents about their experiences with the vaccine. Ran a campaign to encourage parents to schedule their annual check-ups for their child in order to increase the likelihood of parent/pediatrician conversations about the COVID-19 vaccine.

DISCUSSION QUESTIONS AND EXERCISES

1. The authors suggested that you might be surprised that you are two thirds of the way through the planning process and just now getting to what some people think is marketing: promotion. Why is the promotional tool developed after selecting priority audiences; a desired behavior; a positioning statement; and product, price, and place strategies?
2. What are the three major factors contributing to messenger credibility? Give an example of a credible messenger for a campaign you have seen. It can be for a commercial, nonprofit, or social marketing effort.
3. How would you explain the difference between social media and social marketing to someone who thinks they are the same?
4. Share examples of social marketing efforts using social media that you are aware of or have implemented.

PART IV

MANAGING SOCIAL MARKETING PROGRAMS

14 STEP 8: MONITORING AND EVALUATION

LEARNING OBJECTIVES

Upon completion of this chapter, you should be able to:

14.1 Identify the five major components of a comprehensive evaluation plan, and explain the distinction between monitoring and evaluation.

14.2 Choose among the potential reasons for **why** you are conducting an evaluation.

14.3 List the five major categories related to **what** you might measure.

14.4 Identify options for methodologies and techniques for **how** you will conduct measurements.

14.5 Identify three major options for **when** you will conduct measurements.

14.6 Give examples of minimal, moderate, and significant evaluation **costs**.

14.7 Note any major ethical issues related to campaign evaluations.

Now you've reached a step you may not be eager for—developing a plan for monitoring and evaluation. If this is true for you, your experiences and conversations may sound similar to the following common laments:

- "My administrators and additional funders think it's nice I can report on how many PSAs we ran and how many hits we got to our website, but I can see it in their eyes. It's not enough. They want to know how many more people got an HIV/AIDS test as a result of our efforts. And actually, that's not even enough. What they really want to know is how many positives did we find and how much did it cost us to find each one."
- "You think that's hard. In my line of work, they want to know if the fish are any healthier."
- "Most of the evaluation strategies I've looked at could cost as much as the small budget I have for this campaign. I honestly can't justify it. And yet, everyone seems to want it."

- "Quite frankly, my concern is with the results. What if it's bad news—that we didn't reach our goal? They like the plan, are going to fully fund it, and trust that we know what we're doing. Bad news could dampen any further work like this."

This chapter describes the five major components to be included in an evaluation plan, Step 8 in this model:

1. *Purpose.* Why are you conducting this evaluation, and who is the audience?
2. *Results to be measured.* What will you measure in order to achieve the evaluation purpose?
3. *Methods.* How will you conduct these measurements?
4. *Timing.* When will these measurements be made and by whom? Will it include a pretest and/or pilot?
5. *Budget.* How much will it cost?

CASE HIGHLIGHT
CLOSING DUMPSTER LIDS

(Pilot Program Summary—2021)

The following Case Highlight exemplifies the process for conducting a program pilot effort. It is also a testimonial of the benefits of regional collaboration in the development and implementation of a pilot.

In Washington State, in fall 2020, 25 Regional Municipalities who are members of Stormwater Outreach for Regional Municipalities (STORM) participated in the development of a social marketing effort. The group became known as the Dumpster Outreach Group (DOG). The DOG Planning Team consisted of eight participating members who then volunteered to help lead a Pilot Program in 2021, attending regular planning meetings, reviewing materials, and guiding the pilot program and evaluation. The DOG Planning Team engaged a local marketing agency with environmental project and social marketing expertise to assist with pilot phase development.

Background, Purpose, and Focus

A statement by a team lead summarized the "wicked problem" to be addressed. "Puget Sound is in trouble. Toxic runoff causes aquatic habitat damage, putting many of our indigenous aquatic species at risk. Most of the pollution reaching Puget Sound comes from polluted stormwater runoff."[1] A clear purpose was established to *reduce stormwater pollution to surface waters*, with a focus on *dumpster lids*, given the high probability that uncovered and leaking dumpsters will cause pollutants like chemicals, bacteria, and organic matter to end up in stormwater runoff.[2]

TABLE 14.1 ■ Audience Insights Related to Closing Dumpster Lids "Every	
Barriers	Dumpster full so can't close Can't reach the lid Lid is heavy Don't think about it/forget
Benefits	Reduce pests on the property Get rid of smells Reduce illegal use of our dumpsters by others Have cleaner look Keep the rain out
Motivators	Reminder to close the lid Make it easier to put it down Point out what pollution it is causing Being compliant with the law
Influential Others	Business Manager/Boss Property Owners City Inspectors Neighbors

Priority Audience and Desired Behavior

The priority audience for their effort would be those *commercial businesses* within each participating municipality that were not consistently closing their dumpster lids. The desired behavior change was for them to *close dumpster lids every time something is put in the dumpster.*

Audience Insights

Partners in the pilot effort conducted audience research that provided the following inspirational audience insights (see Table 14.1).

Positioning Statement

Based on these insights, the team decided they wanted businesses to see closing lids on dumpsters every time as a simple way to have pest and odor-free dumpster areas that are clean for them and the environment, reduce illegal use, and be compliant with regulations.

Marketing Intervention Strategies

Inspired by their audience research, the team brainstormed potential components of an intervention tool kit, conducted research to pretest strategies such as slogans, and then tested the following strategies in the 2021 Pilot.

Product:

- *Core*: Pest and odor-free dumpsters with no rain inside
- *Actual*: Permanent signage and stickers; Site visits
- *Augmented*: Stepstools; Tool for pulling down lids; Consulting

FIGURE 14.1 ■ Dumpster Lid Pilot Pledge

Source: Washington Stormwater "Dumpster Outreach Group".

Price:

- *Monetary Incentives*: Free stepstool
- *Monetary Disincentives*: Cost to dispose of illegal dumping; Staff having to clean up around dumpsters or pay someone to do the cleaning, being required to have their storm system cleaned
- *Nonmonetary Incentives*: Pledges (see Figure 14.1); Visible window clings, stickers, and signage on site for taking the pledge; Rewards (e.g., chocolate fish)
- *Nonmonetary Disincentives*: Reminder letter for those not following behavior; Photos of unclosed lids

Place:

- *Tangible goods*: Distributed at business dumpster locations
- *Site visit*: One-on-one conversation

Promotion:

- *Messages*: Cleaner, less odors, fewer pests
- *Messengers:* Municipal staff; Consultants
- *Creative Elements:* Slogans including KEEP THE LID SHUT (see Figure 14.2) with visual images representing "Less Smell. Fewer Pests. No Rain Inside."
- *Communication Channels:* Permanent signage on dumpsters and sites; door/area leading to dumpster site

Evaluation Strategy

Pilot implementation included participation from 30 municipalities. Team members were provided a starter packet of campaign materials, including stickers, signs, and posters and then:

FIGURE 14.2 ■ Dumpster Sticker and Sign

Source: Washington Stormwater "Dumpster Outreach Group".

- Attended training meetings;
- Conducted baseline field surveys to identify businesses in their jurisdiction with open lids;
- Communicated with their waste hauler and other local stakeholders as needed before putting stickers on dumpsters;
- Implemented the campaign in their jurisdiction with at least two businesses;
- Conducted field surveys to collect all evaluation data within the timeline;
- Entered evaluation data into a Survey Monkey survey and provide additional information and feedback as requested.

Evaluation components were rigorous including collecting data at baseline, start, and six months after implementation as well as in some of the jurisdictions, selecting, and monitoring a control group of similar businesses. Evaluation measures were comprehensive:

- *Inputs Measured:* Staff time; money spent for tool kit materials; partner contributions; consultant expenses
- *Outputs Measured:* Number of site visits/businesses; materials disseminated; materials posted/put in place; implementation of program elements were on track and on budget
- *Outcomes Measured:* Behavior adoption; change in knowledge and beliefs; campaign awareness
- *Impact Measured:* Cleaner dumpster areas, reduced odors, and vermin; cleaner appearance in downtown and commercial areas, impacting economic development health, which would lead to reduction in polluted runoff from dumpster areas

Pilot Results and Next Steps

Key findings from the 6-month pilot effort in over 100 dumpster areas across the Puget Sound that were evaluated before and after the pilot campaign implementation, were encouraging:

- Dumpster lid closure rose from 49% during the baseline evaluation to 77% during the pilot evaluation, a 57% increase.

FIGURE 14.3 ■ Dumpster Lid Pilot Sticker on a Commercial Dumpster

Source: Washington Stormwater "Dumpster Outreach Group".

- Municipalities participating in the program realized substantial cost savings due to economy of scale through joint funding, distribution of tasks, data sharing, and leveraging the experience and knowledge of regional E&O staff.

As of May 2022, a webpage is active (Dumpster Outreach Group—Washington Stormwater at wastormwatercenter.org) where dumpster lid details and access to tool kits are made available. Quarterly dumpster lid meetings are hosted for municipal staff who took part in the campaign, or want to, to meet and discuss progress, the National Pollutant Discharge Elimination System Permit, and new ideas. Participating municipalities are now rolling out the campaign on a broader scale in each of their individual communities, with additional program components including the development of materials in multiple languages and more public recognition for participating municipalities (Figure 14.3).

STEP 8: DEVELOP A PLAN FOR EVALUATION

We recommend that you take time to develop a plan for monitoring and evaluating your social marketing effort before creating your budget in Step 9 and implementation plan in Step 10. You will want your final budget to include funding for this critical activity and your implementation plan to include action items to ensure that it happens.

This chapter will guide you in determining these funding needs and identifying related activities. It is intended to help by outlining components of a monitoring and evaluation plan mentioned earlier, posed in the form of questions you'll want to answer sequentially—starting with the toughest one, of course:

- Why are you conducting this measurement, and who is the audience for the results?
- What will you measure?
- How will you conduct these measurements?
- When will these measurements be taken?
- How much will it cost?

One distinction is important to clarify up front: the difference between the term *monitoring* and the term *evaluation.*

Monitoring refers to measurements conducted sometime after you launch your social marketing effort but before it is completed. Its purpose is to help you determine whether you need to make midcourse corrections that will ensure that you reach your ultimate marketing goals.

Evaluation, on the other hand, is a measurement and final report on what happened, answering the following bottom-line question: Did you reach your goals for changes in behaviors, knowledge, and attitudes among your priority audiences? Additional questions are also likely to be addressed in the evaluation. Were activities implemented on time and on budget? Were there any unintended consequences that will need to be addressed now or in future projects? Which program elements worked well to support outcomes? Which ones didn't? Was there anything missing? What will you do differently next time if there is a next time?[3]

WHY ARE YOU CONDUCTING THIS MEASUREMENT?

Your purpose for this measurement often shapes what you measure, how you measure, and when you measure. Consider the differing implications for your plan for each of the following potential reasons for your effort. Notice that audiences for the measurement results will also vary, depending on your purpose.

- To fulfill a grant requirement;
- To do better the next time you conduct the same campaign;
- To (hopefully) get continued or even increased funding;
- To help you decide how to prioritize and allocate your resources going forward;
- To alert you to midcourse corrections you need to make to achieve your goals.

To fulfill a grant requirement. Sometimes the nature of the monitoring and/or evaluation will be predetermined by specifications in a grant. Consider an example you will read about further in this chapter where a city receives a grant from a state department of transportation (DOT) to increase the use of pedestrian flags in the city's eight crosswalks in a downtown corridor. Assume the DOT is hoping that this city's campaign strategies are successful and that these strategies can then be shared by the DOT with other cities in the state. The campaign's evaluation plan will certainly include measuring levels of flag usage before and after the campaign. And the funder (primary audience for the measurement) will need to be assured that the data were collected using a systematic, reliable, and verifiable methodology that can be replicated in other cities.

To do better next time. What if, instead, you are sincerely interested in measuring what happened so that you can improve results in your next similar effort? Perhaps it is a pilot and you want to evaluate the campaign elements to decide what worked well and should be repeated, what could be improved, and what elements should be "dropped" next time around. Imagine a countywide effort to reduce smoking around children in cars. A pilot is carried out the first year to help determine what elements of the campaign should be used when it is rolled out countywide in Year 2. The pilot includes a packet of materials sent home with children from the elementary schools and contains a secondhand tobacco smoke information card, a plug to replace the cigarette lighter, a smoke-free pledge card, and an air freshener with the campaign's slogan, "Please Smoke Outside." Follow-up surveys with parents will then measure changes in parents' levels of smoking around their child in the car as well as their ratings on which of the materials in the packet they noticed, used, and felt were influential. Imagine further that the results indicated that some of the parents thought the air freshener would reduce the harmful effects of the smoke, so they didn't change their habits. This finding, of course, would then lead the county (the primary audience for this measurement) to eliminate the $1.50 item when the campaign was rolled out countywide.

To get support for continued funding. Often the purpose of an evaluation is to persuade funders to reinvest in the project to sustain it into the future. As you can imagine, key to the success of this endeavor is identifying criteria the funders will use to make their decisions and then creating an evaluation plan that includes measures to provide this information. Consider the Road Crew case in Wisconsin, mentioned in Chapter 9, in which a service using limousines and other luxury vehicles picks up people at their home, business, or hotel; takes them to the bars of their choice; and returns them home at the end of the evening—all for about $15 to $20 an evening. A key statistic that funders of the program (the primary audience for this measurement) were interested in was a cost-benefit analysis, and the program's evaluation methodology provided just that. You may recall that it showed an estimated cost of $6,400 to avoid a crash through Road Crew compared with $231,000, the estimated costs incurred from an alcohol-related crash.

To help determine resource allocation. Management may also, or instead, want to use an evaluation effort to help decide how resources should be allocated in the future. In King County, Washington, for example, the Department of Natural Resources and Parks wanted an evaluation survey to help decide which of some 30 community outreach efforts should receive more funding and which, perhaps, should be pulled back. This objective led to a plan to measure household behaviors that each of these 30 programs sought to influence (e.g., leave grass clippings on the lawn). The programs with the greatest potential market opportunity for growth were then considered first for increased support, with market opportunity being determined by the percentage of

FIGURE 14.4 ■ Original PedFlags Were Orange and Had to be Inserted Carefully in the Pole Holder

Source: Author photo.

households doing the behavior sometimes but not on a regular basis (the in-action stage of change) or not doing the behavior at all but considering doing it (the contemplation stage of change).

To decide if course corrections are needed. This purpose will lead to a monitoring effort, measuring sometime after an effort launches but before completion, to determine whether goals are likely to be met based on how the market is responding.

Example: Pedestrian Flags. In 2007, the City of Kirkland in Washington State was interested in knowing the difference their 12-year PedFlag program was making. In 1995, in an effort to increase the visibility of pedestrians in crosswalks, they had installed pole holders with orange flags for pedestrians to carry when crossing streets in 37 locations around the city (see Figure 14.4). City officials estimated that about 5% of pedestrians used the flags, but no formal measure had confirmed this. They were interested in knowing what they could do to increase usage to a desired level of 40% by 2011. Observation research of more than 3,000 pedestrians over a 20-day period estimated usage at 11%, and barriers research with those not using the flags provided inspirational feedback. Many did not know what the orange flag was for, thinking it either was intended to alert drivers to a pedestrian crosswalk or signaled a construction zone—a *product* problem. Others noted that often there were no flags on their side of the street—a *place* problem. And the vast majority indicated they felt safe and were sure drivers could see them—a *promotion* problem. Enhancements to the program included redesigning the flags so that they had an immediate connection with pedestrian crosswalks and making them easy to grab by placing them in buckets instead of pole holders (see Figure 14.5). The number of flags at each crosswalk was increased from six to 18, and local businesses were engaged in notifying the city when they saw supplies running low. New promotional strategies included a slogan, "Take It to Make It," and messages intended to increase perception of risk (see Figure 14.6). Five months after the enhanced strategies had been implemented, the monitoring research methodology was replicated and indicated that usage had increased by 64% (from 11% to 18%).

WHAT WILL YOU MEASURE?

What you will measure to achieve your evaluation purpose is likely to fall into one or more of five categories: *inputs, outputs, outcomes, impacts,* and *return on investment* (ROI). As you will read, required efforts and rigor vary significantly by category.

Overview of a Modified Logic Model

A logic model is a visual schematic that organizes program evaluative measures into categories that can be measured and reported using a "logical" flow, beginning with program inputs and outputs, moving on to program effects in terms of outcomes and impact, and ending with (ideally) reporting on returns on investment (see Table 14.2). The difficulty of reporting increases the further one moves to the right on the model.

FIGURE 14.5 ■ Enhanced PedFlags Were Yellow and Were Easy to Grab and Then Replace in a Bucket

Source: Author photo.

FIGURE 14.6 ■ Campaign Messages Were Intended to Increase Risk Perception as Well as the Benefits of Taking a Flag

Source: Author photo.

TABLE 14.2 ■ A Modified Logic Model for Reporting on Social Marketing Efforts

Inputs	Outputs	Outcomes	Impact	Return on Investment
Resources allocated to the campaign or program effort	Program activities conducted to influence audiences to perform a desired behavior	Audience response to outputs	Indicators that show levels of impact on the social issue that was the focus for the effort	Value of changes in behavior and the calculated rate of return on the spending associated with the effort
• Money • Staff time • Volunteer hours • Existing materials used • Distribution channels utilized • Existing partner contributions	• Number of materials disseminated, calls made, events held, websites created, social media tactics employed • Reach and frequency of communications • Free media coverage • Number of special events held • Paid media impressions and cost per impression • Implementation of program elements (e.g., whether on time, on budget)	• Changes in behavior • Numbers of related products or services "sold" (e.g., safer pesticides) • Changes in behavior intent • Changes in knowledge • Changes in beliefs • Engagement with campaign elements (e.g., YouTube videos shared, Facebook postings shared, Twitter followers, number of attendees at special events) • Campaign awareness • Customer satisfaction levels • New partnerships and contributions created • Policy changes	• Improvements in health • Lives saved • Injuries prevented • Water quality improved • Water supply increased • Air quality improved • Landfill disposal reduced • Animal cruelty reduced • Crimes prevented • Financial well-being improved • Increased college admissions	• Cost to change one behavior • For every dollar spent, dollars saved or generated • After subtracting expenses, the rate of return on investment

Input Measures

The easiest and most straightforward measures are those itemizing resources used to develop, implement, and evaluate the campaign. The most common elements include money spent and staff time allocated. In many cases, there will also be additional contributions to the effort to report on, including any volunteer hours, existing materials, distribution channels utilized, and/or existing partner contributions (Developing new partnerships for the effort would be noted in program outcomes.). The quantification of these resources will be especially important when determining return on investment, as they represent the amount invested.

Output/Process Measures

The next-easiest measures are those describing your campaign's outputs, sometimes referred to as process measures, which focus on quantifying your marketing activities as much as possible. They represent how you utilized program inputs and are distinct from outcome measures, those focusing on your priority audience's response to these activities. Many are available in your records and databases.[4]

- *Number of materials distributed and media channels utilized.* This measure refers to the numbers of mailings, brochures, flyers, key chains, bookmarks, booklets, posters, or coupons put forth. This category also includes numbers and types of additional outreach activities, such as calls made, events held, websites created, and social media tactics deployed. Note that this does not indicate whether posters were noticed, brochures were read, or events were attended, YouTube videos were viewed—only the numbers "put out there."

- *Reach and frequency.* Reach refers to the number of different people or households exposed to a particular image or message during a specified period. Frequency is the number of times within this time frame, on average, that the target audience is exposed to the communication. It is a predictor of audience response but not an indicator of such.

- *Media coverage.* Measures of media and public relations efforts, also referred to as earned media, may include reporting on numbers of column inches in newspapers and magazines, minutes on television and radio news, and paid ads on websites and special programs, and people in the audience attending a planned speaker's events. Efforts are often made to determine and report what this coverage would have cost if it had been paid for.

- *Total impressions/cost per impression.* This measurement combines information from several categories, such as reach and frequency, media exposure, and material dissemination. Typically, these numbers are combined to create an estimate of the total number of people in the priority audience who were exposed to campaign elements.

Taking this to the next level of rigor to achieve a cost per impression, total campaign costs associated with this exposure can be divided by the estimated number of people exposed to the campaign. For example, consider a state-wide campaign prioritizing mothers to increase children's fruit and vegetable consumption; the campaign may have collected exposure information from media buys (e.g., parenting magazines) and any additional efforts (e.g., messages on grocery bags). Let's assume they were able to estimate that 100,000 mothers were exposed to these campaign efforts and that the associated costs were $10,000. Their cost per impression would be $0.10. These statistics can then be used over time to compare the cost efficiency of varying strategies. Suppose, for example, that in a subsequent campaign, efforts reached 200,000 mothers after funds were redirected to sending messages from childcare centers and preschools, thus reducing the cost per impression to $0.05.

- *Cost-per-click.* Online (search and digital), mobile, and social ads are typically priced either by impressions delivered or per each "click" to an advertiser's website that the ad delivers. The cost per click (CPC) is calculated by dividing the total media budget by the number of clicks delivered. You can compare the effectiveness of your campaign by comparing your CPC to industry CPC benchmarks for your subject area or for reaching your same audience. In some cases (e.g. search ads), the media can be purchased at a predetermined cost per click and the ads can be turned off when the budget has been expended.
- *Implementation of program elements.* An audit of major activities planned and implemented (or not) may shed light on campaign outputs and outcomes. Did you do everything you planned to do? Did you complete activities on time and on budget? This audit can help address the tendency many of us have to expect campaign goals to be achieved, even though we did not implement all planned activities or spend originally allocated funds in planned timeframes.

Outcome Measures

Measuring outcomes is a little more rigorous, as you are now assessing customer response to your outputs, most likely involving some type of primary research surveys. Other items included in outcome measures are any partnerships formed as a result of the campaign, as well as any policy changes a campaign might have intended to influence. Ideally, these measures were determined by the goals you established in Step 4, the specific measurable results you want your program to achieve—one or more of the following types:

- *Changes in behavior.* These may be measured and stated in terms of a change in percentage (e.g., adult binge drinking decreased from 17% to 6%) and/or a change in numbers (e.g., 40,000 new households signed up for food waste recycling bins, increasing the total number of households participating from 60,000 to 100,000). In 2011, for example, results of a research study conducted by Michael Slater at Ohio State

University regarding behavior outcomes for the U.S. federal antidrug campaign Above the Influence were encouraging:

A study of more than 3,000 students in 20 communities nationwide found that by the end of 8th grade, 12 percent of those who had not reported having seen the campaign took up marijuana use compared to only 8 percent among students who had reported familiarity with the campaign.[5]

Slater believed that the successful outcomes were due in part to the fact that the campaign appears to "tap into the desire by teenagers to be independent and self-sufficient." He cited, for example, one television ad in the campaign ending with the line "Getting messed up is just another way of leaving yourself behind."[6]

- *Changes in behavior intent.* This measure might be appropriate for campaigns with minimal exposure or when campaigns have been running for only short periods of time. It may be the most appropriate measure for campaigns prioritizing those in the precontemplation stage, when the social marketer's goal is to move them to contemplation and then (eventually) to the action stage. This was illustrated during the COVID-19 pandemic with rapid changes in the intent to get vaccinated in the U.S. increasing rapidly from the Fall of 2020 into the Spring of 2021 as public health officials educated the public about the safety and efficacy of the COVID-19 vaccines.
- *Changes in knowledge.* This may include changes in awareness of important facts (e.g., five drinks at one sitting is considered binge drinking), information (e.g., an estimated 75,000 people are on waiting lists for organ transplants), or recommendations (e.g., eat five or more servings of vegetables and fruit daily for better health).
- *Changes in belief or attitudes.* Traditionally, a belief refers to what people think is true, whether "proven" or not by facts (e.g., childhood immunizations can cause autism), and attitudes are personal evaluations/viewpoints on the issue (e.g., I'd rather not take a chance so I will avoid several of the immunizations).
- *Responses to campaign elements.* Here you may be counting hits to your website, times a video was shared, social media engagements, calls to an 800 number (e.g., for a booklet on natural gardening), attendees at an event, coupon redemptions (e.g., for a bike helmet), or orders or requests for more information (e.g., for a free consultation on home earthquake preparedness).
- *Campaign awareness.* Though not necessarily an indicator of impact or success, measures of awareness of campaign elements provide some feedback on the extent to which the campaign was noticed and recalled. Measurements might include levels of unaided awareness (e.g., what you have seen or heard lately in the news about legal limits for blood alcohol levels while driving); aided awareness (e.g., what have you

FIGURE 14.7 ■ The New Approach Driving Positive Action

Source: Photo courtesy of Patricia McLaughlin.

seen or heard lately in the news about your state's new 0.08% legal limit); or proven awareness (e.g., where you read or hear about this change in the law).

- *Norms creation.* One of the **Truth Initiative** campaigns to reduce youth tobacco use was branded "Finish It", rallying a volunteer army of youth and young adults to use their influence and creativity to denormalize smoking among their peers. The campaign sought to connect smoking and the effects of tobacco to the things young people really care about, such as relationships. Figure 14.7 exemplifies their normalizing approach.[7]
- *Customer satisfaction levels.* Customer satisfaction levels range from those related to experiences of benefits from engaging in the behavior to ones associated with goods (e.g., Fitbits) and services (e.g., auto leak tests) offered or promoted during the campaign. These measures provide important feedback for analyzing results and for planning future efforts (e.g., ratings on levels of satisfaction with counseling at Supplemental Nutrition Program for Women, Infants, and Children [WIC] clinics).
- *Partnerships and contributions created.* Levels of participation and contributions from outside sources are significant and represent positive responses to your campaign, even though they may not be a reflection of the impact on target audience behaviors. These may include numbers of hours spent by volunteers, partners, and coalition members participating in the campaign, as well as amounts of cash and in-kind contributions

received from foundations, media, and businesses. It should be noted that these contributions would be included in determining returns on investment measures.

- *Policy changes.* A legitimate campaign goal may focus on causing an important change in policies or infrastructures that will encourage and/or support behavior change. In the interest of reducing gun violence, for example, efforts to increase rigor of background checks would be considered a success if changes were made to existing relevant laws.

Impact Measures

This measure is the most rigorous, costly, and controversial of all measurement types. In this category, you are attempting to measure the impact that the changes (outcomes) in behavior you have achieved (e.g., more homeowners using natural fertilizers) have had on the social issue your plan is addressing (e.g., water quality). It would indeed be great to be able to report on the following types of impact measures in addition to outputs and outcomes:

- Lives saved (e.g., from reducing drinking and driving);
- Diseases prevented (e.g., from increased physical activity);
- Injuries avoided (e.g., from safer workplace practices);
- Water quality improved (e.g., from taking prescription drugs back to pharmacies);
- Water supply increased (e.g., from increased purchases of low-flow toilets);
- Air quality improved (e.g., from use of fewer leaf blowers in a community);
- Landfill reduced (e.g., from composting food waste);
- Animal cruelty reduced (e.g., from increases in spaying and neutering);
- Crimes prevented (e.g., from increases in the use of motion sensors for outdoor lighting);
- Financial well-being improved (e.g., from microcredit loans for farm animals);
- College admissions increased (e.g., from decreasing high school dropouts through tutoring).

The reality is that not only are these measures rigorous and costly to determine, but it may, in fact, be inappropriate and inaccurate to try to connect your campaign activities with these impacts, even though they were designed with them in mind.

Several key points can assuage you and others. First, you need to trust, or assume, that the behavior that was chosen for your campaign is one that can have an impact on the issue (e.g., that folic acid can help prevent some birth defects). Credible resources for statistics and other facts of interest include agencies with a focus on the social issue and behavior being addressed, ones in the United States such as CDC, EPA, and U.S. Departments of Transportation,

Health and Human Services and Education. Second, you may need to wait longer to measure, as there may be a lag between adopting the behavior and seeing the impact (e.g., increased physical activity to lower blood pressure levels). Finally, your methodology for measurement may need to be quite rigorous, controlling for variables that may also be contributing to the social issue (e.g., there may not be an improvement in water quality in a lake if during your campaign a new manufacturer in the area started polluting the same waters). You will need to be diligent and forthright about whether you believe you can even determine and claim this victory.

Return on Investment

Determining and reporting on return on investment (ROI) has several benefits. It can provide a solid rationale for *continued funding* for successful programs, funding that might be cut if it is perceived that the program is too costly or is a large-budget item. This will help agency directors address tough budget questions from policymakers, peers, constituents, and the media. Second, findings can help administrators *allocate resources*, providing a "disproportionate" share to programs with the highest ROI based on a rational, "apples-to-apples" comparison. And finally, if more and more programs calculate this, we can build and share a *database of ROIs* that will assist in evaluating programs' efficacy as well as replicating the most cost-effective ones.

Most ROIs can be determined with five simple (but not necessarily easy) steps:[8]

1. *Money spent.* Determine total costs of the campaign/program, including the value of staff time spent as well as direct expenses associated with research, development, implementation, and evaluation of the program. In other words, calculate total inputs.

2. *Behaviors influenced.* Estimate how many people were influenced to adopt the targeted behavior as a result of the campaign/intervention. Hopefully, this was determined when conducting outcome research.

3. *Cost per behavior influenced.* This is the simpler step, completed by dividing the dollars spent by the numbers of behaviors influenced (Step 1 divided by Step 2).

4. *Benefit per behavior.* This step answers the question, "What is the economic value of this changed behavior?" This is the most challenging step for many, as it is most often stated in terms of costs avoided as a result of the behavior adoption (e.g., healthcare costs, response to injuries, landfill costs avoided, and environmental cleanup efforts). In some cases, it may be revenue generated by behavior adoption (e.g., from home energy audits conducted by a utility). The problem is that reliable data on the economic benefit of one changed behavior are not often readily available, and many are reluctant to use even reasonable estimates. This concern might be assuaged by being up front with audiences and presenting information as a "best estimate," explaining the rigor that was taken to create the estimates.

5. *ROI.* This takes three calculations:

a. Number of behaviors influenced (from Step 2) *times* economic benefit per behavior (from Step 4) *equals* the gross economic benefit (#2 × #4 = gross economic benefit).
b. The gross economic benefit *minus* the amount spent (Step 1) *equals* the net benefit.
c. The net benefit divided by the investment costs (Step 1) times 100 *equals* rate of return on the investment.

Example: A Positive ROI for Public Health. The American Public Health Association's National Public Health Week in 2013 had a bold new theme—that "Public Health is ROI: Save Lives, Save Money"—supporting "the notion that spending a small amount of money on preventive efforts can avert a much larger expenditure years later."[9] Examples were featured in a two-minute animated YouTube video that included the calculated potential economic value of seatbelts, for example, reporting that every $1 invested in a child safety seat has a potential for a $42 return in avoided medical costs.[10]

Example: Reducing Deaths and Injuries on Roads in the United Kingdom and Saving Society Money. In 2010, the U.K. Department for Transport launched a comprehensive program to reduce the number of deaths and injuries on the road, with an in-depth case summary provided in the 2011 *Social Marketing Casebook*, coauthored by Jeff French, Rowena Merritt, and Lucy Reynolds.[11] The campaign, branded "THINK!," utilized a 3Es approach: enforcement, education, and engineering, an intervention mix focused on enhancing the physical environment to promote safe road use (e.g., speed cameras and traffic-calming measures); strategies to increase awareness and understanding; and an emphasis on enforcement and punishment for inappropriate and unsafe behaviors. Of interest relative to ROI, the authors provided an inspiring recap:

> Based on the difference between the number of road deaths in 2008 and the 1994–8 baseline average, 1,040 lives have been saved and there have been 18,044 fewer serious injuries and 69,939 slight injuries, saving society £5.1 billion, or £4.2 billion if only killed or seriously injured (KSIs) are taken into account. This means that a reduction of only 418 KSIs is needed to cover all of "THINK!" costs.[12]

HOW WILL YOU MEASURE?

Our third step in developing an evaluation and monitoring plan is to identify methodologies and techniques that will be used to actually measure indicators established in the first step. Chapter 3 outlined typical research methodologies available to you, a few of which are most typical for evaluation and monitoring measures. In general, audience surveys will be the primary technique used in measuring outcomes, given your focus on the actual influence you have had on your priority audience in terms of behavior, knowledge, and beliefs. Records will provide information for determining inputs; outputs will rely on records as well but will also tap information from contact reports, anecdotal comments, and project progress reports. Outcome measures usually require quantitative surveys, whereas impact measures may require more scientific or technical surveys.

FIGURE 14.8 ■ Hypothetical Illustration of a Randomized Controlled Trial to Test a Strategy to Increase the Number of High School Graduates Who Go to College

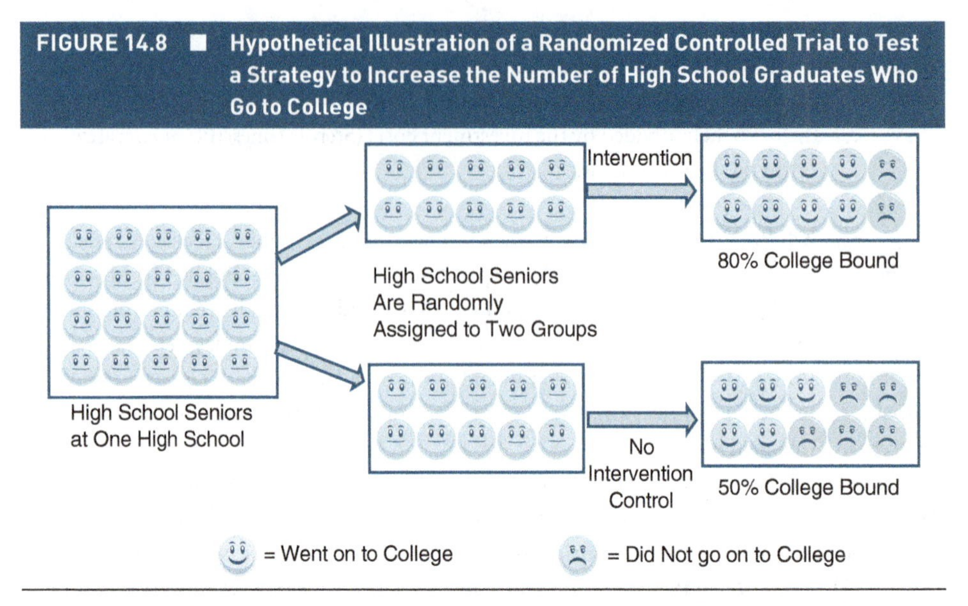

Source: Schematic adapted from Laura Haynes, Owain Service, Ben Goldacre, and David Torgerson,"Test, Learn, Adapt: Developing Public Policy With Randomised Controlled Trials" (Cabinet Office Behavioral Insights Team, June 2012).

It is important to note that some audiences tend to have lower participation rates in certain evaluation methodologies, meaning your results may not be representative of all your priority audience groups. For example, older people and people with lower literacy levels are less likely to participate in online surveys. Younger people are less likely to participate in phone surveys. Historically marginalized communities may not trust sharing information through surveys but may be more likely to share information with trusted community groups. People that have English as a second language are less likely to participate in all research types. If these types of dynamics impact your priority audience groups, you should seek out other ways to reach them for your evaluation purposes. This could be through one-on-one interviews, by partnering with a community-based organization to distribute a survey, or by participating in a preexisting event to have a discussion with audience members.

Quantitative surveys are needed when reliable data are key to evaluation (e.g., percentage increase in levels of physical activity) and are most commonly conducted using telephone surveys, online surveys, self-administered questionnaires, and/or in-person interviews. These may be proprietary or shared-cost studies in which several organizations have questions for similar populations. They may even rely on established surveys, such as the Behavioral Risk Factor Surveillance System (BRFSS) presented in Chapter 6.

Randomized controlled trials (RCTs) are rigorously designed and implemented experiments to determine the effectiveness of one or more interventions by comparing results with a similar control group that didn't receive the intervention (see Figure 14.8 for a schematic that illustrates this systematic process.). Sometimes a new intervention (e.g., providing one-on-one assistance in completing a college application) is compared against the status quo (e.g., not providing this one-on-one assistance). Other times the objective is to compare different levels of "dosage" (e.g., pregnant mothers receiving a text message encouraging healthy behaviors once a week compared with those receiving them daily).

Nonrandomized control groups used in combination with quantitative and scientific or technical surveys will further ensure that results can be closely tied to your campaign and program efforts. A drug and alcohol prevention campaign might be implemented in high schools in one community but not in another similar community. Extra precautions can even be taken to ensure the similarity of the control groups by conducting surveys prior to the selection of the groups and then factoring in any important differences. Results on reported drug use in the control group of high schools are then compared with those in the other (similar) communities.

Qualitative surveys should be considered when evaluation requirements are less stringent or more subjective in nature and include methodologies such as focus groups, informal interviews, and capturing anecdotal comments. Focus groups might be appropriate for exploring with childcare providers which components of the immunization tracking kits were most and least useful and why. This information might then refocus efforts for the next kit reprint. Informal interviews might be used to understand why potential consumers walked away from the low-flow toilet display, even after reading accompanying materials and hearing testimonials from volunteers. Anecdotal comments regarding an advertising campaign might be captured on phone calls to a sexual assault resource line.

Observation research is often more reliable than self-reported data and, when possible, the most appropriate technique for highly visible behaviors. It can be used for evaluating behaviors such as wearing a life vest, washing hands before returning to work, or topping off gas tanks. It may also provide more insight for assessing skill levels and barriers than self-reported data (e.g., observing people sorting garbage and placing it in proper containers or observing a WIC client finding their way around a farmers' market for the first time). An example of this method was carried out in Vancouver, British Columbia, in 2014 where there was a problem at one of the TransLink bus stops that most cities would envy: It was too popular. Commuters leaving the adjacent train station to catch a bus experienced long waiting lines, which curled around the block, creating safety hazards as well as blocking the sidewalks for pedestrians. Past efforts to manage the long lines had not always turned out well, with riders ignoring interventions or cutting through them. This time, they tried a "real-time" observation approach where one morning they tested several interventions, video-recorded crowd response, and then reviewed results to determine the most effective strategy. This observation approach enabled the consulting firm Nelson/Nygaard to make recommendations to TransLink without undergoing a lengthy and more costly data gathering and analysis. They discovered, in part, that sidewalk tape was as effective as fences for keeping the sidewalk clear; stanchions (sturdy upright fixtures) were needed for switchbacks; and arrows on the ground worked better than posted signs. A senior associate at the consulting firm confirmed the benefits that observation research can have:

> Sometimes it's easy for us to be armchair planners and look at maps and this other stuff and attack a problem. But this is one of those cases that just by being there and observing over the course of a couple hours how people react to something it became clear what was going to work and what wasn't.[13]

Scientific or technical surveys may be the only sure methodology to assess the impact of your efforts. If you are charged with reporting back on the difference your efforts have made in reducing diseases, saving lives, improving water quality, and the like, you will need help designing and conducting reliable scientific surveys that not only are able to measure changes in these indicators but can also link these changes to your social marketing campaign.[14]

Records and databases will be very useful for several indicators, particularly those measuring responses to campaign elements and dissemination of campaign materials. This may involve keeping accurate track of number of visits to a website and length of time spent, numbers of calls (e.g., to a tobacco quitline), comments on Facebook (e.g., regarding tips to avoid the flu), views of a YouTube video (e.g., of a PSA persuading viewers to wear seatbelts), numbers of requests (e.g., for child care references), numbers of visits (e.g., to a teen clinic), numbers of people served (e.g., at car seat inspections), or numbers of items collected (e.g., at a needle exchange). This effort may also involve working with suppliers and partners to provide similar information from their records and databases, such as numbers of coupons redeemed (e.g., for trigger locks), tangible goods sold (e.g., compost tumblers featured in the campaign), or requests received (e.g., organ donation applications processed).

Comparative effectiveness research is a relatively new approach and is utilized primarily to inform healthcare decision-making by providing evidence on the effectiveness, benefits, and potential harms of various treatment options. According to the U.S. Department of Health and Human Services, there are two ways this evidence is found. Researchers can look at all available evidence on the benefits and harms of each choice for different groups of people from existing clinical trials, clinical studies, and other research. They might also, or instead, conduct studies that generate new evidence of effectiveness or comparative effectiveness of a test, treatment, procedure, or healthcare service.[15] For social marketers, implications are similar to those of controlled experiments, where one or more interventions are evaluated based on a comparison of results.

Pilots, as Doug McKenzie-Mohr suggests, could be thought of as a "test run," providing an opportunity to work out any bugs in the program before broad-scale implementation.[16] He offers six principles as guidelines in conducting a pilot, with more detail on pilots also available on his website Fostering Sustainable Behavior: Community-Based Social Marketing:

1. Don't mix barrier and benefit research with piloting, as this could impact behavior change levels.
2. Use a minimum of two groups to conduct a pilot, with one a control group.
3. Use random assignment to assign participants to groups.
4. Make measurements of behavior change a priority, ideally not relying on self-reports, which can be unreliable.
5. Calculate return on investment, strengthening your opportunity for broad-scale implementation.
6. Revise your pilot until it is effective.[17]

FIGURE 14.9 ■ These Information Cards Outline the Benefits of Reduced Engine Idling and Are Suitable for Distribution at Schools and Other Community Locations

You can use energy more wisely and help improve air quality by turning off your engine when parked.

Conserve energy – You'll help reduce needless greenhouse gas emissions.

Breathe easier – You'll breathe more easily by combatting problems like poor air quality and smog.

Save money – You'll save over 80 litres of gasoline per year if you reduce your idling by only 10 minutes a day.

Idling for over 10 seconds uses more fuel than restarting your engine.

idling gets you

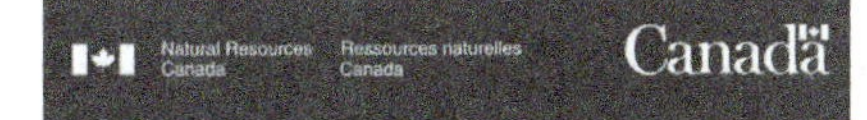

Source: Natural Resources Canada.

As an example, Doug shared the following pilot effort in Canada: "Turn It Off: An Anti-idling Campaign."

This pilot project in 2007 sought to decrease both the frequency and duration of motorists idling their vehicle engines. The project involved staff approaching motorists at Toronto schools and Toronto Transit Commission Kiss and Ride parking lots and speaking with them about the importance of turning off their vehicle engines when parked and sitting in their vehicles. Approached motorists were provided with an information card (see Figure 14.8), and signs

FIGURE 14.10 ■ A Sign Used at Schools and Kiss and Ride Sites

Source: Doug McKenzie-Mohr and William Smith, *Fostering Sustainable Behavior: An Introduction to Community-Based Social Marketing*, 2nd ed. (Gabriola Island, BC, Canada: New Society, 1999).

reminding motorists to turn off their engines were posted at both the schools and the Kiss and Ride sites (see Figure 14.9). As part of the conversation, each motorist was asked to make a commitment to turn off the vehicle engine when parked. To assist motorists with remembering to turn off their engines, they were asked to place a sticker on their front windshields. The sticker both served as a prompt to turn off their engines and facilitated the development of community norms with respect to engine idling (the sticker, which was static-cling, could be pulled off, was transparent, and was placed on the front windshield of the vehicle with the graphic and text viewable from both inside and outside the vehicle). Over 80% of the motorists who were asked to make a commitment to turn off their engines did so, and 26% placed the sticker on their front window (see Figure 14.10).

This project had three separate conditions. Two Kiss and Ride sites and two schools served as controls and received none of the above materials. In a second condition, two Kiss and Ride sites and two schools received only the signs. Finally, in the third condition, the personal conversations, which involved providing an information card and the sticker described above, were used in conjunction with signs. Note that the signs alone, which are what most municipalities would gravitate toward using, were completely ineffective. Motorists in the sign-only condition were no more likely to turn off their engines than those in the control group. However, the combination of signs, stickers, and information cards (third condition) dramatically affected idling. In this condition, there was a 32% reduction in idling and over a 70% reduction in the duration of idling. These results are based on over 8,000 observations of vehicles in the various parking lots. With the support of NRCan, this pilot project was subsequently implemented across two Canadian cities, Mississauga and Sudbury, with similar results. Most important, NRCan has made the materials from the project freely available to communities so that they can

FIGURE 14.11 ■ Stickers Given to Motorists for Their Windows

Source: Doug McKenzie-Mohr and William Smith, *Fostering Sustainable Behavior: An Introduction to Community-Based Social Marketing*, 2nd ed. (Gabriola Island, BC, Canada: New Society, 1999).

quickly and inexpensively implement their own anti-idling campaigns. As a consequence, municipalities across North America have implemented anti-idling programs based on this case study.

For further information, visit the Government of Canada's Idle Free Zone website (http://www.nrcan.gc.ca/energy/efficiency/communities-infrastructure/transportation/idling/4397). This site provides further details on delivering effective anti-idling programs as well as downloadable materials that can be used in a local program (Figure 14.11).

WHEN WILL YOU MEASURE?

Earlier, we distinguished between evaluation and monitoring, referring to final assessments of efforts as *evaluation* and ongoing measurements as *monitoring*. Timing for measurement efforts is likely to happen as follows:

1. *Prior* to campaign launch, sometimes referred to as precampaign or baseline measures.
2. *During* campaign implementation, thought of as tracking and monitoring surveys; this may occur at one time only or over a period of years (i.e., longitudinal surveys).
3. *Postcampaign* activities, referring to measurements taken when all campaign elements are completed, providing data on short-term outcomes and long-term impact.

Baseline measures are critical when campaigns have specific goals for change, and future campaign efforts and funders will rely on these measures for campaign assessment. These are then compared with postcampaign results, providing a pre and postevaluation measure. Monitoring efforts during campaigns are often conducted to provide input for changes midstream and to track changes over time. Postcampaign (final) assessments are the most typical evaluations, especially when resources and tight time frames prohibit additional efforts. A few programs will use all points in time for evaluation, most common when significant key constituent groups or funders require solid evidence of campaign outcomes.

An example of a pre and posttest study appeared in the *Social Marketing Quarterly* in 2016, "Eat Your Greens: Increasing the Number of Days That Picky Toddlers Eat Vegetables."[18] Authors Eiskje Clason and Denise Meijer described the development of a social marketing intervention called "the vegetable box" with a purpose to increase the number of days per week that toddlers in the city of Rotterdam in the Netherlands eat vegetables. The vegetable box was wrapped in attractive packaging and included contents such as cookie cutters that could be used with carrots and cucumbers for having fun with toddlers and a booklet with stickers to help mothers track the number of vegetable tastings (product). Boxes were free (price) and were distributed at public playgroups and the child Health Center in Rotterdam (place). Key messages highlighted how "vegetables will make children grow tall and strong" and to "have fun with your child as you play with food." The effect of the vegetable box project was evaluated by an experimental study with a pre and posttest design and control group. Results indicted a significant increase in the number of days per week in which parents served vegetables and children ate them.[19]

HOW MUCH WILL IT COST?

Costs for recommended monitoring and evaluation activities will vary from *minimal* costs for those that simply involve checking records and databases or gathering anecdotal comments to *moderate* costs for those involving citizen surveys or observation research, to potentially *significant* costs for randomized controlled trials and those needing scientific or technical surveys. Ideally, decisions to fund these activities will be based on the value they will contribute to your program. If such an activity will assist you in getting support and continued funding for your program, it may be a wise investment. If it helps you refine and improve your effort going forward, payback is likely in terms of return on your investment. Once a methodology is determined based on your research purpose, you can assess these potential costs versus potential benefits.

ETHICAL CONSIDERATIONS IN EVALUATION PLANNING

Ethical considerations for monitoring and evaluation are similar to those discussed regarding research and focus mostly on the respondents surveyed for the evaluation.

One additional issue worthy of mention is the extent to which you should (or can) measure and report on unintended outcomes (consequences) as well, both positive and negative. For example, many program managers are now reporting concerns with their success in encouraging recycling. Although volumes of materials are being recycled that might otherwise have been put in landfills, managers believe the use of recyclable materials has significantly increased. Anecdotal comments such as these confirm their fears: "I don't worry about printing extra copies anymore because I'm using recycled paper and I'll put any copies not used in the recycling bin" and "I don't worry about buying small bottles of water to carry around because I can recycle them." As a result, environmentalists in some communities are now beginning to direct more of their efforts to the other two legs of their "three-legged stool"—reduce use and reuse.

COVID-19 Social Marketing Example

In the U.S., several key outcomes have been reported frequently in national and local news including:

- Number of new cases;
- Number of hospitalizations;
- Number of deaths;
- % vaccinated, often by major age groups, ethnic groups, and geographic locations.

This frequent and visible monitoring and subsequent promotion of outcome measures has potential for influencing persuasive factors such as perceived norms (e.g., % vaccinated) as well as increasing perceived risks of harm (e.g., number of hospitalizations) that would be potential motivators for practicing "safe" behaviors (e.g., wearing a mask).

In addition, this level of data tracking around COVID-19 allows for impact measures to be evaluated. Vaccine campaign results can be measured by vaccine rates and can then be correlated with death and hospitalization rates showing impacts on saving lives and reducing serious illness.

CHAPTER SUMMARY

As Philip Kotler proclaims: "Marketing is a learning game. You make a decision. You watch the results. You learn from the results. Then you make better decisions."[20]

Key components of an evaluation and monitoring plan are determined by answers to the following questions:

- Why are you conducting this measurement, and who is the audience for the results?
- What will you measure?
- How will you conduct these measurements?
- When will these measurements be taken?
- How much will it cost?

Reasons *why* you are measuring will guide your research plan, as methodologies will vary according to your reason for measurement. Is it to fulfill a grant requirement? To do better the next time you conduct this same campaign? To (hopefully) get continued or even increased funding? To help you decide how to prioritize and allocate your resources going forward? Or to alert you to midcourse corrections you need to make in order to achieve goals?

What you will measure to achieve your evaluation purpose is likely to fall into one or more of five categories: inputs, outputs, outcomes, impacts, and return on investment. Input measures report on program resources expended. Output measures report on campaign activities, outcomes on priority audience responses and any partnerships formed or desired policy changes, and impacts on improvements in social conditions as a result of adoption of the targeted behavior. The final, ideal metric to report on is return on investment.

Optional techniques for *measurement* include randomized controlled trials and surveys that are quantitative, qualitative, observational, or scientific/technical in nature, as well as ones that use control groups and rely on records and databases.

In this plan, you will also determine *timing* for evaluations, considering opportunities to carry out measurements prior to campaign launch, during campaign implementation, and once the campaign has ended.

Finally, you will determine *costs* for your proposed efforts, which should be weighed in light of potential benefits (See worksheet in Appendix A on potential evaluation measures.).

RESEARCH HIGHLIGHT

IN MOTION—EVERY TRIP COUNTS

(2004–2018)

Information for the following Research Highlight was provided by Sunny Knott at King County Metro Transit and Erin Cawley-Morse at C+C. This case was chosen in part to illustrate an evaluation plan design (Step 8) to address and report on program goals (Step 3). A more in-depth version of this case study and a case study of the overall *In Motion* program can be found at *Tools of Change*.[21]

Background

In Motion is a program of King County Metro in Washington State created in 2004 with a *purpose* to reduce drive-alone trips by engaging citizens in alternative modes of travel including mass transit, ridesharing, biking, and walking. For many years, in support of the state Commute Trip Reduction Law,[22] Metro had offered programs with a *focus* on reducing work-related commute trips. When transportation planner Carol Cooper realized that 80% of trips were actually nonwork-related trips, though, she proposed a shift in this focus, proclaiming, "the County would not meet its goals if they continued to focus solely on commute trips."[23]

An important element of the *In Motion* program is its innovative approach to developing behavior change strategies tailored to specific neighborhoods in the county (*priority audience*). This case presents the specific strategies utilized in one Seattle neighborhood, Capitol Hill, a densely populated residential district well-served by transit, evidenced by the fact that 70% of the residents were already commuting using transportation options other than driving alone. Good data are not available on nonwork trips, but many people still own cars in this neighborhood. They may not be using the cars to commute to work but are using them for nonwork trips, which make up 80% of all trips, so there were still trips that could be shifted. The challenge this effort took on was "how do we get people to use alternative modes for non-work trips?" A Link light rail station had recently opened in Capitol Hill, which created a great opportunity to talk with people about considering shifting their travel away from driving.

As you will read, audience insights regarding barriers and motivators, and a commitment to a tailored intervention mix, were key to reaching specific program goals to:

1. Enroll 1,000 car-owners in the *In Motion* program, representing ten percent of the 10,000 households on Capitol Hill.
2. Motivate 75% of participants to pledge to reduce their drive-alone trips.

TABLE 14.3 ■ Intervention Tools to Reduce Barriers

Barrier	Intervention Tool
Concern with increased effort: Concern with walking and biking given the hilly neighborhood and often rainy Seattle weather	• Enrollment programs ran during good weather, making it easier to have a positive first experience trying travel options. • Branded umbrellas were offered as an incentive at events.
Lack of awareness of convenient options: Many new residents were unfamiliar with transportation options, as well as had current perceptions that options were inconvenient.	• Registration materials enabled customized communications, with information that was specific to needs identified by participants. • Local travel map identified local bus routes including frequencies, on-street bike facilities, community amenities, and more.
Lack of perceived positive norms: Many new, as well as existing, residents were unaware of the community's participation and enthusiasm for alternative transportation modes.	• Social norming tactics included: ○ Highlighting stories and photos of neighbors using alternative transportation options ○ Messages including "Join 1,500 Capitol Hill neighbors" ○ Local businesses promoting the program and displaying posters and window slicks
Perceiving costs greater than benefits: Some residents believed alternatives would take more time and/or they were already "doing all they can"	• Local travel map showed how many minutes (little time) it took to walk to surrounding locations. • Program call-to-action emphasized reducing a few more trips: pledge to shift just two (or more) round trips per week driving alone to another option. • Materials highlighted the variety of popular, nonwork neighborhood destinations accessible by transit, including museums, parks, retail outlets, and classes. • Program incentives included free bus passes and opportunities to win prizes (e.g., Fitbit).

3. Reduce drive-alone trips by 10% among program participants.

A robust, multifaceted evaluation approach tracked the results of the program.

Marketing Intervention Mix

Program planners conducted in-depth stakeholder interviews and discussion groups to identify major barriers to alternative transportation modes, as well as to inspire an intervention mix based on what priority audiences saw as most motivating to address each barrier. Table 14.3 displays how intervention tools were aligned with major audience barriers, and Figure 14.10 highlights a program mailer.

Program Evaluation

Highlights of an evaluation report in November 2016 were encouraging and included process, output, outcome, and impact measures (Figure 14.12):[24]

FIGURE 14.12 ■ Program Mailer to Learn More, Enroll, and Make a Pledge

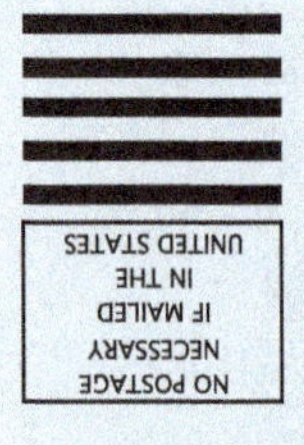

FIGURE 14.12 ■ Program Mailer to Learn More, Enroll, and Make a Pledge (Continued)

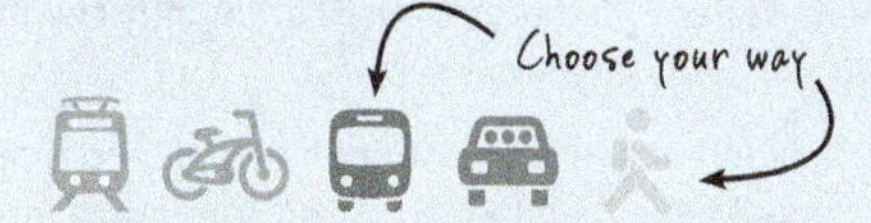

How will you get In Motion?

This summer, King County Metro is here to help you explore Capitol Hill and beyond by walking, bicycling, carpooling, riding the bus, taking light rail, and traveling on the First Hill Streetcar.

Here's how it works:

- **Sign up** online or below, and request information about how you can reduce your driving, plus get an ORCA card good for **two weeks of unlimited travel to help get you started.*** We'll send this all right to your door at no cost to you!
- **Pledge** to shift two or more round trips per week from driving alone to another option.
- **Track** your trips online or by postcard, and you'll be entered into ongoing drawings for rewards to local businesses!

Who is eligible?

You must live, work, or go to school in Capitol Hill, be 16 or older, and have at least one car in your household.

No car? No problem!

If you've already chosen a car-free lifestyle, we still want you involved! Register to find out more about rewards and information just for you!

Track your trips, win a Fitbit!

Along with a FREE ORCA card good for two weeks of travel, we're holding drawings throughout the program for great prizes like a Fitbit and gift cards to local businesses (while supplies last).

**ORCA card valid for two weeks from when you receive it; for use on regional buses, light rail, Seattle Streetcar, and water taxi. Offer available through August 7, 2016*

King County In Motion

inmotion@kingcounty.gov

(206) 477-2005

kingcounty.gov/inmotion

King County METRO

We'll Get You There

TEAR HERE AND MAIL

Sign me up! I want to get in motion! Or sign up online at **www.kingcounty.gov/inmotion** before August 8, 2016

1 Check one or more of the boxes ☑

☐ I live in Capitol Hill ☐ I work in Capitol Hill ☐ I go to school in Capitol Hill

2 Your pledge to drive less (☑ Please check one box)

☐ I pledge to reduce my drive alone trips by two or more round trips each week by walking, biking, transit or carpooling.

I will log my trips ☐ online ☐ by postcard

☐ No car? No problem! Check this box and fill out your information in section 6, and we'll be in touch with more details.

If you're not ready to pledge, go to step 3

3 Choose your rewards (☑ Please check one box)

☐ ORCA card good for two weeks of unlimited travel on regional buses, light rail, Seattle Streetcar, and water taxi.

☐ In Motion tote bag

4 Tell us how you get around

How many cars are there in your household? ____

How many drivers are there in your household? ____

In general, how much of your travel around town is by...? (Please make sure your answers add up to 100%)

Drive alone: ___ % Bus/Light Rail: ___ %

Bicycle: ___ % Carpool/Shared Rides: ___ %

Walking: ___ %

5 Send me information about... (☑ Please check appropriate boxes)

☐ Bus and ORCA Card	☐ Bicycling
☐ Metro Bus Schedules	☐ Carsharing
☐ Light Rail	☐ Bikesharing
☐ First Hill Streetcar	☐ Carpool, Vanpool and Vanshare
☐ Walking	☐ NE Seattle / Capitol Hill Map
☐ ACCESS (For people unable to take the bus)	☐ ORCA LIFT (Reduced transit fare)

6 Tell us where to send your information

Name: ____

Address: ____

Apt/Unit: ____

City: ____ Zip: ____

Phone: ____

Email: ____

Ready to get In Motion? Program partners Zipcar and Pronto are offering special discounts for In Motion participants. Keep an eye on your inbox for a special offer code after taking our pledge!

Source: King County Metro.

Registration analysis: Program goals were exceeded, with a total of 1,874 individuals enrolled in the program and 1,707 (91%) pledging to reduce their drive-alone trips. When participants registered for the program, a web form gave them an option to specify how they heard about the program. Top-cited sources were community events (35%), materials mailed to their home (33%), and social media (24%).

Trip logging: Throughout the program, participants were encouraged by email and mail to log their weekly trips (online or on mailed cards) and incentivized with entry into weekly prize drawing. In total, 427 participants (22.7%) logged their trips, reporting shifting 4,049 round trips to modes other than driving alone.

Driving impact: A postprogram survey, distributed to all participants, asked respondents to indicate the weekly number of reduced trips completed during the program. A total of 55% of the respondents reported a weekly reduction in driving of two or more trips. Importantly, in terms of long-term impact, nearly all survey respondents (94%) reported they are likely to continue using their new travel patterns.

Bus ridership: The postprogram survey asked respondents about their bus ridership before and after signing up for the program. An impressive 84% of respondents reported increasing their bus rides by one to six trips per week after signing up for the program.

Trip mode: By the end of the 12-week pilot, surveys of 321 participants indicated the following mode shift results: drive-alone trips decreased from 39% to 23%; bus/light rail usage increased from 22% to 31%; bicycling increased from 7% to 12%; carpooling increased from 7% to 11%; and walking increased from 26% to 31%.

Participation analysis: A postprogram survey of participants identified major perceived benefits gained from the program included opportunities to: reduce impact on climate change (73%); decrease transportation costs (68%); improve personal health (61%); improve neighborhoods (59%); and earn rewards and prizes (55%).

DISCUSSION QUESTIONS AND EXERCISES

1. Why is establishing the purpose of the evaluation the recommended first step in developing an evaluation plan?
2. Explain the difference between output and outcome measures.
3. Give an example of an actual or hypothetical randomized controlled trial, using the schematic presented in the chapter.

15 STEP 9: BUDGET AND FUNDING PLANS

LEARNING OBJECTIVES

Upon completion of this chapter, you should be able to:

15.1 Describe the importance of budgeting, major considerations to plan for, and the major phases of budgeting.

15.2 List the major approaches to determining and justifying campaign budgets.

15.3 Identify potential sources for additional campaign funding.

15.4 Illustrate the process for appealing to potential funders.

15.5 Revise plans when funding levels are not adequate.

15.6 Verify whether a corporate partner has potential ethical concerns.

In this chapter, not only will you read about how to determine and justify budgets for your proposed plans, but you will also explore options for additional funding. You will read that we encourage you to seriously consider opportunities for corporate support for your initiatives, such as ones mentioned in the opening Case Highlight. In the ethical considerations section of the chapter, we will ask you to think back on your reaction to the following examples of corporate initiatives related to decreasing childhood obesity:

Sesame Street. A press release from the Sesame Workshop in September 2005 presented findings from a research study titled "The Effectiveness of Characters on Children's Food Choices" (the "Elmo/Broccoli Study"). It indicated that

> intake of a particular food increased if it carried a sticker of a *Sesame Street* character. For example, in the control group (no characters on either food), 78% of children participating in the study chose a chocolate bar over broccoli, whereas 22% chose broccoli. However, when an Elmo sticker was placed on the broccoli and an unknown character was placed on the chocolate bar, 50% chose the chocolate bar and 50% chose the broccoli. Such outcomes suggest that the *Sesame Street* characters could play a strong role in increasing the appeal of healthy foods.[1]

Nickelodeon. In October 2005, Nickelodeon held its second annual Worldwide Day of Play, a part of its larger Let's Just Play initiative. The network went dark that Saturday for the first time in its 25-year history, from 12 p.m. to 3 p.m., replacing its usual programming with a broadcast message that encouraged kids to go outside and play. More than 60,000 kids registered online to get a number to wear to Day of Play events, and 40,000 kids attended events organized by Nickelodeon in selected American cities and abroad.[2] The annual campaign continued five years later. On Saturday, September 25, 2010, a special message was shown on the Nick channel screen: "Today is Nickelodeon's Worldwide Day of Play! We're outside playing, and you should be too! So, turn off your TV, shut down your computer, put down that cell phone, and go ALL OUT! We'll be back at 3!"[3] The annual event celebrated its 19th season in April of 2022.

CASE HIGHLIGHT

Increasing Funding Through Corporate Social Marketing

In Kotler, Hessekiel, and Lee's book *GOOD WORKS!*, six major initiatives under which most corporate social-responsibility-related activities fall are identified. Three are developed and managed primarily by the corporation's marketing function: *cause promotion, cause-related marketing*, and *corporate social marketing*. And three are most often developed and managed by other corporate functions, including community relations, human resources, foundations, and operations: *corporate philanthropy, workforce volunteering*, and *socially responsible business practices*.[4]

This Case Highlight focuses on describing corporate social marketing and making the case that when it comes to gaining a market edge while supporting a social cause, a social marketing effort is the "Best of Breed."[5]

"Corporate Social Marketing uses business resources to develop and/or implement a behavior change campaign intended to improve public health, safety, the environment, or community well-being."[6] It is most distinguished from other corporate social initiatives by this behavior change focus. And, as illustrated in the following seven examples, many of the potential benefits for the corporation are connected to marketing goals and objectives.

1. *Supporting brand positioning:* SUBWAY Restaurants

If you were the marketing director at SUBWAY, responsible for securing a brand positioning as the healthy fast-food option, you would be grateful for the long-term partnership the company has had with the American Heart Association, sponsoring many initiatives including Start! Walking at Work, Jump Rope for Heart, and the American Heart Walks. You would have also been pleased with the announcement in January 2014 from First Lady Michelle Obama that SUBWAY has committed to promoting healthier choices for kids through a fresh marketing campaign and additional restaurant offerings. Adding to the applause, a follow-up press release from the American Heart Association also praised the effort:

> For almost 15 years, we have worked with SUBWAY to develop and provide healthier meals to adults and children. Today is another example of SUBWAY's leadership and its commitment to kids' health. This represents a great step toward marketing only healthy foods and beverages as well as promoting fruits and vegetables to children.[7]

2. *Creating brand preference with a priority audience*: Macy's *Go Red for Women Campaign*

The American Heart Association's signature women's initiative, *Go Red for Women*, is a platform designed to reduce heart disease among women by inspiring risk-reduction behaviors. Macy's, a department store chain that offers a wide variety of women's apparel, was a founding national sponsor of this movement and has helped raise more than $69 million[8] to support *Go Red For Women* since 2004, a contribution that is estimated to have helped the movement save 285 lives each day.[9] Recognition of Macy's partnership with the American Heart Association continues in 2022 and is visible in multiple venues including their Red Dress Collection that is featured in annual runway shows, highlighted at *Go Red For Women* luncheons, and is noted by actresses and models on social media.

3. *Building traffic: Lowe's*

   In 1999, the Water—Use it Wisely campaign was launched to respond to a sentiment among Arizona residents to "Don't tell us to save water. Show us how." Partners included local city governments, private and public utilities, Arizona Department of Water Resources, Arizona Municipal Water Users Association, and, in 2005, Lowe's, a partner in the private sector, joined and is still a partner in 2022.[10] As part of a radio campaign, the partners scheduled radio broadcasts every Saturday at prominent Lowe's locations to help drive traffic and purchases of water-saving devices. Conservation workshops were presented by Lowe's employees on those Saturdays, using a curriculum created by the water conservation experts from the cities. Promotions included water-saving tips appearing on aisle, register, and door signs. Outcomes for the program as well as Lowe's were impressive, with Lowe's reporting a 50% increase in workshop attendance over prior similar workshops and sales of water efficient merchandise increasing by an average of 30%.[11]

4. *Increasing sales:* Energizer and "Change Your Clock, Change Your Battery"

   According to the U.S. Fire Administration, every year more than 3,400 Americans die in fires and approximately 17,500 are injured, with the majority of these fires occurring in the home, but adding a working smoke alarm can double the chances of survival.[12] Influencing homeowners to ensure the battery in their smoke alarm is functional, and to then replace it is a natural social marketing campaign for a brand like Energizer to support. And linking this action to another routine behavior, changing your clock in the spring and fall, is an even smarter idea, functioning as a sustainable prompt. For 29 years (as of 2017), Energizer, the International Association of Fire Chiefs, and more than 6,400 fire departments have partnered to remind people of this simple life-saving habit.[13] And this annual promotional reminder continues in 2022, now encouraging the use of social media to help spread the word and remind friends and family to ensure their batteries are functioning.

5. *Improving profitability:* Allstate and Teen Driver Pledges

   Given the statistics put forth by the Centers for Disease Control and Prevention (CDC) indicating that motor vehicle crashes are one of the leading causes of death for U.S. teens, it might not be surprising that Allstate Insurance is interested in promoting safer teen driving.[14] And given that teens have the highest proportion of distraction-related fatal crashes, it also isn't surprising that reducing texting and driving among teens is a priority for one of Allstate's corporate social marketing efforts, carrying the potential to reduce their claims as well. Their strategic focus is on encouraging teens to pledge not to text and drive, supporting the *IT CAN WAIT* campaign. The movement began in 2009, and by 2021, the campaign had received more than 40 million pledges (all ages).[15] Social media are a primary channel for making the pledge, with teens being encouraged on Facebook to add their thumbprint to an oversized pledge banner.

6. *Attracting credible partners:* Clorox and the CDC's "Say Boo to the Flu"

   Because of their behavior change focus and potential, corporate social marketing initiatives, perhaps more than the other five initiatives identified, are likely to be welcomed and supported by public sector agencies. A partnership between Clorox and CDC is a notable example. The *Say Boo to the Flu* program was created in 2004 to increase the number of families vaccinated against the flu and to promote additional simple prevention behaviors. On the campaign's website, for example, a section on "Where is the Flu Virus Hiding in Your House?" identifies five germ "hot spots" and recommends using sprays and wipes that are disinfectant cleaning products, such as Clorox. Since the fall of 2013, Clorox has sponsored annual *Say Boo! to the Flu* events across the country, offering parents opportunities to get their families the flu vaccination and incorporating a fun Halloween theme and a "Boo-mobile" that crisscrossed the country.[16] In 2021, during the COVID-19 Pandemic campaign, messages reassured the public that flu vaccine was still important. "The CDC has determined that it is safe to receive both the flu and the COVID-19 vaccine at the same time."[17]

7. *Having a real impact on social change*: Pampers' "Back to Sleep" campaign

   SIDS is a term used to describe the sudden, unexplained death of an infant younger than one year of age. In the United States, it is the leading cause of death in infants between one month and one year old.[18] One behavior to help reduce SIDS is to place infants on their backs to sleep. The Back to Sleep campaign, launched in 1994 by the National Institute of Child Health and Human Development, included an early partner, Pampers, one that helped expand the reach of the campaign message by printing the Back to Sleep logo across the fastening strips of its newborn diapers (see Figure 15.1). This prompt helped ensure that every time caregivers changed a baby's diaper, they would be reminded that back sleeping is best to reduce a baby's risk of dying from SIDS. In 2021, it was announced by the U.S. Department of Health and Human Services that since the campaign had been launched, the percentage of infants placed on their backs to sleep had increased dramatically, and the rate of SIDS had declined by almost 50%.[19]

FIGURE 15.1 ■ A Just-in-Time Reminder on Pampers Newborn Diapers

Source: National Institutes of Child Health and Human Development, Back to Sleep Campaign, "Safe Sleep for Your Baby: Ten Ways to Reduce the Risk of Sudden Infant Death Syndrome" (n.d.), accessed October 31, 2006,

STEP 9: BUDGETS AND FUNDING SOURCES

Step 9, the budgeting process, is "where the rubber hits the road." You are now ready to determine price tags for strategies and activities that you have identified in your plan, those you believe are key to reaching quantifiable behavior change goals. Once this number is totaled, you will evaluate this potential cost by referring to anticipated benefits from targeted levels of behavior change, comparing this with current funding levels and, if needed, identifying potential additional resources.

It is also important to note that it is not always appropriate to take the lowest-cost-per behavior change approach. Social marketers need to be aware of diversity, equity, and inclusion (DEI) considerations for their programs. While for some issues, it may be easier and less costly to spur behavior change among a majority white priority audience group, BIPOC, LGBTQ+, and other historically marginalized communities deserve the same programs and should be "caught up" for programs that have traditionally ignored them. If these audiences are less familiar with the issue or behavior change, you will have to do more work to establish your program and support these communities to spur the desired behavior changes. This is a budgeting consideration you should plan for and be prepared to justify when seeking budget approval.

This chapter section will take you through each of these budgeting phases: Determining the Budget; Justifying the Budget; and Finding Additional Funding.

DETERMINING BUDGETS

In the commercial as well as nonprofit and public sectors, several approaches are often cited as possibilities to consider in determining marketing budgets.[20] The following four have the most relevance for social marketing:

The affordable method. Budgets are based on what the organization has available in the yearly budget or on what have been spent in prior years. For example, a county health department's budget for teen pregnancy prevention might be determined by state funds allocated every two years for the issue, and a local blood bank's budget for the annual blood drive might be established each year as a part of the organizational budgeting process.

The competitive-parity method. In this situation, budgets are set or considered based on what others have spent for similar efforts. For example, a litter campaign budget might be established based on a review of media expenses from other states that have been successful at reducing litter using social marketing campaigns.

The objective-and-task method. Budgets are established by (a) reviewing specific objectives and quantifiable goals, (b) identifying the tasks that must be performed to achieve these objectives, and (c) estimating the costs associated with performing these tasks. The total is the preliminary budget.[21] For example, the budget for a utility's marketing effort for recycling might be based on estimated costs for staffing a new telephone service center to answer questions on what can be recycled, providing plaques for recognizing homeowner participation and promotional strategies, including social media and television ads, radio spots, statement stuffers, and flyers. These total costs are then considered with any projections of increased revenues or decreased costs for the utility.

Cost per sale. Commercial marketers often set budgets based on sales goals, having (what may seem to social marketers) the luxury of knowing what it has cost in the past to generate leads and then convert to sales. In this case, costs are typically those associated with promotional activities. A company wanting to sell 5,000 more of one of their products may have historic data indicating it takes $10 of advertising to generate one sale, a rate meeting targeted profit margin. This metric would be used to establish the advertising budget for the campaign (e.g., $50,000). For social marketers, the math is similar, with "cost per behavior" substituting for "cost per sale." Consider this example, a Fish & Wildlife campaign to increase usage of crab gauges to determine whether a crab should be retained. Program managers would, ideally through a pilot, divide the total promotional costs for an effort by the number of crabbers they observed, or determined, used a crab gauge because of the promotional effort. Future efforts could then use this amount to estimate budgets for desired behavior change goals (though you need to factor in DEI considerations here realizing that it may cost more per behavior when you factor in the costs of reaching new diverse audiences).

The most logical of these approaches, and one consistent with our planning process, is the objective-and-task method. In this scenario, you will identify costs related to your marketing intervention mix strategy (product, price, place, and promotion) as well as evaluation and monitoring efforts. This becomes a preliminary budget, one based on what you believe you need to do to achieve the goals established in Step 4 of your plan. In subsequent sections of this chapter, we discuss options to consider when this preliminary budget exceeds currently available funds, including sources to explore for additional funding as well as the potential for revising strategies and/or reducing behavior change goals.

The following brief example is included to further illustrate the nature of identifying strategies with budget implications. In this example, assume a hospital has developed a draft marketing plan to decrease the number of employees commuting to work in single-occupant vehicles (SOVs). The campaign *objective* is to influence employees to use public transportation, carpools, or van pools or walk or bike to work, with the *goal* being to decrease the number of SOVs on campus by 10% (100 vehicles) over a 12-month period. The hospital is motivated by a desire to build a new wing, an effort that will require land use permits granted, in part, based on impacts on traffic congestion in the surrounding neighborhoods.

Product-related costs are most often associated with producing or purchasing any accompanying *tangible goods* and developing or enhancing associated *services* needed to support behavior change. Costs may include direct costs for providing these goods and services, or they may be indirect costs, such as staff time. Product-related cost considerations for the hospital will include the need to lease additional vans from the county's transit system, install new bike racks, and construct several additional showers for employee use if marketing goals are, in fact, met. Incremental service charges because of increased efforts might include costs for temporary personnel to provide ride share matching or to build and maintain a special online software program for ride sharing.

Price-related costs include those associated with incentives, recognition programs, and rewards. In some cases, they include net losses from sales of any goods and services associated with the marketing effort. Price-related costs for the hospital may include incentives, such as cash incentives for carpooling, reduced rates for parking spots close to the building, free bus passes, and occasional free taxi rides home promised to staff if they need to stay late. The draft plan also includes providing recognition pins for name tags, a strategy anticipated to make members of the program "feel good" as well as spread the word about the program to other employees during meetings, in the cafeteria, and the like. The hospital might also decide to reward those who have stuck with the program for a year with a free iPad to make their ride home on the bus or in the van more pleasant and encourage others to stick with the program.

Place-related costs involve providing new or enhanced access or delivery channels, such as telephone centers, online purchasing, extended hours, and new or improved locations. There may be costs related to distribution of any tangible goods associated with the program. In our example, there may be costs for creating additional parking spots for carpools close to the main entrance of the hospital or for staffing a booth outside the cafeteria for distributing incentives and actual ride share sign-up.

Promotion-related costs are the costs associated with developing, producing, and disseminating communications including transcreation or translation into other languages. Promotion-related costs for the hospital might include developing and producing fact sheets on benefits, posters, special brochures, and transportation fairs.

Evaluation-related costs include any planned measurement and tracking surveys. Evaluation-related costs for the hospital might include conducting a baseline and follow-up survey that measures employee awareness of financial incentives and ride share matching programs, as well as any changes in attitudes and intentions related to alternative transportation.

Justifying the Budget

First, consider how those in the commercial marketing sector look at marketing budgets—it's all about the return on investment. We begin with a story from *Kotler on Marketing* that illustrates the marketing mindset, as well as a potential budget analysis:

> The story is told about a Hong Kong shoe manufacturer who wonders whether a market exists for his shoes on a remote South Pacific island. He sends an *order taker* to the island who, upon cursory examination, wires back: "The people here don't wear shoes. There is no market." Not convinced, the Hong Kong shoe manufacturer sends a *salesperson* to the island. This salesperson wires back: "The people here don't wear shoes. There is a tremendous market."
>
> Afraid that this salesperson is being carried away by the sight of so many shoeless feet, the Hong Kong manufacturer sends a third person, this time a *marketer*. This marketing professional interviews the tribal chief and several of the natives, and finally wires back: "The people here don't wear shoes. However, they have bad feet. I have shown the chief how shoes would help his people avoid foot problems. He is enthusiastic. He estimates that 70 percent of his people will buy the shoes at the price of $10 a pair. We

probably can sell 5,000 pairs of shoes in the first year. Our cost of bringing the shoes to the island and setting up distribution would amount to $6 a pair. We will clear $20,000 in the first year, which, given our investment, will give us a rate of return on our investment (ROI) of 20 percent, which exceeds our normal ROI of 15 percent. This is not to mention the high value of our future earnings by entering this market. I recommend that we go ahead."[22]

As described in Chapter 14 in the section on ROI, consider the marketing budget as an investment, one that will be judged based on *outcomes* (levels of behavior change) relative to financial *inputs*. Theoretically, you want to calculate your costs for the targeted levels of behavior change and then compare them with the potential economic value of the behaviors influenced. The following examples are the types of simple, but not necessarily easy, questions you will want to answer for yourself and others:

- What is it worth in terms of medical and other societal costs for a health department to find 50 HIV-positive men in one city because of their testing efforts in gay bathhouses? How does that compare with the proposed marketing budget of $150,000 to support this effort? Is each "find" worth at least $3,000 ($150,000 ÷ 50)?
- What is the economic value of a 2% increase in seatbelt usage in a state? How many injuries and deaths would be avoided, and how do savings in public emergency and health care costs compare with a $250,000 budget for promotional activities proposed to achieve this increase?
- If a county's campaign to increase spaying and neutering of pets is previsioned to persuade five hundred more pet owners this year, compared to last year, how does a budget of $50,000 sound? Is it worth $100 for each "litter avoided"?

You may be surprised how grateful (even delighted) colleagues, funders, and management will be when you provide estimates on these returns on investment. This is possible only when you have estimated dollars saved for a specific behavior change; established specific, measurable, attainable, relevant, and time-sensitive (SMART) goals for behavior changes; developed calculated strategies to support these goal levels; and then determined a budget based on each marketing-related expense. In Chapter 9, the case branded *Road Crew* was presented. This can be used as an example of the ROI calculation process.

As noted, by 2008, the program was operating in 32 communities in rural Wisconsin and had provided more than 97,000 rides. Five steps to determining the ROI would be:

1. Resources allocated: $870,000 (2000–2007)
2. Behaviors changed: 140 alcohol-related crashes prevented
3. Cost per behavior change: $870,000 ÷ 140 = $6,214
4. Benefit per behavior change: $231,000 public-related costs per alcohol-related crash

5. ROI:

   - Gross economic benefit: 140 × $231,000 = $32,340,000
   - Net economic benefit: $32,340,000 – $870,000 (campaign costs) = $31,470,000
   - ROI: $31,470,000 ÷ $870,000 = 36.2 × 100 = 3,620% return on investment

FINDING SOURCES FOR ADDITIONAL FUNDING

What if the costs for the marketing activities you propose—ones you believe are needed to reach the agreed-upon goal—are more than is currently available in your agency's budget? Before reducing the goals, you have options for additional funding to explore. Each option will be illustrated with an example, and we use this as an opportunity to recall several of the cases highlighted in this text.

Government Grants and Appropriations

Federal, state, and local government agencies are the most common sources of funds and grants for social marketing efforts. Potential sources, especially for nonprofit organizations, include national, state, and local departments of health, human services, transportation, ecology, traffic safety, natural resources, fish and wildlife, parks and recreation, and public utilities.

Example: The Puget Sound Partnership. Puget Sound, in Washington state, is the second largest estuary in the United States. The Puget Sound Partnership is a Washington state agency serving as the backbone organization for Puget Sound recovery, coordinating the efforts of citizens, government, tribes, scientists, businesses, and nonprofits to set priorities, implement a regional recovery plan, and ensure accountability for results.[23] In 2014, the agency coordinated more than $650 million to help fund over 800 projects to improve natural resources around Puget Sound; many of those are projects of nonprofit organizations, local governments, and tribes.[24] About $11 million is currently devoted to developing and implementing social marketing efforts that protect water quality and fish and wildlife habitats and to building regional capacity, such as training, technical assistance, and practitioner networks to implement and evaluate such projects.[25] Examples include increased planting of native plants on shorelines, disposing of farm animal waste properly, using commercial car washes versus washing on driveways, removing invasive plants on streams, properly maintaining septic systems, purchasing safer pesticides, preventing abandonment and assisting in recovery of derelict marine vessels, and testing and fixing vehicle oil leaks (see Figure 15.2).

Nonprofit/Foundations

There are more than 127,595 active independent corporate, community, and grant-making foundations operating in the United States alone (2021) with missions to contribute to many of the same social issues and causes addressed by social marketing efforts.[26] Kotler and Andreasen identify four major relevant groups: *family foundations*, in which funds are derived from

FIGURE 15.2 ■ Counter Card for Don't Drip & Drive, a Campaign That Won a Silver Anvil Award in 2014 From the Public Relations Society of America

Source: Courtesy of Washington State Department of Ecology.

members of a single family (e.g., Bill and Melinda Gates Foundation); *general foundations*, usually run by a professional staff awarding grants in many different fields of interest (e.g., Ford Foundation); *corporate foundations*, whose assets are derived primarily from the contributions of a for-profit business (e.g., Bank of America Foundation); and *community foundations*, set up to receive and manage contributions from a variety of sources in a local community, making grants for charitable purposes in a specific community or region.[27]

Example for a Nonprofit Organization: World Bicycle Relief. To the nonprofit organization World Bicycle Relief, a bike is not a bike; "it's an engine for economic and cultural empowerment."[28] The organization envisions a world where distance is no longer a barrier to education, health care, and economic opportunity, and as of 2014, the organization has trained more than 900 field mechanics and provided more than 180,000 specially designed, locally assembled bicycles to disaster survivors, health care workers, students, and entrepreneurs (see Figure 15.3).[29] The bikes are engineered to increase load capacity as well as to withstand

FIGURE 15.3 ■ Rugged Bicycles Are Engineered Specifically for Rural African Terrain and Load Requirements

Source: World Bicycle Relief.

rugged terrains. In rural Zambia, for example, where children are at risk for extreme poverty and high HIV/AIDS infection rates, only 60% enrolled in primary school go on to complete high school.[30] It is not uncommon for students to have to walk two or three hours each way to get to school, an effort exposing them further to harassment, sexual abuse, poor nutrition, and inability to provide critical family support. High school students must travel even farther and often end up having to rent rooms near their school, putting them at risk for dangers of living away from parental supervision. The Zambian Ministry of Education identified safe, reliable transportation as one way to increase school enrollment, and in partnership with local communities and relief organizations, implemented World Bicycle Relief's Bicycles for Educational Empowerment Program, providing approximately 50,000 purpose-designed locally assembled bicycles to children, teachers, and community supporters.[31]

Example Corporation and Foundation: Drink Wiser

Inspired by a global target set by WHO to reduce the harmful use of alcohol by 2025, Anheuser-Busch InBev (AB InBev) launched in 2015 the Global Smart Drinking Goals program with a mission, in part, to reduce the harmful consumption of alcohol across the globe[32] and created the AB InBev Foundation to support the implementation, measurement, and evaluation of this program around the world. AB InBev committed to investing at least USD$1 billion across their markets in dedicated social marketing campaigns and programs to influence social norms and individual behaviors to reduce harmful use of alcohol.[33]

Budweiser is the largest beer brand in the United States, and in 2018 and 2019, AB InBev implemented its *Drink Wiser* social marketing campaign with commercials at the Super Bowl and other major sporting events.[34] Additional tactics included communications on packaging during holidays, public service announcements on radio, and out-of-home advertising, with one behavior objective to influence beer drinkers to **"Hydrate between Buds"** (see Figure 15.4).

FIGURE 15.4 ■ Encouraging the Desired Behavior

Source: AB InBev and AB InBev Foundation

A Smart Drinking Toolkit was developed to guide marketing teams, and as part of the campaign, hydration stations (*product*) were to be set up during Major League Baseball All-Star games (*place*), where 15,000 water bottles were distributed. The Drink Wiser Challenge gave NBA fans who pledged to hydrate between Buds a chance to win prizes such as tickets to the NBA Finals and autographed memorabilia (*monetary and nonmonetary incentives*).

An analysis, published by Business for Impact at Georgetown University's McDonough School of Business in June 2021, reported that "Consumers planning to always or most of the time drink non-alcohol beverages between beers after taking the Drink Wiser Challenge increased from 41% to 66%."[35]

Advertising and Media Partners

Advertising agencies often provide pro bono services to support social causes, with contributions ranging from consulting on media buying and creative strategies to developing and producing promotional campaigns. Several factors motivate their choices, including opportunities to contribute to issues in the community, give their junior staff more experience, have more freedom to be in charge in developing creative strategies, and make new and important business contacts.[36]

The Ad Council, formed in 1942 as the War Ad Council to support efforts related to World War II, has played a significant role in producing, distributing, promoting, and evaluating public service communication programs. Familiar campaigns include Smokey Bear's "Only You Can Prevent Forest Fires," "Friends Don't Let Friends Drive Drunk," and McGruff the Crime Dog's "Take a Bite Out of Crime." Each year the council supports approximately 40 campaigns to enhance health, safety, and community involvement; strengthen families; and protect the environment, chosen from several hundred requests from nonprofit organizations and public sector agencies. Factors used for selection include criteria that the campaign must be noncommercial, nondenominational, and nonpolitical in nature. It also needs to be perceived as a prominent issue and national in scope. When a proposal is selected, the council then organizes hundreds of professional volunteers from top advertising agencies, corporations, and the media to contribute to the campaign.[37] Television and radio stations are often approached to provide free or discounted ("two for one") airtime for campaigns with noble causes. Even more valuable, they may be interested in having their sales force find corporate sponsors for campaigns, who then pay for media placement (e.g., for a campaign promoting bicycling, a media partnership between an outdoor equipment retailer, a health care organization, and a local television station). In this win-win-win situation, the social marketing campaign gets increased frequency and guaranteed placement of ads on programs that appeal to their priority audience; the local corporations get to "do good" and "look good" in the community; and the television or radio stations get paid, which might not occur with public service advertising.

Coalitions and Other Partnerships

Many social marketing campaigns have been successful, at least in part, because of the resources and assistance gained from participating in coalitions and other similar partnerships. Coalition members may be able to pool resources to implement larger-scale campaigns. Networks of individual coalition members can provide invaluable distribution channels for campaign programs and materials (e.g., the local department of license office airs a traffic safety video in the lobby, where a captive audience waits for their number to be called).

As evidenced by a tally of the cases and examples highlighted in this text, support from coalitions and public/private/nonprofit partnerships appears to be the norm, illustrated by the following examples, to name a few:

- Chapter 1: Although *Hope Not Handcuffs* was initiated by a sheriff's department, multiple community partners were key to delivering on the promise including treatment centers, local drug stores, and health care providers.
- Chapter 2: *WaterSense* is an inspiring example of a public-private partnership program, with EPA relying on coordination and support from manufacturers, water utilities and third-party certifiers, as well as retail outlets.
- Chapter 7: Washington's Departments of Fish and Wildlife and Natural Resources' *Shore Friendly* program, which featured face-to-face interactions and assistance for waterfront homeowners, was clearly reliant on coordination with local permitting

offices, homeowner associations, realtors, and technical assistance from engineers and shoreline armoring services.

- Chapter 10: We doubt that the F'Poon, developed by the Diabetes Association of Sri Lanka, would have the dissemination it needed for impact without its partnership with tea houses and major restaurants, making access convenient and a perceived norm.
- Chapter 11: The Sea Tow Foundation's efforts to influence *Designated Skippers* would not have experienced the same levels of visibility and behavior change without the involvement of marinas distributing wristbands, waterfront restaurants providing incentives, marine supply stores displaying promotional materials, and local police patrols supporting the program in local media.

Corporations

Bill Shore, Founder and CEO of Share Our Strength, stresses how critical it is that supportive partners, like corporate partners, get as well as give. He goes on to say, "To find the intersection of public interest and private interest that will work for your partners, begin by sitting down with them to learn about their needs before telling them about yours."[38] As Kotler and Lee describe in their book *Corporate Social Responsibility: Doing the Most Good for Your Company and Your Cause*, three trends in corporate giving are noteworthy, especially for social marketers: First, the good news is that giving is on an upward trend, with a report from Giving USA indicating that giving by for-profit corporations rose from an estimated $9.6 billion in 1999 to $18.9 billion in 2012[39] and to $46.4 billion in 2021.[40] Second, there is an increased shift to strategic versus obligatory giving, with a desire, even expectation, for "doing well and doing good." An increased number of corporations are picking a few strategic areas of focus that fit their corporate values. Shareholders expect that corporations both have Corporate Social Responsibility plans and that they report back at least annually on their progress toward those plans. They are selecting initiatives that support their business goals, choosing issues more closely related to their core products, and expressing more interest in opportunities to meet marketing objectives, such as increased market share, better market penetration, or building a desired brand identity.[41] And this brings us to the third relevant trend. Many corporations are discovering (and deciding) that supporting social marketing initiatives and campaigns can be one of the most beneficial of all corporate social initiatives, especially for supporting their marketing efforts. In an article titled "Best of Breed" in the *Stanford Innovation Review* in the spring of 2004, Kotler and Lee described why corporations find this so attractive:

- It can support brand positioning (e.g., SUBWAY partnering with the American Heart Association to influence healthy eating).
- It can create brand preference (e.g., Pampers' support of the SIDS Foundation to influence parents and caregivers to put infants to sleep on their back).
- It can build traffic in stores (e.g., Best Buy's recycling events at store locations).

- It can increase sales (e.g., Mustang Survival's partnership with Seattle Children's Hospital and Regional Medical Center to help the company capture a share of the toddler market).
- It can have a real impact on social change, and consumers make the connection (e.g., 7-Eleven's participation in the Don't Mess with Texas litter prevention campaign that has helped decrease litter by more than 50% in that state).[42]

Corporations have several ways to support your campaigns, as described in the following sections: cash grants and contributions, cause-related marketing campaigns, in-kind contributions, and use of their distribution channels.

Cash Grants and Contributions

Cash contributions from corporations (as opposed to their foundations) are awarded for a variety of purposes, including sponsorship mentions in communications, potential for building traffic at retail or Internet sites, and opportunities for visibility with key constituent groups.

Example: Child Care Resources. Child Care Resources is a nonprofit organization in Washington state providing information and referral assistance to families seeking childcare, training, and assistance for childcare providers and consulting and advocacy for quality childcare. In the mid-1990s, Safeco, an insurance company based in Seattle, provided a generous grant to Child Care Resources to strengthen the ability of childcare providers to promote and track immunizations of children in their care. Formative research with childcare providers provided input for developing training and a kit of materials that included immunization-tracking forms, posters, flyers, stickers, door hangers, and brochures for parents, with refrigerator magnets and immunization schedules (see Figure 15.5). In partnership with numerous local and state health agencies, Child Care Resources developed and disseminated more than 3,000 kits to childcare providers in the first year of the grant. An evaluation survey among approximately 300 of the providers indicated that 94% felt the materials helped them encourage parents to keep their children's immunizations up to date. The grant was extended for a second year, and trainings and kit distribution were taken statewide under the direction of the Washington State Child Care Resource and Referral Network.

Cause-Related Marketing

Cause-related marketing (CRM) is an increasingly popular strategy with a win-win-win proposition. In the typical scenario, a percentage of sales of a company's product is devoted to a nonprofit organization. The strategy is based on the premise that buyers care about the civic virtue and caring nature of companies. When market offerings are similar, buyers have been shown to patronize the firms with better civic reputations. Carefully chosen and developed programs help a *company* achieve strategic marketing objectives (e.g., sell more product or penetrate new markets) and demonstrate social responsibility, with an aim of moving beyond rational and emotional branding to "spiritual" branding. At the same time, CRM raises funds and increases exposure for a *social issue or cause* and gives *consumers* an opportunity to be involved in improving the quality of life.[43] Well-known partnerships include programs such as American Express and Charge

FIGURE 15.5 ■ Door Hanger Used at Childcare Centers to Remind Parents to Check Immunization Status

Source: Materials developed by Child Care Resources and Safeco Insurance.

Against Hunger, Yoplait yogurt and breast cancer, Lysol and Keep America Beautiful, and Ethos Water* sold at Starbucks to support water, sanitation, and hygiene education programs. National surveys indicate that many consumers would be influenced to buy, or even switch and pay more for, brands when the product supports a cause, especially when product features and quality are equal. However, if the promotion rings hollow or lacks authenticity, customers may be cynical; if the charitable contribution doesn't amount to much or the promotion doesn't run long enough, customers may be skeptical; if the company chooses a cause of less interest to their customers, it will gain little; and if the company chooses a cause and other causes feel miffed, it may lose out.

In-Kind Contributions

For some corporations, in-kind donations are even more appealing than cash contributions. Not only do they represent opportunities to off-load excess products or utilize "idle" equipment such as that used for printing, but they also provide opportunities to connect consumers with the company's products and to connect the product with the organization's cause. The following example illustrates this opportunity well.

Example: Mustang Survival. Drowning is the second leading cause of unintentional injury-related death for children in the United States.[44] In Washington state alone, 90 children under the age of 15 drowned from 1999 to 2003. Sadly, in too many cases, drowning deaths could have been avoided if the child had been wearing a properly fitted life jacket. Although Washington state regulations require that children 12 years and younger wear a properly sized U.S. Coast Guard–approved life jacket on any boat under 19 feet long, not all children are wearing life jackets or ones that are properly fitted. In 1992, Mustang Survival, a life vest manufacturer, made a three-year commitment to a partnership that included Seattle Children's Hospital and Regional Medical Center and other members of a drowning prevention coalition. In addition to contributing free life jackets for unique events, they also provided financial support, discount coupons, bulk buy programs, and in-kind printing (see Figure 15.6). Financial support was used to develop a parent's guide, children's activity booklet, and interactive display.

Use of Distribution Channels

Companies can provide tremendous visibility and support for your efforts by giving you space in their stores for such things as car seat safety checks (at car dealers), flu shots (at grocery stores), energy-saving events like light-bulb exchanges (at hardware stores), and pet adoptions (at pet stores). In some cases, this can have a profound impact, as it did in the following example.

Example: Best Buy". No matter where you bought it, we'll recycle it" is a headline Best Buy uses frequently, and in recognition of this effort, Best Buy received the first-ever eCycling Leadership Award from the Consumer Electronics Association in 2013, recognizing consumer electronics companies that are recycling above and beyond any level mandated by government.[45]

FIGURE 15.6 ■ Coupon Used to Promote Life Vest Use

Source: Reprinted from Seattle Children's Hospital and Regional Medical Center.

As of 2022, two billion pounds of electronics and appliances have been recycled at Best Buy stores.[46] No doubt this success is due in part to the fact that they make this easy and "cheap" for consumers, offering kiosks just inside the door of their U.S. stores for easy drop-off and taking them at no charge, and in 2022 launched home pick-up recycling service for unwanted electronics and appliances.[47] Although their annual sustainability reports do not comment on the traffic and sales these customer contacts generate, we can imagine it would be substantial, as those bringing their used and unwanted items in are likely looking for replacements.[48]

APPEALING TO FUNDERS

The same principles we have outlined for influencing priority audiences are applicable for influencing potential funders as well. They could be viewed simply as another type of audience, and the same steps and customer orientation are called for:

- Begin by identifying and prioritizing segments (potential funders) that represent the greatest opportunities for funding your program. Several criteria may guide this prioritization, with a special focus on organizations where you have existing contacts and relationships, shared areas of focus and concern, and similar priority audiences, publics, or constituent groups.
- Reach out to a contact at the company briefly describing your planned campaign purpose, focus, audience, and desired behavior change. Suggest a brief meeting to describe further.
- Prior to meeting formulate clear, specific potential requests (e.g., coupons for discounts on life vests).
- Spend time in person deepening your understanding of the funders' wants, needs, and perspectives. What are potential benefits of and concerns with your proposal? Who is the competition, and what advantages and disadvantages do you have?
- Based on this information, refine and finalize your specific request. Your preliminary inquiries, for example, may reveal that a large request (risking the "door in your face") may in fact make it more likely that you will receive funding for a smaller one.
- Develop a strategy using all elements of the marketing intervention mix, a proposal that (a) articulates clear value for the funder (what's in it for them) and benefits to the cause (priority audiences), (b) addresses concerns and barriers, (c) ensures a smooth and responsible administrative process, and (d) provides assurance of measurable outcomes.

It is helpful to keep in mind that corporations evaluating an opportunity to support a social marketing effort are likely to consider the following questions:

- Is there a natural bond between the cause and the company?
- Is it an issue that their priority audience cares about?

- Is there an opportunity for staff to be involved?
- Can they own or at least dominate the position of corporate partner?
- Can they stick with the program for at least two to three years?
- Is there cooperation with their current distribution channels?
- Does it provide enhanced media opportunities?
- Can they develop an optimal donation model that provides sales incentives at an economically feasible per-unit contribution?
- Will they be able to absolutely measure their return on investment?

And, to underscore additional points made in the "Best of Breed" article in the *Stanford Innovation Review*, these partnerships must "pass the smell test."[49] It is crucial that the social issue being addressed avoids any appearance of inauthenticity or hidden agendas. A tobacco company promoting parent–teen dialogue on the dangers of smoking, for example, is likely to be viewed as inauthentic. Cynical consumers know the tobacco industry counts on early uptake among the youth population for a sustainable customer base. If there is the potential for even the appearance of a conflict of interest, companies should choose a different issue, and social marketers should choose a different partner.

REVISING YOUR PLAN

What happens if funding levels are still inadequate to implement the desired plan? In this familiar scenario, you have several options to make ends meet:

Develop campaign phases. Spread costs out over a longer period, allowing for more time to raise funds or to use future budget allocations. Options for phasing could include selecting only one or a few priority audiences the first year, launching the campaign in fewer geographic markets, focusing on only one or a few communication objectives (e.g., using the first year for awareness building) or implementing some strategies the first year and others in subsequent years (e.g., waiting until the second year to build the demonstration garden using recyclable materials).

Strategically reduce costs. Options might include *eliminating strategies and tactics* with questionable potential impact, *choosing less expensive options* for noncritical executional strategies (e.g., distributing materials online rather than printing) and, where feasible, *bringing some of the tasks in-house* (e.g., social media posts and response and organization of special events).

Adjust goals. Perhaps the most important consideration is the potential need to return to Step 4 and adjust your goals. Clearly, in situations where you have chosen to spread campaign costs over a longer period, goals will need to be changed to reflect new timeframes. In other situations where time frames cannot be adjusted and additional funding sources have been explored, and you have decided you need to eliminate one or more key strategies (e.g., television may not be an option, even though it was identified as key to reach and frequency objectives), you will then need to adjust the goal (e.g., reach 50% of the priority audience instead of the 75% that television was anticipated to support). You are encouraged to then return to your managers, colleagues, and team members for frank discussions about the need to adjust preliminary goals, so that "promises" are honest and realistic.

ETHICAL CONSIDERATIONS WHEN ESTABLISHING FUNDING

Ethical considerations regarding budgets and funding are probably familiar and include issues of responsible fiscal management, reporting, and soliciting of funds. Consider, though, the following additional dilemmas that could face a social marketer: What if a major tobacco company wanted to provide funding for television spots for youth tobacco prevention but didn't require the company's name to be placed in the ad? Is that okay with you? What if a major lumber and paper manufacturer wanted to provide funding for a campaign promoting recyclable materials and wanted the name of the company associated with the campaign? Any concerns? What if a fast-food chain wanted to be listed as a sponsor of magazine ads featuring the food guide pyramid? Is it okay to accept pro bono work from an advertising agency for a counter-alcohol campaign if the parent company has clients in the alcohol industry?

COVID-19 Social Marketing Example

Corporate support for influencing COVID-19 protective behaviors has been abundant, with examples for each of the 4 P's illustrated in Table 15.1.

TABLE 15.1 ■ Examples of Corporate Support for Reducing the Spread of COVID-19

Products	Restaurants offering hand sanitizing dispensers at tables Retailers installing plexiglass shields at checkout counters Banks providing single-use pens and pencils for signing documents
Price	Uber offering free rides to vaccine clinics A Donut shop offering a free donut with proof of vaccination Amazon offering free delivery of at-home tests
Place	Shopping centers offering space for vaccine sites Grocery stores offering special hours for seniors and other vulnerable populations Restaurants encouraging takeout orders
Promotion	Businesses posting prompts at entrances to wear a mask Daily news reports on numbers of new cases and deaths Grocery stores installing markers prompting six feet distancing

CHAPTER SUMMARY

Preliminary budgets are best determined by using the *objective-and-task method* in which budgets are established by (a) reviewing specific objectives, (b) identifying the tasks that must be performed to achieve these objectives, and (c) estimating the costs associated with performing these tasks. These costs will include those related to developing and implementing elements of the marketing intervention mix, as well as funds needed to support the evaluation and monitoring plan. And to justify them, you are encouraged to quantify the intended outcomes you are targeting for these outputs to produce, and ideally the return on investment.

When preliminary budgets exceed current funding, several major sources for additional funds are identified: government grants and appropriations, nonprofit organizations and foundations, advertising and media partners, coalitions and other partnerships, and corporations. You are also encouraged to consider more than cash grants and contributions from corporations, with cause-related marketing initiatives, in-kind contributions, and the use of their distribution channels being excellent opportunities as well.

If proposed budgets exceed funding sources even after exploring additional sources, you can consider creating campaign phases, strategically reducing costs, and/or adjusting the campaign goals you established in Step 4.

RESEARCH HIGHLIGHT

INCREASING PROGRAM EFFECTIVENESS AND EFFICIENCIES BY EXPLORING AND REPLICATING PRIOR SUCCESSFUL EFFORTS

(2022)

This Research Highlight is intended to inspire program planners to identify and review prior and existing campaigns addressing similar "wicked problems." Not only can this effort inspire campaign strategies, but it can also reduce costs associated with budgets for audience research and development of interventions, the focus of this chapter. One of the "luxuries" that those in the public and nonprofit sectors can experience is the opportunity to replicate successful public campaigns, with relevant permissions and references, of course.

On May 23, 2022, the elementary school shooting in Uvalde, Texas, that took the lives of 19 children and 2 teachers, left many with thoughts and desires to know what should be done to prevent this from happening again. One option would be to explore existing and prior programs developed to address mass school shootings. This case highlights a program that could clearly inform potential strategies for future efforts, with most information for this highlight found at the Sandy Hook Promise website https://sandyhookpromise.org/who-we-are/about-us/

Background, Purpose, and Focus

Sandy Hook Promise is a national nonprofit organization founded and currently (as of 2022) led by several family members whose loved ones were killed at Sandy Hook Elementary School on December 14, 2012. With a *purpose* to reduce mass school shootings, and historic data indicating that "in 4 out of 5 school shootings, at least one other person had knowledge of the attacker's plan but failed to report it,"[50] the program *focused* on influencing reporting of possible threats of violence; in their words, "*Say Something*." Similarly, in Mark Follman's book *Trigger Points: Inside the Mission to Stop Mass Shootings in America*, he reported results from a research study of 37 mass school shootings between 1999 and the mid-70s that indicated that "in almost all thirty-seven cases, the shooters had told other kids about what they intended to do."[51]

Priority Audience and Desired Behaviors

The *Say Something* program seeks to influence middle and high school students to recognize the warning signs of someone at-risk of hurting themselves or others and to then say something to a trusted adult to get help. Two examples of more than a dozen warning signs noted on the website include seeing someone's share on social media about a planned attack and bragging about access to guns.[52]

Relative to the Uvalde school shooting, a *New York Times* article confirmed evidence of similar relevant warning signs. "About 30 minutes before arriving at the school, the shooter posted on Facebook that he was going to shoot his grandmother, Governor Abbott said. In a second post on Facebook, the shooter said he had shot his grandmother, the governor said. In a third post, the shooter said he was going to shoot an elementary school."[53] In addition, a press release on May 26, 2022, from Sandy Hook Promise stated that "he also posted cryptic messages along with photos of the two automatic weapons he purchased."[54]

Marketing Interventions

Sandy Hook Promise's *Know the Signs* program (*product*) provides curriculums that instruct youth in grades 4–12, as well as adults, on how to "Recognize the Signs" and to then "Say Something" to get help, including the option to chat anonymously online with a crisis counselor. Each program offers 30–40 minutes of student training that can be delivered in-person or online (*place*). Resources also include a Training Guide and an Educator's Guide for adults. Programs are made available to schools and youth organizations nationwide at no cost (*price*). A pledge program (*nonmonetary incentive*) includes an online portal to confirm an agreement that "I promise to do all I can to protect children from gun violence by encouraging and supporting solutions that create safer, healthier homes, schools and communities."[55]

One additional tool available to select school districts and state-wide partnerships is an anonymous reporting system for youth using a downloadable **mobile app** branded *Say Something*. After information is provided, a crisis counselor reviews and then replies to the tip with a private chat message and then chats anonymously with the youth, providing answers to any follow-up questions.

Results

The Sandy Hook Promise website, in 2021, reported the following engagements, outcomes, and impact of the program from its beginning in 2013.[56]

- *Know the Signs Program*: 14+ million participants nationwide
- *Get "Back to School Essentials"* : 8.3 million You Tube video views
- *Promise*: Over 8 million pledges to "Say Something"
- *Report*: 82,000+ tips anonymously reported

- *Prevent Violence*: 60+ acts of violence with a weapon prevented
- *Plots Averted*: 8 planned school shootings prevented
- *Saving Lives*: 296 confirmed lives saved with crisis interventions

DISCUSSION QUESTIONS AND EXERCISES

1. Discuss responses to the questions posed in the opening examples, as well as those in the ethical considerations section.
2. What ideas do you have for a potential corporate partner for a campaign influencing women to know the signs of a heart attack? What about one for literacy?
3. Give an example of a social marketing campaign that has a visible corporate sponsor, one not mentioned in this chapter.

16 STEP 10: IMPLEMENTATION AND SUSTAINING BEHAVIORS PLANS

LEARNING OBJECTIVES

After reading this chapter, you should be able to:

16.1 Summarize the key components of an implementation plan.

16.2 Describe the 11 options for developing campaign phases.

16.3 Discuss the major strategies for campaign sustainability.

16.4 Create an effective approach to selling and sharing your plan.

16.5 Summarize the International Social Marketing Association (iSMA) code of ethics.

We envision a world where people are healthy and safe, involved in protecting the environment, engaged in their communities, financially secure, reaching educational milestones, and living in inclusive and equitable communities. We have written this book for the thousands of current and future practitioners on the front lines responsible for behavior change for social good to help create this reality.

After reading the prior 15 chapters, we hope you see social marketing as a disciplinary process with a priority audience behavior change focus and an intervention toolbox (4Ps) containing more tools than the promotion "P," ones you'll need to get the job done. We hope you appreciate the rigor involved in achieving success and that you picked up on principles that will help ensure your desired outcomes—ones worth repeating and reviewing:

- Take advantage of prior and existing successful campaigns.
- Start with priority audiences most ready for action.
- Make sure to include diverse audiences and take equity considerations into account.
- Promote single, simple, doable behaviors, ones that will have the most impact, greatest audience willingness, and largest market opportunity.
- Identify and help remove barriers to behavior change.

- Bring real benefits to the present.
- Ask your priority audience what would motivate them to do the behavior.
- Highlight costs of competing behaviors.
- Search for, or develop and promote, tangible goods and services that will help your priority audience perform the behavior.
- Consider nonmonetary incentives in the form of recognition and appreciation, commitments, and pledges.
- Make access to products and to performing the behavior easy.
- When appropriate, have a little fun with your messages.
- Use communication channels at the point of decision-making.
- Try for social and entertainment media channels.
- Use prompts for sustainability.
- Create plans for social diffusion.
- Track results and make adjustments.

CASE HIGHLIGHT
HOW CAN SOCIAL MARKETING REDUCE HOMELESSNESS?

The following case highlights social marketing components of one of the major program models adopted worldwide to reduce homelessness, a program model branded *Housing First*. A literature review of this program did not reveal the use of the term *social marketing*, but this highlight identifies the application of many, if not most, of the major principles for success including: selecting a priority audience; determining a desired behavior change; identifying audience barriers, benefits, and motivators; developing a compelling positioning and strategic marketing intervention mix; and utilizing a systematic and informative evaluation process.

By Reviewing Background Data and Establishing a Clear Purpose and Focus

The U.S. Department of Housing and Urban Development's Annual Homeless Assessment Report to Congress in February 2022 reported that on a single night in 2021, more than 326,000 people were experiencing homelessness, a term used by HUD to describe a person who lacks a fixed, regular, and adequate nighttime residence, with major subgroups including:[1]

- 60% were *individuals*
- 40% were *families with children*

- 45% were *Black*; 44% were *White*; 5% were *Multiple Races*; 2% were *Native American*; 1% were *Asian*; and 1% were *Pacific Islander*

Housing First, as a model to address homelessness, was developed in the early 1990s in New York City as an alternative to what some refer to as a *staircase* model where individuals are required to abandon drug use, accept treatment, and complete a series of steps in order to access housing, progressing, for example, from the streets to a public shelter and from a public shelter to a transitional, time-limited housing program. By contrast, the Housing First model recommends *leaping over* the steps and going *straight* into a regular self-contained dwelling, often with a rental contract.[2] This approach is guided by the belief that people need the safety and stability of a home to best address circumstances that may have led to or are perpetuating their homelessness including substance abuse issues, mental health problems, broken relationships, and lack of employment.

By Selecting a Priority Audience

The program uses a data-driven assessment system for matching people experiencing homelessness with approaches tailored to unique audience needs.[3] For example, one program model prioritizes households who became homeless due to a temporary personal or financial crisis and has limited service needs, only wanting and needing help accessing and securing permanent housing.[4] Other programs focus on high need populations, such as chronically homeless individuals with chronic illnesses, disabilities, mental health issues, or substance use disorders, and have experienced long-term or repeated homelessness, and want help. With each priority audience, however, the goal is to help them quickly secure permanent housing.

By Determining a Desired Behavior Change

Though a literature review of the program did not reveal a clear desired behavior change, it is surmised that what housing program managers, staff, and volunteers want these homeless individuals and families to do is *accept help in identifying permanent housing* that best meets their situation and needs, a process that would likely begin with one-on-one interviews with candidates sharing detailed background information, current circumstances, and a desired future.

By Identifying Audience Barriers

The Housing First model was designed to overcome common concerns and, in some cases, misperceptions that homeless individuals and families have considering shelters in general:

- Concerned they will be required to give up their drugs, convert to their host's religion, or enter into counseling and treatment services.
- Concerned that by disclosing personal information and belongings, they could be arrested (e.g., drug possession, property crime).
- Perceptions that shelters will be dangerous (e.g., housing drug dealers) and that they could face discrimination (e.g., for LGBTQ populations); they could be exposed to contagious diseases (e.g., hepatitis, COVID-19 and tuberculosis) or pests (e.g., bed bugs); they could be victims of theft (e.g., shoes); they won't be able to take their "best friend" with

them (e.g., a dog or cat); or they will face restrictions (e.g., single fathers with children, requiring the dad to sleep outside).[5]

By Crafting a Compelling Positioning

Housing First is positioned to be seen as a housing option for the homeless that provides a foundation for life improvement, offering access to permanent housing *without prerequisites or conditions beyond those of a typical renter, with supportive services offered, but not required, in order to obtain and retain housing.*[6]

By Developing a Strategic Marketing Intervention Mix

The Housing First *product* platform includes housing and support services, either on-site or in the community.[7] Housing units are typically individual units in a single building, with some structures and floor plans resembling downtown apartment or condominium buildings where there are common indoor/outdoor spaces for community activities and 24-hour front-desk reception. Supportive services most often include case management, psychiatric services, medical and/or nursing care, substance-use counseling, connections to external service providers, and assistance with access to basic needs such as food. A best practice is for communities to provide a unified and streamlined process for applying for rapid rehousing, supportive housing, and/or other housing interventions (*place*).[8]

Housing First programs often provide rental assistance, with amounts varying depending on the household's needs (*price*). Some provide long-term rental assistance and supportive services, while other models provide only short-term rental assistance and services. In Finland, for example, tenants pay rent depending on their income and are entitled to receive housing benefits. Depending on their income, they may contribute to the cost of the services, with the rest covered by municipalities; provide support services themselves; or buy support from other service providers including NGOs.[9]

By Developing Partnerships for Interventions

Housing First, as noted, is a model, one in which a unified and community-wide (total market) approach is seen as key to the success. A variety of organizations play a variety of roles with street outreach workers and emergency shelters connecting candidates to housing providers; NGOs providing resources for basic needs such as food and clothing; service providers such as community clinics offering mental, addiction, and health care services; and federal, state, and city governments providing funding support.

By Measuring Results

In 2017, The U.S. Department of Housing and Urban Development developed a Housing First Assessment Tool, available to encourage communities to assess and measure progress of homelessness projects relative to the Housing First model of best practice standards.[10] Individual projects can use this tool to identify what they are doing well and where improvements can be made.

The National Alliance to End Homelessness reported in 2016 the following outcomes from programs using the Housing First model:

- Consumers in a Housing First model are *accessing housing faster* and are *more likely to remain stably housed*, with a variety of studies indicating that between 75% and 91% of households remain housed a year after being "rapidly re-housed"[11] (see Box 16.1).

- Housing First programs have been found to result in *cost savings for communities* as housed people are less likely to use emergency services: hospitals, jails, and emergency shelter. "One study found an average cost savings on emergency services of $31,545 per person housed in a Housing First program over the course of two years. Another study showed that a Housing First program could cost up to $23,000 less per consumer per year than a shelter program."[12]

In 2022, it was published that the Housing First model has also "been proven to be cost efficient, which benefits entire communities. By providing access to housing, communities save money on emergency services like jails, hospitals and emergency shelters."[13]

BOX 16.1 SUCCESS STORY REDUCING HOMELESSNESS IN UTAH[14]

In 2005, the state of Utah set an ambitious goal to end chronic homelessness, estimated at the time to be nearly 2,000 people in their state.[15] Their core strategy is a model developed by Pathways National branded Housing First (*product*), one with the premise that permanent housing comes first and services come later. Housing is typically in a dedicated apartment complex, and services are in the areas of mental and physical health, substance abuse, education, and employment, and are focused on supporting people with psychiatric disabilities and addiction disorders to keep their housing and avoid returning to homelessness. Clients do pay some rent—either 30% of income or up to $50 a month, whichever is greater (*price*). Utah's program was launched in Salt Lake City with a pilot project that housed 17 of the hardest cases and provided them with services. The fact that two years later they all remained housed was indication of success and then expanded to other areas in the state. Under Utah's Housing First model, candidates are selected by a group that assesses the list of potential candidates and prioritizes those who are the best match for the apartment complex (e.g., gender and family composition), as well as not dealing in drugs.

The Results

In 2015, Utah could just about declare victory, with the population of chronically homeless people dropping by 91%, from the nearly 2,000 people in 2005 to fewer than 200 in December 2015. And in 2021, an article in *The Salt Lake Tribune* reported that "For the last several years, roughly 95% of people placed into permanent housing in Utah stayed there or moved into another housing situation."[16]

STEP 10: COMPLETE AN IMPLEMENTATION PLAN

For some, the implementation plan *is* the marketing plan, one that will reflect all prior decisions and is considered your final major step in the planning process. It functions as a concise working document to share and track planned efforts. It provides a mechanism to ensure that you and your team do what you said you wanted to do, on time, and within budget. It provides the map that charts your course, permitting timely feedback when you have wavered or need to take corrective actions. It is not the evaluation plan, although it incorporates evaluation activities. It is also not the same as a marketing plan for an entire program or organization, as the emphasis in this book has been on developing a marketing plan for a specific social marketing campaign.

Kotler and Armstrong describe *marketing implementation* as "the process that turns marketing strategies and plans into marketing actions in order to accomplish strategic marketing objectives."[17] They further emphasize that many managers think *doing things right* (implementation) is just as important as *doing the right things* (strategy). In this model, both are viewed as critical to success.

Key components to a comprehensive implementation plan include addressing the classic action-planning elements of what will be done, by whom, when, and for how much:

- *What will we do?* Key activities necessary to execute strategies identified in the marketing intervention mix and the evaluation plan are captured in this document.
- *Who will be responsible?* For each of these major efforts, you will identify key individuals and/or organizations responsible for program implementation. In social marketing programs, typical key players include staff (e.g., program coordinators), partners (e.g., coalition members or other agencies), sponsors (e.g., a retail business or the media), suppliers (e.g., manufacturers), vendors (e.g., an advertising agency), consultants (e.g., for evaluation efforts), and other internal and external publics, such as volunteers, citizens, and lawmakers.
- *When will it be done?* Time frames are included for each major activity, typically noting expected start and finish dates.
- *How much will it cost?* Expenses identified in the budgeting process are then paired with associated activities.
- *Are sustainability tactics supported in the implementation plan?* Strategies to sustain behaviors (e.g., prompts, permanent signage, websites, recognition and feedback mechanisms) may have been noted in the marketing intervention plan and/or there may be ones that emerge during the design of the implementation plan (e.g., working with retail outlets to have an annual event to promote high efficiency light bulbs).

Most commonly, these plans represent a minimum of one year of activities and, ideally, two or three years. In terms of format, options range from simple plans included in executive summaries of the marketing plan to complex ones developed using sophisticated software programs. Box 16.2 presents a summary of one section of a social marketing plan developed for the Mental Health Transformation Grant Social Marketing Initiative in Washington State, a section focusing on influencing policymakers. Also see Appendix B for an additional example of two social marketing plans with detailed implementation plans.

BOX 16.2 A SOCIAL MARKETING PLAN FOR ELIMINATING THE MENTAL HEALTH STIGMA: SPECIAL SECTION FOR INFLUENCING POLICYMAKERS, AN UPSTREAM AUDIENCE

1.0 Background, Purpose, and Focus

The purpose of this initiative is to reduce the stigma surrounding mental illness and the barriers it creates in the work setting, at home, within the health care system, and in the community. The focus is on increasing the understanding that people with mental illness can and do recover and live fulfilling and productive lives.

2.0 Situation Analysis and Review of Prior Similar Efforts

Strengths. Statewide transformation initiative with executive support, multiagency work-group commitment, and marketing task group with strong consumer participation; recent legislative action on mental health issues, including PACT teams, parity, and increased funding for children's mental health.

Weaknesses. Limited budget, unrealistic expectations for a communications solution, and lack of consensus on the use of social marketing.

Opportunities. Grant funding, governor endorsement, emerging coalitions, provider interest and support, and political curiosity.

Threats. Competing projects/staff time limitations, constituent expectation that "campaign" can be all things to all people, and skepticism that marketing is a legitimate method for social change.

This initiative will be built around the framework set forth by Patrick Corrigan, professor of psychiatry at Northwestern University, whose research suggests a target-specific stigma change model, identifying and influencing groups who have the power to change stigma and support adoption of the recovery model. Policymakers, the focus of this section of the plan, were identified as one of three priority audiences and will be addressed in Year 3 of the social marketing initiative. The full marketing plan includes sections focused on consumers and providers.

3.0 Priority Audience Profile

- State legislators who are responsible for state-level policies and funding
- State agency officials who set reimbursement rules for the types of services that can be covered
- Local elected officials who are responsible for local policies and allocating funds to regional service providers

4.0 Marketing Objectives and Goals

4.1 We want this plan to influence policymakers to

- Pass legislation that enables "recovery" and "mental health transformation."
- Reallocate existing funds to put more resources into recovery, resulting in a decreased need for crisis intervention.

- Interpret regulations affecting people with mental illness using a "recovery" lens.
- Ensure adequate funding to support recovery-oriented mental health services, including consumer participation.
- Support the provision of employment opportunities for consumers.
- Eliminate stigmatizing language and views and adopt a language and process that promotes recovery.

4.2 Goals

- Conduct a minimum of four speaking engagements with local elected officials.
- Conduct a minimum of six speaking engagements with state legislators.
- Conduct a minimum of five speaking engagements with state agency officials.

5.0 Priority Audience Barriers, Benefits, Motivators, and Competition

5.1 Barriers

Perceived barriers to desired behaviors include: (a) lack of knowledge about mental illness and funding/resource issues, (b) uncertainty that successful recovery is how the consumer defines it, and (c) uncertainty that recovery-oriented treatment systems can be devised where people with mental illness pose no greater violence risk to the community than people without mental illness.

5.2 Benefits/Motivators

Potential motivators include consumer success stories and proof that the recovery model works and is an efficient way to spend tax dollars.

5.3 Competing Behaviors

Responding to public fear and belief in stereotypes; providing funding for crisis intervention before funding recovery-oriented self-help programs.

6.0 Positioning Statement

We plan to develop a speakers' bureau consisting of providers and consumers of mental health services that will educate policymakers about recovery and serve as living examples of success. We want them to view these speaking engagements as an opportunity to hear success stories from consumers and as a good source of information about mental health issues, including recovery and stigma. We will also develop white papers, in partnership with consumers and providers, and want policymakers to see these as a credible source of information about mental illness, recovery and resiliency, and stigma, and as a source of empirical evidence that the recovery model works, can be economical and is a good investment.

7.0 Marketing Intervention Mix Strategies (4Ps)

7.1 Product

Core: Increased knowledge of mental illness and Washington's Mental Health Transformation Project.

Actual: Strategic speaking engagements and presentations throughout the state, highlighting consumer success stories and the recovery model.

Augmented: White papers on the transformation effort in Washington state.

7.2 Price

Speaking engagements and white papers will be free. Media coverage will address public fear and instill hope for recovery. Advocacy awards will honor policy "heroes" who contribute to recovery and the breaking down of myths and stereotypes.

7.3 Place

Speaking engagements will be scheduled at locations and times throughout the state that are convenient for policymakers. White papers will be available on the Internet and downloadable for print. Hard copies will be mailed out individually and made available at speaking engagements.

7.4 Promotion

Speaking engagements will be promoted in association newsletters, on listserves, and at sessions at related conferences. White papers will be promoted via direct mail. A news bureau will be used to publicize awards, conduct editorial board meetings to discuss mental health transformation, and stimulate feature stories. Availability of the speakers' bureau will be promoted through ongoing conversations with elected officials and their staff.

8.0 Evaluation Plan

Purpose and audience for evaluation: Speakers' bureau evaluation will measure change in policymaker knowledge of mental illness and recovery, change in belief that people with mental illness can live fulfilling lives in the community, disposition toward changing regulations and funding to support recovery-oriented services, and actual changes in policies, regulations, and funding. The marketing team will use evaluation findings to determine continuation, improvement, and expansion of speakers' bureau and policymaker strategies.

Output measures: Numbers of speaking engagements conducted, white papers distributed, news articles and editorials printed, news stories aired, and editorial board meetings conducted.

Outcome measures: Number of policymakers at speaking engagements, number of visits to website, increased knowledge about mental illnesses, increase in knowledge about Washington's Mental Health Transformation Project, and decrease in stigmatizing attitudes and beliefs by policymakers attending speaking engagements.

How and when to measure: Pre- and postworkshop questionnaires by speakers' bureau participants and audience members. Tracking of policy, regulation, and funding changes.

Media monitoring for number of letters to the editor, retractions of stereotypical portrayals, feature stories on recovery, and media coverage of award recipients.

9.0 Budget

Budget estimate is for Year 3 for the speakers' bureau and news bureau, aimed at three target audiences—consumers, providers, and policymakers—and does not include all planned activities for Year 3. The project is funded by a Mental Health Transformation State Incentive Grant from the Substance Abuse and Mental Health Services Administration of the U.S. Department of Health and Human Services.

Speakers' bureau $70,000

Recovery and stigma materials (print and web) $20,000

News bureau $15,000

Professional education $10,000

Management and coordination $20,000

Total for speakers' and news bureaus $135,000

10.0 Implementation Plan

Key Activities	Responsibility/Lead	Timing	Budget
Project coordination and oversight	DOH	Ongoing	$30,000
Speakers' bureau coordination and scheduling	Washington Institute for Mental Illness Research and Training; finalize schedule for speaking engagements	1st quarter Quarterly	$70,000
Continuing availability of recovery and stigma materials in print and on the web	DOH	Ongoing (started in Year 2)	$10,000
Policy white papers	Mental Health Transformation staff with DOH	1st quarter: Draft for review 2nd quarter: Finalize and print 2nd–4th quarters: Publicity and distribution	(Included in project coordination)

Source: Heidi Keller and Daisye Orr, Office of Health Promotion, Washington State Department of Health with Washington's Mental Health Transformation Project, Office of the Governor, 2006.

PHASING

As mentioned earlier in our discussion on budgeting in Chapter 15, when funding levels are inadequate to implement the desired plan, one tactic to consider is spreading costs over a longer period of time, allowing more time to raise funds or use future budget allocations. Natural options include creating phases that are organized (driven) by some element of the marketing plan: priority audience, geographic areas, campaign objectives, campaign goals, stages of change, products, pricing, distributional channels, promotional messages, or communication channels. The following provide examples of situations in which a particular framework might be most appropriate.

Phases Organized by First Piloting

Conducting a pilot prior to broad-scale implementation is strongly recommended. As Doug McKenzie-Mohr writes, "Think of a pilot as a 'test run,' an opportunity to work out the bugs before committing to carrying out a strategy broadly."[18] And the "bugs" that may be identified can range from discovering that something about the offer (product, price, place) was not sufficient to overcome barriers and provide valued benefits, or that some element or elements of promotional strategies (messages, messengers, creative elements, communication channels) were insufficient to reach and inspire priority audiences. The Iron Fish project described in Chapter 10, for example, began as a pilot in Cambodia, with several subsequent phases:

Phase 1: Pilot prior to 2011, testing different shapes of the iron for pots including the lotus flower shape, with disappointing results.

Phase 2: In 2011, a new shape (the Lucky Fish) was found to be appealing, and women put them in their pots.

Phase 3: Broad-scale implementation in 2013 when the program was disseminated worldwide.

Phases Organized by Priority Audience

In a differentiated strategy in which several market segments are identified for the campaign, each phase could concentrate on implementing strategies for a distinct segment. This would provide a strong focus for your efforts as well as increase resources behind them. For the Monterey Bay Aquarium's Seafood Watch program intended to decrease the purchasing of endangered and/or contaminated fish, deliberate phases include:[19]

Phase 1: Influencing consumers to ask for and purchase "green fish."

Phase 2: Equipping restaurants and grocery stores to favor suppliers of "green fish."

Phase 3: Developing a recognition and certification program that recognizes "green fisheries."

Phases Organized by Geographic Area

Phasing by geographic area has several advantages. It may align with funding availability as well as offer the ability to pilot the campaign, measure outcomes, and then make important refinements prior to implementation. When a program includes several unique geographic areas that will be focused on, this also provides input for tailored community approaches. The following example confirms these advantages.

The Clean River Coalition (CRC) is a voluntary group based in Oregon State comprised of more than 60 stakeholders from governmental and nonprofit agencies, watershed councils, and soil and water conservation districts, including ones in southwest Washington. In 2020, CRC created a campaign branded *Follow the Water-Connect the Drops* with a vision to "get more people to feel connected to the local waterways, learn about them, touch them, and appreciate the wildlife that live there."[20] The *purpose* of the effort is to reduce water pollutants, with a *focus* on those of highest concern, ones determined by an innovative "Pollutant Risk Tool[21]" that enables comparing toxic pollutants by type (e.g., consumer products, pesticides, metals), that then generates ranking scores to compare pollutants. This effort then informed a pilot program to be implemented in 2023 to influence safe weed control practices (e.g., spot spraying vs. applying pesticides over the entire lawn). A statewide survey (n = 1,000) of residents pointed to a *priority audience* of white residential gardeners, ages 34–55, earning more than $50,000 per year, who were using pesticides on their lawns but, importantly, were open to change.

The survey found statistical correlation between those who felt "connected" to their local waterway and an understanding that their personal actions could harm waterways via storm drains. As such, the CRC commissioned the production of a three-part river film series (*product*) describing "Connection", one highlighting Native American history and values.

Focus group research provided *audience insights* that people will try new behaviors as long as they are proven effective, leading to the creation of a series of three-minute lawn care videos highlighting turf expert recommendations for best practices, including pesticide use. Both video series are being *promoted* with a $100,000 allocation for digital advertising. Based upon demographic research, priority audience *communication channels* will include Facebook and YouTube. An additional outreach tool, to be tested during the first Pilot, is the delivery of lawn care outreach workers going door to door to engage in conversations that will inspire best practices. Timing and objectives of the first two phases of the program include:

> Phase 1: Pilot testing of safe lawn care practices will take place in several communities across the state of Oregon during a full lawn season, one from Spring to Fall 2023. Strategies will be tailored for each city based upon several factors, including community partners and delivery locations. Meaningful data will be gathered to determine the lowest cost delivery strategies, lessons learned, and to make any recommended changes, especially for unique communities.
>
> Phase 2: The lawn care model will be replicated across a variety of cities over time based upon their available resources.

Phases Organized by Objective

In a situation in which a campaign has identified important objectives related to knowledge and beliefs as well as behavior, campaign phases can be organized and sequenced to support each objective. A litter prevention campaign in Washington state used this strategy, allowing more time to gain the support of partners (e.g., law enforcement), secure sponsors (e.g., fast-food restaurants), and establish important infrastructures (e.g., identifying broad distribution channels for litterbags and incorporating questions on fines for litter in driver education tests). In this example, phases reflect the process of moving priority audiences from awareness to action—over time.

Phase 1: Creating awareness of laws and fines.

Phase 2: Altering the belief that "no one's watching and no one cares" by implementing a toll-free hotline for reporting littering.

Phase 3: Changing littering behavior.

Phases Organized by Goal

Campaigns may have established specific benchmarks for reaching interim goals in which case, activities and resources would then be organized to support desired outcomes. The advantage of this framework is that funders and administrators "feel good" that the program will achieve targeted goals—eventually. Similar to phasing by geographic area, this approach does not require altering the marketing strategy you developed for the program. For example, a social marketing effort in Japan to increase breast-screening rates from 30% in 2008 set the following milestones:[22]

Phase 1: To 40% by 2010

Phase 2: To 50% by 2012

Phases Organized by Stage of Change

In keeping with the objective of moving audiences through stages of change, it may make the most sense to phase a campaign effort by prioritizing those "most ready for action" and then using this momentum to move on to other markets. In a campaign encouraging food waste composting, for example, efforts might be made to set up demonstration households in neighborhoods with eager volunteers, who can then be influenced and equipped to spread the word to neighbors. In this case, phases might appear as follows:

Phase 1: Influence households with consistent participation in all curbside recycling (maintenance segment).

Phase 2: Influence households participating in paper and glass curbside recycling, but not yard waste recycling (in action segment).

Phase 3: Influence households that have responded to and inquired about information in the past but are not regular curbside recyclers (contemplator segment).

Phases Organized by Introduction of Products

When new or improved services and tangible goods have been identified for a program plan, it may be necessary, even strategic, to introduce these over a period of time. A Supplemental Nutritional Program for Women, Infants, and Children (WIC) clinic, for example, might phase the introduction of service enhancements by starting with those perceived to have the most potential impact on increasing use of farmers' markets and then move on to those providing added value:

Phase 1: Counselor training and support materials

Phase 2: Market tours and transportation vouchers

Phase 3: Clinic classes on freezing and canning

Phases Organized by Pricing Strategies

A program may plan a pricing strategy in which significant price incentives are used early in the campaign as a way to create attention and stimulate action. In subsequent phases, efforts may rely on other elements of the marketing mix, such as improved distribution channels or targeted promotions. In the case of a utility promoting energy-efficient appliances, pricing strategies might change over time as follows:

Phase 1: Rebates for turning in old appliances

Phase 2: Discount coupons for energy-efficient appliances

Phase 3: Pricing similar to competing appliances and increased emphasis on contribution to the environment

Phases Organized by Distribution Channels

A campaign relying heavily on convenience of access might begin with implementing distribution channels that are the quickest, easiest, or least expensive to develop and then move on to more significant endeavors over time. Launching a prescription drug medication return program might progress over time as follows, allowing program managers to develop procedures that ensure secure as well as convenient return locations:

Phase 1: Pilot the program by accepting medications at the county sheriff's office.

Phase 2: Expand to major medical centers and hospitals.

Phase 3: Expand to pharmacies.

Phases Organized by Messages

When multiple campaign messages are needed to support a broad social marketing program (e.g., decreasing obesity), behavior change may be facilitated by introducing messages one at a time. This can help your priority audience spread costs for change over a period of time as well as feel less overwhelmed (self-efficacy). The Ad Council's Small Steps campaign for the U.S. Department of Health and Human Services could phase its 100 recommended actions in the following clustered way:

Phase 1: Steps at Work: Walk during your lunch hour. Get off a stop early and walk. Walk to a coworker's desk instead of emailing or calling.

Phase 2: Steps When Shopping: Eat before grocery shopping. Make a grocery list before you shop. Carry a grocery basket instead of pushing a cart.

Phase 3: Steps When Eating: Eat off smaller plates. Stop eating when you are full. Snack on fruits and vegetables.

Phases Organized by Communication Channels

At the onset of major threats such as COVID-19, mass shootings, and wildfires, you may need to first reach broad audiences in a very short time. Once this phase is complete, efforts may shift to priority audiences through more targeted communication channels. For COVID-19, for example, we have seen channels progress as follows:

Phase 1: Mass communication channels: ads on TV, radio, social media, and digital channels and news stories on a wide range of media channels.

Phase 2: Segmented channels to reach specific audiences: community media, paid social media microinfluencers, in-language paid media (social and banner ads), Google search, blogs and website tools (such as vaccine locators).

Phase 3: Personal contact and partnerships: materials for health care providers and businesses (e.g., stickers, buttons, signage, handouts), expert panel webinars, and partnerships with organizations such as community-based organizations, sports teams, colleges and universities, religious organizations.

Phases Organized by a Variety of Factors

In reality, it may be important, even necessary, to use a combination of phasing techniques. For example, campaign priority audiences may vary by geographic area (e.g., farmers are more important priority audiences for water conservation in rural areas than they are in urban communities). As a result, different communities may have different priority audience phasing in their campaigns. As most practitioners will attest, campaigns will need to be meaningful to their specific communities, or they will not receive the necessary support for implementation.

Phase 1: Rural communities prioritize farmers and urban communities prioritize large corporations for water conservation.

Phase 2: Rural communities prioritize businesses and urban communities prioritize public sector agencies.

Phase 3: Rural communities and urban communities prioritize residential users.

A Note About Including Equity in Phasing Decisions

An important overlay to consider when evaluating how to phase your implementation is equity and inclusion. As social marketers, if we always focus on the cheapest, quickest, and easiest priority audiences to influence or strategies to reach our goals, we may inadvertently leave large swaths of our communities out of our programs. It is important to apply an equity lens to your phasing decisions knowing that sometimes it may take more effort, time, and resources to reach diverse or historically marginalized members of the community. But to advance equity, that investment may be imperative to further racial equity and justice in the community.

SUSTAINABILITY

At this point in the planning process, most strategies have been identified and scheduled to support desired behavior change objectives and goals. It is a worthwhile exercise, however, to give last-minute consideration to any additional tactics to include in the plan that will keep your campaign visible and behavior change messages prominent after ads go off the air and news stories die down.

It is possible that elements for sustainability were identified when developing marketing intervention mix strategies: a laminated card in the shower as a reminder to conduct monthly breast exams (*augmented product*); a message in a monthly bill from a utility providing feedback on your energy consumption last month compared to neighbors' (*nonmonetary incentive*); establishment of an annual take-back medications event (*place*); or reminders in a public service announcement twice a year to check smoke alarm batteries when changing clocks (*promotion*).

This is a point in the planning process for last minute consideration of any additional mechanisms you could include in the campaign that will help your priority audience sustain their behavior over the long-term. In keeping with our stages of change theory and model, you should be specifically interested in ensuring that those in the action stage don't return to contemplation and that those in the maintenance stage don't return to irregular actions. In the following sections, ideas including the use of prompts, commitments, plans for social diffusion, dissemination, and utilizing public infrastructures are presented.

Prompts

Doug McKenzie-Mohr highlights the value of prompts. "Numerous behaviors that support sustainability are susceptible to the most human of traits: forgetting. Fortunately, prompts can be very effective in reminding us to perform these activities."[23] In their book *Fostering Sustainable Behavior*, McKenzie-Mohr and Smith offer insights, guidelines, tools, and checklists for the social marketer to consider for supporting continued behavior change. They describe prompts as

> visual or auditory aids which remind us to carry out an activity that we might otherwise forget. The purpose of a prompt is not to change attitudes or increase motivation, but simply to remind us to engage in an action that we are already predisposed to do.[24]

They have four recommendations for effective prompts:

1. Make the prompt noticeable, using eye-catching graphics.
2. Make the prompt self-explanatory, including all information needed to take the appropriate action.
3. Place the prompt as close as possible to where and when the action is to be taken.
4. Use prompts to encourage positive behaviors rather than to avoid harmful ones.

Anchoring is similar to prompting, where the desired behavior (e.g., flossing) is "anchored" or closely linked to a current established behavior (e.g., brushing your teeth). Examples of both are illustrated in Table 16.1, and as a planning note, any new or additional prompts that you identify at this point should be noted in the appropriate 4Ps section of your marketing plan.

Commitments and Pledges

Gaining commitments, or pledges, from priority audiences has also proven surprisingly effective. "Individuals who agreed to a small initial request were far more likely to agree to a subsequent larger request."[25] Examples include a backyard wildlife sanctuary program in which homeowners sign the application promising to follow the natural gardening guidelines, and WIC clinics in which clients who sign a receipt for farmers' market coupons state they are interested in using these in the next three months. For an effort to sustain a physical activity program commitment, social media is a great option, one such as Everymove.org where participants post their exercise activities and see what their friends have been doing as well. Evidently, as McKenzie-Mohr and Smith report, "when individuals agree to a small request, it often alters the way they perceive themselves."[26] Any commitments you decide to add to your plan at this point should be noted in the price strategy section. We consider it a form of a nonmonetary incentive,

TABLE 16.1 ■ Sustaining Behaviors and Campaign Efforts

Issue	Using Prompts to Sustain Behavior
Tobacco cessation	Electronic alerts during vulnerable times in the day that signal, "Come on, you can do it."
Binge drinking	Small posters in bar restrooms encouraging a nonalcoholic beverage between drinks.
Physical activity	Wearing a Fitbit to make sure you get 10,000 steps a day.
Unintended pregnancies	Keeping a condom in a small case on a key chain.
Fat intake	Detailed data on food labels indicating fat grams and percentage of calories.
Fruits and vegetables	Placing fruits and vegetables in glass bowls at eye level in refrigerators.
Water intake	Stickers at water coolers saying, "Have you had your 8 glasses today?"
COVID-19	Masks available at retail store entrances.
Breast cancer	Shower nozzle hanger reminding about monthly breast self-exams.
Folic acid	Keeping vitamin pills by the toothbrush as an established habit.
Immunizations	Emails recognizing and reminding parents of when a child's immunizations are due.
Diabetes	Using a reminder app on a phone for blood glucose monitoring.
Car seats	Keeping a car seat in all cars used frequently by a child.
Drinking and driving	Making Breathalyzers available in bars.
Booster seats	Air fresheners for cars with reminders about booster seats.
Drowning	Providing loaner life vests for toddlers at public beaches.
Smoke alarms	Placing reminder stickers in planning calendars for checking batteries in smoke alarms.
Waste reduction	Label on a bathroom towel dispenser suggesting, "Take only what you need. Towels are trees."
Food waste composting	Stickers on recycling containers recognizing a homeowner who also composts food waste.
Reducing use	Messages at coffee stands suggesting that "the regulars" bring their own cups.
Air pollution	Stickers inside car doors reminding car owners when it is time to get their tires inflated.
Organ donation	Lawyers asking their clients who are organ donors if they have talked to their families about their wishes.

since making this commitment has been shown to act as an incentive to follow through with the behavior.

In McKenzie-Mohr's 2011 edition of *Fostering Sustainable Behavior*, the following four guidelines for designing effective commitments are among those emphasized:[27]

1. Make commitments as public as possible (e.g., signs on lawns or signatures on a petition).
2. Seek commitments in groups (e.g., members of a church congregation pledging to conserve energy).
3. Engage the audience in performing the activity initially to increase their perception of commitment (e.g., having homeowners check the thermostat on their hot water heater will likely lead them to take the next step, setting it at 120°).
4. Use existing, related contact points to solicit commitments (e.g., when customers purchase paint, ask for a commitment to dispose of unused paint properly).

Plans for Social Diffusion

Before wrapping up the planning process, also take time to consider additional tactics to facilitate social diffusion—the spread of the adoption of a behavior from a few to many, a concept introduced in Chapter 6. McKenzie-Mohr suggests guidelines for this as well, including:[28]

1. Make support for behavior adoption visible (e.g., affix a decal to a recycling container indicating that "We compost").
2. Use durable versus temporary indicators (e.g., a Mutt Mitt station in a neighborhood vs. yard signs encouraging picking up pet waste).
3. Engage well-known and well-respected people to make their support for a desired behavior visible (e.g., a city mayor speaking frequently about the advantages they see from taking mass transit to city hall).
4. Make norms visible, especially when "most of us" are engaged in the behavior (e.g., a sign at the entrance to a grocery store stating that 60% of shoppers bring their own bags at least once a month).

Utilizing Public Infrastructure

If you are working in the public sector, you have numerous opportunities for sustained visibility, as you often have access to public places and signage at public agencies. Those working on traffic safety can negotiate for signage on roadways; those working on flu prevention have access to public restrooms for signage reminding people to wash their hands; those working

FIGURE 16.1 ■ A Durable Sign at the Entrance to a Playground Provided to Recognize Cities That Support Active Play

Source: Author photo.

on pedestrian safety can negotiate for tougher tests for getting a driver's license; those working on decreasing secondhand tobacco smoke can work with school districts to send home "smoke-free home" pledge cards with the children; and successful programs can benefit from sustained visibility. An example is Playful City USA, a national recognition program honoring cities that champion efforts to make play a priority through establishing policy initiatives, infrastructure investments, and innovative programming (see Figure 16.1).[29] These are resources and opportunities that many in commercial marketing would envy and most would have a hard time paying for.

SHARING AND SELLING YOUR PLAN

Several techniques will help increase buy-in, approval, and support for your plan. First, include representatives from key internal and external groups on the planning team. Consider those who have a role in approving the plan as well as those key to implementation. For a litter prevention campaign with an emphasis on enforcement, it would be critical that a member of the state patrol have input in the planning process; to increase WIC clients' use of farmers' markets, it would be important to have a representative from the farmers' market association present, especially to hear the results of research with clients on their experiences of shopping at the market; and a city developing a pedestrian safety plan will benefit from having a police officer, an engineer, someone from the communications department, someone from a local business, and a citizen at the planning table.

Second, share a draft plan with decision makers and those key to implementation before finalizing your plan. Identify their concerns and address them. Be prepared to share the background data that led to your recommended strategies, and be prepared to compromise or modify a strategy based on their feedback. And surprise them with the targeted quantifiable goals you are proposing and how you plan to evaluate and report on campaign outcomes.

Finally, once the plan is finalized, consider developing and disseminating a concise summary of the plan. It could be as simple as a one-pager that presents the purpose, focus, priority audience, objectives, key audience insights, essential strategies, and evaluation plan.

ETHICAL CONSIDERATIONS WHEN IMPLEMENTING PLANS

In most of the chapters in this book, we have presented ethical considerations related specifically to each phase in the planning process. As you have seen, ethical considerations will come into play throughout your social marketing planning process. In 2020, the International Social Marketing Association (iSMA) adopted a code of ethics[30] to guide social marketing practitioners. The principles were created after a two-year process to gather input from social marketers from around the world. The iSMA code of ethics includes the following six social marketing ethical principles:

Respect and sensitivity: Respect for people's privacy, autonomy, diversity, free and informed choice and rights to participation and nonparticipation, inclusion and exclusion, and control over their lives.

Social justice and fairness: Promotion of social justice and avoidance of unfair distribution of benefits and burdens.

Openness and transparency: Transparency of goals, methods, intended and achieved outcomes, data ownership, and potential or apparent benefits and risks to target group(s) and society.

Avoidance of conflicts of interest: Avoidance of potential or apparent conflicts of interest, including opportunity for personal and reputational gain or avoidance of loss; promote public trust in social marketing.

Duty of care and nonmaleficence: Endeavor to do no physical, psychological or environmental harm and exercise a duty of care, integrity and professional and scientific responsibility.

Serve public interest: Fulfill social and political mandate and identify responsibilities and accountabilities for all stakeholders.

You are encouraged to adopt these principles as you work on the development and implementation of social marketing programs.

COVID-19 Social Marketing Example

In the United States, on June 17, 2022, a new phase for COVID-19 vaccinations was introduced. The CDC announced that children ages six months to five years old are now eligible for the COVID-19 vaccine, and that doctor's offices, pharmacies, and other providers such as health departments will start administering the shots in the coming week.

Interestingly, and perhaps not surprising to social marketers, the CDC Director noted in a CNN interview that a survey indicated the following potential vaccine adoption rates, with statistics similar to the "Show Me. Help Me. Make Me." model:[31]

- 18% of parents of children under 5 said they would vaccinate their child against COVID-19 as soon as a vaccine became available.
- 40% said they would "wait and see" before vaccinating their young children.
- 11% would get the vaccine for their kids only if required.
- 27% would "definitely not" get the vaccination.

CHAPTER SUMMARY

Developing an implementation plan is Step 10, the final step in the social marketing plan model. It turns strategies into actions and is critical to *doing things right*, even if you've planned *the right things*. An implementation plan functions as a concise working document that can be used to share and track planned efforts. It provides a mechanism to ensure that you do what you said you would do, on time, and within budgets. Key components of the plan include the following: What will you do? Who will be responsible? When will it be done? How much will it cost?

Formats for plans vary from simple plans incorporated in the executive summary of the social marketing plan to complex plans using software programs. The ideal plan identifies activities over a period of one to three years.

Plans are often presented in phases, usually broken down into months or years. Several frameworks can be used to determine and organize phases, including priority audiences, geographic areas, campaign objectives, campaign goals, stages of change, products, pricing, distribution channels, promotional messages, and communication channels. Often it will be a combination of these factors, and it is important to factor equity considerations into these decisions.

Typical strategies to sustain visibility for your campaign include the use of prompts and commitments, social diffusion, and existing infrastructures. Prompt tactics and mechanisms include signage, stickers, mailings, electronic reminders, labels on packaging, messages on social media, and email alerts. As noted, these may have already been identified in one or more of the marketing intervention strategies. New or additional prompts you identify at this stage in the planning process can and should be then incorporated in those sections of the plan.

Several techniques may be used to increase buy-in, approval, and support for your plan. First, include representatives from key internal and external groups on the planning team. Second, share a draft plan with decision makers and those key to implementation before finalizing your plan. Third, once the plan is finalized, consider developing and disseminating a concise summary of the plan. It could be as simple as a one-pager that presents the purpose, focus, priority audience, objectives, key audience insights, essential strategies, and evaluation plan.

RESEARCH HIGHLIGHT
INCREASING HIGH SCHOOL GRADUATION RATES FROM 55% TO 89%

(2010–2019)

Some may wonder why and how this case highlighting a success story of increasing high school graduation rates is an example of a social marketing effort. As you will read, it "qualifies" as there is a clear priority audience (those at risk for dropping out), a desired behavior that will benefit the individual as well as society (completing graduation requirements), and an intervention mix custom designed to help the audience perform.

It is included in this chapter on implementation as it demonstrates the power of monitoring progress toward a goal, analyzing the impact of program components to date, and using research findings to prioritize resources going forward to help ensure end point goals are realized.

Background

The City of Tacoma, in Washington state, and the Tacoma Public Schools, are a diverse community, with, as of 2018, 60% students of color, 58% students in poverty, 15% special education students, and 10% English language learners.[32]

In 2016, an article regarding high school student graduation rates described the following situation: "Not long ago, the reputation of public education in Tacoma, Washington, was as bleak as the gray skies that often blanket the city. A 2007 national study dubbed the 30,000-student Tacoma Public School district's five high schools as "dropout factories," where many freshmen never made it to graduation. As recently as 2010, just 55% of the district's high school students—well below the national average of 81%—earned their diplomas on time.[33] The Superintendent of Tacoma schools called it "shameful" and declared the community had "had enough."[34] They then set a bold 10-year goal to increase this rate by 50%, from 55% four-year on time rates to 83% by 2020.[35] A 2018 report indicated they had "arrived early," with high school four-year on time graduation rates for 2017 at 86%.[36] And by 2018, they were at 89%.[37] How did this happen? Some declared higher expectations and a laser-like focus on individual student needs were key to this success, described further in this next section.

Program Highlights

The Foundation for Tacoma Students served as an organizational hub, aligning goals, data, resources, and collective impact, with *Graduate Tacoma*, created as a partnership movement among more than 260 community organizations and citizens, including parents and educators, early learning and higher education, business and labor, youth and community service, civic and philanthropy, local governments and communities of faith, all aligning with Tacoma schools to impact student success.[38]

One of the most recognized intervention strategies contributing to this success started with a radical vision: "What if teachers and principals had *analytical tools* to look at the data surrounding a student and then could predict whether or not a student was likely to disengage and ultimately drop out?"[39] With this data, teachers and support staff would be able to intervene earlier and work closely with those at-risk students. The district then started exploring various business intelligence technologies, ultimately working with Microsoft to develop a data warehouse solution that captured recent data including student grades, attendance, health records, and other data. Then, based on historic data that correlated these data points with graduation outcomes, those at risk were identified and seen as a priority for attention. The end goal was a scenario in which a teacher or principal can log into a portal each morning to see a data view of each student, and then be proactively alerted by the system when a particular student is at risk of failing a course or dropping out.

An additional component seen as contributing to improved outcomes and reduced disparities was the commitment and participation of community partners, referred to by program managers as Collaborative Action Networks. Four stakeholder groups, several downstream from high school students and a few upstream, were considered key to "covering every student from cradle to graduation" and included Early Learning and Reading Network, Out of School and Summer Learning Network, Tacoma STEAM Learning Network (Science, Technology, Engineering, Arts, Math), and Tacoma College Support Network.[40]

Monitoring Results

As noted in the introduction, four-year on time graduation rates had risen from 55% in 2010 to 89% in 2018.

DISCUSSION QUESTIONS AND EXERCISES

1. Describe, in your own words, the difference between the "staircase" housing model and the "leap" to a home model discussed in the opening case. What concerns, if any, do you have with the "leap" approach?
2. Share an example of a midcourse correction, either one you are aware of or one you can imagine might be needed.
3. What is your impression of the analytical tool strategy described in the Research Highlight to increase graduation rates? Why, if it works, might other schools not adopt it?

EPILOGUE

We envision a world where people are healthy and safe, involved in protecting the environment, engaged in their communities, financially secure, reaching educational milestones, and living in inclusive and equitable communities. We believe that the discipline of *Social Marketing: Behavior Change for Good* is a key strategic model to help make this a reality.

What we want is for Social Marketing to become institutionalized (in Orbit), with the following indicators, as of the summer of 2022, that it has at least been launched:

- 8 Global Professional Social Marketing Membership Associations
- Estimated 2,500 Social Marketing Association Members Around the Globe
- 2 Global Academic Journals
- 10–12 Recurring Global Conferences
- Workshops and Training Opportunities Available Frequently and Globally
- Online Professional Certificate Courses Offered by the International Social Marketing Association
- Continued Expansion from Primarily Public Health Topics to Other Major Social Issues
- Several Active Professional Listserves
- More than 40 Books with Social Marketing Titles
- Academic Global Course Offerings with Social Marketing Content Doubled in 10 Years, from 54 in 2012 to 106 in 2022.[1]

Several factors, however, stand out as indicators we are not in Orbit including:

- Confusion with social media
- More recognition of, and reference to, Behavioral Economics
- Equating social marketing with promotions/communications
- Lack of inclusion in most relevant academic degree programs: Public Health, Environmental Studies, Public Administration
- Lack of awareness and understanding among policymakers of the social marketing option for citizen behavior change

- Misunderstanding among some policymakers and decision makers that social marketing is "social engineering"

In 2021, the International Social Marketing Association (iSMA) formed 12 Orbit Subcommittees to help achieve its institutionalization:

1. Increase Academic Course Offerings
2. Provide More Online Courses for Professional Certificates of Completion
3. Provide One Central Accessible Resource for Evidence-Based Case Studies
4. Advocate with Public Sector Agencies for Social Marketing Job Titles and Mentions in RFPs
5. Increase Awareness Among Elected Officials of the Social Marketing Option for Citizen Behavior Change
6. Consider More Partnerships with Corporations to Increase Visibility and Funding
7. Explore More Funding from Foundations, Associations, and Nonprofit Organizations
8. Increase Social Media and Internet Presence
9. Increase Membership in Current Social Marketing Professional Associations and Launch New Associations in Regions Not Currently Represented
10. Increase Presentations at Related Professional Association Conferences and Submission to Related Academic Journals
11. Ensure Campaigns Labeled Social Marketing Exemplify Core Social Marketing Concepts
12. Create a Stronger Brand Identity and Awareness

There are, thankfully, more than 50 social marketers currently (2022) participating in these subcommittees, and we encourage you to contact iSMA (https://isocialmarketing.org/volunteer/) if you are interested in knowing more about how you can join any of these efforts. We hope that this book has inspired you to use social marketing principles to help create more sustainable, healthy, and equitable communities by encouraging people to change behaviors for good.

Nancy Lee, Philip Kotler, and Julie Colehour

Note

International Social Marketing Link: 20211122 Social marketing education and trainings—Google Sheets

APPENDIX A

Social Marketing Planning Worksheets

Note: A free downloadable version of these worksheets in Word format can be accessed at https://www.socialmarketingservice.com/, or by emailing Nancy Lee who will send them via an email attachment to you (nancyrlee@msn.com).

STEP 1: DESCRIBE THE SOCIAL ISSUE, DEI CONSIDERATIONS, ORGANIZATION(S), BACKGROUND, PURPOSE, AND FOCUS OF YOUR PLAN

1.1 Briefly identify the social issue, sometimes referred to as the "wicked problem," your plan will be addressing (e.g., gun violence, youth suicide, air pollution, water contamination, homelessness, voting).

1.2 Note any Diversity, Equity, and Inclusion (DEI) considerations relevant to the social issue being addressed.

1.3 Identify the organization(s) involved in developing and implementing the plan.

1.4 Summarize key *background* information leading to the development of this plan, ideally using reliable statistics (e.g., percent decrease in salmon populations).

1.5 What is the *purpose of this effort*, the intended impact (e.g., reduced teen pregnancies, increased protection of salmon habitats)?

1.6 What is the plan's *focus*, the approach you will be using to contribute to your plan's purpose (e.g., residential gardening practices)? Areas of focus may be solution-oriented (e.g., soft shore buffers), population-based (e.g., homes on streams), or product-related strategies (e.g., native plants).

Refer to Chapter 5 for a detailed description of the process.

STEP 2: CONDUCT A SITUATION ANALYSIS

(Identify Two to Three Bullet Points for Each)

Organizational Factors: Organizational Resources, Service Delivery Capabilities, Expertise, Management Support, Issue Priority, Internal Publics, Current Alliances and Partnerships, Past Performance

2.1 What organizational *strengths* will your plan maximize?

2.2 What organizational *weaknesses* will your plan minimize?

External Forces: Cultural, Technological, Demographic, Natural, Economic, Political/Legal, External Publics

2.3 What external *opportunities* will your plan take advantage of?

2.4 What external *threats* will your plan prepare for?

Prior and Similar Efforts

2.5 What findings from *prior and similar efforts* are noteworthy, those of yours and others?

Refer to Chapter 5 for a detailed description of the process.

STEP 3: SELECT PRIORITY AUDIENCES

3.1 Describe the *priority audience* for your program/campaign in terms of size, problem incidence and severity, and relevant variables, including demographics, psychographics/values and lifestyles, geographics, related behaviors, and/or readiness to act (e.g., homeowners on shoreline properties engaged in landscaping and interested in protecting the environment).

3.2 If you have *additional important audiences* that you will need to influence as well, describe them here, to keep them in mind as you develop strategies. They may end up being messengers or distribution channels (e.g., garden centers and nurseries).

Refer to Chapter 6 for a detailed description of the process and Worksheet A in this Appendix.

STEP 4: SET BEHAVIOR OBJECTIVES AND TARGET GOALS

Objectives

4.1 Behavior Objective:
What, very specifically, do you want to influence your priority audience to *do* as a result of this campaign or project (e.g., plant native plants)?

4.2 Knowledge Objective:
Is there anything you need them to *know* in order to be more likely to act (e.g., how to identify native plants at the nursery)?

4.3 Belief Objective:

Is there anything you need them to *believe* in order to be more likely to act (e.g., native plants can be beautiful and easier to maintain)?

Goals

4.4 What quantifiable, measurable goals are you targeting? Ideally, these are stated in terms of *behavior change* (e.g., increase in sales of native plants). Other potential target goals are campaign awareness, recall, and/or response and changes in knowledge, belief, or behavior intent levels.

Refer to Chapter 7 for a detailed description of the process and Worksheet B in this Appendix.

STEP 5: IDENTIFY PRIORITY AUDIENCE BARRIERS, BENEFITS, AND MOTIVATORS; THE COMPETITION; AND INFLUENTIAL OTHERS

Barriers

5.1 Make a list of *barriers* your priority audience may have to adopting the desired behavior. These may be related to something, physical, psychological, cultural, economic, skills, knowledge, awareness, or attitudes. (Try for a list of 5–10.)

Benefits

5.2 What are the key *benefits* your priority audience wants in exchange for performing the behavior (e.g., a yard that's easier to maintain and increased wildlife on their property)? This answers the question "What's in it for me?" (Try for a list of 2–3.)

Motivators

5.3 What does your priority audience say will make it more likely that they would do the behavior? Ask them if there is something you can *give* them, *say* to them, or *show* them that would help them (e.g., an easy way to know which nurseries sell native plants and to identify plants at the nursery).

Competition

5.4 What are the major competing *alternative behaviors* (e.g., planting nonnative plants)?

5.5 What *benefits* do your audiences associate with these behaviors (e.g., easier to find)?

5.6 What *costs* do your audiences associate with these behaviors (e.g., requires more fertilizing)?

Influential Others

5.7 Relative to the desired behavior, who does your priority audience listen to, watch, and/or look up to?

5.8 What do you know about what these midstream audiences are currently saying and doing regarding the desired behavior (e.g., staff at nurseries)?

Refer to Chapter 8 for a detailed description of the process and Worksheet C in this Appendix.

STEP 6: DEVELOP A POSITIONING STATEMENT

Positioning Statement

6.1 Write a statement similar to the following, filling in the blanks:
"We want [PRIORITY AUDIENCE] to see [DESIRED BEHAVIOR] as [ADJECTIVES, DESCRIPTIVE PHRASES, SET OF BENEFITS, OR HOW THIS BEHAVIOR IS BETTER THAN THE COMPETITION]." (e.g., "We want shoreline property owners engaged in landscaping to see native plants as beautiful, easy to find, less hassle to maintain, and a way to protect water quality and wildlife habitats.")

Refer to Chapter 9 for a detailed description of the process.

STEP 7: DEVELOP MARKETING STRATEGIES

Product: Creating the Product Platform

7.1.1 *Core* Product: What is the major perceived benefit your priority audience wants from performing the behavior that you will highlight? (Choose one or a few from those identified in 5.2.)

7.1.2 *Actual* Product: What, if any, tangible goods and services will you be offering and/or promoting (e.g., 100 native plants to choose from, fruits and vegetables, life vests, blood monitoring equipment, low-flow showerheads, 988 mental health hotline)?

7.1.3 *Augmented* Product: Are there any additional tangible goods or services that would assist your priority audience in performing the behavior (e.g., workshop on designing a native plant garden)?

Refer to Chapter 10 for a detailed description of the process.

Price: Fees and Monetary and Nonmonetary Incentives and Disincentives

7.2.1 If you will be including tangible goods and services in your campaign, what, if anything, will the priority audience have to *pay* for them (e.g., cost of native plants, life vests)?

7.2.2 Describe any *monetary incentives* for your priority audience (e.g., coupons, rebates).

7.2.3 Describe any *monetary disincentives* you will highlight (e.g., fines, increased taxes, higher prices for competing products).

7.2.4 Describe any *nonmonetary incentives* (e.g., pledges to have toddlers wear a life vest on the beach).

7.2.5 Describe any *nonmonetary disincentives* (e.g., negative visibility, a website with photos of properties where migratory birds have disappeared).

Refer to Chapter 11 for a detailed description of the process.

Place: Develop the Place Strategy

As you determine each of the following, look for ways to make locations closer and more appealing, to extend hours, and to be there at the point of decision-making.

7.3.1 *Where* will you encourage and support your priority audience to *perform the desired behavior* and *when*?

7.3.2 *Where* and *when* will the priority audience acquire any related tangible goods?

7.3.3 *Where* and *when* will the priority audience acquire any associated services?

7.3.4 Are there any groups or individuals in the distribution channel that you will engage to support efforts (e.g., nursery owners and their staff)?

Refer to Chapter 12 for a detailed description of the process.

Promotion: Decide on Messages, Messengers, Creative Strategies, and Communication Channels

7.4.1 *Messages*: What key messages do you want your campaign to communicate to priority audiences?

7.4.2 *Messengers:* Who will deliver the messages and/or be the perceived sponsor?

7.4.3 *Creative Strategies*: Summarize, describe, or highlight elements such as logos, taglines, copy, visuals, colors, script, actors, scenes, and sounds in broadcast media.

7.4.4 *Communication Channels*: Where will messages and creative elements appear?

Refer to Chapter 13 for a detailed description of the process.

STEP 8: DEVELOP A PLAN FOR MONITORING AND EVALUATION

8.1 What is the *purpose* of this evaluation? Why are you doing it?

8.2 For *whom* is the evaluation being conducted? To whom will you present it?

8.3 *What inputs, outputs, outcomes, and impact* will be measured?

8.4 *What techniques and methodologies* will be used to conduct each of these measurements?

8.5 *When* will these measurements be taken?

8.6 *How* much will this cost?

Refer to Chapter 14 for a detailed description of the process and Worksheet D in this Appendix.

STEP 9: ESTABLISH BUDGETS AND FIND FUNDING SOURCES

9.1 What costs will be associated with *product*-related strategies?

9.2 What costs will be associated with *price*-related strategies?

9.3 What costs will be associated with *place*-related strategies?

9.4 What costs will be associated with *promotion*-related strategies?

9.5 What costs will be associated with *evaluation*-related strategies?

9.6 If costs exceed currently available funds, what potential additional funding sources can be explored?

It should be noted that formative research costs are not included in this plan. It is included in plan development costs. Costs in Step 9 are ones associated with Plan implementation. Refer to Chapter 15 for a detailed description of the process.

STEP 10: COMPLETE AN IMPLEMENTATION PLAN

10.1 Sample Implementation Plan

What	Who	When	How much

10.2 If you are conducting a pilot or plan with several phases, complete a grid for each phase.

Refer to Chapter 16 for a detailed description of the process. For an electronic version of this plan, visit www.socialmarketingservice.com.

WORKSHEET A

Selecting Priority Audiences

1 Potential Priority Audiences	2 Size	3 Problem Incidence	4 Readiness to Act	5 Ability to Reach	6 Match for the Organization	7 Average Score (From 2, 3, 4, 5)

1. **Potential Priority Audiences:** Relative to a campaign purpose (e.g., improve water quality) and focus (e.g., yard care), brainstorm and then list potential priority audiences. A priority audience is a segment of a population that has similar characteristics. Potential audiences may be grouped based on one or more variables, including demographics, geographics, values and lifestyles, or current related behaviors (e.g., homeowners with large lawns).
2. **Size:** As a segment of a population, what is the actual or relative size of this segment?
3. **Problem Incidence:** How significant is the contribution that this audience makes to the problem this plan is addressing (e.g., shoreline properties or frequency of fertilizing)?
4. **Readiness to Act**: How concerned is the priority audience with the problem issue/behavior?
5. **Ability to Reach:** Can you identify this audience, and do you have efficient ways to reach them?
6. **Match for the Organization:** Does this audience support your organizational mission, expertise, and positioning?
7. **Average Score:** This can be a "weighted average" to give increased significance to one or more of the items, or it can be an "unweighted average," with each aspect being considered equally important.

A variety of scales have been used to rank these items: (a) high, medium, low; (b) scale of 1–10, (c) scale of 1–7, (d) scale of 1–5. The one used will depend on how much verifiable information is available.

WORKSHEET B

Prioritizing Behaviors

Priority Audience ______________________________

1 Potential Behaviors to Rank	2 Impact on the Social Issue	3 Willingness of Priority Audience to do This Behavior	4 Measurability	5 Market Opportunity	6 Market Supply	7 Average Score (From 2, 3, 4, 5, 6)

1. **Potential Behaviors to Rank:** Relative to a campaign purpose, focus, and priority audience, brainstorm and then list potential single, simple behaviors to promote (e.g., replacing half of lawn with native plants).

2. **Impact on the Social Issue:** What potential impact do scientists, technical staff, and/or engineers determine that this desired behavior will have on the environment relative to other behaviors (e.g., using natural vs. chemical fertilizers vs. reducing lawn in half)?

3. **Willingness:** How willing is the priority audience to do this? In the diffusion model, this would be the percentage or number or relative size who are in the *Help Me* group versus the *Show Me* or *Make Me* group.

4. **Measurability:** Can the behavior be measured through either observation, record keeping, or self-reporting?

5. **Market Opportunity**: Estimate the percentage and/or number of people in the priority audience/population who are not already doing the behavior. (Note: The higher the number, the higher the score.)

6. **Market Supply:** Does the behavior need more support? If some other organization or organizations are already addressing this behavior, perhaps a different behavior would be more beneficial to the social issue.

7. **Average Score:** This can be a "weighted average," to give increased significance to one or more of the items, or it can be an "unweighted average," with each aspect being considered equally important.

A variety of scales have been used to rank these items: (a) high, medium, low, (b) scale of 1–10, (c) scale of 1–7, (d) scale of 1–5. The one used will depend on how much verifiable information is available.

(Adapted from Doug McKenzie-Mohr, www.cbsm.com.)

WORKSHEET C

Marketing Intervention Tools: Using the 4Ps to Reduce Barriers and Increase Benefits, Inspired by Audience Motivators

Desired Behavior: ______________________________

Priority Audience: ______________________________

For each of the priority audience's perceived barriers and potential benefits, consider whether one or more of the 4Ps would help reduce the barrier and provide desired benefits.	Potential strategies using the 4Ps to reduce barriers and increase benefits			
	PRODUCT Goods or services to promote or to provide to help the audience do the behavior	PRICE Incentives and disincentives (includes use of pledges and commitments)	PLACE Where goods and services can be accessed or behavior will be performed	PROMOTION Messages, messengers, creative strategies, and communication channels (includes use of prompts)
Perceived Barriers to Desired Behaviors				
Desired Benefits				

WORKSHEET D

Potential Evaluation Measures

Inputs	Outputs	Outcomes	Impact	Return on Investment
Resources allocated to the campaign or program effort: • Dollars • Incremental staff time • Existing materials • Existing distribution channels • Existing partners	*Program activities conducted to promote a desired behavior. These measures do not indicate whether the audience "noticed" or responded to these activities. They represent only what was "put out there," including:* • Number of materials disseminated • Number of calls made • Numbers and types of distribution channels for any products or services • Number of events held • Websites created/utilized • Social media tactics • Reach and frequency of communications • Free media coverage • Paid media impressions • Implementation of program elements (e.g., whether on time, on budget)	*Audience responses to outputs, including:* • Changes in behavior • Changes in numbers of related products or services "sold" (e.g., native plants) • Changes in behavior intent • Changes in knowledge • Changes in beliefs • Responses to campaign elements (e.g., hits on a website) • Campaign awareness • Customer satisfaction levels • Policy changes • Partnerships and contributions created	*Indicators that show levels of impact on the social issue that constituted the focus of the effort:* • Lives saved • Diseases prevented • Injuries avoided • Water quality improved • Water supply increased • Air quality improved • Landfill reduced • Wildlife and habitats protected • Animal cruelty reduced • Crimes prevented • Financial well-being improved	*Economic value of changes in behavior and calculated rate of return on the spending associated with the effort:* • For every dollar spent, dollars saved or generated • After subtracting expenses, rate of return on investment

APPENDIX B

Sample Social Marketing Plan

RESTORING SALMON HABITATS

Lake Washington/Cedar/Sammamish Watershed (WRIA 8) King County, Washington

STEP 1: BACKGROUND, ORGANIZATION, PURPOSE, FOCUS

The Lake Washington/Cedar/Sammamish Watershed (WRIA 8) is a collaborative effort of 27 local governments, community groups, and businesses. Together they developed and adopted a plan to conserve and restore salmon in the watershed and work together to implement the plan. In 2010 and 2011, WRIA 8 conducted an analysis of changes in forest cover and riparian buffers in the watershed. The analysis found that many riparian areas lost forest cover and all gained impervious cover between 2005 and 2009, despite regulations designed to protect these areas. WRIA 8 has decided to make riparian areas a higher priority for plan implementation and is developing a strategy to address the many small actions of streamside property owners that reduce forest cover and streamside vegetation.

The *purpose* of this plan is to improve salmon habitats along streams in WRIA 8 watershed.

Its *focus* is on increasing planting of native plants and trees along streams in suburban residential neighborhoods along high-priority (Tier 1) spawning areas.

STEP 2: SITUATION ANALYSIS

Similar prior and existing efforts suggest that workshops can be effective, as can contacting property owners and assisting them with physical labor and finding ways to help them cover or discounting costs.

Organizational Factors	External Forces
Strengths: • Broad coalition of local governments, NGOs, state agencies, and interested citizens • Data that support the need • Several strong NGOs already working with streamside property owners and doing riparian restoration • Existing marketing materials from prior projects • Existing success stories to highlight/share • Strong expertise in watershed for designing a program	**Opportunities:** • Existing programs would benefit from support • Increase in community volunteerism from students needing community service credit • Families seeking family-friendly activities • Companies wanting team-building events • Riparian planting benefits several water quality issues, which can lead to increased partnerships and funding • New home owners are more willing to change landscaping
Weaknesses: • Limited funding/cuts to programs • Property owner concerns about volunteers on private property • Lack of monitoring of effectiveness of outreach efforts • High maintenance needed for plantings/lack of long-term funding • Lack of infrastructure for ongoing riparian restoration	**Threats:** • Economy • Budget cuts in local governments and NGOs • "Save the Salmon" fatigue • People love their lawns

STEP 3: PRIORITY AUDIENCE

Property owners along the Cedar River, Bear Creek, and Issaquah Creek, especially those with lawn extending to the edge of the stream who are contemplating (or open to) making a change to their landscaping.

Additional important audiences that may warrant separate marketing plans include homeowner associations that may have concerns about replacing lawns and misperceptions regarding native plants, and jurisdictions that own public land along streams that also need restoration. These sites can be good demonstration areas and could be used for kick-off planting events.

STEP 4: SET BEHAVIOR OBJECTIVES AND GOALS

Behavior objective: Streamside property owners will plant and maintain native trees and plants along their streamside property.

Knowledge objectives: How to prepare the site, what nonnative invasive plants need to be removed and how, and where to buy and how to choose, plant, and care for native plants.

Belief objective: Native plants are beautiful and benefit birds, salmon, and other wildlife. They are easy to maintain, save money, conserve water, save time, and are safe for pets and kids, since no pesticides are needed.

Goals: Contact 500-plus streamside property owners, of whom 165 will agree/pledge to remove nonnative plants and plant native trees and plants. Among these 165 willing property owners, 50 will agree to have supervised volunteers assist them with restoring riparian areas. In the end, restore 10–15 acres of riparian area, planting 10,000-plus native trees and shrubs.

STEP 5: BARRIERS, BENEFITS, MOTIVATORS, COMPETITION, AND INFLUENTIAL OTHERS

Barriers that property owners may have to replacing lawns with native trees and plants along the shorelines include:

- "I want to see/interact with the creek."
- "I don't think my lawn to the creek matters/hurts the stream."
- "I don't want to sign anything."
- "I don't like the government telling me what to do with my property."
- "I don't like the look of native plants—too scraggly, messy."
- "It costs too much."
- "I'm concerned about stream bank eroding, flooding."
- "I don't know how to do it, where to start."
- "I need lawn for my kids' play area."
- "It's too much to do. I'm too busy and overwhelmed."
- "The homeowner association won't let me."
- "The social norm around here is a neat, tidy yard."
- "I think that's critical area by code. I can't touch it."
- "I don't know native plants or where to buy them."
- "I'm not the problem; ___ is the problem."
- "I don't trust government, the messenger."
- "There's no technical assistance available to help."

- "We have a large bulkhead and would need a permit to change anything."
- "I need to have access to my dock/boat."

Benefits desired include increased property value and improved water quality and wildlife and salmon habitats.

Motivators include knowing and believing that native plants are a beautiful, low-maintenance landscaping choice and that property owners will be a part of the community/neighborhood effort to improve their stream.

The *competition* is tidy yards that fit in with their neighborhood and provide space for kids and pets to play.

Key *influencers* include environmental scientists and neighbors experiencing desired benefits.

STEP 6: POSITIONING STATEMENT

We want streamside property owners in WRIA 8 watershed to see planting native plants as easy, beautiful, and beneficial to their property values as well as to bird, fish, and other wildlife.

STEP 7: MARKETING INTERVENTION MIX: 4PS STRATEGIES

Product Strategies

Core product: A beautiful, low-maintenance yard

Actual product: Native plants and trees

Augmented product:

- Technical assistance to develop planting plan and actual support for planting
- Workshop for streamside property owners in each watershed

Price Strategies

Monetary incentives:

- Free or discounted plants and compost
- Potentially, compost buckets full of gifts (e.g., Brown Bear car wash coupons, Cedar Grove compost discounts)

Nonmonetary incentives:

- Recognition signage similar to Backyard Wildlife Sanctuary sign

Place Strategies

Workshops will be held in a convenient location in the neighborhood, where property owners can also sign up for technical assistance/support for planting and receive free plants, compost, and discount coupons.

Technical assistance and planting support will be provided at homes, arranged at a time convenient for the property owner.

Promotion Strategies

Key Messages:

- Planting native plants and trees along streams will create a beautiful, low-maintenance yard.
- In fact, it is the Northwest look.
- It will also improve water quality and habitats for salmon, birds, and other wildlife.

Key Messengers:

- NGOs in each target watershed area
- WRIA 8 and local jurisdictions in watersheds will be cosponsors and help to promote events/services

Creative Strategies:

- "Easy for Salmon and Me" tagline
- Incorporate into the Puget Sound Starts Here brand and messaging

Communication Channels:

- *Special event:* Kick off a volunteer planting event in each watershed on publicly owned property
- *Outreach materials:* Door hangers for neighborhood canvassing by NGO partners to contact property owners one on one; letters inviting property owners to neighborhood workshops; flyers and electronic invitations to promote volunteer stewardship events; materials for workshops (PowerPoint presentations, planting instructions, plant identification—reuse good existing materials as much as possible); recognition signage; thank-you gifts of donated items for participating landowners

STEP 8: DETERMINE AN EVALUATION PLAN

Inputs	Outputs	Outcomes	Impact	Return on Investment
• Dollars spent • Staff time • Volunteer hours • Partners' contributions (business donations, jurisdictions helping to promote events and workshops, donation of meeting space)	• # of streamside property owners contacted • # of events held • # of partners assisting with program • # of articles/ media messages promoting events/ program	• # of streamside property owners attending events • # of streamside property owners pledging • # of streamside property owners removing nonnative plants and planting native trees and plants	• # of square feet/acres of invasive plants controlled • # of trees/ shrubs planted • # of square feet/acres of riparian area plantings	• For every dollar spent, # of households that removed nonnative plants and planted native trees and plants • For every dollar spent, # of square feet/acres of riparian area plantings

STEP 9: ESTABLISH A CAMPAIGN BUDGET AND FIND FUNDING

Product-Related Costs	Staff time, printing, workshop/stewardship event refreshments
Price-Related Costs	Native plants, compost to give away
Place-Related Costs	Travel costs, room rental for workshops
Promotion-Related Costs	Staff time, postage
Evaluation-Related Costs	Staff time
TOTAL	At least $250,000; program is scalable based on funding available.

STEP 10: OUTLINE AN IMPLEMENTATION PLAN

What	Who	When	How Many
Volunteer stewardship kick-off events to help create buzz around restoring riparian areas along Cedar River, Bear Creek, and Issaquah Creek	NGO in each basin with assistance from WRIA 8 staff, WRIA 8 jurisdictions, King County Noxious Weeds	Beginning of campaign	3+, at least one per basin
Letters to prioritized property owners inviting them to workshops and offering technical assistance with restoring their riparian vegetation	NGO in each basin	Before workshops	All property owners along each targeted stream
Workshops for property owners on how to identify and control noxious weeds and plant native plants	NGO in each basin with assistance from WRIA 8 staff, WRIA 8 jurisdictions, King County Noxious Weeds	After kick-off event	3+, at least one per basin
Door-to-door canvassing of property owners in targeted reaches of streams offering technical assistance	NGO in each basin	After workshops	All property owners along each targeted stream
Technical assistance with planning riparian restoration and assistance with actual plantings by volunteers	NGO in each basin	After canvassing	30+ willing property owners

Case information was provided by Jean White, King County WRIA 8.

APPENDIX C

Additional Planning Models

Community-Based Social Marketing (Doug McKenzie-Mohr)	Aligning With the 10-Step Planning Model Presented in This Text
Step 1: Selecting behaviors	Step 4: Set behavior objectives and goals
Step 2: Identifying barriers and benefits	Step 5: Identify audience barriers, benefits, motivators, influential others, and the competition
Step 3: Developing strategies	
o Commitment/pledges	Step 7: Price (a nonmonetary incentive)
o Social norms	Step 7: Promotion (messengers, messages, communication channels)
o Social diffusion	Step 3: Select priority audience Step 7: Promotion
o Prompts	Step 7: Product and/or promotion
o Communication	Step 7: Promotion
o Incentives	Step 7: Price (monetary and/or nonmonetary incentives)
o Convenience	Step 7: Place
Step 4: Piloting	Step 10: Implementation plan
Step 5: Broad-scale implementation and evaluation	Step 9: Evaluation plan Step 10: Implementation plan Postimplementation and evaluation

Source: Doug McKenzie-Mohr, *Fostering Sustainable Behavior: An Introduction to Community-Based Social Marketing*, 3rd ed. (Gabriola Island, BC, Canada: New Society Publishers).

BEHAVIORAL ECONOMICS

The following examples are derived from author notes taken during the "Workshop on Behavioral Economics: Exploring Applications and Research Methods", July 28–29, 2022, sponsored by the National Academies of Sciences, Engineering and Medicine in Washington, DC.

Behavioral Economics (Richard Thaler and Others)	Aligning With the 10-Step Planning Model Presented in This Text
Audience Segments Noted	**Step 3: Segmentation by Stage of Change**
Nudge Group (Has Intention to Act)	Help Me Group
Shove Group (No Intention to Act)	Make Me Group
Educate Group (Ready to Act)	Show Me Group
Audience Insight Examples Noted	**Step 5: Audience Insights**
Sludge (A mental burden associated with performing a desired behavior)	Barriers
Value (Why might perform behavior)	Benefits
Major Interventions & Examples Noted	**Marketing Intervention Tools**
Make It Easy (e.g., assistance with completing college admissions forms)	Step 7.1: Product (Service)
Offer Valued Incentives (e.g., bonuses for teachers based on student performance)	Step 7.2: Price (Monetary Incentive)
Make It Convenient (e.g., opt-out vs. opt-in for automatic deductions for retirement savings)	Step 7.3: Place (Application Process)
Highlight Costs of Not Performing (e.g., number of days of incarceration that can happen if don't show up for court appearance)	Step 7.2: Price (Monetary Disincentive) Step 7.4: Promotion (Messages)
Provide Reminders (e.g., court date)	Step 7.4: Promotion (Prompts)
Sustain Behaviors (e.g., report on accumulated cost savings from using energy efficient appliances)	Step 7.4: Promotion (Feedback)

COMMUNITY-BASED PREVENTION MARKETING

Community-Based Prevention Marketing (CBPM) (Carol Bryant)	Aligning With the 10-Step Planning Model Presented in This Text
Step 1: Creating foundation for success—Creation/engagement of community coalition.	Step 1: Social issue, organization(s), background, purpose, and focus Step 2: Situational analysis
Step 2: Review of existing evidence-based interventions and review of community assets.	Step 1: Social issue, organization(s), background, purpose, and focus

Community-Based Prevention Marketing (CBPM) (Carol Bryant)	Aligning With the 10-Step Planning Model Presented in This Text
Step 3: Select behavioral focus.	Step 4: Behavior objectives and target goals
Step 4: Selection of priority population(s).	Step 3: Priority audiences
Step 5: Listen—conduct formative research.	Step 5: Priority audience barriers, benefits, motivators, the competition, and influential others.
Step 6: Develop integrated marketing strategy.	Step 6: Positioning Step 7: Marketing intervention mix (Product, price, place, promotion)
Step 7: Develop monitoring evaluation plan.	Step 8: Plan for monitoring and evaluation
Step 8: Implement and evaluate.	Step 9: Budget Step 10: Plan for implementation and sustaining behaviors

- Mahmooda Khaliq, Samantha Boddupalli, Claudia Parvanta, and Carol Bryant, "Community-Based Prevention Marketing (CBPM): Evolution from Programming to Policy Development to Systems Change," in *The Palgrave Encyclopedia of Social Marketing*, ed. (Cham: Springer International Publishing, 2021), 1–9.
- Carol A. Bryant, Kelli R. McCormack Brown, Robert J. McDermott, Melinda S. Forthofer, Elizabeth C. Bumpus, Susan A. Calkins, and Lauren B. Zapata, "Community-Based Prevention Marketing: Organizing a Community for Health Behavior Intervention," *Health Promotion Practice* 8, no. 2 (2007): 154–63.
- Carol A. Bryant, Anita H. Courtney, Robert J. McDermott, James H. Lindenberger, Mark A. Swanson, Alyssa B. Mayer, ... Brian J. Biroscak, "Community-Based Prevention Marketing for Policy Development: A New Planning Framework for Coalitions," *Social Marketing Quarterly*, 20, no. 4 (2014): 219–46.

SCOPE, TEST, ENACT, LEARN (STEL)

STEL (Jeff French)	Aligning With the 10-Step Planning Model Presented in This Text
Stage 1: Scope	
Task 1: Setting goals and SMART objectives	Step 1: Purpose and focus Step 3: Select priority audience Step 4: Set behavior objectives and goals

STEL (Jeff French)	Aligning With the 10-Step Planning Model Presented in This Text
Task 2: Analyzing situation and influencing factors	Step 2: Situation analysis
Task 3. Understanding target audience(s)	Step 5: Identify audience barriers, benefits, motivators, influential others, and the competition
Task 4: Developing exchange proposition(s)	Step 6: Positioning Step 7: Promotion
Task 5: Selecting marketing interventions	Step 7: Product, price, place, and promotion
Stage 2: Test	
Task 6: Pretesting and piloting	Step 9: Evaluation plan
Stage 3: Enact	
Task 7: Planning implementation	Step 10: Implementation plan
Task 8. Initiating and managing implementation	Step 10: Implementation plan
Stage 4: Learn & Act	
Task 9. Evaluating and reporting	Implementation of evaluation plan and summary report on results
Task 10. Reviewing and building learning	Inclusion of recommendations in evaluation and summary report

Source: Jeff French, *Social Marketing and Public Health: Theory and Practice*, 2nd ed. (Oxford University Press).

CBE FRAMEWORK

CBE Framework (Sharyn Rundle-Thiele)	Aligning with the 10 Step Planning Model Presented in This Text
Co-Creation	Establish a Campaign Budget & Find Funding. Describe Background, Purpose, and Focus for the Effort. Conduct a Situation Analysis. Select and Describe the Priority Audience. Set Behavior Objectives and Goals. Audience Insights: Barriers, Benefits, Motivators, Competition & Influencers. Craft a Desired Positioning Statement. Determine an Evaluation Plan. Outline an Implementation Plan.
Build	Build the Strategic Marketing Intervention Mix (4Ps).
Engage	Implementation.

HANDS-ON SOCIAL MARKETING

Hands-On Social Marketing (Nedra Kline Weinreich)	Aligning With the 10-Step Planning Model Presented in This Text
Step 1: Analysis	Step 1: Purpose and focus Step 2: Situation analysis
Step 2: Strategy development	Step 3: Select priority audience Step 4: Set behavior objectives and goals Step 5: Identify audience barriers, benefits, motivators, influential others, and the competition Step 7: Marketing intervention mix Step 10: Implementation plan
Step 3: Program and communication design	Step 7: Marketing intervention mix
Step 4: Pretesting	Step 5: Identify audience barriers, benefits, motivators, influential others, and the competition Step 7: Pretest 4Ps prior to Step 8: Budget
Step 5: Implementation	Step 10: Implementation of plan
Step 6: Evaluation and feedback	Postimplementation of plan

APPENDIX D

Social Marketing Resources

Compiled by Mike Newton-Ward, Adjunct Assistant Professor, Public Health Leadership Program, UNC Gillings School of Global Public Health (2022)

ACCESS TO CASE STUDIES

Social Marketing Case Studies Online. Want to find out what's been done before and how well it worked? Looking for inspiration, evidence to support your planning, or examples for your research, writing, or lessons? Find social marketing case studies with measured impacts for a range of topics and locations around the globe. You can also help social marketers worldwide by submitting your own case study. Covered topics include some of the worlds' most pressing problems.

- *International Social Marketing Association and affiliated regional social marketing associations*- A global portal for social marketing case studies is under development at the time of publication; look for the "Case Studies" tab at https://isocialmarketing.org/
- *ShowCase.* The first collection of fully researched case studies to enhance social marketing success, ShowCase features projects that have used social marketing to achieve real changes in behavior. https://www.thensmc.com/resources/showcase/browse
- *Tools of Change*- The most extensive, freely accessible collection of full-length voluntary behavior change, social marketing and CBSM case studies available on the web. Formative research, implementation, and program impacts included. www.toolsofchange.com

BLOGS

Brooke's Two Cents	http://brooketully.com
Have Fun, Do Good	https://brittbravo.com/blog/
International Social Marketing Association	https://isocialmarketing.org/blog/
Marketing for Change	https://funeasypopular.com/

BOOKS

Andreasen, A. (1995). *Marketing social change: Changing behavior to promote health, social development, and the environment*. San Francisco, CA: Jossey-Bass.

Andreasen, A. (2006). *Social marketing in the 21st century*. Thousand Oaks, CA: SAGE.

Bearden, W. O., Netemeyer, R. G., & Haws, K. L. (2011). *Handbook of marketing scales: Multi-item measures for marketing and consumer behavior research* (3rd ed.). Thousand Oaks, CA: SAGE.

Berger, W. (2010). *Glimmer: How design can transform your world*. Toronto, ON: Vintage Canada.

Berger, J. (2016). *Contagious: Why things catch* on. Toronto, ON, New York, NY: Simon and Schuster.

Brennan, L., Binney, W., Parker, L., Aleti, T., & Nguyen, D. (2016). *Social marketing and behavior change: Models, theory and applications*. Cheltenham: Edward Elgar.

Bruner, G. C. (2019). *Marketing scales handbook: Multi-item measures for consumer insight research*. Fort Worth, TX: GCBII Productions, LLC.

Buros Center for Testing. (2021). *The twenty-first mental measurements yearbook*. Lincoln, NE: University of Nebraska Press.

Cheng, H., Kotler, P., & Lee, N. (2009). *Social marketing in public health: Global trends and success stories*. Sudbury, MA: Jones & Bartlett.

Deshpande, S., & Lee, N. (2014). *Social marketing in India*. Thousand Oaks, CA: SAGE.

Diaz, M. G., & Basil, M. D. (2019). *Social marketing in action: Cases from around the world*. Cham: Springer.

Dietrich, T., Rundle-Thiele, S., & Kubacki, K. (2017). *Segmentation in social marketing: Process, methods and application*. Singapore: Springer.

Donovan, R., & Henley, N. (2010). *Principles and practice of social marketing: An international perspective*. Victoria: Cambridge University Press.

Duhigg, C. (2014). *The power of habit: Why we do what we do in life and business*. New York, NY: Random House.

Evans, D. W. (2016). *Social marketing research for global public health: Methods and technologies*. New York, NY: Oxford University Press.

French, J. (Ed.). (2017). *Social marketing and public health: Theory and practice* (2nd ed.). Oxford: Oxford University Press.

French, J., & Gordon, R. (2019). *Strategic social marketing: For behavior and social change* (2nd ed.). UK: SAGE Publications Ltd.

Fourali, C. (2016). *The promise of social marketing: A powerful tool for changing the world for good* (1st ed.). London: Routledge.

Fourali, C., & French, J. (2020). *The palgrave encyclopedia of social marketing.* Cham: Palgrave Macmillan.

Harvey, P. D. (1999). *Let every child be wanted: How social marketing is revolutionizing contraceptive use around the world.* Westport, CT: Auburn House.

Hastings, G., & Domegan, C. (2018). *Social marketing: Rebels with a cause.* Oxford: Routledge.

Hastings, G., Angus, K., & Bryant, C. (2011). SAGE *handbook of social marketing.* Thousand Oaks, CA: SAGE.

IDEO. (2015). *The field guide to human-centered design.* Palo Alto, CA: IDEO.

Kotler, P., & Lee, N. (2006). *Marketing in the public sector: A roadmap for improved performance.* Philadelphia, PA: Wharton School.

Kotler, P., & Lee, N. (2009). *Up and out of poverty: The social marketing solution.* Philadelphia, PA: Wharton School.

Kreuger, R. A., & Casey, M. A. (2014). *Focus groups: A practical guide for applied research* (5th ed.). Thousand Oaks, CA: SAGE.

Lee, N., & Kotler, P. (2019). *Social marketing: Behavior change for social good.* Thousand Oaks, CA: SAGE.

Lee, N. (2017). *Policymaking for citizen behavior change: A social marketing approach.* New York, NY: Routledge.

Lee, N., & Kotler, P. (2022). *Success in social marketing: 100 case studies from around the Globe.* New York, NY: Routledge.

Lefebvre, C. (2013). *Social marketing and social change: Strategies and tools for improving health, well-being, and the environment.* San Francisco, CA: Jossey-Bass.

McKenzie-Mohr, D. (2011). *Fostering sustainable behavior: An introduction to community-based social marketing* (3rd ed.). Gabriola Island, BC: New Society Publishers.

McKenzie-Mohr, D., Lee, N., Schultz, P. W., & Kotler, P. (2011). *Social marketing to protect the environment: What works.* Thousand Oaks, CA: SAGE.

Meyer-Emerick, N. (2016). *Using social marketing for public emergency preparedness: Social change for community resilience.* New York, NY: Routledge.

Ramsey, T. Z. (2015). *Introduction to neuromarketing & consumer neuroscience.* Taastrup: Neurons Inc.

Resnick, E. A., & Siegel, M. (2012). *Marketing public health: Strategies to promote social change* (3rd ed.). Boston, MA: Jones & Bartlett.

Stewart, D. W. (2015). *The handbook of persuasion and social marketing*. Santa Barbara, CA: Praeger, an imprint of ABC-CLIO, LLC.

Weinreich, N. K. (2010). *Hands-on social marketing: A step-by-step guide to designing change for good*. Thousand Oaks, CA: SAGE.

Wymer, W. W. (2015). *Innovations in social marketing and public health communication: Improving the quality of life for individuals and communities*. Cham: Springer.

CONFERENCE OPPORTUNITIES

1. *Australian and New Zealand Marketing Academy (ANZMAC)*
   https://anzmac.wildapricot.org/
2. *Agents of Change Summit*
   https://agentsofchangesummit.com/
3. *International Social & Behavioral Change Summit*
   https://sbccsummit.org/
5. *Social Marketing Conference* June, University of South Florida, Sand Key, Florida (biennially in May/June)
   https://thesocialmarketingconference.org/
6. *World Social Marketing Conference* (Locations and dates rotate) http://wsmconference.com/
7. *SPARKS* Annual Conference sponsored by the Pacific Northwest Social Marketing Association
   https://www.pnsma.org/Events2

JOURNALS AND MAGAZINES

Advertising Age

Crain Communications, Inc.

http://adage.com/

Adweek

VNU, Inc.

http://www.adweek.com/

Health Marketing Quarterly

Haworth Press

https://www.tandfonline.com/loi/whmq20

Journal of Consumer Research

Journal of Consumer Research, Inc.

http://www.ejcr.org/

Journal of Health Communication

Taylor & Francis

http://www.tandfonline.com/toc/uhcm20/current#.U8CRDah2fs0

Journal of Marketing

American Marketing Association

https://www.ama.org/publications/JournalOfMarketing/Pages/Current-Issue.aspx

Journal of Philanthropy and Marketing

John Wiley & Sons

https://onlinelibrary.wiley.com/journal/1479103x

Journal of Public Policy and Marketing

American Marketing Association

https://www.ama.org/publications/JournalOfPublicPolicyAndMarketing/Pages/current-issue.aspx

Journal of Social Marketing

Emerald Group Publishing Limited

http://www.emeraldgrouppublishing.com/products/journals/journals.htm?id=JSOCM

SOCIAL MARKETING QUARTERLY

Sage Journal

https://journals.sagepub.com/home/smq

LISTSERVES, FORUMS, AND EMAIL DIGESTS

Dispatches: Insights on Brand Development From the Marketing Front (Email Digest)

Brand Development Network International

http://bdn-intl.com/summer-schedule-for-dispatches

Fostering Sustainable Behavior Listserv

https://cbsm.com/forum_posts

Knowledge at Wharton (Email Digest)

The Wharton School at the University of Pennsylvania

https://knowledge.wharton.upenn.edu/category/marketing/

LinkedIn International Social Marketing Association

https://www.linkedin.com/company/international-social-marketing-association/

LinkedIn Marketing for Change Network

www.linkedin.com/groups/4621758

LinkedIn Social Marketing Quarterly

www.linkedin.com/groups/4621758

Social Marketing Association of North America Listserve

https://smana.org/

MAJOR EMPLOYERS FOR SOCIAL MARKETERS

The following list represents major job sectors where social marketing professionals are most commonly employed, with examples of areas of specific focus. In addition to these three, some commercial sector companies support or engage in social marketing efforts but do not often have social marketing professionals as employees.

Governmental Agencies at National and Local Levels

- Public Health
- Environmental Protection
- Department of Natural Resources and Parks
- Department of Fish and Wildlife
- Traffic Safety
- Public Safety
- Injury Prevention
- Education
- Public Utilities
- City Governments
- County Governments
- Public Schools & Universities

Consulting Firms

- Communications
- Research & Evaluation
- Strategic Planning

Nonprofit Organizations and Foundations

- Healthcare
- Donors (e.g., Blood, Organs)
- Suicide Prevention
- Drug Abuse
- Homeless
- Pet Shelters
- Foodbanks
- Youth & Family Services

MEMBERSHIP ORGANIZATIONS

African Association of Social Marketing

https://www.linkedin.com/groups/7409325/

Australian Social Marketing Association

www.aasm.org.au

European Social Marketing Association

http://www.europeansocialmarketing.org/

International Social Marketing Association

https://isocialmarketing.org/

Latin American Social Marketing Association (Asociación Latinoamericana de Mercadeo Social)

http://www.mercadeosocial.org/

Pacific Northwest Social Marketing Association

https://www.pnsma.org/

Social Marketing Association of North America

https://smana.org/

iSMA is currently (2022) in discussion with a number of other developing regional associations including Asia and Oceania. iSMA is also in discussion with a number of single country associations regarding direct affiliation or membership via existing or new regional associations. These countries include Japan, Indonesia, Vietnam, Moldova, Bangladesh, France, and the UK.

NETWORKING OPPORTUNITIES

Social Marketing Association of North America Meetup Groups

https://smana.org/events/

ONLINE PLANNING TOOLS AND E-LEARNING

B-HUB, (Behavioral Evidence Hub)	http://www.bhub.org/
Community Based Prevention Marketing for Policy Prevention University of South Florida	https://health.usf.edu/publichealth/prc/cbpm
Design Kit (Human-Centered Design, IDEO)	http://www.designkit.org/
European Center for Disease Control (ECDC) Technical Guide to Social Marketing	http://ecdc.europa.eu/en/publications/Publications/social-marketing-guide-public-health.pdf
Health Communication Theory Picker	http://www.orau.gov/hsc/theorypicker/index.html
Introduction to Social Marketing for Public Health (Free) University of S. Florida -WHO Collaborating Center & Pan American Health Organization	https://www.campusvirtualsp.org/en/course/introduction-social-marketing-public-health-course-1-self-learning (free)
Smart Chart 4.0 SPITFIRE	https://smartchart.org
Social Marketing Planning Guide and Toolkit, National Social Marketing Centre, United Kingdom	https://www.thensmc.com/toolkit
Tools of Change Webinars, Cullbridge Marketing and Communications	https://www.toolsofchange.com/en/home/

SAMPLE JOB DESCRIPTION

Template Instructions: This template is intended to provide a strong foundation for attracting and hiring applicants with the requisite skills to oversee social marketing programs that align with best practices. The template may be tailored to suit the specific needs and requirements of those utilizing it. Note that the qualifications listed below represent desired experiences, but many can be learned based on a candidate's interests, background, or other qualities. Applicants should be considered based on their potential as well as their experience.

JOB DESCRIPTION: SOCIAL MARKETING PROGRAM MANAGER

About the Company/Organization/Agency

[BRIEFLY DESCRIBE THE HISTORY, MISSION, FUNCTION, STRUCTURE, AND SERVICES, AND FOCUS, AS APPROPRIATE.]

[BRIEFLY DESCRIBE THE SOCIAL MARKETING FOCUS OF THE ORGANIZATION, INCLUDING TOPIC AREAS, AUDIENCES, GEOGRAPHIES, ETC.

INCLUDE A STATEMENT ABOUT THE ORGANIZATION'S COMMITMENT TO BEHAVIOR CHANGE FOR SOCIAL GOOD.]

Position Summary

This position is intended to guide and oversee the development, implementation, and evaluation of the [COMPANY/ORGANIZATION/AGENCY]'s social marketing programs.

Minimum Qualifications

- Bachelor's degree in marketing, business, public health, social science, communications, behavioral science, or closely related discipline; Relevant lived and work experience acceptable instead of a degree;
- 5–10+ years of experience developing and/or overseeing the implementation of behavior change campaigns for government, nonprofit, or private sector entities;
- Strong understanding of a wide range of behavior change theories, models, and frameworks and their application;
- Demonstrated knowledge and experience across multiple media channels and platforms;
- Experience with delivery of programs that extend beyond communication-only efforts;
- Demonstrated knowledge and experience in establishing and maintaining partnerships with a diverse array of stakeholders;
- Demonstrated excellence in written and verbal communication skills;
- Strong project management skills.

Preferred Qualifications

- Specific technical knowledge and experience in [HEALTH/SAFETY/ENVIRONMENT] field(s) or [BEHAVIOR/AUDIENCE];
- Degree, coursework, or work experience in social marketing and/or behavioral science;
- Experience in statistics, survey design, user experience, and/or randomized control trials;
- Training and certification in social marketing;
- Experience with multicultural practices and awareness of culturally appropriate data collection and presentation considerations.

POSITION RESPONSIBILITIES

Program Planning and Strategy

- Work with key stakeholders to identify key outcomes, purpose, and focus for campaigns.
- Conduct internal and external audits to identify factors that support or inhibit success.
- Gather insights from evidence reviews and peer-reviewed articles, technical reports, case studies, and other relevant documents.
- Identify audience segments using theory, audience insights, and relevant data and evidence.
- Identify and define clear behavior change objectives and measurable goals.
- Develop and oversee the implementation of appropriate methodologies for identifying barriers, benefits, and relevant audience insights, including co-design, systems methods, observations, surveys, focus groups, and interviews.
- Develop and oversee the implementation of a variety of qualitative and quantitative research tools.
- Develop strategic positioning statements for public health/safety/environment campaigns.
- Oversee the development of a social marketing intervention strategy that aligns with positioning statements and draws from audience insights and best practices.
- Work with designers, copywriters, and other creative team members to translate the marketing intervention strategy into clear and engaging communications, products, and services utilizing a range of communication channels.
- Create and oversee pilots for first-time program implementation and adapt program elements as needed before implementation.
- Create and/or oversee methodologies for evaluating behavior change campaigns through observations, self-report methods, randomized control trials or field trials, and other methods as appropriate.

Program Implementation and Evaluation

- Develop a plan for evaluation that includes inputs, outputs, outcomes, and impact.
- Define metrics that adequately assess success at changing behavior.
- Develop actionable recommendations for broad-scale implementation.
- Present program outcomes to internal and external stakeholders.
- Disseminate program outcomes and lessons learned through reports, journal submissions, conference presentations, and press releases.

Business and Professional Development

- Actively stay on top of recent trends and emerging best practices in social marketing and related fields, including systems social marketing, human-centered design, and behavioral economics.

- Maintain membership in professional organizations such as the International Social Marketing Association and regional associations (e.g., Social Marketing Association of North America).
- Respond to grant applications or requests for proposals to acquire funding.

General

- Maintain strict adherence to established ethical guidelines and standards for social marketing and human subjects research.
- Integrate Diversity, Equity, and Inclusion principles into social marketing program planning and implementation.
- Build and maintain relationships with stakeholders.

Employment Details

Location: [E.G., REMOTE; or ONSITE (COUNTRY; STATE/PROVINCE; CITY); or HYBRID]

Class: [E.G., TEMPORARY/REGULAR/INTERNSHIP]

Full-Time Equivalent: [E.G., FULL TIME/PART-TIME]

Reports to: [CEO/PRESIDENT/DEPARTMENT HEAD]

Benefits: [DESCRIBE ANY BENEFIT PACKAGES INCLUDING PAID TIME OFF, MEDICAL, RETIREMENT PLANS, PROFIT SHARING, ETC.]

Other Work Details

- **Work Environment.** [DESCRIBE WORK ENVIRONMENT. EXAMPLE: Normal office work conditions with a computer workstation; Telecommute with daily videoconferencing; etc.]
- **Travel.** [DESCRIBE TRAVEL EXPECTATIONS. EXAMPLE: May include occasional domestic and international air travel; Monthly travel with extended stays of 5–7 days; etc.]
- **Physical Requirements.** [DESCRIBE ANY PHYSICAL REQUIREMENTS SUCH AS MOBILITY, SEEING, HEARING, GRASPING, or LIFTING. EXAMPLE: Must be able to read from a computer or laptop monitor; Able to sit for prolonged periods.]
- **Equal Opportunity Employer.** [INSERT LANGUAGE AS APPLICABLE TO ORGANIZATION AND AS REQUIRED BY FEDERAL, STATE, and LOCAL LAWS.]

This job template was developed by Jennifer Tabanico, Owner and President of Action Research. She can be reached at tabanico@actionresearch-inc.com

SAMPLE RFP FOR SOCIAL MARKETING EFFORTS

Request for Proposals

Kitsap County Public Works Department, Stormwater Division for
Social Marketing Campaign Development
Response Deadline: Thursday, October 4, 2018, at 3:00 p.m.

Project Description

Kitsap County is accepting proposals for the development and implementation of a behavior change campaign that includes a social marketing strategy to address polluted stormwater runoff. This strategy will include development of a three-year social marketing plan to address a targeted behavior and specific audience that would reduce polluted runoff in the participating areas. Social marketing is the practice of using commercial marketing strategies to drive behavior change around a social issue. The contract period may begin November 1, 2018. The anticipated budget for this project may not exceed $30,000 in 2018 and $50,000 for each of the subsequent years.

Background

The WSSOG is a multijurisdictional partnership between Kitsap County, the Cities of Bainbridge Island, Bremerton, Gig Harbor, Poulsbo, Port Angeles, Port Orchard, and the US Navy. These agencies share an interest in improving water quality by reducing pollutants in stormwater runoff, which are a major source of pollution to local waterways and Puget Sound. The partnership has a successful existing behavior change program (Pet Waste in Public Places) and desires to meet the requirements of the upcoming NPDES (National Pollution Discharge Elimination System) permit, which takes effect in July 2019, by establishing a new behavior change campaign aimed at a new topic.

Regional Influence

While the campaign will focus on specific local communities, it is also important that it be designed to be easily modified and scaled to other communities (or jurisdictional consortiums similar to the WSSOG group) in the Puget Sound region or beyond.

Scope of Work

The consultant will work with Kitsap County and a small, established workgroup ("Workgroup") comprised of members of the West Sound Stormwater Outreach Group (WSSOG) to accomplish these objectives based on the scope of work outlined. The Workgroup will meet regularly with the consultant to both direct and make critical decisions. Utilizing social marketing best practices, consultant will:

- Facilitate the Workgroup in determining the program focus and targeted behavior change that will result in a benefit to water quality, including reviewing past and similar efforts.
- Prepare a brief summary report on marketing and outreach research and analysis.
- Facilitate the Workgroup in identifying target audience(s) and tools for reaching those audiences.
- Prepare a summary report of any original audience research performed for this campaign.
- Develop objectives and goals and an intervention mix strategy.
- Create a timeline for implementing plan over three years.
- Test creative concepts and other components with community stakeholders and target populations using focus groups, surveys, or other evaluation strategies.
- Implement pilot of selected tools and techniques in a defined population/area with the support of Kitsap County and the WSSOG.
- Create an evaluation strategy for tracking success of the pilot in driving behavior change, including evaluation of near term campaign success utilizing benchmarks and a plan for long-term program evaluation.
- Prepare final report, including lessons learned, recommendations for next steps, and scalability assessment.
- Provide quarterly reports and invoices.

Proposal Requirements

Proposals should not exceed 25 pages and should be prepared in such a way as to provide a straightforward, concise description of capabilities to satisfy the requirements of this RFP.

Specific Requirements & Expertise Desired

In your Statement of Qualifications, discuss how you plan to meet the requirements:

- Consultant (or consultant team) should demonstrate notable experience developing and managing social marketing strategies for a range of topical areas including best management practices relating to stormwater and water quality, experience working with a multi-jurisdictional client, and with a proven ability to accomplish deliverables on time and within budget.

- Experience working with existing programs/campaigns/brands/partnerships and building upon such efforts to improve outcomes.

RFP/SOW Questions

Additional questions regarding this solicitation and/or the scope of work must be submitted *in writing via e-mail* no later than **3:00 PM September 19, 2018** and should be directed to:

Michelle Perdue, Education & Outreach Coordinator Kitsap County Public Works Stormwater Division, mperdue@co.kitsap.wa.us

Source: Information for this RFP example is an edited version of an RFP that was provided by Kitsap County Public Works Department, Stormwater Division.

TRAINING OPPORTUNITIES

International Social Marketing Association (iSMA)

iSMA's Professional Development Opportunities as of July 2022 include the online courses listed below. Students receive a Professional Certificate of Completion from iSMA when they complete the course. More in-depth information, including how to register, can be found at https://isocialmarketing.org/trainings/:

- *Key Concepts in Social Marketing;*
- *Researching Your Audience;*
- *Developing a Strategic Social Marketing Plan.*

iSMA has provided a link to additional Social Marketing Education and Trainings at https://isocialmarketing.org/trainings/. At this link, you can find info on academic trainings, as well as professional development opportunities such as workshops.

Community-Based Social Marketing

Fostering Behavior Change Workshops: If you design or fund programs to encourage environmental, health, or safety behaviors, you will find the trainings provided by Dr. Doug McKenzie-Mohr invaluable. Held virtually over Zoom, his workshops consist of three four-hour sessions spread over three days. Dr. McKenzie-Mohr is an award-winning author and presenter and founder of community-based social marketing. Over 75,000 have attended his workshops! https://nam12.safelinks.protection.outlook.com/?url=https%3A%2F%2Fcbsm.com%2Ftraining%2Fworkshops&data=05%7C01%7C%7Cb40c5539522540b0e4ea08da6fea9a5e%7C84df9e7fe9f640afb435aaaaaaaaaaaa%7C1%7C0%7C637945350649099955%7CUnknown-%7CTWFpbGZsb3d8eyJWIjoiMC4wLjAwMDAiLCJQIjoiV2luMzIiLCJBTiI6Ik1haWwiLCJXVCI6Mn0%3D%7C3000%7C%7C%7C&sdata=mdTKZSoTbydVpfDbggmv306FFcZtDbdjIBDC4a35JNc%3D&reserved=0

University of South Florida

Social Marketing in Transportation Certificate (University of South Florida—Center for Urban Transportation Research): https://www.commuterservices.com/training/social-marketing-in-transportation-certificate/ (nominal fee)

Introduction to Social Marketing for Public Health (University of South Florida—WHO Collaborating Center on Social Marketing and Social Change & Pan American Health Organization): https://www.campusvirtualsp.org/en/course/introduction-social-marketing-public-health-course-1-self-learning (free)

Making Moves

"Making Moves: Creating Conservation Movements" is an 8-week, live course that guides conservation practitioners through the exact steps for designing an outreach plan that motivates action. Through weekly lessons and worksheets, participants clarify behavior goals and audiences, dive into the psychology behind why people will or won't take action, and identify practical strategies for motivating change. Get your conservation movements started here: https://brooketully.com/making-moves/

Center for Behavior & the Environment

Rare's Center for Behavior & the Environment offers several training opportunities in social marketing and behavior-centered design. They range from online, self-paced courses to live, multiday workshops. https://behavior.rare.org/training/

Additional Resources

National Social Marketing Centre	https://www.thensmc.com/training-courses
Nedra Kline Weinreich, Social Marketing University	https://socialmarketingu.com/ChangeforGood/
Griffith University, Social Marketing at Griffith	https://www.griffith.edu.au/griffith-business-school/social-marketing-griffith/training
Rescue Agency	https://rescueagency.com/webinars
Tools of Change	https://www.toolsofchange.com/en/workshops/
Pacific Northwest Social Marketing Association	https://www.pnsma.org/events

Twitter Feeds about Social Marketing and Communication

Nathaly AP, @AP_Nathaly (Spanish)

Australian Association of Social Marketing, @AASM_Aus

The Behavior Change Collaborative, @TheBCC_Org

Brian Cugelman, @cugelman

Brooke Sadowsky Tully, @brooke2cents

Carlos Santos, @CarlosOSantos4

CDC e-Health, @CDC_eHealth

Carla Rodriguez-Sanchez @CarlaRod_UA

Center of Excellence for Public Sector Marketing, @CEPSM

Craig Lefebvre, @chiefmaven

Doug McKenzie-Mohr, @dougcbsm

Dr Fiona Spotswood, @FiSpotswood

Erik Cateriano, @erikcateriano

European Social Marketing Association, @europeansma

Giuseppe Fattori, @mktsociale

Hamilton Carvalho, @PublicHamilton (Portuguese)

International Social Marketing Association, @isma_org

Jeff French, @JeffFrenchSSM

Jeffrey W. Jordan, @jeffreywjordan

Kelley Dennings, @kdennings

Latin American Social Marketing Association, @LAMSO (Spanish)

Luke van der Beeke, @LukevanderBeeke

Marketing for Change, @m4changeco

Mike Newton-Ward, @sm1guru

Nedra Kline Weinreich, @nedra

Neil Hopkins, @interacter

Nicholas Goodwin, @nickgoodwin

Osocio Social Advertising, @osocio

Pacific Northwest Social Marketing Association, @thePNSMA

Peter Mitchell, @M4Change

Pew Research Internet, @pewinternet

Prof Ross Gordon, DrRossGordon

R. Russell-Bennett, @DrBekMarketing

Rescue Agency, @RescueAgency

Sameer Deshpande, @sameerdpande

Sharyn Rundle-Thiele, @rundlesr

Social Marketing Association of North America, @SMANAorg

Social Marketing at Griffith University, @SMGriffith1

Susannah Fox, @SusannahFox

Vilarmina Ponce, @Vili_pl

World Social Marketing Conference, @WSMConference

WEBSITES

Ad Council	www.adcouncil.org/
American Marketing Association	https://www.ama.org/
Association of Consumer Research	www.acrwebsite.org
Australia and New Zealand Marketing Academy	www.anzmac.org
CDCynergy Lite	http://www.cdc.gov/healthcommunication/cdcynergylite.html
Center of Excellence for Public Sector Marketing	http://cepsm.ca/home/
Co-Design, Griffith University	https://www.griffith.edu.au/griffith-business-school/social-marketing-griffith/co-design
Community-Based Prevention Marketing, Florida Prevention Research Center, University of South Florida	https://health.usf.edu/publichealth/prc/cbpm
FHI360, Social Marketing and Communication Center	http://www.fhi360.org/services/social-marketing
Fostering Sustainable Behavior, Community-Based Social Marketing	www.cbsm.com/
FrameWorks Institute	www.frameworksinstitute.org/

Goodman Center: Where Do-Gooders Learn to Do Better *Free-Range Thinking* *Storytelling as Best Practice* *Why Bad Ads Happen to Good Causes*	http://www.thegoodmancenter.com
IDEO	www.ideo.org/
Institut du Marketing Social (France)	https://institutdumarketingsocial.org/
How to Increase Behavior Change, Griffith University	www.griffith.edu.au/griffith-business-school/social-marketing-griffith/how-to-increase-behavior-change
Institute for Social Marketing, University of Stirling, Scotland	www.ism.stir.ac.uk/
Marketing Social Portugal	http://marketingsocialportugal.net/
Marketing sociale e comunicazione per la salute (Italian Social Marketing Association)	www.marketingsociale.net/
The Market Research Society (UK)	www.mrs.org.uk/
National Centre for Health Marketing	www.nsmcentre.org.uk/
Neuromarketing	www.neurosciencemarketing.com
Social Change UK	https://social-change.co.uk/
Social Marketing Behavior Change Institute (Greece)	https://www.social-marketing.gr/?lang=en
Social Marketing Services, Inc.	https://www.socialmarketingservice.com
Stanford Social Innovation Review	https://ssireview.org
Stanford University Persuasive Technology Lab	https://behaviordesign.stanford.edu/
Tools of Change	www.toolsofchange.com/
University of South Florida, Social Marketing and Social Change Graduate Certificate	https://catalog.usf.edu/preview_program.php?catoid=15&poid=6068&returnto=2536

APPENDIX E

History Annex

(Updated 2022)

Jeff French

The table set out in this annex attempts to capture significant events and publications associated with the development of the application of social marketing since the 1960s. The chronology table does not attempt to represent the development of the social marketing concept itself. The table does, however, illustrate that social marketing has developed into a broad community of practice and research with global reach. For the sake of brevity, the table does not record the opening of every specialist academic center or every major social marketing program or even the many key academic papers that have helped to shape contemporary practice. Readers interested in a fuller exploration of the significance and development of social marketing theory and practice may wish to read:

Jeff French, "The Unfolding History of the Social Marketing Concept," in David W. Stewart (ed.), *The Handbook of Persuasion and Social Marketing* (Vol. 2: Conceptual, Theoretical and Strategic Dimensions; Santa Barbara, CA: Praeger, 2015).

Jeff French, "The Importance of Social Marketing History," *Social Marketing Quarterly*, 21, no. 4 (2015): 191–3.

Merritt, R. k., Kamin, T., Hussenöder, F., and Huibregtsen, J, "The History of Social Marketing in Europe: The Story So Far," *Social Marketing Quarterly*, 23, no. 4 (2017): 291–301.

A CHRONOLOGY OF KEY EVENTS IN THE DEVELOPMENT OF SOCIAL MARKETING THEORY AND PRACTICE

(Updated July 2022)

Pre 1960	Marketers and social program planners begin to debate the application of marketing to social issues.
1964	Chandy et al. from the Indian Institute of Management are commissioned by the Indian Government Central Family Planning Board to develop and publish proposals for family planning promotion using marketing as the core of the plan.

1967	USAID's International Contraceptive Social Marketing Project is initiated in India and subsequently introduced to other countries around the world in the 1970s including Jamaica in 1974.
1969	Levy and Kotler's article "Broadening the concept of Marketing" is published making the case for marketing to be applied to solving social issues and the idea of Social Marketing is introduced. Luck challenges Levy and Kotler and makes the case for not stretching the marketing concept to include Social Marketing.
1969	USAID, DIFID, and other donor agencies begin to commission and fund Social Marketing programs in developed countries. Social Marketing begins to be applied to health programs in the developed world.
1970	Population Services International is formed and rapidly develops and applies a Social Marketing approach to health development project implementation.
1971	The phrase "Social Marketing" is discussed and defined for the first time by Kotler and Zaltman in the paper "Social Marketing: An Approach to Planned Social Change" in the *Journal of Marketing*.
1973	The RARE Social Marketing organization is founded which applies Social Marketing interventions to environmental programs.
1974	The Canadian Federal Minister of Health, Marc Lalonde publishes 'A New Perspective on the Health of Canadians' which sets out the need for government action focused on modifying behavior. It leads to the development of several sustained Social Marketing programs.
1974	The Social Marketing Company, a not-for-profit agency is set up by the Bangladeshi Government to deliver Social Marketing health and development related interventions.
1978	AED, the Academy for Educational Development, begins its prolonged program of implementing Social Marketing programs with its oral rehydration program in Africa.
1979	Rothschild's paper "Marketing Communications in Non-Business Situations" is published in the Journal of Marketing.
1980	World Bank, World Health Organisation and Centres for Disease Control, Health Canada, and the Australia Government start to apply and promote interest in Social Marketing. USAID, DIFID, and other national development agencies continue support for Social Marketing programmes.
1981	Health Canada becomes the first government agency to set up a Social Marketing Unit to lead its health programs.
1984	UNICEF task force report on the application of Social Marketing to enhance child survival rates.
1985	"Social Marketing New Imperatives for Public Health" is published giving a rationale for Social Marketing as part of public health and also tips for marketing and communication planning, plus example case studies.
1986	The first time Social Marketing is included in a training program offered by the CDC. The course on Social Marketing: Theory into Action. Community Intervention Skills: The Essentials, is staged.

1988	Social Marketing principles are used to inform the delivery of key Australian Social Marketing programs such as Quit, Anti-tobacco, and "Slip, Slop, Slap" skin cancer prevention.
1988	1988: "Social Marketing and Public Health Intervention," an article in *Health Education Quarterly*, is published by Lefebvre and Flora, reviewing social marketing application of social marketing in the field of public health.
1989	Publication of Kotler and Roberto's book *Social Marketing: Strategies for Changing Public Behaviour.*
1990	Academic Social Marketing programs are established in the US, Australia, UK, Canada, New Zealand. Social Marketing begins to be incorporated into developed countries health and environmental programs.
1990	The Health Sponsorship Council is established in New Zealand with Social Marketing as one of its core functions.
1991	The Centre for Social Marketing is launched at Strathclyde University. The Centre grew from the Advertising Research Unit at the University which was launched in 1980.
1991	The first University of South Florida Conference on Social Marketing and Public Health. Over 20 events have now been run.
1993	The first Social Marketing web site at Health Canada is launched.
1994	The Social Marketing Quarterly is launched, based at the University of South Florida.
1994	The Center for Social Marketing was created at Carleton University.
1994	An new journal, *Social Marketing Quarterly* by Best Start Inc. and the Department of Public Health, University of South Florida, is launched.
1995	The Canadian Social Marketing Network website was launched to house public resources generated by Health Canada's Social Marketing division, and to offer a forum and network for those interested in Social Marketing.
1995	The first edition of the *Tools of Change* workbook by Jay Kassirer and Doug McKenzie-Mohr is published.
1995	Andreasen's book, *Marketing Social Change* is published which includes a focus on strategic thinking and customer centric planning.
1995	The first "Innovations in Social Marketing"' conference is held in Atlanta. Subsequent events are staged in 1996, 1997, 1999, 2003, and 2007.
1996	The Consensus Conference on the "Future of Social Marketing" is hosted by Porter Novelli.
1996	A simple solution is published by Mushtaque, Chowdhury, and Cash focused on using social marketing in low-income countries.
1996	Tamborini edits and published Marketing Social Communication in Italy.
1997	The US Social Turning Point Social Marketing National Excellence Collaborative is launched and runs until 2006. A partnership of local, state, and national public health organizations to develop guidance and good practice in Social Marketing.
1997	The Social Marketing "List serve" goes live, launched by George Washington University.

1998	"Marketing Public Health" is published by Siegel and Doner, making the case and giving examples about how Social Marketing can be applied to chronic and acute public health issues.
1998	The Open University distance learning Level 3 Social Marketing course (B324 Marketing and Society) is offered for the first time and continues to the present day.
1998	Joint UN, Aids "Social Marketing. An effective tool in the global response to HIV/AIDS" guidance is published.
1998	The "Tools of Change" website is created, offering specific community-based social marketing tools and case studies.
1998	CDCynergy social marketing planning tool is launched by CDC.
1999	The Social Marketing Institute is formed in Washington D.C. Alan Andreasen acts as executive director and launches the Social Marketing email list server, the first online Social Marketing network.
1999	Rothschild's paper "Carrots Sticks and Promises" is published setting out a conceptual framework that includes Marketing influencing social behavior.
1999	Epstein's book, *A Manual for Culturally Adapted Social Marketing*, is published which sets out the case and suggestions for ensuring that Social Marketing interventions are developed via cocreation and engagement.
1999	McKenzie-Mohr and Smith publish *Fostering Sustainable Behaviour*; 3rd edition published in 2011. Introduces the notion of Community Based Social Marketing and the application of Social Marketing to environmental issues.
1999	*Hands on Social Marketing* is published by Weinreich giving step by step guidance on running a social marketing program. 2nd Edition is published in 2011.
1999	Social Marketing begins to be embedded into mainstream social policy programs and systems.
2000	The Social Marketing National Excellence Collaborative is set up by a grant from the Robert Wood Johnson Foundation. The task was to grow the capacity of Social Marketing in the US public health system.
2000	The Robert Wood Johnson Foundation sponsors three pioneering Non-profit Marketing Summits and again in 2001.
2001	WHO launch its development of COMBI Social Marketing planning model for communicable disease. Final guidance published in 2012 following years of field testing and development.
2001	The University of South Florida offers a social marketing certificate program.
2001	Andreasen's book *Ethics in Social Marketing* is published and is the first book to deal exclusively with this issue.
2001	University of Lethbridge Canada launches the Centre for Socially Responsible Marketing.
2002	A. Andreasen publishes the six benchmark criteria for Social Marketing.
2002	Mendive publishes the first book on *Social Marketing in Argentina*.

2002	Hastings and Donovan call for a Social Marketing focus on "up-stream" policy, social and environmental behavioral determinants as well as individual and group influences on behavior.
2002	Kotler, Roberto, and Lee's book *Social Marketing: Improving the Quality of Life* is published.
2002	**In Italy MKTS The Association of Social Promotion, social marketing and health communication is established.**
2003	Rob Donovan's book *Social Marketing, Principles and Practice* is the first Social Marketing text book published in Australia.
2003	CDCynergy-Social Marketing Edition planning tool is launched, the 2nd edition is launched in 2006. CDCynergy was an interactive training and decision support tool designed to plan Social Marketing and communication programmes.
2004	Mukherji publishes *An Introduction to Social Marketing*, the first book on Social Marketing to be published by an Indian author based on case studies and examples from India.
2004	The first Canadian SMART Conference was held (Social Marketing Advances in Research and Theory), and the first "tools of change" webinar is held.
2004	EPODE a community-based approach to healthy living is launched in France with Social Marketing as one of its key component strategies. In 2011, the schemes international network is formed with 25 participating countries.
2004	The Centre for Social Marketing becomes The Institute for Social Marketing and moves to Stirling University.
2004	The National Coordination of Social Marketing is established in Italy with **Giuseppe Fattori leading the program**.
2004	The first national governmental Social Marketing Strategy is developed in the UK.
2005	The UK National Social Marketing Centre is formed in London with a remit to develop good practice and capacity in Social Marketing.
2005	The 10th annual conference on Innovations in Social Marketing and 16th annual Social Marketing in Public Health conferences are held.
2005	The Centre of Excellence for Public Sector Marketing is opened in Canada.
2005	The 10th annual conference for Innovations in Social Marketing is held in Baltimore the USA.
2005	The 16th annual Social Marketing in Public Health conference is held in Florida.
2006	*Social Marketing in the 21st Century*, by Alan Andreasen, describes the expanding role of Social Marketing.
2006	Social Marketing is included in the UK Environmental agency DEFRA strategic plan.
2006	"It's our Health," the UK Government sponsored first national review of Social Marketing is published.
2007	The UK Government publish the first national policy on Social Marketing.

2007	The National Institute for Health and Clinical Effectiveness begins to publish a series of systematic reviews that indicate that Social Marketing should form part of generic attempts at population level behavior change in a number of specific areas including premature death, smoking, and alcohol and accident prevention.
2007	French and Blair-Stevens publish the eight UK National Benchmark criteria for Social Marketing.
2007	The First UK Social Marketing Conference is held in Oxford, UK.
2007	Hasting's book *Social Marketing, Why Should the Devil Have All the Best Tunes* is published.
2007	The Institute of Social Marketing publish reviews of evidence demonstrating Social Marketing's effectiveness.
2008	The WHO Healthy Cities Conference focuses on Social Marketing.
2008	The 3rd Edition of Kotler and Lee's book *Social Marketing Influencing Behaviours for Social Good* is published.
2008	The First World Social Marketing Conference is held in Brighton, UK.
2008	The UK government published the first National Social Marketing Strategy called Ambitions for Health.
2009	US Government health strategy 2020 includes requirements for Public Health departments to develop Social Marketing Capacity.
2009	The UK National Occupational Standards for Social Marketing is published.
2009	Operational Guide to Social Marketing is translated into Italian French, Blair-Stevens **Giuseppe Fattori.**
2009	The Institute of Social Marketing (ISM-Open) is launched at the main campus of the Open University in Milton Keynes, UK.
2009	The Australian Association of Social Marketing is formed.
2009	Kotler and Lee publish their book *Up and Out of Poverty.* It is focused on using Social Marketing to address poverty, social exclusion, and inequality.
2009	The National Social Marketing Centre published its economic evaluation/value for money tools for Social Marketing.
2010	Cheng, Kotler, and Lee publish their book *Social Marketing for Public Health: Global Trends and Success Stories.*
2010	Donovan, R. J. and Henley, N. (2003). *Principles and Practice of Social Marketing an International Perspective* 2nd Edition Published by Cambridge University Press.
2010	French et al. publish *Social Marketing and Public Health, Theory and Practice* setting out new thinking re Strategic Social Marketing theory and how to apply Social Marketing in the policy field.
2010	The Australia National Preventative Health Agency established with a specific remit to coordinate across states and build Social Marketing capacity.

2010	The requirement that public health staff should receive Social Marketing training and capacity on Social Marketing should be increased is included for the first time in US Government policy as part of the National Health Promotion and Disease Prevention Objectives for the 2020 "Healthy People" strategy.
2010	The Australian International Social Marketing conference is held and repeated in 2012.
2010	The International Social Marketing Association is launched.
2011	The 2nd World Social Marketing Conference is held in Dublin, Ireland.
2011	The Journal of Social Marketing is launched by Emerald Publishing.
2011	WHO Healthy Cities Programme for action recognizes Social Marketing as a key tool for increased impact.
2011	French, Merritt and Reynolds book *Social Marketing Case Book* is published setting out the Total Process Planning Model and the Value Cost Exchange matrix plus case studies from around the world.
2011	Hastings, Angus, and Bryant's book, *Handbook of Social Marketing* is published containing a collection of seminal chapters by a wide range of leading thinkers and practitioners in the field.
2011	CDC systematic review of "Health Communication & Social Marketing" is published endorsing the efficacy of applying the approach.
2011	The UK Government publish the second National Strategy for Social Marketing called "Changing Behaviour Improving Outcomes."
2011	The World Marketing Summit is held in Bangladesh with a major focus on Social Marketing.
2011	The University of South Florida offers an online social marketing certificate program.
2011	The 4th Edition of Kotler and Lee's book *Social Marketing Influencing Behaviours for Social Good* is published.
2012	The UK House of Lords review on behavior change is launched which endorses the application of Social Marketing as part of a broader approach to social behavior change.
2012	The first European Social Marketing Conference is held in Lisbon, Portugal.
2012	The European Social Marketing Association is launched.
2012	Launch of the African Social Marketing Forum.
2012	The first-in-the-world MBA in social marketing and behavior change program is launched from the University of Stirling, Scotland.
2012	Hasting's book, *Marketing Matrix* is published.
2012	WHO Europe published a new 2020 Health Strategy with commitment to the application of Social Marketing principles.
2012	Carlos Santos book, *Melhorar a Vida Um Guia De Marketing Social.* The first Social Marketing text book in Portuguese is published.
2012	McKenzie-Mohr, Lee Schultz, and Kotler publish *Social Marketing to Protect the Environment.*

2012	iSMA and ESMA begin work on developing a consensus definition of Social Marketing. The final definition is published in 2013.
2012	The Pacific Northwest Social Marketing Association is formed in the US.
2013	The Third World Social Marketing Conference held in Toronto, Canada.
2013	Eagle, Dahl, Hill, Bird, and Spotswood's book on Social Marketing is published.
2013	Lefebvre's book *Social Marketing for Social Change* is published.
2013	The first consensus definition of Social Marketing is agreed by International Social Marketing Association, the European Social Marketing association, and the Australian Association of Social Marketing.
2013	A special issue of the *European Journal of Marketing* is published dedicated to Social Marketing edited by Dibb and Carrigan.
2013	The international Conference of Social Franchising and Social Marketing takes place in Cochin, India.
2013	The first consensus definition of Social Marketing is agreed by the iSMA, AASM, and the ESMA (Subsequently endorsed by the North American Social Marketing Association in 2016).
2013	*Social Marketing in India* is published by Deshpande and Lee.
2013	The First global conference on Social Marketing and Social Franchising is held in Cochin, India.
2014	The Second European Social Marketing Conference is Held in Rotterdam.
2014	Social marketing research center launched at Griffiths University, Australia.
2015	The Third World Social Marketing Conference is Held in Sydney, Australia.
2015	Three volume *Persuasion and Social Marketing* edited by Stewart is published.
2015	*Strategic Social Marketing* is published by French and Gordon.
2015	The book *Segmentation in Social Marketing* edited by Dietrich, Rundle-Thiele and Kubacki is published.
2015	iSMA publish academic course competency criteria.
2016	First technical Guide to Social Marketing published by the European Center for Disease Control, Authors French and Apfel
2016	The book *Social* Marketing, *From Tunes to Symphonies* by Hastings and Domegan is published.
2016	The Third European Social Marketing Conference is Held in Espoo, Finland.
2016	First Agents of Change Summit is held in San Diego.
2016	North American Social Marketing Association is formed.
2016	The 5th Edition of Lee and Kotler's book *Social Marketing Influencing Behaviours for Social Good* is published.
2017	4th World Social Marketing Conference is held in Washington, USA.

2017	Segmentation in social marketing is published, edited by Rundle-Thiele, and Kubacki.
2017	First set of consensus Social Marketing principles is endorsed by iSMA and all other Social Marketing Associations.
2017	*Policy Making for Citizen Behavior Change* by Lee is published.
2017	The Second Edition of *Social Marketing and Public Health*, edited by French is published.
2017	African Social Marketing conference is held.
2018	Latin American Social Marketing Association is formed.
2018	4th European Social Marketing Conference is held in Antwerp, Belgium.
2018	4th Australian and Pacific Social Marketing conference is held in Singapore.
2018	Second Agents of Change Summit is held in San Diego, USA.
2018	iSMA and all federated social marketing associations begin work of developing social marketing ethics principles.
2018	The BEST Centre for Behavioural Economics, Society and Technology is launched at Queensland University of Technology, Australia that combines expertise form behavioral sciences and Social Marketing.
2019	5th World Social marketing conference is held in Edinburgh, Scotland.
2019	The First Social Marketing research center is established in France at the Université Paris-Saclay.
2020	Hay *Broadening Cultural Horizons in Social Marketing* is published by Eagle & Bhati.
2020	Social marketers around the world make contributions to local, national, and regional Covid-19 pandemic programs.
2020	F French and Gordon publish second edition of *Strategic Social Marketing*' repositioning social marketing as a systems intervention process.
2020	The 6th Edition of Lee and Kotler's book *Social Marketing Influencing Behaviours for Social Good*' is published.
2021	WHO Behavioural Working group is formed and includes social marketing experts and explicit reference to the role of social marketing in developing and delivering effective behavioral influence programs.
2021	The First Social Marketing research center is established in Japan at Doshisha University.
2021	UN, UNITAR training organization launches training modules of applying social marketing planning processes to reduce road traffic accidents and increase Covid vaccine uptake.
2021	African Social Marketing Association is formed.
2021	WHO publish technical guidance on principles of effective behavioral influence including inputs form Social Marketing.
2021	Social Marketing professional standards group and code of ethics working group are established by the International Social Marketing Association.

2022	Social Marketing encyclopedia published Fourali and French.
2022	5th European social marketing conference held in Thessaloniki, Greece.
2022	6th World social marketing conference held in Brighton, UK.
2022	***Success in Social Marketing: 100 Case Studies Form Around the Globe*** **is published by Lee and Kotler.**
2022	**First Drafts iSMA Ethics principles guide published.**
2022	**iSMA Professional standards statement published for consultation.**
2022	**African Social Marketing association is formed.**
2022	**Social Marketing networks established in Moldova, Indonesia, Vietnam, Japan, Spain, Portugal, Slovenia, and Italy.**

All updates and suggested amendments to this chronology should be sent to:
Jeff.French@strategic-social-marketing.org

APPENDIX F

Academic Course Offerings

The International Social Marketing Association maintains a listing of academic course offerings on its website at https://isocialmarketing.org/trainings. As an update to previous studies (Kelly, 2009, 2013), research was conducted to develop this listing and assess the global landscape and trends associated with social marketing formal education (Foote, 2022; Foote, Kelly, Lee, & AbrashWalton, 2022). An upward trend in course availability was evident. In 2022, a total of 104 courses were available, housed at 70 different universities within 20 countries. Of these courses, 80 focused primarily on social marketing, while 24 included it as a component (less than half of course content). The majority of academic course offerings are available in Global North countries. Approximately half of the courses were offered at the graduate level (48%), with slightly fewer (41.3%) offered at the undergraduate level, and much fewer (7.8%) offered as part of a postgraduate certificate; several courses were offered at multiple levels, either graduate and undergraduate or graduate and postgraduate certificate. For the "primary disciplinary area" of the courses, a third (33.7%) were classified as "Health" (which includes these "other" responses written in by respondents: "Health Communication," "Public Health," "Global Public Health," and "Behavioral Science & Health Communication") and followed by "Marketing" (28.8%). "Communications" and "Business" each made up 12.5% of the total. Nearly 10% of the courses can be classified as "Environment & Conservation," which includes examples within "Environmental Studies" and "Conservation Sciences, General." Other disciplinary areas include "Public Administration," "Political Science," "Psychology," and "Humanities," each represented by one course.

REFERENCES

Foote, L. (2022). *The diffusion of a discipline: The institutionalization of social marketing as an innovative practice within environmental contexts*. Environmental Studies Department, Antioch University New England.

Foote, L., Kelly, K. J., Lee, N. R., & Abrash Walton, A. (2022). Academic course offerings in social marketing: Snapshot and trends as the discipline marks 50 years. *Social Marketing Quarterly*.

Kelly, K. J. (2009). Social marketing education: The beat goes on. *Social Marketing Quarterly, 15*(3), 129–141.

Kelly, K. J. (2013). Academic course offerings in social marketing: The beat continues. *Social Marketing Quarterly, 19*(4), 290–295.

APPENDIX G

International Social Marketing Association's Academic Competencies September 2014

The academic competencies for social marketing outlined in this document are intended as guidance for **instructors of academic courses and designers of academic and nonacademic certificate programs** in social marketing. They provide a set of participant-focused benchmarks for the development of course curricula and certificate completion requirements. These competencies are not meant to prescribe or restrict the content of academic social marketing degree programs. It is anticipated that degree-granting programs in social marketing may have more competencies than are outlined here.

The development of these competencies was formally begun at a collaboratory held at the Social Marketing Conference in Clearwater Beach, Florida, in June 2012. Since then, the full list of competencies generated by that discussion has been reviewed and revised, and was approved in September by the International Social Marketing Association, Australian Association of Social Marketing, and European Social Marketing Association.

Comments about these competencies can be sent to Nancy Lee (nancyrlee@msn.com).

It should also be noted that in 2023, additional standards will be published including ones for Professional Standards. This will then be available on the International Social Marketing Association website at https://isocialmarketing.org/.

ACADEMIC COMPETENCIES IN SOCIAL MARKETING (AUGUST 2014)

Upon completion of a social marketing certificate or academic course, a participant should be able to:

1. Describe social marketing to colleagues and other professionals and differentiate it from other approaches to influencing behaviors and social change.
2. Work with colleagues and stakeholders to identify community, state, province, national, regional, and/or international priorities, and identify those for which a social marketing approach may be appropriate.
3. Identify and segment affected populations and select appropriate, high priority segments.
4. Prioritize and select measurable behaviors (not just awareness or attitudes) of individuals, organizations, and/or policymakers to influence.

5. Design and conduct situational analysis and formative research, employing mixed methodologies needed to understand current audience barriers and benefits, as well as competing behaviors and direct and indirect competition.
6. Select and apply relevant social marketing, behavioral, exchange and social science theories, models, frameworks, and research to inform development of a social marketing strategic plan, one that meet the needs and wants of the intended audience.
7. Create an integrated social marketing mix strategy that extends beyond communications only campaigns, with consideration of all appropriate evidence-based tools and theory needed to influence a desired behavior.
8. Critically reflect and test the effectiveness, acceptability, and ethics of potential social marketing strategies with representatives of target audiences and stakeholders and adapt as necessary.
9. Finalize an implementation plan, incorporating opportunities for scaling up and sustainability.
10. Design and implement an evaluation plan, including a monitoring system to assure programs are on track to achieve goals and meet agreed quality and efficiency standards.
11. Apply ethical principles to the conduct of research, developing, implementing, and evaluating a social marketing plan.
12. Document and communicate the results of social marketing initiatives to colleagues, stakeholders, communities, and other relevant organizations and groups.

REFERENCES

CHAPTER 1 TABLE NOTES

a. Centers for Disease Control and Prevention, "Current Cigarette Smoking Among Adults in the United States," n.d., accessed October 19, 2021, https://www.cdc.gov/tobacco/data_statistics/fact_sheets/adult_data/cig_smoking/index.htm.

b. National Institute on Alcohol Abuse and Alcoholism, "Binge Drinking," May 2021, accessed October 19, 2021, https://www.niaaa.nih.gov/publications/brochures-and-fact-sheets/binge-drinking.

c. March of Dimes, "Street Drugs and Pregnancy," n.d., accessed October 19, 2021, https://www.marchofdimes.org/pregnancy/street-drugs-and-pregnancy.aspx.

d. Centers for Disease Control and Prevention, "Exercise or Physical Activity," n.d., accessed October 19, 2021, http://www.cdc.gov/nchs/fastats/exercise.htm.

e. Centers for Disease Control and Prevention, "Condom and Contraceptive Use Among Sexually Active High School Students 2019," Morbidity and Mortality Weekly Report, August 21, 2020, accessed October 19, 2021, https://www.cdc.gov/mmwr/volumes/69/su/su6901a2.htm.

f. Centers for Disease Control and Prevention, "HIV in the United States: At a Glance," n.d., accessed October 19, 2021, https://www.cdc.gov/hiv/statistics/overview/ataglance.html.

g. Centers for Disease Control and Prevention, "Division of Nutrition, Physical Activity, and Obesity," n.d., accessed October 19, 2021, https://www.cdc.gov/nccdphp/dnpao/division-information/media-tools/adults-fruits-vegetables.html.

h. Centers for Disease Control and Prevention, "Cholesterol," September 17, 2021, accessed October 19, 2021, https://www.cdc.gov/cholesterol/index.htm.

i. Centers for Disease Control and Prevnetion, "Breastfeeding," August 24, 2021, accessed October 19, 2021, https://www.cdc.gov/breastfeeding/data/facts.html.

j. Centers for Disease Control and Prevention, "National Center for Health Statistics: Mammography," 2019, accessed October 19, 2021, https://www.cdc.gov/nchs/fastats/mammography.htm.

k. USA FACTS, "US Coronavirus Vaccine Tracker," October 18, 2021, accessed October 19, 2021, https://usafacts.org/visualizations/covid-vaccine-tracker-states/.

l. Centers for Disease Control and Prevention, "Colorectal (Colon) Cancer," June 8, 2021, accessed October 19, 2021, https://www.cdc.gov/cancer/colorectal/statistics/.

m. WebMD.com, "CDC to Young Women: Take Folic Acid," 2008, accessed October 19, 2021, http://women.webmd.com/news/20080110/cdc-to-young-women-take-folic-acid.

n. Centers for Disease Control and Prevention, "National Center for Health Statistics," August 23, 2021, accessed October 19, 2021, https://www.cdc.gov/nchs/fastats/immunize.htm.

o. Centers for Disease Control and Prevention, "Adolescent and School Health: Youth Risk Behavior Surveillance System (YRBSS)," n.d., accessed October 19, 2021, http://www.cdc.gov/HealthyYouth/yrbs/index.htm.

p. Centers for Disease Control and Prevention, "National Center for Health Statistics," 2021, accessed October 19, 2021, https://www.cdc.gov/nchs/fastats/dental.htm.

q. Centers for Disease Control and Prevention, "Diabetes," October 5, 2021, accessed October 19, 2021. https://www.cdc.gov/diabetes/library/features/truth-about-prediabetes.html.

r. Centers for Disease Control and Prevention, "High Blood Pressure," September 27, 2021, accessed October 19, 2021, https://www.cdc.gov/bloodpressure/facts.htm.

s. National Eating Disorders Association, "National Eating Disorders Association Announces Results of Eating Disorders Poll on College Campuses Across the Nation," September 26, 2006, accessed October 20, 2006, http://www.edap.org/neda Dir/files/documents/PressRoom/CollegePoll_9-28-06.doc.

t. Centers for Disease Control and Prevention, "Youth Risk Behavior Surveillance," 2019, accessed October 20, 2021, https://nccd.cdc.gov/Youthonline/App/Results.aspx?TT=A&OUT=0&SID=HS&QID=QQ&LID=XX&YID=2017&LID2=&YID2=&COL=S&ROW1=N&ROW2=N&HT=QQ&LCT=LL&FS=S1&FR=R1&FG=G1&FA=A1&FI=I1&FP=P1&FSL=S1&FRL=R1&FGL=G1&FAL=A1&FIL=I1&FPL=P1&PV=&TST=False&C1=&C2=&QP=G&DP=1&VA=CI&CS=Y&SYID=&EYID=&SC=DEFAULT&SO=ASC.

u. Ibid.

v. Ibid.

w. Centers for Disease Control and Prevention, "Child Passenger Safety," September 2021, accessed October 20, 2021, https://www.cdc.gov/transportationsafety/child_passenger_safety/cps-factsheet.html.

x. National Vital Statistices Reports, "State Suicide Rates Among Adolescents," September 11, 2020, accessed October 20, 2021, https://www.cdc.gov/nchs/data/nvsr/nvsr69/nvsr-69-11-508.pdf.

y. Social Solutions, "20 Alarming Domestic Violence Statistics," n.d., accessed October 20, 2021, https://www.socialsolutions.com/blog/domestic-violence-statistics/#:~:text=Every%20year%2C%20more%20than%2010%20million%20men%20and,by%20an%20intimate%20partner%20in%20their%20lifetime.%20%28source%29.

z. Nationwide Children's, "Gun Safety," 2021, accessed October 20, 2021, https://www.nationwidechildrens.org/research/areas-of-research/center-for-injury-research-and-policy/injury-topics/general/gun-safety.

aa. Centers for Disease Control and Prevention, "Youth Risk Behavior Surveillance."

bb. National Fire Protection Association, "Smoke Alarms in US Home Fires," 2021, accessed October 20, 2021, https://www.nfpa.org/News-and-Research/Data-research-and-tools/Detection-and-Signaling/Smoke-Alarms-in-US-Home-Fires.

cc. Centers for Disease Control and Prevention, "Home and Recreational Safety," 2016, accessed October 20, 2021, https://www.cdc.gov/homeandrecreationalsafety/falls/adultfalls.html.

dd. SAFE KIDS Worldwide, "Medication Safety," 2021, accessed October 20, 2021, https://www.safekids.org/medicinesafety.

ee. EPA, "Facts and Figures About Materials, Waste and Recycling," July 29, 2021, accessed October 20, 2021, https://www.epa.gov/facts-and-figures-about-materials-waste-and-recycling/frequent-questions-regarding-epas-facts-and. U.S. Environmental Protection Agency, "Municipal Solid Waste—Recycling and Disposal in the United States," 2012, accessed November 1, 2017, https://archive.epa.gov/epawaste/nonhaz/municipal/web/pdf/2012_msw_fs.pdf.

ff. EcoWatch, "Fish Stocks Depleted to 'Alarming' Levels," 2016, accessed October 20, 2021, https://www.ecowatch.com/one-third-of-commercial-fish-stocks-fished-at-unsustainable-levels-1910593830.html.

gg. National Interagency Fire Center, "National Fire News," October 2021, accessed October 20, 2021, https://www.nifc.gov/fire-information/nfn.

hh. U.S. Environmental Protection Agency, "Pesticides Impact on Indoor Air Quality," March 2021, accessed October 20, 2021, https://www.epa.gov/indoor-air-quality-iaq/pesticides-impact- indoor-air-quality.

ii. Conservation Mart, "Leaking Toilet Tank," 2021, accessed October 20, 2021, https://www.conservationmart.com/t-leaking-toilet-tank.aspx#:~:text=Toilet%20leaking%20results%20in%20a%20tremendous%20amount%20of,translates%20to%20money%20spent%20on%20higher%20water%20bills.

jj. U.S. Census Bureau, "United States Commuting at a Glance," 2019, accessed October 20, 2021, https://www2.census.gov/programs-surveys/commuting/guidance/acs-1yr/DY2019-Percent-drove-alone.pdf.

kk. U.S. Environmental Protective Agency, "At Home," October 2021, accessed October 20, 2021, http://epa.gov/climatechange/wycd/home.html.

ll. U.S. Environmental Protection Agency, "Composting at Home," April 2021, accessed October 20, 2021, https://www.epa.gov/recycle/composting-home.

mm. National Park Service, "Wildfire Causes and Evaluations," 2017, accessed October 20, 2021, https://www.nps.gov/articles/wildfire-causes-and-evaluation.htm.

nn. Keep America Beautiful, "END LITTERING," 2020, accessed October 20, 2021, https://kab.org/goals/end-littering/.

oo. Pet Poo Skiddoo, "Pet Waste Removal," 2015, accessed October 20, 2021, https://www.petpooskiddoo.com/blog/top-10-reasons-why-people-dont-pick-up-dog-poop/.

pp. HRSA, "Organ Donation Statistics," 2021, accessed October 20, 2021, https://www.organdonor.gov/learn/organ-donation-statistics.

qq. American Red Cross, "Importance of the Blood Supply," 2021, accessed October 20, 2021, http://www.redcrossblood.org/learn-about-blood/blood-facts-and-statistics.

rr. U.S. Census Bureau, "Voting in America: A Look at the 2016 Presidential Election," May 2017, accessed October 20, 2021, https://www.census.gov/newsroom/blogs/random-samplings/2017/05/voting_in_america.html.

ss. Centers for Disease Control and Prevention, "Screen Time vs. Lean Time," January 2018, accessed October 20, 2021, https://www.cdc.gov/nccdphp/dch/multimedia/infographics/getmoving.htm.

tt. USA FACTS, "Homeless Population," 2021, accessed October 20, 2021, https://usafacts.org/data/topics/people-society/poverty/public-housing/homeless-population/?utm_source=bing&utm_medium=cpc&utm_campaign=ND-StatsData&msclkid=6a08e6a2e3031c68c99b87d2860a5f74.

uu. ASPCA, "Pet Statistics," 2021, accessed April 21, 2021, https://www.aspca.org/animal-homelessness/shelter-intake-and-surrender/pet-statistics.

vv. Identity Theft Info, "Identity Theft Victim Statistics," n.d., accessed October 20, 2021, http://www.identitytheft.info/victims.aspx.

ww. CNBC, "Make It," 2021, accessed October 20, 2021, https://www.cnbc.com/2020/10/19/7point1-million-american-households-didnt-have-a-bank-account-last-year.html/.

xx. FBI, "Scams and Safety," n.d., accessed October 20, 2021, https://www.fbi.gov/scams-and-safety/common-scams-and-crimes/elder-fraud.

CHAPTER 1

1. CDC, "Drug Overdose Deaths in the U.S. Up 30% in 2020," July 2021, accessed November 17, 2021, Drug Overdose Deaths in the U.S. Up 30% in 2020 (cdc.gov).

2. NBC News, "Drug Overdoses Killed 50,000 in U.S., More Than Car Crashes,"

December 2016, accessed November 17, 2021, http://www.nbcnews.com/health/health-news/drug-overdoses-killed-50-000-u-s-more-car-crashes-n694001?cid=sm_fb.

3. Ibid.
4. CNN, Dr. Sanjay Gupta on Your Health, "Help, Not Handcuffs for Addicts," December 21, 2015, accessed October 23, 2017, www.cnn.com/videos/us/2015/12/23/heroin-in-america-new-hampshire-dnt-gupta-ac-part-2.cnn/video/playlists/sanjay-gupta-health/.
5. Chris Sweeney, "Police Chief Leonard Campanello' s New Fight Against the Heroin Crisis," Boston Magazine, October 2015, accessed October 23, 2017, http://www.bostonmagazine.com/news/article/2015/09/29/leonard-campanello-heroin-crisis/.
6. Ibid.
7. Ibid.
8. Police Assisted Addiction and Recovery Initiative [website], accessed October 23, 2017, http://paariusa.org/about-us/.
9. Ibid.
10. James David Dickson, "Hope Not Handcuffs Changes Landscape for Addicts," The Detroit News, February 2017, accessed October 23, 2017, http://www.detroitnews.com/story/news/local/macomb-county/2017/02/12/hope-handcuffs/97817574/.
11. Personal Communication From Alan Andreasen to Philip Kotler, April 28, 2011.
12. American Marketing Association, "AMA Definition of Marketing," December 17, 2007, accessed July 24, 2013, http://www.marketingpower.com/aboutama/pages/definitionofmarketing.aspx.
13. Robert J. Donovan and Nadine Henley, Social Marketing: Principles and Practices (Melbourne, VIC: IP Communications, 2003).
14. Message Posted to the Georgetown Social Marketing Listserve, March 16, 2006.
15. Ibid.
16. Philip Kotler and Gerald Zaltman, "Social Marketing: An Approach to Planned Social Change," Journal of Marketing 35 (July 1971): 3–12.
17. Philip Kotler, My Adventures in Marketing: The Autobiography of Philip Kotler (IDEA BITE PRESS, 2017), 51.
18. Richard P. Bagozzi, "Marketing as Exchange: A Theory of Trans-ctions in the Marketplace," American Behavioral Science 21, no. 4 (March/April 1978): 535–56.
19. Smith, "Social Marketing and its Potential Contribution."
20. Philip Kotler, "Marketing is the Original Behavioral Economics," July 2020, accessed November 17, 2021, Philip Kotler: Marketing is the Original Behavioral Economics - Evonomics.
21. Richard H. Thaler and Cass R. Sustein, Nudge: Improving Decisions About Health, Wealth, and Happiness (New York, NY: Penguin Books, 2009).
22. Doug McKenzie-Mohr, Fostering Sustainable Behavior: An Intro-duction to Community-Based Social Marketing (Gabriola Island, BC: New Society, 2011).
23. Craig R. Lefebvre, Social Marketing and Social Change: Strategies and Tools for Improving Health, Well-Being, and the Environment (San Francisco, CA: Jossey-Bass, 2013).
24. Robert Hornik, "Some Complementary Ideas About Social Change," Social Marketing Quarterly 8, no. 2 (Summer 2002): 11.
25. Max Marchione, "Doctors Test Anti-Smoking Vaccine," 2006, accessed July 31, 2007, http://www.foxnews.com/printer_friendly_wires/2006Ju127/0,4675,TobaccoVaccine,00.html.
26. Distraction.gov: Official U.S. Government Website for Distracted Driving, "State Laws," n.d., accessed November 1, 2017, http://www.distraction.gov/con tent/get-the-facts/state-laws.html.

27. Ira Teinowitz, "Pediatricians Demand Cuts in Children-Targeted Advertising: Doctors' Group Asks Federal Government to Impose Severe Limits," Advertising Age, December 4, 2006, accessed June 29, 2011, http://adage.com/print?article_id=113558.

28. NBC Connecticut, "Dozens of Girls Rescued in Cross-Country Sex-Trafficking Sweep," July 2013, accessed July 29, 2013, http://www.nbcbayarea.com/news/national-international/Dozens-of-girls-rescued-in-cross-country-child-sex-trafficking-sweep-217421071.html.

29. World Health Organization, "Tobacco," May 2017, accessed November 1, 2017, http://www.who.int/mediacentre/factsheets/fs339/en/.

30. Alan R. Andreasen and Philip Kotler, Strategic Marketing for Non-profit Organizations, 6th ed. (Upper Saddle River, NJ: Prentice Hall, 2003), 490.

31. Alan R. Andreasen, Social Marketing in the 21st Century (Thousand Oaks, CA: SAGE, 2006), 11.

32. Philip Kotler and Nancy R. Lee, Marketing in the Public Sector: A Roadmap for Improved Performance (Upper Saddle River, NJ: Wharton School, 2006).

33. Nancy R. Lee, Michael L. Rothschild and William Smith, A Declaration of Social Marketing's Unique Principles and Distinctions (unpublished manuscript, March 2011).

CHAPTER 2

1. Personal Communication From Heidi Keller, Keller Consulting, 2016.

2. EPA, "WaterSense2020 Accomplishments Report," accessed December 4, 2021, https://www.epa.gov/sites/default/files/2021-06/documents/ws-aboutus-2020-watersense-accomplishments-report.pdf.

3. EPA, "About WaterSense," accessed December 4, 2021, http://www.gao.gov/products/GAO-14-430.

4. EPA WaterSense, "Every Drop Counts: 2006 Accomplishments," accessed December 4, 2021, https://www.epa.gov/watersense/watersense-accomplishment-reports.

5. New Reference Will be Provided by March 2022.

6. Responsible Bathroom, "The Stream-Blue Success Stories. The Results Are in: Serenbe WaterSense Conversion Reduces Household Water Usage 27%," accessed August 1, 2013, http://responsiblebathroom.com/education/stream/blue-success-stories/serenbe-watersense-conversion-reduces-household-water-usage/.

7. EPA, "Start Saving," accessed December 2021, https://www.epa.gov/watersense/start-saving#save-indoors.

8. EPA, "Residential Toilets," accessed November 22, 2017, https://www.epa.gov/watersense/residential-toilets.

9. EPA WaterSense, "Start Saving," accessed December 4, 2021.

10. EPA, "Residential Toilets," accessed December 22, 2020, https://www.epa.gov/watersense/residential-toilets.

11. EPA, "WaterSense2020 Accomplishments Report," accessed December 4, 2021.

12. Idid.

13. Sonya A. Grier and Sonja Martin Pool, "Will Social Marekting Fight for Black Lives? An Open Letter to the Field," Social Marekting Quarterly 26, no. 4 (December 2020): 378–87.

14. Philip Kotler and Nancy R. Lee, Marketing in the Public Sector (Upper Saddle River, NJ: Wharton School, 2006), 283–84.

15. Washington State Department of Ecology, "Litter Campaign," 2006, accessed October 10, 2006, http://www.ecy.wa.gov/programs/swfa/litter/campaign.html.

16. Washington State Department of Ecology, Washington 2004 State Litter Study: Litter Generation and Composition Report (Olympia, WA: Author, March 2005).
17. Al Ries and Jack Trout, Positioning: The Battle for Your Mind (New York, NY: Warner Books, 1986), 2.
18. Philip Kotler and Nancy Lee, Marketing in the Public Sector, 113.
19. Alan R. Andreasen, Marketing Research That Won't Break the Bank (San Francisco, CA: Jossey-Bass, 2002).

CHAPTER 3

1. Alan R. Andreasen, Marketing Research That Won't Break the Bank (San Francisco, CA: Jossey-Bass, 2002), 6–11.
2. League of Women Voters of the St. Petersburg Area, "Behavior Change Marketing Campaign: Democracy Starts at Home (VOTE-BY-MAIL)," 2020, accessed December 30, 2021, https://lwvspa.org/wp-content/uploads/Election-2020-Report-1.pdf.
3. Ibid.
4. Philip Kotler and Gary Armstrong, Principles of Marketing, 9th ed. (Upper Saddle River, NJ: Prentice Hall, 2001), 140.
5. Ibid.
6. Ibid.
7. WA Traffic Safety Commission, "Seat Belt Use in Washington State, 2019," accessed April 7, 2022, http://wtsc.wa.gov/wp-content/uploads/dlm_uploads/2020/02/Washington-2019-Seat-Belt-Use-Report.pdf.
8. Alan R. Andreasen, Marketing Social Change: Changing Behavior to Promote Health, Social Development, and the Environment (San Francisco, CA: Jossey-Bass, 1995), 120.
9. Ibid., 127.
10. Philip Kotler and Gary Armstrong, Principles of Marketing, 141.
11. Craig R. Lefebvre, Message Posted to the Georgetown Social Marketing Listserve, January 21, 2007.
12. Philip Kotler and Gary Armstrong, Principles of Marketing, 152.
13. Caitlin Roper Science, "The Human Element: Melinda Gates and Paul Farmer on Designing Global Health," 2013, accessed November 28, 2017, https://www.wired.com/2013/11/2112gatefarmers/.
14. Philip Kotler and Gary Armstrong, Principles of Marketing, 146.
15. Ibid., 144.
16. Philip Kotler, Marketing Insights From A to Z (New York, NY: Wiley, 2003), 117–8.
17. OlsonZaltman Associates, "Success Stories," n.d., accessed August 9, 2013, http://www.olsonzaltman.com/process.htm.
18. Philip Kotler and Nancy R. Lee, Marketing in the Public Sector: A Roadmap for Improved Performance (Upper Saddle River, NJ: Wharton School, 2007), 259.
19. Hyunyi Cho and Kim Witte, "Managing Fear in Public Health Cam-paigns: A Theory-Based Formative Evaluation Process," Health Promo-tion Practice 6, no. 4 (2005): 483–90.
20. Kim Witte, "Putting the Fear Back Into Fear Appeals: The Extended Parallel Process Model," Communication Monographs 59 (1992): 329–49.
21. Hyunyi Cho and Witte Kim, Managing Fear, 484.
22. Ibid., 484–89.
23. Alan R. Andreasen, Marketing Social Change, 101.
24. Judit Sarai Alvarado, et al., "Using Formative Research to Develop a Social Marketing Campaign to Understand Food Shopping Behaviors in Young Mothers," Social Marketing Quarterly 28, no. 1 (2022): 44–56. Using Formative Research.
25. Ibid., 47.
26. Alan R. Andreasen, Marketing Research That Won't Break the Bank, 75.
27. Ibid., 108.

28. Ibid., 120.

29. Ibid., 167.

30. Information Provided November 2017, to Nancy Lee by Sigrid Reinert, Suicide Prevention Specialist, Injury & Violence Prevention, Washington State Department of Health.

31. Washington State Department of Health, "Healthy Youth Survey," 2014, accessed November 24, 2017, https://www.doh.wa.gov/DataandStatisticalReports/DataSystems/HealthyYouthSurvey.

32. Ibid.

33. Washington State Department of Health, "We All Make Us Strong," 2021, accessed December 30, 2021, https://medium.com/wadepthealth/for-native-americans-connection-and-identity-help-protect-against-suicide-a5c7f8aad3ed.

CHAPTER 4

1. Naohiro Matsumura, Renate Fruchter, and Larry Leifer, "Shikakeology: Designing Triggers for Behavior Change," October 2014, accessed January 24, 2018, https://link.springer.com/article/10.1007/s00146-014-0556-5.

2. Ibid.

3. Richard H. Thaler and Cass R. Sustein, Nudge (New York, NY: Penguin Books, 2009), 268.

4. Craig R. Lefebvre, Social Marketing and Social Change (San Francisco, CA: Jossey-Bass, 2012), 98.

5. Stephanie Simon, "The Secret to Turning Consumers Green," The Wall Street Journal, October 18, 2010, accessed July 16, 2011, http://online.wsj.com/article/SB10001424052748704575304575296243891721972.html.

6. James O. Prochaska and Carlo C. DiClemente, "Stages and Processes of Self-Change of Smoking: Toward an Integrative Model of Change," Journal of Consulting and Clinical Psychology 51 (1983): 390–95.

7. James O. Prochaska, John C. Norcross, and Carlo C. DiClemente, Changing for Good (New York, NY: Avon Books, 1994), 40–1.

8. Ibid., 40–1.

9. Ibid., 40–1.

10. Ibid., 41–3.

11. Ibid., 43.

12. Ibid., 44.

13. Dikla Shmueli and Judith J. Prochaska, "Resisting Tempting Foods and Smoking Behavior: Implications From a Self-Control Theory Perspective," Health Psychology 28, no. 3 (2009): 300–6.

14. Bonnie Spring, et al., "Randomized Controlled Trial for Behavioral Smoking and Weight Control Treatment: Effect of Concurrent Versus Sequential Intervention," Journal of Consulting and Clinical Psychology 72 (2004): 785–96.

15. Edwin A. Locke, "Toward a Theory of Task Motivation and Incentives," Organizational Behavior and Human Performance 2, no. 3 (1968): 157–89.

16. Doug McKenzie-Mohr, Fostering Sus-tainable Behavior: An Introduction to Community-Based Social Marketing (Gabriola Island, BC: New Society, 2011), 45.

17. Ibid., 45.

18. CDC, "About Social Determinants of Health," 2021, accessed January 3, 2021, https://www.cdc.gov/socialdeterminants/about.html.

19. K. R. M. Brown, "Health Belief Model," 1999, accessed April 2, 2001, http://www.hsc.usf.edu/-kmbrown/Health_Belief_Model_Overview.htm.

20. United States Department of Health and Human Services, National Institutes of Health, National Heart Lung and Blood Institute, "National High Blood Pressure Education Program (NHBPEP)," n.d., accessed September 18, 2001, http://hin.nhlbi.nih.gov/nhbpep_kit_about_m.htm.

21. Ibid.

22. Ibid.

23. Ibid.

24. Icek Ajzen, "The Theory of Planned Behavior," Organizational Behavior and Human Decision Processes 50 (1991): 179–211.

25. Karen Glanz, B. Rimer, and K. Viswanath, Health Behavior and Health Education: Theory, Research, and Practice, "Introduction," 4th ed., n.d., accessed February 5, 2018, http://www.med.upenn.edu/hbhe4/part2-ch4-introduction.shtml.

26. Alan R. Andreasen, Marketing Social Change: Changing Behavior to Promote Health, Social Development, and the Environment (San Francisco, CA: Jossey-Bass, 1995), 266–8.

27. Ibid., 266–8.

28. Service-Dominant Logic [website], http://www.sdlogic.net/.

29. "Interview With Mechai Viravaidya," July 23, 2007, CNN.com/Asia, accessed December 17, 2013, http://edition.cnn.com/2007/WORLD/asiapcf/07/22/talk asia.viravaidya/index.html? iref=allsearch.

30. ChangingMinds.org, "Social Norms," n.d., accessed December 18, 2013, http://changingminds.org/explanations/theories/social_norms.htm.

31. Personal communication, 2001.

32. Carolyn Moore "Research Improves Handwashing Programs by Uncovering Drivers of Behavior Change," October 2017, accessed January 25, 2018, https://globalhandwashing.or g/research-improves-handwashing - programs-by-uncovering-drivers-of-behavior-change/.

33. Ibid.

34. Lisa Schuster, Krzysztof Kubacki, and Sharyn Rundle-Thiele, "Community-Based Social Marketing: Effects on Social Norms," Journal of Social Marketing 6, no. 2 (2016): 193–210.

35. Walk Safely to School Day (website), July 1, 2020, accessed April 7, 2022, https://www.walk.com.au/WSTSD/images/elements/contentpics/2020/2020_Walk_Safely_to_School_Day_Media_Release.pdf.

36. Jay Grizzell, "Behavior Change Theories and Models," n.d., accessed June 9, 2008, http://www.csupomona.edu/~jvgriz zell/best_practices/betheory. html#Ecological%20Approaches.

37. Philip Kotler and Nancy R. Lee, Up and Out of Poverty: The Social Marketing Approach (Upper Saddle River, NJ: Wharton School, 2009), 151.

38. Bill Smith, "Behavioral Economics and Social Marketing: New Allies in the War on Absent Behavior," Social Marketing Quarterly XVI, no. 2 (Summer 2010): 137–41.

39. Philip Kotler, "Behavioural Economics or Social Marketing? The Latter!," The Sunday Times, May 22, 2011, accessed December 28, 2013, http://www.sundaytimes.lk/110522/BusinessTimes/bt36.html.

40. Richard H. Thaler and Cass R. Sunstein, Nudge: Improving Decisions About Health, Wealth, and Happiness (New York, NY: Penguin Group, 2009), 180–1.

41. Jeff French, "Why 'Nudges' Are Seldom Enough," Strategic Social Marketing (2010).

42. Personal communication from Daniel Read, February 6, 2018.

43. Ibid.

44. Duhigg Charles, "Warning: Habits May Be Good for You," The New York Times, July 13, 2008, accessed July 16, 2011, http://www.nytimes.com/2008/07/13/business/13habit.html.

45. Learn Marketing.net, "Hierarchy of Effects Model," n.d., accessed December 17, 2013, http://www.learnmarketing.net/hierarchy_of_effects_model.html.

46. College of Natural Sciences, Tri-Ethnic Center, "Community Readiness Model," n.d., accessed December 17, 2013, http://triethniccenter.colostate.edu/communityReadiness.htm.

47. Carol A. Bryant, et al., "Community-Based Prevention Marketing: A New Planning Framework for Designing and Tailoring Health Promotion Interventions," in Emerging Theories in Health Promotion Practice and Research: Strategies for Improving Public Health, 2nd ed., eds. DiClemente, R., Crosby, R.A., Kegler, M.C. (San Francisco, CA: Jossey-Bass, 2009).

48. Carol A. Bryant, et al., "A Social Marketing Approach for Increasing Community Coalitions' Adoption of Evidence-Based Policy to Combat Obesity," Social Marketing Quarterly 20, no. 4 (2014): 219–46.

49. Brian J. Biroscak, et al., "Social Marketing and Policy Making: Tools for Community-Based Policy Advocacy," Social Marketing Quarterly 21, no. 4 (2015): 249–59, doi: 10.1177/1524500415609880.

50. Brian J. Biroscak, et al., "From Concept to Action: Integration of Systems Thinking and Social Marketing for Health Disparities Elimination," in Social Marketing: From Tunes to Symphonies, 3rd ed., eds. G. Hastings and C. Domegan (New York, NY: Routledge, 2017).

51. Washington State Department of Health, "Emergency Language and Outreach Service Contracts," n.d., accessed January 14, 2002, https://www.doh.wa.gov/Emergencies/COVID19/CommunityOutreachContracts.

52. Michael L. Rothschild, "Carrots, Sticks, and Promises: A Conceptual Framework for the Management of Public Health and Social Issue Behaviors," Journal of Marketing 63 (October 1999): 24–37, accessed December 31, 2013, http://www.social-marketing.org/papers/carrot article.pdf.

53. Ibid, 24.

54. Ibid., 25–26.

55. Matsumura, Fruchter, and Leifer, "Shikakeology."

56. Martin Fishbein, in Developing Effective Behavior Change Interventions (pp. 5–6), as quoted in The Communication Initiative, Summary of Change Theories and Models (Slide 6), accessed April 2, 2001, http://www.comminit.com/power_point/change_theories/sld005.htm.

57. World Bank, "Population 2016," n.d., accessed January 29, 2018, http://databank.worldbank.org/data/download/POP.pdf.

58. Marie Ng, et al., "Global, Regional, and National Prevalence of Overweight and Obesity in Children and Adults During 1980–2018: A Systematic Analysis for the Global Burden of Disease Study 2013," The Lancet 384, no. 9945 (August 30, 2014): 766–81.

59. I. Ajzen, "Theory of Planned Behavior."

CHAPTER 5

1. Kimberly S George, et al., "Our Health Is in Our Hands: A Social Marketing Campaign to Combat Obesity and Diabetes," American Journal of Health Promotion 30, no. 4 (2016): 283–6. doi:10.1177/0890117116639559.

2. Sharpe, "U.S. Obesity Rate Climbing in 2013," Gallup, November 1, 2013, accessed January 31, 2022, https://news.gallup.com/poll/165671/obesity-rate-climbing-2013.aspx.

3. J. Harris and W. Frazier III, Rudd Center and Council on Black Health, "Increasing Disparities in Unhealthy Food Advertising Targeted to Hispanic & Black youth," January 2019, accessed January 31, 2022, https://media.ruddcenter.uconn.edu/PDFs/TargetedMarketingReport2019.pdf.

4. Ibid., page 2.

5. Ibid., page 2.

6. Ibid., page 2.

7. Edward Wong, "China's Plan to Curb Air Pollution Sets Limits on Coal Use and Vehicles," The New York Times, September 12, 2013, accessed September 19, 2013, http://www.nytimes.com/2013/09/13/world/asia/china-releases-plan-to-reduce-air-pollution.html?_r=0.

8. Ibid.

9. Ibid.

10. REUTERS, "China Says Average National Smog Levels Down 9/1% in 2021," January 2022, accessed April 11, 2022, China says average national smog levels down 9.1% in 2021 | Reuters.

11. C. Qide, "Campaign to Teach Kids About Road Safety," China Daily, April 1, 2004, accessed November 20, 2006, http://www.chinadaily.com.cn/english/doc/2004-04/01/content_319588.htm.

12. David Foster Wallace, "Plain Old Untrendy Troubles and Emotions," 2008, accessed July 2016, https://www.theguardian.com/books/2008/sep/20/fiction.

13. Personal communication from Christine Domegan, February 21, 2018.

14. U.S. Energy Information Administration, "International Energy Outlook 2013," July 25, 2013, accessed September 19, 2013, http://www.eia.gov/forecasts/ieo/world.cfm.

15. Q. Quanlin, "Campaign Aims to Smoke Out Young Addicts," China Daily, May 30, 2006, 1–5.

16. CHINA CDC WEEKLY, "Current Progress and Challenges to Tobacco Control in China", February 11, 2022, accessed Aprill 11, 2022, https://www.ncbi.nlm.nih.gov/pmc/articles/PMC8844520/.

17. L. Qi, "Pets Bring Host of Problems," China Daily, May 29, 2006, 5.

18. Feng, "Current Anti-smoking Efforts," 1, 5.

19. K. Holder, "China Road," UCDAVIS Magazine Online, 2006, accessed November 28, 2006, http://www-ucdmag.ucdavis.edu/current/feature_2.html.

20. Personal Communication from Christine Domegan referencing a case study: "Waves of Change: Collaborative Design for Tomorrow's World."

21. NIH, "Our Health Is in Our Hands: A Social Marketing Campaign to Combat Obesity and Diabetes," March 2016, accessed January 31, 2022, Our Health Is in Our Hands: A Social Marketing Campaign to Combat Obesity and Diabetes - PubMed (nih.gov).

22. Julia E. Carins, Sharyn R. Rundle-Thiele, and Joy E. Parkinson, "Delivering Healthy Food Choice: A Dual-Process Model Enquiry," Social Marketing Quarterly 23 (September 2017): 266–83.

23. Ibid.

24. Julia E. Carins, Sharyn R. Rundle-Thiele, and Joy E. Parkinson, "A Picture Says a Thousand Words: A Food Selection Observational Method," Health Promotion Journal Australia 27, no. 2 (2016): 94–101.

25. Julia E. Carins, Sharyn R. Rundle-Thiele and Joy E. Parkinson, "Delivering Healthy Food Choice: A Dual-Process Model Enquiry," Social Marketing Quarterly 23 (September 2017): 279.

CHAPTER 6

1. State of Oregon, DEQ "Food Environmental Impacts and Actions," January 2022, accessed January 13, 2022, https://www.oregon.gov/deq/mm/food/Pages/Food-Rescue.aspx.

2. DEQ, "Oregon DEQ Strategic Plan for Preventing the Wasting of Food," March 2017, accessed January 13, 2022, https://www.oregon.gov/deq/FilterDocs/foodstrategic.pdf.

3. Tools of Change, "Fork It Over!," 2005, accessed January 13, 2022, https://www.toolsofchange.com/en/case-studies/detail/166.

4. Ibid.

5. Ibid.

6. Waste Not Food Taxi, "Our Work," n.d., accessed January 13, 2022, www.wastenotfoodtaxi.org/our-work.html.

7. Tools of Change, "Fork it Over!," 2005, accessed January 13, 2022, https://www.toolsofchange.com/en/case-studies/detail/166.

8. Ibid.

9. DEQ, "Oregon DEQ Strategic Plan for Preventing the Wasting of Food," March 2017, 14.
10. StopWaste, "4Rs Student Action Projects," n.d., accessed January 13, 2022, http://www.stopwaste.org/recycling/schools/4rs-student-action-project.
11. West Coast Climate & Materials Management Forum, "Fork it Over in the Portland Public School System," n.d., accessed January 13, 2022, https://westcoastclimateforum.com/cfpt/fork-it-over-portland-public-school-system.
12. Philip Kotler and Gary M. Armstrong, Principles of Marketing (Upper Saddle River, NJ: Prentice Hall, 2001), 265.
13. Ibid., 244.
14. Philip Kotler and Gary M. Armstrong, Principles of Marketing, 253–9.
15. James O. Prochaska and Carlo C. DiClemente, "Stages and Processes of Self-Change of Smoking: Toward an Integrative Model of Change," Journal of Consulting and Clinical Psychology 51 (1983): 390–5.
16. James O. Prochaska, John C. Norcross, and Carlo C. DiClemente, Changing for Good (New York, NY: Avon Books, 1994), 40–56.
17. Ibid., 40–1.
18. Ibid., 40–1.
19. Ibid., 41–3.
20. Ibid., 44.
21. Ibid., 45.
22. Ibid., 46.
23. Ibid., 47.
24. Personal communication from Edward Maibach to Nancy Lee, October 30, 2013.
25. Leiserowitz Anthony and Edward W. Maibach, Global Warming's "Six Americas": An Audience Segmentation (Fairfax, ON: George Mason University, Center for Climate Change Communication, 2010).
26. Philip Kotler and Kevin Lane Keller, Marketing Management (Upper Saddle River, NJ: Prentice Hall, 2006), 251–2.
27. Benjamin M and W. Tsui, "Generation Next," Advertising Age 72, no. 3, (January 1, 2001): 14–6; Anna Liotta, Resultance Incorporated, www.resultance.com.
28. Wikipedia, "Generation Alpha," n.d., accessed January 19, 2022, Generation Alpha - Wikipedia.
29. Philip Kotler and Kevin Lane Keller, Marketing Management, 251–2.
30. Philip Kotler and Eduardo L. Roberto, Social Marketing: Strategies for Changing Public Behavior (New York, NY: Free Press, 1989), 149.
31. Alan R. Andreasen, Marketing Social Change: Changing Behavior to Promote Health, Social Development, and the Environment (San Francisco, CA: Jossey-Bass, 1995), 148.
32. Ibid., 177–9.
33. ABC News, "As Variant Rises, Vaccine Plan Targets 'Movable Middle,'" June 27, 2021, accessed January 17, 2022, As variant rises, vaccine plan targets 'movable middle' - ABC News (go.com).
34. Police Executive Research Forum, "Reducing Gun Violence: What Works, and What Can Be Done Now," March 2019, accessed January 19, 2022, https://www.policeforum.org/assets/reducinggunviolence.pdf.
35. Ibid., 4.
36. Ibid., 4.
37. Ibid., 17.
38. Ibid., 3.
39. Ibid., 28.
40. Ibid., 35.
41. Ibid., 41.
42. Ibid., 46.

CHAPTER 7

1. Washington State Department of Natural Resources Website, accessed March 3, 2022, https://www.dnr.wa.gov/news/commissioner-franz-kicks-%E2%80%98wildfire-ready-neighbors%E2%80%99-spokane-county-help-protect-homes.
2. Pacific Northwest Social Marketing Association Fall Forum: Reducing Wildfire Risk Through Community Action, September 8, 2022, presenters: Hilary Franz, Washington State Commissioner of Public Lands and Molly Brumley, Senior VP at C+C.
3. Project Smart, "Smart Goals," n.d., accessed August 11, 2007, http://www.projectsmart.co.uk/smart-goals.html.
4. National Social Marketing Centre, Effectively Engaging people: Views From the World Social Marketing Conference 2008 (2008), 8, accessed July 15, 2011, http://www.tcp-events.co.uk/wsmc/downloads/NSMC_Effectively_engaging_people_conference_version.pdf.
5. Climate Crisis, "Ten Things to Do," n.d., accessed 2006, http://www.climatecrisis.net/pdf/10things.pdf.
6. Personal communication from Doug McKenzie-Mohr, January 27, 2018.
7. Sonya A. Grier and Sonja Martin Pool, "Will Social Marketing Fight for Black Lives? An Open Letter to the Field," Social Marketing Quarterly 26, no. 4 (December 2020): 378–87.
8. U.S. Department of Health and Human Services, Office of Disease Prevention and Health Promotion, Healthy People 2020, ODPHP Publication No. B0132, November 2010, www.healthypeople.gov.
9. Shore Friendly, "Protecting Your Property and Puget Sound," n.d., accessed December 28, 2017, http://www.shorefriendly.org/.
10. Personal communication from Margaret McKeown, Washington Department of Fish and Wildlife, February 8, 2018.
11. Washington Department of Fish and Wildlife, "Shore Friendly Grant Program," 2022, accessed January 27, 2022, Shore Friendly Grant Program | Washington Department of Fish & Wildlife.

CHAPTER 8

1. CDC, "Surgeon General's Advisory on E-cigarette Use Among Youth," April 9, 2019, accessed March 1, 2022, https://www.cdc.gov/tobacco/basic_information/e-cigarettes/surgeon-general-advisory/index.html.
2. Kaitlyn M. Berry, et al., "Association of Electronic Cigarette Use With Subsequent Initiation of Tobacco Cigarettes in US Youths," JAMA Network Open 2, no. 2 (2019): e187794. https://doi.org/10.1001/jamanetworkopen.2018.7794.
3. Tracy T. Smith, et al., "Intention to Quit Vaping Among United States Adolescents," JAMA Pediatrics 175, no. 1 (2021): 97–9. https://doi.org/10.1001/jamapediatrics.2020.2348.
4. Personal communications from Rescue Agency, March 2022.
5. Richard P. Bagozzi, "Marketing as Exchange: A Theory of Transactions in the Marketplace," American Behavioral Scientist 21 (March/April 1978): 535–56.
6. Philip Kotler, "A Generic Concept of Marketing," Journal of Marketing 36 (April 1967): 46–54.
7. Philip Kotler and Sidney J. Levy, "Broadening the Concept of Marketing," Journal of Marketing 33 (January 1999): 10–5.
8. Richard P. Bagozzi, "Marketing as an Organized Behavioral System of Exchange," Journal of Marketing 38 (1974): 77–81; Bagozzi, "Marketing as Exchange.".
9. Doug McKenzie-Mohr, "Community Based Social Marketing: Quick Reference," (n.d.), accessed January 30, 2007, http://www.cbsm.com/Reports/CBSM.pdf.

10. Philip Kotler and Nancy R. Lee, Marketing in the Public Sector: A Roadmap for Improved Performance (Upper Saddle River, NJ: Wharton School, 2006), 199.

11. Adapted from the Marketing Highlight, "Save the Crabs. Then Eat 'em (2005–2006)," by Bill Smith, in the 3rd edition of this book (pp. 4–7).

12. U.S. Department of Health and Human Services, "Public Service Campaign to Promote Breast-feeding Awareness Launched," [Press release], June 4, 2007, accessed April 6, 2007, http://www.hhs.gov/news/press/2004pres/20040604.html.

13. U.S. Department of Health and Human Services, "National Breastfeeding Awareness Cam-paign: Babies Are Born to Be Breastfed," 2005, accessed April 2007, http://www.4woman.gov/breastfeeding/index.cfm? page=campaign.

14. The National Women's Health Information Center (womenshealth.gov), a service of the Office on Women's Health in the U.S. Department of Health and Human Services.

15. Centers for Disease Control and Prevention, "Breastfeeding Report Card–United States, 2016," n.d., accessed February 22, 2018, https://www.cdc.gov/breastfeeding/pdf/2016breastfeedingreportcard.pdf.

16. Sue Peattie and Ken Peattie, "Ready to Fly Solo? Reducing Social Marketing's Dependence on Commercial Marketing Theory," Marketing Theory Articles 3, no. 3 (2003): 365–85.

17. Doug McKenzie-Mohr and William Smith, Fostering Sustainable Behavior: An Introduction to Community-Based Social Marketing (Gabriola Island, BC: New Society, 1999), 5.

18. The Humane Society, Tacoma and Pierce County, "Kittenkaboodle," n.d., accessed October 25, 2006, http://thehumanesociety.org/2006/09/kittenkaboodle/.

19. Case source: Nancy Lee, Social Marketing Services, Inc.

20. Philip Kotler and Eduardo L. Roberto, Social Marketing: Strategies for Changing Public Behavior (New York, NY: Free Press, 1989), 102.

21. Alan R. Andreasen, Marketing Social Change: Changing Behavior to Promote Health, Social Development, and the Environment (San Francisco, CA: Jossey-Bass, 1995), 108–9.

22. March of Dimes, "United States: Quick Facts: Folic Acid Overview," 2001, accessed December 23, 2010, http://www.marchofdimes.com/peristats/tlanding.aspx?reg=99&top=13&l ev=0&slev=1%20.

23. Personal email communication from Michael Jortner, May 2013.

24. This case was taken from a draft of a social marketing plan for the Washington Department of Health, 2006. Ilene Silver, lead project manager.

25. "25Institutional Review Board," Wikipedia, n.d., accessed January 16, 2007, http://en.wikipedia.org/wiki/Institutional_Review_Board.

26. Seattle Times, "Most of Seattle Area's 200,000 Unvaccinated Adults Say They Will 'Definitely Not' Get COVID Shots", January 2022, accessed February 22, 2022, "Most of Seattle area's 200,000 unvaccinated adults say they will 'definitely not' get COVID shots | The Seattle Times.

27. Ibid.

28. John A. Staley, "Get Firefighters Moving: Marketing a Physical Fitness Intervention to Reduce Sudden Cardiac Death Risk in Full-Time Firefighters," Social Marketing Quarterly XV, no. 4 (2009): 85–98.

29. Ibid. 85.

30. Ibid. 96–7.

CHAPTER 9

1. Al Ries and Jack Trout, Positioning: The Battle for Your Mind (New York, NY: Warner Books, 1982), 3.

2. https://climate.nasa.gov/effects/.

3. https://www.energystar.gov/sites/default/files/tools/ES_20th_Anniv_brochure_spreads.pdf.
4. https://www.energystar.gov/sites/default/files/tools/ES%20Anniv%20Book_508compliant_toEPA051412.pdf.
5. Ibid.
6. Ibid.
7. Ibid.
8. https://www.energystar.gov/about/origins_mission/impacts.
9. Ibid.
10. https://cee1.org/content/national-awareness-energy-star-surveys.
11. https://www.energystar.gov/partner_resources/utilities_eeps/es_partnership.
12. Adapted from Philip Kotler and Kevin Lane Keller, Marketing Management, 12th ed. (Upper Saddle River, NJ: Prentice Hall, 2005), 320.
13. Philip Kotler and Kevin Lane Keller, Marketing Management.
14. Ibid., 312–3.
15. Nancy R. Lee, Policymaking for Citizen Behavior Change: A Social Marketing Approach (London: Routledge, 2018), 96–7.
16. Washington State Department of Health, "Tobacco Quitline," 2007, accessed January 22, 2007, http://www.quitline.com/.
17. Nancy R. Lee, Policymaking for Citizen Behavior Change, 78–9.
18. Michael L. Rothschild, The Impact of Road Crew on Crashes, Fatalities, and Costs, June 2007, available upon request from roadcrew@mascomm.net; Show Case, "Road Crew," n.d., accessed July 29, 2011, http://www.thensmc.com/resources/showcase/road-crew?view=all.
19. Philip Kotler and Gary M. Armstrong, Principles of Marketing, 9th ed. (Upper Saddle River, NJ: Prentice Hall, 2001), 273–5.
20. Michael Moss, "Broccoli's Image Makeover," The New York Times Magazine, November 13, 2013, 30–5.
21. Ibid., 32.
22. Bill Smith, "Social Marketing: Marketing With No Budget," Social Marketing Quarterly 5, no. 2 (June 1999): 7–8.
23. CIVIQS National Black Lives Matter Poll, April 25, 2017 – April 18, 2022, accessed April 19, 2022, https://civiqs.com/results/black_lives_matter?annotations=true&uncertainty=true&zoomIn=true.
24. Axios, "Black Lives Matter Co-founder Explains "Defund the Police" Slogan," June 7, 2020, accessed April 19, 2022, https://www.axios.com/defund-police-black-lives-matter-7007efac-0b24-44e2-a45c-c7f180c17b2e.html.
25. Media Cause, "The Problem With "Defund the Police" Isn't Policy, it's Branding," June 20, 2020, accessed April 19, 2022, https://mediacause.com/the-problem-with-defund-the-police-isnt-policy-its-branding/.
26. Carley N Gemelli, et al., "Evaluation of the Impact of a Personalized Postdonation Short Messaging Service on the Retention of Whole Blood Donors," Transfusion 58, no. 3 (March 2018): 701–9.
27. Ibid., 702.
28. Ibid., 708.
29. Ibid., 705.
30. ABC NEWS, "Blood Texts Aim to Encourage People to Donate More Often to Save Lives," April 29, 2017, accessed March 3, 2022, https://www.abc.net.au/news/2017-04-30/blood-texts-encourage-donors-to-give-again-red-cross-brisbane/8482366.
31. Ibid. 707.

CHAPTER 10

1. Matt Bershadker, "Animal Shelter Outcomes Are Improving," Huffington Post, March 20, 2017, accessed March 14, 2018,

https://www.huffingtonpost.com/entry/are-animal-shelter-outcomes-improving_us_58cfff2ae4b0537abd957323.

2. Ibid.
3. The Humane Society of the United States, "Pets by the Numbers," n.d., accessed March 14, 2018, https://www.animalsheltering.org/page/pets-by-the-numbers.
4. American Society for the Prevention of Cruelty to Animals, "Pet Statistics," n.d., accessed January 8, 2014, http://www.aspca.org/about-us/faq/pet--statistics.aspx.
5. Priority Ventures Group, "Animal Impact," n.d., accessed January 16, 2014, http://priorityventures.com.
6. Maddie's Fund, "The Shelter Pet Project by the Numbers—and Something More," 2009, accessed January 10, 2014, http://www.maddiesfund.org/Maddies_Institute/Articles/The_Shelter_Pet_Project_By_the_Numbers.html.
7. ASPCA, "Meet Your Match," n.d., accessed March 14, 2018, https://www.aspcapro.org/research/meet-your-match-0.
8. ASPCA, "Meet Your Match Pet Program," n.d., accessed March 9, 2022, https://www.aspcapro.org/resource/meet-your-match-pet-adoption-program.
9. Meet Your Match Saves Lives, accessed January 16, 2014, http://aspcapro.org/meet-your-match-saves-lives.
10. Philip Kotler and Kevin Lane Keller, Marketing Management, 12th ed. (Upper Saddle River, NJ: Prentice Hall, 2005), 372.
11. Ibid.
12. Philip Kotler and Gary M. Armstrong, Principles of Marketing, 9th ed. (Upper Saddle River, NJ: Prentice Hall, 2001), 291.
13. Ibid., 294.
14. Ibid.
15. Centers for Disease Control and Prevention, "Infant Mortality," n.d., accessed January 6, 2014, http://www.cdc.gov/reproductivehealth/maternalinfanthealth/infantmortality.htm.
16. Centers for Disease Control and Prevention, "National Prematurity Awareness Month," n.d., accessed January 6, 2014, http://www.cdc.gov/features/prematurebirth/.
17. Philip Kotler and Eduardo L. Roberto, Social Marketing: Strategies for Changing Public Behavior (New York, NY: Free Press, 1989), 156.
18. Business Standard, "Global Handwashing Day: Low-Cost 'Social' Robot Teachers Kerala Children Hygiene Lessons," October 15, 2019, accessed April 27, 2022, https://www.business-standard.com/article/pti-stories/global-handwashing-day-low-cost-social-robot-teaches-kerala-children-hygiene-lessons-119101500859_1.html.
19. Edelman Adam, "Engineers in India Create Electronic Rape-Preventing Underwear, GPS Included," New York Daily News, April 2, 2013, http://www.nydailynews.com/life-style/health/engineers-create-rape-preventing-underwear-article-1.1305842.
20. N. Garun, "Three Engineer Students Invent an Electronic Anti-rape Undergarment," Digital Trends, April 3, 2013, accessed January 6, 2014, http://www.digitaltrends.com/home/three-engineer-students-invent-an-electrifying-anti-rape-undergarment/.
21. Information for this example was provided by Ingrid Donato, chief of the Mental Health Promotion Branch of the Center for Mental Health Services (CMHS) at the Substance Abuse and Mental Health Services Association (SAMHSA) under Task Order No. HHSS2832007000271/HH SS28342001T, directed by contracting officer's representative Anne Mathews-Younes. Contri-buting authors include Ingrid Donato, SAMHSA, CMHS; James Wright, SAMHSA, CMHS; Erin Reiney, HRSA; Katie Gorscak, ASPA; Stephanie Rapp, Department of Justice; Sharon Burton, Department of Education; and Alana Vivolo, CDC. SAMHSA has assisted in the development of the

SAMHSA Bullying Prevention App by IQ Solutions, Inc.

22. "Don't Turn a Night Out into a Nightmare," n.d., accessed March 15, 2018, http://www.drinkingnightmare.gov.au/internet/drinkingnightmare/publishing.nsf/Content/game.

23. B. Chakravorty, as quoted in B. Chakravorty, "Product Substitution for Social Marketing of Behaviour Change: A Conceptualization," Social Marketing Quarterly (1996): 5, accessed July 19, 2011, http://degraysystems.com/aedmichael/Vol%203/3-2/Full%20Text/III.2.Chakravorty.pdf.

24. Philip Kotler and Eduardo L. Roberto, Social Marketing, 155–7.

25. Philip Kotler, My Adventures in Marketing: The Autobiography of Philip Kotler (Chicago, IL: Idea Bite Press, 2017), 169–72.

26. KidZania, "What is KidZania?" 2021, accessed March 24, 2022, https://kidzania.com/en.

27. Doug McKenzie-Mohr and William Smith, Fostering Sustainable Behavior: An Introduction to Community-Based Social Marketing, 2nd ed. (Gabriola Island, BC: New Society, 1999), 156.

28. Opower, "About Us," n.d., accessed January 26, 2011, http://www.opower.com/Company/AboutUs.aspx.

29. Opower, "Special Delivery: Energy Savings," n.d., accessed January 26, 2011, http://www.opower.com/Products/HomeEnergyReport.aspx.

30. M. Trost, "A Call for 'Design Thinking': Tim Brown on TED.com," TED Blog, July 2009, accessed January 7, 2014, http://blog.ted.com/2009/09/29/a_call_for_desi/.

31. Philip Kotler and Gary Armstrong, Principles of Marketing, 301.

32. "Drug Test Kits a Bargain for Parents," Chicago Sun-Times, January 22, 2011, accessed January 26, 2011, http://www.suntimes.com/lifestyles/3412644-423/parents-drug-kids-schools-test.html.

33. "Canadian's Lucky Iron Fish Saves Lives in Cambodia," TheRecord.com, November 12, 2011, accessed January 20, 2014, http://www.therecord.com/news-story/2591989-canadian-s-lucky-iron-fish-saves-lives-in-cambodia/.

34. Lucky Iron Fish, "It's Our Anniversary," December 2017, accessed March 5, 2018, https://luckyironfish.com/blogs/news/happy-anniversary.

35. Lucky Iron Fish, "Why We Give," 2022, accessed March 24, 2022, https://luckyironfish.com/pages/social-impact.

CHAPTER 11

1. Nancy R. Lee and Philip Kotler, Social Marketing: Behavior Change for Social Good, 6th ed. (Thousand Oaks, CA: SAGE, 2019), 273.

2. Boating Safety Resource Center [website], accessed January 11, 2018, https://bard.knightpoint.systems/PublicInterface/Report1.aspx.

3. Personal communication from Derek Franklin, January 22, 2018.

4. Sea Tow Foundation's Sober Skipper Campaign Final Grant Report – Grant 1192, provided April 18, 2022, by Gail Kulp, Sea Tow Foundation Executive Director, www.boatingsafety.com.

5. Ibid., 10.

6. Philip Kotler and Gary M. Armstrong, Principles of Marketing (Upper Saddle River, NJ: Prentice Hall, 2001), 371.

7. Richard O'Connor, et al., "Financial Incentives to Promote Smoking Cessation: Evidence From 11 Quit and Win Contests," Journal of Public Health Management and Practice 12, no. 1 (2006): 44–51, accessed March 10, 2007, http://www.ncbi.nlm.nih.gov/entrez/query.fcgi?cmd=Retrieve&db=pubmed&dopt=Abstract&list_uids=16340515&query_hl=6&itool=pubmed_docsum.

8. Nancy R. Lee and Philip Kotler, Social Marketing: Behavior Change for Social God, 5th ed. (Thousand Oaks, CA: SAGE, 2916), 286–9.

9. Xavier Gine, Karlan Dean, and Jonathan Zinman, "Put Your Money Where Your Butt Is: A Commitment Contract for Smoking Cessation," American Economic Journal: Applied Economics 2, no. 4 (October 2010): 213–335.
10. Diane Rich, "Humane Society Adoptions Hit Record," Mercer Island Reporter, September 17, 2013, 8, accessed October 7, 2014, http://www.mi-reporter.com/opinion/letters/224089501.html.
11. Information in this example is from Harborview Injury Prevention and Research Center, University of Washington, Seattle, accessed October 1, 2001, http://www.hiprc.org.
12. Karen F. Fox, "Time as a Component of Price in Social Marketing," in Marketing in the '80s, ed. Richard P. Bagozzi (Chicago: American Marketing Association, 1980), 464–7; as cited in Philip Kotler and Eduardo L. Roberto, Social Marketing: Strategies for Changing Public Behavior (New York, NY: Free Press, 1989).
13. Ibid.
14. Hans Georg Gemunden, "Perceived Risk and Information Search: A Systematic Meta-Analysis of the Empirical Evidence," International Journal of Research in Marketing 2 (1985): 79–100; as cited in Kotler and Roberto, Social Marketing, 182–3.
15. Alan R. Andreasen, Social Marketing in the 21st Century (Thousand Oaks, CA: SAGE, 2006), 153.
16. Ibid., 102.
17. Driven to Distraction Task Force, "Frequently Asked Questions/Cell Phone Legislation Proposed by Senator Tracey Eide and Representative Reuven Carlyle," n.d., accessed January 28, 2011, http://www.nodistractions.org/The_Evidence.html.
18. thinkSPAIN, "Dog-Mess Not Cleared Up Hand-Delivered Back to Owners as 'Lost Property'," April 2013, accessed February 3, 2014, http://www.thinkspain.com/news-spain/22852/dog-mess-not-cleared-up-hand-delivered-back-to-owners-as-lost-property.
19. City of Tacoma, "The Filthy 15," 2007, accessed March 21, 2007, http://www.cityoftacoma.org/Page.aspx?nid=167.
20. Bulletin, "Thread: Offenders Sentenced to Barry Manilow Music," November 2008, accessed March 30, 2018, http://filmdope.com/forums/94483-offenders-sentenced-barry-manilow-music.html.
21. NIH, "Abstinence and Abstinence-Only Education," October 2007, accessed May 9, 2022, https://www.ncbi.nlm.nih.gov/pmc/articles/PMC5913747/.
22. Students received creative and production assistance from Cynthia Hartwig (creative director), Shelley Baker (art director at Cf2Gs Advertising), Marlene Liranzo (Mercer Island High School teacher), Gary Gorland (Teen Aware program manager), and Nancy Lee (consultant).
23. Personal communication from Jennifer Tabanico, April 27, 2022.
24. stickK commit, "FAQ-About Stick," n.d., accessed April 26, 2022, https://www.stickk.com/faq/about/About+stickK.
25. Texan By Nature, "Thinking Outside the Tackle Box: Recycling Fishing Line to Protect Wildlife Along the Texas Cost," n.d., accessed April 26, 2022, https://texanbynature.org/2020/04/recycling-fishing-line-to-protect-wildlife/.
26. National Academies of Sciences, Engineering, and Medicine, Increasing Uptake of COVID-19 Vaccination Through Requirement and Incentive Programs (Washington, DC: The National Academies Press, 2022), accessed April 21, 2022, https://doi.org/10.17226/26545.
27. Reshmaan Hussam, et al., "Habit Formation and Rational Addiction: A Field Experiment in Handwashing," December 13, 2016, accessed March 23, 2018, http://www.communityledtotalsanitation.org/sites/communityledtotalsanitation.org/files/HabitFormation_and_RationalAddiction.pdf.
28. Carmen Nobel, "How to Get People Addicted to a Good Habit," Harvard Business School: Working Knowledge,

January 24, 2018, accessed March 23, 2018, https://hbswk.hbs.edu/item/how-to-get-people-addicted-to-a-good-habit?cid=wk-rss.

29. Ibid.
30. Ibid.
31. Ibid.
32. Ibid.
33. Ibid.
34. Ibid.

CHAPTER 12

1. U.S. Environmental Protection Agency, Facts and Figures About Materials, Waste and Recycling, 2018, accessed May 3, 2022, https://www.epa.gov/facts-and-figures-about-materials-waste-and-recycling.
2. Pet Poo Skiddoo, "Top 10 Reasons Why People Don't Pick Up Dog Poop," October 2015, accessed April 13, 2018, https://www.petpooskiddoo.com/blog/top-10-reasons-why-people-dont-pick-up-dog-poop/.
3. Centers for Disease Control and Prevention, "Current Cigarette Smoking Among Adults—United States," n.d., accessed May 3, 2022, https://www.cdc.gov/tobacco/data_statistics/fact_sheets/adult_data/cig_smoking/index.htm.
4. Howard M. Nathan, et al., "Organ Donation in the United States," American Journal of Transplantation 3, no. 4 (2003): 29–40, accessed February 11, 2007, http://www.blackwell-synergy.com/links/doi/10.1034/j.16006143.3.s4.4.x/full/?cookieSet=1.
5. Verena Tiefenbeck, et al. "Overcoming Salience Bias: How Real-Time Feedback Fosters Resource Conservation," Management Science 64, no. 3 (2018): 1458–76; Verena Tiefenbeck, "Shower Feedback in Switzerland," 2016, accessed April 5, 2018, http://www.toolsofchange.com/en/case-studies/detail/697.
6. Ibid.
7. American Cancer Society, "Key Statistics for Melanoma Skin Cancer," May 19, 2016, accessed April 5, 2018, https://www.cancer.org/cancer/melanoma-skin-cancer/about/key-statistics.html.
8. National Cancer Institute, "Sun-Protective Behavior," April 2022, accessed May 2, 2022, https://progressreport.cancer.gov/prevention/sun_protection.
9. Krutika Pathi, "More Cities Are Doubling Down on Free Sunscreen," CITYLAB, May 26, 2017, accessed April 5, 2018, https://www.citylab.com/life/2017/05/free-sunscreen-dispensers/528315/.
10. Megan Wood, Tom Raisanen, and Ingrid Polcari, "Observational Study of Free Public Sunscreen Dispenser Use at a Major U.S. Outdoor Event," Journal of the American Academy of Dermatology, July 2017, accessed April 5, 2018, http://www.jaad.org/article/S0190-9622(17)30285-2/fulltext.
11. Impact Melanoma, "Martinis for Melanoma," May 2022, accessed May 19, 2022, https://impactmelanoma.org/event/m4m-ri/.
12. Velib, "Bikes for Everyone," n.d., accessed May 4, 2022, https://www.velib-metropole.fr/en_GB/service.
13. Uganda Health Marketing Group, Meeting the Unmet Need for Family Planning Through Workplace Acti-vations, October 2017, Abstract #072 Uganda Social Marketing Conference 2017.
14. Ibid.
15. Delta Dental: Washington Dental Service, "SmileMobile," n.d., accessed May 3, 2022, https://www.smilemobilewa.org.
16. "Oregon Voter Turnout 85.76% in November," The Oregonian, December 4, 2008, accessed February 1, 2011, http://www.oregonlive.com/news/index.ssf/2008/12/oregon_voter_turnout_8567_in_n.html/.
17. Secretary of State, "Voting in Oregon," n.d., accessed May 3, 2022, https://sos.oregon.gov/elections/Pages/voteinor.aspx.

18. DanceSafe [website], accessed March 14, 2014, http://www.dancesafe.org/about-us/.

19. Ibid.

20. City of Los Angeles, California [website], http://www.lacity.org/index.htm.

21. Personal communication from Michelle. mowery@lacity.org, May 20, 2014.

22. PetKeen, "14 Animal Shelter Statistics and Facts to Know in 2022," February 2022, accessed May 4, 2022, https://petkeen.com/animal-shelter-statistics/.

23. Sacramento Society's Prevention of Cruelty to Animals, "Pets on the Net," n.d., accessed October 31, 2001, http://www.sspca.org/adopt.html.

24. Department of Defense, "Special Report: Elections 2016-Americans Can Vote. Wherever They Are," January 2016, accessed April 13, 2018, https://www.defense.gov/News/Article/Article/644482/special-report-elections-2016-americans-can-vote-wherever-they-are/.

25. Amber Smith, "How Smart Is Your School Cafeteria? 12 Small Lunchroom Changes that Make a Big Nutritional Difference," November 16, 2010, accessed July 23, 2011, http://blog.syracuse.com/cny/2010/11/how_smart_is_your_school_cafeteria_12_small_lunchroom_changes_that_make_a_dig_nutritional_difference.html.

26. J. Bott, "Karmanos Site to Offer Mammograms at Mall," Detroit Free Press, April 28, 1999, http://www.freep.com/news/health/qkamra28.htm. Reprinted with permission.

27. J. Kowal, "Rapid HIV Tests Offered Where Those at Risk Gather: Seattle Health Officials Get Aggressive in AIDS Battle by Heading to Gay Clubs, Taking a Drop of Blood and Providing Answers in 20 Minutes," Chicago Tribune, January 2, 2004, accessed July 23, 2011, http://www.aegis.com/news/ct/2004/CT040101.html.

28. Personal communication, March 2007. Data from the HIV/AIDS Program, Public Health–Seattle & King County.

29. Club Z, "A Private Bathhouse for Men," n.d., accessed May 5, 2022, https://www.thezclub.com/.

30. N. Rytter, "Few Takers for Free Heroin," The Week, January 28, 2011, 19.

31. Health Products Stewardship Association, Annual Report to the Director: 2018 Calendar Year, June 30, 2019, accessed May 5, 2022, https://www2.gov.bc.ca/assets/gov/environment/waste-management/recycling/recycle/batteries/hpsa_2018_bcmrp_ar_2019-06-25.pdf#:~:text=Volumes%20of%20post%20-consumer%20health%20products%20collected%20in,total%20of%2095%25%20of%20licenced%20BC%20community%20pharmacies.

32. Greenstar Social Marketing [website], accessed May 19, 2022, http://www.greenstar.org.pk/.

33. International Centre for Social Franchising, "About," n.d., accessed March 12, 2014, http://www.the-icsf.org/.

34. National Trust for Nature Conservation, "Annapurna Con-servation Area Project," n.d., accessed April 16, 2018, http://www.ntnc.org.np/project/annapurna-conservation-area-project.

35. D. Ahlert, et al., "Social Fran-chising: A Way of Systematic Replication to Increase Social Impact," Bundesverband deutscher Stiftungen, 2008, accessed April 16, 2018, https://www.stiftungen.org/fileadmin/bvds/de/Projekte/Projekttransfer/Social_Franchise_Manual_Englisch.pdf.

36. Ibid.

37. Philip Kotler and Eduardo L. Roberto, Social Marketing: Strategies for Changing Public Behavior (New York, NY: Free Press, 1989), 162.

38. Malcolm Gladwell, From the Tipping Point: How Little Things Can Make a Big Difference (Boston, MA: Little, Brown,

2000; copyright by Malcolm Gladwell), 203–6. Reprinted by permission of Little, Brown and Company, Inc.

39. ABC News "Unexpected Places Now Offering COVID-19 Vaccines," May 3, 2021, accessed May 6, 2022, https://abcnews.go.com/Health/creative-places-vaccinated-popping-country/story?id=77461117.

40. NIH: National Institute on Drug Abuse, "Opioid Overdose Crisis," March 2018, accessed April 9, 2018, https://www.drugabuse.gov/drugs-abuse/opioids/opioid-overdose-crisis.

41. Ibid.

42. National Institute of Health, "NIH Launches HEAL Initiative, Doubles Funding to Accelerate Sci-entific Solutions to Stem National Opioid Epidemic," April 4, 2018, https://www.nih.gov/news-events/news-releases/nih-launches-heal-initiative-doubles-funding-accelerate-scientific-solutions-stem-national-opioid-epidemic.

43. We Are the Drug Policy Alliance, "Supervised Injection Facilities," n.d., accessed April 9, 2018, http://www.drugpolicy.org/issues/supervised-injection-facilities.

44. Walmart, "Walmart Supports State of Emergency Declaration on Opioids," October 26, 2017, accessed April 9, 2018, https://news.walmart.com/2017/10/26/walmart-supports-state-of-emergency-declaration-on-opioids.

45. A. Kunkler, "Narcan, the Eastside and How to Curb the Overdose Epidemic," Mercer Island Reporter, November 22, 2017, 1–7.

46. THE HILL, "NYC Vending Machines Will Give People Syringes, Opioid Overdose Treatment," January 3, 2022, accessed May 5, 2022. NYC vending machines will give people syringes, opioid overdose treatment - the Hill.

CHAPTER 13

1. Kevin Lane Keller and Philip Kotler, Marketing Management, 12th ed. (Upper Saddle River, NJ: Prentice Hall, 2005), 536.

2. Rosser Reeves, Reality in Advertising (New York, NY: Knopf, 1960).

3. Lynne Doner and Michael Siegel, Marketing Public Health: Strategies to Promote Social Change (Gaithersburg, MD: Aspen, 1998), 332–3.

4. Ibid., 321.

5. Syracuse University, Newhouse School of Public Communications, "The Stupid Drink," July 29, 2009, accessed February 5, 2011, http://www.slideshare.net/prceran/syracuse-universitys-the-stupid-drink-campaign-book?from=ss_embed.

6. Siegel and Doner, Marketing Public Health, 314–5.

7. "Pioneering S.F. Program Puts Bank Accounts in Reach of Poor," Irvine Quarterly, n.d., accessed July 24, 2011, http://www.irvine.org/publications/irvine-quarterly/current-issue/947; City and County of San Francisco, Office of the Treasurer & Tax Collector, "Mayor Gavin Newsom and Treasurer José Cisneros Announce Over 24,000 Accounts Opened for Bank on San Francisco Clients," [Press release], Irvine Quarterly, November 20, 2008, accessed July 24, 2011, http://www.sftreasurer.org/ftp/uploadedfiles/tax/news/PR%20Bank%20on%20SF.pdf.

8. Barack Obama, "Race Against Time—World AIDS Day Speech," December 1, 2006, accessed April 11, 2007, http://obama.senate.gov/speech/061201-race_against_time_world_aids_day_speech/index.html.

9. Philip Kotler and Kevin Lane Keller, Marketing Management, 12th ed., 547.

10. Ruth C. Browne, "Most Black Women Have a Regular Source of Hair Care—But Not Medical Care," Journal of the National Medical Association 98, no. 10 (October 2006), 1652–3.

11. Sesame Street Store, Healthy Habits, "Ready, Set, Brush Pop-Up Book,"

[Product description], n.d., accessed February 4, 2011, http://store.sesamestreet.org/Product.aspx?cp=21415_21477_21532&pc=6EAM0196.

12. Herbert C. Kelman and Carl I. Hovland, "Reinstatement of the Communication in Delayed Measurement of Opinion Change," Journal of Abnormal and Social Psychology 48 (1953): 327–5; as cited in Kotler and Keller, Marketing Management, 12th ed., p. 546.
13. David J. Moore, John C. Mowen, and Richard Reardon, "Multiple Sources in Advertising Appeals: When Product Endorsers Are Paid by the Advertising Sponsor," Journal of the Academy of Marketing Science (Summer 1994): 234–43; as cited in Kotler and Keller, Marketing Management, 12th ed., 546.
14. Montana Meth Project [website], accessed March 26, 2007, http://www.montanameth.org/About_Us/index.php.
15. Doug McKenzie-Mohr and William Smith, Fostering Sustainable Behavior: An Introduction to Community-Based Social Marketing, 2nd ed. (Gabriola Island, BC: New Society, 1999), 101.
16. K. Roman and J. M. Maas, How to Advertise, 2nd ed. (New York, NY: St. Martin's, 1992).
17. Personal communication from Mary Shannon Johnstone, March 24, 2014.
18. Siegel and Doner, Marketing Public Health, 335–6.
19. Posting on Georgetown Social Marketing Listserve, March 3, 2012.
20. Brian Sternthal and C. Samuel Craig, "Fear Appeals: Revisited and Revised," Journal of Consumer Research 3 (1974): 23–34; as summarized in Philip Kotler and Eduardo L. Roberto, Social Marketing: Strategies for Changing Public Behavior (New York: Free Press, 1989), 198.
21. Jerold L. Hale and James Price Dillard, "Fear Appeals in Health Promotion Campaigns: Too Much, Too Little, or Just Right?" in Designing Health Messages: Approaches From Communication Theory and Public Health Practice, eds. Edward Maibach and Roxanne Parrott (Thousand Oaks, CA: SAGE, 1995), 65–80.
22. Doug McKenzie-Mohr and William Smith, Fostering Sustainable Behavior, 101.
23. Ibid., 85.
24. Ibid., 86.
25. Shawn M. Burn, "Social Psychology and the Stimulation of Recycling Behaviors: The Block Leader Approach," Journal of Applied Social Psychology 21 (1991): 611–29.
26. Chip Heath and Dan Heath, Made to Stick: Why Some Ideas Survive and Others Die (New York, NY: Random House, 2007).
27. Pew Research Center, "Social Media Factsheet," April 7, 2021, accessed May 23, 2022, https://www.pewresearch.org/internet/fact-sheet/social-media/.
28. Mental Health America of Montana, "Catchy Vegetable Names Increase Affinity for Greens," September 18, 2012, accessed April 27, 2018, http://montanamentalhealth.org/eblast/eblast091812.html.
29. Health Affairs, "Interview: From Family Planning to HIV/AIDS Prevention to Poverty Alleviation: A Conversation With Mechai Virabaidya," Web Exclusive, September 25, 2007, Glenn A. Melnick, gmelnick@usc.edu.
30. Philip Kotler and Gary Armstrong, Principles of Marketing, 9th ed. (Upper Saddle River, NJ: Prentice Hall, 2001), 548.
31. Vince Carducci, "The Big Idea," n.d., accessed March 28, 2007, http://www.popmatters.com/books/reviews/h/how-brands-become-icons.shtml.
32. Porter Novelli, "The Big Idea: Death by Execution," 2006, accessed March 28, 2007, http://www.porternovelli.com/site/pressrelease.aspx?pressrelease_id=140&pgName=news.
33. Ibid.

34. Eric R. Spangenberg, et al., "Mass-Communicated Prediction Requests: Practical Application and a Cognitive Dissonance Explanation for Self-Prophecy," Journal of Marketing 67 (July 2003): 47–62, http://www.atyponlink.com/AMA/doi/abs/10.1509/jmkg.67.3.47.18659.

35. M. Guido, "A More Effective Nag," Washington State Magazine, Spring 2004, accessed July 28, 2011, http://researchnews.wsu.edu/society/33.html.

36. Ibid.

37. Philip Kotler and Kevin Keller, Marketing Management, 12th ed. (Upper Saddle River, NJ: Prentice Hall, 2005), 546.

38. J. Dunn, "Denver Water's Ads Already Working Conservation Angle," Denver Post, July 13, 2006, accessed April 22, 2007, http://www.denverpost.com/portlet/article/html/fragments/print_article.jsp?articleId=4043. Ads developed by Sukle Advertising and Design.

39. Denver Water, "Thank You for Using Even Less," n.d., accessed April 21, 2014, http://www.den.verwater.org/Conservation/UseOnlyWhatYouNeed/.

40. Personal communication from Robert John, June 4, 2018.

41. J. Weaver, "A License to Shill," MSNBC News, November 17, 2002, accessed July 25, 2011, http://www.msnbc.msn.com/id/3073513/.

42. Pew Research Center, "Social Media Factsheet," April 7, 2021, accessed May 23, 2022, https://www.pewresearch.org/internet/fact-sheet/social-media/.

43. Adapted from the Centers for Disease Control and Prevention's "The Health Communicator's Social Media Toolkit," https://www.cdc.gov/healthcommunication/toolstemplates/socialmediatoolkit_bm.pdf.

44. Pew Research Center, "Social Media Factsheet," April 7, 2021, accessed May 23, 2022, https://www.pewresearch.org/internet/fact-sheet/social-media/.

45. Lifebuoy, "Lifebuoy Helps More Children Reach Their 5th Birthday," n.d., accessed April 23, 2014, http://www.lifebuoy.com/socialmission/help-childreach5/helpchild.

46. Unilever, "Lifebuoy Launches 'High Five for Handwashing' Campaign," October 14, 2016, accessed May 17, 2018, https://www.unilever-ewa.com/news/press-releases/2016/lifebuoy-launches-high-five-for-handwashing-campaign.html.

47. Pew Research Center, Social Media Factsheet, April 7, 2021, accessed May 23, 2022, https://www.pewresearch.org/internet/fact-sheet/social-media/.

48. Information for this case was provided by Michael Miller of Brown-Miller Communications, March 8, 2011.

49. Pew Research Center, Social Media Factsheet, April 7, 2021, accessed May 23, 2022, https://www.pewresearch.org/internet/fact-sheet/social-media/.

50. Personal communication from Meghan Sansivero May 30, 2018.

51. Pew Research Center, "Mobile Fact Sheet," April 7, 2021, accessed May 24, 2022, https://www.pewresearch.org/internet/fact-sheet/mobile/.

52. Pop!Tech,"Project Masiluleke: A Breakthrough Initiative to Combat HIV/AIDS Utilizing Mobile Technology & HIV Self-Testing in South Africa," n.d., accessed April 29, 2014, http://poptech.org/system/uploaded_files/27/original/Project_Masiluleke_Brief.pdf.

53. Ibid.

54. Ibid.

55. Pew Research Center, "Social Media Factsheet," April 7, 2021, accessed May 23, 2022, https://www.pewresearch.org/internet/fact-sheet/social-media/.

56. Personal communication from Carrie Clyne, May 17, 2018.

57. Philip Kotler and Kevin Lane Keller, Marketing Management, 556.

58. "How One Man Has Fought to Clear the Air Over China's Polution," Toronto Star, April

23, 2013, accessed April 23, 2014, http://www.thestar.com/news/world/2013/04/23/environmentalist_ma_jun_fights_for_change_to_clean_up_chinas_pollution.html.

59. "Cleaning Up China," Time Magazine, June 24, 2013, accessed April 23, 2014, http://content.time.com/time/magazine/article/0,9171,2145500,00.html.
60. "How One Man Has Fought," Toronto Star.
61. "Cleaning Up China," Time Magazine.
62. Philip Kotler and Nancy R. Lee, Marketing in the Public Sector (Upper Saddle River, NJ: Wharton School, 2006), 152.
63. Lynne Doner and Michael Siegel, Marketing Public Health: Strategies to Promote Social Change (Gaithersburg, MD: Aspen, 1998), 393.
64. Ibid., 394.
65. Ibid., 396.
66. Ad Council Website, accessed March 23, 2022, https://www.adcouncil.org/.
67. Prevent Cancer Foundation, "Prevent Cancer Super Colon Exhibit," n.d., accessed March 7, 2011, http://www.preventcancer.org/education2c.aspx?id=156&ekmensel=15074e5e_34_38_btnlink.
68. Prevent Cancer Foundation, "Prevent Cancer Super Colon Exhibit," n.d., http://preventcancer.org/what-we-do/education/super-colon/.
69. Philip Kotler and Kevin Lane Keller, Marketing Management, 613.
70. For more information, go to http://www.petwaste.surfacewater.info.
71. E. M. Rogers, et al., Proceedings From the Conference on Entertainment Education for Social Change (Los Angeles, CA: Annenberg School of Communications, 1989).
72. Alan Andreasen, Marketing Social Change: Changing Behavior to Promote Health, Social Development, and the Environment (San Francisco, CA: Jossey-Bass, 1995), 215.
73. John Davies, "Preventing HIV/AIDS With Condoms: Nine Tips You Can Use," n.d., accessed April 12, 2007, http://www.johndavies.com/johndavies/new2html/9tips_print.htm.
74. M. Miller, "Messages From a Mexican Soap Opera-Making Financial Education Entertaining International Finance Corporation," May 2014, accessed May 17, 2018, http://www.worldbank.org/en/results/2014/09/04/using-a-soap-opera-as-a-vehicle-for-financial-education-in-mexico.
75. Keep America Beautiful, "I'm Not Your Mama: Mississippi's War Against Highway Litter," n.d., accessed April 13, 2007, http://www.kab.org/aboutus2.asp?id=642.
76. Centers for Disease Control and Prevention, "Entertainment Education: Overview," n.d., accessed October 10, 2006, http://www.cdc.gov/communication/entertainment_education.htm.
77. Community Idea Stations, "Art and Social Marketing Address Rising Problem of Ocean Plastics," April 6, 2017, accessed May 17, 2018, http://ideastations.org/radio/news/art-and-social-marketing-address-rising-problem-ocean-plastics.
78. Philip Kotler and Gary Armstrong, Principles of Marketing (Upper Saddle River, NJ: Prentice Hall, 2001), 552.
79. CISION PR Newswire, "FDA Launches Public Education Campaign to Encourage Adult Smokers Trying to Quit Cigarettes," December 11, 2017, accessed May 17, 2018, https://www.prnewswire.com/news- releases/fda-launches-public-education-campaign-to-encourage-adult-smokers-trying-to-quit-cigarettes-300569546.html.
80. Philip Kotler and Gary Armstrong, Principles of Marketing, 513–7.
81. Ibid.
82. Ad Council, "Drunk Driving Prevention (1983–Present)," n.d., accessed April 18, 2007, http://www.adcouncil.org/default.aspx?id=137.

83. Ibid., "Campaign Description."

84. Ibid.

85. Ad Council, "Drunk Driving Prevention," n.d., accessed May 18, 2018, https://www.adcouncil.org/Our-Campaigns/The-Classics/Drunk-Driving-Prevention.

86. Matching Donors [website], accessed March 7, 2011, http://www.matchingdonors.com/life/index.cfm?page=main&c fid=12265246&cftoken=12950547.

87. S. Satel, "Is It Wrong to Advertise for Organs?" National Review Online, April 13, 2007, 16.

CHAPTER 14

1. Washington Stormwater, "Dumpster Outreach Group," 2022, accessed June 9, 2022, https://www.wastormwatercenter.org/permit-assistance/municipal/dumpster-outreach-group/.

2. Ibid.

3. Philip Kotler and Nancy R. Lee, Marketing in the Public Sector: A Roadmap for Improved Performance (Upper Saddle River, NJ: Wharton School, 2006), 266.

4. Ibid., 268–269.

5. Ohio State University, "National Anti-drug Campaign Succeeds in Lowering Marijuana Use, Study Suggests," Research News, n.d., accessed March 14, 2011, http://researchnews.osu.edu/archive/aboveinfluence.htm.

6. Ibid.

7. Truth Initiative, "truth® Campaign Successful in Saving Lives and Preventing Youth Smoking," December 7, 2017, accessed May 25, 2018, https://truthinitiative.org/news/truth-campaign-successful-saving-lives-and-preventing-youth-smoking.

8. Adapted from an article that first appeared in the Journal of Social Marketing, Vol. 1, Issue 1, Emerald Group Publishing Limited (February 2011): Nancy R. Lee, "Where's the Beef? Social Marketing in Tough Times," 73–5.

9. Charlotte Tucker, "National Public Health Week Highlights Return on Investment," Nation's Health, July 2013, accessed May 5, 2014, http://thenationshealth.aphapublications.org/content/43/5/1.3.full.

10. Ibid.

11. Jeff French, Lucy Reynolds, and Rowena Merritt, Social Marketing Casebook (Thousand Oaks, CA: SAGE, 2011), 129–39.

12. Ibid., 138.

13. E. Jaffe, "Watch 'Real-Time' Transit Planning Help North America's Busiest Bus Line," March 26, 2014, accessed May 5, 2014, http://www.the atlanticcities.com/commute/2014/03/watch-real-time-transit-planning-helps-north-americas-busiest-bus-line/8725/.

14. Philip Kotler and Nancy R. Lee, Marketing in the Public Sector, 266.

15. U.S. Department of Health and Human Services, "What is Comparative Effectiveness Research," n.d., accessed March 15, 2011, http://www.effectivehealthcare.ahrq.gov/index.cfm/what- is-comparative-effectiveness-re search1/.

16. Doug McKenzie-Mohr, Fostering Sustainable Behavior: An Introduction to Community-Based Social Marketing, 3rd ed. (Gabriola Island, BC: New Society Publishers, 2011), 137.

17. Ibid., 140–42.

18. Eiskje R. Clason and Denise Meijer, "Eat Your Greens: Increasing the Number of Days that Picky Toddlers Eat Vegetables," Social Marketing Quarterly 22, no. 2 (2016): 119–37.

19. Ibid.

20. Philip Kotler, Kotler on Marketing: How to Create, Win and Dominate Markets (New York, NY: Free Press, 1999), 185.

21. Tools of Change, "King County in Motion," n.d., accessed May 28, 2018, http://www.toolsofchange.com/en/case-studies/detail/688/.

22. Washington State Department of Transportation, "Commute Trip Reduction," n.d., accessed June 21, 2018, http://www.wsdot.wa.gov/transit/CTR.

23. Tools of Change, "King County in Motion."

24. In Motion Capitol Hill, "Final Report November 2016," King County Metro, 18–26.

CHAPTER 15

1. Sesame Workshop, "If Elmo Eats Broccoli, Will Kids Eat it Too? Atkins Foundation Grant to Fund Further Research," [Press release], September 20, 2005, accessed July 26, 2011, http://archive.sesameworkshop.org/aboutus/inside_press.php?contentId=15092302.

2. Leonard L. Berry, Kathleen Seiders and Albert C. Hergenroeder, "Regaining the Health of a Nation: What Business Can Do About Obesity," Organizational Dynamics 35, no. 4 (2006): 341–56.

3. "Worldwide Day of Play," Wikipedia, n.d., accessed March 16, 2011, http://en.wikipedia.org/wiki/Worldwide_Day_of_Play.

4. David Hessekiel, Nancy Lee and Philip Kotler, GOOD WORKS! Marketing and Corporate Initiatives That Build a Better World... and the Bottom Line (New York, NY: Wiley, 2012).

5. Philip Kotler and Nancy R. Lee, "Best of Breed," Stanford Social Innovation Review, Spring 2004.

6. Philip Kotler, et al., GOOD WORKS!.

7. American Heart Association, "American Heart Association Applauds SUBWAY's Com-mitment to Marketing Healthy Foods to Kids," January 23, 2014, accessed May 23, 2014, http://newsroom.heart.org/news/american-heart-association-applauds-subways-commitment-to-marketing-healthy-foods-to-kids.

8. Macy's, Inc. "Macy's Honors America Heart Association's Go Red for Women This February by Motivating Women to Get Active and Take Action Against Heart Disease, accessed January 28, 2019, Macy's Honors American Heart Association's Go Red for Women® this February by Motivating Women to Get Active and Take Action Against Heart Disease :: Macy's, Inc. (M) (macysinc.com).

9. MRO Magazine, "Macy's Inspires and Ignites Action This February in Support of Go Red For Women," January 27, 2016, accessed June 3, 2022, https://www.mromagazine.com/press-releases/macys-inspires-and-ignites-action-this-february-in-support-of-go-red-for-women/.

10. Water—Use It Wisely, "Campaign History," n.d., accessed June 16, 2022, http://wateruseitwisely.com/jump-in/campaign-history/.

11. Philip Kotler, et al., GOOD WORKS! 130–132.

12. U.S. Fire Administration, "Home Fire Prevention and Safety Tips," n.d., accessed May 23, 2014, http://www.usfa.fema.gov/citizens/home_fire_prev/.

13. Energizer, "Change Your Clock Change Your Battery," n.d., accessed June 7, 2018, https://www.energizer.ca/responsibility/change-your-clock-change-your-battery.

14. Centers for Disease Control and Prevention, "Teen Drivers: Get the Facts," October 2021, accessed June 7, 2022, https://www.cdc.gov/transportationsafety/teen_drivers/teendrivers_factsheet.html.

15. AT&T: It Can Wait, "Take the Pledge," 2022, accessed June 7, 2022, https://about.att.com/csr/itcanwait.

16. Say Boo to the Flu, "Vaccine Info," n.d., accessed June 7, 2018, http://sayboototheflu.com/events/.

17. Florida Health, "Say Boo To The Flu: Get Your Vaccine Before Halloween," October 2021, accessed June 7, 2022, https://pinel

las.floridahealth.gov/newsroom/2021/10/flu-shots-10-14-2021.html.

18. National Institute of Child Health and Human Development (NICHD), "Safe to Sleep," n.d., accessed May 23, 2014, http://www.nichd.nih.gov/sts/Pages/default.aspx.
19. U.S. DHHS and NIH, "Safe to Sleep," 2021, accessed June 7, 2022, https://safetosleep.nichd.nih.gov/.
20. Philip Kotler and Gary Armstrong, Principles of Marketing (Upper Saddle River, NJ: Prentice Hall, 2001), 528–9.
21. Ibid., 529.
22. Philip Kotler, Kotler on Marketing: How to Create, Win and Dominate Markets (New York, NY: Free Press, 1999), 31.
23. PugetSound Partnership, "About the Puget Sound Partnership," n.d., accessed June 2, 2014, http://www.psp.wa.gov/aboutthepartnership.php.
24. Personal communication from Dave Ward of the Puget Sound Partnership, May 2014.
25. Ibid.
26. Candid, "Key Facts: U.S. Nonprofits and Foundations 2021 Edition," 2021, accessed June 28, 2022, https://www.issuelab.org/resources/38265/38265.pdf.
27. Alan Andreasen and Philip Kotler, Strategic Marketing for Nonprofit Organizations (Englewood Cliffs, NJ: Prentice Hall, 1991), 285.
28. World Bicycle Relief [home page], accessed May 30, 2014, https://www.worldbicyclerelief.org/.
29. Ibid.
30. World Bicycle Relief, "Mobility= Education. Bicycles for Educational Empowerment Program," 2011, accessed May 30, 2014, https://www.worldbicyclerelief.org/stor age/documents/wbr_education_field_report.pdf.
31. Ibid.
32. Business for Impact at Georgetown University McDonough School of Business, "AB InBev & Smart Drinking: An Analysis of How the World's Largest Beer Company Contributes to the Reduction of Harmful Alcohol Use," June 2021, accessed June 16, 2022, AB-InBev-Smart-Drinking-Case-Study-2021.pdf (georgetown.edu).
33. Ibid.
34. Ibid.
35. Ibid., 18.
36. Hamish Pringle, Marjorie Thompson, and Brand Spirit, How Cause-Related Marketing Builds Brands (New York, NY: Wiley, 1999); Richard Earle, The Art of Cause Marketing (Lincolnwood: NTC Business Books, 2000).
37. Ad Council [website], accessed October 10, 2001, www.adcouncil.org, www.adcouncil.org/body_about.html.
38. "Surprising Survivors: Corporate Do-Gooders," CNN Money.
39. Charity Navigator [website], accessed June 4, 2014, http://www.charitynavigator.org/index.cfm?bay=content.view&cpid=42#.U49Hc3l3uUk.
40. Philanthropy Roundtable, "Early Analysis Shows 2021 A Record Year for Charitable Giving," April 13, 2022, accessed June 14, 2022, https://www.philanthropyroundtable.org/early-analysis-shows-2021-a-record-year-for-charitable-giving/#:~:text=The%20Blackbaud%20Institute%E2%80%99 s%20%E2%80%9C%202021%20Charitable%20Giving%20Report ,giving%20also%20increased%209%25%20over%20the%202020%20total.
41. Philip Kotler and Nancy R. Lee, Corporate Social Responsibility: Doing the Most Good for Your Company and Your Cause (New York, NY: Wiley, 2006), 9.
42. Philip Kotler and Nancy R. Lee, "Best of Breed," Stanford Social Innovation Review (Spring 2004): 14–23.
43. Pringle and Thompson, Brand Spirit; Earle, Art of Cause Marketing.

44. Extension, "Protecting Children From Unintentional Injuries," n.d., accessed June 28, 2022, https://extension.missouri.edu/publications/gh6026

45. Best Buy, "Best Buy Gets Top Recycling Honors," (n.d.), accessed May 23, 2014, http://www.bby.com/best-buy-gets-top-recycling-honors/.

46. Best Buy "Best Buy Launches Home Pick-Up Recycling Service," April 2022, accessed June 14, 2022, https://corporate.bestbuy.com/best-buy-launches-home-pick-up-recycling-service/.

47. Ibid.

48. T. Granger, "Best Buy Targets 1 Billion Pounds of Electronics Recycling," April 27, 2010, accessed July 26, 2011, http://earth911.com/news/2010/04/27/best-buy-targets-1-billion-pounds-of-electronics-recycling/.

49. Philip Kotler and Nancy R. Lee, "Best of Breed."

50. Sandy Hook PROMISE, "About Our Programs," 2021, accessed June 1, 2022, https://www.sandyhookpromise.org/who-we-are/about-us/.

51. Mark Follman, Trigger Points (New York, NY: HarperCollins, 2022), 97–8.

52. Sandy Hook PROMISE, "About Our Programs," 2021, accessed June 1, 2022, https://www.sandyhookpromise.org/who-we-are/about-us/.

53. The New York Times, "Famlies in Texas Grieve Loss of 19 Children in Shooting," May 29, 2022, accessed June 2, 2002, https://www.nytimes.com/live/2022/05/25/us/shooting-robb-elementary-uvalde?smid=url-share#d69253a4-b974-58e7-af1c-d55cb2f0882d.

54. Sandy Hook PROMISE, "Know the Signs" Could Have Saved Lives in Uvalde," May 26, 2022, accessed June 1, 2022, https://www.sandyhookpromise.org/press-releases/know-the-signs-could-have-saved-lives-in-uvalde/.

55. Sandy Hook PROMISE "About Our Programs," 2021, accessed June 1, 2022, https://www.sandyhookpromise.org/who-we-are/about-us/.

56. Ibid.

CHAPTER 16

1. The U.S. Department of Housing and Urban Development, "The 2021 Annual Homeless Assessment Report (AHAR) to Congress," February 2022, accessed June 22, 2022, https://www.hud.gov/press/press_releases_media_advisories/HUD_No_22_022.

2. Housing First, Europe Hub, "1.2 The History of Housing First," n.d., accessed June 18, 2018, http://housingfirsteurope.eu/guide/what-is-housing-first/history-housing-first/.

3. United States Interagency Council on Homelessness, "Deploy Housing First Systemwide," June 5, 2018, accessed June 18, 2018, https://www.usich.gov/solutions/housing/housing-first.

4. National Alliance to End Home-lessness, "Fact Sheet: Housing First," April 2016, accessed June 18, 2018, http://endhomelessness.org/wp-content/uploads/2016/04/housing-first-fact-sheet.pdf.

5. Care2, "Reasons Homeless People Sleep Out in the Cold," December 10, 2017, accessed June 18, 2018, https://www.care2.com/causes/10-reasons-homeless-people-sleep-out-in-the-cold-and-die.html.

6. National Alliance to End Homelessness, "Fact Sheet: Housing First."

7. Coalition for the Homeless: Proven Solutions, "We Can End the Homelessness Crisis," n.d., accessed June 18, 2018, http://www.coalitionforthehomeless.org/ending-homelessness/proven-solutions/.

8. United States Interagency Council on Homelessness, "Deploy Housing First Systemwide."

9. Dawn Foster, "What Can the UK Learn From How Finland Solved Homelessness," The Guardian, March 22, 2017, accessed June 20, 2018, https://www.theguardian.com/housing-network/2017/mar/22/finland-solved-homeless ness-eu-crisis-housing-first.

10. U.S. Department of Housing and Urban Development, "Housing First Assessment Tool," September 2017, accessed June 20, 2018, https://www.hudexchange.info/resource/5294/housing-first-assessment-tool/.

11. National Alliance to End Home-lessness, "Fact Sheet: Housing First."

12. Ibid.

13. JOIN, "Understanding & Implementing The Housing First Model," August 13, 2019, accessed June 23, 2022, Understanding & Implementing The Housing First Model - Join PDX

14. Nancy R. Lee, Policymaking for Citizen Behavior Change: A Social Marketing Approach (London: Routledge, 2018), 109.

15. NPR, "Utah Reduced Chronic Homelessness by 91 Percent; Here's How," December 10, 2015, accessed June 20, 2018, http://www.npr.org/2015/12/10/459100751/utah-reduced-chronic-homelessness-by-91-percent-heres-how.

16. The Salt Lake Tribune "Utah's 'Housing-first' Model is Keeping People Off the Streets. So Why Are Auditors Worried?," November 2021, accessed June 22, 2022, https://www.sltrib.com/news/politics/2021/11/16/utahs-housing-first-model/.

17. Philip Kotler and Gary Armstrong, Principles of Marketing (Upper Saddle River, NJ: Prentice Hall, 2001), 71.

18. McKenzie-Mohr, Fostering Sustainable Behavior: An Introduction to Community-Based Social Marketing, 3rd ed. (Gabriola Island, BC: New Society Publishers, 2011), 137.

19. Nancy R. Lee and Philip Kotler, Social Marketing: Changing Behaviors for Good, 5th ed. (Thousand Oaks, CA: SAGE, 2011), 339–42.

20. Personal communication from Keri Handaly, and information at "Clean Rivers Coalition," November 2020, https://gaftp.epa.gov/region10/columbiariver/WWTRP/Meeting-2020-11-18/Presentation-Iwai-Handaly-CRC-Healthy-Waters.pdf.

21. Alix Danielsen and Keri Morin Handaly. "Oregon Pollutant Toxicity Ranking Database." 2018, Portland State University Graduate Thesis Project supported by the City of Gresham.

22. Nancy R. Lee and Philip Kotler, Social Marketing: Influencing Behaviors for Good, 4th ed. (Thousand Oaks, CA: SAGE, 2011), 406–9.

23. Doug McKenzie-Mohr, et al., Social Marketing to Protect the Environment: What Works (Thousand Oaks, CA: SAGE, 2011), 13.

24. Doug McKenzie-Mohr and William Smith, Fostering Sustainable Behavior, 61.

25. Ibid., 61.

26. Ibid., 48.

27. Doug McKenzie-Mohr, Fostering Sustainable Behavior.

28. Doug McKenzie-Mohr, Fostering Sustainable Behavior, 70.

29. KaBOOM!, "Playful City USA Program Details," accessed June 24, 2014, https://kaboom.org/take-action/playful-city-usa/program-details.

30. "iSMA Social Marketing Statement of Ethics," February 2020, accessed July 9, 2022, https://isocialmarketing.org/wp-content/uploads/sites/5/2022/05/Statement-of-Ethics-Multilingual-2020.pdf.

31. CNN Health, "The FDA has Authorized Covid-19 Vaccines for Children Under 5. What Should Parents Know?," June 2022, accessed June 22, 2022, https://www.cnn.com/2022/06/18/health/children-under-5-covid-vaccine-explainer-wellness/index.html.

32. Graduate! Tacoma, "2018 Community Impact Report," n.d., accessed June 21, 2018, https://graduatetacom

a.org/wp-content/uploads/2018/05/ImpactReport18_040618-lo-res_FNL.pdf.

33. Microsoft, "Tacoma Public Schools," August 10, 2016, accessed June 21, 2018, https://customers.microsoft.com/sv-se/story/tacomapublicschoolsstory.

34. Graduate! Tacoma, 2018 Commu-nity Impact Report.

35. Ibid.

36. Ibid.

37. Graduate! Tacoma, "Tacoma Graduation Rates Are at a Record High, But Budget Challenges Pose Threat," January 2019, accessed June 22, 2022, https://www.graduatetacoma.org/tacoma-graduation-rates-record-high-budget-challenges-pose-threat/.

38. Ibid.

39. Microsoft, "Tacoma Public Schools."

40. Graduate! Tacoma, 2018 Commu-nity Impact Report.

INDEX

B

C

D

G

H

N

S

W

Y

Z